Philodemus and Poetry

PHILODEMUS AND POETRY

Poetic Theory and Practice
in Lucretius, Philodemus,
and Horace

Edited by
DIRK OBBINK

New York   Oxford
OXFORD UNIVERSITY PRESS
1995

Oxford University Press

Oxford   New York
Athens   Auckland   Bangkok   Bombay
Calcutta   Cape Town   Dar es Salaam   Delhi
Florence   Hong Kong   Istanbul   Karachi
Kuala Lumpur   Madras   Madrid   Melbourne
Mexico City   Nairobi   Paris   Singapore
Taipei   Tokyo   Toronto

and associated companies in
Berlin   Ibadan

Copyright © 1995 by Oxford University Press, Inc.

Published by Oxford University Press, Inc.,
200 Madison Avenue, New York, New York 10016

Library of Congress Cataloging-in-Publication Data
Philodemus and poetry : poetic theory and practice in Lucretius, Philodemus, and Horace / edited by Dirk Obbink.
p.   cm.
Includes bibliographical references and indexes.
ISBN 0-19-508815-8
1. Philodemus, ca. 110-ca. 40 B.C.—Aesthetics.   2. Classical poetry—History and criticism—Theory, etc.
3. Classical poetry—History and criticism.   4. Lucretius Carus, Titus—Aesthetics.   5. Horace—Aesthetics.
6. Aesthetics, Ancient.   7. Poetics.   I. Obbink, Dirk.
PA4271.P4P45   1994
881'.0109—dc20   93-39253

1 3 5 7 9 8 6 4 2

Printed in the United States of America
on acid-free paper

In Memory of Cecilia

οὔπω γεγονυίας τριάκοντα ἔτη,
οὐκ ἔςτι φύςις ἐν ὅλῃ τῇ Ἑλλάδι ἀμείνων.

Preface

Philodemus and poetry have been on the lips of the intelligentsia in the same breath since at least the year 55 B.C. when Cicero paired them in his speech *Against Piso* (68–72):

> There is a certain Greek who virtually lives with him, a man whom, to tell the truth, I have found to be a very gentlemanly fellow, at any rate as long as he is in other company than Piso's, or is by himself. This man met our young friend Piso who even then went about with eyebrows raised, and was not averse to his friendship, especially as the other eagerly sought him; he so far gave himself up to his company that he absolutely lived with him and scarcely ever left his side. I am speaking not to an ignorant audience, but, as I think, in an assembly of learned and accomplished gentlemen. . . . Now the Greek of whom I speak was refined (*perpolitus*) not only in philosophy but also in other accomplishments which Epicureans are said commonly to neglect; he composes, furthermore, poetry so witty, neat, and elegant, that nothing could be cleverer. . . . In response to request, invitation, pressure, he wrote reams of verse to Piso and about Piso, sketching to the life in lines of perfect finish all his lusts and immoralities, all his varied dinners and banquets, all his adulteries; and in these poems anyone who wishes can see the fellow's life relected as in a mirror. I would read you a copious selection from these (they have often been read and listened to before), were it not that I am afraid that, even as it is, my present subject is out of keeping with the traditions of this place, and at the same time I do not wish to cast any slur upon the character of their author.

No one in antiquity ever doubted whom Cicero meant. "Philodemum significat," comments Asconius (ad *In Pisonem* 68, adding that Philodemus was also the leading Epicurean philosopher of the day): so well known was he as an expert in the field of poetics. Later in the speech (74), in defense of his own poetry against Piso's criticism of it, Cicero indicates that he would defer to this critic's judgement about poetry, bidding Piso: "Ask your friend the Greek poet; he will recognize my figure of speech, and will feel no surprise at your lack of discernment."

   In the Renaissance, an age that might have hoped to add Philodemus' complete prose writings on poetics, rhetoric, and music to their canon of classical texts recovered from oblivion, Philodemus' elegant epigrams (known from the Greek anthologies) and his relationship with his famous patron Piso so intrigued readers that learned epigrams were forged around data gleaned from Cicero and other sources about his activities and circle of friends and associates (e.g. Epigram 9 Brunck, vol. 2, p. 85). In the mid-eighteenth century such a discovery accidentally came to pass: over a thousand papyrus rolls from a library consisting largely of Philodemus' writings were recovered from where they lay buried beneath the mud and ash of Vesuvius on the Bay of Naples. More recent developments, as outlined in the following chapters, in the wake of two hundred years of painstaking editorial work on the papyri, have occasioned the present volume.

Philodemus of Gadara (ca. 110–ca. 40 B.C.) shares with his contemporaries Lucretius and Horace the fact that all excelled in the production of poetry, while all three were (at least at some stage in their careers) students of Epicurean philosophy. Interest in the philosophical aspects and background of their poetry and poetic theory and method has increased dramatically in recent years. Thanks largely to the efforts of Marcello Gigante and his students, newly published and re-edited papyrus texts of Philodemus' treatises on poetry and the related subjects of rhetoric and music have reawakened scholarly awareness in the philosophical status and historical importance of these Epicurean treatises. From long stretches of shipwrecked text, a welter of reference numbers, critical signs, asterisks, dots, brackets, and exegetical expansions—a semblence of order begins to emerge. In spite of fluctuations in the text, and new readings supplanting old ones in the face of constantly deteriorating or disappearing papyri, the general trend is toward greater stability, clarification, and comprehension. The result is an improved text.

The recent discovery of copies of Ennius and Lucretius among the papyrus rolls recovered from Herculaneum, and the publication of an Oxyrhynchus papyrus showing that a collection of Philodemus' Epigrams circulated in Roman Egypt, hastens the demand for further investigation of Philodemus as a poet and literary theorist. Philodemus presents us with poetry of repute (he is often compared with Asclepiades and Meleager), together with a poetic theory that may be described as a precursor to modern formalist theories of poetry, one which contrasts markedly with those known to us from received literary sources (Plato, Aristotle, rhetorical technicians). As a literary critic, Philodemus embraced a formalism which denied both the moral utility of poems and separability of content from poetic form, while eschewing dogmatic claims for aesthetic criteria. In *On Piety* he presents he offers the earliest detailed exposition of the application of allegory in the interpretation of poetry, attacking the method and refuting the Stoics in their claims that traditional poetry embodies moral and physical truths about the world. At the same time, several of Philodemus' treatises (e.g., *On the Good King According to Homer*) provide case studies, especially for the benefit of Philodemus' patron Piso, of the convergence of the Epicurean and the traditionally poetic, of how traditional poetry like Homer's, for example, could be seen as providing moral and political paradigms and personal guidance for the potential ruler. How Philodemus proposed to square this position with standard Epicurean views on poetic practice, theology, participation in political affairs, and his own rejection of the moral utility of poetry are questions explored by most of the essays in this book.

To these ends the present volume has been designed to offer a critical survey of recent trends and developments in recent scholarship on Philodemus in particular and Hellenistic literary theory in general. The critical works from Herculaneum treated in the studies which follow, it should be stressed, were not selected and transmitted through the standard routes by which we have come to know and understand the literary criticism of, say, Plato or Aristotle. Rather, they were preserved at random and were not subject to the same criteria of selection for transmission as our canonical authors and texts. As such they provide a valuable control, by way of comparison with our received texts, and indications of the procedures and criteria for selection and preservation. In addition to the findings of individual contributors, the volume performs the modest task of collecting and synthesizing some most important work done on Philodemus' aesthetic works to date, from the *disegnatori* of the papyri in the late eighteenth and early nineteenth centuries to the editorial Renaissance of the last three decades. Wherever possible, an English translation of an otherwise difficult passage is given, and crucial problems of the text are reported in a footnote.

From time to time the authors of the studies which follow cite comparisons from other works preserved among the Herculaneum papyri. In light of the problems of working on the papyri set out in this volume, the reader will no doubt wonder how secure their texts are. Some degree of indulgence is clearly called for in dealing with texts which, in spite of two hundred years of editorial care, are still relatively uncharted water. We should be the first to admit that working on such a corpus without the benefit of a searchable concordance like TLG is, from the point of view of modern textual studies, at times like working in the dark. Other major *desiderata* remain unfilled: a photographic or digitized archive of the papyri; a replacement of the now outdated but fundamental study of the morphology of the Greek of the Herculaneum papyri by Crönert 1903; continuing investigation of the hands and palaeographical dating of the papyri building on Cavallo 1983 (ground-work on the Latin papyri from Herculaneum cannot even be said to be in its infancy); a comparative study of the physical typology of the rolls; a thoroughgoing analysis of Philodemus' prose style —not to mention reliable editions of many texts—in the absence of all of which the texts from Herculaneum remain infinitely re-editable.

The studies which follow were delivered in numerous earlier incarnations at various locations around the world; three were revised specifically for the present volume; four grew from presentations at a meeting of the American Philological Association. Chapters 2 and 3 were originally published elsewhere, and are reprinted here with minor changes by permission of their authors in order to make them grouped with like material. Three were commissioned specifically for the the present volume, as was the translation of *On Poems* 5 (Appendix 1). With characteristic generosity, Diskin Clay agreed to contribute an overview of the volume (Chapter 1) and discussed its contents with me.

A note of thanks is due to Wesley Trimpi, who first drew to my attention the importance of Philodemus' poetics, was presumptuous enough to entrust me with his questions, and has been nothing if not patient in awaiting the answers. On behalf of the contributors, I wish to extend thanks to Marcello Gigante, without whose assistance and expert advice this volume could not have been contemplated, for making available the resources of the Centro per lo studio dei papiri ercolanesi and the Officina dei papiri ercolanesi in the Biblioteca Nazionale in Naples; and to Richard Janko and the NEH Philodemus Translation Project. Individual chapters were greatly enhanced through the assistance of Francesca Longo Auricchio, Giovanni Indelli, and Gioia Rispoli. For expert typography we are indebted to Jeffrey Dean of Manchester, England. Over several years, Albert Henrichs, Elaine Fantham, André Laks, Anna Angeli, The Pinto Storey, Knut Kleve, Costantina Romeo, Mario Capasso, Annick Monet, Jürgen Hammerstaedt, Tiziano Dorandi, Daniel Delattre, an anonymous reader for Oxford University Press, and Daniella Reinhard all contributed an essential aspect of this book. Where special admiration and gratitude is due, I must not leave unacknowledged Cecilia Mangoni, who never saw the book between two covers, and whose precosity and memory flourish in its contents.

Barnard College, Columbia University   *D.O.*
and Center for Hellenic Studies, Washington D.C.
March 1994

Contents

Abbreviations

A & R	Atene e Roma
AAT	Atti della Accademia delle Scienze di Torino, Classe di Scienze morali, storiche e filologiche
A.Class.	Acta classica: proceedings ot the Classical Association of South Africa
AJPh	American Journal of Philology
ANRW	Aufstieg und Niedergang der römischen Welt
APAW	Abhandlungen der Preussischen Akademie der Wissenschaft, Berlin
ASNP	Annali della Scuola Normale Superiore di Pisa, Classe di Lettere e Filosofia
BICS	Bulletin of the Institute of Classical Studies of the University of London
BMCR	Bryn Mawr Classical Review
CA	Classical Antiquity
CErc	Cronache Ercolanesi
CFC	Cuadernos de Filologia clásica
CPh	Classical Philology
CQ	Classical Quarterly
CR	Classical Review
CSCA	California Studies in Classical Antiquity
G & R	Greece and Rome
GB	Grazer Beiträge
GRBS	Greek, Roman and Byzantine Studies
HV¹	Herculanensium Voluminum quae supersunt. Collectio Prior 1–11 (Naples 1799–1855)
HV²	Herculanensium Voluminum quae supersunt. Collectio Altera 1–11 (Naples 1863–76)
HSCPh	Harvard Studies in Classical Philology
JRS	Journal of Roman Studies
LCM	Liverpool Classical Monthly
MH	Museum Helveticum
NGG	Nachrichten von der Gesllschaft der Wissenschaften zu Göttingen, Philol.–Hist. Klasse
OSAP	Oxford Studies in Ancient Philosophy
P.Herc.	Catalogo dei papiri ercolanesi (Naples 1979)
P.Oxy.	The Oxyrhynchus Papyri (London 1898–present)
QUCC	Quaderni Urbinati di Cultura classica
RAAN	Rendiconti dell'Accademia di Archeologia, Lettere e Belle Arti di Napoli
REA	Revue des Études Anciennes
RE	Wissowa, G., Kroll, W., and Misttelhaus, K., edd., Paulys Realencyclopädie der classischen Altertumswissenschaft (Stuttgart 1893–1972)

REL	*Revue des Études Latines*
RhM	*Rheinisches Museum*
RIL	*Rendiconti dell'Istituto Lombardo, Classe di Lettere, Scienze morale e storiche*, Milan
R.Ph.	*Revue de philologie*
RSF	*Rivista critica di Storia della Filosofia*
SIFC	*Studi Italiani di Filologia Classica*
TAPA	*Transactions of the American Philological Association*
WJA	*Würzburger Jahrbücher für die Altertumswissenschaft*
WS	*Wiener Studien*
Zeits. f. philos. Forsch.	*Zeitschrift für Philosophische Forschung*
ZPE	*Zeitschrift für Papyrologie und Epigraphik*

Other abbreviations follow *L'annee philologique.*

Philodemus and Poetry

1

Framing the Margins of Philodemus and Poetry

Diskin Clay

An Epicurean Schism

Socrates alludes to an ancient quarrel between poetry and philosophy in his sustained assault on the cognitive status and ethical dangers of poetry in Book 10 of the *Republic* (607B). Plato knew well of what Socrates spoke, for according to one tradition Plato began his career as a poet, and the voice of poetry can be heard in almost every one of the dramatic dialogues Plato wrote. Nevertheless, he banished poetry from his heavenly city, since he heard no voice raised in her defense. But Aristotle soon appeared as the advocate of exiled poetry, and, by the end of the fourth century B.C., the quarrel between poetry and philosophy seems to have spent some of the energies that had fed it on the side of philosophy. Aristotle, who was himself a poet, turned his serious and sympathetic attention to the study of poets and poetry, and led poetry back into the city of philosophy after her brief banishment. But the situation becomes complicated once again with the emergence towards the middle of the first century B.C. of a poet who was also a philosopher. So far as we know, none of his contemporaries was shocked by Lucretius' decision to write poetry, but the students of Epicureanism in the twentieth century have discovered an antinomy in the precept and example of Lucretius' "master," Epicurus, and his powerful Latin hexameter poem of six books, *On the Nature of Things*.

For there to be an antinomy there must be a law, and this antinomy within Epicureanism is created by three extraordinary sentences of Epicurus, which were excerpted in antiquity, and are now difficult to integrate into a plausible context. They are:

1. "It is only the wise who can converse properly of music and poetry . . . . And the sage would not compose poems as an activity" (Diogenes Laertius 10.121b = Epicurus frr. 568 and 569 Usener)

2. Epicurus writing to Pythocles: "Hoist the sails of your ship and, my blessed man, steer clear of every form of conventional education" (Epicurus fr. 89 Arrighetti).

3. Epicurus writing to Apelles: "I count you blessed, Apelles, because you have started out pure of every form of conventional education" (Epicurus fr. 43 Arrighetti).

Other considerations have made this antinomy seem more extreme. One is Epicurus' practice. He was said to have avoided citations (from prose as well as from poetry) in his writings. But whoever reads his *Letter to Menoeceus, Kyriai Doxai,* or *Vatican Sayings,* will recognize quotations from the poetry of conventional education as well as sayings that recognize the wisdom of poets precisely in order to recast it. There is also the weight of the slighting remarks of Greeks and Romans of literary culture and traditional education directed against the uncultured Epicureans as a group. One example of attitude towards an uncouth Epicurus is Cicero's characterization of the poetry of Philodemus of Gadara in his *Against Piso* 70. And finally, there is Lucretius' fierce attachment to Epicurus and his emphatic claim to be following in his footsteps (*On the Nature of Things* 3.3–4)—a claim he makes in his own hexameter poetry and a claim that ignores the law decreeing the antinomy.

If the long road taken in the quarrel between philosophy and poetry (to change Socrates' terms) leads us to Lucretius, we find him in good company. One of the Epicureans whom we discover on this road is Lucretius' older contemporary, Philodemus of Gadara (ca. 110–ca. 40 B.C.). Philodemus was not only a critic of rhetorical theory, poetry, and music, but a poet himself. It is to his criticism and his poetry that this volume is dedicated. In the essays of *Philodemus and Poetry* the antinomy that has so exercised law abiding critics of Lucretius' *On the Nature of Things* is abolished at last and in its place we have a critical account of theories of poetry from the seemingly barren critical centuries between Aristotle's *Poetics* and Horace's *The Art of Poetry.*

The combined achievement of the essays of this volume is not to annul the long standing article of faith that Lucretius broke with Epicurean "orthodoxy" in writing his philosophical poem *On the Nature of Things.* Its combined achievement is that it draws our attention to the much more interesting critical debate that was being engaged by one of Lucretius' older contemporaries. At the same time, these essays place Lucretius' poem and Philodemus' epigrams and literary, rhetorical and even theological criticism in the large and largely unfamiliar context that allows us to appreciate the world in which poetry was discussed and written in the first century B.C. and in the two centuries preceding. We move decisively away from what had become the dead center of the well-intentioned casuistry justifying Lucretius' *On the Nature of Things* in terms of Epicurus' few and isolated pronouncements on poetry and traditional education (*paideia*) to take into our view the implicit poetics of Democritus in the first generation of Greek atomism, and finally to consider the consequences of an Epicurean poetics in the satires and odes of Horace. At the center of these investigations stands the figure of Philodemus, the critic and poet, whose poetry and criticism permit and provoke a fresh assessment of the criticism and practice of the Hellenistic age.

The Case of Epicurus

Epicurus' attitude towards poetry has a strange history. I have produced three of his comments on poetry and education as an introduction to the critical problem that has exercised critics of Lucretius. There are a few other pieces of evidence for this attitude, some of which report the attitudes of the Epicureans as a group (Epicurus fr. 229 Usener; Cicero, *De finibus* 2.4.12). But Epicurus' isolated, scattered, and global comments on poetry and education do not provide us with a developed opinion out of which an orthodoxy can develop. Nor does Epicurus' practice. He cites poetry in his more exoteric writings—Theognis (frr. 425/427 West), in his *Letter to Menoeceus* (Diogenes Laertius 10.126), and in his ethical sayings he recognizes the authority of poets in order to serve his own purposes: Solon in *Kyriai Doxai* 7 (Solon fr. 12 West); and even Sousarion's notorious lines on the necessity of living with women (*Vatican Saying* 9; cf. Sousarion fr. 1 West). The weight of the evidence for an orthodoxy deriving from Epicurus is pretty slight and unsupported by any larger theoretical foundation.

In her "Epicurean Poetics" (Chapter 2), Elizabeth Asmis considers the two pieces of evidence extracted from the excerpts in the short section of Diogenes Laertius illustrating Epicurus' conception of how the philosopher should live his life (10.117–121b). The claim that the philosopher alone can converse about music and poetry causes no problem; here the issue is theory not practice. The problem arises in the next sentence fragment Diogenes attaches to this. As David Sider suggests in his response to Asmis, this sentence originally had a protasis that read something like "[If a philosopher wanted tranquility,] he would not write poetry." There is one word still unaccounted for: the infinitive ἐνεργεῖν, which Usener emended to ἐνεργείᾳ.[1] This Asmis interprets plausibly as practicing energetically, that is, as a serious pursuit. In her view, Epicurus viewed poetry as an innocent form of entertainment (as heard or viewed), but of no educational value.

Energeia is likely to be the real issue for Epicurus. Sextus Empiricus reports that the Epicureans advertised that they could impart an art of living and "for this reason Epicurus used to say that philosophy was an activity (*energeia*) which, by words and arguments, produces the happy life" (fr. 219 Usener; cf. *Letter to Herodotus* 37). Words and arguments, but no indication of whether these words and arguments could take the form of poetry. Art for the Epicureans was a method of producing (ἐνεργοῦcα) what is beneficial to life (Epicurus fr. 227[b] Usener = 231 Arrighetti).

The results of Asmis' study (and Sider's response, Chapter 3) are disarming. No orthodoxy or reasons for holding a right opinion concerning poetry emerge from the testimony to Epicurus' attitude towards hearing and writing poetry. Indeed, it seems that Odysseus' words on poetry in the context of a banquet in Phaeacia (*Odyssey* 9.5–11) were cited by Epicurus with approval. The scattered injunctions concerning poetry and education in Epicurus bear the same relation to an Epicurean edict against

---

[1] Note, however, that the MSS reading τε ἐνεργεῖν is defended by J. Bollack, *La pensée du plaisir. Épicure: textes moraux, commentaires* (Paris 1975), 28, 45f. with 29: "Il est le seul, l'homme sage, qui serait capable de discuter justement des arts et de la poétique, et il ne fera pas agir les œuvres elles-mêmes."

the writing of poetry as the sentence concerning Onan in Genesis 38.9 bears to the prohibition against birth control. And both Epicurus' precept and practice left wide open the question of whether, "in some circumstances" (as he liked to say in his work *On Lifecourses*), poetry might serve not only as a source of entertainment but as a method of producing what is of benefit to life.

The Case of Lucretius

There is no doubt that the Roman Epicurean Lucretius recognized that his own Roman context and audience presented just such a situation. He tells us that he made his decision to convey his philosophy in poetry "not without good reason" (*id quoque non ab nulla ratione videtur*: *On the Nature of Things* 1.935). Part of the difficulty of communicating his philosophy to a Roman audience is the grim and unpalatable nature of its teachings; and part the "obscurity" of his theme of a world formed of atoms and void (1.943-50; 933-34). And, even as he begins his poem with an invocation to Venus, he recognizes that the elements of his philosophy might seem impious to the Roman novice (1.80-82). The Greek situation of Epicurus was radically different. In his own intellectual context, Epicurus had to demonstrate that an invisible atom could not exist; Lucretius had to demonstrate the existence of invisible bodies, and to cope, as he did brilliantly, with the poverty of his native language (*patrii sermonis egestas*, 1.832; 3.260). And Epicurus wrote in an age when the very name Epicurus did not cause alarm.

One of the many bright points Elizabeth Asmis makes in her "Epicurean Poetics" is that, in writing poetry radiant with its evocations of the sensuous world that illuminate the invisible workings of nature, Lucretius is following, in his own manner, Epicurus' insistence on clear expression (*caφήνεια*); to which one could add that Lucretius' followed Epicurus' advice on being aware of the primary or current meaning of words (cf. *Letter to Herodotus* 37 and the comment *iure*, "with good reason," on the rightness of the Roman term *perire*: 2.1132).

Michael Wigodsky pursues the case of Lucretius in his essay, "The Alleged Impossibility of Philosophical Poetry" (Chapter 5), and returns us to the views of Epicurus and Epicureans on poetry, mainly as these views are reported in uniformly hostile sources. Wigodsky's purpose is to address the strong form of the view that the Epicurean school was united in its belief that poetry was not a suitable vehicle for philosophy. And he notes the discovery of what might prove to be a copy of Lucretius' *On the Nature of Things* in the library of the Villa dei Papiri (published by Kleve 1989). This papyrus roll might bear silent witness to Philodemus' view of the matter. But it is not sure that Lucretius' poem was part of the library assembled there for study of Philodemus or his patron Lucius Calpurnius Piso Caesoninus. Before the library and villa were invested in the volcanic mud flowing off Vesuvius, the library had acquired an historical poem on the battle of Actium (*P.Herc.* 817, sometimes attributed to Gaius Rabirius).[2] Wigodsky centers not on Epicurus but on a passage

---

[2] The question of the authorship of this historical poem is taken up by Marcello Gigante in Gigante 1991.

from Book 5 of Philodemus' *On Poems*, where Philodemus judges that no poet had ever written or was likely to write a poem that would satisfy the philosophical requirement of utility. Philodemus' judgment is difficult to understand. In his *On Piety*, he quotes the philosophical poets Xenophanes and Parmenides, and he also refers to Hermarchus' tract *Against Empedocles* (542–46 and 997–1001 Obbink). If Philodemus had read Lucretius he would know that Lucretius made a strong claim on the utility of his sweet verse (*On the Nature of Things* 1.333; 4.25). Wigodsky explains Philodemus' attitude by invoking the empiricism of Epicurean science (vividly illustrated in Philodemus' own *On Methods of Inference*), which had the tendency to declare the unexampled as impossible. Thus, the limits of Philodemus' own experience of philosophical poetry constitute a frontier beyond which poetry cannot pass. He knew of no "common conception" (κοινὴ ἔννοια) of a philosophical poet. The interesting consequence of this reading of Philodemus' judgment on the impossibility of philosophical poetry is that Philodemus, who knew Empedocles and still other philosophical poets, must have judged that these philosophical poets did not offer the utility required by his rival critic.

The Critic of Critics

Rival critic is perhaps not an accurate term, for as the essays on Philodemus' *On Poems* make clear, it is difficult to individuate the positive critical theory of Philodemus himself in his criticism of other critics; and it is unclear too what Philodemus owed to his teacher, Zeno of Sidon, whom Philodemus acknowledges at *On Poems* 5 col. xxvi 19 Jensen (= col. xxix 19 Mangoni). In the absence of evidence, critics have retained the hope that he made his own position clear in the first book of his *On Poems*. But in Richard Janko's reconstruction of Philodemus' *On Poems* there is still no sign of a positive theory of poetry in Book 1. It is fair to say that when he published his edition of Book 5 of Philodemus' *On Poems* (Jensen 1923), Christian Jensen opened up a new chapter in the history of literary criticism in antiquity. This book has now been reedited by Cecilia Magnoni.[3] This book and the more scantily preserved Book 4 hold the focus of four of the studies of this volume. Book 4 of Philodemus' *On Poems* has just been published in a new edition by Richard Janko (Janko 1991a), who offers us here his reconstruction of this treatise as a whole.

Richard Janko provides us with a context for the four essays on Philodemus as a critic of critics. In his "Reconstructing Philodemus' On Poems" (Chapter 6), he attempts to reconstruct the character of Philodemus' *On Poems* as a whole, and for the first time we can consider an attempt at reconstruction which has some chance of success. What makes such an attempt possible now, when it was doomed at the time of Jensen's 1923 edition, is not the discovery of new rolls or fragments but the discovery, made independently by Daniel Delattre and Dirk Obbink, of how the papyri recovered in the excavations of the Villa dei Papiri in 1752–1754 were opened and recorded. Once a roll was cut in half, its contents, beginning with its end represented by two hemispheres of papyrus, were transcribed and numbered by draughtsmen

---

[3] Mangoni 1993. I give in brackets the equivalents for the new numeration of columns in her edition.

who had good eyes and steady hands but, in the case of the Neapolitans, no Greek. Janko gives an admirably clear account of what this method has meant for our recovery of the ordering of individual columns and fragments and what can be gained from the Delattre/Obbink method of reordering our fragments. The second advance in our understanding of the evidence comes from the study of the scribal hands at work in the texts preserved in the Villa dei Papiri by Guglielmo Cavallo (Cavallo 1983).

The Delattre/Obbink method of recovering the original order of columns in the papyri from Herculaneum reveals an order in the *disegni* or copies that is often, but not always, the reverse of the roll as a reader would unroll it from its beginning (and outer *scorza* or "bark") to its inmost end (*midollo* or "marrow"). Scribal hands also help identify and associate fragments that have been detached from their volumes. Some conclusions concerning the contents and sequence of themes of the five books (or more) of *On Poems* will probably change, as they have since Janko's 1991 article. But Janko has reconstructed a scaffolding on which to build and a structure that will allow us to house, at least provisionally, the scattered fragments of our knowledge of Hellenistic poetics before Philodemus. We can now speak confidently of Book 1 of Philodemus' *On Poems*. As it turns out, what we now know of Book 1 does not vindicate the long cherished hope that at the beginning of this ambitious book Philodemus would set out his own poetic theory in a positive fashion. He does not. Rather, we find him taking up Crates' criticisms of the *kritikoi*, whom Janko identifies as Heracleodorus and Pausimachus. We also have an argument for Book 4 of *On Poems* and possibly the first fragments that can be assigned to Books 2 and 3.

These essays on Philodemus, critic of critics, far transcend the borders of the criticism of poetry in the Hellenistic age, even as they offer a reconstruction of Philodemus' *On Poems* and a history of literary criticism between Aristotle's *Poetics* and Horace's *The Art of Poetry*. We encounter the early critics, Xenophanes and Heraclitus, both stern moralists with a sharp eye to the content of poetry; the atomist poetics and theory of language implicit in Democritus, explicit in Lucretius, and illustrated in the syntax of Horace; Aristotle not only of the *Poetics*, but of the *Rhetoric*, *De Anima*, and *Metaphysics*; and the critics of the Hellenistic age who had survived as mere names and, in one case (Heracleodorus, named in *On Poems* 5 col. xxi [xxiv] 28), not even that before Philodemus' *On Poems* was published.

One of these critics was Neoptolemus of Parium, once known only from Porphyrion's commentary on Horace's *The Art of Poetry* and the claim that Horace had followed Neoptolemus in his most salient precepts. In his "Content and Form in Philodemus: The History of an Evasion" (Chapter 7), James Porter offers us a delicate and surgical presentation of Neoptolemus' "aspectual" theory of poetics that allowed him to view poetry in three perspectives: *poema*, or choice and order of words in a poem, *poesis* or the conception or plot governing the poem, and the poet (*poetes*) of both. Porter excises Neoptolemus' theory from the enveloping tissue of Philodemus' criticism. His formal and autonomous analysis of poetry, which evokes but does not deploy the category of *poetes*, "the poet," is seen as a development of Aristotle's *Poetics*, which itself occludes from view the poet, the performance, and even the text, as it views the plot of tragedy in abstraction as if it were the "soul" of a play. Porter also calls attention to what Philodemus owes to Aristotle of the *Rhetoric* in his attachment to a doctrine of there being an appropriateness of style to a poet's matter.

In her "Philodemus on Censorship, Moral Utility, and Formalism in Poetry" (Chapter 8), Elizabeth Asmis allows us to appreciate the larval personalities brought back to life by the intensity of Philodemus' hostile gaze: the Stoics Ariston of Chios and Crates of Mallos, and a critic thoroughly canvassed by Philodemus, Heracleodorus. What emerges is that, for all his carping criticism of this critic, whose statements are never given in context, Philodemus and Heracleodorus seem to have shared the attitude that literary and moral judgments are distinct and that the "virtue" of a good poet could well be discovered in writing well and movingly about bad things. In its Greek context, and even in the context of Cicero's rhetorical writings, this view is paradoxical. This constitutes the Machiavellian paradox of ancient literary criticism (*se del male è licito dire bene*, *Principe* 9). To do bad well translates into writing well about bad things. In divorcing literary and ethical judgments, after a marriage of centuries' duration, our critics argue that Euripides, who portrays base characters uttering base thoughts, is a "better" poet than Chaeremon, who portrays good men unsuccessfully (*P.Herc.* 1081 fr. h 13–26 Sbordone).

As both Elizabeth Asmis and James Porter argue, Philodemus might have taken a less uncompromising view. In his *On the Good King According to Homer* (*P.Herc.* 1507, addressed to Lucius Calpurnius Piso), Philodemus leads Homer back from his long exile from Plato's Kallipolis to introduce him to the readers of Greek in Roman Italy. The question of censorship remains an issue for Philodemus, and it is addressed by Elizabeth Asmis in her essay (Chapter 8). Philodemus scornfully echoes the stern judgment of Heraclitus that Homer and Archilochus should be expelled from poetic competitions and beaten (presumably with their own staffs, fr. 22 B 42 Diels–Kranz = XXI Kahn) as he deals with the moralism of Heraclides of Pontus, who would drive out the most beautiful poems (*On Poems* 5 xxxiii [xxxvi] 8–22). Asmis and Porter engage this issue on two fronts: one is the history of moralism as the force driving literary judgments and the countervailing attempt, by critics such as Philodemus, Heracleodorus, and Eratosthenes, to emancipate poetry from the despotism of morality; the other front is drawn along the fault opened up by the critical distinction between style and content—an antithesis of Protean terminology that can be traced to Socrates' distinction between *logos* (subject matter) and *lexis* (the manner of treatment) in his primer on literary criticism (in *Republic* 3.392c). Both a poet's subject and his style leave him open to censure, because both can harm an audience.

An illuminating disagreement emerges on this front between James Porter and David Armstrong: the issue is how did Philodemus regard the relation between style and content, if indeed he drew such a distinction. It is clear to both that Philodemus did not consider style to be a garment or a sweetener (in the metaphors of an old critical vocabulary); he did insist that style (or composition) and meaning are inseparable in poetry (*On Poems* 5 xxv [xxviii] 33–xxvi [xxix] 7). The metrical rearrangement of the words of a poem by metastasis creates a new meaning. The issue that divides Porter and Armstrong is this: Porter detects in Philodemus a strong and clear trace of Aristotle's requirement of appropriateness (τὸ πρέπον), by which style must be appropriate to matter. Divine themes require a high style (cf. *On Music* 4 xxviii 5–14 Neubecker). But Armstrong looks in another direction to the atomist poetics of Democritus and Lucretius, which does not accommodate a doctrine of levels of style.

Shift the order of the letters of the Roman alphabet in a line of Lucretius' *On the Nature of Things* and you create a new world of meaning. By this linguistic atomism the word "word" can become the world and *lignum* (wood) *ignis* (fire). This is Lucretius' claim: *verum positura discrepitant res* (2.1018). The application of this principle to Lucretius' poetics and the poetics of Horace, both of the *Odes* and of *Satire* 1.4, comes as the last chapters of this volume (Chapters 11 and 12).

Philodemus on Rhetoric and Theological Poetry

David Blank and Dirk Obbink enlarge the scope of this volume in their contributions on "Philodemus and the Technicity of Rhetoric" (Chapter 9) and "How to Read Poetry about the Gods" (Chapter 10). They enlarge our frame for understanding Philodemus the critic of critics by concentrating on the issues he addresses in his *Rhetoric* and *On Piety*. In the *Rhetoric* Philodemus is engaged with the question: Is rhetoric an art or a mere knack? In his treatise *On Piety* he gives us a survey of poetic and philosophical conceptions concerning the gods and offers an alternative in Epicurean piety. In doing so, Philodemus allows us to recover Epicurus' approach to the anthropology of religious beliefs and his genealogy of theology. In his *On Piety* we have his study of the poetry in which theological beliefs were expressed and codified.

In an agreement that is not coincidental but reflects an Epicurean attitude towards human progress, both of these studies reveal something about Epicurus and Philodemus. What they reveal about Epicurus is that he viewed the early stages of human literacy as natural and as benign for human civilization in its infancy. He also accepted sophistic rhetoric as art; but he denied that status to political rhetoric–that is to speeches made in the assembly and in courts of law. Epicurus also found in a parallel fashion that the earliest conceptions of the gods were natural and clear: "The gods exist. For our knowledge of them is clear and distinct" (*Letter to Menoeceus* 123). It is only at the point that human beings attribute disturbingly human characteristics to these gods—anger, need, and, connected with need, gratitude—that in the evolution of society our conception of the gods undergoes a devolution.

David Blank canvasses Book 2 of Philodemus' *Rhetoric* and other Epicurean texts for an explanation of Philodemus' odd judgment that sophistic rhetoric is an art. As we have seen, for Epicurus and for the Epicureans, art is "a method of producing what is of advantage to life" (Epicurus fr. 205 Arrighetti). Most of our evidence for the Epicurean attitude towards the arts comes from Sextus Empiricus and the book of his treatise *Against the Professors* devoted to the "grammarians" (*Adv. math.* 1.49–53, 270, and 279–80). Some of Sextus' evidence must have come from Epicurus' treatise *On Gifts and Gratitude*, where Epicurus seems to have made a distinction between *grammatistike* and *grammatike*, that is, between the art of reading and writing and what we would call philology. One problem with the single minded absorption of the professional—and the scientist—is the upset that comes from failure—or from even success (cf. Diogenes of Oenoanda fr. 205 Smith). Philology also arrogates to itself judgments that belong to the philosopher. Blank points for an analogue to this conception of two stages of development, one primary and beneficial, the next secondary and harmful, to Lucretius' history of the development of human civilization (*On the Nature of Things* 5.1028–1457).

Which brings us to the art of poetry. Lucretius makes *gramatistike* or literacy a precondition for the emergence of poetry, just as Epicurus had made it the precondition for the transmission of any philosophical argument (*On the Nature of Things* 5.1444–45, Sextus *Adv. math.* 1. 49–53). He makes his own poetry the means to his reader's happiness (1.921–50; 4.1–21). David Blank's intricate argument brings us back to the problem of Lucretian heresy and a possibility never envisaged by Epicurus or even by Philodemus. Lucretius' own language was, as he confesses, rudimentary compared with the resources of philosophical Greek (1.136–45; 830–33; 3.258-60). As a poem, *On the Nature of Things* promised what one of Philodemus' rival critics, Heracleides of Pontos, asked for—utility. Its rhetoric was neither political (although it was addressed to a politician) nor forensic. Nor was it sophistic, except perhaps for the clarity it offered his reader. If it is the province of the philosopher to judge the thought contained in words set to music (Philodemus, *On Music* 4 col. ii 9–15 Neubecker), the *On the Nature of Things*, although composed by a philosopher, is not meant to be judged by a philosopher. It is meant, rather, to persuade—by a kind of rhetoric not yet named in Greek rhetorical theory—a non philosophical reader.

Dirk Obbink makes the attractive and original argument that the considerable interest in poetry to be detected in the Epicurean tradition is "a natural outcome of [Epicurus'] views on the development of human culture, particularly as regards formation of language and ideas about the gods." Obbink is particularly well qualified to speak on this subject. His argument is based on the arrangement he has recovered for the fragments of Philodemus' treatise *On Piety* 1, and his new edition of the difficult and reconstituted text of this precious document reveals the syntax of Philodemus' argument. In the Greek tradition, poetry was intimately connected with theology, and Aristotle spoke of poets as the first theologians (*Metaphysics* A 983^{b}29). In order to establish contact with early forms of religious belief, Epicurus and Epicureans after him consulted poetry. So much is clear from Lucretius' representation of how Greek poets portrayed the cult of Cybele: *haec veteres Graium docti cecinere poetae* (*On the Nature of Things* 2.600). After humans formed their first conceptions of the divine, there comes another stage, when philosophers reinforce a respect for justice and the social order by introducing a conception of angry gods who punish wrongdoing (Philodemus, *On Piety* 1176–1217 Obbink). Epicurus needed to have studied a peculiar form of poetry to have found a poetic articulation of this hypothesis. Dirk Obbink is right, I think, when he suggests that Epicurus knew this view from Critias' satyr play, the *Sisyphus* (*Tragicorum Graecorum fragmenta*, vol. 1, 43 F 19). It does not appear, at any rate, that the *Sisyphus* was digested in the philosophical prose of the fourth century and that Epicurus would have known of Critias' views indirectly. He in fact names him in his *On Nature* 12 (fr. [27] 2.8 Arrighetti).

This interest in poetry, so evident in Philodemus and Lucretius and now more evident in Epicurus, is not solely an autonomous feature of the Epicurean tradition. The Stoics also evinced a remarkable interest in poetry, and it is clear from this volume just how they were recognized by Philodemus. Their interest is dramatically illustrated by Chrysippus, who occasionally spoke in iambic verse and who quoted so much of Euripides' *Medea* in one of his books that one ancient reader called the book "Chrysippus' *Medea*" (Diogenes Laertius 7.179–81).[4]

By unrolling and piecing together the some 80 (out of 140) columns that contain Philodemus' review of theology in the first part of *On Piety*, Dirk Obbink affords us with more than a view of Philodemus' literary criticism. In *On Piety* Philodemus remains a critic of critics (the Stoic Ariston of Chios is named in the first surviving column); but he is also a critic of Greek theological poetry and in this he belongs to the same age as Lucretius. He is also a witness to Epicurus' interest in poetry.

Dirk Obbink's contribution to this volume reminds the reader of the recent and excellent editorial work that has made the volume possible: his own forthcoming edition of Philodemus' *On Piety* 1; Francesca Longo Aurrichio's edition of Philodemus, *Rhetoric* 2 (Longo 1977); A. J. Neubecker's edition of Philodemus, *On Music* 4 (Neubecker 1986); Daniel Delattre's edition of cols. 40*–109* of this same book (Delattre 1989); Richard Janko's edition of Book 4 of Philodemus, *On Poems* (Janko 1991a); and Cecilia Mangoni's edition of book 5 of Philodemus, *On Poems* (Mangoni 1993). Philodemus' *On Poems* 5 and its translation for this volume by David Armstrong below (Appendix 1) point us to Horace.

Horace's mosaic syntax

Steven Oberhelman and David Armstrong's development of Armstrong's "The Impossibility of Metathesis: Philodemus and Lucretius on Form and Content in Poetry" in "Satire as Poetry and the Impossibility of Metathesis in Horace's Satires" (Chapters 11 and 12). On the surface of what Lucretius says about his own poetry and the poetry of cult and erotic hyperbole (*On the Nature of Things* 1.921–50; 2.600–660; 4.1153–70) there appears to be a strict separation and antithesis between poetry and content. Lucretius presents his verse as a coat of honey on the rim of a cup containing bitter medicine. He does not follow Horace's prescription and mix the sweet and the useful, but he coats the utility of his Epicurean teaching with the sweet honey of the Muses (1.934–50). Attracted by this coating his reader will be brought to perceive the usefulness of the doctrine disguised by this sweet surface (4.24–25). But these are not the only terms for presenting the relation between poetry and content employed by Lucretius. Heraclitus falls under his attack for the dissonance between the obscure content of his thought and its gaudy, deceptive surface. It might be significant that Lucretius' metaphor for the inane appeal of Heraclitus' style confuses sound and sight: his words please the ear as they strike it and are daubed with a charming ring (*quae belle tangere possunt / auris et lepido quae sunt fucata sonore*, 1.643–44). This criticism has the ring of Philodemus arguing against the euphonists. Despite the deceptive terms Lucretius chooses to describe his own poetry, he expects a clear and direct relation between the thought and expression of a philosopher. His Calliope wears no cosmetics.

---

[4] The Stoic interest in poetry is now well illustrated by Martha C. Nussbaum in the Stoic chapters of her *The Therapy of Desire: Theory and Practice in Hellenistic Ethics* (Princeton 1994).

In his first essay, Armstrong argues against the venerable representation of poetry as clothing that can be removed to reveal its content, a content that is then open to interrogation—a view represented by Socrates in Book 10 of the *Republic*. In this final discussion of imitation (*mimesis*), Socrates proposes to strip a poem of its poetic clothing and he speaks in another metaphor of the "sweetened Muse" (601B and 607A). Armstrong argues convincingly that there is an atomist poetics implicit in *On the Nature of Things* that is antithetical to the mode of analysis of the "critics." Change the letters within a word, add to them, subtract from them, or change the order of words, and the result is not only a new sound apparent to the ears but a new meaning apparent to the mind. In this atomist poetics of *On the Nature of Things*, sound and meaning are strictly associated. Add or remove letters in a line of verse and the word wood (*lignum*) becomes fire (*ignis*, 1.814–29 and 911–12, for which Pliny offers an interesting parallel at *Natural History* 1.37.42).

In their collaborative essay on "Satire as Poetry and the Impossibility of Metathesis in Horace's Satires" Oberhelman and Armstrong show this atomistic poetics at work in a passage from Horace, *Satires* 1.4.39–52, where Horace presents himself as a poet and engages his reader in a conversation on poetry and poetics that will conclude in the last satire of this book (1.10) and his *The Art of Poetry* (addressed fittingly to Piso's descendants). In this final essay on Philodemus as a critic, the topic of the poet (*poetes*) and his art and nature are addressed in the last in a series of disjunctions between form and content, style and subject, *ars* and *ingenium*. These disjunctions are all collapsed in a poetics that is strikingly unitarian. And the reader wonders with Rostagni (in his *Scritti minori* II) if Cicero did not read his excellent and learned friend's treatise *On Poems* (cf. *De finibus* 2.119). If he did, he remained friendly, but unpersuaded that *ars* and *ingenium* were inseparable, for he agrees with his brother Quintus' judgment of Lucretius, which is cast in the disjunctive style: *Lucreti poemata, ut scribis, ita sunt: multis luminibus ingenii, multae tamen artis (Ad Quintum fratrem* 2.9).

Poema facit

Like Lucretius, Philodemus was a poet as well as an Epicurean. But his epigrams seem to belong to another universe from that occupied by his philosophical writings and criticism. If a copy of Lucretius' *On the Nature of Things* was shelved in the Villa dei Papiri with the works of Philodemus on poetry that have been unrolled in this volume (see Kleve 1989, cf. id. 1990), no slim volume of Philodemus' epigrams has yet been discovered there. Cicero's urbane and forensic representation of Philodemus' poetry is worth reviewing, for it sets David Sider's presentation of Philodemus' poetics at work in his epigrams in a context that is now familiar: that of antinomy ("The Epicurean Philosopher as Hellenistic Poet," Chapter 4). In his speech against Philodemus' patron, Lucius Calpurnius Piso Caesoninus, Cicero works on the theme of Piso's disreputable companion and tutor, an Epicurean he never names in his *Against Piso*. Unlike other Epicureans, this Epicurean writes poetry. Interestingly, Cicero uses the term *poema* and stresses first Philodemus' style: *poema porro facit ita festivum, ita concinnum, ita elegans, nihil ut fieri possit argutius.* He then turns in the manner of the moralist to consider the content of Philodemus' poetry. We would not censure him for being corrupt, scandalous, impure; the proper terms of criticism are milder: he is one of your Greeks, a flatterer, a poet. He goes on, in his best invective manner, to catalogue the content of Philodemus' poetry, which was the mirror to Piso's debauched life and household: *omnis . . . libidines, omnia stupra, omnia cenerarum genera conviviorumque, adulteria denique eius delicatissimis versibus expressit* (*Against Piso* 70–71). The disjunction between style and subject matter could not be greater; and this might have been Cicero's point.

But David Sider considers one of Philodemus' extraordinary feasts and one group of extraordinary guests that seem to have impressed Cicero, and he demonstrates in his reading of Philodemus' invitation poem to Piso (*Palatine Anthology* 11.44) just how serious and allusive the Epicurean Philodemus can be as a poet. The occasion is the feast of Epicurus, held by Epicureans on the twentieth of each month. The guests are Epicureans, who will provide the Roman aristocrat Piso dinner conversation more enchanting than the song of the Sirens (which, as we have seen, fascinated Epicurus himself); and Piso is being invited for one of his annual visits. Sider also demonstrates how deep and eclectic Philodemus' literary and philosophical culture is in still other poems, and suggests how he should be read as a poet not only of literary but also of philosophical allusion.

One of Philodemus' allusions is striking for a poet of Philodemus' critical attitudes and for an Epicurean. By casting the object of his epigrammatic passions in the role of Xanthippe (and also Xantho), Philodemus casts himself in the role of Socrates, the very critic whose conception of poetry was in so many respects antagonistic to his own. His Xanthippe epigrams (1, 11, 14, and 17 in Gow and Page 1968) might have had an unintended consequence. By implicitly casting himself in the role of Socrates, Philodemus might have inspired Catullus to cast him as Socration in his infamous libel of Piso and two of his close companions: *Porci et Socration, duae sinistrae / Pisonis, scabies famesque mundi* (Catullus c. 47). So much for another disjunction—that between life and poetry.

> nam castum esse decet pium poetam
> ipsum, versiculos nihil necesse est.
> (c. 16.5-6)

But this was not Cicero's forensic manner of reading Philodemus.

2

Epicurean Poetics

Elizabeth Asmis

If one were to ask people to rank the contributions made by the Epicureans to philosophy, I would not be surprised if poetic theory were near the bottom of most people's lists, or altogether missing, whereas poetry itself might well be at the top. The ancient quarrel between philosophy and poetry seems to have played itself out in an extreme paradox in Epicureanism. Epicurus has the reputation of being the most hostile to poetry of any Greek philosopher. But some of his later followers were clearly devoted to poetry, and one of them, Lucretius, achieved a remarkable reconciliation between philosophy and poetry.

In this paper, I propose to investigate the road between Epicurus and Lucretius. What were Epicurus' views, and to what extent did his followers adopt, modify, or jettison his views? We know that in other areas Epicurus' followers went to great lengths to show that their views were consistent with those of their leader. The more innovative they were, it seems, the more they insisted on their orthodoxy. The problem of orthodoxy became especially acute at the time when Zeno of Sidon was head of the Epicurean school at Athens, about the end of the second century to the early seventies B.C.[1] The period of Zeno and his immediate followers is also a time when the Epicureans showed an especially strong interest in poetry. Zeno and his student Philodemus of Gadara both offered comprehensive criticisms of poetic theories; and while Lucretius' great poem on the nature of the universe overshadows all contemporary poetry, Philodemus' epigrams are among the most elegant examples of this genre. There are just a few, well known bits of evidence about Epicurus' views on poetry. But these testimonies, in conjunction with the much larger and partially

---

[1] The problem of orthodoxy is well attested in the areas of epistemology and ethics, as well as rhetoric and poetry. On epistemology, see E. Asmis, *Epicurus' Scientific Method* (Ithaca 1984), esp. 220–24. When Zeno of Sidon was head of the Epicurean school there was a very acrimonious debate among Epicureans on who observed Epicurus' teachings about whether rhetoric is a craft. This debate is discussed in detail by David Sedley (Sedley 1989); see also Asmis 1990a, 2400-2. In his work Περὶ παρρηςίας (fr. 45.8–11 Olivieri), Philodemus sums up the loyalty of Epicurus' followers in a statement which is virtually an oath of loyalty: καὶ τὸ cυνέχον καὶ κυρι|ώτ[α]τον, Ἐπικούρωι, κα|θ' ὃν ζῆν ἡ⟨ι⟩ρήμεθα, πει|θαρχήcομεν ("the basic and most important [principle] is that we will obey Epicurus, according to whom we have chosen to live").

unfamiliar body of evidence concerning the later period, suggest that there is greater continuity between Epicurus and his followers than has been thought.

The allegorist Heraclitus (about the first century A.D.) pairs Epicurus with Plato as a detractor of Homer, while charging him with deriving his doctrines from the great poet. Heraclitus accuses Epicurus of condemning all of poetry, not just Homer; and he describes Epicurus as "purifying himself (ἀφοσιούμενος) from all of poetry at once as a destructive lure of fictitious stories."[2] He also charges that, although Epicurus condemned poetry, he was a "Phaeacian" philosopher who, by misinterpreting Odysseus' words to Alcinous, stole from Homer the notion that the supreme good is pleasure.[3] Another late author, Athenaeus, associates Epicurus with Plato as someone who expelled Homer from cities.[4]

But Epicurus' hostility to poetry is not as simple a matter as Heraclitus and Athenaeus make out. According to Heraclitus, the Homeric words that Epicurus misinterpreted were:

> . . . ὅταν εὐφροσύνη μὲν ἔχῃ κατὰ δῆμον ἅπαντα,
> δαιτυμόνες δ᾽ ἀνὰ δώματ᾽ ἀκουάζωνται ἀοιδοῦ
> τοῦτό τί μοι κάλλιστον ἐνὶ φρεσὶν εἴδεται.

When joy possesses all the people,
and banqueters throughout the house listen to the singer,
this seems to my mind most beautiful.[5]

Heraclitus has omitted three lines, coming just after mention of the singer, in which Odysseus describes the abundance of food and drink at the banquet. The whole passage is:

> οὐ γὰρ ἐγώ γέ τί φημι τέλος χαριέστερον εἶναι
> ἢ ὅτ᾽ ἐυφροσύνη μὲν ἔχῃ κατὰ δῆμον ἅπαντα,
> δαιτυμόνες δ᾽ ἀνὰ δώματ᾽ ἀκουάζωνται ἀοιδοῦ
> ἥμενοι ἑξείης, παρὰ δὲ πλήθωσι τράπεζαι
> σίτου καὶ κρειῶν, μέθυ δ᾽ ἐκ κρητῆρος ἀφύσσων
> οἰνοχόος φορέῃσι καὶ ἐγχείη δεπάεσσι·
> τοῦτό τί μοι κάλλιστον ἐνὶ φρεσὶν εἴδεται εἶναι.

For I say that there is no more pleasant fulfilment than when joy possesses all the people, and banqueters throughout the house listen to the singer, sitting next to each other, and alongside the tables are full of bread and meat, and the wine-pourer draws drink from the mixing-bowl and brings it and pours it into cups. This seems to my mind to be most beautiful.[6]

According to Heraclitus, Epicurus failed to notice that Odysseus was driven by necessity to praise his host's way of life. What Heraclitus fails to notice himself is that, in the very lines he has cited, Odysseus is praising the joy of listening to the songs of a poet.

---

[2] *Homeric Problems* 79 and 4 (= Epicurus fr. 229 Usener), including at 4: ἅπασαν ὁμοῦ ποιητικὴν ὥσπερ ὀλέθριον μύθων δέλεαρ ἀφοσιούμενος.

[3] *Homeric Problems* 79 = partly at fr. 229 Usener.   [4] *Deipnosophistae* 5.187c = fr. 228 Usener.

[5] *Homeric Problems* 79. These lines correspond to *Odyssey* 9.6–7 and 11.   [6] *Odyssey* 9.5–11.

Odysseus' words to Alcinous are among the most famous passages of poetry in antiquity.[7] Because they were thought to propose a view of the goal ($\tau\acute{\epsilon}\lambda o\varsigma$) of life, they received much philosophical attention. Plato cited only Homer's description of food and drink, omitting the lines dealing with the singer, to illustrate the inadequacy of Homer's ethics.[8] Aristotle cited only the lines dealing with the singer as evidence that Homer believed that music is an appropriate leisure time activity.[9] Later authors associated the whole passage with Epicurean hedonism. Some, like Heraclitus, accused Epicurus explicitly of taking his hedonism from Homer.[10] More perceptively, Seneca derides the attempt to turn Homer into an Epicurean or any other philosopher. Seneca also describes the ostensible "Epicurean Homer" as one who praises peace, banquets, and songs.[11] Implicitly, the entire later tradition associates the full measure of Homeric conviviality, including poetic entertainment, with Epicureanism.

Although the charge of plagiarism is hardly plausible, it is not implausible, as Bignone has argued, that Epicurus cited Odysseus' words in his own writings.[12] Despite his reputation for being unlearned, Epicurus was not averse to citing verses for his own ends. Epicurus seems to have quoted a couple of verses from Sophocles' *Trachinians* to illustrate his claim that we naturally avoid pain.[13] He might well have cited the famous Homeric verses to explain his complementary doctrine that we all naturally seek pleasure. By doing so, he would have staked a position within a philosophical tradition; nor need he have imputed any special insight to either Odysseus or Homer. If Epicurus did cite the passage, it is unlikely that he excluded poetic entertainment from the life of pleasure.

Plutarch is our main witness for Epicurus' attitude to poetry. He subordinates the

---

[7] The history of these verses, dubbed Homer's "golden verses," is discussed by E. Kaiser, "Odyssee-Szenen als Topoi," *MH* 21 (1964), 109–136 and 197–224, esp. 213–23.

[8] *Republic* 3.390A–B.   [9] *Politics* 1338^{a}27–30.

[10] These references have been gathered by E. Bignone, *L'Aristotele perduto e la formazione filosofica di Epicuro*, vol. 1 (Florence 1936), 269-70; see also Kaiser (above, n. 7), 220-21. Athenaeus (*Deipnosophistae* 12.513A–C), quoting the entire passage at *Odyssey* 9.5–12, writes that "Odysseus seems to be the leader for Epicurus' notorious pleasure"; then he cites a defense of Odysseus similar to that of Heraclitus. Likewise, ps-Plutarch (*On the Life and Poetry of Homer* 2.150) claims that Epicurus was misled by Odysseus' words to propose pleasure as the goal of happiness. A scholiast on *Odyssey* 9.28 and Eustathius (p. 1612, 10) also claim that Epicurus took the goal of pleasure from Homer. Exceptionally, the scholiast approves of Epicurus' notion of the goal, with the observation that he extended the Homeric goal to all circumstances of life.

[11] Seneca (*Epistles* 88.5): *nam modo Stoicum illum faciunt . . . modo Epicureum, laudantem statum quietae civitatis et inter convivia cantusque vitam exigentis* ("they sometimes make him a Stoic . . ., sometimes an Epicurean who praises the condition of a government that is at peace and passes life among banquets and songs"). In a lighter vein, Lucian (*Parasite* 10–11), quoting "banqueters sitting next to each other" and "alongside the tables are full of bread and meat," suggests that Epicurus stole from Homer the goal of the parasite.

[12] Bignone (above, n. 10), 270-73 holds that Epicurus cited the verses polemically to show, against Aristotle, that the type of enjoyment praised by Odysseus is not the supreme good; instead, Bignone proposes, Epicurus wished to show that the supreme pleasure is the absence of pain and anxiety, that is, catastematic pleasure. In response to Bignone, Francesco Giancotti argues that Epicurus cited the verses in partial agreement with Odysseus; for Epicurus approves of the kinetic pleasure of listening to songs and consuming food and drink, even though this is not the supreme good, catastematic pleasure (F. Giancotti, "La poetica epicurea in Lucrezio, Cicerone ed altri," *Ciceroniana* 2 [1960], 67–95, esp. 83-84). A passage in *P.Herc.* 1012 (see below, n. 18) suggests that Epicurus cited Odysseus' words as expressing a commonplace opinion.   [13] Diogenes Laertius 10.137 (= fr. 66 Usener).

charge that Epicurus shunned poetry to the general charge that he rejected all intellectual pleasures. In his treatise *That Epicurus Actually Makes a Pleasant Life Impossible,* Plutarch alleges that both Epicurus and Metrodorus berated their intellectual forebears, including the poets, in the most abusive language. Two terms cited by Plutarch, apparently of the milder sort, are "poetic confusion" (ποιητικὴ τύρβη) and "the foolish statements (μωρολογήματα) of Homer."[14] Plutarch accuses the Epicureans of rejecting both historical investigation, including the study of poetry, and the mathematical studies of geometry, astronomy, and harmonics.[15] As an example of Epicurean philistinism, Plutarch cites a statement from Metrodorus' *On Poems*: "Don't worry," Metrodorus said, about admitting that you don't even know "on whose side Hector was, or the first lines of Homer's poetry, or the middle."[16] Plutarch also reports that the Epicureans urged their students to "hoist sail" in order to flee intellectual pleasures. In particular, he notes, Epicurus' entire entourage urged Pythocles not to "envy the so-called liberal education"; and they praised a certain Apelles for having kept himself entirely "pure" (καθαρόν) of learning.[17] These admonitions can be traced to Epicurus' own writings. Epicurus urged Pythocles in a letter: "Flee all education, hoisting sail."[18] According to Athenaeus, Epicurus' words to Apelles were: "I call you blessed, Apelles, because you set out for philosophy, pure of all education." Athenaeus adds that Epicurus was himself "uninitiated in the educational curriculum."[19]

The sail boat in Epicurus' *Letter to Herodotus* is an allusion to the boat in which Odysseus sailed past the Sirens.[20] In another treatise, *How a young person should listen to poets*, Plutarch explicitly associates the Epicurean hoisting of sails with the Homeric episode by asking: Should we protect the young against the deceptions of poetry by plugging their ears with wax (as happened to Odysseus' men), forcing them to flee poetry "by hoisting the sails of an Epicurean boat"; or should we protect them by binding them and straightening their judgment with reason (Odysseus' choice)?[21] The same Siren imagery is implicit in the description of poetry as a "de-

---

[14] 1087A = fr. 228 Usener.   [15] 1092c–1094d.   [16] 1094d–e.

[17] 1094d, including: ὅπως οὐ ζηλώσει τὴν ἐλευθέριον καλουμένην παιδείαν.

[18] 10.6 (= fr. 163 Usener): παιδείαν δὲ πᾶσαν, μακάριε, φεῦγε τἀκάτιον ἀράμενος. Quintilian (12.2.24) also quotes this advice. It is possible, as Bignone (above, n. 10), 282–83, has suggested, that Epicurus included a polemic against Homer in the same letter to Pythocles. *PHerc.* 1012, whose author was conjectured by Crönert (W. Crönert, *Kolotes und Menedemos* [Munich 1906]) to be Demetrius the Laconian, contains an address to Pythocles, together with an attack on Homer, as follows (col. xlviii 8–13): Ὅμη|ρος μὲν γὰρ οὐδὲν πλῆον | περὶ τῶν τοιούτων διέ|γνωκεν ἥπερ ο[ἱ] λοι[πο]ὶ ἀν|-θ[ρω]ποι, ἡμεῖς δ[έ], ὦ Πυθό|κλ[εις . . . ("Homer recognized nothing more about such matters than the rest of mankind, but we, Pythocles . . ."). The text is fr. 70 of Enzo Puglia's new edition of fragments in Puglia 1988; cf. id., "Nuove Letture nei PHerc. 1012 e 1786 (Demetrii Laconis opera incerta)," *CErc* 10 (1980), 25-53 esp. 49. Bignone argued that Demetrius excerpted not only the address to Pythocles from Epicurus' letter (as is generally agreed), but probably also the preceding remarks on Homer. Puglia's new text strongly supports this suggestion. The issue under discussion is Homer's notion of enjoyment, as indicated by the word [ἀπό]|λαυσιν at lines 4–5. The claim that Homer knew no more than the rest of mankind also occurs in the arguments against grammar which are attributed by Sextus Empiricus "especially" to the Epicureans (*Adv. math.* 1.285 and 299, see below).

[19] *Deipnosophistae* 13.588A (= fr. 117 Usener), including: μακαρίζω cε, ὦ Ἀπελλῆ, ὅτι καθαρὸς πάςης παιδείας ἐπὶ φιλοσοφίαν ὡρμήςας.

[20] The Sirens' song was commonly taken to symbolize the attractiveness of learning in general and poetry in particular; see Kaiser 1964 (above, n. 7), 109–36.   [21] *De poetis audiendis* 15D.

structive lure," which the allegorist Heraclitus attributes to Epicurus. Heraclitus' entire description of Epicurus as "purifying himself" (ἀφοςιούμενος) from this lure seems to be based on the same well known core of testimonies cited by Plutarch and others. The purity demanded by Epicurus has a religious aspect; and Athenaeus responds to it by calling Epicurus "uninitiated."

Plutarch shows that Epicurus' opposition to poetry is part of a larger issue, education. Like Plato in the *Republic*, Epicurus believed that the whole traditional educational system, with its teaching of Homer and other poets, was a corrupting influence that prevented a person from achieving happiness. Epicurus also rejected the alternative curriculum proposed by Plato in the *Republic,* with its purged poetry and rigorous program of mathematics. Epicurus aimed to replace both types of education with Epicurean philosophy. Accordingly, he assured his students that it was an advantage not to be educated; and, unlike most philosophers, he welcomed the uneducated, both young and old, to his school.

But Plutarch's testimony, too, is ambivalent. Embedded within his attack is evidence that Epicurus was, in part, hospitable to poetry. On the one hand, Plutarch notes, Epicurus claims in his *Questions* (Διαπορίαι) that the wise person is a "lover of sights (φιλοθέωρον) and enjoys hearing and seeing Dionysiac performances (χαίροντα . . . ἀκροάμαςι καὶ θεάμαςι Διονυςιακοῖς) as much as anyone"; on the other hand, Epicurus does not permit musical or philological inquiry even over drink, but in his work *On Kingship* (Περὶ βαςιλείας) "recommends to even music-loving (φιλομούςοις) kings that they should put up with military narratives and vulgar jesting at parties rather than with lectures on musical and poetic problems."[22] Plutarch thinks that these two positions are contradictory: how can the Epicureans care so much about musical performances, if they shut their ears to discussions about musical and poetic matters, such as musical modes, poetic styles, and so on?[23]

In a manner that is typical of him, Plutarch has juxtaposed two excerpts that are not really in conflict with each other. In his *Questions*, Epicurus challenges a distinction made by Plato in the *Republic*.[24] Socrates argues that ordinary lovers of sights (φιλοθεάμονες) and lovers of hearing (φιλήκοοι) differ from philosophers (φιλόςοφοι) in that the former chase the sights and sounds of sensible things, whereas philosophers seek the wisdom of knowing things in themselves. The lovers of sounds, especially, are strangely unphilosophical, as Glaucon observes: they are unwilling to participate in discussion and "run around all the Dionysiac festivals" instead, "as though they had rented out their ears to listen to all the choruses." True philosophers, Socrates proposes, are lovers of sight in the special sense of being

---

[22] *That Epicurus Actually Makes a Pleasant Life Impossible* 1095c (= frr. 5 and 20 Usener): φιλο-θέωρον μὲν ἀποφαίνων τὸν ςοφὸν ἐν ταῖς Διαπορίαις καὶ χαίροντα παρ' ὀντινοῦν ἕτερον ἀκροά-μαςι καὶ θεάμαςι Διονυςιακοῖς, προβλήμαςι δὲ μουςικοῖς καὶ κριτικῶν φιλολόγοις ζητήμαςιν οὐδὲ παρὰ πότον διδοὺς χώραν, ἀλλὰ καὶ τοῖς φιλομούςοις τῶν βαςιλέων παραινῶν ςτρατηγικὰ διηγήματα καὶ φορτικὰς βωμολοχίας ὑπομένειν μᾶλλον ἐν τοῖς ςυμποςίοις ἢ λόγους περὶ μουςι-κῶν καὶ ποιητικῶν προβλημάτων περαινομένους. ταυτὶ γὰρ ἐτόλμηςεν γράφειν ἐν τῷ Περὶ βαςιλείας . . . . Diogenes Laertius (10.120) paraphrases the first claim as follows: μᾶλλόν τε εὐφραν-θήςεςθαι τῶν ἄλλων ἐν ταῖς θεωρίαις ("[the wise person] delights more than others in spectacles").

[23] *That Epicurus Actually Makes a Pleasant Life Impossible* 1095E–1096c.

[24] *Republic* 5.475D–476B. This attack on Plato is further evidence that Epicurus studied Plato's dialogues.

lovers of the sight of truth.[25] Using φιλοθέωρος as a synonym for φιλοθεάμων, Epicurus responds to Plato's distinction by contending that the wise person loves the sights and sounds of Dionysiac festivals as much as anyone.[26] The Epicurean wise person does not forsake the objects of sense perception in the pursuit of truth; for wisdom consists precisely in enjoying sensory experiences and having correct opinions about them. Epicurus agrees that the wise person loves the sight of truth, but insists that the love of truth encompasses the love of visual spectacles and auditory performances.

In this confrontation with Plato, Epicurus gives clear approval to the enjoyment of musical and poetic performances. In the second half of Plutarch's indictment, Epicurus rejects an entirely different use of leisure time, listening to lectures on musical and poetic problems. These are lectures given by musicologists and grammarians or literary "critics," experts who, according to Epicurus, make no contribution to happiness.[27] By contrast, Epicurus approves of philosophical inquiry about music and poetry. According to Diogenes Laertius, Epicurus held that the wise person "alone would discuss music and poetry correctly."[28] Epicurus himself wrote a book, not extant, *On Music;* and his friend Metrodorus, as we saw, wrote *On Poems.*[29] In advising kings to put up with military talk and buffoonery at parties rather than with musical and literary criticism, Epicurus does not advocate the former kind of entertainment, but suggests merely that it is more tolerable than the latter. Military talk, we may guess, might be useful for kings, even though a party is hardly the proper occasion for it, and buffoonery might be pleasant, whereas musicology and philology are neither. In his work *Symposium,* Epicurus showed that appropriate subjects of discussion at parties are indigestion, fever, wine, and sexual intercourse—all topics that are useful for party-goers to know about.[30] But Epicurus does not imply here or elsewhere that one should fill one's leisure time with nothing but useful discussion. It is significant that he does not advise "music-loving" kings to give up music; he urges them only not to waste their time listening to learned discussions about it.

---

[25] 475D–E.

[26] Pierre Boyancé suggests that Epicurus' attitude to Dionysiac festivals is a concession to established religious practice, rather than an endorsement of poetic performances: the Epicurean, he proposes, will participate in religious festivals, even though he does not share the ordinary person's beliefs (P. Boyancé, "Lucrèce et la poésie," *Revue des Etudes Anciennes* 49 [1947] 88-102, esp. 91-92); cf. Dirk Obbink, "*POxy.* 215 and Epicurean religious ΘΕΩΡΙΑ," *Atti del XVII Congresso Internazionale di Papirologia* (Naples 1984), 607-19. Although the terms φιλοθέωρος, θεωρία, and θέαμα can apply to religious spectacles, there is no reason to suppose that their scope is restricted to religious worship here. As was customary, Epicurus regularly uses forms of θεωρ- to refer to visual or mental viewing in general.

[27] Plutarch pairs the "critics" with the musicologists (*That Epicurus Actually Makes a Pleasant Life Impossible* 1095C, see n. 22 above). There is a fine line between "grammarians" and "critics." As Sextus Empiricus shows (*Adv. math.* 1.93), grammar included poetic criticism. Some who called themselves "critics" held that grammar is subordinate to "criticism"; among them, Crates held that, unlike the grammarian, the "critic" must be experienced in "all knowledge of speech (λογικῆς ἐπιστήμης)" (*Adv. math.* 1.79).   [28] Diogenes Laertius 10.121.

[29] Another friend of Epicurus, Colotes, discussed poetry in his work *Against Plato's Lysis.* It is difficult to extract any information from the few relevant fragments; see Crönert 1906 (above, n. 18), 6-12, and A. Mancini, "Sulle opere polemiche di Colote," *CErc* 6 (1976), 1-67, esp. 61-63.

[30] Frr. 56–63 Usener.

Although Plutarch regards Epicurus' notion of entertainment as incredibly crude, his testimony indicates that Epicurus had a clear-cut position. Epicurus distinguished between two uses of poetry, education and entertainment, and condemned poetry wholesale as education, while welcoming it as entertainment. Plutarch charges Epicurus with just one type of inconsistency: excluding musical and literary learning from the appreciation of music and poetry. But Epicurus' dichotomy suggests a more serious inconsistency. How can the two uses of poetry, education and entertainment, be compartmentalized so neatly as Epicurus supposes? Is it possible for a person to derive enjoyment from poetic performances without being contaminated by morally bad subject matter? Plato did not think so. Epicurus seems to believe optimistically that one can. Presumably, Epicurus held that it is a sufficient protection to come to a poetic performance with a philosophically trained mind. Epicurus adopted an analogous position concerning religious ritual: the Epicurean participates in it freely, while discounting false religious beliefs. Both positions betoken a strong faith in human rationality.[31]

Unlike Plato, Epicurus did not propose to use a purified type of poetry as a propaedeutic to philosophy or happiness. Nor did he consider poetic form appropriate for teaching philosophical doctrines. In his list of things that the Epicurean wise person will and will not do, Diogenes Laertius reports that, although the wise person alone would speak correctly about music and poetry, he would not practice the composition of poems,[32] and that he would leave behind prose writings.[33] As the writings of Epicurus and his circle amply illustrate, the wise person uses prose, not poetry, to instruct others. What prevents Epicurus from making poetry a handmaid to philosophy is again, I suggest, his rationalism. Although there is no doubt that Epicurus and his followers practiced irrational indoctrination, it was Epicurus' aim to persuade his students by an appeal to their intellectual powers, or, as he conceived it, by philosophical examination. He sought to mold their character by undisguised opinions, approved by a mental act of judgment on the part of each person. To this end, he required clarity as the only quality of good speech.[34] It is the function of clear speech to communicate clear opinions that are verifiable by each student on the basis of sensory experience. False tales, mimetic experience, public speeches are all rejected as educational tools because they do not engage a person in a clear vision of the truth.[35] What produces a happy life is "sober reasoning" in all circumstances;[36] and this depends on having a clear view of human nature, as imparted by the clear speech of philosophy.

Granted that the wise person will not use poetry to instruct others, why should he or she not compose poems for private enjoyment? There is some confusion about

---

[31] Ronconi argues that there is an irreconcilable conflict between Epicurus' theory, which makes him repudiate all of poetry, and his practice, whereby he cites poetry and recommends Dionysiac festivals (A. Ronconi, "Appunti di estetica epicurea," *Miscellanea di Studi Alessandrini in memoria di Augusto Rostagni* [Turin 1963], 7-25; reprinted as "Poetica e critica epicurea," in *Interpretazioni letterarie nei classici* [Florence 1972], 64–90).   [32] Diogenes Laertius 10.121 (= Epicurus fr. 568 Usener).

[33] Diogenes Laertius 10.120 (= fr. 563 Usener): συγγράμματα καταλείψειν.

[34] Diogenes Laertius 10.13.

[35] According to Diogenes Laertius (10.120), the wise person "will not make panegyric speeches" (οὐ πανηγυριεῖν). See further P. H. De Lacy, "The Epicurean Analysis of Language," *AJPh* 60 (1939), 86-90.   [36] *Letter to Menoeceus* 132 (νήφων λογισμός).

Epicurus' prohibition in the text of Diogenes Laertius (10.121b). All the manuscripts have: (τὸν coφὸν . . .) ποιήματά τε ἐνεργεῖν οὐκ ἂν ποιῆcαι. Since the combination of the two infinitives is ungrammatical, all editors have accepted Usener's emendation of ἐνεργείᾳ for ἐνεργεῖν. According to Usener, Epicurus' meaning is that, whereas the wise person has poetic ability, he will not use this ability "in actuality."[37] This interpretation makes sense only if we understand the wise person's poetic ability in the very restricted sense of an ability to judge a poem philosophically: the wise person knows all that it is useful to know about poems, but he does not have the expertise that a practicing poet has. The wise person, therefore, does not compose poems "in actuality"—that is, not at all. Epicurus might have justified this absolute prohibition on the ground that the toil of learning the poetic craft outweighs the enjoyment of practicing it; or he might have held that the wise man will have nothing to do with an inherently deceptive mode of expression.

But Diogenes' report admits of another interpretation. This is to take either ἐνεργείᾳ, as emended, or ἐνεργεῖν, understood as a gloss on ποιῆcαι, in the sense of "being busy at," or "making a practice of," or "practicing energetically"—meanings primarily associated with the corresponding adjective ἐνεργός and adverb ἐνεργῶς. In that case, Epicurus is not prohibiting the wise person from dabbling in the composition of poetry, but only from busying himself with it or practicing it in the manner of a professional poet. I shall return to this possibility.

In the centuries after Epicurus, his followers both defended and revised his position that poetry is to be rejected as education and welcomed as entertainment. Cicero signals a major shift in his book *De finibus*. He taunts his young friend Torquatus, a confirmed Epicurean, by pointing out that he, Torquatus, is devoted to history, poetry, and literature in general, whereas his master, Epicurus, shunned these studies and was altogether uneducated.[38] Torquatus comes to Epicurus' defense by asserting that, according to Epicurus, "there is no education except that which contributes to the learning of happiness" (*nullam eruditionem esse . . . nisi quae beatae vitae disciplinam iuvaret*). There is no reason why Epicurus should have spent his time reading the poets, "in whom there is no solid usefulness but only a childish delight" (*in quibus nulla solida utilitas omnisque puerilis est delectatio*) and whom, Torquatus admits, he reads at the urging of Cicero. Nor is there any reason, Torquatus continues, why Epicurus should have wasted his time on the Platonic curriculum of "music, geometry, arithmetic and astronomy." For unlike "the art of life," or practical philosophy, none of these arts contributes anything to happiness. Torquatus concludes that Epicurus is not uneducated (*ineruditus*), but those are who think they should study into old age what it is disgraceful for them not to have learned as children (*pueri*).[39]

---

[37] Usener briefly explained: "copia et facultas poeseos non minus in sapiente est, etsi carmina non facit." The contrast between the sage's ability, including his ability as a poet, and his actual practice is well attested in Stoicism (*SVF* 3.654–56). On the text here, however, see above, Chapter 1 n. 1, and below, p. 33 n. 95, Chapter 3 n. with n. 1, Chapter 5 n. 13.

[38] *De finibus* 1.25–26 and 71–72. Cicero appears to use *indoctus* (1.26 and 72) and *ineruditus* (1.72, cf. *parum . . . eruditus* at 1.71) as synonyms, corresponding to Greek ἀπαίδευτος.

[39] *De finibus* 1.71–72:
> Qui quod tibi parum videtur eruditus, ea causa est quod nullam eruditionem esse duxit nisi quae beatae vitae disciplinam iuvaret. An ille tempus aut in poetis evolvendis, ut ego et Triarius te

Cicero's presentation is based on well known doxographical material. Similarly to Plutarch, he accuses Epicurus of rejecting all learning, as divided into literary studies and mathematics. But there is an important difference: the Roman Torquatus does not shun traditional studies, as Epicurus is said to have done and to have advised others to do. As though aware of his failure to follow Epicurus' example and precept, Torquatus makes Cicero responsible for the deviation.[40] At the same time, Torquatus admits that literary and mathematical studies do not contribute to happiness, and that the study of poetry in particular is without "solid utility" and nothing but a "childish delight" (*puerilis delectatio*). The latter phrase recalls Plato's proposal in the tenth book of the *Republic* to set aside the "childish love" ($\pi\alpha\iota\delta\iota\kappa\acute{o}\nu$ . . . $\acute{\epsilon}\rho\omega\tau\alpha$) of poetry.[41] Torquatus does not set it aside; and he is uncomfortably aware that, whereas Epicurus spent his time in the serious pursuit of philosophy instead of in literary and mathematical studies, he is devoting much of his time to a trivial pursuit.

This difference between Torquatus and Epicurus suits Cicero's polemical purpose. Throughout the discussion, Cicero aims to show that Torquatus' professed Epicureanism is incompatible with robust Roman values, as exemplified by Cicero himself. At the same time, Cicero's literary portrait of Torquatus stands for real Epicureans at Rome who were devotees of Epicurus and poetry at once; and we might expect some of them to resist the charge of deviating from their master. How would they defend their study of poetry, without the help of Cicero? Another look at Cicero's exposition suggests a possible defense.

Cicero's Torquatus presents a tightly constructed argument whose major premise is a definition of "education" (*eruditio*) as "that which contributes to the learning of happiness." Torquatus attributes this definition to Epicurus himself. Accordingly, neither the traditional curriculum nor that of Plato counts as "education"; the only education in the proper sense is philosophy. The other studies, such as the "childish (*puerilis*) delight" of poetry, are properly the pursuits of childhood: it would be disgraceful for children (*pueri*) not to occupy themselves with them; but they do not make a person educated. To put the point in Greek, the curriculum of so-called liberal studies is $\pi\alpha\iota\delta\epsilon\acute{\iota}\alpha$ only in the etymological sense of being the occupation of children, $\pi\alpha\hat{\iota}\delta\epsilon\varsigma$; it is not $\pi\alpha\iota\delta\epsilon\acute{\iota}\alpha$ in the proper sense in which education is a training for happiness.

The definition of education is not exemplified in the extant sayings of Epicurus,

---

hortatore facimus, consumeret, in quibus nulla solida utilitas omnisque puerilis est delectatio, aut se, ut Plato, in musicis, geometria, numeris, astris contereret, quae et a falsis initiis profecta vera esse non possunt et si essent vera nihil afferrent quo iucundius, id est quo melius viveremus;—eas ergo artes persequeretur, vivendi artem tantam tamque operosam et perinde fructuosam relinqueret? Non ergo Epicurus ineruditus, sed ii indocti qui quae pueros non didicisse turpe est ea putant usque ad senectutem esse discenda.

[40] Giancotti holds that there is total agreement between Epicurus and his followers, including Cicero's Torquatus. He suggests that Epicurus and his followers alike condemned only certain poems—those that present myths and appeal to the emotions—as having no utility, whereas they admitted other poems as having utility (F. Giancotti, *Il Preludio di Lucrezio* [Florence 1959], 24, and Giancotti 1960 [above, n. 12], 69-76). This interpretation is in conflict, among other things, with Torquatus' blanket characterization of poetry as having no "solid" utility (as pointed out by P. Boyancé, Review of Giancotti 1959 in *REG* 73 [1960], 442).   [41] *Republic* 608A.

but might be said to capture his intent.[42] It is clearly a philosophical reinterpretation of the commonplace notion of education.[43] Using the new definition, Epicurus' followers could argue that when Epicurus urged Pythocles to "flee all education, hoisting sail" (παιδείαν δὲ πᾶσαν . . . φεῦγε τἀκάτιον ἀράμενος), he meant: don't be misled into thinking that what commonly passes for education *is* education; shun this spurious education and turn instead to real education. According to this interpretation, Epicurus was, in effect, using the term παιδείαν in quotation marks. Plutarch confirms this hypothetical exegesis by paraphrasing Epicurus' command to Pythocles as "do not envy the so-called liberal education."[44] What Epicurus did not mean, on the other hand, according to this exegesis is: avoid so-called liberal studies altogether. So long as a person shuns these studies as an education, he is free to enjoy them as a leisure-time activity or, to use the Aristotelian term, as διαγωγή. Epicurus' admonition to "hoist sail" does not mean, therefore, as Plutarch mistook it, that one should shut one's ears to poetry and all other learning. There is another option: it is possible to flee the Sirens, as Odysseus did, by experiencing the charm of their song while escaping its destructive influence. What one needs as a defense is the only true education, Epicurean philosophy.

It would not be surprising if Cicero was not convinced by this exegesis. The plain meaning of the testimonies is that Epicurus urged his followers to get away from traditional and Platonic education altogether. The hypothetical exegesis, however, proposes nothing that might not be held to agree with Epicurus' views. His approval of poetry as an enjoyment provides an opening for the acceptance of poetry as a leisure-time occupation, or διαγωγή, alongside the serious pursuit of philosophy. Epicureans like Torquatus could argue that they really do emulate Pythocles and Apelles, and even Epicurus, in the only way that matters: they keep themselves pure of so-called education by giving serious attention only to philosophy. Epicurus' followers are quite willing to admit a difference between Epicurus' practice and their own: he did not "waste" his time in poetry and other so-called liberal studies, whereas they spend time in such pursuits. But this difference, as Torquatus shows, does not amount to a difference in the estimation of these studies. Historically, the difference might be explained by the fact that Epicurus is the philosophical leader and they are the followers: as leader, he gave them the protection they need; and as followers, they may exploit it.

Sextus Empiricus provides a further glimpse of how Epicurus' followers related poetry to philosophy. In agreement with Cicero's Torquatus, Sextus reports that Epicurus held that learning (as ordinarily understood) makes no contribution to wisdom.[45] We have already seen that one type of learning rejected by Epicurus is the criticism of poetry as practiced by the grammarians. According to Sextus, the gram-

---

[42] Apart from the testimonies that have been cited, *Vatican Sayings* 45 is the only extant text in which Epicurus uses the term παιδεία. Epicurus shows his contempt for those who flaunt their learning by observing that the study of nature, φυσιολογία, does not make people boast or show off "the education that is an object of rivalry among the many" (τὴν περιμάχητον παρὰ τοῖς πολλοῖς παιδείαν).

[43] Cicero uses the ordinary definition at 1.26, when charging Epicurus with being uneducated: *est enim [Epicurus] . . . non satis politus iis artibus quas qui tenent eruditi appellantur* ("[Epicurus] is not sufficiently polished in those arts whose possession causes people to be called educated").

[44] See above, nn. 17 and 18   [45] *Adv. math.* 1. 1; cf. *Adv. math.* 6. 27 (= fr. 229b Usener).

marians tried to show the usefulness of their discipline by arguing that, whereas poetry contains many "starting-points" (ἀφορμάς) for wisdom and happiness, these truths cannot be discerned adequately without the light shed by the grammarians. The ethical precepts of the philosophers, the grammarians maintained, are rooted in the ethical sayings of the poets; and this is true even of Epicurus, who stole his most important doctrines from the poets.[46] As the allegorist Heraclitus and others confirm, Epicurus had a reputation for stealing from the poets. With obvious reference to the Platonic expulsion of poets from cities, the grammarians also claimed that poetry is useful and even necessary for the welfare of cities.[47]

Against the grammarians, Sextus cites a series of objections which he says are due "especially" to the Epicureans.[48] In these arguments, poetry is analyzed as harmful in three ways. First, although poetry contains some worthwhile statements, these are outweighed by many more statements that are harmful. Since poetry does not supply demonstrative proofs (ἀποδείξεις), which would allow listeners to distinguish between good and bad, listeners incline toward the worse course.[49] Second, whereas philosophers and other prose-writers teach what is useful by pursuing the truth, poets aim at all cost to move the soul (ψυχαγωγεῖν), and since falsehood moves the soul more than truth, poets pursue falsehood rather than the truth.[50] Third, poetry is a "stronghold of human passions," inflaming anger and the desire for sex and drink.[51] These arguments allow that poetry may occasionally be useful. But poetry can be useful only when the language is clear.[52] Moreover, even if it is occasionally useful for cities, it is not necessary to their welfare; nor, if it is useful for cities, does it follow that it is useful for individuals.[53]

Because they view poetry as predominantly false and harmful, we might expect Sextus' opponents of grammar to brand poets in general as corrupters of humankind and to join with Plato in banning all except morally useful poetry. Instead, they recognize a way of rendering poetry harmless: whereas grammar can not bring any aid to poetry, philosophy can cancel out the harm and even extract some utility from it. For philosophy can distinguish the good from the bad in poems by supplying proofs. Whereas poetry unaided is harmful, it is harmless and can even be of some small moral benefit when joined by philosophy.

In this partnership, philosophy extends its help to poetry without being dependent on it in any way. "Genuine philosophers," Sextus' opponents of grammar claim, do not use the poets as witnesses; instead, their own argument is sufficient to persuade.[54] This is an attack not only on the grammarians, but also on the Stoic propensity to cite poets in support of their doctrines. The attack is reinforced by the claim that the assumptions of poets are far worse than those of ordinary individuals. Examples of how bad the beliefs of the poets include the castration of Uranos by Cronos and the subjugation of Cronos by Zeus—stories defended by the Stoics by allegorical interpretation.[55] This implicit attack against the Stoics agrees with the Epicureans' rejection of allegorical explanation. Epicurus, it is argued, did not steal any doctrines from

[46] 1.270–73.   [47] 1.275–76.
[48] 1.299: τὰ μὲν ὑπὸ τῶν ἄλλων λεγόμενα . . . καὶ μάλιστα τῶν Ἐπικουρείων. Sextus distinguishes these arguments from his own Pyrrhonist arguments.   [49] 1.279–80.
[50] 1.296–97.   [51] 1.298.   [52] 1.278.
[53] 1.293–95.   [54] 1.280.   [55] 1.288–91.

the poets: for his teaching is fundamentally different from that of the poets; or, if there is a resemblance, what is admirable is not the mere assertion, but the philosophical proof; or the belief is shared by Epicurus with all of mankind, not just the poet.[56]

Although these arguments are clearly indebted to Plato and although Sextus may well have gathered his material from a variety of sources, the overall content and cohesiveness of the arguments show that the Epicurean school is indeed the main source of the arguments, as Sextus states.[57] The demand for clear speech, the distinction between civic and private life, the view that poetry does much harm, and, in general, the claim that learning is useless for happiness, are all fundamental tenets of Epicureanism. Sextus does not name any particular Epicurean; but we can go a little further in trying to pinpoint his source. The view that there is little or no utility in poems, and that poems inflame the emotions, is argued in detail in the writings of Philodemus of Gadara (ca. 110–ca. 40 B.C.).[58] In his book *On Music*, Philodemus is concerned primarily with the utility of music; but in the course of his discussion he has much to say about the utility of poems. With a systematic review of poems that are sung, he maintains that they have little or no utility, and that they do much harm by intensifying the emotions. Against an opponent, probably the Stoic Diogenes of Babylon, who agreed with Plato that music has the power to produce orderliness or disorder of the soul, Philodemus argues at length that if there is any moral utility in songs, it lies in the poems—or lyrics—not in the musical accompaniment, and then it is small. The harm done by poems, moreover, can be very great. Marriage songs, for example, are no more useful than cookery; if there is a moral benefit, it comes from the poems, not the music, and then it extends to only a few (if indeed marriage can be said to be a good).[59] Love songs do not help the passion of love either by the music or by the poetry; in the case of most people, most poems inflame it.[60] In particular, Ibycus, Anacreon, and the like corrupted the young with the thoughts expressed in their love songs.[61] Also, poems that are sung as dirges generally do not heal grief, but most often intensify it.[62] Concerning poems in general, Philodemus brings his greatest indictment against poetry in his work *On Piety*, where he charges the poets, along with philosophers and others, of holding beliefs about the gods that are impious and harmful to humans.[63]

In the fifth book of *On Poems*, Philodemus extends to all poems the claim that there is little utility in them, while showing that they have a goodness that is independent of the utility of their subject matter. Against Heraclides of Pontus, who followed Plato in demanding that poems be both useful and pleasing, he objects that

> he eliminates (ἐκρ[απ]ίζει, literally "expels with the rod") from goodness the most beautiful poems of the most famous poets because they provide no benefit

---

[56] 1.283–86.

[57] Apart from the general claim that the poets state many morally harmful beliefs, the most conspicuous debt to Plato is the charge that poetry is a stronghold of the passions (as designated by the Stoic term πάθη), with the bipartite division of passions into anger and the desire for food and drink.

[58] Philodemus' views on poetry are discussed in more detail in Asmis 1991b.

[59] *On Music* 4 col. v 25–37 Neubecker.

[60] *On Music* 4 col. vi 5–8; I understand "poems" (from lines 4–5) with ὑπὸ τῶν πλείστων (line 7).

[61] *On Music* 4 col. xiv 7–13. Anacreon is cited likewise by Sextus Empiricus (*Adv. math.* 1.298) as a poet who "inflames" the "lovemaddened."

[62] *On Music* 4 col. vi 13–18.   [63] See below, Chapter 10.

whatsoever; in the case of some poets [he eliminates] most poems, and in certain cases all poems.[64]

Echoing the Presocratic Heraclitus, who demanded that Homer and Archilochus be expelled (ἐκβάλλεϲθαι) from the contests and flogged (ῥαπίζεϲθαι),[65] Philodemus uses the compound verb ἐκραπίζει to show his disapproval of Heraclides' censoriousness. If utility is admitted as a criterion of a good poem, Philodemus argues, a large proportion of the most beautiful poems of the most famous poets will not qualify as good. Philodemus restates his objection later in book 5 in a survey of poetic theories that he owes to his teacher Zeno of Sidon.[66] Using the same verb ἐκραπίζειν, which occurs only in these two places, he now rejects the requirement for poetic utility in general on the ground that it

> eliminates (ἐκραπ[ίζ]ει) many wholly beautiful poems, some containing what is useless, others containing . . ., and prefers many that are worse, as many as contain beneficial or more beneficial thoughts.[67]

Philodemus agrees with Zeno that utility is absent from many utterly beautiful poems and is not a requirement of good poetry. He obviously places a high value on poems that have no utility, and thereby shows why an Epicurean might wish to devote time to poetry, despite its moral deficiencies.

Like Sextus' opponents of grammar, Philodemus considers it the function of prose, not poetry, to be useful. Although the thrust of his argument in *On Music* is that

---

[64] *On Poems* 5 col. i 10–18 Jensen (= col. iv 10-18 Mangoni) in Jensen's text:

10   . . . τὰ κάλ-
        λιϲτ[α] ποιήματα τῶν [δο-
        κιμ[ω]τάτων ποητῶ[ν
        διὰ τὸ μηδ' ἡντινοῦν
        ὠφελίαν παρασκευ[ά-
15   ζειν, ἐνίων δὲ καὶ [τὰ
        πλε[ῖ]ϲτα, τινῶν δὲ πά[ν-
        τα [τ]ῆϲ ἀρετῆϲ ἐκρ[απ]ί-
        ζει.

[65] 22 B 42 Diels-Kranz.

[66] Philodemus introduces his survey by saying that he will refute the opinions found in Zeno (*On Poems* 5 col. xxvi [xxix] 19–23). Zeno classified these opinions for the purpose of criticism and may be assumed to be responsible for the analysis as a whole, including the objections.

[67] *On Poems* 5 col. xxvix (xxxii) 9–17, Jensen's text:

9   . . . πολλὰ τῶν παν[κά-
10   λ[ων] ἐκραπ[ίζ]ει ποιημά-
        των τὰ μέ[ν ἀ]νωφελῆ,
        τὰ [δὲ οὐδ' ἀνωφελ]ῆ περι-
        έχοντ[α, καὶ π]ολλὰ πρ[ο-
        κρίνει τ[ῶ]ν ἡττόνων,
15   ὅϲα τὰς ὠφελίμους ἢ τὰς
        ὠφελιμωτέρας περιείλη-
        φε.

It should be noted, however, that ἐκραπίζει is no longer read at this point. Mangoni 1993 (at her col. xxxii 10) has α]ἰϲχρὰ [ποι]εῖ (but she does read ἐκρ[απ]ί[ζει at her col. iv 17–18, quoted above, n. 64).

any moral benefit associated with music comes from the words of songs, not the music, he does not consider poems suited for moral instruction. One reason, as Philodemus shows in an argument against the Stoic Cleanthes, is that poetic expression blunts any moral message that a poem might have. Against Cleanthes' claim that melody reinforces the moral impact of a poem and makes the thoughts more useful, Philodemus argues that melody not only fails to enhance but actually weakens the moral utility of the thoughts because the pleasure, as well as the special qualities of the sounds, distract the listener, because "the words are expressed continuously and not naturally," and so on.[68] The same argument applies to poems without music; in their case, too, the moral force of a poem is weakened by the attendant pleasure, the peculiarity of the sounds, and the unnatural diction. In general, Philodemus believes, poetic expression is not as clear as prose. He points out in *On Poems* that not every kind of clarity is permitted to poets nor does the permitted kind seem to fit all thoughts.[69] In agreement with Sextus' opponents of grammar, he draws a distinction between poems and "demonstrative discourses" ($\dot{\alpha}\pi o\delta\epsilon\iota\kappa\tau\iota\kappa o\grave{\iota}\ \lambda\acute{o}\gamma o\iota$).[70] The kind of clarity that poems lack most conspicuously is the clarity of philosophical demonstration; and since this is an indispensable tool of moral instruction, the usefulness of poems is severely limited.

It follows that if ever poems are useful, prose would have been more useful. In *On Music*, Philodemus is not at all persuaded that the many examples of how poets stopped civil strife with their songs are historically accurate. But if Stesichorus and Pindar did indeed persuade their fellow citizens to put aside their differences, Philodemus writes, they did so by speech ($\lambda\acute{o}\gamma\omega\nu$) put in poetic form, not by the melodies; and "they would have succeeded better if they had tried to dissuade them by prose."[71] Of prose, the best kind is philosophical prose, whose job it is to teach what is morally correct. Music, Philodemus points out, cannot console the distraught lover at all; only the words ($\lambda\acute{o}\gamma o\varsigma$) can do so.[72] Words, moreover, overpower sexual passion by "teaching what is futile, harmful, and insatiable."[73] The words of a song can do some teaching. But the teaching of moral truths is clearly the special prerogative of philosophical prose, using "demonstrative discourses" to show, among other things, that unless a limit is placed on desires, they are insatiable and cause great unhappiness. Philodemus therefore suggests that instead of contributing music toward the acquisition of "erotic virtue," as Diogenes of Babylon seems to have claimed, the Muse Erato contributed "poetry or, better still, philosophy."[74] Since "everything has been attributed to the Muses," Philodemus reasons, we might as well make Erato responsible for contributing philosophy to the virtue identified as "erotic" by the Stoics. For music does not help one bit toward helping people who are in love. Poetry can help a little; but it can help only to the extent that it agrees with philosophy, which alone can show the full truth about love.

In his own quarrel with poetry, Philodemus agrees with Plato that poets have said "vulgar, bad, and contradictory" things about every virtue. If they were to have

---

[68] *On Music* 4 col. xxviii 16–35; cf. xxvi 9–14. At *On Music* col. xv 5–7 Philodemus claims that music, like sexual pleasure and drink, distracts a person from paying attention to the misfortunes of love.

[69] *On Poems* 5 col. xxviii (xxxi) 26–32.   [70] *On Poems* 5 col. xxix (xxxii) 33–36.

[71] *On Music* 4 col. xx 7–17.   [72] *On Music* 4 col. xv 1–5.

[73] *On Music* 4 col. xiii 16–24.   [74] *On Music* 4 col. xv 15–23.

knowledge about virtue, Philodemus adds, "they would not have this knowledge as poets ([κ]αθ' ὃ ποιηταί), let alone as musicians."[75] Moral knowledge belongs to the philosopher; it belongs to poets—and here Philodemus parts with Plato—to create beautiful poems, whether morally beneficial or not. Drawing the same distinction between the proper function and an incidental attribute of a poem, Philodemus claims in his Zenonian survey of poetic theories in *On Poems* that "even if [poems] benefit, they do not benefit as poems (κα[θὸ πο]ήματ')."[76] Philodemus agrees with Sextus' opponents of grammar that it is not the aim of poetry to present the truth; hence, if poetry does impart moral truths, this is incidental to its function. Because it is not the job of the poet to discover or impart truths, the philosopher will not use the poet as a witness. In his work *On Rhetoric*, Philodemus picks out a favorite poet of many philosophers in order to make this point: "How would a philosopher pay attention to Euripides, especially since he has proof (πίςτιν) whereas Euripides does not even bring in proof?"[77]

These similarities between Philodemus' position and Sextus' account suggest that Sextus may have drawn directly on Philodemus or one of his circle. Such a conjecture receives some support from the fact that in his book *Against the Musicians* Sextus cites a series of arguments that coincide even more closely with arguments found in Philodemus' *On Music*.[78] Philodemus, we know, was strongly indebted to his teacher Zeno, whom he greatly admired; and, as we have seen, in *On Poems* he used a summary of poetic theories prepared by Zeno.[79] Zeno wrote a work *On Grammar*, as well as a work *On the Use of Poems,* which are not extant.[80] A powerful and original thinker, Zeno was remarkably adept at gathering material for his arguments from many sources and marshalling them in tight array against his opponents. It is plausible, therefore, that Zeno was the primary source of Sextus' arguments.[81]

---

[75] *On Music* 4 col. xxvi 1–7, including: οὐ | μὴν ἀλλ' οὐδὲ [κ]αθ' ὃ ποιη|ταὶ ταῦτ' εἰδεῖ[εν] ἄν, οὐχ ὅτι καθ' ὃ μουςικοί.

[76] *On Poems* 5 col. xxix (xxxii) 17–19: κᾶν ὠφελῆ, | κα[θὸ πο]ήματ' οὐκ ὠφε|λεῖ.

[77] *On Rhetoric* in *HV*¹ vol. 5 col. xxvii 10–14 (Sudhaus vol. 1, p. 262): καὶ | πῶς Εὐριπίδει φιλό-coφoc | ἂν προcέχοι καὶ ταῦτα μη|δὲ πίcτιν εἰcφέροντι | πίcτιν αὐτὸc ἔχων; The type of proof used by a philosopher is demonstrative proof, ἀπόδειξιc; πίcτιc is "proof" in a wider sense, which includes the proofs used by rhetoricians and, at times, poets. In Sextus' arguments, Euripides is called "the philosopher of the stage," and he is said to have held more reasonable views about the gods than Homer or Hesiod (*Adv. math.* 1.288–289).

[78] *Adv. math.* 6.19–37. This section consists of the "more dogmatic," non-Pyrrhonist arguments against music (as announced at 6.4). Marcello Gigante showed that there is a close agreement between this section and Philodemus' *On Music*, and conjectured that Sextus is here indebted directly to Philodemus (*Scetticismo e Epicureismo* [Naples 1981], 215–21).

[79] Many of Philodemus' writings contain summaries or transcriptions of Zeno's teachings; and some are derived entirely from him. Zeno had a strong interest in literature as well as in mathematics and logic. In addition to *On Poems*, Philodemus' other major work on literature, *On Rhetoric*, contains extensive excerpts from Zeno's writings.

[80] *P.Herc.* 1005, col. x, contains a list of Zeno's works, including Περὶ γραμματικῆc and Περὶ ποιημάτων χρήcεωc. *P.Herc.* 1012, whose author is thought to be Demetrius the Laconian, contains two references to Zeno that may have been derived from Zeno's *On Grammar*; see A. Angeli and M. Colaizzo, "I Frammenti di Zenone Sidonio, *CErc* 9 (1976), 76. There are no other testimonies about Zeno's *On Grammar*.

[81] Crönert 1906 (above n. 18), 119, previously suggested that Sextus' Epicureans are οἱ περὶ τὸν

Cicero, Sextus, and, above all, Philodemus show that at the end of the second century and in the first half of the first century B.C., the Epicureans reconsidered the relationship between poetry and philosophy. Although we have very little evidence about Epicurus, the testimonies suggest that whereas Epicurus emphasized the harmful educational influence of poetry and the need to replace poetic teaching by philosophy, his followers took the more hospitable view that it is not the function of poetry to teach and that philosophy may form an alliance with poetry, in which both pursuits achieve their own ends. In this partnership, the serious study of philosophy gives license to Epicureans like Torquatus to spend their leisure time in the enjoyable, though fundamentally useless, study of poetry. As a sign of this more conciliatory view, Cicero's Torquatus describes poetry as having "no solid usefulness" (*nulla solida utilitas*). Torquatus recognizes that only philosophy can bring happiness; but since philosophy can render the enjoyment of poetry harmless, there is no reason why he should not indulge in this delight, which may even bring a little incidental moral benefit. Since Epicurus, too, admitted poetry as a form of enjoyment, there is no contradiction with Epicurus' doctrine; but a new place is given to poetry as a study subordinate to philosophy.

Philodemus is the outstanding example of a Greek Epicurean who conjoined the pursuit of poetry with philosophy. But he went considerably further than Cicero's Torquatus in the value he placed on poetry. As we have seen, Philodemus held that poetry can do much harm. In particular, he agreed with Epicurean tradition that Homer said many foolish and harmful things. His book *On Piety* (Περὶ εὐcεβείαc) contains striking examples of how Homer propagated false and pernicious beliefs about the gods.[82] But Philodemus also believed that Homer provides beneficial moral guidance for rulers. In fact, Philodemus devoted an entire treatise to showing that Homer offers good advice on how to rule. The treatise is *On the Good King According to Homer;* and it has generally been regarded as an anomaly among Epicurean texts. In this work, which is dedicated to Piso, the father-in-law of Caesar and a leading politician himself, Philodemus proposes to extract from Homer "starting-points . . . for the correction of positions of power" (ἀφ[ορμῶν] . . . εἰc ἐπανόρθω-cιν δυνα⟨c⟩τε[ιῶν]).[83] With numerous examples from the whole range of human Homeric rulers—Odysseus, Nestor, Agamemnon, Achilles, Hector, Alcinous, Telemachus, the suitors, and others—and even some divine rulers, Philodemus gives a detailed analysis of how a ruler should behave both in peace and in war. It looks as though, contrary to Epicurus' alleged expulsion of Homer from the city, Philodemus has led him back.

Ζήνωνα and that Sextus used Zeno's *On Grammar*. Crönert supposes, unnecessarily in my view, that Sextus derived his knowledge of Zeno's work from Aenesidemus. It is possible that Demetrius the Laconian, an associate of Zeno and Philodemus, also participated in the debate on the usefulness of poetry. *P.Herc.* 1014 is entitled "Demetrius' *On Poems* 2," and has been attributed to the Laconian by the most recent editor, Costantina Romeo (Romeo 1988). It is debatable, however, whether the author is the Laconian or the first century B.C. Peripatetic; see Romeo 1988, 21–25. The extant text shows a detailed acquaintance with Greek poetry and includes excerpts from Homer, Euripides, and others.

[82] For example, he denounces Homer's description of Ares, son of Zeus, as "mindless, lawless, murderous, a lover of strife and of battle" (*On Piety, P.Herc.* 1088 fr. x 22-28: below, p. 205). Other examples of Homeric impiety occur at p. 9 Gomperz; p. 34 Gomperz; and p. 59 Gomperz (1866).

[83] Col. xliii 16-19 Dorandi (1982a).

Whereas Torquatus' devotion to poetry as something pleasurable but fundamentally useless can readily be regarded as an extension of Epicurus' position, the view that Homer is morally useful seems a reversal. Philodemus does bring Homer back into the city—the Roman city—as a politically useful poet; and this is a major turning point in the history of Epicurean poetics. Yet this apparent reversal can also be seen to fit a tradition of interpretation which claims to be faithful to Epicurus' thought. In particular, it fits the view that philosophy may ally itself with poetry in such a way as to illuminate the truths that are found incidentally in poems. Philodemus recognizes that Homeric poetry contains a great deal that is harmful, not just in its theology, but also in its depictions of the misuse of power, notably by Achilles and, most of all, by the suitors. But, according to Philodemus, Homer also shows, through Nestor, Odysseus, and others, how the misuse of power is to be corrected. These "starting points for the correction" of power need to be illuminated by the philosopher—not anyone else; and this is the job that Philodemus undertakes for Piso, a Roman ruler who is in a position to practice what he is taught.[84] As philosophical interpreter of Homer, Philodemus guides Piso through a reading of Homer by drawing attention to statements that are morally beneficial. The treatise is unique as an example of Epicurean literary criticism, according to which the only legitimate critic is the philosopher, distinguishing what is morally valuable from what is morally harmful. Although Philodemus' procedure resembles that of other philosophers, the theoretical underpinning is wholly different. He does not use the poet as a witness for moral truths, but identifies truths on the basis of his own philosophical understanding.

Philodemus, therefore, extends Epicurus' acceptance of poetry by admitting it not only as a pleasant, but also as a morally useful pastime. He also made another extension, which concerns the enjoyment of poetry. For the most part, Philodemus seems to follow Epicurus closely on how poetry is to be enjoyed. Indeed, much of what he says about the pleasure of listening to poetry looks like an amplification of Epicurus' remarks. In his book *On Music*, Philodemus mentions that the Homeric poems "have indicated, as they ought to, that music is appropriate at parties."[85] One obvious piece of evidence is Odysseus' speech to Alcinous. I suggested earlier that Epicurus may have quoted the words; Philodemus surely has them in mind, and may be following Epicurus. Homer, of course, attests that not just music, but the recitation of poems is appropriate at parties; and Philodemus agrees with him. Philodemus approves of Diogenes of Babylon for admitting Homer, Hesiod, and other poets to the entertainment at parties, even though he does not approve of Diogenes' reasons.[86] Philodemus proposes, in effect, to recreate the good cheer of Homeric parties by bringing in Homer himself, together with other early poets and their successors, as singers of tales; and this position is not essentially different from that of Epicurus.

Just as Epicurus recommends the enjoyment of Dionysiac festivals, so Philodemus points out that there is an abundance of public entertainments for one's listening pleasure; indeed, he observes, there is such great scope for participating in them that one can easily get tired of them.[87] Like Epicurus, Philodemus restricts participation

---

[84] At col. xxv 20 Dorandi, Philodemus refers to himself as a "philosopher."

[85] *On Music* 4 col. xvi 17–21. [86] *On Music* 4 col. xvii 2–13.

[87] *On Music* 4 col. xxxvii 16–29.

to being a member of the audience, in the belief that the acquisition of technical musical skill adds nothing to happiness. The availability of public shows, Philodemus points out, makes it futile to toil at learning musical skills oneself; only the small-minded, who have nothing worthwhile to do, think they need to toil at learning music in order to get enjoyment for themselves.[88] Musical learning and practice, Philodemus argues, are toilsome and "shut us out from the things that are most decisive for prospering."[89] What is most decisive for happiness is, of course, the study of philosophy; but Philodemus presumably also has in mind the companionship of friends. The "continuous inactivity of the person who sings in boy-like fashion or is busy at playing the lyre ($\kappa\iota\theta\alpha\rho\iota\zeta o[\nu\tau]oc\ \dot{\epsilon}[\nu]\epsilon\rho\gamma\hat{\omega}c$)," Philodemus implies, excludes the activity of friendly social intercourse.[90] Expertise in musical theory is no less an obstacle to happiness than skill in performance, since it requires practice for its perfection.[91] Philodemus supports Epicurus' ban on musical and literary lectures by commenting that "to have something to say [about music] at parties and other gatherings" is "not demanded of all . . . and may even be laughed at if a philosopher should do it."[92] In general, "it is vastly better to have good cheer ($\epsilon\dot{v}\theta\upsilon\mu\dot{\iota}\alpha\nu$) than uselessness ($\dot{\alpha}\chi\rho\eta c\tau\dot{\iota}\alpha\nu$) by giving a display or working out some other detailed interpretation."[93]

These warnings against musical expertise would seem to apply just as much to poetry. But there is a problem. Philodemus not only studied poetry and wrote about it as a philosopher; he also composed poetry. In one of his epigrams, he calls himself $\mu o\upsilon co\phi\iota\lambda\dot{\eta}c$, "beloved of the Muses"; and although he might well have extended the meaning of this term to include service to the Muse of philosophy, he draws attention specifically to his poetic creativity. For he promises his addressee Piso, to whom he dedicated *On the Good King According to Homer,* that Piso will hear "things far sweeter than [in?] the land of the Phaeacians" at the party to which Philodemus invites him.[94] Piso, we may guess, loved Homer; and Philodemus, it appears, places himself ever so ironically among the successors of Homer himself. Philodemus composed only light epigrams; but he displays considerable poetic skill. How could he justify this activity if Epicurus did indeed prohibit the wise person from composing poems?

At this point I would like to return to the alternative interpretation of Epicurus' prohibition. It is possible that Philodemus and others interpreted Epicurus to mean that the wise person does not make a practice of composing poetry: unlike the lyre-player who plays $\dot{\epsilon}\nu\epsilon\rho\gamma\hat{\omega}c$, keeping himself busy with this activity, the wise person does not busy himself with composing poetry. If he composes poetry, he does so as an

---

[88] *On Music* 4 col. xxxvii 8–15.

[89] *On Music* 4 col. xxxvii 31–34: $\tau\hat{\omega}\nu\ \kappa\upsilon\rho\iota\omega\tau\dot{\alpha}|\tau\omega\nu\ \pi\rho\dot{o}c\ \epsilon\dot{v}\epsilon\tau\eta\rho\dot{\iota}\alpha\nu\ \dot{\epsilon}\kappa\kappa[\lambda]\epsilon\dot{\iota}|o\upsilon c\alpha\nu$.

[90] *On Music* 4 col. xxxvii 36–39.

[91] *On Music* 4 col. xxxviii 22–26; Philodemus claims that the required practice "removes [us] from the things that tend toward happiness." [92] *On Music* 4 col. xxxviii 12–19.

[93] *On Music* 4 col. xxxviii 25–30: $\kappa\alpha\dot{\iota}\ \mu\upsilon\rho\dot{\iota}[\omega\iota\ \kappa]\rho\epsilon\hat{\iota}\tau|\tau[o\nu\ \ddot{\epsilon}\chi]\epsilon\iota\nu\ \tau\dot{\eta}\nu\ \epsilon\dot{v}[\theta\upsilon]\mu\dot{\iota}\alpha\nu\ |\ \ddot{\eta}\ \tau\dot{\eta}\nu\ \dot{\alpha}\chi\rho\eta c\tau\dot{\iota}\alpha\nu\ \dot{\epsilon}[\pi\iota]\delta\epsilon\iota|\kappa[\nu]\upsilon\mu\dot{\epsilon}\nu o\upsilon[c\ \ddot{\eta}\ \tau]\hat{\omega}\nu\ \ddot{\alpha}\lambda\lambda\omega\nu\ |\ \tau\iota\ \tau\hat{\omega}\nu\ \dot{\epsilon}\kappa\ \tau\hat{\eta}c\ \delta\iota\epsilon\xi\dot{o}\delta o\upsilon\ \pi[\epsilon]|\rho\alpha\dot{\iota}\nu o\nu\tau\alpha c$. The verb $\pi\epsilon\rho\alpha\dot{\iota}\nu\epsilon\iota\nu$ is also used by Plutarch in his report of Epicurus' prohibition of musical and poetic lectures (*That Epicurus Actually Makes a Pleasant Life Impossible* 1095c, see n. 22). Although the verb is commonplace, it is possible that Philodemus and Plutarch are drawing on the same text by Epicurus.

[94] *Palatine Anthology* 11.44. David Sider drew my attention to the reference to the Phaeacians (see below, pp. 46–47, and his commentary, forthcoming).

amateur, not a professional. Accordingly, he does not spend a great deal of effort at acquiring the skill, so that the pleasure of exercising the skill is not outweighed by the toil; nor does he deprive himself of any opportunities for happiness, or of any "good cheer" at parties. This interpretation could have been placed on either an original prohibition phrased simply as ποιήματά τε οὐκ ἂν ποιῆcαι or on a prohibition augmented by ἐνεργείᾳ.[95] Whatever the original wording, it is unlikely that Epicurus meant to leave a loophole for poetic composition. But his followers might reasonably have argued that he did not intend his prohibition to apply to the amateur efforts of someone who practices poetic composition only incidentally, not "as a poet."

If Philodemus justified the composition of poems as an amateur pleasure, this is a further extension of the acceptance of poetry as a leisure-time occupation, or δια-γωγή. The amateur composer does not use poetry for the serious purpose of instructing others. To educate others, he uses prose, just as Epicurus demanded. Philodemus' own writings exemplify this demarcation between prose and poetry. His epigrams might have some incidental moral utility, but they are not intended to teach.

Philodemus, then, represents a new kind of Epicurean, who studies poetry with enjoyment and even profit, and who may even compose poems as a pastime. This Epicurean is cast in a new mould, but one which is carefully calculated to fit the standard established by Epicurus. But there is also a wholly different new Epicurean. Lucretius exploited the seductive beauty of poetry to educate others and spared no labor to make poetry a suitable vehicle for philosophical instruction. By combining the two uses of poetry—education and enjoyment—that Epicurus had kept strictly apart, Lucretius seems to preclude any way of reconciling his approach to poetry with that of Epicurus.

Lucretius does not, however, use poetry without offering a defense of his method; and this defense may be regarded as his own, novel exegesis of Epicurus' views on poetry. In a famous image, Lucretius compares himself to a doctor who smears honey around the cup of bitter medicine in order to trick the child into drinking the healing potion. The reason for this trickery, Lucretius explains, is that the doctrine of Epicurus generally seems "too cheerless" (*tristior*) to people who are not acquainted with it.[96] Lucretius proposes to use poetry as a lure to attract the ordinary person to Epicurean philosophy. But this is not all. Lucretius does not regard poetry simply as a necessary device, dictated by the antipathy of his audience. Instead, what makes him so enthusiastic about his work is that poetry makes a positive contribution to the presentation of philosophy. Not only does its sweetness differ from the bitterness of the doctrine, but also its clarity differs from the obscurity of Epicurus' discoveries. Lucretius takes great pleasure in his poetic toil "because I fashion such lucid songs about an obscure subject matter" (*quod obscura de re tam lucida pango / carmina*).[97] As he assures Memmius, he will not spare any labor "in seeking by what words and what song I may be able to spread clear light over your mind."[98] Lucretius

---

[95] If Epicurus wrote the simple prohibition, a later interpreter may have added ἐνεργεῖν as a marginal explanation which subsequently crept into the text (cf. above, Chapter 1, n. 1).

[96] *On the Nature of Things* 1.936–50, including (943–45): *quoniam haec ratio plerumque videtur / tristior esse quibus non est tractata, retroque / volgus abhorret ab hac.*   [97] 1.933–34.

[98] 1.143–44: *quaerentem dictis quibus et quo carmine demum / clara tuae possim praepandere lumina menti.*

aims to dispel the darkness of his listeners' ignorance by illuminating the discoveries of Epicurus with the language of poetry.

In claiming clarity for his verses, Lucretius asserts, paradoxically, a continuity of his method of teaching with that of Epicurus. Whereas Epicurus assigned clarity to prose alone, Lucretius now claims this quality for poetry. If poetry has clarity, it is entirely appropriate for imparting philosophical truths. Lucretius is so intent on proving the suitability of poetry as a philosophical medium that he does not shun any technical difficulties; indeed, he goes out of his way to give a full presentation of philosophically difficult material. His poem is a "demonstrative discourse" (ἀπο-δεικτικὸс λόγοс), aiming to move the soul (ψυχαγωγεῖν) in such a way as to lead it to the truth. In combining what other Epicureans kept apart, Lucretius reaffirms the traditional link between divine inspiration and poetic expression. Lucretius symbol-izes his source of inspiration by Venus, a deity who represents both his love for Epicurus and the expression of this love in his poetry. If called to account by Epi-curus for using poetry to instruct others, he might reply: "You have inspired me to attempt a feat that no one has tried before: to illuminate your teachings in poetry. I do not deviate from your path; but you have shown me a path by which I may lead others to a clear vision of your divine truth."

We do not know whether Lucretius associated with Philodemus and his friends. There is no sign in Philodemus' writings that he ever conceived that a poem such as Lucretius' might be compatible with Epicurus' teachings. Yet I suspect that if he ever came to know Lucretius' poetry, he would have been so impressed by its exceptional beauty and clarity that he would have welcomed Lucretius as an associate in his own efforts to spread Epicureanism to the Romans.

3
Epicurean Poetics: Response and Dialogue

David Sider

The view that Epicurus was himself impervious to the charms of poetry, and that his charge to his disciples was to avoid it absolutely, both the listening and the composing, has become standard in handbooks and histories. Not everyone of course held to this extreme statement of his position, but it was easy enough to believe that anyone who wrote prose on so stylistically plain a level as Epicurus would, almost *a fortiori*, be insensitive to the charms of poetry. Moreover, that the most famous piece of Epicurean literature was itself a poem could be regarded as all the more interesting if Epicurus himself abjured the writing of poetry.

Nor did this view derive *e nihilo*. There seemed to be sufficient ancient testimony to support it. Cicero, for example, says of Philodemus: *non philosophia solum sed etiam ceteris studiis quae fere ceteros Epicureos neglegere dicunt perpolitus*, "he is expert not only in philosophy but also in other skills which almost all other Epicureans are said to neglect" (*Against Piso* 70). As Cicero's very next sentence makes clear, these other skills include, or are coextensive with, the writing of poems, and indeed, Cicero admits, quite elegant ones at that. Thus, for Philodemus as well as his contemporary Lucretius, although one wrote in the slightest of genres, the epigram, while the other wrote in the weightiest of genres, the didactic epic, the very idea of Epicurean poetry would seem to remain something of a challenge, which would have to be confronted before verse composition could begin.

Whereas Cicero speaks of contemporary Epicureans, Diogenes Laertius, not only our most complete ancient source for the teachings of Epicurus but also one of the most sympathetic, seems to have been an unambiguous witness to the hostility of Epicurus himself to poetry. Elisabeth Asmis, however, in the previous study shows that his prohibition was probably not intended to be absolute. She suggests that the unconstruable infinitive ἐνεργεῖν at Diogenes Laertius 10.121b should either be emended as it was by Usener to ἐνεργείᾳ, but with the sense "energetically"; or understood as a gloss with this same sense on the infinitive ποιεῖν. Reading the dative is preferable, as it (or some synonymous expression) would have been written presumably by Epicurus himself and thus have formed an essential part of his original statement. The infinitive as gloss would have to have come from an interpreter

35

later than Diogenes Laertius who, like Elizabeth Asmis, would have reasoned that Epicurus allowed for the writing of poetry by Epicureans. ἐνεργείᾳ could well have appeared as in his *Choices and Avoidances* (Περὶ καὶ αἱρέceωc καὶ φυγῶν), where Epicurus classifies εὐφροcύνη, the very word used by Homer in the Phaeacian passage, and χαρά, "joy," as kinematic pleasures. If, however, as seems likely, ἐνεργεῖν is to be emended, then ἐνεργῶc, which is equally possible paleographically, provides the desired sense unambiguously.[1] Epicurus' statement would thus be noticeably similar to Philodemus' in *On Music* which Asmis cites later where he objects to someone's κιθαρίζοντοc ἐνεργῶc, "being busy [i.e. overbusy] at playing the kithara" (*On Music* 4 col. xxxvii 38f.).

Also in favor of Asmis' interpretation of this Diogenes passage is its general context. Between his transcription of Epicurus' letters to Pythocles and to Menoeceus, Diogenes inserts a number of do's and don'ts for the wise man, who in this parlance is none other than the Epicurean.[2] It is noteworthy that, although drawn from several Epicurean sources, these ethical guidelines often take the following form: The wise man will in general avoid activity X but will engage in it under certain circumstances. He shouldn't marry, for example, but may yet find some reason for doing so. He shouldn't get drunk, but if he does so then let him not babble. He will avoid the usual business of the state but will occasionally sue somebody. And so on. The notion that the Epicurean will not write poetry but if he does he will not do so actively fits perfectly into this Diogenean context. This would seem to provide further confirmation of Asmis' thesis. It should be pointed out, however, that Diogenes seems, in his usual cut-and-paste style of composition, to have suppressed a clause or two. Although commentators and translators usually connect the two clauses under discussion with an "although" or a "but," they are in fact linked by two τε's: Literally, "Only the wise man would converse correctly concerning music and poetry; *and* [to adopt Asmis' sense of the passage] he would not write poems enthusiastically." Ignored is the fact that the infinitive of each clause is accompanied by an ἄν, which makes it unlikely that one clause was subordinate to the other. There would seem to be suppressed protases of future less vivid conditions here, which in turn follow upon suppressed prohibitions: In full, then, we may flesh out Epicurus' original statements as follows: (1) "Nobody should spend time discussing music and poetry, but if it should be done only the wise man would do so correctly." And (2) "The wise man should not write poetry but if he should do so he would not do so too seriously."

This analysis, as I have said, not only fits Diogenes' context, it separates what are too often linked in discussions of Epicurus' views of poetry, the analyzing of poetry and the writing of poems, and leaves open the possibility of an Epicurean doing one, like Lucretius, or both, like Philodemus. And it may be worth noting that Diogenes

---

[1] Cf. Diogenes Laertius 10.136 = Epicurus fr. 2 Usener = 7 Arrighetti ἡ δὲ χαρὰ καὶ ⟨ἡ⟩ ἀπονία κατὰ κίνηcιν ἐνεργείᾳ. See above, Chapter 2 with n. 37. However, for a defense of the transmitted τε and the infinitive ἐνεργεῖν at Diogenes Laertius 121b see above, Chapter 1 n. 1; cf. below, Chapter 5 n. 13.

[2] Strictly speaking, these maxims are attributed to Epicurus or his followers, but nobody I think would argue that a prohibition against poetry was added by a later Epicurean without the master's own authority.

attributes no prohibition to Epicurus concerning the mere listening to poetry. This too supports Asmis' general thesis.

One should also add to her discussion of Lucretius and Philodemus that there were several, some might say many, other poets who considered themselves Epicureans. The earliest of these may be Epicurus' friend Metrodorus of Lampsacus, who has been credited with the philosophical poem credited merely to "Metrodorus" in the Palatine Anthology 9.360, and who has been put forth as the possible author of a recently published hexameter fragment on the birth of Aphrodite.[3] None of this, however, is very secure. We are on surer ground with Titus Albucius in the second century B.C., who is called a *perfectus Epicureus* by Cicero (*Brutus* 131) and an *aridus* [*poeta*] by Fronto (*On Eloquence* 1.2, p. 133 van den Hout[2]). Krebs may be right in thinking that Albucius left behind some sort of *Lehrgedicht*, i.e., a didactic poem with an Epicurean message, although he is more certain than the evidence actually warrants.[4]

In the first century B.C. there are the poets Plotius Tucca and Lucius Varius Rufus, who edited the *Aeneid* after Vergil's death, and who are addressed more than once by Philodemus in his prose treatises, which suggests very strongly that they were regular members of the Epicurean circle which met in and around Naples. Donatus in his life of Vergil furthermore specifically attests to the Epicureanism of Varius.[5] This makes it quite likely, if not certain, that Varius' hexameter poem *On Death* (*De Morte*) dealt with this central Epicurean subject again along Epicurean lines. Our understanding of Lucretius' diatribe against the fear of death would probably be much enhanced were Varius' poem extant.[6] There is also the obscure Pollius Felix, whom Statius credits in his *Silvae* with writing a Hesiodic, i.e., didactic, poem which is worthy of Epicurus (2.2.112ff.):

> huc ubi Pierias exercet Pollius artes
> seu voluit monitus, quos dat Gargettius auctor[7]
> seu nostram quatit ille chelyn seu dissona nectit
> carmina sive minax ultorem stringit iambon.

Less obscure a poet than Pollius Felix is Vergil, who spent time with the two most famous Epicureans in Naples, Siro and Philodemus, and who, I am convinced, wrote at least some of the Epicurean poems in the *Catalepton*, most notably 5, which not

---

[3] G. A. Gerhard, *Phoinix von Kolophon* (Leipzig and Berlin 1909), 104; K. Maresch, *Kölner Papyri* (*P. Köln*) 6 = *Papyrologica Coloniensia* 7 (1987), 26–51, esp. 27, 30f., 35 (text), 46–8 (comm.).

[4] "Albucius (2)," *RE* 1 (1892), 1330f.

[5] Donatus, *Life of Vergil* 68 [*Vergilius*] *audivit a Sirone praecepta Epicuri, cuius doctrinae socium habuit Varium*. Cf. Jerome *Chron.* ad Ol. 140.4 *Varius et Tucca Vergilii contubernales poetae habentur illustres*, although not everyone agrees that Tucca was in fact a poet; cf. H. Naumann, "Suetons Vergil-vita," *RhM* 87 (1938), 364–9.

[6] It does not tell against this interpretation that at least some of the extant fragments of this poem (p. 100 Morel) seem to concern Marc Antony; consolation literature often uses the death of a friend or relative (or in this case a Roman leader) as an obvious point of departure for a disquisition on the nature of death and how it should be borne by those left behind. R. Ungar, *L. Varii de morte eclogae reliquiae* (Halle 1870), 78 argues for its being a *Lehrgedicht*; cf. further A. Rostagni, "Il *De Morte* di Vario," *Virgilio Minore* (Rome 1961), 391–404; *RE* 8A1 (1955), 412, s.v. L. Varius (21). Rufus; M. Gigante, *Filodemo in Italia* (Florence 1990), 56ff.

[7] i.e., Epicurus called after his Attic deme; cf. Diogenes Laertius 10.1, *Suidae vita*.

only refers to Siro (as does 8) but whose point clearly recalls that of Philodemus Epigram 17 (*Palatine Anthology* 11.41).[8] Horace is a different case when it comes to philosophical affiliation, but he too consciously drew upon Epicurean doctrine in some of his poems (as well as many other schools of thought).[9] Nor should we forget that Diogenes Laertius, who seems to have considered himself an Epicurean (10.138), wrote many epigrams.[10] Thus, although this brief census may well be incomplete, there are enough names to show us that however broad the term Epicurean poetics is, allowing as it does for the poetry of Lucretius, Philodemus, and Horace, it is not so oxymoronic as is often thought.[11]

Asmis strengthens her case when she analyzes Epicurus' attitude toward poetry as though it were a form of reader-response criticism. That is, Epicurus' criterion for the acceptability of a particular piece of poetry lies not in its particular content but in how it is received by a particular audience. The ancient testimony brought to the fore by Asmis connecting Epicurus with the Phaeacians and Odysseus is especially pertinent. Whereas earlier scholars looked at the elements of the *telos* listed by Odysseus in isolation, it now seems better to view them as complementary parts of the larger whole that is the proper banquet scene which can serve as model for those held in an Epicurean Garden. Poetry now takes its rightful place, at least in Epicurus' eyes, as but one contributory element of pleasure. But straining too hard for pleasures, we know, can only bring pain; in the case of poetry this would entail too much attention

---

[8] Cf. *AJPh* 108 (1987), 315f. The presence of Vergil and Plotius in the Herculaneum papyri, long conjectured, has been recently confirmed; cf. Gigante and Capasso 1989, 3–6, with frontispiece plate. For ancient literary testimony, cf. W. Crönert, *Kolotes und Menedemos* (Munich 1906, repr. Amsterdam 1965), 126f. Vergil's patron Maecenas also wrote poetry with an Epicurean flavor; cf. J. Ferguson, "Epicureanism under the Roman Empire," *ANRW* II 36.4 (1990), 2263f. Ferguson 2268 also suggests Vergil's friend Octavius Musa, who was in the Naples circle, but we do not know if his poetry was in any way Epicurean.

[9] Horace's use of philosophical themes is far too complex to deal with here; in brief, though, we can say that like Philodemus he uses what in a philosophical treatise would be doctrine as poetical *topoi*. Thus although in one poem he calls himself *Epicuri de grege porcum* (*Epodes* 1.4.16), in another epistle he more truthfully says that he is *nullius addictus iurare in verba magistri* (1.1.14). Cf. N. W. De Witt, "Epicurean doctrine in Horace," *CPh* 34 (1939), 127–34; E. Fraenkel, *Horace* (Oxford 1957), 254–57. Note in particular *Odes* 1.31, which ends with distinctly Epicurean and Philodemean echoes in praise of the simple needs of the good life (cf. Nisbet and Hubbard's commentary, pp. 348, 355f.), including the composing of poetry (*nec cithara carentem*).

[10] That 10.138 indicates Diogenes was an Epicurean, or at any rate more Epicurean than anything else, is argued by O. Gigon, "Das dritte Buch des Diogenes Laertios," *Elenchos* 7 (1986), 137. For an assessment of Diogenes' epigrams, cf. J. Mejer, *Diogenes Laertius and his Hellenistic Background* (Wiesbaden 1978; Hermes Einzels. 40), 46–50; M. Gigante, "Biografia e dossografia in Diogene Laerzio," *Elenchos* 7 (1986), 34–44. At 1.63, Diogenes mentions that his *Pammetros* contained poems on famous men "in all meters and rhythms, in epigrams and in lyrics"; cf. Mejer 48 n. 102 for a list of the meters in the extant poems. Gigante art. cit., 39f. argues that the many epigrams on the death of philosophers earn Diogenes "un posto nella letteratura antica περὶ θανάτου."

[11] After Horace, the Epicurean views found in the poets tend to become more literary motifs and borrowings (often from Philodemus), and hence less meangingful from our point of view. There is little of value in H. Disch, *De poetis Aevi Augusti Epicureis* (diss. Bonn 1921), who discusses Vergil, Horace, Tibullus, Propertius, and Ovid(!). Cf. the remarks of E. Courtney, *The Poems of Petronius* (Atlanta 1991), 11–14, on several seemingly Epicurean poems: "Petronius is in no sense propagating Epicurean doctrine, but is quite willing to allow his characters to justify their acts by recourse to a superficial Epicureanism."

paid to what after all cannot, whatever its claims to do so, contribute to our happiness. Poetry is thus reduced by Epicurus to *Tafelmusik*, to which we should pay no more attention than the music that comes over the phone when we are put on hold.

In more Epicurean terms, poetry is classifiable as a natural but unnecessary pleasure, which adds variety to already existing pleasures without, like a necessary pleasure, ameliorating pains. In a banquet setting it is equivalent to fancy food.[12] If listening to poetry is thus barely tolerated, Epicurus' view of composing it must have been similar to that of Athena who thought that however beautiful the sound of the *aulos*, the playing of the instrument was *infra dignitatem*.

In classifying poetry as a natural but unnecessary pleasure, Epicurus is thus, like Plato, stripping it of any claims made on its behalf to offer valuable ethical precepts that could lead to happiness. Poetry, that is, makes claims that gourmet food does not, so that it is not suprising that Epicurus would have followed Plato in cautiously treating poetry as a rival whose admittance into philosophical society can be allowed only under circumscribed conditions. That he himself knew his Greek poetry well and could make poetical allusions with ease has been recently brought out by Diskin Clay,[13] but the overall impression Epicurus produced in ancient readers is that he depended on no predecessors in his arguments, that "there is no external authority in them; the voice is the voice of Epicurus."[14] The allusions pointed out by Clay and Asmis, therefore, were probably made in passing; it seems unlikely that Epicurus would have based an argument on a poetic passage. As Asmis properly reminds us, poetry formed an essential part of Greek culture and as such demands emotional and critical detachment, however difficult it must have been to maintain *ataraxia* while listening to Homer.

We should not, however, miss the irony of Epicurus' using a literary allusion to Odysseus and the Sirens when he warns Pythocles to set sail and flee all culture. For in couching his admonition to Pythocles in this form, Epicurus demonstrates precisely how literature should be treated: Listen to it, he seems to be saying, and use it, i.e., make allusions to it; but do not succumb to its charms. Epicurus' specific warning to Pythocles had a notable echo in Stokely Carmichael's famous dictum of the 1960s: "When I hear the word 'culture' I reach for my gun." Carmichael's phrase "the *word* 'culture'" makes the same point attributed to Epicurus by Plutarch, that one should not envy τὴν ἐλευθέραν καλουμένην παιδείαν, "the *so-called* liberal education" (Plutarch, *That Epicurus Actually Makes a Pleasant Life Impossible* 1094D = Epicurus fr. 164 Usener), which is all too often used to convince people of their social inferiority. Rather than being the philistine Plutarch says he is, Epicurus seems instead to have been working to break down the social barriers maintained in large part by the ability to parade one's cultural credentials. The line of Metrodorus quoted by Asmis which says in effect, Don't worry if you can't quote Homer at the drop of a hat, reinforces this very point. (All the more so if we believe Epicurus'

---

[12] Cf. *Kyriai Doxai* 29 with scholion: φυcικὰc καὶ ἀναγκαίαc ἡγεῖται ὁ Ἐπίκουροc τὰc ἀλγηδόνοc ἀπολυούcαc, ὡc ποτὸν ἐπὶ δίψουc· φυcικὰc δὲ οὐκ ἀναγκαίαc δὲ τὰc ποικιλλούcαc μόνον τὴν ἡδονήν, μὴ ὑπεξαιρουμέναc δὲ τὸ ἄλγημα, ὡc πολυτελῆ cιτία.

[13] D. Clay, *Lucretius and Epicurus* (Ithaca 1983), 16 with n. 12, 78 n. 58.

[14] Diogenes Laertius 10.26; cf. D. Sedley, "Epicurus and his professional rivals," in J. Bollack and A. Laks (eds.), *Études sur l'Epicurisme antique* (Lille 1976), 119–59.

charge that Metrodorus lacked originality, for he would probably have taken the phrase from Epicurus.)

If thanks to Asmis we now have a good idea of what Epicurean poetics meant to Epicurus himself, we are also better prepared to examine what it meant to his later followers. We can certainly agree with her that the continuity between Epicurus' and Philodemus' poetical theory is unbroken. If nothing else, we should note with Asmis the various Epicurean writings on the subject, from Epicurus' own $Περὶ\ μουcικῆc$ and $Cυμπόcιον$, Metrodorus' $Περὶ\ ποιημάτων$, and Demetrius of Laconia's $Περὶ\ ποιημάτων$, through the many titles on these subjects under Philodemus' name.[15] Many of the statements she quotes from Philodemus' *On Music* could have been said by Epicurus himself. Others, including the famous statement quoted by Asmis—that a poem insofar as it is a poem does not benefit—are sophisticated extensions and elaborations of Epicurus' basic beliefs.

Against this theoretical background, then, of Epicurean *poetics*, what could be the nature of Epicurean *poetry*? Lucretius' is one approach: proselytizing poetry in the service of Epicureanism. If in Philodemus' phrase it is not the poetry as such that benefits, the poetry will nonetheless have justified itself if it turns the reader to a better way of life thanks to its honey-sweet charms. Epicurus himself would not have needed such a poem, so it is probably Philodemus' style of poetry that would have appealed to him more than Lucretius', especially as Lucretius seems to have composed more for the reader whereas Philodemus' epigrams, almost certainly recited viva voce before audiences in Herculaneum, would have fit in better with the dinner parties that Epicurus considered an important part of the good life as lived in the Garden. We can probably get a good idea of Epicurus' ideal banquet from his *Symposium*, which Athenaeus tells us described a banquet whose company, unlike those in Plato and Xenophon, comprised only Epicurean philosophers, whom Athenaeus calls "prophets of atomism" (fr. 56 Usener).[16] It is just such an audience as this that Philodemus had on the bay of Naples, in his and Siro's modest houses and in the more grand villas of their Roman acquaintances who were their students and patrons, sometimes both at the same time. As I have argued at greater length elsewhere,[17] before this sophisticated audience Philodemus could compose and recite poems which were appreciated primarily for their Hellenistic grace. That is, as with much Hellenistic poetry, especially in epigrams, the wit often lies in the striking combination of old and new. This could take several forms, one of which is the ringing new changes on familiar *topoi*. Philodemus could depend upon his particular philosophically inclined audience to catch allusions not only to Epicurus but also to Socrates, Plato, Aristotle, and perhaps even more obscure thinkers. If this is true, then there is no need to look for philosophical consistency let alone Epicurean orthodoxy in the thirty-five or so poems we can credit to Philodemus.

As an example, we could look at the poem alluded to by Asmis in which he calls himself $μουcοφιλήc$, a friend to the muses. We should not lose sight of the fact that this occurs in a poem in which Philodemus invites a wealthy Roman to take part in a dinner party in honor of Epicurus, and thereafter to become Philodemus' patron. In

---

[15] See Dorandi 1990a.

[16] Athenaeus 5.187B = fr. 56 Usener ὁ δὲ Ἐπίκουρος ἅπαντας εἰcήγαγε προφήτας ἀτόμων.

[17] "The Epicurean philosopher as Hellenistic poet," below, Chapter 4.

such a context the -φιλης part of the word along with two other examples of the stem φιλ- in this poem remind us of some other meanings; first the friendship that was to prevail in an Epicurean setting, and second the Latin *amicitia* that, perhaps euphemistically, defined the mutual relationship between patron and poet.[18] Asmis has also alerted us to the likely significance of Philodemus telling Piso that if he comes tomorrow he will hear things things sweeter than the Phaeacians. If Epicurus himself cited the Phaeacian feast in the *Odyssey* as a model of his school's own dinner parties and as a result he was referred to as the Phaeacian philosopher, then Philodemus is almost certainly alluding to this particular Epicurean passage, which in turn alludes to Homer. A perfect example of Hellenistic poetic wit that could also serve as a perfect example of one person's—Philodemus' if not Lucretius'—idea of Epicurean poetic theory in action.

[18] Cf. P. White, "*Amicitia* and the profession of poetry in early imperial Rome," *JRS* 68 (1978), 74–92; R. Saller, "Patronage and friendship in early imperial Rome," in A. Wallace-Hadrill (ed.), *Patronage in Ancient Society* (London 1989), 49–62.

4

The Epicurean Philosopher as Hellenistic Poet

David Sider

Far from merely being a repository of lost Epicurean thought, Philodemus is also of interest for what may well be his own views on the nature of poetry. In the main, these demand our attention because their relation to Epicurus' own views on poetry is unclear if not at first glance outright antithetical. In particular, how can someone who more than once alluded to himself as an orthodox Epicurean write poetry when Epicurus seems to have abjured this very activity,[1] for, whether or not Philodemus's treatises are orthodox in their adherence to Epicurus, they are significant documents in and of themselves.[2] Furthermore, in addition to their philosophical interest, they cannot help but be of interest to students of literary criticism and of Latin literature, for Philodemus had the good luck or good sense to locate himself in Rome and then, it would seem, in the Bay of Naples, where he, along with Siro, came to be regarded as spokesmen for Epicurean dogma by upper-class Romans, in particular L. Calpurnius Piso, the father-in-law of Julius Caesar.[3] And where there are wealthy Romans

[1] Cf. Asmis, Chapter 2 above, who surveys the ancient evidence concerning Epicurus' attitudes towards writing, listening, and commenting on poetry. In brief, Epicurus argued that hearing poems recited (especially at Epicurean dinners) contributed to one's pleasure, but that criticizing what one has heard or composing poetry did not. Cf. Plutarch, *That Epicurus Actually Makes a Pleasant Life Impossible* c.13 (1095c–96c), Diog. Laert. 10.120f. That Epicureans from Metrodorus to Philodemus did in fact write works on the nature of poetry may indicate that Epicurus forbade literary analysis only during dinner on the grounds that it would spoil an otherwise pleasurable evening.

[2] In addition to the articles printed in this volume, cf. Dorandi 1990a, 2341ff., 2362f., for a brief survey of the Philodemean fragments on poetry; and in the same volume, Asmis 1990a, 2400–2406, for an overview of Philodemus' views with bibliographical references. See also M. Gigante, *Filodemo in Italia* (Florence 1990), esp. chapter 3, "Gli epigrammi di Filodemo quali testimonianze autobiografiche," pp. 63–79. As I have already indicated in my review, and as will become clear in what follows, my view is that Philodemus has fashioned a persona for himself in the epigrams which should not be taken at face value for any biographical information: cf. what I have written in *BMCR* 2 (1991), 353–55.

[3] Cicero's speech against Piso provides our most complete account of Philodemus (cc. 68–72); cf. R. G. M. Nisbet, *Cicero In L. Calpurnium Pisonem Oratio* (Oxford 1961) ad loc. and Appendices III and IV. Cicero sums up Philodemus and his poetry as follows: *Est autem hic de quo loquor non philosophia solum sed etiam ceteris studiis quae fere ceteros Epicureos neglegere dicunt perpolitus; poema porro facit ita festivum, ita concinnum, ita elegans, nihil ut fieri possit argutius* (70).

there are Roman poets, so that Philodemus' views on poetry, apart from their independent value as literary theory, would call for study simply because Vergil, Plotius Tucca, Lucius Varius Rufus, Quintilius Varus, Catullus, and others who were to be found in his company (including perhaps the young Horace) were influenced by his theoretical views as much as by his poetry.[4]

This is not the place to review the entirety of this influence and its scholarship (see n. 4 above), but more than a hint of Philodemus' importance for the study of Latin poetry can be gained from a brief look at some recent discoveries suggesting links between him and Vergil. In the first place, we now have *P.Oxy.* 3724, a list of ca. 175 *incipits* of Greek epigrams, at least 27 of them the beginning of known Philodemean poems.[5] This surprising statistic led its editor Peter Parsons and others to entertain the notion that many, perhaps a majority, of the remaining *incipits* of hitherto unknown poems also belong to Philodemus. A number of these *incipits* clearly allude to Roman topics (suggesting that, after the first few words, others of the *incipit*-poems referred to Rome or Italy), a theme we do not find in the Philodemean poems preserved in their entirety by the *Palatine Anthology*, but which is certainly appropriate for a Greek poet who lived in Italy for many years.[6] For our purposes the most interesting are two which begin with the word Παρθενόπης (col. iv 13–14). This is certainly our earliest reference to Naples by its poetic synonym Parthenope,[7] which appears next in extant literature in the *sphragis* to Vergil's *Georgics* (4.563f.):

> illo Vergilium me tempore dulcis alebat
> Parthenope studiis florentem ignobilis oti.

The collocation of Parthenope and *otium* evokes the katastematic pleasures enjoyed by Vergil in the company of Siro and Philodemus.[8] If Vergil can allude here to the

---

[4] The best survey of Philodemus' relation to Latin poetry remains that of Tait 1941. Among more recent articles, the following may be noted: Barra 1973; id. 1977–78, 87–104; M. Gigante, "Virgilio fra Ercolano e Pompei," *A&R* 28 (1983), 31–50; id., "Cercida, Filodemo e Orazio," in *RF* 235–44; id., "Filodemo e Pisone: Da Ercolano a Roma," *ASNP* ser.3 (1985), 855–66; L. Landolfi, "Tracce Filodemee di estetica e di epigrammatica simpotica in Catullo," *CErc* 12 (1982), 137–43; M. Marcovich, "Catullus 13 and Philodemus 23," *QUCC* 11 (1982), 131–38; A. K. Michels, "Παρρησία and the satire of Horace," *CPh* 39 (1944), 173–77; L. P. Wilkinson, "Philodemus and poetry," *G&R* 2 (1932–3), 144–51.

[5] *Oxyrhynchus Papyri* 54 (1987), no. 3724. In addition to the incipits identified as Philodemean by Parsons, cf. my suggestions in *ZPE* 76 (1989), 229–36, and Gigante 1989; and A. Cameron, *The Greek Anthology from Meleager to Planudes* (Oxford 1993), Appendix VII. Only seven poems assigned to Philodemus by one or both of the mss. do not occur among the incipits (which amount to no more than a few words each): *Palatine Anthology* 5.8 (Meleager 69 in *Hellenistic Epigrams*; ascribed to Meleager by P, to Philodemus by Pl), 5.15 (3 GP), 5.124 (10), 6.246 (Argentarius 18; ascribed to Argentarius by Pl, to Philodemus by P), 11.318 (28), 12.173 (16), 16.234 (29). Clearly, the presence or absence of a doubtful poem among the incipits will have to be considered when deciding for or against Philodemean authorship.

[6] It is probably just an accident that none of these have survived: Crinagoras' poems alluding to Roman topics (assigned to the loosely defined declamatory epigrams found in Book 9 of the Anthology) show that there was no anti-Roman bias in Cephalas and later anthologists.

[7] Cf., e.g., Servius ad *Georg.* 563.1–8, who says that Parthenope was the original name for Naples. In fact, however, the original Parthenope, settled by Rhodians (Strabo 14.654, Stephanus of Byzantium, s.v. Παρθενόπη) was later absorbed into the increasingly prosperous Naples. Cf. B. Capasso, *Napoli Greco-romana* (Napoli 1905), M. Napoli, *Napoli Greco-romana* (Napoli 1959), E. Pirovine, *Napoli nella visione classica del Golfo delle Sirene* (Napoli 1977), esp. pp. 9–28.

[8] On Epicurean "pleasure in rest," cf. e.g. Diogenes Laertius 10.136 ἡ μὲν γὰρ ἀταραξία καὶ

Epicurean pleasures to be found in Naples, it is tempting to follow a suggestion of Dirk Obbink and at least entertain the possibility that in beginning a line with *Parthenope* Vergil is alluding to one or more poems of Philodemus that may well also have offered an appreciation of the pleasurable ambience to be found in the Epicurean Gardens of Naples, just as Ovid can clearly allude to Vergil, if not Philodemus as well (*Metamorphoses* 15.711 f.):[9]

> Herculaneamque urbem Stabiasque et in otia natam
> Parthenopen

Precisely what Vergil heard from Philodemus can of course never be recovered in detail, but it may well be significant that Philodemus addresses Vergil, along with Varius Rufus, Varus, and Plotius Tucca, in his work *On Flattery*,[10] where the criterion for distinguishing the true friend from the flatterer is that the former will not hesitate to speak frankly; that is, the virtue opposed to κολακεία is παρρηςία.[11] That this particular group offered friendly advice on each other's poetry is strongly suggested by Horace, *The Art of Poetry* 438–452, where the person who does not hesitate to criticize even trifling matters in a friend's poetry is none other than Quintilius Varus.[12] Brink ad loc. says that "I know of no evidence attesting the conjunction of friendship and criticism in extant Hellenistic writing on literary theory as it is attested in H[orace]," but, given the strong poetic interests of the quartet here addressed[13] and Varus' appearance in both places, it is easy to imagine that the parallel Brink desiderated was located in a now lost passage of Philodemus *On Flattery*.

All of this is by way of saying that in Philodemus we have a theorist and practi-

---

ἀπονία καταστηματικαί εἰςιν ἡδοναί; J. Rist, *Epicurus* (Cambridge 1972), 100–11. For Vergil's association with Siro, cf. Donatus, *Life of Vergil* 68 *audivit a Sirone praecepta Epicuri*; W. Crönert, *Kolotes und Menedemos* (Leipzig 1906; repr. Amsterdam 1965), 125–27. Cicero, *De finibus* 2.119 has Torquatus link Siro and Philodemus: *Sironem dicis et Philodemum, cum optimos viros tum homines doctissimos*. See further *P.Herc.* 312, discussed by Gigante 1984, 74–77.

[9] The incipits may offer another link between Vergil and Philodemus: col. v 19 παρθένιος. This may of course, as Parsons points out, simply be the adjective; but, on the working assumption that any *incipit* of an unknown poem is likely to come from an epigram of Philodemus, we should certainly entertain the possibility that mentioned here is Παρθένιος of Nicaea, Vergil's teacher (Macrobius, *Saturnalia* 5.57). Philodemus names at least eight of his male acquaintances in the extant epigrams (the women's names all seem to be fictitious). But another possibility is that referred to here is none other than Vergil himself, who was called Parthenias (i.e., the maidenly one) by his friends: Donatus, *Life of Vergil* 11; Servius, *Life of Vergil* 8.

[10] Vergil's name, long conjectured in two papyrus fragments of Philodemus, has finally been found: *P.Herc. Paris* 2: Πλώτιε καὶ Οὐά|ρ[ι]ε καὶ Οὐεργ[ί]λιε καὶ Κοιντ[ί]λιε; cf. Gigante and Capasso 1989, 3–6.

[11] Cf. R. Phillipson, "Philodemos," *RE* 19.2 (1938), 2470. Gargiulo 1981, 104 argues that this virtue is φιλία, but it is more accurate to say that friends display virtues toward one another (such as frankness), whereas κακοί display vices (such as flattery). Setting Philodemus' writings on flattery into a historical philosophical context is F. Longo Auricchio, "Per la concezione filodemea dell'adulazione," *CErc* 16 (1986), 79–91.

[12] The whole passage demands attention, but note in particular 438f. *Quintilio si quid recitares*, "*corrige sodes / hoc*" *aiebat*, and 450f. *nec dicet "cur ego amicum / offendam in nugis?"* For more on Horace's debt to Philodemus in regard to frankness, cf. Gigante 1990 (above, n. 2), 29–36.

[13] Cf. Chapter 3 above.

tioner of poetry whose influence on Augustan poetry is clearly extensive. In what follows I will concentrate on the poetry, but will further assume that any philosopher of poetic theory who himself writes poetry invites us to read the latter with the former in view (and perhaps vice versa as well).

Although the Greek Anthology has preserved only thirty or so[14] poems under (or alongside) his name, Horace almost certainly refers to one more, and the Oxyrhynchus incipits suggest that his original output may have run to the hundreds.[15] The question that now arises—and this is the particular thrust of my investigation—is what, if any, relationship exists between his theory of poetry and his own verse compositions. And since his theory is that of an Epicurean a necessary second question is: How Epicurean (if at all) is his poetry? Another question, also related: How can someone who regards himself as an orthodox Epicurean write poetry at all, since Epicurus seems to have abjured this form of activity?[16]

In order to define the relationship between his poetry and his poetic theory, we should obviously look to the theory for guidance. We might, for example, expect to find there statements of a general kind that would be applied or exemplified in his own as well as in other people's poetry. It would then be simply a matter of plugging his poetry into his theory. We are, however, quite far from this ideal situation. First, as with all his prose philosophical treatises, the state of preservation of *On Poems* and *On Music* prevents us at present from having more than a few consecutive sentences whose sense can be be securely deciphered. (*On the Good King According to Homer* is in better shape, and although it is less theoretical than the two other works named will be referred to below.) Second, although we find occasionally several statements of a theoretical character, we should be cautious in trying to adapt theories designed to deal with epic and tragedy to the slighter genre of four- to eight-line epigrams. Although, as we shall see, this very choice of genre accords with Philodemus' view of appropriate Epicurean poetry.

And third, what we do have from *On Poems* tells us that Philodemus was far more concerned with the relationship between form and content and other literary matters than he was with content alone.[17] Indeed, he was quite firm in his belief that the excellence of poetry is to be found in what may be called aesthetic qualities such as

---

[14] His poems are most conveniently located in Gow and Page 1968, 1.351–69 (text), 2.371–400 (commentary). Disagreement of attribution between the two main mss. of the Greek Anthology accounts for the imprecise number given above. Gow and Page gather twenty-nine epigrams under Philodemus' name. In my forthcoming edition I shall argue that four more should be assigned to Philodemus and that one should be ascribed to another claimant; about three remaining I am in doubt. For a study of the formation of the two major collections of epigrams, cf. Cameron 1993 (above, n. 5).

[15] Horace, *Satires* 1.2.119ff. (cited below) almost certainly alludes to a lost poem of Philodemus; cf. *ZPE* 76 (1989), 229.

[16] Epicurus may have employed more literary allusions than he has been given credit for; cf. D. Clay, *Lucretius and Epicurus* (Ithaca 1983), 302 n. 58, but he still seems to have discouraged his associates from the actual writing of poetry. Even if he did not do so actively, the mere fact that the Master did not write poetry could have served as a deterrent. Some Epicureans, however, obviously thought that an exception could be made if the poems they wrote espoused the right philosophical position; in addition to Lucretius, there is Varius' *On Death* and perhaps others; cf. Chapter 3 above.

[17] On the other hand, in *On the Good King According to Homer*, Philodemus extracts his points from content alone; cf. Asmis 1991b.

euphony and word order rather than exclusively in its content.[18] His most famous statement along these lines is that "Poems, insofar as they are poems, do not provide benefit." He also held that bad men can make good poets.[19] These views, antithetical as they are to those expressed in authors from Aristophanes and Plato to Lucretius, may not immediately send us off in the right direction, but they should remain as benchmarks for any conclusions we may reach.

How then are we to interpret the epigrams of Philodemus the Epicurean? One approach is to examine them for signs of Epicurean content, as has been done, for example, by Jane Macintosh Snyder. This is of limited application, however, first because it leaves the stuff of non-Epicurean content out in the cold; and second because we are doing what Philodemus has told us not to do, namely judge a poem by its content. Another approach might be to determine that there can in fact be no join between Philodemus the Epicurean and Philodemus the poet; that the poems emerged from a part of Philodemus' psyche that either had nothing to do with his professed Epicureanism or, worse, was at war with the dictates of his Epicurean beliefs. This last interpretation is maintained by Philip Merlan,[20] who thought that there was some sort of tension existing within the person who was both poet and philosopher. This is an intriguing notion, but one I think far more appropriate to Plato than to the elegant and polished epigrammatist.

Some other answer, I think, will have to be sought: one that is perhaps more comprehensive than the one provided by Snyder and one less *angst*-ridden than the one we find in Merlan. Perhaps if we begin with the poetry rather than with the theory, a picture will develop that will touch upon Philodemus' philosophy. After all, with the exception of his poetic invitation to Piso to attend one of the monthly get-togethers in Epicurus' honor, the epigrams extant make no overt reference to Epicureanism. This poem, though, does provide the obvious point of departure for a study of the philosopher-poet (*Palatine Anthology* 11.44 = 22 Gow and Page):

1   αὔριον εἰς λιτήν ϲε καλιάδα, φίλτατε Πείϲων,
     ἐξ ἐνάτηϲ ἕλκει μουϲοφιλὴϲ ἕταροϲ
     εἰκάδα δειπνίζων ἐνιαύϲιον· εἰ δ' ἀπολείψειϲ
     οὔθατα καὶ Βρομίου Χιογενῆ πρόποϲιν,
5   ἀλλ' ἑτάρουϲ ὄψει παναληθέαϲ, ἀλλ' ἐπακούϲῃ
     Φαιήκων γαίηϲ πουλὺ μελιχρότερα,
     ἢν δέ ποτε ϲτρέψῃϲ καὶ ἐϲ ἡμέαϲ ὄμματα, Πείϲων,
     ἄξομεν ἐκ λιτῆϲ εἰκάδα πιοτέρην.

P Φιλοδήμου, caret Pl   Π iv.4 αυριονειϲλειτην.ε

---

[18] Cf. F. Sbordone, "Filodemo e la teorica dell'eufonia," *RAAN* 30 (1955), 25–51 = Sbordone 1983, 125–53 at 138.

[19] Cf. Philodemus, *On Rhetoric* 1.226, col. xxi 12–15 ὄν[τ]εϲ πονηροί, τ[ε]χνῖται | [δέ] ὅμωϲ οὐ κωλύονται | δ[ιαφορ]ώτατοι π[ά]ν[τ]ων ὑπ[άρχ]ειν. I agree with Grube 1965, 200 that these words apply to poetry as well as to rhetoric.

[20] J. M. Snyder, "The poetry of Philodemus the Epicurean," *CJ* 68 (1972), 346–53; P. Merlan, "Aristoteles' und Epikurs müssige Götter," *Zeitschr. f. philos. Forsch.* 21 (1967), 489f. Cf. also A. Ronconi, "Poetica e critica epicurea," in *Interpretazioni letterarie nei classici* (Florence 1972), 64–90.

2 ἔταρος Salm., ἔταρις P   3 ἐνιαύcιον] ἐπιμήνιος Schmid tent.
ἀπολείψεις Brunck -ψῃις P   6 πουλύ Ppc, πολύ Pac

Tomorrow, friend Piso, your musical comrade drags you to his modest digs at three in the afternoon, feeding you at your annual visit to the Twentieth. If you will miss udders and wine *mis en bouteille* in Chios, yet you will see true-blue comrades, yet you will hear things far sweeter than the land of the Phaeacians. And if you ever turn an eye to us too, Piso, instead of a modest feast we shall lead a richer one.[21]

Although only the one word εἰκάς, "twentieth," overtly signals the Epicurean nature of the next day's dinner, everyone in Philodemus' audience would know that Epicurus himself had established the twentieth of every month as the day on which his followers would meet to remember him.[22] Philodemus identifies himself in the poem only as μουcοφιλής, which in this tight little poem where there is no room for ornamental epithets suggests not only that Philodemus is a poet,[23] but also that poetry will be on the agenda for the next day's festivity. Furthermore, because of the connotation of the word εἰκάς, one can also suspect that Philodemus' calling Piso φίλτατε is designed to evoke the central Epicurean idea of friendship.[24] But if φίλτατε can do this, why can't μουcοφιλής as well?[25] With this one word Philodemus thus elliptically but not very enigmatically alludes to himself as both poet and Epicurean. Philodemus clearly did not suffer mental anguish at the thought that poet and Epicurean could simultaneously occupy the same body.

Piso, the addressee of this poem, can be expected to understand the Epicurean connotation of friendship, but as a Roman statesman, he would know that the friendship alluded to in this poem could also evoke the patron–poet relationship. For Philodemus quite clearly, if not shamelessly, is angling for reciprocal benefits from Piso in the future. In return, as the reference to the Phaeacians indicates, Piso will receive the combined pleasures of poetry and Epicurean companionship. Piso, that is, will

---

[21] For literature on this poem, cf. D. Clay, "The cults of Epicurus," *CErc* 16 (1986), 11–28; Gigante 1990 (above, n. 2), 104f.; O. Hiltbrunner, "Einladung zum epikureischen Freundsmahl," in *Antidosis: Festschrift W. Kraus* (Vienna 1972), 168–72. For its relationship to Latin invitation poetry, especially Catullus, cf. L. Edmunds, *AJPh* 103 (1982), 184–88; Landolfi 1982 (above, n. 4); Marcovich 1982 (above, n. 4) = *Studies in Greek Poetry* (Atlanta 1991), 193–99; G. Williams, *Tradition and Originality* (Oxford 1968), 125f.

[22] The evidence is conveniently available in Clay 1986 (above, n. 21), 20 (T 6–11), 21 (T 16–17). Cf. further K. Alpers, "Epikurs Geburtstag," *MH* 25 (1968), 47–50; D. M. Lewis, *CR* 19 (1969), 121f.

[23] Cf. Callimachus, *Aitia* 1.2 οἳ Μούcης οὐκ ἐγένοντο φίλοι, 37–38 Μοῦcαι γὰρ ὅcουc ἴδον ὄθματι παῖδα / μὴ λοξῷ, πολιοὺc οὐκ ἀπέθεντο φίλουc; Theocritus 1.141 τὸν Μοίcαιc φίλον ἄνδρα (Daphnis), 7.95 φίλος ἔπλεο Μοίcαιc (Lycidas), 11.6 πεφιλημένον ἔξοχα Μοίcαιc (Nikias); Meleager 1.1 (*Palatine Anthology* 4.1) Μοῦcα φίλα; Nossis 11.3 in *Hellenistic Epigrams* (*Palatine Anthology* 7.718; text uncertain).

[24] Cf. J. Rist, *Epicurus: An Introduction* (Cambridge 1972), 127–39; B. Gemelli, "L'amicizia in Epicuro," *Sandalion* 1 (1978), 59–72; P. Mitsis, "Epicurus on friendship and altruism," *OSAP* 5 (1987), 127–53.

[25] The word is a *hapax* in Greek literature; it would seem to be passive in sense, but a simultaneous active sense is possible, especially as *philia* is a reciprocal relationship; on which see further below. (The similarly formed θεοφιλής is not found in an active sense until Philo, but a poet can always force things.)

provide patronage,[26] while Philodemus will provide both Epicurean ambience and poetic delights: Piso and Philodemus will be both *amici*—i.e. patron and poet—and φίλοι, i.e. two members of an Epicurean fellowship.

How balanced will this relationship be? Philodemus after all has invited a wealthy Roman to a humble dwelling where he should not look forward to such delights as grilled sow's udders.[27] But this is to be expected; Epicureans, we know, make a virtue of λιτότης, frugality.[28] Philodemus' use of the word ἐνιαύσιον sheds further light on this point. Although universally taken to modify εἰκάδα, this cannot be correct, for all poets,[29] as well as Plato, Herodotus, Xenophon, Aristotle, Hippocrates, et al., treat this word as an adjective of three terminations. Failure to recognize this has led to the spilling of much ink on the question of what exactly the phrase "year-long" or "annual Twentieth" could mean. This chimaera in the literature arose from another misunderstanding, which once promulgated became an entrenched misinterpretation. I speak of the regular translation of δειπνίζων as "celebrating," with εἰκάδα as its object. In fact, the verb δειπνίζειν means only "to feed (someone) dinner," and hence demands a personal object. With this recognized, it is easy to see that its object is the cε of line one, i.e. Piso.[30] It follows, therefore, that ἐνιαύσιον modifies this cε in the manner of many other temporal adjectives.[31] The personal pronoun was the object of the finite verb of v. 2 and would readily be carried over to v.3 by the transitive nature of δειπνίζων. Philodemus, thus, is inviting Piso to come for *his*, Piso's, annual—or perhaps, merely infrequent—visit to one of the monthly Twentieths. With these grammatical points settled, we can now see that Philodemus' use of ἐνιαύσιον parallels that which obtains in the well-known begging song the

---

[26] W. Allen and P. De Lacy, "The patrons of Philodemus," *CPh* 34 (1939), 59–65, are probably too skeptical of the evidence suggesting that Piso was (for whatever length of time) Philodemus' patron, but they do not deny that in this poem Philodemus is trying to obtain Piso's patronage (they say he failed); cf. Cicero, *Against Piso* 68 *Is [sc. Philodemus] . . . non fastidivit eius [sc. Pisonis] amicitiam . . . ; dedit se in consuetudinem sic ut prorsus una viveret nec fere ab isto umquam discederet.* This passage, which cannot be treated as a complete rhetorical falsehood, strongly suggests that Piso was thought of as Philodemus' patron. Cf. B. Gold (ed.), *Literary and Artistic Patronage in Ancient Rome* (Austin 1982); ead. *Literary Patronage in Greece and Rome* (Chapel Hill 1987).

[27] Which Romans prized far more than Greeks; cf. Athenaeus 9.399c = 14.656E. Note that Piso will not find the unequal distribution common in Roman banquets of food among the guests; instead there will be the more equitable sharing associated with philosophers; cf. Cicero, *To Atticus* 13.52.2, Pliny, *Letters* 2.6.

[28] Cf. Epicurus, *Letter to Menoeceus* 130, Philodemus, *On Death* 4, 30.10, *On Estate Management* 38.7, Cicero, *De finibus* 1.65, Vergil, *Catalepton* 8; Hiltbrunner 1972 (above, n. 21), 169–71; Gigante 1990 (above, n. 2), 106f.

[29] Alcaeus 130.35 L.P.; Ion of Chios 19 F 21, Euripides, *Hippolytus* 37.

[30] Εἰκάδα = "feast of the twentieth" (cf. Pliny, *Natural History* 35 *ferias . . . quas icades vocant*), and is here an internal accusative; cf. Plutarch, *That Epicurus Actually Makes a Pleasant Life Impossible* 1089c (words put in Epicurus' mouth by Carneades:) ποίας εἰκάδας ἐδείπνησα πολυτελέστατα; Matro *Conv. Att.* 1f. δεῖπνα . . . δείπνιcεν ἡμᾶc. The Plutarch passage should not be emended to ποίας εἰκάδοc (as with Bernadakis and De Lacy) and construed as a genitive of time. Since Carneades mocks Epicurus for making lists (οἷον ἐξ ἐφημερίδων) of past pleasures— "ποσάκιc Ἡδείᾳ καὶ Λεοντίῳ" ἢ "ποῦ Θάcιον ἔπιον"—the plural of the mss. should be allowed to remain.

[31] Cf. e.g. Philodemus, Epigram 3.2 ἑcπέριοc; and for the phenomenon in general of adjectives used adverbially, F. Létoublon, "'Ὕcτατον ἐλθεῖν, ἄγγελοc ἐλθεῖν: Prédication, attribut, et apposition," in A. Rijksbaron et al. (eds.), *In the Footsteps of R. Kühner* (Amsterdam 1988), 161–75.

Eiresione, traditionally sung, we are told, during an annual holiday by beggars who gather before the houses of the rich:

δῶμα προϲετραπόμεϲθ᾽ ἀνδρὸϲ μέγα δυναμένοιο,
ὃϲ μέγα μὲν δύναται, μέγα δὲ βρέμει ὄλβιοϲ αἰεί,
αὐταὶ ἀνακλίνεϲθε θύραι· Πλοῦτοϲ γὰρ ἔϲειϲι
πολλόϲ, ϲὺν Πλούτῳ δὲ καὶ Εὐφροϲύνη τεθαλυῖα
Εἰρήνη τ᾽ ἀγαθή.

. . .

νεῦμαί τοι, νεῦμαι ἐνιαύϲιοϲ, ὥϲτε χελιδὼν
ἕϲτηκ᾽ ἐν προθύροιϲ.[32]

Let us turn to the house of a man of wealth and power, who accomplishes much and, prosperous, roars mightily.[33] Open of your own accord, doors; much wealth lies within, and with wealth joy flourishes and gentle peace . . . . I come then, I come yearly, like a light-footed swallow who stands in your forecourt.

At first glance, the situation would appear to be the complete opposite to that of the invitation to Piso. A beggar goes to the house of the rich and powerful, saying "I come [return?], I come on my annual visit." ἐνιαύϲιοϲ is so rarely used in this personal sense,[34] that it does not seem far-fetched to imagine that Philodemus intended Piso to recall the *Eiresione*. Piso, that is, as the epigram points out, is the rich man coming to the home of a poor, or at least frugal, man. But ἐνιαύϲιοϲ suggests that in a certain sense he, like the beggar, comes hat in hand hoping to take away with him something that can be found only at Philodemus' house. If the surface of this invitation poem puts Philodemus in the position of beggar, the subtext suggests that it is Piso himself in need. But the notion that the beggar, if offered something, has the power to bestow benefit on the house, is found in other begging songs. Note how in Phoinix fr. 2 (Powell, *Collectanea Alexandrina* [Oxford 1925]) Ploutos is equated not with the rich man within, as in the *Eiresione*, but with the beggar (v. 8 ὦ παῖ, θύρην ἄγκλινε, Πλοῦτοϲ ἔκρουϲε, "Open the door, slave; Wealth knocked."), who has the power to bestow fecundity and wealth on those in the house:

θεοί, γένοιτο πάντ᾽ ἄμεμπτοϲ ἡ κούρη,
κἀφνειὸν ἄνδρα κὠνομαϲὸν ἐξεύροι,
καὶ τῷ γέροντι πατρὶ κοῦρον εἰϲ χεῖραϲ
καὶ μητρὶ κούρην εἰϲ τὰ γοῦνα κατθείη,

. . .

ἀμείβομαι Μούϲῃϲι πρὸϲ θύρηϲ ᾄδων,
καὶ δόντι καὶ μὴ δόντι, πλεῦνα τῶν ⟨Γύ⟩γεω.

Gods, may the daughter be blameless; may she find a husband both wealthy and of good name; and may she place a son in her father's hands and a daughter in

---

[32] *Vita Homeri Herodotea* 467ff. = *Hom. Ep.* 15. On begging songs, cf. W. Burkert, *Greek Religion* (Cambridge, Mass. 1985), 101f.　　[33] πρέπει (Ilgen) would make better sense.

[34] On the supposed hibernation of sparrows and their return in the spring, cf. D. W. Thompson, *Glossary of Greek Birds* (Oxford 1936), 318ff. In particular, note the Rhodian swallow-song sung by Χελιδονϲταί which begins ἦλθ᾽, ἦλθε χελιδὼν ὥραϲ καλὰϲ ἄγουϲα, καλοὺϲ ἐνιαυτούϲ, and which ends ἂν δὲ φέρῃϲ τι μέγα δή τι φέροιο. ἄνοιγ᾽ ἄνοιγε τὰν θύραν χελιδόνι (Athenaeus 360c = 848 *Poetae Melici Graeci*).

her mother's lap. Singing at the doors with the Muses, I make the wealth of both those who give and those who do not give greater than Gyges'.

Both Philodemus and Piso, then, are each in his own way in need; and each has the power to aid the other. This interpretation sits comfortably with other hints in the epigram that the next day's dinner (like friendship itself) will prove mutually beneficial. In particular, I suggest, Philodemus' comparing Piso to the king of the Phaeacians would seem to entail that Philodemus is comparable to Odysseus, and hence that just as Odysseus and Alkinoos rewarded each other, the former with fine words the latter with gifts of a more material nature, so too will Philodemus and Piso benefit each other. Both, that is, are comparable to Odysseus, whom Philodemus elsewhere compares to a κόλαξ, a parasite.[35] Here, however, the boundary between flatterer and friend is blurred, so that what by Roman standards is an inherently unequal relationship is made to approximate, however obliquely, the equality demanded by Epicurean friendship.

The invitation to dinner thus invites Piso to act—ἐνιαύϲιοϲ entails "continue to act"—as Philodemus' patron.[36] Philodemus' mention of the Phaeacians appears all the more significant when we note, first, that Epicurus and his followers were characterized by their opponents as "Phaeacians," i.e., hedonists,[37] and, next, that the Phaeacians figure significantly in Philodemus' *On the Good King According to Homer*, which is dedicated to none other than Piso.[38] More can be done along these lines in interpreting the invitation epigram,[39] but enough has already been said to show that even here where the reference to Epicureanism is explicit, a good deal of the Epicurean point of the invitation is wedded to its poetic form. And as with many another Hellenistic poem, full understanding comes only with recognition of its allusions to other literary works.

What then of the remaining poems, where we are not given even so much as the one word εἰκάϲ to signal their Epicurean nature. We could begin by classifying them along traditional lines. Thus we would note immediately that a clear majority (twenty-two) of the thirty-seven poems ascribed (doubtfully or not) to Philodemus

---

[35] Cf. Longo 1986 (above, n. 11), 81. Failure to recognize this ambiguity led R. Aubreton in the Bude edition to compare first Piso to Odysseus and then Philodemus. Aubreton was followed by M. Jufresa, "Il mito dei Feaci in Filodemo," in *La Regione sotterrata dal Vesuvio. Studi e Prospetti. Atti del Convegno Internazionale, 11–15 Novembre 1979* (Naples 1982), 509–518, at 517.

[36] ἄξομεν on the last line is not *pluralia tantum*: both Philodemus and Piso will enjoy the true wealth of Epicurean fellowship.

[37] Heraclitus, *Alleg. Hom.* 75 (fr. 229 Usener) ὁ δὲ Φαίαξ φιλόϲοφοϲ Ἐπίκουροϲ ὁ τῆϲ ἡδονῆϲ ἐν τοῖϲ κήποιϲ γεωργόϲ. Cf. Asmis, Chapter 2 above.

[38] The text has been recently edited by T. Dorandi, *Il Buon Re secondo Omero* (Naples 1982). See also Asmis 1991b. Cf. Asmis on Philodemus in *On Music* 4 on the desirability of musical performances at festive dinners (nn. 69–72).

[39] For example, as Asmis shows, a key Homeric passage in ancient Epicurean–Stoic polemics was *Odyssey* 9.5ff.

οὐ γὰρ ἐγώ γε τί φημι τέλοϲ χαριέϲτερον εἶναι
ἢ ὅτ' ἐϋφροϲύνη μὲν ἔχῃ κατὰ δῆμον ἅπαντα,
δαιτυμόνεϲ δ' ἀνὰ δώματ' ἀκουάζωνται ἀοιδοῦ.

For me, the parallels between this passage and the *Eiresione* strengthen the case made above that this poem lies in the background to that of Philodemus.

are erotic.[40] The list of incipits from Oxyrhynchus too clearly has its share of erotic themes (which would be true of almost any selection from the Palatine Anthology), although most of course are indeterminate. But more interestingly the list also suggests that Philodemus (again on the assumption that it contains much by him) wrote often of Rome and Naples.[41] The remaining extant poems are anathematic, sepulchral, skoptic, and sympotic, but these traditional labels do nothing to determine whether Philodemus is or is not alluding to Epicurean doctrine. Epicurus, after all, wrote on many subjects, including love and marriage; and Philodemus, as we have just seen, is a master of allusion. We do not have to imagine that every poem he wrote in Italy was intended for Vergil's ears to grant him an audience thoroughly familiar with (if not actually converted to) Epicurean views, and equally conversant with (if not actually practitioners of) the allusive nature of Hellenistic poetry.

To see the erotic poems in their proper Epicurean setting, however, one must recognize first that many of them should not be read in isolation but rather as the constituent elements of a no-longer completely extant love cycle addressed to one woman, Xanthippe; and, second and more pertinent here, that the woman in question was pictured as a wife who would be the ideal partner for a philosopher.[42] That this wife is the subject of erotic poems comes as something of a surprise: first, wives are generally not to be spoken of at all, let alone in an erotic context; and, second, the traditional genre of erotic poetry is concerned with the winning and losing of someone who can satisfy one's passion, whereas wives are, at least in many husbands' minds, already "won."[43]

---

[40] Cf. n. 14 above.

[41] In addition to the Parthenope incipits discussed above, col. iv 25 may contain the name Καῖcαρ; iv 29 mentions the Roman *palliolum*; vii 23 may contain the Roman name Mucius. Cf. further Parsons 1987 (above, n. 5), 67f.

[42] D. Sider, "The love poems of Philodemus," *AJPh* 108 (1987), 310–24. In addition to the argument presented there and below, a passage in one of Alciphron's Letters of Courtesans is of interest: Epicurus' "girl friend" Leontion complains about the way Epicurus treats her and others: οἷά με Ἐπίκουροc οὗτοc διοικεῖ . . . . καὶ cωκρατίζειν καὶ cτωμυλεύεcθαι, καὶ Ἀλκιβιάδην τινὰ Πυθοκλέα νομίζει καὶ Ξανθίππην ἐμὲ οἴεται ποιήcειν (Alciphron 2.2.1–3 = fr. 142 Usener). How likely is it that Alciphron would have originated the idea of Epicurus' acting like Socrates and treating Leontion like Xanthippe? The Epicureans were frequent and strong critics of Socrates (not least for his irony); cf. M. T. Riley, "The Epicurean criticism of Socrates," *Phoenix* 34 (1980), 55–68; K. Kleve, "Scurra Atticus: The Epicurean view of Socrates," in *ΣΥΖΗΤΗΣΙΣ: Studi . . . a Marcello Gigante* (Naples 1983), 2.227–53; P. A. Vander Waerdt, "Colotes and the Epicurean refutation of Skepticism," *GRBS* 30 (1989), 253ff.; A. A. Long, "Socrates in Hellenistic philosophy," *CQ* 38 (1988), 150–71. Alciphron may have found this comparison in one or more comedies; and if this is so, Philodemus may have used these comedies to shape the relationship between his poetic persona and the woman he calls Xanthippe. (Least likely is the possibility that Alciphron's comparison comes from his reading of Philodemus' epigrams.)

[43] As Philodemus says in a poem outside the Xanthippe cycle, when trying to decide between two women, one a courtesan, the other a protected virgin, οὐ γὰρ ἕτοιμα / βούλομαι, ἀλλὰ ποθῶ πᾶν / τὸ φυλλαccόμενον (*Palatine Anthology* 12.173 = 16 Gow and Page). It is in support of this very *topos* that Horace names Philodemus (*Satires* 1.2.119–22):

> parabilem amo venerem facilemque.
> illam "post paulo," "sed pluris," "si exierit vir,"
> Gallis, hanc Philodemus ait sibi, quae neque magno
> stet pretio neque cunctetur cum est iussa venire.

Cf. further Meleager 18 *Hellenistic Epigrams* (*Palatine Anthology* 12.86), Argentarius 4 Gow and Page

In making my case earlier, I pointed out several philosophical allusions: First, the wife's name, Xanthippe, cannot help but recall Socrates' wife; moreover, Philodemus' choice of this name becomes all the more significant when one notes that in one of his works on poetic theory, now partially preserved in *P. Herc.* 994, he regards certain names as uneuphonic: [   ]ώ, Φοῖ[νι]ξ, Ξανθ[όс], Ζῆθοс.⁴⁴ If space permitted, the third name could be restored as Ξανθώ, but in either case Philodemus' choice of this name for the woman in so many of his poems would have struck his audience as odd, making them look for a reason that would overcome its euphonic shortcomings.

Second, the age at which the narrator—let's call him Philodemus—comes to his senses and realizes that he should give up his life of debauchery and settle down is given in one poem as thirty-seven, the very year Aristotle in the *Politics* determined as the ideal age for a man to marry; the age at which Aristotle thought the woman should marry, eighteen, intriguingly appears as the first and only word of a fragmentary epigram by, almost certainly, Philodemus.⁴⁵ The idea that a woman could be a philosophical partner I tried to show was especially Epicurean, but account must also be taken of the allusions to Socrates and Aristotle.

And to the list Epicurus, Socrates, Aristotle, I want to add a fourth name, that of Polemon, the early head of the Academy. Polemon led a wild life when young, but rejected it all to live the life of philosophy. Many sources attest to this conversion, including Philodemus himself in his history of philosophers: "Polemon," Philodemus says, "is reported to have been an undisciplined chariot driver in his youth, driving while intoxicated through the Kerameikos. His wife brought him up on charges of illicit sexual conduct. He loved boys and he loved lads, and he always made sure to carry some money around with him, so that he could have quick sex with whomever he might meet. But once he was captivated by the lectures of Xenocrates, the head of the Academy, and spent some time with him, he so changed his way of life so as never to alter his manner or even his tone of voice, no matter how provoked."⁴⁶

(*Palatine Anthology* 5.89), Rufinus 5 Page (*Palatine Anthology* 5.18), Ovid, *The Art of Love* 1.717, Propertius 2.23.12 ff., Martial 9.32.

⁴⁴ Col. xxix Nardelli. Cf. Sbordone 1983, 138.

⁴⁵ See above n. 4. It has to be said of course that any epigram beginning thus is statistically far more likely to be in the form of an epitaph which mentions the young age of the girl to increase the pathos; e.g., Dioscorides 40.5 *Hellenistic Epigrams* (*Palatine Anthology* 7.167) ὀκτωκαιδεκέτις δ' αὐτὴ θάνον ἄρτι τεκοῦσα. Cf. *Palatine Anthology* 7.163–66, also on the death of young women in childbirth, each of which specifies at which age (three at 22, one at 20).

⁴⁶ *P.Herc.* 1021, col. iv 13, ed. K. Gaiser, *Philodems Academica* (Stuttgart 1988), 230–33: ἐλέγετο δ' εἶναι τῶν [ἐ]πί τινα χρόνον ἁρματροφηсάντων. ἱστορεῖται δὲ κα[ὶ] νεανίсκ[ος] ἀ[κόλас]τος γεν[έс]θαι τὴν πρώ[την], ὥстε] καὶ διὰ τ[ο]ῦ Κεραμει[κοῦ πο]τε μεθύοντα κω[μᾶс]θαι μεθ' ἡμέραν· φυγεῖν [δὲ] δίκην αἰсχρὰν κακώсεως ὑπὸ τῆс γυναικόс· εἶναι γὰρ φιλόπαιδα καὶ φιλομειράκιον· ὅс γε περιέφερε νόμιсμα παντοδαπόν, ἵνα τῷ сυναντ[ή]сαντ[ι χρῆс θ]αι προχείρως ἔχῃ. θηραсθεὶς δ' ὑπὸ Ξενοκράτουс καὶ сυсτα[θε]ὶс αὐτῷ τοсοῦτο μετήλ[λ]αξε κατὰ τὸν βί[ο]ν, ὥстε μηδέποτε μήτε τὴν τοῦ προсώπου φανταсίαν δια[λῦ]сαι καὶ сχέсιν ἀλλοιῶс[αι] μ[ή]τε τὸν τ[ό]νον τῆс φω[νῆс] ἀλλὰ ταὐτὰ διαφυλάττε[ιν] κἂν δυсκ[ο]λώτερ[ο]ν [ὄντα]. For other testimony on this part of Polemon's life, see M. Gigante, "Polemonis Academici fragmenta," *RAAN* 51 (1976), 106–15, esp. Horace, *Satires* 3.250–57. Others are 17 (*Palatine Anthology* 11.41) and 21 (*Palatine Anthology* 11.34).

The earliest philosophical conversion is credited to Empedocles, who calmed down an unnamed man

Polemon became a paradigm for this kind of philosophical conversion, certainly more so than, say, Plato, who merely gave up the writing of poetry to follow Socrates. Philodemus seems to have liked this picture of the conversion from debauchery to philosophy enough to work it up in several poems. Consider, for example, Epigram 18 Gow and Page (*Palatine Anthology* 5.112):

> 1 ἠράσθην, τίς δ' οὐχί; κεκώμακα, τίς δ' ἀμύητος
> κώμων; ἀλλ' ἐμάνην ἐκ τίνος; οὐχὶ θεοῦ;
> ἐρρίφθω, πολιὴ γὰρ ἐπείγεται ἀντὶ μελαίνης
> θρὶξ ἤδη, συνετῆς ἄγγελος ἡλικίης.
> 5 καὶ παίζειν ὅτε καιρός, ἐπαίξαμεν· ἡνίκα καὶ νῦν
> οὐκέτι, λωϊτέρης φροντίδος ἁψόμεθα.[47]

---

1 κεκώμακα P, -κε P   2 θεοῦ Pl, θῦ P   3 πολιή C, -ιῇ P, πολλή Pl   5 παίζειν] κείνων Lumb   ἡνίκα καὶ νῦν] ἤ. καιρός Herwaerden οὕνεκα καλόν F. G. Schmidt, οὕνεκα καὶ νῦν Desrousseaux   6 λωϊτέρης P, λωοτ- Pl

I fell in love. Who hasn't? I revelled. Who is not an initiate of revels? But whose fault is it I went mad? A god's, isn't it? Let it go, for already grey hair rushes in to take the place of black-grey hair, the proclaimer of the age for wisdom. And when it was right to play we played; and since it is right no longer, we shall lay hold of loftier thoughts.[48]

A more complex poem on this subject is Epigram 17 (*Palatine Anthology* 11.41):

> 1 ἑπτὰ τριηκόντεσσιν ἐπέρχονται λυκάβαντες,
> ἤδη μοι βιότου σχιζόμεναι σελίδες·
> ἤδη καὶ λευκαί με κατασπείρουσιν ἔθειραι,
> Ξανθίππη, συνετῆς ἄγγελοι ἡλικίης,
> 5 ἀλλ' ἔτι μοι ψαλμός τε λάλος κῶμοί τε μέλονται
> καὶ πῦρ ἀπλήστῳ τύφετ' ἐνὶ κραδίῃ·
> αὐτὴν ἀλλὰ τάχιστα κορωνίδα γράψατε, Μοῦσαι,
> ταύτης ἡμετέρης, δεσποτίδες, μανίης.

---

2 βιότου Pl, βρότου P   3 spat. vac. relicto om. Pl   4 Ξανθίππη Salm., -ίπη P, -ίππης Pl   6 τύφετ' ἐνί Pl, τύφετ' ἐν P, τύφεται ἐν Jacobs   7–8 om. Pl.   8 ταύτης scripsi, ταύτην P

---

on the point of murder; he thereafter became the most famous of Empedocles' followers (Iamblichus, *Life of Pythagoras* 11 f = A 15 Diels-Kranz).

[47] In general cf. A. Grilli, *Il problema della vita contemplativa nel mondo Greco-romano* (Milan 1953), esp. ch. 1, "La contemplatività dell'Epicurismo."

[48] On the grounds that this poem offers a pointed contrast with Epigram 17 (to be cited immediately below), A. H. Griffiths, *BICS* 17 (1970), 38, argues that this was the first poem in Philodemus' published epigram book, and that Epigram 17 was the last. Since, however, the *coronis* which Griffiths believes signals that 17 was the last poem has another explanation (see below), these two poems may well have been placed elsewhere in the book. Cf. F. Jacoby, *RhM* 60 (1905), 99f.

Thirty-seven years have come, papyrus columns of my life now torn off; now too, Xanthippe, white hairs besprinkle me, announcing the age of intelligence; but the lyre's voice and revels are still a concern to me, and a fire smolders in my insatiable heart. Inscribe her immediately as the *coronis*, Mistress Muses, of this my madness.[49]

Any audience for Hellenistic poetry would have to be attuned to poetic allusions and *topoi*. Philodemus' audience in particular could also be expected to catch allusions to philosophical passages and traditions which in the context of Philodemus' poetry can now be regarded as new sorts of *topoi*. In this poem, the *topos* of philosophical conversion is overlaid with allusions to various discussions of marriage. The first allusion in the poem is the most oblique: Philodemus' use of an inflected form of τριήκοντα (his is the only example of this word in the dative) could be expected to recall for his learned audience the nearly as rare genitive which they would have seen (so far as we know) only in Hesiod and Callimachus (fr. 714 Pfeiffer). It is possible therefore that Philodemus would have expected his audience to recall as well the Hesiodic context, which argues that a man should marry approximately at age thirty (*Works and Days* 695–97):

ὡραῖος δὲ γυναῖκα τεὸν ποτὶ οἶκον ἄγεϲθαι,
μήτε τριηκόντων ἐτέων μάλα πόλλ' ἀπολείπων
μήτ' ἐπιθεὶϲ μάλα πολλά· γάμοϲ δέ τοι ὥριοϲ οὗτοϲ.

The specific number thirty-seven, however, as I have argued earlier, would have recalled that passage in Aristotle's *Politics* where this very age was declared the proper one for a man to marry (1335a29ff.). Although Aristotle is in accord with most Greek writings on this subject, only he points to a single year (which is not even a round number).[50]

What, therefore, sets Philodemus apart from other Hellenistic poets who ring changes on preexisting *topoi* is that he draws his *topoi* from philosophical literature rather than from earlier poetry. This particular theme of philosophical conversion, where the allusions are to Socrates, Aristotle, and Polemon, as well as to Epicurus, also demonstrates that philosophical orthodoxy, so important in his prose, is of no moment whatsoever in the epigrams. What makes them true to Epicurus is the joy they must have produced in their audience. If we imagine them recited at symposia of like-minded friends, we come close to the picture painted by Epicurus in his *Symposium*.

Although the Xanthippe cycle presents different stages of the relationship, the overall picture is that the man needs her as part of his life as a philosopher. One

[49] ταύτηϲ scripsi, ταύτην cod. P. Whether 7 αὐτήν refers to the *coronis* alone (Gow and Page) or, as I think, to Xanthippe as a metaphorical *coronis* (Dübner, Kaibel, Giangrande), αὐτὴν . . . ταύτην would make for unusual hyberbaton, and the error I posit could readily have arisen after, and below, αὐτήν. Cf. G. Giangrande, "Erklärungen Hellenistischer Stellen," *GB* 1 (1973), 142ff.; Griffiths, op. cit. (n. 48 above), 37f.; Sider, op. cit. (n. 42 above), 315f. As my translation shows, I agree with Dübner, Kaibel, and Giangrande that Xanthippe is the metaphorical *coronis* referred to, who (as wife I further argue) thus marks the end of the manic stage of his life.

[50] Philodemus comes closest to Solon's assignment of the year for a man's marriage to the fifth heptad (27.9): πέμπτῃ δ' ὥριον ἄνδρα γάμου μεμνημένον εἶναι. Other suggestions are 25–55 (Plato, *Republic* 460E), 25–35 (id. *Laws* 772D), 30–35 (ibid. 721B–D, 785B).

particular way in which Xanthippe could contribute towards this end is suggested by Epigram 14 (*Palatine Anthology* 9.570):

1   —Ξανθὼ κηρόπλαστε μυρόχροε μουσοπρόσωπε,
     εὔλαλε, διπτερύγων καλὸς ἄγαλμα Πόθων,
     ψῆλόν μοι χερσὶν δροcιναῖc μύρον· ἐν μονοκλίνῳ
     δεῖ με λιθοδμήτῳ δεῖ ποτε πετριδίῳ
5   εὕδειν ἀθανάτωc πουλὺν χρόνον. ᾆδε πάλιν μοι,
     Ξανθάριον, ναὶ ναὶ τὸ γλυκὺ τοῦτο μέλος.
    —οὐκ ἀίειc, ὤνθρωφ' ὁ τοκογλύφοc· ἐν μονκλίνῳ
     δεῖ cε βιοῦν αἰεί, δύcμορε, πετριδίῳ.

P Φιλοδήμου, caret Pl   Π iv.7 ξανθωκηροπλαcτε

1 Ξανθὼ κηρ- Π Huschke, ξανθοκηρ- P   3 ψῆλόν Ppc (i.e., P adds η alongside in the margin), ψιλον Pac, ψῆξόν Gigante   χερcίν Schneider, χερcί P   4 δεῖ ποτε Kaibel, δέ ποτι P, δήποτε Huschke, δέcποτι Schneider   7 οὐκ ἀίειc Salm., οὐ καὶ εἰc P   τοκογλύφοc Chardon, τοκονγ- P, ἄνθρωπε τόκων γλύφοc Salm.   8 cε βιοῦν αἰεί Chardon, cε βίου ἀεί P, c' ἄβιον ναίειν Brunck ap. Jacobs

Man: Xantho—formed of wax, with skin smelling of perfume, with the face of a Muse, of splendid voice, a beautiful image of the double-winged Pothoi—pluck with your hands dewy with myrrh: "In a solitary rocky bed made of stone I must surely someday sleep a deathlessly long time." Yes, yes, Xantharion, sing again for me this sweet song.

⟨Xantho:⟩ Don't you understand, man, you accountant you? You must live forever, you wretch, in a solitary rocky bed!

The persona Philodemus has fashioned for himself is that of an imperfect Epicurean, who needs Xanthippe to remind him, in none-too-kind language, that death is forever and, by implication, that a proper Epicurean would not allow himself to act in so maudlin a manner. Philodemus as author can make his Epicurean point obliquely by means of the flawed persona he develops in the poems. A very similar point is made by Epigram 20 (*Palatine Anthology* 9.412):

1   —ἤδη καὶ ῥόδον ἔcτι καὶ ἀκμάζων ἐρέβινθοc
     καὶ καυλοὶ κράμβηc, Cώcυλε, πρωτοτόμου
     καὶ μαίνη cαλαγεῦcα καὶ ἀρτιπαγὴc ἁλίτυροc
     καὶ θριδάκων οὔλων ἀφροφυῆ πέταλα·
5   ἡμεῖc δ' οὔτ' ἀκτῆc ἐπιβαίνομεν οὔτ' ἐν ἀπόψει
     γινόμεθ' ὡc αἰεί, Cώcυλε, τὸ πρότερον·
    —καὶ μὴν Ἀντιγένηc καὶ Βάκχιοc ἐχθὲc ἔπαιζον,
     νῦν δ' αὐτοὺc θάψαι cήμερον ἐκφέρομεν.

PPl Φιλοδήμου   Π vii.21 ηδηκαιροδον

2 καυλοί Pl, καυλοῖο P   πρωτοτόμου] πρωτότμοι Gow–Page

3 καὶ μαίνη] καὶ μὴν ἡ Σ ϲαλαγεῦϲα Dilthey, ζαλαγεῦϲα PP1,
ζαγλαγεῦϲα Σ1, λαλαγεῦϲα Σ2, ϲελαγεῦϲα Scaliger, γλαγόωϲα
Kaibel ἁλίτυροϲ PacPl, ἁλὶ τυρόϲ Ppc   4 ἀφροφυῇ] ἀβρο-
vel ἀκρο- Scaliger   6 γινόμεθ᾽ P, γιγν- Pl

Philodemus: Already now the rose and chickpea and first-cut cabbage-stalks are
at their peak, Sosylus, and there are sauteed sprats and fresh cheese curds and
tender curly lettuce leaves. But we neither go on the shore nor are we on the
promontory, as we always did before.

Sosylus: But Antigenes and Bakkhios were playing yesterday; and today we
carry them out for burial.

This poem has always been read as if it were spoken by one voice, presumably that
of Philodemus himself. In this reading, however, it is difficult to make sense of καὶ
μήν beginning v. 7. If, on the other hand, we assign the last distich to Sosylus (addressed in vv. 2 and 6), καὶ μήν appropriately introduces his response, as Sosylus,
like Xanthippe in Epigram 14, tries to restore Philodemus to a proper Epicurean
perspective on the subject of death. That is, of all the possible ways this combination
of particles is used, the most appropriate here is "inceptive-responsive," when "a
person who has been invited to speak expresses by the particles his acceptance of the
invitation."[51] Denniston notes that this usage is "common in Aristophanes and Plato,
and is almost confined to them," but this is just another way of saying that a particular
usage is colloquial, which is entirely appropriate here.

The reply could be spoken only by Sosylus, to whom the preceding words have
been directed. Implicit is the message that the goods of the season are indeed to be
enjoyed, and today, before we too are dead.[52] In having "Xanthippe" and "Sosylus"
criticize himself, Philodemus is engaging in a well-established tradition of personal
lyric, of which perhaps the most famous example is Sappho 1, where Sappho writes
of herself being chastized by "Aphrodite." With this technique, Philodemus allows
himself to be the butt of Epicurean criticism, avoiding in his poetry what he practices
in his prose, the preaching of Epicurean doctrine. Or should we rather say, Pretend-
ing to avoid such preaching? In fact, of course, he simply refracts these teachings
through the skewed persona of an imperfect Epicurean.[53] Poetic pleasure and Epicurean pleasure come together in the literary unpacking of the poem.

Enough, I hope, has been said to demonstrate the thesis of this study, that Philodemus' art is an allusive one, depending not only on poetical allusions, as does much

---

[51] Denniston, *Greek Particles* 355; for the difficulties involved with other interpretations, cf. Gow
and Page 1968, 388, who reluctantly settle for an unparalleled causal use.

[52] Cf. Philodemus, *On Death* 4 col. xxxvii 23ff. πᾶϲ ἄνθρωποϲ . . . ἐφήμερόϲ ἐϲτι . . . καὶ ἄδηλόν
ἐϲτιν οὐ τὸ αὔριον μόνον, ἀλλὰ καὶ τὸ αὐτίκα δή. Cf. Epicurus, *Letter to Menoeceus* 124f. γνῶϲιϲ
ὀρθὴ τοῦ μηθὲν εἶναι πρὸϲ ἡμᾶϲ τὸν θάνατον ἀπολαυϲτὸν ποιεῖ τὸ τῆϲ ζωῆϲ θνητόν. Philodemus
comments on this and other Epicurean passages concering death in *On Death* 4 cols. i–ii et passim; cf. M.
Gigante, "L'Inizio del quarto libro Della Morte di Filodemo," in *Ricerche Filodemee*, 2nd ed. (Naples
1983), 125ff.

[53] Cf. Aristotle, *Rhetoric* 3.1418b24 εἰϲ τὸ ἦθοϲ, ἐπειδὴ ἔνια περὶ ἑαυτοῦ λέγειν ἢ ἐπίφθονον ἢ
μακρολογίαν ἢ ἀντιλογίαν ἔχει, καὶ περὶ ἄλλου ἢ λοιδορίαν ἢ ἀγροικίαν, ἕτερον χρὴ λέγοντα
ποιεῖν, "In regard to moral character, since sometimes, in speaking of ourselves, we render ourselves
liable to envy, to the charge of prolixity, or contradiction, or, when speaking of another, we may be
accused of abuse or boorishness, we must make another speak in our place" (trans. Freese).

of Hellenistic poetry, but also, given an audience of philosophically and poetically inclined Romans, depending on philosophical allusions. Philodemus, that is, has drawn from philosophical literature a number of references and arguments and used them as literary *topoi*. In doing so, he has not only remained true to his theory that poetry does not benefit, he seems even to flaunt his theory. In order to demonstrate as vividly as possible that one should not look to poetry for "benefit," that is, for straightforward philosophical content, he takes not only the tenets of Epicureanism, in whose defense he argues strongly in his prose, but also dogma and even biographical data from other philosophers. The result is a poetic amalgam of philosophy whose overall point is to imply that the only way to incorporate philosophy into poetry is to reduce its doctrines to literary topoi, very much in the Hellenistic fashion. And as such his epigrams are both philosophically correct and poetically satisfying. In a word, Philodemus is μουcοφιλήc.

5

The Alleged Impossibility of Philosophical Poetry

Michael Wigodsky

Among the opinions of the Stoic or Stoicizing thinker called "Aristo"[1] which Philodemus professes to find astonishing is his approval of "good thought found in poems which present good thoughts and actions, or which aim at education"; the Epicurean writer adds, apparently as his own comment, "although no poet has written or is ever likely to write poems containing such thoughts"[2]—a remark which prompted Jensen to wonder "whether Lucretius' poem was not yet known to him when he wrote that."[3] The recent discovery of a text of Lucretius in Philodemus' library[4] does not resolve this chronological question, since it could have been added to the collection after his death; and even if Philodemus saw the poem, we do not know whether his command of Latin was sufficient for him to appreciate its merits. More interesting than such biographical speculations is the question whether he would have felt obliged to condemn Lucretius' poem if he did know it, that is, how broadly his criticism of Aristo is to be interpreted.

It is often claimed that the Epicurean school, apart from Lucretius, was united in condemning the use of poetry as a vehicle for philosophical ideas;[5] but even if that is what Philodemus meant, it cannot simply be taken for granted that his views represent established school orthodoxy. To be sure, he says (*On Rhetoric* 1 col. vii 24–28 p. 21 Longo) that Epicureans who disagreed with views expressed by Epicurus and Metrodorus were guilty of a crime equivalent to parricide; but he makes this often-

---

[1] So called, that is, by modern scholars, following Jensen's supplement [Ἀρίϲτ]ων in *On Poems* 5 col. xiii (xvi) 30 and his identification of this person with Zeno's student Ariston of Chios. I agree with Asmis 1990b, that the arguments for and against the identification are inconclusive, and use "Aristo" only as a conventional designation. I cite *On Poems* 5 by Jensen's text, and give in parentheses the equivalents for the numeration of columns in the new edition by Mangoni 1993.

[2] *On Poems* 5 col. xiv (xvii) 14–24 [τί | δὲ δι]άνοια[ν ϲπο]υδαίαν | [δῆλ]ον ὅτι [τῶν ἐμ]φα[ι]|-ν[ό]ντ[ων] δ[ιανοία]ϲ ἀϲ|τείαϲ καὶ π[ράξ]ειϲ ἢ τῶν | εἰϲ παιδ[εί]α[ν ἐν]τεινόν|των, οὐ γεγραφό-τοϲ τι|νὸϲ τῶν ποιητῶν τ[οι]|αύταϲ περιέ[χοντ]α [ποι]|ήματα διανοίαϲ [οὔ]τ᾽ ἂν | γράψοντοϲ.

[3] Jensen 1923, 133.   [4] Cf. Kleve 1989, 5–27.

[5] For an extreme statement, cf. A. Ronconi, "Appunti di Estetica Epicurea," *Miscellanea di Studi Alessandrini in memoria di A. Rostagni* (Turin 1963), 7–25; more moderately, P. Boyancé, *Lucrèce et l'Épicurisme* (Paris 1963), 57–59.

quoted remark in defense of an opinion which seems to have been an innovation of his teacher Zeno's, namely, that epideictic rhetoric is an art.[6] If protestations of orthodoxy could be used to cloak innovation, then innovation is certainly a possibility where no such protestations are made.

The reason why it is unclear how broadly we should understand Philodemus' condemnation of philosophical poetry is that we do not have any extended account of his own literary theory;[7] instead we find him here mocking his opponents' statements, as he so often does, without bothering to tell us why he thinks them so laughably wrong. Thus it is at least possible that τοιαύτας might mean merely "such thoughts (and in such poems) as are described by Aristo."[8] Philodemus' implied objection might have been that what Aristo considered good thoughts were not in fact good, or that, since the Stoic wise man is an impossibility, no one ever could have thoughts which Aristo would consider good; less plausibly, it has been suggested that Philodemus was objecting to the idea that narrative or dramatic poetry on mythological subjects could be made morally improving.[9] Other passages, however, suggest that his objection to poetic treatment of philosophical subjects was more general, for instance his condemnation of Cleanthes for saying "that, since the language of philosophy is able to deal adequately with things divine and human, but does not in its bare form possess diction befitting the grandeur of the divine, meters, melodies, and rhythms come closest to the true vision of the divine."[10] Both the broad and the narrow interpretations require us to supply something about Philodemus's or his opponents' views. What must decide the question is whether we can give a coherent and convincing account of how either common Epicurean doctrine or his own aesthetics might have led him to issue a sweeping condemnation of philosophical poetry; and the fragmentary character of the texts on which it must be based of course ensures that such an account can be no more than a likely story. I think that a likely story can be told; but it will not be either of the two stories which have been told up to now.

The first of these stories is that Epicurus condemned the reading and writing of any sort of poetry, and that his followers simply followed, seeking no better reason

---

[6] On the failure of his attempt to show that this view is in fact implied in the passages he cites from the founders, cf. most recently Sedley 1989, 107–17.

[7] In view of Janko's recent identification of Sbordone's Treatise B as Book 1 of *On Poems* (Chapter 6, below), it appears unlikely that Philodemus himself can have written anything more than a brief summary of this theory in the lost opening columns; the only fuller exposition must have been that contained in Zeno's work Περὶ ποιημάτων χρήcεωc.

[8] So P. Giuffrida, *L'Epicureismo nella letteratura latina nel I' secolo a.C.* (*U. Torino, Pubbl. fac. magistero, ser.* 1,10, 1940), 97 n. 1.

[9] The last-mentioned view is that of Giuffrida 1940 (above, n. 8) based on Aristo's having said that the poems of Homer and Antimachus could be called good, but only by a misuse of the word "good" (καταχρηcτικῶc, *On Poems* 5 col. xv [xviii] 5–6); for the suggestion of a joke about the impossibility of the Stoic wise man, cf. Asmis 1990b, 168 and above.

[10] *On Music* 4 xxviii 5-14 Neubecker: . . . καὶ τοῦ [λόγ]ου τοῦ τῆc φιλοco|φίαc ἱκανῶc μὲν ἐξαγ[γ]έλ|λειν δυναμένου τὰ θεῖα καὶ | ἀ[ν]θ[ρ]ώ[πινα], μὴ ἔχοντοc δὲ | ψειλοῦ τῶν θείων μεγεθῶν | λέξειc οἰκείαc, τὰ μέτρα καὶ | τὰ μέλη καὶ τοὺc ῥυθμοὺc | ὡc μάλιcτα προcικνεῖcθαι | πρὸc τὴν ἀλήθειαν τῆc τῶν | θείων θ[ε]ωρίαc, οὐ καταγελα|cτότερον οὐ ῥᾁδιον εὑρεῖν; cf. the Epicurean Colotes' criticism of Plato for mixing philosophy with fictions such as the myth of Er (Proclus *in Remp.* 2.105ff. Kroll, Macrobius *Somn. Scip.* 1.2.3-4).

than the master's word; even Philodemus' own composition of epigrams, on this account, would be a relaxation of strict Epicurean orthodoxy.[11] Loyalty to the master's opinions was indeed characteristic of the Epicureans; but so was giving arguments in support both of those opinions and of particular interpretations of them,[12] and we would expect to find somewhere in the remains of Philodemus' writings on poetry arguments purporting to show that his treating the subject at such length was consistent with Epicurus' condemnation, especially if his view about poems "containing good thoughts" was based on that condemnation.

Even apart from the question of Philodemus' orthodoxy, it is far from clear that Epicurus did issue any such unqualified judgment: Diogenes Laertius, it is true, tells us (10.121b) that he said "that only the wise man would discourse correctly about both music and poetry, and elsewhere[13] that he would not in practice compose poems"; but we have no context for either statement, and so no way to tell whether the first means that the wise man will judge poetry at its proper, low value[14] or implies a more positive estimate. As for the second statement, that the wise man would not compose poems, we should be on our guard against interpreting it in the way we would interpret similar statements in the Stoics. For the Stoics, virtue consists in obedience to an objective external norm which is the same for all men, and the way to become a wise man is by performing actions which, if performed by a wise man, that is, out of perfect knowledge and perfectly virtuous intentions, would be virtuous ones. There is no evidence that Epicurus had a similar conception of moral progress, and some evidence that suggests that statements about the wise man do not represent universal norms for the Epicureans: thus Philodemus (*On Poems* 5 cols. xxx-xxxi [xxxiii-xxxiv]) says of the idea that goodness in poetry consists in the proper imitation of Homer that one might as well define justice as the imitation of Aristides, or wisdom as the imitation of Epicurus. I suggest[15] that statements about what the wise man will and will not do implied, in Epicurus' mouth, no more than an evaluation of strategies for living a pleasant life, and that most, if not all of them are subject to the qualification which we find expressed in another part of Diogenes' doxography: "and that the wise man will even marry and father children, . . . but only sometimes, in accordance with exceptional circumstances in his life."[16] It has even been suggested

---

[11] Cf. n. 5 above.

[12] Cf. Sedley 1989, 102 and n. 16: "only the Pythagorean sect . . . stooped to that," i.e., to relying on the founder's authority alone.

[13] That the following statement (fr. 568 Usener) was drawn from a different context is implied by the use of τε rather than δέ; Usener prints the two statements, in reverse order, as two fragments (frr. 569 and 568 Usener).

[14] So F. Giancotti, *Il preludio di Lucrezio* (Messina–Florence 1959), 19-20.

[15] I hope to present further arguments for this view elsewhere, as part of a discussion of the place of mental pleasures in Epicurean ethics.

[16] Diogenes Laertius 10.119 καὶ μὴν καὶ γαμήcειν καὶ τεκνοποιήcειν τὸν coφόν, ὡc Ἐπίκουρος ἐν ταῖc Διαπορίαιc καὶ ἐν ταῖc Περὶ φύcεωc, κατὰ περίcταcιν δέ ποτε βίου [γαμήcειν]. I follow O. Gigon, *Epikur, Von der Überwindung der Furcht*[2] (Zürich 1968), 115, and M. Giusta, "Passi dossografici di morale epicurea nel X libro di Diogene Laerzio," *AAT* 97 (1962–63), 143–44, in deleting the second γαμήcειν; this seems simpler than emending to introduce a negation, and more consistent with the other evidence, since Epicurus allowed the title "wise man" not only to himself, but also to Metrodorus (Cicero, *De finibus* 2.3.7), who both married and fathered children. Cf. most recently R. D. Brown, *Lucretius on Love and Sex*, Columbia Studies in the Classical Tradition 15 (Leiden, 1987), 118–120.

that the exceptional circumstances referred to might include variations in natural disposition;[17] it seems unlikely that κατὰ περίςταςιν βίου could *mean* that, but Epicurus very likely did think that different wise men would behave differently in accordance with such variations, whether or not he said so in the passages excerpted here. On the other hand, though Lucretius says (*On the Nature of Things* 3.320-22) that these variations can be so reduced by reason "that nothing prevents living a life worthy of the gods," Epicurus did not think that all human beings were capable of attaining wisdom ("and that a wise man does not originate from every bodily consti- tution, nor in every nation," Diogenes Laertius 10.117), and we should probably distinguish his concession about marriage from his attitude to pursuits which he may have accepted only as ensuring a life of the least possible unpleasantness, for those people who, because of their constitutions, must settle for something less. His accep- tance of participation in politics for those who are naturally fond of honor and repu- tation probably belongs in the latter category,[18] and he may have taken a similar view of the writing of poetry. If this is right, the statement that the wise man would not compose poems will mean only that, for most people (but not necessarily for some- one like Lucretius), poetic composition is an activity which causes more discomfort than satisfaction. At most, it would also follow that anyone who composes poetry is not a wise man, and this would not mean that his poems could not contain wise thoughts, that is, those of Epicurus.

Other testimonies suggest that Epicurus denied to poetry any utility, at least as a preparation for philosophy,[19] and regarded at least some poems as actually harmful because of the encouragement they gave to undesirable emotions and false beliefs about the gods; what the testimonies do not tell us is whether these were mere empiri- cal judgments on the poems, or some of the poems,[20] known to him, leaving open the possibility of a reformed poetry, or were based on some theory about the nature of poetry which would apply equally to poems as yet unwritten. A similar question is notoriously raised by Plato's similar criticisms of the poets' theology and ethics;[21] and it might seem prudent, in view of Philodemus' apparently untroubled approval of at least some poetry, to suppose that Epicurus' remarks on the subject, even if we had the complete text, would prove to be equally elliptical and ambiguous.

In 1939, nevertheless, Phillip De Lacy suggested that the condemnation of poetry for causing emotional disturbance was part of a general Epicurean theory of

[17] So A. Grilli, "Epicuro e il matrimonio," *RSF* 26 (1971), 51–56.

[18] Plutarch, *Moralia* 465ғ οὐδὲ Ἐπίκουρος οἴεται δεῖν ἡςυχάζειν ἀλλὰ τῇ φύςει χρῆςθαι πολι- τευομένους καὶ πράςςοντας τὰ κοινὰ τοὺς φιλοτίμους καὶ φιλοδόξους, ὡς μᾶλλον ὑπ' ἀπραγμο- ςύνης ταράττεςθαι καὶ κακοῦςθαι πεφυκότας, ἂν ὧν ὀρέγονται μὴ τυγχάνουςιν. Cf. the discussion by Fowler 1989, 126–27.

[19] Metrodorus' adjuration (Plutarch, *Moralia* 1094ᴇ), "Do not be disturbed because, as you say, you do not know on which side Hector fought, or the first lines of Homer's poem," and Epicurus' advice to Pythocles to "flee all forms of culture" (fr. 163 Usener) probably come from such contexts, like the congratulations to Apelles for "coming to philosophy without any taint of culture" (fr. 117 Usener).

[20] The relative clause in Cicero, *De finibus* 1.72, *poetis . . . in quibus nulla solida utilitas omnisque puerilis est delectatio*, is no doubt non-restrictive, as Boyancé argues, "Études Lucrétiennes," *REA* 62 (1960), 442; but Cicero could be generalizing from more particular statements in Epicurus: cf. Giancotti, "La poetica epicurea in Lucrezio, Cicerone ed altri," *Ciceroniana* 2 (1960), 72–73.

[21] Cf. J. Annas, "Plato on the Triviality of Literature," in J. Moravcsik and P. Temko, (eds.), *Plato on Beauty, Wisdom, and the Arts* (Totowa, N. J., 1982), 1–28.

language.[22] According to this account, Epicurus distinguished, like the logical posi-tivists, between cognitive and emotional uses of language, and denied cognitive value to poetic language both because of its emotional character and because of its reliance on metaphors chosen for their aesthetic appeal rather than on the basis of a scientific analysis of similarities and differences. De Lacy thought that this distinc-tion between cognitive and emotional uses of language was implied by the contrast between natural and conventional stages in its development at *Letter to Herodotus* 75–76, taking the natural stage to include only expressions of emotion and the as-signment of names to be purely conventional;[23] but closer analysis seems to show that both Epicurus and Lucretius place at least the beginnings of naming in the first, natural stage.[24] He also cited the fragments of Philodemus referring to the natural values of sounds and the cries of animals; but these all belong to Sbordone's *Treatise B*, which is devoted to questions of euphony and contains no reference to the emo-tions.[25] Epicurus' own discussion of language, in *On Nature* 28, appears to be equally silent on the subject; and it would in fact be very surprising if he had envi-sioned a purely cognitive use of language, since his denial of an intermediate condi-tion between pleasure and pain means that there is no room in his psychology for a cognitive state untinged by emotion.

As for metaphor, Philodemus himself, far from condemning it, says that "all the arts cannot utter a word, if deprived of the aid of metaphors," and that "it is necessary for a poet who has studied philosophy to have considered the nature and origins of both figurative and philosophical language, or else he will choose and avoid (meta-phors) at random."[26] Hostility to metaphor is equally hard to find in *On Nature* 28; on

---

[22] P. De Lacy, "The Epicurean Analysis of Language," *AJPh* 60 (1939), 85–92. Prof. De Lacy has informed me that he no longer holds the views expressed in this article; cf. the revised statement in De Lacy and De Lacy 1978, 184, where the first edition's citation of the 1939 article is omitted.

[23] De Lacy 1939, 87–88; followed by D. Konstan, *Some Aspects of Epicurean Psychology*, Philo-sophia Antiqua 25 (Leiden, 1973), 45–48.

[24] Cf. G. Vlastos, "On the Pre-History in Diodorus," *AJPh* 67 (1946), 53–54 and n. 16; D. Sedley, *Epicurus, On Nature Book XXVIII, CErc* 3 (1973), 17–19; and J. Brunschwig, "Epicure et le problème du 'langage privé'," *Revue des Sciences humaines* 43 (1977), 157–77. τὰ ὀνόματα ἐξ ἀρχῆς μὴ θέσει γενέσθαι (Epicurus, *Letter to Herodotus* 75) is naturally taken to mean that names came into existence from the beginning, but not by convention (rather than "men did not employ names" in the beginning, as suggested by Konstan 1973 [above, n. 23], 46), especially since, in what follows, this first stage is said to have involved responses to φαντάσματα as well as πάθη, and the later, conventional stage is distin-guished, not as bringing an entirely new use of language, but only as making communication less am-biguous and more concise (τὰς δηλώσεις ἧττον ἀμφιβόλους . . . καὶ συντομωτέρως δηλουμένας). Lucretius *may* be referring to the second stage in 5.1029 *utilitas expressit nomina rerum* (cf., against this interpretation, H. Offermann, "Lukrez V 1028–1090," *RhM* 115 [1972], 150–56; in defense of it, P. H. Schrijvers, "La pensée de Lucrèce sur l'origine du langage [*DRN*. V 1019–1090]," *Mnemosyne* 27 [1974], 340–46); but in any case he also associates naming with the *beginnings* of language in 5.71-72:

  quove modo genus humanum variante loquela
  coeperit inter se vesci per nomina rerum

(and probably also in 1089–1090, *tum potuisse . . . res voce notare*), as does Demetrius of Laconia (*P.Herc.* 1012 col. lxvii 9-12 Puglia φύσει δὲ τὰς πρώτας τῶν | ὀνομάτων ἀναφωνήσεις | γεγονέναι λέγομεν).

[25] The texts cited from Hausrath's edition in De Lacy 1939 (above, n. 22), 88 nn. 13 and 15, are Sbordone frr. B 7, 11, 23, and 26.

[26] *On Rhetoric* 4 col. xv 15-18 vol. 1 p. 175 Sudhaus καὶ πᾶσα τέχνη | φων[ῆ]ν οὐ δύναται προ[ίεc]||θαι cτερ[η]θεῖcα τῆc ἐκ τῶν | μεταφορῶν εὐχρηc[τίαc]; ibid. col. xxi 8–15 p. 180 Sudhaus

the contrary, we may perhaps find there some hints about the reasons for Philodemus' approval of it. Unlike some philosophers of other schools, Epicurus claims, "we do not use words in ways that violate linguistic conventions nor change them with regard to objects of perception."[27] Even where innovations are permissible, he says, "it is not possible to alter many words or words of all kinds; it is possible to alter a few of those which are connected with sense-perceptions—the ones which we previously defined in the non-image-making manner, but which we altered when upon some further reflection (on sense-data) we saw that they were not of this kind; but most of the words which might be (shown to be mistaken ?) in the perceptual mode . . . ."[28] The text unfortunately breaks off here, and our uncertainties about the meanings of technical terms, as well as such gaps, leave much obscure, but it seems clear at least that by "changing words" Epicurus means the introduction of new words for abstract ideas, coined on the basis of analogies with perceptible objects or actions, as for instance his own coinage of πρόληψις, which had been based on the analogy with "taking beforehand."[29] When no such analogies offered themselves, he remained content with common usage; but many such common expressions are themselves metaphorical, and they need not be on that account less satisfactory than the metaphors of philosophers, at least for denoting particular aspects of τὰ ἄδηλα. Thus Sextus Empiricus reports (*Adv. math.* 10.2) that "according to Epicurus, the so-called "intangible substance" is sometimes named void (κενόν), sometimes place (τόπος) or room (χώρα), the names varying according to the different applications, since the same substance when it is empty of any body is called "void," and when occupied by a body it is termed "place," and when bodies roam (χωρούντων) through it, it becomes "room." From such reflections on the metaphorical character of ordinary language, it is only a step to Philodemus' observation that a poet who has studied philosophy ought to be particularly careful in his choice of metaphors.

If, then, the Epicureans disapproved neither of metaphor nor of the emotional use of language as such, what reason do we have for interpreting Philodemus' criticism of Aristo broadly, as a general condemnation of the use of poetry to express philosophical ideas? De Lacy has a further suggestion, that Philodemus objected to emotional effects when they are used not for their own sake, as part of the indissolubly complex working of poetry, but, as in rhetoric, for persuasion.[30] If so, the objection

---

[καὶ ἐπεσκέφθαι]‖ φιλοc[οφήcαν]τι ποιη[τῆι ἀν]αν‖[καῖον, π]ῶc καὶ π[όθ]εν [τ]ρ[οπικὴ | ἅμα λέξι]c καὶ κ[α]τὰ [τί]ν[α τρό|πον ἵcτ]αντ[αι] φυcικοὶ [λόγοι, ἢ]‖ μάταιον δ[ὴ] θεω[ρ]εῖν, [πῶc]‖ τὸ μ[ὲ]ν ἐκλέγητα[ι] τ[ὸ δ᾿ ἐ]κ[κλ]είνῃ.

[27] *On Nature* 28 fr. 13 col. v sup. 8–12 p. 48 Sedley: . . . οὐκ ἔξω τῶν | ἐθιcμένων λέξεων ἡμῶν | χρωμένων οὐδὲ μετατιθέν[των ὀνόματα ἐπὶ τῶμ φανε‖[ρ]ῶν . . . .

[28] *On Nature* 28 fr. 8 col. v 1–10 p. 41f. Sedley [οὐκ ἔξεcτι ποιῆcαι πολλῶν]‖ καὶ παντο[ί]ω[ν] ὀνομάτωμ | μεταθ[έc]ε[ιc]· ὀλίγα γὰρ ἔξ[ε]‖cτιν τῶ[ν c]ὺν ταῖc αἰcθήcεcιν | ἃ πρότερον [ο]ὕτωc δ[ι]ο[ρί]ζον|τεc κατὰ τὸν οὐ φανταcτι[κ]ὸ]ν τρ[όπομ] μετεθέμεθα | cυνιδόντεc οὐ [τοια]ῦτα ἔκ | τινοc ἐπιλ[ογ]ιcμ[ο]ῦ· τὰ δὲ | πλεῖcτα τῶν ἐ[μ πε]ρι[λ]ηπτι|κῶι τρόπωι [ἐ]λ[εγχο]μένων ἂν . . . . I follow H. Usener, *Glossarium Epicureum* (Rome 1977), 534–35, and R. Philippson, "Neues über Epikur und seine Schule," *NGG* (1929), 142–43, on the meaning of περιληπτικός. Sedley, *CErc* 3 (1973), 25–26, interprets it as referring to a "conceptual . . . process" involving the "test of conceivability"; *alii alia*.

[29] Cf. Sedley 1973 (above, n. 24), 58, on "changing words," and, on *prolepsis*, 14–15, 34, and 60.

[30] De Lacy 1939 (above, n. 22), 89-90. On his supporting claim, 89 n. 22, that the "Epicureans deny

is unlikely to derive from Epicurus' own writings, since both Philodemus' views on rhetoric and his holistic idea of poetic excellence are probably no older than Zeno;[31] the natural historical development would be from dissatisfaction with theories like those of Aristo and the euphonists, in which form and content were considered in isolation, to a more unified view. But the texts do not really support the view that Philodemus' objection to rhetoric was its use of emotional appeals; he probably viewed irrational and emotional means of persuasion not as illegitimate, but simply as too unreliable to be useful. He could nevertheless have held that poetic ornamentation, while adding nothing to a philosophical exposition *qua* exposition, might be a source of pleasure in itself even when applied to such material. His statement that "the composition proper to poets results when their experience of life has supplied the interconnection of thoughts and a copious flow of expressions"[32] does not suggest an intention to restrict poetry to such light subjects as those of his own epigrams, and his concept of imitation[33] could have been generalized into a theory in which all poetic utterances were regarded as implicitly dramatic, with didactic poetry included as an imitation of the act of giving instruction. But if anything like this occurred to Philodemus, his next question would surely have been about the proper style for such an imitation. If, as he thought, the one naturally fine style is a simple one,[34] and the slightest change even in the order of words produces a completely different effect,[35] then poetic form not only adds nothing to the effectiveness of a philosophical discourse, but must in fact destroy it.

He might nevertheless have allowed the pleasures of poetry at least a protreptic function, as representing the *feelings* of a learner,[36] though this would not help the argumentative parts of a poem like that of Lucretius. If he did not do so, it was, I suggest, for a reason which is indeed rooted in basic Epicurean doctrine, though not in doctrine about language or poetry as such. An empiricist philosophy, if it is to deal with anything outside immediate experience, requires a strong faith in the uniformity of nature (Hume's argument against miracles is the obvious example); and it is only too easy to slip from the claim that there are limits to the possibility of variation to the claim that our experience extends to those limits, or, lacking a mathematics of prob-

---

that good poetry has anything to do with persuasion through emotional apppeal (ψυχαγωγία)," see the Appendix to Chapter 5 below.

[31] Cf. on rhetoric, n. 6 above.

[32] *On Poems* Treatise C col. xvii 16–21 Sbordone τ[ὴν τῶ]ν διαν[οιῶ]ν ἀλ[λη]||λουχία[ν, ἔτι] δὲ καὶ τὴν χύ|ϲιν τῶ[ν] λέξεων τοῦ βί|ου χορη[γής]αντοϲ ἡ ϲύνθε|ϲιϲ ἰδ[ία γε]ίνεται τῶν πο|ητῶν. See Romeo 1992b, however, who reports tentative corrections to several readings in this text (ἀλ[λη]||-λουχία[ν, for example, is no longer read): cf. below, pp. 138f., 163, 245.

[33] I am not convinced by the arguments of Janko 1991a, 17–18 and 31, that *mimesis* in Philodemus' usage always has a narrow meaning according to which words can imitate nothing but other words and sounds; and even if Janko is right about the *word*, Philodemus accepted that poetry aims at *similarity* (Treatise C col. xvi 14–16 on which cf. Asmis, Chapter 2 above and Chapter 8 below).

[34] *On Rhetoric* 4 col. vii 7–8 vol. 1 p. 151 Sudhaus φ[υ]|ϲικῶϲ καλ[ὸ]ϲ λόγοϲ, explained at col. x 2–12 vol. 1 pp. 153f. Sudhaus as that of γραμματικοὶ καὶ | φ[ι]λ[ό]ϲοφοι . . . |[το]ύϲ τε λόγουϲ | ἀπ[λῶϲ ϲυ]νάπ[τ]ο[ντ]εϲ |[οὐ κ]ατὰ [τὰϲ] τεχνολ[ογί]αϲ καταγελαϲτοτ[ά]||τουϲ [ἔ]γδεδωκότ[εϲ].

[35] Cf. N. A. Greenberg, "Metathesis as an Instrument in the Criticism of Poetry," *TAPA* 89 (1958), 262–70.

[36] Cf. *On Poems* 5 col. xxiii (xxvi) 1–4: τῆι | μὲν λέξει τὸ μ[εμι]μῆϲ|θαι τὴν ὠφέλι[μα] προϲ|διδάϲκουϲαν.

ability, from the claim that in an infinite universe ruled by chance everything that can happen must happen at some time to the claim that everything that can happen must have happened in the time known to us. We learn from the treatise *On Signs* (or what we might call "methods of inference") that the Epicureans' tendency to exaggerate the uniformity of nature was so conspicuous that their critics could pretend that the existence of giants and pygmies was an embarrassment for them; and although Philodemus acknowledges in reply that it would be a mistake for someone who had never seen an Ethiopian to assume that all human beings are white, he does not himself hesitate to assert the impossibility of human beings who live on hay.[37] Epicurus himself appears to have supposed that the animal and plant species which chance has brought into existence in our world would appear in any other world that could support life at all;[38] and the argument that the gods must have human form because in our experience only human beings are rational (*On signs* col. xxii 17-28, Cicero, *On the Nature of the Gods* 1.48) extends the principle into the *intermundia*. Lucretius' claim that men had already reached the highest peak in the arts (*On the Nature of Things* 5.1457 *artibus ad summum . . . venere cacumen*) suggests that the Epicureans underestimated the varieties of culture as well as those of DNA. To them there was nothing mere about a merely empirical judgment.

That, for Philodemus, "no poet is every likely to write such poems" followed almost trivially from "none has ever written them" is confirmed by his striking use of the verb προλαμβάνειν for our recognition of poetic merit: his opponents' definition, he says, "has nothing to do with the general concept, nor is this the idea we have previously formed of poetic excellence."[39] The goodness of poetry is the subject of something like the *prolepsis* of a natural kind, similarly based on past experience and on the confidence that other members of the species will not differ greatly from those we already know—in the case of good poems, from those of Homer and the other classics. In effect, he imagined human nature as saying, like Lucretius' universal Nature, "there is nothing further that I can devise and discover to give you pleasure."[40]

Appendix
The Meaning of Ψυχαγωγία in Philodemus

De Lacy's translation of ψυχαγωγία as "persuasion through emotional appeal"[41] seems *prima facie* plausible if one merely considers the word's etymological meaning; but history is the realm of the contingent, and words often develop meanings which could hardly be predicted from their etymologies. Thus *psuchagogia* and *psuchagogein*, though they may be

---

[37] *On Signs* col. ii 3-25, xxx 20–27, and xxvi 6-9.

[38] *Letter to Herodotus* 74, on which cf. E. Asmis, *Epicurus' Scientific Method*, Cornell Studies in Classical Philology 42 (Ithaca, 1984), 314.

[39] *On Poems* 5 col. xxx [xxxiii] 32–36 [καὶ μ]ὴν οὔτε παρε|φάπτεται τ[ῆς κ]οινῆς | ἐννο[ί]ας [οὔτε] προει|λήφαμεν ταύτην ἀρετὴν | ποιήματος . . . . Asmis 1984 (above, n. 38), 25 n. 13, points out that the verb implies the noun.

[40] *On the Nature of Things* 3.944–5, *tibi praeterea quod machiner inveniamque / quod placeat nil est*.

[41] See n. 30 above.

used of many kinds of mental influence, and sometimes occur in contexts involving persuasion and appeals to the emotions,[42] more often in later Greek mean no more than "entertain."[43] Since most of Philodemus' uses of the words are clearly echoes of his opponents' language, we must examine usage, and ask not what Philodemus, or the Epicureans in general, thought about *psuchagogia*, but what he thought about what his opponents said about, and meant by, "*psuchagogia*"; and the choice between the translations "emotional influence" and "entertainment" may depend on whether we think that *psuchagogia* was more like the English "glamor," whose etymological meanings, whether "grammar" or "enchantment," are seldom present to the mind even of speakers of English who know the word's history, or, rather, like "charm," whose meaning "magical incantation" is easily revived by a suitable context.

The analogy with "glamor" and "charm" was not chosen casually, since in fact the original meaning of *psuchagogein* and related words does not seem to have been "influence the mind"; the earliest occurrences refer rather to calling up the ghosts of the dead,[44] and although the meaning "enchant the minds of the living" soon followed (as when Xenophon says in *Memorabilia* 3.10.6 that what most *psuchagogei* us about statues is their appearance of being alive), a passage in which Plato juxtaposes the two meanings suggests that it was the latter one which was felt as metaphorical.[45] Among the earliest examples of the words' application to literature, Plato's definition of rhetoric as "a kind of *psuchagogia* by means of speeches" (*Phaedrus* 261A, echoed in 271C) might seem to support De Lacy's translation; but immediately after the first passage cited, Socrates corrects Phaedrus' supposition that the scope of rhetoric is confined to forensic and deliberative oratory, and two passages in Isocrates (both wrongly listed under "inveigle, delude" in LSJ) suggest that Plato, like Philodemus later, was using the language of his opponents,[46] and that these opponents were not concerned exclusively with the *persuasive* power of rhetoric. In one of these passages (col. ii 42-49), Isocrates argues that people "consider those poems and prose writings which contain good counsel the most useful, but do not derive the most pleasure from them;[47] instead they react just as they do to those who reproach them, for these too they praise, but prefer to associate with those who share their vices, not those who warn against them," and concludes that those who wish to please the crowd must choose not the most useful things to say, but the most marvellous (μυθωδεϲτάτουϲ), as Homer and the early tragic poets did: "from their examples it is clear that those who wish to *psuchagogein* their hearers must refrain from giving advice and must say instead the

---

[42] Clear examples of the meaning "persuade" include Lycurgus 33 and Polybius 13.8.3; for emotional appeals in general, cf. the scholium on Euripides, *Orestes* 241, ψυχαγωγεῖ τὸν ἀδελφὸν ὑπομιμνήϲκουϲα τοῦ πατρὸϲ καὶ ἐλπίδαϲ ἀγαθὰϲ ὑποτίθεται διὰ τοῦ θείου (cited by Gudemann on Aristotle, *Poetics* 1450a33, along with other interesting examples).

[43] The Anti-Atticist in Bekker's *Anecdota* (1.116) defines the verb as τὸ τέρπειν, οὐ μόνον ἐπὶ τοῦ ἐξαπατῶντα πιπράϲκειν, perhaps indicating that the meaning "deceive" remained current longer; on Hellenistic usage, cf. generally P. M. Fraser, *Ptolemaic Alexandria* (Oxford 1972) vol. 1, 757–758 and vol. 2, 1063–1064, and see below.

[44] ψυχαγωγόϲ (adj.) in Aeschylus, *Persians* 687 and the title of a lost play; Aristophanes, *Birds* 1555.

[45] *Laws* 909B, καταφρονοῦντεϲ δὲ τῶν ἀνθρώπων ψυχαγωγοῦϲι μὲν πολλοὺϲ τῶν ζώντων, τοὺϲ δὲ τεθνεῶταϲ φάϲκοντεϲ ψυχαγωγεῖν καὶ θεοὺϲ ὑπιϲχνούμενοι πείθειν . . . .

[46] R. Hackforth, *Plato's Phaedrus* (Cambridge 1952), 123 n. 1, suggests that Plato was influenced by Isocrates 2.49; W. Süss, *Ethos. Studien zur älteren griechischen Rhetorik* (Leipzig 1910), 77–79, argues from the echoes in 268B–C and 270B–D of Gorgias' comparison between rhetoric and medicine (*Helen* 14) that both Plato and Isocrates are borrowing a Gorgianic catchword, and F. Wehrli, "Der erhabene und der schlichte Stil in der poetische-rhetorischen Theorie der Antike," in O. Gigon et al., *Phyllobolia für P. von der Mühll* (Basel 1946), 15–21, traces back to Gorgias all the ideas later associated with the term.

[47] οὐ μὴν ἥδιϲτά γ᾽ αὐτῶν ἀκούουϲιν.

sort of thing at which they see mobs taking the most pleasure."[48] In 9.10, he says that the poets have the advantage over orators, since even if they fall short in style and thought, they *psuchagogousin* their hearers by means of rhythm and proportion alone. Clearly, the metaphor from magic was already in the first half of the fourth century being weakened to mean no more than "entertain."

Aristotle's usage is somewhat harder to interpret. At *Poetics* 6.1450a33–35 he observes that "the most important means by which tragedy *psuchagogei* are parts of the plot, namely reversals and recognitions," and a little later (1450b16–18) he calls spectacle "*psuchagogikon*, but the least artistic and least connected with the art of poetry" of the elements of tragedy. Many scholars have been tempted to see in these passages a reference to appeals to pity and fear, the emotions proper to tragedy;[49] but in his *Rhetoric* Aristotle describes reversals and narrow escapes from danger as pleasant objects of imitation because of their surprising character,[50] and *psuchagogei* in the *Poetics* probably means "gives pleasure," or more generally "makes an impression" or "is effective," rather than "has an emotional effect." He may nevertheless have meant the word to indicate both the calmer and the more emotional pleasures given by tragedy: in later criticism ἔκπληξιc and ἡδονή (or χάριc) are frequently paired to describe the range of effects aimed at by the various genres, and although ψυχαγωγία sometimes figures as the second item of this pair,[51] it has been suggested that when the word is used for the aim of poetry in general, as it was by Eratosthenes,[52] it was meant to cover this wider range.[53] This may also be true of Neoptolemus' statement that poetry aims at benefit along with *psuchagogia*, even though in Philodemus' citation this is immediately followed by the paraphrase τέρπειν (*On Poems* 5 col. xiii [xvi] 9-14):[54] though Horace renders the idea with *delectare, iucunda,* and *dulci* (*The Art of Poetry* 333–34 and 343–44), he also applies the more literal translation *animum auditoris agunto* (ibid. 100) to a variety of emotional effects.

No clear reference to emotional effects can be found among Philodemus' other uses of the words. "Persuade" and "persuasion" are probably the right translations at *On Rhetoric* 4 col. iii 1-14 vol. 1 p. 148 Sudhaus, "if by fine (diction) they mean that which introduces apparently advantageous matters and has the capacity to *psuchagogein*, because . . . we will insert similar language for *psuchagogia*," and *Index Academicorum* col. xxxvi 3–5 p. 172 Dorandi, where a certain Phanostratus is described as "well trained for all kinds of *psuchagogia*." On the other

[48] τοῖc ἐπιθυμοῦcιν τοὺc ἀκρροωμένουc ψυχαγωγεῖν . . . τὰ δὲ τοιαῦτα λεκτέον, οἷc ὁρῶcι τοὺc ὄχλουc μάλιcτα χαίροντεc.

[49] So, e.g., F. Susemihl, "Zu Aristotle's Poetik," *RhM* 18 (1863), 471–72, responding to "X." (Bernays, according to Bonitz, *Index Aristotelicus* s.v.), ibid. 156; G. F. Else, *Aristotle's Poetics: The Argument* (Cambridge, Mass. 1957), 278–79, who interprets ὄψιc as referring mainly to masks and costumes, and cites Aeschylus' Furies and Euripides' ragged heroes.

[50] *Rhetoric* 1.1371b6-12, ἡδέα . . . καὶ αἱ περιπέτειαι καὶ τὸ παρὰ μικρὸν cώζεcθαι ἐκ τῶν κινδύνων· πάντα γὰρ θαυμαcτὰ ταῦτα, cited by J. Vahlen in his fundamental discussion, "Aristoteles Lehre von der Rangfolge der Theile der Tragoedie," *Symbola Philologorum Bonnensium in Honorem F. Ritschelii* (Leipzig 1864), 168 n. 33.

[51] See Polybius 2.56.11, Ps.-Plutarch, *Life of Homer* 5.

[52] Strabo 1.1.10 ποιητὴc πᾶc cτοχάζεται ψυχαγωγίαc, οὐ διδαcκαλίαc.

[53] So H. Mutschmann, "Das Genesiscitat in der Schrift ΠΕΡΙ ΥΨΟΥΣ," *Hermes* 52 (1917), 191–93; W. Kroll, "Die historische Stellung von Horazens Ars poetica," *Sokrates* 72 (n. F. 6) (1918), 89 n. 2; *contra*, R. Heinze, *Virgils Epische Technik* 3 (Berlin 1915), 466–67.

[54] Note also the anticipation in Timocles 6.5–7 (of the effects of tragedy):

ὁ γὰρ νοῦc τῶν ἰδίων λήθην λαβὼν
πρὸc ἀλλοτρίῳ τε ψυγαγωγηθεὶc πάθει,
μεθ' ἡδονῆc ἀπῆλθε παιδευθεὶc ἅμα,

where "entertained" or "consoled" is clearly the translation required.

hand, the meaning is clearly "charmed" or "beguiled" in the quotation from Epicurus at *On Rhetoric* 3 col. iii 7-17 vol. 2 p. 256 Sudhaus and col. iv 20-25 p. 257–58 (= Epicurus fr. 20.4 Arrighetti, reedited by J. Hammerstaedt, *CErc* 22 [1992] 26f.; also paraphrased at *On Rhetoric* 2 col. x 30–xi 18 p. 63 Longo), "When they hear them in display speeches at festivals, and *psuchagogethosi* because the subject is not some contract nor something advantageous, as is the case in assemblies and law-courts . . . *psuchagogoumenoi* by the mere sound and the periods and *parisa* and antitheses and *homoeoteleuta* . . . ." Just as clearly, *psuchagogia* when applied to music (*On Music* 4 cols. xi 19–20, xvii 29, xix 33–34) means simply "entertainment." In *On Poems*, besides the citation of Neoptolemus mentioned above, the terms are used repeatedly in the polemics against Heracleodorus and an anonymous opponent discussed by Asmis in this volume,[55] and in reference to the effects of thought at Treatise B fr. 16, 9 Sbordone, plot at Treatise B fr. 25 col. i 15–20, and diction at Treatise D fr. 7 col. i 18–19 Nardelli, in all these passages clearly reporting the opponents' language. They are applied to the effects of *synthesis* and rhythm at Treatise A fr. c 19 and col. i 8, of repetition at Treatise A fr. e 1ff., and of sounds in general at Treatises B fr. 15, 24 and C fr. a col. ii 10.

Finally, there is an interesting group of fragments, in one of which (Treatise D fr. 20) Philodemus mentions opponents who "would not shrink from saying without qualification that the many are influenced (*psuchagogeisthai*) by the kind of (diction?) that is thought to befit poets, and what is more, influenced rationally, not irrationally; on this account they will despise the test of the things which make an effect on (*psuchagogounton*) the crowd,[56] and on this point I agree with them. For (I maintain?) that fine diction is not one of the things which exist naturally, but rather . . . ."[57] The same opponents are probably the target of fr. 21, where he refers to "metaphors; and you might add the things which ornament and those which offend the ears. But anyone can see that everything which the ears perceive has no effect on the hearing and does not move the soul irrationally but rationally, by means of its artistry."[58] As Nardelli has seen,[59] what is at issue in these passages is not a contrast between different kinds of *psuchagogia* or favorable and unfavorable views of *psuchagogia*, but rather between theories which attributed effectiveness to only one aspect, rational or irrational, of poetry, and Philodemus' theory, according to which the irrational effect of sounds and the rational effect of content are inseparable.

---

55 See Chapters 2 and 8.

56 Cf. Treatise D fr. 18.2–12: ". . . writing that the sophist ought to seek truth, but the poet, what is pleasing and charming to the many; and therefore he wrote that the finest poetry is that which entertains (*psuchagogousan*) the mobs, not that which suits and is admired by the few"; Treatise E fr. 1, where a similar contrast between truth and what pleases the many is followed by a reference to "tickling the hearing;" and Treatise D fr. 19, 1–5, "to charm the souls of the educated, and in general that one ought to *psuchagogeisthai* with reason, not irrationally . . . ."

57 Philodemus, *On Poems* Treatise D fr. xx 10-24 p. 27 Nardelli ἡμῖν [ἁ]|πλῶς ο[ὑ]κ ἂν ἀπεστή-ca[ν|το] λ[έ]γειν ψυχαγ[ωγεῖc|θαι τ]ὸν πολὺν ὑπὸ τῆc |[νενο]μιcμένηc τοῖc πο|ηταῖc προcήκειν, καὶ |[λογι]κῶc ἀλλ' οὐκ ἀλόγωc |[ψ]υχαγωγεῖcθαι. διὸ | καὶ τῆc βαcάνου τῶν | ψυχαγωγούντων τὸν | ὄχλον καταφρονήcου|cι κἀγὼ μετ' [αὐ]τῶν. | οὐ γὰρ τὸ τὴν καλὴν | λέξιν ἕν τ[ι] τῶν φυcικῶν |[ὑπ]άρχειν, [ἀλλ]ὰ μᾶλλον . . . .

58 Philodemus, *On Poems* Treatise D fr. xxi 21-24 . . . κ[α]λοῦ τ[ὰ μετα]|φορικά, προcδ[οί]ηc ἄ[ν]| τὰ κοcμοῦ[ν]τα καὶ τὰ | παρακ[ρού]οντα τὰ[c | ἀ]κοάc· ὅ[cα δ]έ ποθ' αἱ ἀ|κοαὶ [προcδέχ]ον-ται | βλέ[πε]ται κα[ὶ] τοῖc τ[υ]|χοῦcιν ὅτι πρὸc τὴν | ἀκοὴν οὐθέν ἐcτιν | οὐδὲ τὴν ψ[υ]χὴν ἀλό|γωc ἀλλὰ τῶι τεχνι|κῶι λογιcτικῶc κε[ι]|νεῖ . . . .   59 Nardelli 1983, 115–17.

6

Reconstructing Philodemus' *On Poems*

Richard Janko

foliis tantum ne carmina manda,
ne turbata uolent rapidis ludibria ventis.

When Aeneas requests an oracle from the Sibyl at Cumae, he asks her not to entrust her reply to the leaves on which her oracles were traditionally inscribed, in case the winds should blow them into confusion (*Aeneid* 6.74f.). Vergil might well have been describing the fate of the writings of his teacher, Philodemus of Gadara; for a very basic obstacle to understanding the philosopher's writings has been that many sequences of detached fragments make no sense at all. Editors have usually arranged these in an arbitrary order according to apparent associations of ideas; this has often led them to emend, in order to create joins where there are none. This method was followed, for example, in the editions of the *On Poems* by F. Sbordone[1] and M. L. Nardelli;[2] yet it never gave the works as a whole any satisfactory structure. Others

An earlier version of parts of this paper, which has been substantially revised to take account of developments up to June 1993, appeared in the *Proceedings of the XXth International Congress of Papyrology* (Copenhagen 1993, 367–81); it appears here with the kind permission of A. Bülow-Jacobsen. I am grateful to T. Dorandi for commenting on a draft of it, to D. Delattre, J. Hammerstaedt, C. Mangoni, D. Obbink, and C. Romeo for helpful discussion, and to audiences at Yale University and UCLA, where earlier versions were delivered. The section on Crates will form part of Chapter 3 of *From Aristotle to Longinus: The Invention of Critical Theory* (The Martin Classical Lectures), to appear. An Italian translation of an abbreviated version of this paper will appear in *Atti del Congresso Internazionale 'L'Epicureismo greco e romano'* (Naples forthcoming). Places where either the column-number or the line-number is provisional are marked with asterisks: thus col. 118* is tentatively assumed to be col. 118 in my proposed reconstruction, while line 23* is taken to be line 23 because the top of the column is lost and the number of lines per column is conjectural. These numbers differ from those used in my previous publication (Janko 1991b), because progress in the reconstruction has continued; they are intended for purposes of illustration only, and will no doubt be altered again by the time when I bring out a complete text and translation of Book 1 in *Philodemus: The Aesthetic Works*. 1. *On Poems, Book I* (to appear). Where my text differs from that of Sbordone, Nardelli, or Mangoni, this is owed to my own editorial decisions; it would consume too much space to give a full critical apparatus here.

[1] Sbordone 1976 contains the Treatises A, B and C discussed below.
[2] Nardelli 1983 contains Treatises D and E.

have retained the numeration of the *disegni*, as in Nardelli's publication of *P.Herc.* 1581,[3] yet this too yielded no continuous sense.

In this essay I shall first give an account of a newly developed papyrological method for determining the order of such *feuilles volantes*, and show what it has already accomplished. Secondly, I shall survey all the known papyri of Philodemus' *On Poems* in the light of recent work, to show how the entire treatise is likely to look when it has been reconstructed, a task which will be completed during the coming decade. Thirdly, I shall suggest that Philodemus' technique of argumentation will help to solidify the papyrological results and clarify the structure of his treatise. In conclusion, I shall offer a preliminary interpretation of the structure of *On Poems* 1, and in particular of the euphonic theories of the noted Pergamene critic and literary theorist Crates of Mallos.

1. The Delattre/Obbink method of reconstruction

The new papyrological method offers exciting prospects of progress in the many cases where only the transcripts survive. The basis of this method will be familiar to the papyrologists working on the approximately thirty-eight papyrus-rolls which constituted the official archive of Bubastos in Lower Egypt; these texts, carbonized in A.D. 232, are currently being published by J. Frösén and D. Hagedorn.[4] However, its application to the Herculaneum texts is very recent, and differs in interesting ways from the case of the Bubastos papyri.

To understand the procedure, we need to imagine the original discovery. The charred *volumina* resembled logs in appearance. They were at first opened in the following manner. Each roll was incised with a knife down either side, and the parts outside were peeled off. These formed concave surfaces like the bark of a tree, with writing on the inside; hence such a fragment from the outside was called a *scorza* ("bark"). The interior of the *volumen*, the narrow cylinder left after the removal of the *scorze*, was called the *midollo* ("marrow"). The *midolli*, less completely carbonized, retained some elasticity, and could with relative ease be unrolled as continuous texts. They turned out to contain the ends of the treatises, often with a *subscriptio* giving the author and title.[5] The continuous texts from the *midolli*, up to perhaps forty columns in length, are still extant; although substantial, they rarely represent more than about a quarter of the original roll, some 150 to 200 columns long.[6] The breakthrough described below does not affect texts derived only from the *midolli*, but rather those

---

[3] Nardelli 1978.

[4] Frösén and Hagedorn 1990. See especially pp. 97f. on *Pap. Bub.* 4, with Taf. 15–32, for how the shapes of the successive layers of papyrus from either side of the roll resemble each other. The following several paragraphs develop my earlier remarks in Janko 1991b, esp. 274–83.

[5] For examples see Cavallo 1983, Plates XXIX, XLI, XLIII, LII.

[6] On the average length of the *volumina* see Cavallo 1983, 16. *On Poems* 5 was so lengthy that one copy of it was divided into two rolls (*P.Herc.* 1538); a second exemplar (*P.Herc.* 1425) was perhaps 245–269 cols. in extent (cf. Janko 1991a, 62 n. 346). If the ω reported by Mangoni 1993 ad loc. as in the margin above *P.Herc.* 1425 col. xxi were to stand for "24," one could hypothesize that such a letter marked every tenth column, in which case this would be col. 240, and the length of the entire roll would be 257 columns. There is no exact parallel for this, but cf. Cavallo 1983, 14–15.

known only from the *scorze*. Since the outer layers had been cut down either side with a knife, they could not be unrolled to obtain continuous text: rather, they would yield in an ideal case a set of alternating fragments, one from one side of the papyrus-roll, the next from the other. This situation prevails in the case of many of the Bubastos papyri, where the rolls were flattened and therefore broken down each side; the editors are reconstructing these rolls by interleaving two sets of fragments, one from each side. However, the Herculaneum papyri present a more complicated puzzle.

First, the fact that the two or more sets of *scorze* and a single *midollo* formed, respectively, the outer layers and the core of a single papyrus-roll was forgotten. *Scorze* derived from opposite sides of the same roll were separated and assigned different and often unrelated inventory numbers; thus *P.Herc.* 460 and *P.Herc.* 1073 belong to the same roll of *On Poems* (Treatise B Sbordone). Hence one must first try to match up the outsides and insides of the same roll, if they survive. Second, the layers of the *scorze* could not simply be lifted off and preserved in the correct order. The standard procedure was that the first layer of writing (layer A) visible on the concave interior of the *scorza* was copied down by a draughtsman, and the drawing would be numbered 1. This layer of writing was then removed to expose the layer beneath (layer B). Layer A was usually destroyed in the process. Layer B was then transcribed as *disegno* number 2, and was then peeled away to expose layer C below it, which was then transcribed as *disegno* number 3 and removed to expose layer D, and so on. This process of transcription and destruction ("*scorzatura*") would continue until the last layer was reached, when no further layers could be separated. The result of this procedure was a set of numbered *disegni* and a single *scorza*, the bottommost layer of writing, usually a mass of jumbled letters melted into each other.[7] Editors of the many texts preserved in the *scorze* alone faced difficulties so great that over two centuries elapsed before appropriate techniques of reconstruction could be devised.

The resultant sets of *disegni* yielded no continous sense, until, in recent years, two scholars reconstructing different texts solved the puzzle independently: they are D. Obbink, working on the *On Piety*,[8] and D. Delattre, working on the *On Music*.[9] Their central insight is brilliantly simple. Ancient book-rolls were normally read from the outside in: the reader began at the outside, and continued until he reached the middle. Since the middle of the roll contained the end of the work, with a closing *subscriptio*, the *scorze* must contain earlier portions, further from the end. Moreover, the numeration of the *disegni* must be kept—but in reverse! The first layer which the draughtsman saw and drew, layer A (= *disegno* 1), is in fact the layer nearest the end of the work. The second one, layer B (= *disegno* 2), was one circumference further back towards the beginning; the third, layer C (= *disegno* 3) would be yet earlier in the text, and so on. We had been reading much of Philodemus' work backwards!

The insight basic to the Delattre/Obbink method is simple, but a few further steps are needed. First, a given set of *disegni* represents only one side of the roll; each set of *scorze* needs to be reunited with its missing other half. Cavallo's fine study[10] of the scribal hands is fundamental in helping one decide which papyri can belong together;

[7] On the process of *scorzatura* see Sbordone 1983, 199f.
[8] Obbink 1986, 24–43.   [9] Delattre 1989.
[10] Cavallo 1983.

so is attention to the number of lines per column. If one can find the other half, the two series of *scorze* must usually be *interleaved in reverse order* to obtain a coherent text.

Secondly, sometimes the sequence of fragment-numbers must *not* be reversed. It seems that, for reasons still obscure, the numbers can go forwards if the papyrus is still fully extant. Thus, of the eight papyri of *On Music* 4, the only ones which still exist are *P.Herc.* 225 and 1094, and these alone must be read in forwards order.[11] But this principle does not always apply, e.g., in the case of *P.Herc.* 1581.[12]

Thirdly, the columns of writing rarely coincide with the vertical incisions made down the sides of the roll in order to open it. Frequently, the knife has cut away the left half of one column and the right half of the next. Often the draughtsmen did not draw columns containing only a few letters per line. Sometimes, however, when a single *scorza* contained fragments of two columns, they did draw both, but in two separate drawings. They might indicate the relationship between them by numbering them "A" and "B" (e.g., 10A to the right, 10B to the left, or vice versa), but often they would number the drawings as if they represented successive layers of writing, when in fact they do not. Thus the surviving fragment 5 of *P.Herc.* 460 corresponds to parts of two *disegni* of *On Poems* Treatise B, *disegno* 4 lines 7–10 (= fr. 28 Sbordone) on the left and *disegno* 5 lines 2–10 (= fr. 4 col. i Sbordone) on the right. Hence these *disegni* are adjacent. Such cases can be detected from study of the outlines of the *disegni*, whence one can see which is the left-hand column and which is the right-hand. The successive layers are similar in shape, and the *disegno*-numbers generally decline as the text advances. This is exemplified in Table 6.1, where I have indicated whether each *disegno* is of a left-hand or a right-hand fragment.

Fourthly, the papyrus may have suffered horizontal as well as vertical breakage. This means that further skill is needed in arranging the tops and bottoms of the columns in their correct sequence. This too is seen in Table 1, where the upper and lower parts of *P.Herc.* 1073 (numbered a and b respectively) in fact form two different series from the same side of the roll.

Let me now illustrate this method. C. Mangoni[13] in her study of *P.Herc.* 228, from *On Poems*, already noted that the order of the *disegni*, if reversed, yielded a sequence of quotations parallel to those in *On Poems* 5 cols. xxiii–xxiv, xxvi and xxvii–xxx, where Philodemus refutes the same doctrines in the same order. However, *P.Herc.* 228 consists of disconnected *scorze* from one side of the roll; the other side of it has not been identified.[14] The best demonstration comes from cases where both halves of the same roll are known. Thus Delattre has reconstructed 109 columns of the *On Music*, from eight papyri with different inventory numbers.[15] By reversing and inter-

---

[11] The papyri are nos. 225, 411, 424, 1094, 1497, 1572, 1575, 1578, 1583. Delattre 1989, 66, wrongly states that *P.Herc.* 1583 is to be read in this direction: contrast his chart at ibid. 142.

[12] See Janko 1991a, 59–61. The rolls of *On Rhetoric* 3, the second half of which is published by J. Hammerstaedt (Hammerstaedt 1992), show even greater disordering in the numbering of their fragments than the Delattre/Obbink method would predict.   [13] Mangoni 1989.

[14] For a proposal that *P.Herc.* 228 derives from the same *volumen* as the *scorze P.Herc.* 403, 407, and 1581 and the *midollo P.Herc.* 1425, and therefore from *On Poems* 5, of which *P.Herc.* 1425 contains the end, see Janko 1991a, 59–63, with the valuable comments of C. Mangoni (Mangoni 1992a), esp. 136f, developed in Mangoni 1993, 32–36.

[15] Delattre 1989. Delattre's results are endorsed by Pöhlmann 1991, esp. 484f.; cf. also Janko 1992a and D. Delattre, "Speusippe, Diogène de Babylone et Philodème," *CErc* 23 (1993), 67–86.

leaving various sets of *disegni*, he has shown that the fragments acribed to Books 1, 3 and 4 of the *On Music* all belong to a single *volumen* 154 columns long; they all derive therefore from Book 4, of which the *midollo* preserves the closing *subscriptio*. His reconstruction is confirmed by internal evidence. Philodemus first summarises the opinions of his opponent, Diogenes of Babylon, and then refutes these same opinions in the same sequence. Delattre found a series of twenty-six parallels between the summary of Diogenes' views, which filled at least cols. 2* to 39* in his reconstructed text, and Philodemus' refutation of these arguments in cols. 57* to 146 (the asterisk signifies that the column-number is provisional). I have established a similar set of parallels between *On Poems* Treatises A and B Sbordone, which have helped me confirm my reconstruction of Treatise B, tentatively calculated as sixty-eight columns long (allowing for lacunae). I cannot discuss these in detail here,[16] but append a table of part of my reconstruction (Table 6.1), to show how the parallels with Treatise A, where the order of the columns is securely established, confirm the new sequence of the *disegni*. This lists, first, the column-number, marked as provisional with an asterisk; then, the papyrus and *disegno*-number; then, Sbordone's fragment-numbers, which bear little relation to the true sequence; then the shape of the *scorza*, to show whether we are dealing with a left-hand or a right-hand fragment; and lastly, the extensive series of parallels with Treatise A. Note how the numbers of the *disegni* descend within each series.

A project is currently underway, with the help of a major grant from the Texts and Translations Division of the National Endowment for the Humanities, to fill one of the most serious lacunae in this field—the lack of a collected edition of these materials, together with a facing English translation and explanatory notes. This collaborative effort (the Philodemus Translation Project) is limited to Philodemus' most substantial extant works, those on aesthetics. These are the *On Poems*, in at least five books (by my count, ca. 25,000 words survive); the *On Music*, in at least four books (ca. 18,000 words), and the *On Rhetoric*, in about seven books (ca. 33,000 words). These amount to around 80,000 words, about half of his extant prose writings. The final product will consist of seven volumes with indices.

2. The Papyri of the *On Poems*

Before we can discuss the contents of the *On Poems* as a whole, we need first to assign the papyri to the correct books of it and to establish its overall structure. This will require a rather technical discussion of the papyri, but this is an essential preliminary to finding out what the texts say. Let me therefore review the papyri of the *On Poems*, according to current information.[17] The reader is asked to bear in mind that this is work very much in progress.

[16] See further Janko 1991b, 285–99, with an earlier and less accurate version of Table 6.1 at 291f., composed before I realised that *P.Herc.* 1073 must have fractured laterally.

[17] For earlier overviews cf. Greenberg 1955, esp. 266–70; Sbordone 1983, 1–19 (first published 1956); T. Dorandi, "Per una ricomposizione dello scritto di Filodemo *Sulla poetica*," *ZPE* 91 (1992), 29–46. This version of the Table is further modified in the light of Dorandi's article "Precisizioni su papiri della Poetica di Filodemo," *ZPE* 97 (1993), 81–86.

Table 6.1. Partial reconstruction of Philodemus' *On Poems* Treatise B

col. no.	papyrus/*disegno*	Sbordone fr. no.	shape of *scorza*	parallels with Treatise A and comments
72*	460/23	30	left half	
73*	460/24	19	right half	
74*	1073/12 + 1073/18	34 + 32	opposite side, torn laterally	2–8 cf. Tr. A col. a 6–14; 20*–22* cf. Tr. col. a 24–5
75*	460/21	29	left half	2–7 cf. Tr. A col. a 27–b 12; 18–26 cf. Tr. col. b 19–c 1, c 5–6, e 3–8
76*	460/22	7 col. i	right half	23–4 cf. Tr. A col. b 23, col. d 25–e 8
77*	1073/11	7 col. ii	opposite side, top only	
78*	460/20	12	left half	4 cf. Tr. A col. e 17, f 7
79*	460/19 + 460/14b	5 col. i	right half, + *sovrapposto*	stichometric letter μ in margin
80*	1073/10a + 1073/16b	5 col. ii + 33	opposite side, torn laterally	join with 79* (in a quotation of Euripides)
81*	460/17	11 col. ii	left half	6–8 cf. Tr. A col. iv 19–20, xiv 22–3
82*	460/18	3	right half	19–20 cf. Tr. A fr. 24b 26
83*	1073/9a + 1073/15b	23 col. i + 10 col. i	opposite side, torn laterally	22–4 cf. Tr. A fr. 24b 26, col. i sin. 6–7, col. dext. 24*–ii 1
84*	460/16	10 col ii	opposite side	1–20 cf. Tr. A col. i dext. 24*–ii 1
85*	1073/10b	37	left half, bottom only	
86*	1073/8a	4 col. ii	right half, top only	
87*	460/15	23 col. ii	opposite side	3–6 cf. Tr. A col. vi 4–8; 13–15 cf. Tr. A col. vi 11–12; 15–26 cf. Tr. A cols. v 5–1 22–6
88*	1073/6	23 col. iii	left half, top only	1–2 cf. Tr. A col. v 16–17
89*	1073/7a	9 col. i	right half, top only	
90*	460/14a	6 col. i	opposite side	21–6 cf. Tr. A cols. ix 24–x 7, xi 3 (both c Homer, *Iliad* 5.838)
91*	1073/5	6 col. ii	opposite side, top only	3 cf. Tr. A col. ix 7; 3–7 cf. Tr. A col. x 23–
92*	460/not drawn	—	[left half -- lost]	
93*	460/13	2	right half	(on Homer, *Od.* 11.207)
94*	1073/4	31	opposite side, top only	(on Homer, *Od.* 11.207)
95*	460/12	13	left half	1–9, 19 cf. Tr. A col. xi 20–xii 1, 7–9 (bot on Homer, *Iliad* 21.260–1)
96*	460/11	16	right half	
97*	1073/9b	23 col. i	torn laterally	16–21* cf. Tr. A cols. xiv 20–3, xv 4–6
98*	460/9	26 col. i	opposite side	ref. back to col. 87*; 18, 26, cf. Tr. A col. x 13, 24; 24 cf. Tr. A col. xvii 18
99*	1073/3 + 460/10	26 col. ii + 15	left side, torn laterally	6–7 cf. Tr. A col. xvii 11–12
100*	1073/8b	38	torn laterally	
101*	460/8	20 col. i	opposite side	5–6 cf. Tr. A col. xix dext. 10–13; 7–16 c Tr. A col. xix dext. 21–5; 16–21 cf. Tr. col. xix dext. 24–xx 11; 24–5 cf. Tr. col. xxi 8–10

Table 6.2 illustrates how it seems likely that we will be able to reconstruct the entire work. The papyri are listed by book and then by scribal hand. Within each hand, the papyri are arranged according to the order which I believe that they will be found to follow within each roll; a "+" indicates one or more joins with the next entry. There follows the title of the work to which the papyrus is assigned or the name of Philodemus' opponent, its latest editor, the group and scribal hand as determined by Cavallo, the number of lines per column (or the maximum number of lines preserved,

Table 6.2. The papyri of Philodemus' *On Poems*

P.Herc.	title/opponent, ed.	group, hand	lines/col. (cols.)	comments

Book 1 (total cols. represented: ca. 115; = group β Crönert)

466+	Treatise E/Nardelli	I, xiii	14+ (tops, 15)	summary on euphony; marginal Δ
444	ed. Sbordone	I, xiii	14+ (bots., 17)	summary on euphony
460+	Treatise B/Sbordone	I, xiii	25–28 (35)	summary on euphony; has accents; marginal M
1073+	Treatise B/Sbordone	I, xiii	25–26 (c. 19)	summary on euphony; has accents
1074c+	Treatise D/Nardelli	I, xiii	26–28 (c. 20)	start of refutation on euphony
1081a+	Treatise D/Nardelli	I, xiii	c. 24 (c. 20)	refutation on euphony
1074a	Treatise D/Nardelli	I, xiii	23–24 (13)	refutation on euphony; end of book?

Book 2 (total cols. represented: ca. 120; = group γ Crönert)

1074b+	Treatise C/Sbordone	E, viii	26–28 (9)	refutation on euphony
1677a+	*liber incertus*/Romeo	E, viii	26–28 (14)	refutation on euphony
1081b+	Treatise C/Sbordone	E, viii	26–28 (21)	refutation on euphony
1676	Treatise C/Sbordone	E, viii	26–29 (25)	refutation on euphony
994	Treatise A/Sbordone	E, viii	26–28 (72)	refutation on euphony; end of book, title lost

Book 3 (total cols. represented: 13+?)

?1087a	ed. Dorandi	G, x	17+ (tops, 13?)	mentions Homer, Euripides
?1403	ed. Spina	G, x	? (?)	mentions Choerilus, Euripides

Book 4 (total cols. represented: ca. 35–46?; = group α Crönert)

207	Aristotle?/Janko	Q, xxviii	24+ (ca. 35?)	(refutation) on genre; end of book

Book 5 exemplar 1 (total cols. represented: max. 67; = group α Crönert)

?1087b	?/Dorandi	?N, ?xix	? (2)	*disegni* only; mentions Theodectes
?1581	Aristotle?/Nardelli	N, xix	15+ (top, 11)	(summary) on good poet; Γ in margin
?403	Ariston?/Sbordone	N, xix	18+ (top, 10)	(summary) on good poet; Υ in margin
?407	Ariston?/Mangoni	N, xix	14+ (top, 4)	(summary) on good poet
?228	Crates/Mangoni	?N, ?xix	22+ (top, 12)	*disegni* only; (summary) on good poet
1425	Bk. 5/Mangoni	N, xix	34–36 (39)	(refutation) on good poet; end of book

Book 5 exemplar 2 (total cols. represented: 14)

1538	Bk. 5/Mangoni	M	ca. 30 (14)	second of two rolls; end of book

Probably not relevant:

230	ed. Dorandi	?	16+ (2?)	not on poetry; hand too early to be by Philodemus (Dorandi)
1113a	unpublished	?	?	on style; hand too early to be by Philodemus (Dorandi)
1275	unpublished	Q, xxviii	22+ (ca. 37?)	cites Homer; end of book; title lost
1736	ed. Dürr	Q	+11+ (many)	mentions Euripides

given as e.g. "15+"), followed in brackets by the approximate number of columns represented, and comments on the content and special features of the text. My method and conclusions are in gratifyingly close agreement with the recently published studies of Greenberg[18] and of Dorandi,[19] but were at first independent of the latter's.

---

[18] Greenberg 1955.   [19] Dorandi 1992 and 1993 (above, n. 17).

Book 1

W. Crönert[20] assigned precisely these papyri, and no others, to his "Group β." The major part of this roll (including a column with a marginal stichometric letter M, which should, given the average number of lines per column, be around column 80) is made up of the so-called Treatise B, which consists of a summary of the doctrines of an adversary or adversaries. As Crönert[21] noted, the only Herculaneum papyri with accents are the two papyri of Treatise B, viz. *P.Herc.* 460 and 1073; not coincidentally, they discuss the euphonic effects of accentuation. The accents are limited to a specific stretch of the papyrus, which helps to confirm the sequence of the *disegni*.[22]

I assigned to the beginning of this roll Treatise E (*P.Herc.* 466) and *P.Herc.* 444.[23] The same proposal has been advanced by Greenberg[24] and Dorandi.[25] *P.Herc.* 466 fr. 9 col. i has a stichometric $\varDelta$ in the margin, which, on the plausible assumptions that the columns contained about 27 lines and that such a letter appeared every 180 or 200 lines, must be around col. 28*. Both these texts summarize a discussion of euphony; to judge by the *disegni*, they may be in the same hand and may derive from the same *volumen*.[26] The writing is very similar to that of the rest of the roll, but distinctly smaller in size. *P.Herc.* 444 discusses accentuation (fr. 7), using the terms employed in Treatise B (*epitasis* and *anesis*). There is no continuous text, since only one side of the roll is preserved here. Now these papyri are incomplete at the bottom (Treatise E) and top (*P.Herc.* 444) respectively. The progression of topics is the same in both. The hypothesis that they were originally the tops and bottoms of the same columns can now be confirmed by two joins within the series. First, the bottom line of the damaged *P.Herc.* 444 fr. 10 col. i joins verbally with the top line of *P.Herc.* 466 fr. 8 col. ii (fr. 11 col. ii Nardelli):

$$[\ldots \ldots \ldots \ldots \ \ \tau]\hat{\omega}\nu \ \check{\alpha}\lambda||\lambda\omega\nu \ \mu[\ldots \ldots \ldots \ldots \ ]$$

Secondly, *P.Herc.* 444 fr. 3 appears almost to join in the middle of the column with Treatise E fr. 1 (fr. 6 Nardelli); the similarity between the two fragments was already remarked by Schächter[27] and Sbordone.[28] The opponent is attacking a *kritikos* who believed that the excellence of verses lies in *synthesis* alone. Since all verses are composed of letters, and some of these are bound to have good qualities, this view

---

[20] Crönert 1903, 6. B. Quaranta had assigned *P.Herc.* 444, 460, 463, 1073 and 1074 to the same roll; cf. E. Martini, *Catalogo generale dei Papiri Ercolanesi*, in D. Comparetti and G. De Petra, *La Villa ercolanese dei Pisoni. I suoi monumenti e la sua biblioteca* (Turin 1883, repr. Naples 1972), 100 n. 1.

[21] Crönert 1903, 8f.

[22] They occur only in cols. 78*–82*, with an outlier in col. 70* (the isolation of this fragment might suggest that it has been misplaced in the reconstruction). My suggestion (Janko 1993, 376) that there are two accents elsewhere in the roll turns out, after checking of the originals in Naples, to have been mistaken. The "circumflex" in $\hat{\eta}\tau\iota\varsigma$ at *P.Herc.* 1074 fr. 7.9 (Tr. D fr. 33.9 Nardelli) turns out to be a trace of a *sovrapposto*, and the *disegno* of *P.Herc.* 1081 fr. 36.21 (Tr. D fr. 14.21 Nardelli) should probably be interpreted as $'\omega\nu$ (i.e., an interpunct) rather than as $\acute{\omega}\nu$ corrected to $\hat{\omega}\nu$.

[23] F. Sbordone, "Il papiro ercolanese 444," *RAAN* 35 (1960), 99–110, reprinted in Sbordone 1983, 239–50.

[24] Greenberg 1955, 215ff.   [25] Dorandi 1992 (above, n. 17), 42f.

[26] *Pace* Sbordone 1983, 18.   [27] Schächter 1926, 15f.

[28] Sbordone 1960 (above, n. 23), 109f. Cf. Nardelli 1983, 145f. with nn.

will blur the distinction between good and bad verses (ποήματα). The column runs as follows:

P.Herc. 466 fr. 1 (lineae 1–12) + 444 fr. 3 (lineae 15*–27*)

οὐδὲ καθ᾽ ὅcον κακ[ὸν ἐπαι-
νοῦμεν. καὶ δεή[cειν ἅ-
παcιν ἀγαθὸν κακίαc ἀν-
τικοινώνητον εἶναι πά-
5   cηc], κα[ὶ] ὅταν προcγένη[ται
τὸ κακόν], ἐξ ἀνάγκηc ἐν
ὀνόμαcι]ν ψεκ[τό]ν, ὃ καὶ ἐπ[αι-
νετὸν ἐ]ν πο[ή]μαcιν. ἀτὰ[ρ
ἐπειδὴ] μόν[ον] τοῦθ᾽ ὑ[πό-
10   κειται τ]ῶι ἐπαινουμέ[νωι
ποήμα]τι, ἔcτιν [κα]κὸν κ[αὶ
ἐν τῶι ψ]εκτῶι καὶ [ἐν τῶι
[ἐπαινουμένωι, καθάπερ]
[ἔcτιν καλὸν καὶ ἐν τῶι]
15*   ἐπαινου]μένω[ι καὶ ἐν
τῶι ψεκ]τῶι. ἃ δὲ ὁμοί[ωc
μὲν τ]ῶι ἐπαινουμένωι τ[ί-
θεται], ὁμοίωc δὲ τῶι ψε-
κτῶι, οὔ]τε τοῦ ἐπαινου-
20*   μένου] ἴδια οὔτε τοῦ ψε-
κτοῦ ἔ]cται. ὑπόκ[ε]ιται γά[ρ,
ὅταν τ]ἀγαθὸν προcγέν[η-
ται, ἐ]ξ ἀνάγκη[c] τῶν ἐπαι-
νε]τῶν εἶναι ἐ[κ]εῖνο, καὶ
25*   ὅτα]ν τὸ κακόν, τῶν ψε-
κτ]ῶν. καὶ τὸ γε[ν]ομέν[ων
τι]νῶν ἄλλω[ν τ]ὰ διαλε[

fragmenta coniunxit Janko   1 Caini   2 Janko (δεή[cει iam Caini):
δέδ[οκται Sbordone   5 init. Janko:]ΥΑ[N, πά|[λ]ιν [δ'] Sbor-
done   5 Sbordone   6 Janko   7 init. Janko (fort. ποήμαcι]ν),
cetera Nardelli (]N-EK[N)   6–8 ἐπ[αι|νοῦμε]ν ἐκ[εῖ]νο, καὶ ἐν |
[πᾶcι]ν perperam Sbordone   8 init. Nardelli, cetera Sbordone
9 Janko: ἐπεὶ οὐ] μόν[ον] Schächter   10 Nardelli: ὑ|[πάρχει
Schächter cetera Schächter   11 Janko (fort. ὀνόμα]τι): οὐδ᾽ εἰ]

Sbordone   [κα]κὸν Schächter   12 ἐν Janko (bis) τῶι ψ]εκτῶι
Schächter   12–13 τῶι ἐπαινουμένωι Schächter   13–14* Janko
15* init. Sbordone, cet. Janko: εἶναι καὶ Sbordone   16–26* Schächter, Gomperz, Sbordone   26–27* Janko   27* ἄλλω[ν τ]ὰ Janko:
ἄλλω[ν καὶ] Sbordone

. . . ⟨He says that⟩ it will be necessary for all ⟨poets?⟩ that a good ⟨verse?⟩ have
a share in every ⟨kind of⟩ baseness, and ⟨that⟩, when baseness is added, it follows of necessity that that which is praiseworthy in verses is blameworthy in its
words. But since only this (*sc.* excellence*)* has been posited for the verse that is
praised, there is something bad ⟨both in the blameworthy verse and ‖ in the
praiseworthy verse, just as there is something good both in the⟩ praiseworthy
⟨verse⟩ and in the blameworthy ⟨verse⟩. Those ⟨letters⟩ which are posited likewise in the praiseworthy ⟨verse⟩ and likewise in the blameworthy ⟨verse⟩ will
be particular neither to that ⟨verse⟩ which is praised nor to that ⟨verse⟩ which is
blamed. For it has been assumed that, when (?) excellence is added, that ⟨verse⟩
is of necessity among the praiseworthy, and when (?) badness ⟨is added, that
verse is of necessity⟩ among the blameworthy . . .

The argument of *P.Herc.* 460 fr. 28.2–15, from early in Treatise B, is similar:

τούτων γὰ[ρ οὐδέν]‖ ἐπαινετὸν εἶναι μ[ᾶλλον]‖ ἢ ψεκτό[ν, ο]ὐδὲ ἴδ[ιον
τῶν]‖ εὖ γεγραμμένων ἢ καὶ | φαύλως. οὐκ ἀδύνατον | μέν⟨τοι⟩ τὸ καλὸν
αὐτοῖς πᾶ|cιν ἐνυπάρχειν. οὐ μὴν | ἐξ ἀνάγκης ἀκολουθεῖν | ταῦτα, καθά-
περ τῇ ἐπαι|νετῶc cυγκειμένηι λέ|ξει, cυμπαρεπομένων | ὁμοίωc πάντων
καὶ τοῖc | καταγεγραμμένοιc φαύ|[λωc καὶ τοῖc εὖ . . .

. . . For ⟨he says that⟩ "none of these ⟨elements⟩ is praiseworthy rather than
blameworthy, nor particular to works that are well or even badly written. However it is not impossible that the beautiful exists in them all. Yet these ⟨ele-
ments⟩ do not follow of necessity, just as ⟨they follow⟩ for diction that is
composed in a praiseworthy manner, since (?) all these ⟨elements⟩ likewise
accompany works written in an inferior way also . . . ."

I tentatively placed Treatise D at the end of the same roll, and have now found two
very probable joins between Treatise B and Treatise D. Dorandi[29] at first ascribed
these Treatises to different *volumina*, on the ground that Treatise B has 25–27 lines
per column, whereas Treatise D has only 23–24, except in two fragments with 26 and
28 lines (*P.Herc.* 1074 frr. 7–8 respectively), which he tentatively assigned to Treatise
B. However, these fragments belong to what we must recognize as a distinct
sub-set within *P.Herc.* 1074a, namely frr. 1–10, which are, unlike the rest, largely
extant;[30] they derive from the middle of this same roll, but go in forwards order.
Accordingly, I have called them *P.Herc.* 1074c. The bulk of Treatise D, however, runs
in backwards sequence. It may represent the end of its *volumen*, since Dorandi[31] has
acutely suggested that *P.Herc.* 1074a fr. 22, left blank after the first nine lines and

---

[29] Dorandi 1992 (above, n. 17), 36. A sublinear asterisk marks letters corrected from the apograph.

[30] This fact was left obscure by Nardelli when she published these *disegni* without comparing the
originals, although she refers to their existence (Nardelli 1983, xviii n. 10).

[31] Dorandi 1992 (above, n. 17), 37f.

ending with a complete sentence, could conclude the roll. In a preliminary reconstruction of Treatise D using the new method, I had independently placed this fragment near the end of the Treatise.[32] But I prefer to think that there was once a *midollo*, containing perhaps a further 40 columns or so, which has since been lost. Since the roll represented by the extant fragments must have contained about 180 columns, this would yield a total length of about 220 columns, which seems reasonable.

I initially ascribed Treatises B and D to the same roll because they are in the same hand and on the same topic—euphony in verses, with much discussion of what makes a verse (*poema*) good. But further study shows that Treatise B is a summary of the doctrines of an adversary or adversaries, whereas Treatise D contains Philodemus' refutation of opposing views. Treatise B ends, in my reconstruction, with a summary of the views of the critic Andromenides (in *P.Herc.* 460 fr. 2 and 1073 fr. 1); the same doctrine of Andromenides is restated early in Treatise D at *P.Herc.* 1081 fr. 44.[33] Accordingly, I suspected that Treatise D would be found to follow Treatise B without much of a gap. Joins discovered in Naples in May 1993, between two pairs of fragments which had already been joined to each other on grounds of shape, seem to confirm but also to complicate this hypothesis. These joins are as follows:

> col. 114*: *P.Herc.* 460 fr. 2 = Treatise B fr. 25 col. iii Sbordone (lines 26–7 quoted)
> col. 115*: sup., *P.Herc.* 1074c fr. 1 = Treatise D fr. 13 Nardelli (quoted in its entirety)
> inf., *P.Herc.* 1073 fr. 1b = Treatise B fr. 25 col. ii Sbordone (ll. 17–27 quoted)
> col. 116*: sup., *P.Herc.* 1074c fr. 2 = Treatise D fr. 42 Nardelli (lines 1–4 quoted)

(col. 114*) (excerpta doctrinae Andromenidis) . . . κἀ]κ τῶν ποι|ῶν καὶ ποcῶ[ν] γραμμά- || **(col. 115*)** [των] ἀποτελεῖcθαι τὰ κάλ|λη, καὶ τὸν Ὅμηρον ἐγλο|[γῆι τοι]ούτων ἄπ[αcαν] ἀ|[περιγ]άcθαι τὴν πό[ηcιν, | καὶ φθ]όγγοιc ἡμᾶc [.̣.̣]εν|[.̣.̣.̣.̣.̣.̣.̣] τὰc ὀν[ομαc].̣[|[αc . . . (desunt lineae fere iv, post quas incipit *P.Herc.* 1073 fr. 1b) . . . ἀπο]φηναμένου |[καὶ Κράτ]ητοc ἡγεμο|νίαν διδόcθαι το[ῖc] ἔπε|[cι, τοῖc δὲ] ἤθεcιν cυμμάχοιc χρῆcθαι τὴν πόη|cιν, καὶ τόν τε ποιητήν, |[καθάπερ] Ἀνδρομενί|[δηc, τό τε πόημα] τήν τε |[πόηcιν ὡc ε]ἶδοc ἡγεῖcθαι τῆc τέχνηc. ὁ δ' ἔξω || **(col. 116*)** τῆc τέχνη[c εἶναι τοὺc]| λόγουc καὶ [τὰ διανο]|ήματα κα[.̣.̣.̣.̣ .̣.̣.̣.̣.̣]||λείπει μαλ[. . .

(col. 114*) (Andromenides says that) "beautiful effects are achieved as a result of letters **(col. 115*)** of a ⟨certain⟩ quality and quantity, and that Homer has perfected all his poetry by the choice (*ekloge*) of such ⟨letters⟩, and that by means of the sounds we . . . the words . . ." (*lacuna of about 4 lines, after which begins* P.Herc. *1073 fr. 1b, of which only the end is quoted*) . . . since Crates too declared that "a commanding role must be given to the words, but that poetry must use the characters (?) as allies," and that "I deem both the poet, as does

---

[32] The only two fragments which I had placed after this column, *P.Herc.* 1074 frr. 17–18, are distinct in both shape and numeration from the others in the series and may well derive from another part of the roll.

[33] Cf. Nardelli 1983, xxviii–xxx, discussing her fr. 23. She assigned Treatises D and E to Book 2 (ibid. xxxiv).

Andromenides, and the verse and the poetry to be an aspect of the art." But he (sc. Crates) ⟨declares that⟩ "the (**col. 116***) arguments and the thoughts are external to the art . . . ."

With this last doctrine we may compare the passage in Book 5 of *On Poems*[34] where Philodemus reports that Crates held that the thought was external to the art of poetry:

τόδ᾽ εἴπερ ἔτ᾽ εἶπε, τὸ μ[ὴ]‖ πιθανὸν εἶναι τὴν δι|άνοιαν ἐπαινεῖν, ἀτέ|χνου
γε δὴ τοῦ τοιούτου | ὄντος, ὃ πρὸς τοὺς κριτι|κοὺς λέγει, παραιτο[ῖτ᾽ ἄ]ν,
| ὁμολογούντων ἄτεχνον | εἶναι ⟨οὐδ᾽ εἶναι³⁵⟩ λόγωι, τ[ε]τριμμέ|νηι δ᾽
ἀκο[ῆι] γνωcτόν.

If Crates added this claim, that "it is implausible to praise the content, since the latter is external to the art," which he makes against the *kritikoi*, he would be refuted, since they agree that it is external to the art ⟨and is⟩ knowable ⟨not⟩ by reason, but by the trained ear.

This parallel confirms that the join is likely to be correct. The consequence is that the series which I have called *P.Herc.* 1074c, of which the originals are nearly all preserved, forms the missing link between Treatises B and D. What is more, study of the pattern of folds in the upper halves of the columns proves beyond doubt that the higher-numbered fragments of *P.Herc.* 1074c and the one extant fragment of *P.Herc.* 1074a[36] come from the same side of the same roll, and are relatively close to each other within that roll.

By good fortune, a fragment from this part of the roll appears to mark the transition between the summary of the doctrines of Philodemus' adversaries and his refutation of those doctrines, taking each adversary in turn. This is *P.Herc.* 1074c fr. 3 dext. (my col. 118*):

δεῖ |[δ᾽] ὅμωc πρὸς ἕκας[τον αὐ|τῶ]ν λέγειν. ὁ τοίν[υν Ἡ|ρ]ακλείδης, ὑπὸ
μὲ[ν |]τος ἀλογώτατα παρ[ὰ | πλ]είcτουc ἀκοῆι τη[|] τοῦ ποήμα-
τος ἁ[ρ|μο]γὰc cυνώcθη, πρ[ὸc | τὸ]ν ἀφωριcμένον [ἐν | τῆι περι]οχῆι
θείων [ἢ ἡ|ρ]ωικῶν] cωμάτων . . .

All the same, we must argue against each of them. So Heraclides was most

---

[34] Col. xxvii 4–8 Mangoni.

[35] This is my supplement, which would explain how the phrase came to be lost through a simple haplography; cf. the earlier supplements ἄτεχνον | ⟨οὐκ⟩ εἶναι λόγωι (Gomoll), ἄτεχνον | εἶναι ⟨τὴν cύνθεcιν καὶ οὐ⟩ λόγωι (Mette), ἄτεχνον | εἶναι ⟨τὴν διάνοιαν καὶ οὐ μὲν⟩ λόγωι (Mangoni). Mangoni concludes that there is no lacuna (Mangoni 1993, 290–91); but in this case her translation of λόγωι as "as far as reason is concerned" seems very difficult.

[36] I have named this unpublished fragment *P.Herc.* 1074a fr. 31, because it contains parts of *P.Herc.* 1074a fr. 30 as a *sovrapposto*, and must therefore be one circumference earlier than the latter fragment. It may contain the letters]ΝΔ in the upper margin, which could be restored as Ρ]ΝΔ, which would mean that it is in fact col. 154 (it is currently numbered col. 149* in my reconstruction). As usual, when a single fragment survives, as in this case, it turns out to contain parts of the text seen in the highest-numbered *disegno* of its series: the same phenomenon is found in *P.Herc.* 1081 fr. 47 and *P.Herc.* 1081 fr. 34, which represent the outermost layers of the lower and upper halves respectively of the opposite side of Treatise D. These were the fragments which were left after the process of *scorzatura*, representing the point when the "unrollers" found they could separate no further layers underneath the last one which they had drawn.

illogically forced by . . .³⁷ in most ⟨poets⟩ . . . the harmonies of the verse with the hearing, with regard to the ⟨verse ?⟩ defined by (?) its containing (?) divine or heroic (?) personages . . . .³⁸

The part of the text represented by *P.Herc.* 1074c is unlikely to yield continuous text, since only one side of the roll seems to be represented. However, it is possible that some of the higher-numbered fragments of 1074c may turn out to join with *P.Herc.* 1081. In fact one such join seems very likely. This is between *P.Herc.* 1081 fr. 41 and 1074c fr. 9,³⁹ which would become cols. 136*–137*:

(col. 136*) . . . . ο[ὔτ]ε "τ[ῶν χ]ρυσῶν [λη]‖κύθων" [οὔτ᾽ "ἀ]ργυρῶν," | οὐδὲ "τὰ [λαμ]πρὰ τῶν | Βάκτρων," ἀλλὰ τὸ δ[η]‖λούμενον πρᾶγμα, [ὡς]‖ ἥρωcι κα[ὶ] βαcιλε[ύcι]‖ πρεπωδέcτερον. ὅθ[εν], | ἐπειδὰν ἐξ ἑκατέ-ρο[υ]‖ γένουc cω[ρε]ύcαc ἐπ[ε]‖νέγκη⟨ι⟩ "[το]cοῦτο δύ|ναcθαι κατὰ Μοῦ-cα[ν], | ὅταν τιc οὕτωc τ[ὴν]‖ γῆρυν ἐξ εἰλικρινῶ[ν]‖| (col. 137*) ὀνομάτων cυνταξῆται, | καὶ τὰc ἀκοὰc δοκεῖν ἡ|ρωϊκῶν cωμάτων ἀ|κούειν, καὶ κα[λλίcτη]ν εὑ|ρεῖν ὀνομαcία[ν, ἥτιc μ]ᾶλ|λον χρυcοῦ κ[αὶ ἀργύρ]ου {ν} | χρωματίcαc[α λαμπρ]ὰν | ἀπειργάcθαι τ[αύτην ⟨τὴν⟩ τέ]‖χνην . . .

(col. 136*) . . . neither "of the golden vessels" nor "of the silver ones," nor "the splendours of Bactra," but the action that is portrayed (?), as being more appropriate to heroes and kings. Whence, when, after heaping up ⟨instances⟩ from both genres, he subjoins that "so great is the power ⟨of a poet⟩ according to the Muse, when someone puts together his ‖ (col. 137*) discourse out of pure words in this way," and that "the ears seem to be hearing heroic personages," and ⟨that poets ?⟩ "invent a most beautiful vocabulary, which by adding colour more than gold and silver renders this (?) art splendid (?) . . . .

The remainder of Treatise D consists of *P.Herc.* 1074a (a series of only nine fragments)⁴⁰ and *P.Herc.* 1081a. Whereas 1074a, like *P.Herc.* 460 in Treatise B, tends to consist of entire columns, 1081a has been fractured horizontally, like *P.Herc.* 1073 in Treatise B and *P.Herc.* 466 and 444 at the opening of the roll. It is possible that this damage occurred before the roll was even opened, and likely enough that the fractured papyri all come from the same half of the *volumen*. Such damage makes this part of Book 1 harder to put together, but by following the basic principle that these fragments need to be arranged in interleaved backwards order, allowing for left and

---

³⁷ My tentative supplement Κρά|τη]τοc seems long for the space, but would certainly fit my hypothesis that Crates of Mallos is the source for the entire summary (see below). Any other name, e.g., Πλά-|τω]νοc, is even longer, and the traces only match tau or pi. In support of my idea, cf. the following passage from Treatise C (*P.Herc.* 1677a col. vi ll. 3–19), from which it seems possible that the opponent there similarly discussed the theory of Heraclides: παράδοξοc | [ε]ἄ[ν φ]α{ι}νείη τοῖc ἐφιcτᾶ|cιν ὅταν, διαπορήcαc ‖[τί αἴ]τιον γείνεται τού|του, τὸ παρ᾽ Ἡρ[.]ακλείδηι | κεῖcθαι νομιζόμενον ‖[ἀ]ποδιδῶι (see Romeo 1992c, 193–202, but also Mangoni 1993, 44–47).

³⁸ The end of this fragment, which I read for the first time from autopsy in Naples in May 1993, awaits interpretation: Nardelli's edition of it (Nardelli 1983) is based entirely on the *disegno*, although the original survives.   ³⁹ These are respectively Treatise D frr. 3 and 15 Nardelli.

⁴⁰ These are *disegni* 22–30, plus the unpublished fr. 31 mentioned above. The placement of the isolated *disegni* 17–18 is obscure; they may represent fragments which had fallen off the edge and drawn separately, as was *P.Herc.* 1081a fr. 4 (which is in fact the right edge of *P.Herc.* 1081a fr. 25).

right halves derived from the same side, I have already been able to make great progress towards reconstructing even this section. Further help should come from the likelihood that here Philodemus is refuting in the same sequence the doctrines which were presented in Treatise E; some parallels between Treatises D and E are already apparent, but their full extent has yet to be established. To summarize the arguments of the last part of the roll would be premature, as they are still being worked out. But at least it is clear that, by the end of Treatise D, Philodemus' opponent is no longer Heraclides of Pontus but a certain Heracleodorus, whom we shall consider briefly below.

My identification of this roll as Book 1 is based on Philodemus' discussion of euphony in Treatise A, *P.Herc.* 994 col. xxxi 4–10 Sbordone, where he refers back to a Book 1 on euphony, as follows:

οὐ μὴν [οὐ̣]δ̣' (*conieci:* ἀ̣[λ̣]λ̣' Sbordone), ὡc προ]επέδ[ει]ξα ἐν τῶι |
πρώτωι περὶ [ε]ὐφ[ωνί]]αc ἐπακολ[ούθων γραμ̣|μά]των [κα]ὶ ὁμ̣[ο]ί̣ων,
κει̣|[ν]ῆϲαί τι δύναται τῶν ἐπιλελογιϲ[μ]ένων.

. . . nor indeed, as I showed previously in Book 1 on the euphony of sequential letters and the like, can any of the considerations which he advanced move us.[41]

Treatise A cannot be Book 1, since it refers back to it. I deduce that Treatise B represents Book 1.[42] The doctrines of Philodemus' opponents are first summarised and then refuted, apparently in the same order; the refutation began in Book 1 but continued into Book 2.

Book 2

Except for *P.Herc.* 1677, Crönert classified all the papyri here allotted to Book 2 as his 'Group γ'.[43] Nardelli was the first to assign *P.Herc.* 1074b, 1081b, 1676 and 994, all in hand viii, to the same roll.[44] *P.Herc.* 1677 is in fact parts of three rolls, 1677a (frr. 3, 4, 6, 10, 11, 13b, unnumbered, coll. i–vii), 1677b (frr. 1, 2, 5, 8, 9, 12, unnumbered next to col. vii, *subscriptio*) and 1677c (frr. 7, 13a, 14, 15).[45] These are, respectively, written by hands of group E (anonymous viii), group H (anonymous xi) and group I, as Cavallo recognized.[46] *P.Herc.* 1677b is from *On Rhetoric* 4, 1677c is of obscure content, but 1677a is certainly from the *On Poems*.[47] Given Cavallo's identification of its hand, Dorandi recognized *P.Herc.* 1677a as belonging to this roll.[48] A new edition by Romeo of the whole *volumen* is promised.[49] She and I have made

---

[41] Cf. also Janko 1991b, 304–5.

[42] Dorandi 1992 (above, n. 17), 39 has interpreted this as a reference to Treatise D; he thinks Treatise B is Book 2, and Treatises C + A form Book 3, because the overlap between their contents suggests that they are closely related and successive Books. This latter argument is cogent; if Treatises D and B do not form a single roll, Dorandi's reconstruction is likely to be correct. Greenberg 1955, 269f. assigns Treatises D and B to a single roll, but holds that no papyri of Book 1 survive; he too thinks Treatise B is Book 2, and assigns Treatises C + A to Book 3.   [43] Crönert 1903, 6.   [44] Nardelli 1979, 137–40.

[45] Romeo 1992a, 173–74; cf. Romeo 1992c and id., "Ancora un contributo alla ricostruzione di un rotolo della *Poetica* filodemea," *CErc* 23 (1993), 99–106 (in which she presents a join between *P.Herc.* 1677a fr. 4 and *P.Herc.* 1081b fr. 10).   [46] Cavallo 1983, 32, 34, 35, 45.

[47] So Romeo 1992a, 173–74.   [48] Dorandi 1992 (above, n. 17), 36.

[49] Cf. her articles cited above (n. 45), and Romeo 1992b.

independently several of the same joins between the *scorze* from this *volumen* represented by *P.Herc.* 1074b and 1081b (notably, *P.Herc.* 1081b frr. 1 and 5b, and 1074b fr. 13, make up a single column).

I identify this roll as Book 2 because of the following backward reference in Book 5, col. xxix 7–18 Mangoni:

τὰ δὲ | περὶ τῶν cτοιχείων, ἐ|ν ο[ἷc] τὴν κρί[c]ιν εἶναί φη|cι (sc. ὁ Κράτηc)
τῶν cπου[δ]α[ίων] ποι|ημάτων, τίνοc αὐτῶι | καὶ πόcηc ἡδονῆc γέ|με[ι
π]αρεcτακότεc ἐν | τ[ῶ]ι δευτέρωι τῶν ὑ|πομνημάτων, διὰ τὸ | καὶ περὶ
ποιήματοc εἶ|ναι κοινῶc, ἀποδοκιμά|[ζομ]εν παλιλλογε[ῖ]ν, | ὧc[τε] τὰc
παρὰ Ζήνωνι | δόξαc ἐπικόψαντεc | ἤδη μεμηκυcμένον | τὸ cύνγραμμα
καταπαύ|cομεν.

But as for his remarks on the letters, in which he (sc. Crates) claims that the judgment of good verses resides, we have shown in his regard in the second of our treatises (since it is also about verse in general) of what and of how much absurdity they are full,[50] and we decline to repeat it, so that, after refuting the opinions found in Zeno (sc. of Sidon), we can bring to a close a work that has already become long.

If this argument holds, then Treatise A is the end of Book 2, and the other texts in this hand come from earlier in the same Book.

Book 3

Comparetti[51] assigned *P.Herc.* 1087 to the *On Poems*. We owe to Dorandi[52] the recognition that the surviving *scorze* and the *disegni* to which this number was assigned are in different hands: I shall call these 1087a and 1087b respectively. Dorandi has determined that *P.Herc.* 1087a, which mentions Homer and Euripides, was written by scribe x, from group G; hence he has proposed that it comes from the same roll as *P.Herc.* 1403, which is in the same hand. *P.Herc.* 1403 has been investigated by L. Spina[53] and T. Dorandi.[54] Their readings, and Cavallo's studies of the hand,[55] strongly suggest that this derives from Philodemus' *On Poems*, as Dorandi now agrees.[56] The text mentions Euripides and Choerilus, whose epic poetry is cited also, alongside that of Anaximenes, at *On Poems* Treatise A Sbordone (*P.Herc.* 994 col. xxv 5–14). Since there is a parallel mention of Anaximenes in Treatise E, at *P.Herc.* 466 fr. 5.1, I at first suggested that *P.Herc.* 1403 could derive from a second exemplar of Book 1 or Book 2. Dorandi[57] has now proposed that these two papyri represent Book 1, of which, in his view, no other exemplar exists (he calls my Book 1 Book 2,

---

[50] For this translation I am indebted to J. Hammerstaedt, who kindly drew my attention to two parallels in Philodemus' *Rhetoric*, at 1.206.23f. Sudhaus and in Book 3 in *P.Herc.* 1426 col. xi 1–2 (see Hammerstaedt 1992, 39 with commentary). Cf. also Mangoni 1993, *ad loc.*

[51] Comparetti and De Petra 1883 (above, n. 20), 78 n. 1.

[52] Dorandi 1993 (above, n. 17), esp. 81–84.　　　　　　　　　　　[53] Spina 1988.

[54] Dorandi 1993 (above, n. 17).　　　　　　　　　[55] Cavallo 1983, 33f., 45, 87.

[56] Dorandi 1993 (above, n. 17), 81–82; he had been doubtful (Dorandi 1992 [above, n. 17], 33). As he notes, the other texts in the same hand, that of group G scribe x, viz. *P.Herc.* 479, 862, 1005 and 1485, are not on poetry.　　　　　　　　　[57] Dorandi 1993 (above, n. 17), 84.

and my Book 2 Book 3). If these papyri do represent an otherwise unknown roll, I would assign them to Book 3; but their uniqueness requires verification. If they are not from Book 3, there may well be no surviving papyri from this book.

Book 4

P.Herc. 207 is identified as the end of Book 4 by its *subscriptio*. We are unlikely to find *scorze* from the outside of this roll, since it appears to have been unrolled continuously for its whole length even though the outer layers were stuck together (it may eventually prove possible to separate them). Thus the fragments fill ten trays (*cornici*), yet separate columns can only be distinguished towards the end of the seventh *cornice*. I have argued[58] that the extant portion is an attack on Aristotle's dialogue *On Poets*, and in particular on his definition of the genres of epic and tragedy; compare the earlier view of Greenberg.[59]

Book 5[60]

Crönert[61] classified many of the papyri here assigned to the first exemplar (*P.Herc.* 228, 403, 407, 1425 and 1581) within his group α, along with *P.Herc.* 207. *P.Herc.* 1425 represents the end of the roll; the other papyri have all been argued to derive from earlier in the same *volumen*.[62] Jensen[63] discerned that 228 fr. 6 presents the theories of Crates which appear in 1425 cols. xxiii 25–xxiv 25, and 228 fr. 4 gives in summary form the arguments which Philodemus attacks in 1425 cols. xxviii 7–xxx 4. Relying on these correspondences, Mangoni rightly reversed the order of the fragments in her edition of them;[64] this reversal can now be explained by means of the Delattre/Obbink method. Jensen deduced that 228 is from early in *On Poems* 5; his conclusion is shared by Greenberg[65] and Dorandi[66] but not Mangoni.[67] He also argued that *P.Herc.* 403 and 407 stand in a similar relation to 1425.[68] Greenberg[69] has shown that *P.Herc.* 403 fr. 3 uses the terms κυρίως and καταχρηςτικῶς, which are also used by the Stoic "Aristo" in *P.Herc.* 1425 col. xv 5–6.[70] This latter term also appears in *P.Herc.* 407 fr. 3, which suggests that 403 and 407 are closely connected, a view shared by Mangoni in her new edition of 407.[71] If this shows that Philodemus did indeed first summarize and then refute the same doctrines in the same order in Book 5 (as he did in *On Music* 4), then *P.Herc.* 403 and 407 must precede 228.

I also assigned to this exemplar *P.Herc.* 1581, which, as Nardelli argued in her

---

[58] Janko 1991a.

[59] Greenberg 1955, 129: "the general nature of papyrus #207 seems clear. It is part of an attack against the Peripatetic divisions of poetry into epic, tragedy, comedy, iambic, and lyric."

[60] For an exemplary new edition of papyri 1425 and 1538 of this Book see Mangoni 1993, which replaces that of Jensen 1923.   [61] Crönert 1903, 6.   [62] Cf. Janko 1991a, 61f.

[63] Jensen 1923, 53, 55, 63, 65, 67, 94, 154–56.   [64] Mangoni 1989.

[65] Greenberg 1955, 119.   [66] Dorandi 1992 (above n. 17), 39–42.

[67] Mangoni 1989, 186, and Mangoni 1993, 32–36. She assigns *P.Herc.* 228 to the *On Poems*, but not necessarily to Book 5.   [68] He is followed by Dorandi 1992 (above, n. 17), 39f.

[69] Greenberg 1955, 119–23, esp. 123.   [70] On these parallels see also Janko 1991a, 61 n. 335.

[71] Mangoni 1992a.

editio princeps, presents an Aristotelian theory of catharsis.[72] She assigned it to the early part of Book 4, but it is in fact in the same hand as this copy of Book 5. Accordingly, I have argued elsewhere[73] that it may derive from the opening of Book 5. That it exhibits no parallels with *P.Herc.* 1425 fits the hypothesis that it is from the outermost layers of the roll, and precedes *P.Herc.* 403, 407, and 228. The stichometric letters preserved in the margins of *P.Herc.* 1581 fr. V 7 (*Γ*) and 403 fr. 3 col. ii 6 (*Υ*) are compatible with this arrangement.[74]

Sbordone[75] considered *P.Herc.* 1087b, on the basis of the two Neapolitan *disegni*, to be in the same hand as this exemplar, i.e., group N, scribe xix. Dorandi[76] at first ascribed these *disegni* to the *On Rhetoric* because they mention Theodectes, but this orator also wrote tragedies. Dorandi[77] now agrees with Sbordone about the hand, and with my tentative proposal[78] that these fragments too derive from the opening of *On Poems* 5.

The second known exemplar of Book 5, *P.Herc.* 1538, is unlikely to yield further detached *scorze*, since it, like the *volumen* of Book 4, was unrolled continuously even though the outer layers were adhering to each other (these strata too may eventually prove to be separable). Mangoni[79] has published some new fragments from these outer layers. Her first fragment (fr. 1) discusses the same topic as the last fragment of *P.Herc.* 228 (fr. 1, = fr. 6 in Mangoni's reversed order); this matches the sequence of papyri proposed here. Book 5 was so long that only the latter half of the entire book was accommodated in this roll, as the *subscriptio* informs us.

Book 6 and subsequent books

We cannot entirely exclude that there were once further Books of the *On Poems*. One passage in Book 5 might look forward to further discussion, namely col. xxx 34–xxxi 7 Mangoni:

καὶ τὴν διάνο[ια]ν μέντοι | ποίαν τινὰ τοῖc ποι|ήμαcιν ἀξιουμένην ‖ ὑποτάτ[τ]εcθαι καὶ ὅ|[λωc] οὖ[τ]οι καὶ πολλ[οὶ | τῶν πρό]τερον ἐξη-{c}τ[αc]||μ[έ]νων καὶ τῶν ὕcτε|ρον θεωρηcομένων | πολὺ [δ]έουcιν ἀποχα-|[ρ]άττειν.

However, as for what kind of content is worthy to be included in verses, both these critics, and many of those who have been examined before, and who will be considered later, are far from specifying it.

This may simply indicate the brief survey of views still to come. Were it a reference to another Book, it would not necessarily be contradicted by Philodemus' reference at Book 5 col. xxix Mangoni (cited in the discussion of Book 2 above) to the need to conclude his *cύγγραμμα*, already very long: he may be referring to the length of this particular tome. Dorandi[80] sees a distinction in the latter passage between

[72] Nardelli 1978. For an English translation with notes see R. Janko, *Aristotle: Poetics* (Indianapolis 1987), 61, 187–90, and further Janko 1992b, 346f.   [73] Janko 1991a, 61–63.
[74] For further discussion see Janko 1991a, 62 n. 346 and Mangoni 1992a, 136f.
[75] Sbordone 1983, 18f.   [76] Dorandi 1992 (above, n. 17), 34.
[77] Dorandi 1993 (above, n. 17), 81–82.   [78] Janko 1993, 379.
[79] Mangoni 1991. See now Mangoni 1993, 112–17, 129.   [80] Dorandi 1992 (above, n. 17), 35.

cύγγραμμα as a multi-volume treatise and ὑπόμνημα as a single volume of it, but perhaps Philodemus could have used cύγγραμμα to avoid repeating ὑπόμνημα. Hence, although it would be satisfying to exclude the possibility that further books of the *On Poems* existed, I do not think we can as yet do so. However, it seems unlikely, because Philodemus was in the habit of making vague references to future work, even at what is demonstrably the end of a complete treatise.[81]

Papyri which are probably irrelevant

- *P.Herc.* 128, referred to the *On Poems* by Crönert,[82] was found to belong to group C of hands by Cavallo.[83] Since the scribes of Group C copied only the writings of Demetrius Laco, not those of Philodemus, Cavallo assigned the text to Demetrius' *On Poetry*.[84] Romeo argues, on the basis of a parallel with Philodemus, *On Rhetoric* 2 cols. xlvii f., that it should be assigned to a work of Demetrius on rhetoric.[85]

- *P.Herc.* 230, doubtfully assigned to the *On Poems* by W. Scott,[86] has now been published by Dorandi.[87] It is hard to tell whether it is on poetry or not, but according to Dorandi its hand is archaic, and it may therefore belong to the *On Poetry* or *On Rhetoric* of Demetrius Laco.

- *P.Herc.* 986, in the same hand (group Q, hand xxviii) as *On Poems* Book 4, is not on poetics.[88]

- *P.Herc.* 1113a (= *P.Herc.* 1113 frr. 1–4) was ascribed by Crönert[89] to Demetrius Laco's *On Poetry*. However, Romeo suggests on orthographic grounds that it is not by Demetrius but by Philodemus,[90] and would presumably derive from the latter's *On Poems*. But Dorandi[91] is emphatic that its hand can scarcely postdate the second century B.C., in which case Crönert seems likely to have been correct.

- I had doubtfully assigned the unpublished *P.Herc.* 1275 to Book 3 simply because it is the end of a roll with a *subscriptio* (but the title is lost) and cannot be Books 2, 4 or 5. It contains a number of Homeric quotations. It is in the same hand as *P.Herc.* 1507, our sole copy of *On the Good King according to Homer*.[92]

- Lastly, E. Dürr[93] has tentatively suggested that *P.Herc.* 1726, a *midollo* written by a scribe in group Q (but not scribe XXVIII), may derive from the *On Poems*, because its only legible passage refers to Euripides' *Electra*. However, the state

---

[81] Cf. Delattre 1992, 185–87, with E. Puglia, "La duplice soscrizione del *P.Herc.* 1497," *CErc* 22 (1992), 175–78.

[82] "Fälschungen in den Abschriften der Herculanensischen Rollen," *RhM* 53 (1898), 585–95, esp. 589 n. 4.   [83] Cavallo 1983, 30.   [84] Cavallo 1983, 59.

[85] Romeo 1988, 39. Her conclusion is endorsed by Dorandi 1992 (above, n. 17), 30.

[86] W. Scott, *Fragmenta Herculanensia* (Oxford 1885), 49.

[87] Dorandi 1993 (above, n. 17), 85.

[88] See M. Capasso, "Una pretesa allusione di Filodemo a Cicerone (*P.Herc.* 986, fr. 19)," *CErc* 22 (1992), 169–72.   [89] Crönert 1903, 102, 107.   [90] Romeo 1988, 79f.

[91] Dorandi 1992 (above, n. 17), 33.

[92] On its contents see Dorandi 1992 (above, n. 17), 34, who is extremely doubtful about its assignation to the *On Poems*.   [93] Dürr 1990, 41f.; Dürr 1992.

of this papyrus is so poor that a definite ascription to the *On Poems* in general, let alone any specific part of it, will be very hard to confirm.[94]

3. The structure of Philodemus' *On Poems*

It is now time to turn from the dry but fundamental task of establishing which papyri belong to the *On Poems* and in which order, to the altogether more exciting process of trying to make sense, for the first time ever, of the entire work. One possible key to understanding it may be sought in the Hellenistic tripartite division of poetics into *poema, poesis,* and *poetes*. This classification is modified from a bipartite division— the *ars/artifex* arrangement common in Hellenistic works of introduction (*eisagogai*). The latter division goes back to Aristotle's lost dialogue variously entitled *On Poetics* or *On Poets*. Thus Heraclides Ponticus wrote a work entitled *On Poetics and Poets* (Περὶ ποιητικῆς καὶ τῶν ποιητῶν), and Praxiphanes' treatise on poetics seems to have been called *On Poems* and *On Poets*. Similarly, Varro's *On Poems* (*De Poematis*) was, I hold, the same work as his *On Poets* (*De Poetis*).[95] The tripartite division derives from Neoptolemus of Parium, as Philodemus reveals at *On Poems* 5 col. xiv 5–11 Mangoni:

ἀτόπως δ[ὲ] κα[ὶ τὸν] τὴν | τέχνην κ[αὶ τὴν] δ[ύν]α|μιν ἔχοντα τὴ[ν ποι]ητι|κὴν ε[ἴ]δος [π]αρίς[τη]ϲι | τῆ[ϲ] τέ[χ]νη[ϲ μ]ετὰ τοῦ | ποήμα-το[ϲ] καὶ τῆϲ πό|ηϲεωϲ.

But it is bizarre when he (sc. Neoptolemus) presents the person who possesses the poetic art and its potential as an aspect of the art of poetry alongside the verse (*poema*) and the poetry.[96]

It was also adopted by Andromenides and Crates, as we learned from Book 1 (quoted above).[97] Horace adopted Neoptolemus' schema for his own purposes in *The Art of Poetry*, although the details are controversial and the poet has artfully concealed its structure.[98]

The order of topics in Neoptolemus, Andromenides and Crates (as quoted by Philodemus), and in Horace's *The Art of Poetry* is always first *poema*, then *poesis*, and lastly *poetes*. But this does not after all seem to be the key to the overall structure of Philodemus' *On Poems*. Books 1 and 2 are certainly on the *poema* (verse), including the *compositio verborum* and euphony; however, the same seems to be true of Book 5, although the latter book also discusses the good poet. Our knowledge of Books 3 and 4 is much slighter, but the discussion of genre in the extant portion of the latter would probably fall under *poesis* in Horace's *The Art of Poetry*.[99]

---

[94] Similarly Dorandi 1992 (above, n. 17), 86.   [95] See Janko 1991a, 58.

[96] Philodemus' critique of this division continues to col. xiii 4. See further Greenberg 1955, 42–50; Brink 1963, 55, 58, 60–70; Mette 1981, 16–21; Asmis 1992c; Mangoni 1993, 229–33.

[97] Cols. 114*–115* (*P.Herc.* 460 fr. 2 + 1074a fr. 1 + 1073 fr. 1, = Tr. B fr. 25 col. iii Sbordone + Tr. D fr. 13 Nardelli + fr. 25 col. ii Sbordone). On this passage see Romeo 1988, 46, 50.

[98] The best analysis is that of Brink 1963, 213–38.

[99] Cf. Brink 1963, 246, who identifies *Ars Poetica* 153–294 (on drama) as the nucleus of this section.

Although Philodemus ridicules Neoptolemus' division in *On Poems* 5, the title of his entire work, *On Poems*, strongly suggests that the whole dealt specifically with poetic diction (*poema*); indeed, a good case could be made for translating the title as *On Verse*. Philodemus could conceivably have inherited the tripartite structure as the basis of his own work from predecessors such as Demetrius Laco. The first two books of Demetrius' *On Poems* are on subjects very similar to those in Philodemus' Books 1–2, and share the opponent Andromenides.[100] However, Demetrius' concluding formula in his *On Poems* 2 col. lxvi probably marks the close of the entire work.[101] One suspects that Demetrius was, like Zeno of Sidon, one of Philodemus' teachers; his books apparently formed the nucleus of Philodemus' library.[102] Economy of hypotheses would suggest that, if Demetrius too moved to Italy (as his addresses to his patrons Quintus and Nero suggest), he may have emigrated together with Philodemus as teacher and pupil or indeed simply as friends in the Epicurean tradition of friendship.

Philodemus' approach seems to have entailed the simple expedient of summarizing the arguments of his opponent or opponents, and then refuting them in exactly the same sequence, point by point. As we saw, this method was followed in the *On Music* 4, and apparently also in *On Poems* 5. Whether Books 3–4 of the latter treatise followed the same pattern is unknown, but far from unlikely. Books 1–2 represent a more startling variation of this system. As was argued above, the extensive summary of opponents' views in Treatises E and B of Book 1, filling columns 1*–118*, is followed by a refutation which not only occupies the remaining 64+ columns of Book 1 (Treatise D, cols. 118*–182*) but also continues to the end of Book 2 (Treatises C and A), which consisted of at least 120 columns more. That Philodemus' refutation is almost exactly twice as long as the summary is paralleled in *On Music* 4; but for this structure of summary and refutation to occupy more than one book-roll is, so far as is now known, a unique occurrence.

We can gain further insight into Philodemus' method of work from considering how he came to know about the views of his various opponents. References in Book 5[103] show that he there relied on summaries made by two Epicurean predecessors—first Philomelus, and then Zeno of Sidon. Similarly, a strong case can be made that in Books 1–2 Philodemus relied for his information on another predecessor. However, this time his source was not an Epicurean, but a very different thinker—none other than Crates of Mallos, head of the great library at Pergamum and a personal rival of Aristarchus, librarian at Alexandria in the first half of the second century B.C. When in Book 5 Philodemus refutes other aspects of Crates' literary theory, he adds, as we saw above in discussing Book 2: "as for his remarks on the letters, in which Crates

---

•

[100] Romeo 1988, 50, holds that all the material which I assign to Book 1 concerned with Andromenides' doctrines, by which she means portions of Treatises D, E, and B (*P.Herc.* 460 fr. 2), derives from that part of Andromenides' work which deals with the *poetes*, but in fact it represents his discussion of *poema*. This is shown by the parallels between these doctrines and Demetrius Laco, *On Poems* 1, where Demetrius refutes Andromenides' doctrine of the *poema* (so, rightly, Romeo, loc. cit.).

[101] So tentatively Romeo 1988, 57, 317f., following Crönert and opposing Philippson. It is conceivable that he is only signalling the end of Book 2, and that further books followed; yet the fact remains that Demetrius refers to a second book at the end of Book 1, but does not refer to any subsequent book at the conclusion of 2.

[102] Cavallo 1983, 58–60. On Demetrius' life and work see Romeo 1988, 26–32; Puglia 1988, 37–48; Sedley 1989.   [103] Cols. xii 10, xxix 19 Mangoni.

claims that the judgement of good verses resides, we have shown in Book 2 . . . how absurd they are, and we decline to repeat it" (col. xxix 7–14 Mangoni). This back-reference to *On Poems* 2 matches the contents of Treatise A, which, as we saw, should be Book 2. So Crates' views must have been discussed in Book 2. Now the opponents named in Treatise A are a certain Pausimachus and, although the reading needs confirmation, Crates.[104] Since, as we saw, Treatise A refutes the doctrines summarized in Treatise B, then Treatise B must be Book 1. This is supported by the passage in Treatise A where Philodemus says that Book 1 discussed "the euphony of sequential and similar letters."[105] In fact this is precisely the content of Treatise B, where Philodemus' adversary discusses the effect of repetitions of sounds and words, especially when conjoined with certain accents. For instance, the opponent demands that poets should not repeat words with circumflex accents combined with ugly sounds, like *skhêma* "shape," nor phrases with the same accent on successive words. Now it follows from the argument that at least some of the views summarized in Book 1 must be those of Crates. In fact several of the relevant passages in Treatises A and B have recently been ascribed to Crates by N. Greenberg,[106] F. Sbordone,[107] G.M. Rispoli[108] and Elizabeth Asmis,[109] independently of my proposed reconstruction.

There are suggestions in *On Poems* 5[110] that Philodemus knew of reports by Crates of the views of several of his predecessors. At the start of his critique of Crates, the Epicurean makes some interesting distinctions:

. . . τὰ [παρὰ] τῶι Κράτ[η]τι καὶ]ρὸ[c θ]εωρῆcαι. ἀπο[τυγ]χάνει τοιγα-
[ρ]|οῦν [τῆ]c Ἡρακλεοδώρου | καὶ τῶν ὁμοίων δόξηc — |[οὐ γ]ὰρ τὴν
cύνθεcιν, ἀλ|λὰ τὴν ἐπιφαινομένην |[α]ὐ[τῆι] φωνὴ[ν] ἐπ[αι]ν[εῖ — | ὡc
κ]αὶ τῆc Ἀνδρομενίδ[ου, | πά]ντη⟨ι⟩ γε νομίζων ὁ|[μολ]ογεῖν αὐτὸν καὶ
διὰ |[πα]ντὸc τοῖc εἰρημένοιc.

. . . It is time to consider the views in Crates. He diverges from the opinion of Heracleodorus and those like him, since ⟨Crates⟩ praises not the word order (*synthesis*) but the sound that supervenes upon the word order, just as ⟨Crates⟩ also ⟨diverges⟩ from the view of Andromenides, although ⟨Crates⟩ believes that he is totally in accord with what ⟨Andromenides⟩ said.

The opening sentence has always been translated as "it is time to consider the views *of* Crates"; however, this is inaccurate, since the expression certainly includes the views of Crates, but it is not limited to them. When Philodemus begins his critiques of the views found in the summaries by the Epicureans Philomelus and Zeno, he each time uses the same prepositional phrase.[111] This passage proves beyond doubt that

---

[104] *P.Herc.* 994 fr. 17 = Tr. A col. z 22* Sbordone.

[105] *P.Herc.* 994 col. xxxi 4–10 Sbordone; see above on Book 1.

[106] Greenberg 1955, 227–28 (on *P.Herc.* 460 fr. 26 = Tr. B fr. 17 Sbordone and *P.Herc.* 460 fr. 8, = Tr. B fr. 20 col. i Sbordone), 240–41 (on *P.Herc.* 460 fr. 9, = Tr. B fr. 26 col. i Sbordone), 256 (on *P.Herc.* 1074 fr. 30 = Tr. D fr. 10 Nardelli, on *P.Herc.* 460 fr. 5 = Tr. B fr. 4 col. i Sbordone, and on other fragments on euphony).   [107] Sbordone 1983, 148.

[108] Rispoli 1986, 118–34; Rispoli 1987, 472ff.

[109] Asmis 1992b, 163–69 on *P.Herc.* 460 frr. 26, 24, and 8.

[110] Cols. xxiv 25–xxv 1 Mangoni. See n. 170 below.

[111] Philodemus uses παρά with the dative in all three contexts: cf. τῶν το[ί]νυν παρὰ τῶι Φι|λομή-[λω]ι [γ]εγραμμένων (col. xii 10–12 Mangoni), and τὰc παρὰ Ζήνωνι | δόξαc (col. xxix 19–20 Mangoni). For the standard translation see e.g. Mangoni 1993, 175.

Crates discussed the theories of others, and that Philodemus knew of these theories through his work. This is clearest in the case of the obscure Andromenides, as is confirmed by that passage in Book 1[112] which forms the junction of Treatises B and D, where, as we saw, Philodemus names Crates and has him refer approvingly to the views of Andromenides, who, in fact, upheld the importance of word choice in poetry (ἐκλογή). It follows that, whether or not Philodemus is right about the difference between the views of Crates and those of Heracleodorus and company, who held that word order (cύνθεcιc) was paramount in verse, he also knew of the latter's doctrines through Crates. It has been plausibly suggested[113] that Philodemus invented this distinction, in order to drive a wedge between Crates and a group of theorists with very similar views; but he may well have found the point made in Crates' writings. That Crates was his source is supported by the drift of the argument in the newly reconstructed Book 1. In Treatise E and the opening of Treatise B, Philodemus is apparently reporting the views of an opponent who is criticizing the opinions of those who held that the excellence of verse lies in *synthesis* alone. The opponent grants to these critics that the excellence of a poem lies in *synthesis*, but complains that they do not specify what combinations of sounds poets should seek or avoid.[114] Good poets are best, and their work endures, only by virtue of the quality of their sounds;[115] so he 'will now discuss sounds in themselves'.[116] He continues by doing so in great detail, discussing various consonants, vowels, accents and syllables. This is precisely the difference which, as Philodemus claims in Book 5 col. xxiv Mangoni, lies between the views of Heracleodorus and company on the one hand, and those of Crates on the other. As we also saw, in col. xxix Mangoni, quoted in the discussion of Book 2 above, Philodemus makes clear that Crates went on to prove his point by considering the sounds in themselves. Moreover, in Book 1 the account of the phonetic properties of different sounds and syllables is soon followed by the passage in which Crates refers to the views of Andromenides. The sequence of topics is therefore the same as that in Book 5. It surely follows, firstly, that Crates himself is the source for the views of Heracleodorus and his ilk; and, secondly, that one reason why Book 1 has proved so hard to reconstruct is because Philodemus is summarizing Crates' views about several of the latter's predecessors!

Now in refuting Crates in *On Poems* 5,[117] Philodemus makes it clear that Crates addressed a group of literary theorists called the *kritikoi*:

τόδ᾽ εἴπερ ἔτ᾽ εἶπε, τὸ μ[ὴ]‖ πιθανὸν εἶναι τὴν δι|άνοιαν ἐπαινεῖν, ἀτέ|χνου
γε δὴ τοῦ τοιούτου | ὄντος, ὃ πρὸς τοὺς κριτι|κοὺς λέγει, παραιτο[ῖτ᾽ ἄ]ν,

---

[112] Cols. 114*–115* = *P.Herc.* 460 fr. 2 (Tr. B fr. 25 col. iii Sbordone) + *P.Herc.* 1074c fr. 1 (= Tr. D fr. 13 Nardelli) + *P.Herc.* 1073 fr. 1b (= Tr. B fr. 25 col. ii Sbordone).

[113] Porter 1989, 165, cf. 174ff.; similarly Mangoni 1993, 277. See n. 170 below.

[114] Col. 72* = *P.Herc.* 460 fr. 25.4–18 (= Tr. B fr. 18 Sbordone): "οὐ πα[............ | ο]ὐδὲ ποιητικὴν [............] | ὅλως, εἰ μή," φηcί, "περὶ [τῆς]‖ πλοκῆς τῆς κατὰ τὴν | διάλεκτον αἱρετῆς τε | καὶ φευκτῆς μεθοδικὴν | παραγγελίαν ἐκτιθέα|cιν, ἐπειδήπερ ἐν αὐτῆι | μόνη⟨ι⟩ τὸ cπουδαῖόν τ[ε]‖ καὶ φαῦλον. ἀcθενὲc γάρ, | παρατιθέντας ἄλλων | ἐπιτυχίας καὶ ἀποτυ|χίας, cυμβου[λε]ύειν τὰς | μὲν διώκειν, τὰς δὲ | φεύγειν. πῶς δ᾽ ἂν διώ|κοι τις ἢ φεύγοι, μηδὲν | ὑπογράφων;"

[115] Col. 75* = *P.Herc.* 460 fr. 24.11–14 (= Tr. B fr. 19 Sbordone).

[116] Col. 75* = *P.Herc.* 460 fr. 24.22–24 (= Tr. B fr. 19 Sbordone): νῦν δὲ | περὶ τῶν ἤχων α[ὐτ]ῶν | διαλέξεcθαι.   [117] Col. xxvii 4–8 Mangoni.

| ὁμολογούντων ἄτεχνον | εἶναι ⟨οὐδ᾽ εἶναι⟩ λόγωι, τ[ε]τριμμέ|νηι δ᾽ ἀκο[ῆι] γνωϲτόν.

If Crates added the following claim, that "it is implausible to praise the content, since the latter is external to the art," which he makes against the *kritikoi*, he would be refuted, since they agree that the content is external to the art ⟨and is⟩ knowable ⟨not⟩ by reason, but by the trained ear.

Since the sole group of theorists mentioned during Philodemus' critique of Crates is "Heracleodorus and those of similar views," it seems reasonable to infer that Heracleodorus and his friends are precisely the *kritikoi* who advocated the importance of *synthesis*. Although much has been written from divergent perspectives on this group, there is wide agreement on this central point.[118] The repeated mentions by the opponent in Book 1 (Treatises E[119] and B) of the views of a group of theorists supports my inference that Philodemus is there summarizing a work by Crates in which the latter attacked the *kritikoi*. Indeed, the opponent in Treatise E is addressing precisely a group who praise *synthesis*:[120]

καὶ παρα[πληϲίωϲ]|| τοὺϲ τὴ[ν] ϲύνθεϲιν [ἐπαι]|νοῦντ[αϲ] ἐρωτᾶν [πρὸϲ τί]|| βλέπ[ον]τεϲ ἐπ[αινοῦϲιν]|| ἢ τί ἐρ[γ]άϲεται [ϲύνθε]|ϲιϲ.

"Likewise," (?) ⟨he says,⟩ "I ask those who praise the composition with regard to what criterion they praise it or what the composition achieves."

Slightly later[121] the opponent draws a distinction, analogous in my view to that between Andromenides and the *kritikoi*, between those who seek poetic excellence in word choice (*ekloge*) and those who seek it in word-order (*synthesis*):

καί |[φηϲιν τιν]ὰϲ λέγειν ἐκ |[καλῶν κ]αὶ ποιητικῶν |[ῥημάτω]ν τὸ χρη-ϲτὸν |[ἢ πονηρὸν] πόημα, κατά |[τιναϲ δὲ διὰ τ]ὸ πολλάκιϲ |[τὰ ποιημά-τ]ων φαῦλα γί|[νεϲθαι ἐ]ξ ἰδιωτικῶν |[καὶ ἐξ ἐ]ὐτελῶν, ϲυ[γ]κει|[μένων] δὲ καλῶϲ, χ[ρ]ηϲ|[τά. διδ]άϲκει δὲ καὶ τὸ . . .

He also says that "some claim that a good or bad verse arises from fine and poetic words, but that according to others ⟨it arises⟩ on account of the fact that bad verses often arise from ordinary and commonplace words, but when ⟨such words⟩ are put together well, good ⟨verses arise⟩." He also teaches that . . . .

A reference to Crates' doctrine that poetic excellence arises from the euphony which supervenes upon the *synthesis* actually appears in Treatise E:[122]

πορίζη⟨ι⟩ϲ ε[ὐφωνίαν ἐ]|πιφαίνεϲθαι διὰ τὴν [ϲύν]|θεϲιν, μετατ[εθείϲηϲ]|| τῆϲ "πίων" φ[ωνῆϲ]|πειρ[ ] δ᾽ εὐτ[ελ τὴν ἡδο]|νὴν ἀποβαν[.... . εὐ]|φωνίαν.

---

[118] See most recently Mangoni 1993 on *On Poems* 5 col. xxiv 27–32, with further references to Heracleodorus.

[119] Critics are mentioned in the plural at *P.Herc.* 466 fr. 10.2 (= Tr. E fr. 13 Nardelli), 466 fr. 6.2–4 (Tr. E fr. 9 Nardelli) and especially 444 fr. 8.19*–26*, quoted below.

[120] Col. 37* = *P.Herc.* 444 fr. 8.19*–24*.   [121] Col. 49* = *P.Herc.* 444 fr. 4.16*–26*.

[122] Col. 34* = *P.Herc.* 466 fr. 7.1–5 (Tr. E fr. 10 Nardelli).

⟨if ?⟩ you provide (?) that euphony (?) appears on the surface on account of the composition, when the word 'fat' [*pion*] is altered (?), but . . . ⟨it appears ?⟩ ordinary . . . the pleasure . . . turn out . . . euphony.

I originally identified the opponent of Book 1 as a figure whose name, like that of Crates himself, appears in Book 2, viz. the otherwise unknown Pausimachus; but I now incline to believe that Pausimachus and Heracleodorus were in fact the *kritikoi* whose doctrines Crates discussed, and that Crates himself is the main opponent in Books 1 and 2.

4. A sampling of Crates' euphonic theory

Let us provisionally accept that Crates is Philodemus' source for the opinions of all the critics which are summarized at the opening of *On Poems* 1. The very beginning, Treatise E, still awaits a conclusive reconstruction, but my work on the bulk of the summary, in Treatise B, is sufficiently advanced for me to hazard a preliminary interpretation, albeit subject to the proviso that this is still work in progress and may turn out to need much revision. This field is changing rapidly, but at least we can be confident that enormous progress is being made, even if what follows should turn out to differ considerably from my final conclusions. Because of the damaged state of the new text of Treatise B, I mingle paraphrase and quotation; I also omit fragments which are as yet incomprehensible or too badly damaged, but adhere scrupulously to the original order of the columns as established according to the new method.

"No excellence of plot or character will make up for poor *synthesis*.[123] The diction and the content are merely the material (*hyle*) of poetry, and only offer potential; that which actualizes (*energein*) the material, the sound, is both primary and particular to a poet. One can introduce any sort of character and creature into a poem; but only if artistic excellence is added will that character be recognizable as such.[124] It doesn't matter in which genre the best poets compose: what Archilochus and Euripides have in common with Homer is the quality of their diction.[125] 'There is no content so beautiful that it can make a work praiseworthy if the composition is *not* beautiful, and no content so ugly that it can make a work blameworthy if the composition *is* beautiful.'[126] Good poets excel and endure only on account of their sounds, regardless of whether they compose different genres of poetry, like Homer, Archilochus, and Euripides, or a mixture of genres, like Timotheus."[127]

After this boldly defiant manifesto, Crates promises to speak of "sounds in themselves"[128] and goes into detail, drawing his often recherché examples from Homer, tragedy, and lyric. For instance, earlier in the treatise he rewrote *Iliad* 16.112–14, while keeping all the same words, so as to make one hexameter entirely full of long

[123] Col. 60* = *P.Herc.* 460 fr. 29 col. ii (= Tr. B fr. 24 Sbordone).
[124] Col. 66* = *P.Herc.* 460 fr. 27 (= Tr. B fr. 21 Sbordone) + *P.Herc.* 1073 fr. 17 (= Tr. B fr. 20 col. i Sbordone).
[125] Col. 69* = *P.Herc.* 460 fr. 26 (= Tr. B fr. 17 Sbordone).
[126] Col. 71* = *P.Herc.* 1073 fr. 15a (= Tr. B fr. 11 col. i Sbordone).
[127] Col. 75* = *P.Herc.* 460 fr. 24 (= Tr. B fr. 19 Sbordone).
[128] Col. 75* = *P.Herc.* 460 fr. 24.22–24 (= Tr. B fr. 19 Sbordone).

syllables, but the next entirely dactylic:[129] this was meant to prove that word–order was vital to the effect of these verses. Crates' technique of rearrangement (*metathesis*) was to be applied to prose by the Augustan critic Dionysius of Halicarnassus, in what is usually considered his most original work, the treatise *On Composition*. In fact I suspect that Dionysius borrowed this technique from Crates via Philodemus,[130] along with much of his theory of euphony, just as he may have plagiarized Philodemus' *Rhetoric* for a quotation from Hieronymus of Rhodes.[131] Again, Crates asks why it pleases us when Homer repeats the word *lotos*,[132] but the poet displeases the ear if he repeats the letters sigma or xi too often, e.g. in *rhexe sakos* "ripped the shield,"[133] or in "she at once exited out through the shining doors,"[134] when no harsh effect is intended.[135] Crates argues that words with unaspirated stops and liquids, light, open syllables and acute accents, like *hóplon, kúklos,* and *plátanos*, are more attractive than those with aspirated stops, heavy, closed syllables, and grave or circumflex accents, like *khàlkon* or *skhêma*: he uses cases where such words are repeated to prove his point. Thus he faults Euripides for repeating *skhêma* at *Ion* 237–40.[136] Crates praises Homer, on the other hand, for varying his phrasing to avoid juxtaposing words with the same accentual pattern: thus Homer says *teíkheos ektós*[137] but *halòs éxo*[138] rather than *teíkheos éxo* and *halòs ektòs*, as Crates rewrites the verses.[139] His rewriting pairs what Crates calls "tense" (acute) and "lax" (grave) accents respectively, using the terms *epitasis* and *anesis*. His remarks on the aesthetic effects of accentuation are paralleled, along with the terminology, only in a third-century Peripatetic writer on rhetoric, Hieronymus of Rhodes.[140] The terms derive, as Crates makes clear, from the musical pitch of a lyre-string or a bow:[141] the analogy is apt, since Greek still had a sing-song pitch-accent in his time, like modern Serbo-Croatian or Swedish. He continues that when the sound is "invented" correctly, in terms of accents, aspirates, vowel length and word formation, good Greek

---

[129] Col. 65* = *P.Herc.* 1073 fr. 19 (= Tr. B fr. 35 Sbordone).

[130] Cf. N. A. Greenberg, "Metathesis as an instrument in the criticism of poetry," *TAPA* 89 (1958), 262–70, who concludes that critics prior to Dionysius had used this device to draw more sweeping conclusions than Dionysius did.

[131] Fr. 52 Wehrli, which is cited first by Philodemus at *On Rhetoric* 4 (*P.Herc.* 1007) col. xvia 13–xviiia 8 Sudhaus, and then by Dionysius of Halicarnassus at *Isocrates* 13.3–5, who seems to have derived it from Philodemus, as was proposed by G. Aujac, *Denys d'Halicarnasse, Opuscules rhétoriques* 1, (Paris [Budé] 1978, 194–95. See now G. Indelli, "Testimonianze su Isocrate nel *P.Herc.* 1007," *CErc* 23 (1993), 87–92.

[132] Col. 77* = *P.Herc.* 460 fr. 21 (= Tr. B fr. 29 Sbordone). He refers to Homer, *Odyssey* 9.92–97.

[133] *Iliad* 20.268 or 21.165.   [134] *Odyssey* 10.230.

[135] Col. 78* = *P.Herc.* 460 fr. 22 (= Tr. B fr. 7 col. i Sbordone).

[136] Cols. 80–83*, = *P.Herc.* 460 fr. 20 (= Tr. B fr. 12 Sbordone) + *P.Herc.* 460 fr. 19 (= Tr. B fr. 5 col. i Sbordone) + *P.Herc.* 1073 fr. 16b (= Tr. B fr. 33 Sbordone) + *P.Herc.* 460 fr. 17 (= Tr. B fr. 11 col. ii Sbordone).   [137] *Iliad* 9.67 = 20.49.   [138] *Iliad* 17.265.

[139] Col. 85–86*, = *P.Herc.* 1073 fr. 15b (= Tr. B fr. 10 col. i Sbordone) + *P.Herc.* 460 fr. 16 (= Tr. B fr. 10 col. ii Sbordone).

[140] The case mentioned above (n. 131) of the quotation from Hieronymus found both in Philodemus and in Dionysius of Halicarnassus may therefore indicate that Hieronymus was quoted by Crates, on whom both later writers would therefore be directly dependent, rather than that, as was suggested above, that Dionysius borrowed from Philodemus.

[141] Col. 85* = *P.Herc.* 1073 fr. 15b.21* (= Tr. B fr. 10 col. i Sbordone), where we should read βιῶι and not βίωι.

(*hellenismos*) and a kind of harmony ensue.[142] Crates agrees with the *kritikoi* that a person of thin speech (*iskhnophonos*) will not be a good poet. This may be a hit at Callimachus and similar poets who aspired to writing that was, according to their enemies, "thin" (*katiskhnon*).[143]

Nor, argues Crates, must we let the demands of the sense distract us from choosing the right sounds. In human speech the sound creates what is particular in terms of the sense; it is because of the sounds that Greek is Greek, rather than some other language. Even when Sophocles[144] says "the sailors raised the fig-iron (*iskhas*) of the ship" we understand that he means its anchor, and not the fruit, but the particularly apt expression is maintained: it seems that *iskhas*, normally "fig," evoked *iskhein*, "hold fast."[145] The sound prevails over the sense, and good sound should determine word-choice. For instance, when Homer says "axle of oak-wood"[146] (*pheginos axon*) rather than (as he might have said) "axle of holm-oak" (*prininos axon*), phrases deemed by Crates to be equivalent in sense and in metre, he does so because he wishes to avoid long iota, which is "narrow and hard to pronounce," whereas eta is better.[147] Verses are good when their sound imitates the sound which is being described. For instance, when Homer describes how Patroclus' ghost flits away "gibbering"[148] (*tetrigyia*), the long iota is effective.[149] Conversely, Homer's verse "the pebbles are jostled as the brook flows along"[150] would have been less effective if, instead of saying *okhleuntai* "jostled," he had said *kinountai* "stirred" with a long iota.[151] Homer derives his sounds from the correct words (*ortha onomata*); it would be dreadful if the sound were deprived of its particular nature (*idion*) because one considered the sense in choosing one's words. The sound is more vital than the sense for the effect on the listeners: "it is the sound itself, distinct from the underlying meanings, that enchants those who listen to verses, and when someone mixes both these things and dominates us he arouses us to exaltation." That sound is paramount can be seen in the case of birds. In their case "a kind of articulated voice is produced, distinct from the sound which pours forth, just as is held to be true of the nightingale." But the bird's underlying intention, the sense, is irrelevant: "a parrot does not know whether it is reciting a line from a tragedy, but it can produce the sounds all the same, just as a human being does."[152] The sound, in other words, exists even without

---

[142] Col. 86* = *P.Herc.* 460 fr. 16 (= Tr. B fr. 10 col. ii Sbordone).

[143] Schol. Flor. on *Aetia* fr. 1.1–12.   [144] Fr. 694 Nauck = 761 Radt.

[145] Col. 89* = *P.Herc.* 460 fr. 15 (= Tr. B fr. 23 col. ii Sbordone). The verse is also cited by Athenaeus (3.99d), in a catalogue of bizarre expressions, where the etymological explanation appears. At Athenaeus 14.652b–653b there is a discussion of ἰϲχάϲ immediately before an account by Crates (fr. 68a Mette) of the related terms βότρυϲ and ϲταφύλη. Hence there is a case on external grounds that Crates was interested in this word. Athenaeus' source in Book 14 was Crates' *Attike dialektos*, which discussed the claim of various words to belong to the Attic dialect rather than to be *barbarismoi*. In the work summarized in *On Poems* 1 there is a similar interest in *hellenismos* and *barbarismos* (cf. cols. 86–87* = *P.Herc.* 460 fr. 16.23 + 1073 fr. 10b.17*–18*, col. 89* = *P.Herc.* 460 fr. 15.8–12, and col. 92* = *P.Herc.* 460 fr. 14.18.   [146] *Iliad* 5.838.

[147] Cols. 92–93* = *P.Herc.* 460 fr. 14 (= Tr. B fr. 6 col. i Sbordone) + *P.Herc.* 1073 fr. 5 (= Tr. B fr. 6 col. ii Sbordone).   [148] *Iliad* 23.100–101.

[149] Cols. 95–96* = *P.Herc.* 460 fr. 13 (= Tr. B fr. 2 Sbordone) + *P.Herc.* 1073 fr. 4 (= Tr. B fr. 31 Sbordone).   [150] *Iliad* 21.261.

[151] Col. 97* = *P.Herc.* 460 fr. 12 (= Tr. B fr. 13 Sbordone)

[152] Col. 100–101* = *P.Herc.* 460 fr. 9 (= Tr. B fr. 26 col. i Sbordone) + *P.Herc.* 1073 fr. 3 (= Tr. B fr. 26 col. ii Sbordone).

the sense, and is therefore logically prior to it; it exists even though the parrot can't understand it. The claim is as outrageous as it is unparalleled, but the avian examples are paralleled in the linguistic theory of Crates' contemporary, Diogenes of Babylon. Thus Diogenes[153] said that "a human being differs from other animals by using not speech which is pronounced (for crows, parrots and jays can pronounce articulated words), but speech which is internalized," i.e. speech which corresponds to the speaker's mental concepts. Diogenes developed his important theory of language from that found in Aristotle's biology,[154] where Aristotle had classified the sounds made by different animals, including ourselves, into noise, voice and articulate speech.[155] I find highly significant this parallel between Crates and the contemporary head of the Stoa, who revolutionized the study of grammar.

After a gap, we find Crates again arguing that the different genres exist by convention and not by nature, because the sound is paramount. "Talented poets succeed by becoming alike in their sounds. Poets of lampoon compose tragic verses, and conversely tragic poets compose lampoons . . . . So one must say that a poet composing a lampoon or some other genre exists not by nature, but by convention. Poets compose by nature when they name something by coming upon a word that is nobly born and primary and always apt, and when the same rational account prevails in every genre of verse."[156] As Asmis[157] has seen, Crates accepted the Stoic doctrine of a name-giver who first assigned names to everything, names which somehow reflect the properties of the objects named, but may since have been altered in human parlance. According to this theory, language has meaning by nature and not by convention: the word "table" must somehow evoke the material properties of a table, just as "twitter" evokes the material properties of the sound which a bird makes, and the best poets have a natural ability to hit upon precisely those names which are most in accord with nature. Crates' acceptance of this theory of language, which goes back to Cratylus in Plato's dialogue of that title,[158] makes him more a Stoic than anything else. Moreover, the idea that words may have hidden "natural" meanings offered a parallel to the allegorical criticism of Homer which Crates himself practised.[159]

After another gap, Crates has returned to euphony, moving on from letters to syllables.[160] He claims that syllables ending with simple vowels are better than those which end with consonants, since they are easier to pronounce and to understand.[161] His theory suits Greek better than Latin or English, which are by this criterion very unpronounceable and unintelligible languages. This claim accords with Crates'

---

[153] Ap. Sextus Empiricus *Adv. math.* 8.275 (= *SVF* 2 fr. 135, p. 43.18–22 von Arnim): ἄνθρωπος οὐ τῶι προφορικῶι λόγωι διαφέρει τῶν ἄλλων ζώιων (καὶ γὰρ κόρακες καὶ ψίττακοι καὶ κίτται ἐνάρθρους προφέρονται φωνάς), ἀλλὰ τῶι ἐνδιαθέτωι.

[154] Cf. W. Ax, *Laut, Stimme und Sprache: Studien zu drei Grundbegriffen der antiken Sprachtheorie*, Hypomnemata 84 (Göttingen 1986), 183; Obbink and Vander Waerdt 1991, 355 n. 2.

[155] Cf. Janko 1991a, 43 with n. 195, for a detailed discussion and further references.

[156] Col. 103* = *P.Herc.* 460 fr. 8 (= Tr. B fr. 20 col. i Sbordone).   [157] Asmis 1992b,161–67.

[158] Esp. *Cratylus* 383a, 425d–426b. See now T. M. S. Baxter, *The* Cratylus*: Plato's Critique of Naming* (Leiden 1992), esp. 8–15.

[159] On this, and on Crates' wider literary theory, see now J. I. Porter, *Hermeneutic Lines and Circles: Aristarchus and Crates on the Exegesis of Homer*, in R. Lamberton and J.J. Keaney (eds.), *Homer's Ancient Readers: the Hermeneutics of Greek Epic's Earliest Exegetes* (Princeton 1992), 67–114, esp. 85ff.

[160] For this procedure cf. Plato, *Cratylus* 424b–c, Aristotle, *Poetics* ch. 20, and Dionysius Thrax, *Ars Grammatica* 6–7.11.   [161] Col. 105* = *P.Herc.* 460 fr. 7 (= Tr. B fr. 8 col. i Sbordone).

interest in Phrygian and other non-Greek tongues, evident from earlier in Book 1,[162] and also with his encounter with Latin: we know that, while on a diplomatic mission to Rome, perhaps in 168 B.C., he fell into an open drain, broke his leg and had to stay there, giving lectures, until it healed.[163] Crates continues that lambda is a very pleasant letter, especially when conjoined with unaspirated stops like *p, k* or even *g,* as in *plaka, kladoi* or *glaukopin,* but aspirated letters are ugly.[164] (Much of this theory of euphony was taken over by Dionysius of Halicarnassus in *De Compositione* 14–16.) We may completely fail to perceive the sense of a verse, and yet still notice the cacophony of clashing consonants. For instance, we understand Homer's word *linxe* "twanged,"[165] even though it occurs nowhere else in Greek. But words that overtly resemble sounds are a special case. In general bad sound arises from difficulty in pronunciation, since "the ears do not welcome whatever one cannot pronounce,"[166] After some damaged columns, Crates goes on to consider the views of Andromenides,[167] and soon afterwards Philodemus begins his lengthy refutation of the entire summary.[168]

These massive new extracts of Crates' work resemble the picture of his doctrines formed by H. J. Mette,[169] with close and extensive parallels in Varro, Dionysius of Halicarnassus, Sextus Empiricus and the scholia to Dionysius Thrax; but Crates' views on poetic euphony and on genre are wholly new. When fully reconstructed, Book 1 will add a quite unexpected dimension to our view of Hellenistic and Augustan literary theory and poetry. We may well find that Crates was, with the possible exception of Philodemus himself, the strongest Greek influence on Roman thought about poetry and language. However, for the clarification of such wider questions we must wait and see what conclusions are suggested by the continuing work of reading and reconstructing the library from Herculaneum.[170]

---

[162] Cf. col. 83* = *P.Herc.* 460 fr. 17.12 (= Tr. B fr. 11 col. ii Sbordone), and the references to *hellenismos* and *barbarismos* cited above.   [163] Suetonius, *De gramm.* 2.

[164] Cols. 106–107* = *P.Herc.* 1073 fr. 2a (= Tr. B fr. 8 col. ii Sbordone) + *P.Herc.* 1073 fr. 7b (= Tr. B fr. 36 Sbordone) + *P.Herc.* 460 fr. 6 (= Tr. B fr. 9 col. ii Sbordone).   [165] *Iliad* 4.125.

[166] Cols. 109–110* = *P.Herc.* 460 fr. 4 (= Tr. B fr. 28 Sbordone) + *P.Herc.* 460 fr. 5 (= Tr. B fr. 4 col. i Sbordone).

[167] Cols. 114–16* = *P.Herc.* 460 fr. 2 (= Tr. B fr. 25 col. iii Sbordone) + *P.Herc.* 1074a fr. 1 (= Tr. D fr. 13 Nardelli) + *P.Herc.* 1073 fr. 1b (= Tr. B fr. 25 col. ii Sbordone) + *P.Herc.* 1074a fr. 2 (= Tr. D fr. 42 Nardelli).   [168] Col. 118* = *P.Herc.* 1074a fr. 3 dext. (= Tr. D fr. 40 Nardelli).

[169] *Parateresis. Untersuchungen zur Sprachtheorie des Krates von Pergamon* (Halle 1952).

[170] An unpublished supplement by Annick Monet (*On Poems* 5 col. xxi (xxiv) 32–33 ἐπ[αι]ν[οῦ]ϲιν κ]αὶ) makes Philodemus claim that Crates in fact misunderstood the views of Heracleodorus (see below, p. 263 with n. 38).

7

Content and Form in Philodemus: The History of an Evasion

James Porter

What is important is to recover our senses. We must learn to *see* more, to *hear* more, to *feel* more. Our task is not to find the maximum amount of content in a work of art, much less to squeeze more content out of the work than is already there. Our task is to cut back content so that we can *see* the thing at all.

Susan Sontag, "Against Interpretation" (1964)

1. Ancient Aesthetics and the Discourse of Criticism

Jensen's publication, in 1923, of the remains of a book from *On Poems* by Philodemus brought to light one of the richest sources we currently have on the state of poetic theory during the Hellenistic period, and on the connections between those developments and their classical antecedents in Plato and Aristotle. Figures known only by name or for obscure achievements, such as Neoptolemus of Parium and Crates of Mallos, were drawn out of their prior darkness and isolation and restored to an importance that subsequent research has only reaffirmed. The so-called "heretic" member of the Stoa, Aristo of Chios, emerged (if the attribution is right) as an expositor of a challenging theory of aesthetic value which appears to have been unique.[1] Shadowy extras, like the so-called *kritikoi* ("Critics"), were revealed as having occupied an influential place in the field of ancient literary criticism, prior to Crates and Aristo. In Jensen's wake, it can now be shown that fields of inquiry as remote as physics, epistemology, music, and literary criticism consorted together in the Hellenistic era with an intensity that ought to make us wonder afresh about some of the better known examples of literary criticism from antiquity, where such cross-disciplinary connections are less obviously apparent (e.g., Dionysius of Halicarnassus

---

[1] On the controversial Aristo and his poetic theory, see Asmis 1990b, and J. Porter, "Stoic Morals and Poetics in Philodemus, *CErc* 24 (1994).

and ps.-Longinus). This convergence of disparate inquiries can be traced, however tentatively, back to the late fifth century and its nascent philology.[2]

While more work needs to be done and is in progress, it is fair to say that when the information that is to be had is finally put together, a fresh picture of ancient poetics will emerge, featuring new elements and new stress lines. The spectrum of critical approaches in antiquity will be expanded beyond its recognized limits. Even the very meaning of "criticism" and "critical discourse" will be a matter of renewed debate. It will be increasingly important to look beyond the official, mainstream, institutional, and academic style of criticism, which the Peripatos sanctioned, and which the Museum at Alexandria later enshrined.[3] Non-canonical critical forms and literary canons existed outside the main stream and in opposition to it. It pays to recall that the Alexandrian scholar-critics were controlling the transmission of texts in more ways than one. It is reassuring to know that they did not wholly succeed.

The aim of the present paper is to sketch out, in effect, three pictures or versions of this ancient critical spectrum, from Aristotle down to Philodemus, around one of the several organizing principles that have been used to characterize it in the past: the issue of content and form. The first picture will be done in stark contrasts: content will be opposed dichotomously to form; and Aristotelianism will be challenged by the clarion call of anti-Aristotelianism. The second picture will not efface all the oppositions, but it will yield a more complex set of nuances, by reintroducing more appropriate, and all-too-neglected, ancient criteria: *matter* versus form. Materialism could find its way into aesthetic theory too. The final picture will merge without completely synthesizing the first two pictures and (it is hoped) will complicate even further our image of ancient poetic theories on all sides of all the equations: here we can begin eroding our nuances, and start talking, as modern aestheticians sometimes do (and as ancient poeticians might be understood to have done), about "content of form" versus "form of content"; or about such paradoxical objects as "material form"; or about all of these things—form/content, form/matter, etc.—as epiphenomena, or illusory mental constructs. But before reaching such heady conclusions, we must first get as clear as we can on the distinction between content and form.

2. "Content" or "Form"?

We may begin by considering the dichotomy in all its naked simplicity. It is one to which many of us commonly make appeal in our literary judgments, whenever we

---

[2] Cf. Philodemus, *On Poems* 5 cols. i–iii, Jensen (iv–vii Mangoni [see below, n. 9]; cf. col. v 19-20 Mangoni) which recalls Crates of Mallos, whose forebears include the fifth-century Metrodorus of Lampsacus. Connections between physics, music, and philology are likely in the cases of Democritus and Hippias of Elis.

[3] Cf. esp. R. Pfeiffer, *History of Classical Scholarship from the Beginnings to the End of the Hellenistic Age* (Oxford 1968). But we should perhaps also try harder to separate "mainstream" criticism from its received images. See further J. Porter, "Hermeneutic Lines and Circles: Aristarchus and Crates on the Exegesis of Homer," in *Homer's Ancient Readers: The Greek Epic's Earliest Exegetes*, ed. Robert Lamberton and John J. Keaney (Princeton 1992).

gesture toward the "form" of a work or to its "content," whatever those are, or whatever we take them to be. The pedigree of this contrast is unassailable, but we too often forget that it is no less artificial for having been around for so long, and for having become, so to speak, second nature. Conventionally, the contrast between content and form, however "well intentioned," tends, in the words of one recent essayist, to "make content essential and form accessory":

> [I]t is the defence of art which gives birth to the odd vision by which something we have learned to call "form" is separated off from something we have learned to call "content," and to the well-intentioned move which makes content essential and form accessory.[4]

On the other hand (and this too is easily forgotten, as it is by Sontag herself in the course of her essay), just to posit the distinction at all, even in the form of its denial— as in the claim, "form is inseparable from content"—is to make fatal concessions to the very separation that is being, simultaneously, denied. If even to deny the dichotomy is to surrender to it all over again, the dichotomy at this point becomes a dilemma.

Sontag's immediate inspiration is Victor Shklovsky, a literary theorist who in the early part of this century crusaded in the name of what might be called perceptual form, whereby form, "defamiliarized" as a concept, becomes the very stuff of sensory awareness. Choosing examples from Homer to Sterne, Shklovsky held that "awareness of form *constitutes* the subject matter" of an artwork, the purpose of which "is *not* to make us perceive meaning, but to create a special *perception of the object*" (emphases added). Art, which is the sum of its techniques, has only one aim: "to make forms difficult."[5] Making forms difficult in this way makes accounting for form as it is traditionally received difficult too. Few treatments of ancient literary poetics risk so bold a challenge. Most of these, in fact, accept what appear to be the ancient dichotomizations of poetry into content and form as unproblematically given. This is prima facie odd, since the Greek critical lexicon utterly lacks any satisfying equivalents for our words "content" or "form": *morphe, eidos,* and *schema* do not obviously lend themselves to a juxtaposition with "content" in our sense of the term, nor does a Greek equivalent for "content" readily come to mind. The issue is not the lack of Greek equivalents for "containment"-metaphors; it is the "failure" in Greek thinking to find a way to get the categories of containment to cut neatly across those of language. Even so, something like the distinction between content and form could, in point of fact, be expressed in antiquity, and even, in the most interesting critical circles, evaded. One might even venture to say that from Aristotle to ps.-Longinus the major lines of ancient literary criticism, and especially its internal dissensions, were determined by the ways in which critics variously sought to *avoid* positing a content/form dichotomy, a dichotomy which Plato made notorious and a

---

⁴ Susan Sontag, "Against Interpretation" in *A Susan Sontag Reader*. With an Introduction by Elizabeth Hardwick (New York 1982), 95–104 at 96. See also her essay "On Style" and the first pages of her *Salmagundi* interview in the same volume.

⁵ Quotations drawn from *Russian Formalist Criticism: Four Essays*, translated and with an introduction by Lee T. Lemon and Marion J. Reis (Lincoln, Nebraska 1965), 12, 19, and 35.

cause célèbre.[6] This history of avoidances is a subject worthy of at least a brief survey, and Philodemus is ideally positioned to give us a glimpse into it.

How do you express the difference, which you may sense, between content and form, if you are a Greek critic? The classic approach to the content/form contrast is to divide up a poetic text into two strata: the underlying "ideas" (meanings, intentions, or referents: all three could be implied) and the surface of "words"—in Greek, the "thoughts" (*dianoemata*) and the "expression" (*lexis*). Here is how Plato puts it in the *Ion*:

[1a] Plato, *Ion* 530B10–C4

It is enviable to be able to understand Homer's meaning (τὴν τούτου διάνοιαν ἐκμανθάνειν), and not just his words (or: verses, μὴ μόνον τὰ ἔπη). One would never be a good rhapsode, if one didn't understand (ϲυνείη) what the poet meant (τὰ λεγόμενα). For the rhapsode must become the interpreter of the poet's meanings (διανοίαϲ) for the audience. (Cf. *Hippias minor* 365D1.)

Plato is certainly not the first to use it (see below, on Aristophanes), but he may well be the first to put the dichotomy so strongly. The *hyponoiai* or subtexts "discovered" by the allegorists of the fifth-century or earlier, a form of meaning that Plato also disparaged, are altogether a different affair (cf. *Republic* 378D); for the dichotomy in question touches the very possibility of whether poetry can be meaningful. In Plato's hands the disjunction is fatal: it subjects the poet to a division beyond his control. By contrast, Aristotle's *Poetics* can be read as largely an attempt to counteract Plato's having reduced poetry to its intelligibility as an idea and that idea to nothing (Plato's poet is "mindlessly" inspired, ὁ νοῦϲ μηκέτι ἐν αὐτῷ ἐνῇ: *Ion* 534B5). But the disjunction stuck, being rooted perhaps in ordinary language and in common intuition, and so even Aristotle is prone to talking in terms of the rhetor's language or style (*lexis*) as opposed to his more valuable attribute, his thought or meaning (*dianoia*), and subsequent criticism would rarely move entirely away from the rhetorical perspective on literary language.[7] Hence the dichotomy's reappearance in the commonplace distinction between figures of speech (*schemata tes lexeos*) and figures of thought (*schemata tes dianoias*), or between verbal composition (*synthesis*, the arrangement of letters and words) and selection (*ekloge*, which conventionally implicates meaning).[8] Or its prevailing, day to day appearance in less esoteric forms, as in passages like the following:

---

[6] Compare the two formulations of the Aristarchan maxim, conveniently reproduced in Pfeiffer 1968 (above, n. 3), 226–27; and Philodemus, *On Poems* 5 col. xxv (xxviii) 26–29 (Crates of Mallos); further, Porter 1992 (above, n. 3).

[7] Aristotle, *Rhetoric* 3.1 1404a18–19: "The effect of written speeches is owed more (μεῖζον ἰϲχύουϲι) to *lexis* than to meaning (*dianoian*)." This is not a blanket endorsement of *lexis*, but a lamentable fact about rhetoric, as the sequel (1404a24–28) shows. Cf. *Rhetoric* 1.13 1374b12–13. On subsequent rhetorically-based criticism, see Russell 1981, ch. 9, and e.g. pp. 4, 15, 129, and 146; and T. Cole, *The Origins of Rhetoric in Ancient Greece* (Baltimore 1991), 35.

[8] Cf. Dionysius of Halicarnassus, *De compositione verborum* c. 3: "composition is to *selection* what words are to *ideas*" (καὶ ϲχεδὸν ἀνάλογόν τι πεπονθέναι δόξειεν ἂν ἡ ϲύνθεϲιϲ πρὸϲ τὴν ἐκλογήν, ὃ πάϲχει τὰ ὀνόματα πρὸϲ τὰ νοήματα, p. 9, 9–11 Usener-Radermacher, trans. Carpenter).

[1b] Philodemus, *On Poems* 5 col. xxix (xxxii) 11[9]

τὰ μὲ[ν ἀ]νωφελῆ, τὰ [δὲ οὐδ' ἀνωφελ]ῆ περιέχοντ[α]; cf. *ibid.*, xiv (xvii) 20–24

Some poems *contain* useless meanings/ideas [*dianoemata*; col. xxix (xxxii) 1–5], some [not even useless meanings/ideas]

[1c] *Scholia on Dionysius Thrax's On the art of Grammar* 449, 21–23 Hilgard (Theophrastean)

Poetry is a recounting of events (ἀπαγγελία πραγμάτων) through meters and rhythms, with some kind of elaboration (μετά τινος κατασκευῆς), *containing* (περιέχουσα) mythical subject-matter (τὸ μυθῶδες), sometimes [spliced] with truth and with fact, in some kind of *lexis* (ἐν ποιᾷ λέξει); cf. Theophrastus fr. 65 Wimmer = 78 Fortenbaugh.

While these last examples bring us a few steps closer to the notion of "containment," the question of how "form" fits into all of this remains something of a mystery. Our content/form distinction does not quite seem to overlap with the ancient critical vocabulary. Is it even relevant? Consider another critic's claim, characteristic of the common run of critical aperçus, that *poems* can "have" both *synthesis* (of *lexis*) and some meaning:

[1d] [Aristo of Chios], apud Philodemus, *On Poems* 5 col. xiv (xvii)12

⟨sc. τὰ ποιήματα⟩ καὶ τὴν cύν[θεc]ιν ἀc|τείαν ἔχοντα [κ]αὶ τὴν | διάνοιαν [cπουδαίαν] . . .

poems having both good *synthesis* and good meaning . . .

This remark, typical of everything seen so far, hardly approaches saying that *lexis* gives or is the "form" or "shape" of anything (least of all, of a poem's "contents," viz. meaning).[10] So perhaps we have reason to doubt whether the content/form dichotomy, problematic in any language, is even being expressed at all whenever Greek critics oppose "thought" or "meaning" to "language." Even so, the dichotomy of meaning and expression, whenever it figures in later criticism, never quite figures with the virulent simplicity that it had in Plato (where a poet's "thoughts" are emptied of all content), or with the same reductiveness that our modern "content/form"

---

[9] Quotations from *On Poems* 5 throughout are based on Cecilia Mangoni's revision (Mangoni 1993) of Jensen's edition, *Philodemos über die Gedichte*; Jensen's column numeration has been retained for ease of reference, with Mangoni's given in parentheses. I was fortunate to consult her much improved text before it was published. For that part of *On poems* preserved as *P. Herc.* 1676, I have drawn where noted on the new readings of Romeo 1992b.

[10] It might be objected that in Latin criticism, "*forma*" captures the Greek term *synthesis* (as in Varro, fr. 398 Bücheler): *poema est lexis enrythmos, id est verba plura modice, in quandam coniecta formam*, "A poem is *lexis* in some rhythm, that is, words varied rhythmically, thrown [or "joined together"] into some shape." But here it is *coniecta* that most nearly captures *synthesis*, which is first and foremost a putting together, viz., a compositional act. Perhaps *synthesis* can be said to have a "form." But such talk in ancient sources is rare; neither does it give us the form of a "content."

distinction still enjoys (even when its validity is being denied for us, but reapplied to the ancients). Not, that is, until we reach Neoptolemus of Parium (sometime in the third century B.C.), in the writings of Philodemus.[11]

3. *Poema* and *Poesis*

Neoptolemus' view of poetry is highly schematic, and so will my overview of Neoptolemus be too. He is generally assumed to have worked in the Peripatetic and Alexandrian tradition, and this appears to be largely correct, although "in" conceals a number of ambiguities (as was already seen above). His poetics exhibits a formalism run rampant, and this is not merely explicable as a regular feature of Alexandrian criticism. "Poetics," ἡ ποιητική, is now divided into three "elements," "parts," or "species" (*eide*)—although it is more in keeping with Neoptolemus' theory, and the theory from which it draws its power (namely, Aristotle's), to translate *eide* by "formal (qualitative) aspects," and not to view them as quantitative components.[12] Philodemus has difficulties with this dissection, but his reactions are revealing. The text most revelatory of Neoptolemus' biases, which also happens to be extremely difficult papyrologically, runs as follows:

[2a–b] Philodemus, *On Poems* 5 col. xii (xv) 1–17

[2a] καὶ τὸ πόη[ματος μό-   1
νον τὴν [σύνθεσιν τῆς
λέξεως μ[ετέχειν, ± 5]
νας διανοί[ας ±7]

[2a] And [astounding is the claim] that[13] only the *synthesis* of the *lexis* [is] of the *poema*, [but that] thoughts, actions, and characterizations [are not].[14]

---

[11] For Neoptolemus' dates, see Brink 1963, 45 and 52. These are highly conjectural. Apart from the one certain *terminus ante quem* (c. 180 B.C.), the best argument that can be made is that Neoptolemus is contemporary with or antedates Aristo of Chios, and possibly postdates Heraclides of Pontus and the "Peripatetic" Demetrius of Byzantium, if Philodemus' treatment in *On Poems* 5 is chronologically sequenced, as it appears to be, and if Aristo is indeed the next opponent after Neoptolemus in *On Poems* 5. Neoptolemus' name has been partly restored in col. x (xiii), where it appears for the first and last time in Philodemus. Doubt still swirls around the earlier columns, which Jensen originally ("Neoptolemus und Horaz," *APAW* [1918] and Jensen 1923) gave to Neoptolemus, and then later (1936) gave to Heraclides (cf. "Herakleides"). I have excluded the earlier columns from discussion in the present paper.

[12] Brink 1963 (in his *Prolegomena*, the best treatment of the topic) fluctuates between "aspects" (58–59) and "elements or parts" (58, 92–93); neither is, evidently, meant quantitatively (68 n. 1), but they are strongly correlated with "style and content" (69, 72, 144, et *passim*), but not, evidently, "identified" with these things (60 and n. 3). Ancient criticism generally tends to fluctuate between aspectual and part/whole criteria. Aristotle's *eide* in the *Poetics* are, variously: "species" of the genus poetry (1.1447a8); distinct "kinds" of tragedy (18.1455b32); the "quantitative parts" of tragedy (12.1452b14); or just "qualitative parts" that can only be mentally distinguished from one another and from the play that exhibits them even as they in turn constitute the play (e.g., action, character, and thought; 6.1450a13). The latter are best understood as "aspects" or as "aspectual distinctions." On Aristotle's *eide* as modulating between "parts" and "wesenhafte inhärentia" (*contra* the Platonic usage) see F. Solmsen, Review of Rostagni's *La Poetica di Aristotele,* Gnomon 5 (1929), 402 n. 1.

[13] θ[α]υμα[στὸ]ν δ' αὐτοῦ from xi (xiv) 26 carries down to xii (xv) 1, and then again to col. xii (xv) 13 ([2b] here).

[14] For a supplement at col. xii (xv) 3 μ[± 12], μέροc-words come to mind, but Jensen's μ[ετέχειν

καὶ πράξεις καὶ π[ροcω-   5
ποποιί[αc]. **[2b]** εἰ δ' ἐν [τῆι
λέξει πεποιῆcθαί τ[ι
λέ]γει, κἀνταῦθ[α νὴ Δι' ο]ὐ-
κ ἔcτι τι πεποι[ῆcθαι το]ύ-
των χωρίc, ἀλλ' [ἴδι]ο[ν το]ῦ   10
cυνκεῖcθαι [τὴν] λέξιν τὸ
cυ]νκεῖcθαι [τὴν πρᾶξ]ιν εἶ-
ν]αι φαίνεταί μ[οι· τὸ δὲ] καὶ
τοῦ ποιητοῦ ταῦ]τα καὶ
δὴ] καὶ τὴν ὑπ[όθ]εcιν καὶ   15
τ[ὴν c]ύνθ[ε]cιν. [οὐ γ]ὰρ πάν-
τ[α ποι]ῶν οὗτ[όc ἐc]τιν.

[*paragraphos*]

[2b] But if [Neoptolemus] says (or: agrees)
that something has been (or: that these
have been) composed in *lexis*, even here,
surely, it isn't possible for anything to be
composed apart from these elements [sc.,
thought, *praxis*, and characterization], but
rather the *praxis*'[15] being composed appears to me to be a defining characteristic
of a *lexis*' being composed. [Astounding
too is the claim that] these things [are] also
[of the poet], viz., the *hypothesis* and the
synthesis. For the poet isn't responsible for
making (i.e. inventing) everything[16]

1-2 Jensen   **4** *vac* legit Mangoni: παc O μ[ετέχειν, ἀλλὰ μή] | τὰc
διανο[ίαc καὶ τάξεις Jensen   **5-6** Kenntenich π: O   **7-8** τ[ι |
λέ]γει Mangoni: τ[ι | πρέ]πει Jensen, qui]πει in P legit τ[αῦτα | λέ]γει
Asmis τ[ι ὁμο|λο]γεῖ e.g. Porter   **8-12** Kentenich et Jensen
10 [ἴδι]ο[ν το]ῦ·]ο[.᛬.]υ P]ο[.᛬.]υ O   **13-14** Jensen: φαίνεται,
μ[ᾶλλον δὲ] καὶ |[τοῦ ποιητοῦ ταῦ]τα Mangoni   **15** Kentenich et
Jensen   **16-17** οὐ γ]ὰρ πάν|τ[α ποι]ῶν Porter τ[ὴν c]ύνθ[ε]cιν·
[ὁ γ]ὰρ πάν|τ]α τηρ]ῶν οὗτ[όc ἐc]τιν Mangoni: τ[ὴν c]ύνθ[ε]cιν
[εἶν]αι παν|τ[ὶ δῆλ]ον οὗτ[όc φηc]ιν Jensen

First, a quick sketch of Neoptolemus' position is needed. Any reconstruction of
his system will inevitably have to be incomplete, as it seems certain that Philodemus,
at least in this section, is looking only for contradictions, not coherencies.[17] But the
major outlines ought to be recoverable just the same. The three *eide* of the "[poetic]
techne" (col. xi [xiv] 6, 22) Neoptolemus dubs "poet," *poema*, and *poesis*.[18] On the

---

is supported by the *Scholia to Dionysius Thrax's Art of Grammar* cited infra n. 24. The negative contrast
with διανοί[αc (supplied in line 4 by Jensen), is inevitable given the overall context and the objection
in **[2b]**.

[15] Cf. col. xiv (xvii) 17–18 (the same terms, partially conjectured); and col. ix (xii) 26–27 (*lexis*
versus *pragmata*). More of the same (Aristotelian) terminology appears earlier in col. ix (xii) 13–20:
mythoi, ethopoiia, lexis.

[16] I.e., many plots are traditional, and not the invention of the poet. Elsewhere Philodemus expresses
the same view (cf. text **[7]** below). For the use of ποιῶν in this exact sense, cf. Aristotle, *Poetics* 17.
1455b1; cf. *On Poems* 5 col. vii (x) 22 and col. viii (xi) 26–27 for the usage ὁ εὖ ποιῶν; and Appendix
B to this chapter. (In lines 13f. Mangoni in her edition reads ἐὼ δὲ] καὶ |[τὸ] ποι[ητοῦ ταῦτ]α, and in
16f., where she prints ὁ γ]ὰρ πάν|τ[α ποι]ῶν, in her commentary (p. 236) line 14 is given as [τὸ
ποιητοῦ ταῦτ]α and this is said to be an alternative restoration, while the papyrus at line 16, she writes,
does not exclude οὐ γ]άρ.)

[17] A fuller exposition may have been given in earlier columns of *On Poems* 5, as Jensen assumed; but
see Mangoni 1989, 131 n. 4.

[18] *Poema* and *poesis* will be used as transliterations for ποήμα (ποίημα) and πόηcιc (ποίηcιc)
throughout, reflecting the simplified orthography that for the most part appears in connection with the
theory of Neoptolemus of Parium.

face of it, the categories are emphatically exclusive. Moreover, it would seem that the last two categories carve up the substance of poems into two separate entities, "form" and "content," each implying separate skills which are to be mastered in sequence. This is the way in which Neoptolemus' scheme is universally taken.[19] As we shall see below, there are several reasons to doubt this easy reduction. The very formal nature of the distinctions being made should alert us to this danger.

1. By *poema*, or rather under *poema*, Neoptolemus meant to include "only" (μόνον) the *synthesis* of the *lexis*" ("verbal arrangement," often rendered as "form" or "style"),[20] and to exclude everything else ([2a]), which is to say, everything that falls under categories (2) and (3).[21]

2. Likewise, *poesis*: it is narrowly tied to the *hypothesis* (roughly equivalent to Aristotle's "plot");[22] in Philodemus' quotation or paraphrase, *poesis* covers "only the *hypothesis*," i.e, plot, *praxis*, characters and "thought," or if one prefers, content or "subject matter" (καὶ [τὸ] τῆ[ϲ] ποήϲεω[ϲ]‖ εἶναι τ[ῆ]ν ὑπόθεϲιν [μ]ό|νον, col. xi [xiv] 27).

3. Finally there is the "poet," who stands independently of his creation. To think for a moment with Neoptolemus: logically, the poet cannot be *identified* with the two above-named aspects of his poetry, and so, Neoptolemus reasons, he is yet one more *eidos* of the poetic art. Philodemus finds this mind-boggling, and it is. But Neoptolemus is not quite through. Having erected these neat logical partitions, he goes on to merge them together—to what extent is not entirely clear, thanks in part to a number of interpretive ambiguities (not to mention omissions) in Philodemus' account, and in part to the lacunae that stand at some of the crucial passages of these columns. It was once possible to assume that *poema* is somehow "linked" or "joined" to *poesis* (col. xii [xv] 35f.); a new reading of the text has taken away the textual support for this assumption, but not its logical force, which can be demonstrated in other ways.[23] It is just possible that *poema* is "of" *poesis*, in the sense that it pervades that which *poesis* also pervades at every moment (even if this resembles the view which Philodemus would claim as his own, on different grounds, at col. xi [xiv] 29).

[19] E.g., Jensen 1923, 105; Brink 1963, 68, 69; and, despite momentary hesitations, N. Greenberg, "The Use of *POIEMA* and *POIESIS*," *HSCPh* 45 (1961), 263–89 at 270, followed by Asmis 1992c, 213, 215, 217.

[20] "Style," Brink; "Gestalt," Jensen; but see Porter 1989, 149–150; and, correctly, Greenberg 1961 (above, n. 19), 268: "A *poiema* is a series of words embodying certain formal features, . . . not style, or form."

[21] *Poema*—like all of Neoptolemus' special terms—designates a category, but it also resembles a predicative mass term, as Thomas Rosenmeyer reminds me.

[22] Cf. col. vii (x) 25 for their apparent equation.

[23] εἰ δ[έ]‖ τὸ βέλ[τι]ϲτον, πῶϲ μᾶλλον | τῆϲ ποήϲεωϲ, ἦ καὶ τοῦτο ‖ [προϲ]ῆψεν; (Jensen). Mangoni's text reads at col. xi (xiv) 34ff., "If [he was claiming that] *poema* is [first in the sense of] better, how is it better than *poesis*, which [encompasses] it [sc. *poema*]?" (ἦ καὶ τοῦτο [πε‖ριείλ]ηφεν;). The thought is Philodemus' own, not Neoptolemus', and it refers to their quarrel over "containment" in col. xi (xiv) 29–35 (to be discussed below), if Mangoni's conjecture points in the right way. Alternatively, [εἴλ]ηφεν (?), which could simply mean *poesis* "receives this [label]," namely of being "better" (this claim would likewise be a contribution by Philodemus).

This could even follow from Philodemus' objection at col. xi [xiv] 35 ("the first thirty lines of the *Iliad* are *poema*, but surely not (οὐ μέντοι) *poesis*"), implying Neoptolemus' opposite view that the first thirty lines of the *Iliad* are simultaneously *poema* and *poesis*. If Jensen's conjectures in [2b] (col. xii [xv] 13–14) are right (and they arguably match the overall flow of Philodemus' exposition), both *hypothesis* and *synthesis* are, in a different sense (to be examined below), "of" the poet. Finally, and more securely, all three (*poetes, poema,* and *poesis*) are equally "of" the poetic *techne*, in the sense that they converge with the poetic *techne* they jointly comprise, as its three *eide*.

The various faces that Neoptolemus' poetic system presents appear to be held both together and apart by a series of more or less loosely constructed genitives (as in, "only the *hypothesis* is 'of' the *poesis*"; compare μ[ετέχειν? col. xii [xv] 3, "partake of"; and μ]ὴ κοινωνε[ῖν col. xii [xv] 19, "(not) share in"),[24] constructions which can be (and have been) filled out in different ways, depending on how one conceives the system as a whole. Obviously, if you believe that *poesis* encompasses *poema* (for instance, if you believe that the features defining *poesis* imply those defining *poema*, but not the reverse) you must also hold—in the face of Neoptolemus' own wording—that whatever belongs to (is found in) *poema* at the same time belongs to *poesis* (without defining the latter). Neoptolemus is clearly doing his best to block this move. He is not, however, describing three different objects. He is looking at the same object in three different ways. And if we wish to sort out his various distinctions we will need to attend closely to the shifting level of his gaze. Let us take as our starting-point the premise, derived from the language in which the *poema, poesis, poetes* distinctions are couched, that Neoptolemus' genitives isolate the defining, *logical* properties of the elements of the poetic art (*techne poetike*) and their interrelations; that these properties are *aspectual*; and that the "of's" are both *stipulative*, signalling aspectual inclusions and exclusions, and *variable*, permitting elements (or aspects) to be viewed as standing distinct at some levels, and as coextensive or merged together at others. The triad is, in other words, triune.

It is easy to assume that Philodemus does not present us with the actual definitions which Neoptolemus gave to his trio of terms (at least, not in these columns), and that therefore we cannot be certain what they were.[25] But Neoptolemus could not have been any clearer than he was:

[2c] Philodemus, *On Poems* 5 col. xi (xiv) 5–11

ἀτόπως δ[ὲ] κα[ὶ τὸν] τὴν | τέχνην κ[αὶ τήν] δ[ύν]α|μιν ἔχοντα τὴ[ν ποι]ητι|κὴν ε[ἶ]δος [π]αρίς[τη]ςι | τῆ[ς] τέ[χ]νη[ς μ]ετὰ τοῦ | ποήματος καὶ τῆς πο|ήςεως.[26]

He absurdly juxtaposes [or represents] the person who posseses the art of

---

[24] These are confirmed from a distance by the *Scholia on Dionysius Thrax's Art of Grammar* (*Scholia in Dionysii Thracis Artem Grammaticam*, ed. Alfred Hilgard, in *Grammatici Graeci* 1.3 [Leipzig, 1901]), 449,23–26, where Neoptolemic definitions (though not his emphases) reoccur: ποιητὴς δὲ ὁ κατὰ μετουςίαν τῆς ποιητικῆς ⟨τὸ⟩ ὄνομα ἐςχηκὼς τεχνίτης; and 481, 13: μετέχων. "Participation" here is logical "belonging," nothing more.

[25] Greenberg 1961 (above, n. 19), 278.　　　　[26] Trans. Brink 1963, 58 with modifications.

writing poetry and has the power to do so [i.e., the 'poet'] as an *eidos* along with the *poema* and the *poesis*.

The term *eidos*, vouched for as Neoptolemus' own in col. xi (xiv) 24 ("it is risible to call the poet an '*eidos* of the *techne*'") and in col. xii (xv) 28 (see [5]), can only mean what it does elsewhere: species, kind, form or (by logical extension) aspect.[27] *Eidos* for Neoptolemus is in fact all these things, but most powerfully and simply of all it denotes, on Neoptolemus' theory, "aspect."[28]

Neoptolemus' theory, like Aristotle's own formalism, tends toward sharp aspectual rather than quantitative distinctions. But unlike Aristotle and in contrast to him, Neoptolemus follows the logic of Aristotelian essential distinctions without adopting Aristotle's essentialism. It should be stressed that for Neoptolemus these distinctions are logical fictions and methodological conveniences; they can be "evidenced" *in* parts or wholes of poems or poetic processes (what Neoptolemus ranges under the poetic art, and what he "concretizes," again aspectually, as *ergasia*, the actual workmanship in a poem; see below), but they are not identical *with* either the parts or the wholes of poems or their being composed. All of this may account in part for Neoptolemus' roundabout definitions of *poema* and *poesis*. Philodemus in any case finds this logic-chopping baseless: if the "poet," who is endowed with art and "poetic capacity" (*poetike dynamis*), is ridiculously designated as an *eidos,* "how are these latter (viz., *poema* and *poesis*) [*eide* of the *techne*] too?" (col. xi [xiv] 11–12). Philodemus has simply missed the point. It is not that there is more forthcoming in the way of new and fuller definitions; Neoptolemus' definitions are self-sufficiently contained in the sequel of col. xi (xiv) (see nos. 1 and 2 above, p. 104), which gives the answer to Philodemus' question. *Poema* and *poesis* are eide of the poetic art because Neoptolemus has stipulated them to be so.

If this description of Neoptolemus' definitions is correct, then it follows that *poema* is identifiable in (but not identical with) any part and in the whole of whatever *poesis* is another aspect of (namely, a poem or a poem's *techne*), but it is that poem viewed *just in respect of* its verbal composition—in view of its rhythm, meter, etc., in short, in view of the *synthesis* of its *lexis*, as this came to be defined in the tradition of the "*synthesis*-doctrine" which finally achieved text-book status in Dionysius' *De compositione verborum* (Περὶ ϲυνθέϲεωϲ ὀνομάτων). *Poesis* is identifiable in (but not identical with) whatever *poema* is another aspect of, but it is that poem viewed *just in respect of* plot or plot-related items (i.e., in respect of *hypothesis*). *Poesis*, in other words, picks out an *eidos* (formal aspect) of *poetike*; *hypothesis* gives us the contents of that category. Similarly, the category of *poema* is specified by *synthesis*. And the poet is neither of these things, that is, neither of these categories nor their

---

[27] *Eidos* is frequently a synonym for formal and final cause in Aristotle (Bonitz, *Index* s.v. 4). On the logical extension from this to "aspect," see A. Code, "Aristotle: Essence and Accident," *Philosophical Grounds of Rationality*, eds. R. Grandy and R. Warner (Oxford 1983), 411–39 at 412–13 and 438 with n. 80.

[28] If the "*synthesis* of *lexis*" indicates the contents of the category picked out by *poema* (see also Benvenga, "Per la critica e l'estetica di Filodemo," *RAAN* 26 [1951], 246), it is no less significant that "*synthesis*" can be used interchangeably with *poema* to refer more or less abstractly either to that category or to its contents (as in [4] below, where the triad comes out as *poetes, hypothesis, poema*).

contents. If this is all that can be squeezed out of Neoptolemus' definitions, it is because there was nothing left to say about them.

If we recall, additionally, that Neoptolemus radically sunders the *synthesis* of the *lexis* (the *poema*) from the "thoughts" (**[2ab]** and **[2d]**), which is to say, from a poem's structuring ideas or meanings, his criteria suddenly take on a richer sense, and their latent (and unsettling) implication looms into view. The distinction that Neoptolemus intends by opposing *poema* to *poesis* is, inevitably, a distinction between a poem viewed as a vehicle of meaning or as a structure of intelligibility (*hypothesis*) and that *same* poem now viewed as devoid of, or divorced from, meaning and intelligibility (*synthesis*). Certainly, *hypothesis* connotes much more than "theme" or "plot," as the presence of "thought" (*dianoia*) in **[2a]** shows. *Hypothesis* signifies poetic discourse *qua* bearing meaning—at the very least, characters' meaning, or "reasoning" (which may be all that *dianoia* stands for in this plainly Aristotelian context). But under any description, Aristotelian or Hellenistic, *hypothesis* covers meaning generally (the meanings expressed in or by a poetic composition), which is to say all that poetry's compositional properties fail to account for. And the reverse holds for *synthesis*, which just is defined as what *hypothesis* is not.

Taken together, Neoptolemus' twin concepts define poems (compositions) viewed as wholes. Thus, *hypothesis* and *synthesis* are both mutually exclusive (at the level of their definition) and mutually exhaustive of what is to be found in any instance of poetry. Just to view *synthesis* "alone" (*μόνον*) without taking in *hypothesis* (and vice versa) is to make this very isolation of meaning: in Hellenistic criticism, *synthesis* regularly denotes the arrangement of euphonic elements without regard for meaning; the division between non-semantic and semantic, or between sound and sense, is a straightforward consequence of the *synthesis*-doctrine that was embraced (along with its consequences) within a tradition of criticism in which *synthesis* was promoted at the cost of all else. Neoptolemus' own theory reflects this tradition, though to what extent remains to be decided (see Appendices B and C to this chapter).[29] In any case, an isolation like this is surely one of Philodemus' prime targets in the columns on Neoptolemus, and the more so when we recall the way in which Philodemus puts us in mind of the problem at the very outset of his critique, in the same breath as he mentions Neoptolemus' name:

[2d] Philodemus, *On Poems* 5 cols. x (xiii) 33–xi (xiv) 1

ἀ]λλὰ | μὴν ὅ [γε Νεοπ]τόλεμος | οὐκ ὀρ[θῶς ἔδοξ]ε τὴν σύν|θεcιν [τῆc λέξε]ω[c τ]ῶν ||[xi] διανοημ[άτων χωρί]|ζειν . . .

Now, Neoptolemus wrongly [seemed] to separate the *synthesis* of the *lexis* from the thoughts [or: meanings] . . .

Surely the idea of "separation" (*χωρίζειν*) attacked here[30] is meant to encapsulate,

---

[29] See however Greenberg 1961, 281: "There is no reason to believe that Neoptolemus explicitly espoused the theory that the *poiema* could be evaluated apart from its content." (For the same argument, cf. Asmis 1992c, 222.) On the contrary, there is every reason to do so, if Neoptolemus' distinction is purely aspectual.

[30] The thought of "separation" is suggested by the genitives and the context; the word itself has to be conjectured (based on *χωρίc* in col. xii [xv] 10 **[2b]**).

like a header, the most disreputable features of Neoptolemus' poetic theory, just as the identical theme (the threat of isolation, χωρίc) saliently obtrudes again into the foreground at the crucial moment represented in [2a] (irrespective of the possibly restricted sense of διανοίαc there). Philodemus has understood a central implication of Neoptolemus' theory, whether he found this in the form of a claim parallel to [2d] or whether he saw it in the mutual divorcement of *synthesis* and *hypothesis*, which as we saw requires this very separation. Philodemus is not objecting to the separation per se (it is one he is capable of making himself). What is objectionable, on his view, must be the failure to coordinate these two aspects of poetry in an acceptable way. As we shall see below, Neoptolemus' divisions, which are of a purely logical kind, exist as it were only to suspend their relations to one another: they are utterly separate, as Philodemus complains. Only insofar as they have no existence (no real existence outside their logical definition) do they come back into contact with one another, indistinguishably, in actual poems. But in order to see just what Neoptolemus' theory amounts to we will need to turn briefly to a parallel theory from another context altogether. It is one that is often adduced in connection with Neoptolemus.

Posidonius' much-cited definition of poetry, from the close of the Hellenistic age of criticism, brings out the very sort of distinction that Neoptolemus has in mind (but which he did not invent). It also sets up a useful contrast:

[3] Posidonius (Diogenes Laertius 7.60 = F 44 Edelstein-Kidd)

ποίημα δέ ἐcτιν . . . λέξιc ἔμμετροc ἢ ἔνρυθμοc μετὰ ⟨κατα⟩cκευῆc τὸ λογοειδὲc ἐκβεβηκυῖα· [τὸν MSS: del. Kaibel] ἔνρυθμον δὲ εἶναι τὸ 'γαῖα μεγίcτη καὶ Διὸc αἰθήρ.' ποίηcιc δέ ἐcτι cημαντικὸν ποίημα, μίμηcιν περίεχον θείων καὶ ἀνθρωπείων.

Poema, as Posidonius writes in his introductory work *On Lexis*, is "*lexis* in meter or lexis with rhythm and with poetic elaboration, departing [in either case] from the form of prose." An example of rhythmic [verse] is "Greatest Earth and Aether of Zeus" [Eur. fr. 839, 1 Nauck]. *Poesis* is "*poema* conveying meaning, containing a mimesis of things divine and mortal."

Posidonius is clearly borrowing familiar terms. And the points of interest go beyond the contrast, which one might be tempted to apply here, between content and form. It has been suggested that the presence, in Posidonius, of cημαντικόc ("conveying meaning") "reflects the division of dialectic into cημαίνοντα [signifiers] and cημαινόμενα [signifieds]," and that this reflection is idiosyncratically Stoic.[31] But the link with dialectic is tenuous, and it sends us down the wrong path. The division reflected is not between signifiers and signifieds, but, first, between sense-bearing and non-sense bearing *lexis*, in other words between *lexis qua* significant (cημαντική) and *lexis qua* measured or rhythmic (ἔμμετροc ἢ ἔνρυθμοc).[32] Nor is the reflection uniquely Stoic, let alone original with the Stoa. It is generically poetic (literary-critical) in nature.[33] Observe that Posidonius is not isolating his specimen

---

[31] I. G. Kidd, *Posidonius*, vol. 2.1 *The Commentary* (Cambridge 1985), 198, in the wake of Brink 1963, 66 n. 1.   [32] See M. Gigante, "cημαντικὸν ποίημα," *PP* 16 (1961), 40 with n. 1.

[33] Kidd's comment (rather, his paraphrase), "ποίημα represents style, metre and artistic form," is closer to the mark (1988 [above, n. 31], 198). "Things divine and human" is usually cited as attesting to

poema because "it conveys no complete sense," while *poesis* does.[34] The decisive response to such a view is to point out that a completed syntactical sense unit with a self-contained meaning will hardly satisfy Posidonius' requirements for "meaningful," as the second half of his stipulations makes plain: a significant *poema* will be "a *mimesis* of things divine and human" and not just any mimesis, let alone any meaningful *poema*. Nor is Posidonius concerned to show that the fragment from Euripides' *Chrysippus* carries an incomplete sense. On such a view, *semantikon poema* would be either a contradiction in terms or a pleonasm. (A *poema* cannot be both semantically incomplete by definition and semantically complete.) *Semantikon* in Posidonius' text can not, therefore, just mean "linguistically meaningful" or "syntactically meaningful" (either of which count as a dialectical distinction in the Stoic theory of grammar).[35] The distinction being drawn by Posidonius is, to reverse a phrase by Dionysius of Halicarnassus, evidently a literary-critical and not a dialectical one.[36]

So, far from isolating his specimen *poema* because it conveys no complete sense, Posidonius is isolating the sample because (or rather, insofar as) it conveys no sense whatsoever. A combination of two anapaests, and thus likely to be perceived as a complete metrical unit from a choral ode, the fragment is pure *synthesis* of *lexis*, in the way that Neoptolemus and other literary critics used that term: it is *lexis* exhibiting rhythmical and euphonic properties considered "apart from the ideas (or: meaning)," and these "lexic" properties give no immediate link to the poetic properties of a poem viewed as signifying as a whole (as a *mimesis*, with all that being a *mimesis* entails); indeed, in the extended Peripatetic way of thinking, *noema* ("thought") can be used in this quite different sense of completing a whole, namely as a unifying principle of intelligibility in a poem (*Scholia on Dionysius of Thrax's Art of Grammar* 481, 16 Hilgard). The *synthesis* that is opposed to this, on one view of *synthesis*

"a Stoic description of the world or universe" (see Brink 1963, 66 n. 1), but the Stoa surely held no monopoly on this blanket formula. Here it has a greater proximity to Euripides' *ipsissima verba*; cf. the verse that follows in the same fragment, ὁ μὲν ἀνθρώπων καὶ θεῶν γενέτωρ. For the relevance of Theophrastean precedents, see R. Janko, *Aristotle on Comedy: Towards a Reconstruction of Poetics II* (Berkeley and Los Angeles 1984), 49–50 and 112 n. 35. Boyancé sees in Posidonius nothing more remarkable than the influence of Aristotle ("A Propos de l'*Art poétique*," *RPh* 10 [1936], 27). Cf. *Scholia on Dionysius' Thrax's Art of Grammar* 481, 10–11 Hilgard: ὑποκειμένων ⟨μὲν⟩ θείων τε καὶ ἀνθρωπίνων (not a hint of Stoicism).

[34] Kidd 1988 (above, n. 31), 198; cf. Brink 1963, 66 ("so long as its sense is complete"). The word "complete" may have insinuated itself into the discussion from two sources: the contrast with "whole poem" (suggested by Philodemus and by any quantitative reading of *poesis*), or the (Aristotelian) designation of *poesis* as a teleologically (i.e., *formally*) complete and coherent *hypothesis*: ποίησις δὲ κυρίως ἡ διὰ μέτρων ἐντελὴς ὑπόθεσις (*Scholia on Dionysius of Thrax's Art of Grammar* 449, 24 Hilgard).

[35] Compare the *Scholia on Dionysius of Thrax's Art of Grammar* given below, n. 81, where *poema* is labelled a *phrasis* "prior" to syntactic sense, but where being "prior" does not rule out the co-presence of sound and sense. Posidonius' formal definition seems, moreover, to be lurking in the background (*Scholia on Dionysius of Thrax's Art of Grammar* 481, 10–11 Hilgard).

[36] *De compositione verborum*, c. 4, p. 22, 13 Usener-Radermacher. A poem's meaningfulness is a concept that recurs repeatedly in Philodemus' battle against his opponents. Cf. *P.Herc.* 994 col. xxxiii 12 (p. 103 Sbordone): ἑρμηνείαν πρᾶγμα σημαίνουσαν; *P.Herc.* 1074 fr. xii 17 (p. 197 Sbordone): σημα[ίνε δια|ν]οήμασιν; *P.Herc.* 1074 fr. xxi 9 + 1081 fr. viii 9 (p. 201 Sbordone): λέξεις ἐκ τοῦ [π]ως συντί|θεσθαι διανόημα σημαι|νούσας, "*lexeis* which signify a meaning as a result of being composed in a certain way."

(which is not the content/form view), is the linguistic equivalent of musical sounds, "sounds with absolutely no meaning at all" (φθόγγοι . . . οὐδὲν ἁπλῶς cημαίνον-τεc), but powerfully evocative of strong emotions nonetheless, as ps.-Longinus sets out the subject (varying the traditional theme) in *On the Sublime* cc. 39–40 (here, 39.2). This is an aspectual distinction which divorces sound (words as phonic) from sense (words as sense-bearing).

It should be noted what this divorcement of sound and sense does *not* entail. The phonic aspects presuppose the semantics to which, *qua* aspects, they are opposed. "Words as phonic" are not debarred from being, in the end, "semantic" too.[37] For ps.-Longinus, they are simply to be contrasted with words that may have the same meaning, but without the same rhythmically produced and physically perceived effect —and it is this latter, not the meaning, which gives the "criterial" difference. In principle, the contrast does not even have to involve different words or ordering: the difference can be perceptual, or imagined. A quick reference to Aristotle is again useful here. At *Poetics* 4.1448b18 Aristotle draws a solid line between visual images appreciated not *qua* imitation (ᾗ μίμημα) but *qua* (on account of their) workmanship (διὰ τὴν ἀπεργαcίαν), their color, finish, etc. Aristotle knew how to posit, abstractly, the separation of a "purely" material, sensuous, or aesthetic realm. But he nowhere makes the concession to literary objects that he makes to visual objects here, namely that they can be enjoyed (which is not to say, conceptualized) *qua* "the forms, textures, patterns and sounds of art, apprehended in and for themselves and not as the medium of mimetic significance."[38] There was simply no room for such a conception in his view of poetics. Not so for poetic theories in another vein.

As with Neoptolemus, the contrast with *poesis* in Posidonius' definition is there to bring out this very conceptual difference. Boyancé's gloss on *semantikon* ("qui a un sujet et une signification") and his subsequent expansion ("ou encore simplement [la présence] d'une *hypothesis* au sens large") are exactly to the point.[39] *Poesis* for Posidonius is distinguished by the very feature that is distinctive of Neoptolemus' *hypothesis*. But the similarities with Neoptolemus do not stop here. Posidonius' *poesis* can be viewed in at least two ways: as "signifying" in the largest poetic sense, however he defined that to be;[40] and as continuing to exhibit the non-significant, poetic and euphonic properties that define *poema*. Being a "significant *poema*" thus carries a two-fold burden: it is to be both "significant" *and* to be *poema*, in the technical senses that these terms could assume. And by now it should be obvious that if *poesis* can exhibit these two contrastive and opposed kinds of quality, then Posidonius must be applying them aspectually: the self-same object (*poesis*) can be both

---

[37] Nor are they debarred from being "complete" in another sense: the phrase from Euripides forms a complete metrical unit (constituting a verse, in anapaests, from a choral stasimon; cf. "*mele* and *stasima*," Sextus Empiricus, *Adv. math.* 6.17), as the full text of the fragment shows.

[38] S. Halliwell, *Aristotle's Poetics* (Chapel Hill, NC 1986), 67.

[39] Boyancé 1936 (above, n. 33), 26 and 27. Boyancé's overtranslation of τὸ λογοειδὲς ἐκβεβηκυῖα, "qui sort des limites du raisonnable" (26) adds an intriguing emphasis to the difference that is clear in any case: see *On Poems* 5 col. xv (xviii) 19–22: τὴν δὲ διά|[νοι]αν ἀλλόκοτον καὶ πα[ρ]|ἐκβεβηκυῖαν τὸν κοι|νὸν νοῦν, where the distinction at stake is a *poetic* meaning that diverges from a usual (viz., unpoetic) meaning. Cf. also Gigante 1961 (above, n. 32), 43.

[40] See Kidd 1988 (above, n. 31), 199 for a few suggestions that tie Posidonius' definition more closely and plausibly to Stoic orthodoxy and that modify the meaning of "complete sense" from p. 198.

significative (*qua hypothesis*) and non-significative "au sens large" (*qua synthesis*, viz., *qua poema*), and it can be both of these simultaneously, but only when beheld from two competing perspectives which have to be superimposed on one another. In Neoptolemus' somewhat differently weighted terms: a poem can be simultaneously viewed as *poesis* and as *poema*. This further explains why Posidonius, unlike Philodemus, can accept that the whole *Iliad* may be regarded as *poema*, albeit as *semantikon poema*. It is a powerful, logical maneuver which entitles Posidonius to the claim.[41] Philodemus, by contrast, is unwilling to grant this strong, aspectual claim any validity. *Poema*, for him, is not defined by the qualitative features it has for Neoptolemus or for Posidonius.

Having established the aspectual basis of Posidonius' *poema/poesis* distinction (it is not quite a dichotomy in the sense that it is for Neoptolemus, for whom it is actually part of a trichotomy), it is easy to see how the one set of terms (*synthesis/hypothesis*) is convertible to the other ("without regard for thoughts [meanings]"/ "with regard for thoughts [meanings]"); and how the second set of terms more explicitly brings out the contrast between semantic and non-semantic in poems that is involved in the first. The latter contrast is aspectual in the way that the former is too, and this holds true for both Posidonius and Neoptolemus. But here a crucial difference sets in. For Posidonius, the aspectual distinction cuts across the *synthesis/hypothesis* axis only; for Neoptolemus, it simultaneously cuts across the *poema/poesis* axis as well. Both would have agreed that the Euripides fragment is an example of *synthesis* of *lexis*. Neoptolemus would undoubtedly have conceded that the individual *lexeis*, the words or expressions, have a recognizable meaning. But if the reading of his poetics given so far has any chance of being consistent, he would not have accepted the fragmentary *synthesis* (or the first thirty lines of the *Iliad*) as a specimen example of *poema*, nor would he have countenanced the idea of *semantikon poema*: that would have represented a contradiction to his system. On Neoptolemus' scheme, *poema* is a category that helps isolate *synthesis*, which is to say, the relevant material features of a poem; but *poema* has no material existence per se. The same holds mutatis mutandis for *poesis*, which cannot be confused with the category of *poema*, and still less identified with the idea of *semantikon poema*. A little more background will be needed to see why this is so.

Posidonius is embroiling himself in a controversy that may well have stemmed from Neoptolemus. But it was a controversy that was fuelled by other, related literary debates, and one of these is directly relevant to the issues at hand. From Philodemus (*P.Herc.* 1676 fr. ii p. 223 Sbordone) we know that it was an open question amongst literary critics whether the "meanings," the *semainomena* (or the "signifying words," *semainonta*; the text is uncertain) of Homer's *Iliad* began from the "first word" (*menin*, "I sing of the *wrath*..."), and accordingly whether the allegorical meanings (the *hyponoiai*) underlying the surface meanings also began from there too. Wherever they failed to agree, it follows that the text untouched (as yet) by signifiers and

---

[41] And not, as it could be objected, an inconsistent terminology, which would allow *poema* a "Neoptolemic" sense in its first occurrence (or else "single verse"), and "poem" in the second: *semantikon poema* by itself proves that we are in the ambit of stipulative, and uncommon, definitions. περιέχον shows that what is *poema* is being viewed *qua* conveying mimesis. At this level, *poema* and *poesis* coalesce into one again.

signifieds would have given a footing merely to letters, sounds, and any poetic patterns based on these (i.e., *synthesis*), with no obvious relation to meaning. Alternatively, if "meaningfulness" has to do with only the largest signifying patterns that are to be found in poems (*à la* Posidonius' epic and even cosmic definition), then the first verses of the *Iliad* give us meaning, but not yet Meaning. "Meaning," however we define it, seems here to be tied in some essential way to the semantics of poetic wholes (i.e., *hypothesis*), and not just to the semantics of individual words: why else would the "significance" of the first words of the *Iliad* have been disputed? *Semainomena* is of course ambiguous between these two kinds of meaning (upper and lower case meaning), and it may have been just this ambiguity which touched off the debate. A similar ambiguity could have as easily swirled around *menis* itself. Did the word, hotly contested in the scholia for its moral implications anyway, by itself "signify" the thematic *hypothesis* it was traditionally taken to announce emblematically as well?[42] Or was it to be viewed either as semantically incomplete or worse still as semantically surd, detached from all sense whatsoever and yet (in either case) susceptible of metrical, rhythmical and euphonic analysis? Undoubtedly some (like Crates, in the wake of certain *kritikoi,* or Critics) would have cheerfully latched onto both positions, depending on the focus of their analysis: meaning could be required or provisionally dispensed with (or one could try to conjoin these two kinds of analysis). But for these amphibian Critics, the difference was aspectual (and hence, controversial): *all* words could at *one* level be analyzed independently of their semantic and poetic meanings, which is to say in terms of their phonic values alone (i.e., their *synthesis*). Posidonius' testimony is unique, then, not in raising the issue of the range of signification (that was bequeathed to him in the critical tradition, in an assortment of forms), but in explicitly bringing together *poema* and *poesis* into a single entailment, *semantikon poema* (with the latter, *poesis,* involving the former, *poema,* necessarily). Such an entailment has been denied to obtain in the case of Neoptolemus.[43] But if his system has been correctly laid out here, Neoptolemus not only held that *poesis* entails *poema,* but that the entailment is reciprocal. Let us follow this thread to its end.

Neoptolemus could have said, with Posidonius and some modern scholars, that *poema* just is *poesis* viewed under the aspect of *synthesis* (in a one-way implication: *poesis* implies *poema,* though the reverse implication does not hold).[44] But this would have been an imprecise gloss, for the *poema/poesis* distinction for Neoptolemus takes on meaning only in relation to some third entity, like a poem or the poetic art, which in turn motivates the aspectual identities of the pair of terms.[45] In this respect, then, *poema* and *poesis* are rigidly distinct, and can not be identified *with* one

---

[42] This emerges in the sequel (fr. v), where the epics are said to announce (ἀπαγγελεῖν) their themes: the wrath of Achilles, the much-wandering and suffering Odysseus. The view that *proemia* broadcast themes was a traditional conceit of literary criticism. Cf. Homer, Schol. A 1a (Erbse).

[43] He "does not appear to make *poesis* entail *poema*" (Brink 1963, 69); cf. Kidd 1988 (above, n. 31), 198.

[44] Schmidt, "Nugae Herculanenses," *RhM* 92 (1943), 51, 54 n. 55; Greenberg 1961 (above, n. 19), 280 and 281; Brink 1963, 69 and 70 n. 1.

[45] Motivates, but not necessarily grounds them in some hierarchical relationship. This difference is clearer in the case of Aristotle, where *mythos* is not only an aspect: it is causally prior to a tragedy (its formal and final cause). More on this below.

another. But by the same token, each of the terms is meaningful only relative to its congeners. So here it must be true that *poema* implies *poesis*, and vice versa; one cannot be had without the other; they enjoy no independent existence. But neither do they exist "independently" in a poem. Hence, we must say, there can be no *examples* of a *poema* either, only the signs of its presence, of its "applicability," if you will. Moreover, each of the aspects must be projected onto the background assumption of a whole poem, even when none is at hand (as in the exemplary cases of a fragment or excerpt). The very idea of *hypothesis* by itself presumes an integral poem,[46] and *poema* is thinkable only in relation to the presumption of *hypothesis*. It should be noted in passing, since this issue too has been confused, that the standard guiding criterion in the realm of *poesis* is the integrity of plot (the quality of a poem's *semainomena* or "meanings"); bulk (quantity) is a secondary concern, subordinated to the first. In order to clarify the priorities, one might say with Aristotle that the poem must have a minimum of magnitude (τι μέγεθος), just enough to allow for the suitable development of a "whole action" from beginning (to middle) to end (*Poetics* 7. 1450b25). (Philodemus, in contrast, will settle for a quantity large enough to embrace substance [ideas, plots, etc.] and important enough to subordinate style.) I leave aside the question concerning that whole category of poems which lack any clear "emplotment," e.g., lyric poems. Neoptolemus would have had all the materials he needed to defend his schematism even here, had he so wished.[47] In any event, it should be clear that Neoptolemus would never have endorsed the concept of *semantikon poema*. For Posidonius, *poesis* and *poema* can be predicated of each other; for Neoptolemus, they can only be predicated of the poetic art.

Now to complete the schema, we turn to the third leg of the tripod. *Poema* and *poesis* have already been accounted for. The poet fits neither of these categories, but he or she is also undeniably part of the poetic activity[48] and, in some sense too, part (a contributing part) of the poetic result of which *poema* and *poesis* are aspectually parts too: the poet falls out of the picture whenever we focus intensively and exclusively upon either of the other categories, and comes back into view whenever we adopt a more natural (or more familiar) perspective, and regard the poet as necessarily involved in "his" or "her" poem at all of its moments. In the same way, the poem *qua poema* draws our focus away from the *poesis and* from the *poetes*. Any "weakening" concessions to these partitions, to the extent that Neoptolemus may or simply

---

[46] Cf. *Scholia on Dionysius of Thrax's Art of Grammar* 449, 24–26 Hilgard: "*poesis* properly speaking is a self-contained subject (*hypothesis*) expressed in verse, with a beginning, middle, and end" (ποίησις δὲ κυρίως ἡ διὰ μέτρων ἐντελὴς ὑπόθεσις ἔχουσα ἀρχὰς καὶ μέσα καὶ πέρατα).

[47] Neoptolemus evidently developed his system with the Homeric poems in mind (col. xiii [xvi] 13), read perhaps formally as tragedies (as in all Aristotle-based criticism); and of course Aristotle was notoriously thin on lyric poetics. But Neoptolemus' escape clause is the range of interpretations to which "plot," "thought" (or "meaning"), and "characterization" can be subjected (Greek lyric poems standardly imply a situation or context which minimally involves these elements). See further A. Carson, "'Just for the Thrill': Sycophantizing Aristotle's *Poetics*," *Arion*, 3rd Series, 1 (1990), 142–54; and the discussion of Sappho in Greenberg 1961, 269.

[48] "The *poet* is the craftsman who gets his name from *being part of the poetic art*" (ποιητὴς δὲ ὁ κατὰ μετουσίαν τῆς ποιητικῆς ⟨τὸ⟩ ὄνομα ἐσχηκὼς τεχνίτης, *Scholia on Dionysius of Thrax's Art of Grammar* 449, 23 Hilgard). Primarily male poets are envisaged, as is usually the case in ancient poetics.

could have allowed his categories to run together, suggest nothing more than what common sense dictates. They do not efface the logic of the aspectual distinctions; they simply reinforce the idea that those distinctions are just logical aspects.[49]

If Neoptolemus' system is rigorously aspectual, Philodemus' objections are consistently partitive, converting the aspects back into part/whole relations. A pair of instances will serve as illustrations. In col. xi (xiv) Philodemus remarks, "It is astounding of him to claim that the *hypothesis* is of the *poesis* only, (1) *since both poema and everything* [*else*] *are entirely of poesis* (καὶ τοῦ ποήματο[ς καὶ]‖ πάν-των ὅλως τῆς ποής[ε]‖ως ὄντων), for (2) a *poesis* is also a *poema*, like the *Iliad*, while the first thirty lines are a *poema* but surely not a *poesis*" (cols. xi [xiv] 26–xii [xv] 1). The italicized portion (1) is a contested clause. Grammatically, the genitive absolute could express the view of either Neoptolemus or Philodemus, although the general flow of the argument speaks more in favor of Philodemus here; which doesn't rule out a superficial overlap in views, left uncredited by Philodemus. Elsewhere, he may show a willingness to state the content/form distinction in an aspectual and hence non-partitive way, but his concessions here point up how differently he construes the force of that distinction from the way Neoptolemus does. Neoptolemus held *poema* and *poesis* to be mutually entailing: if Neoptolemus stated (i), he had nothing more in mind than this; Philodemus could not quite bring himself to this admission. "Entirely" (literally, "wholly") earmarks Philodemus' conception. The part/whole schema is how grammarians would later construe the difference ("*poema* is part of *poesis*," *Scholia on Dionysius Thrax's Art of Grammar* 449, 26 Hilgard); more relevantly here, Philodemus holds that *poesis* somehow "contains" *poema*: it designates the greater "whole." But this is not Neoptolemus' view, as the objection by itself shows. It is Philodemus who has (reductively) fastened onto quantitative distinctions with all the hierarchical differences they imply, not Neoptolemus, who on this head, so far as we can tell, makes no claims as to quantity, containment, or subordination. Brink states it for the most part well:

> Neoptolemus alone . . . pays attention to the abstract features of style and matter. He does not identify *poema* with a small poem or with part of a larger, nor does he identify *poesis* with a larger and unified epic poem such as the *Iliad*. All he is doing, at any rate in the . . . relevant excerpts . . ., is to discuss poetic features—wording and content.[50]

Brink, too, is making the likely assumption that the genitive absolute ("since . . .") in (1), and the following sentence in (2) introduced with γάρ in col. xi (xiv), are Philodemus' interventions. Philodemus is disregarding Neoptolemus' usage, in order to refute his meaning. In (1), *poema* is an individually crafted line or unit, like a proem; it "belongs to" *poesis* (a whole poem like the *Iliad*, dignified by its thematic unity) in the sense that a part belongs to a whole, and in the further sense that the special features it displays ("stylistic" features) are subordinate to the larger concerns of the whole. The relation is not reversible, and it is exhaustive (ὅλως). This

---

[49] See Brink 1963, 70 on one of these re-conflations: "It makes sense that he then proceeded to put together again what he had first put asunder." But I doubt that Neoptolemus is guilty of "logical inconsistency" (*ibid.*).   [50] Brink 1963, 68.

sense of *poema* conflates the category with its contents, and presumes that *synthesis* must be localized somehow "within" *poesis* (and that it is not, on the contrary, coextensive with it). When Philodemus states, on the other hand, that "*poesis* is a *poema*, like the *Iliad*," viz. (2), he is reverting, confusingly, to a non-stipulative, non-Neoptolemic, and commonplace meaning of "poem": *poesis* simply defines for him the essential elements of what any poem contains. A reader of the Philodemus columns has to be on the alert for sudden shifts of terrain like this.[51]

Appearances notwithstanding (especially those appearances that Philodemus would have us regard), it is Neoptolemus who achieves the greater degree of conceptual power, by making *hypothesis* into an abstract particular (or as he would say, into an *eidos*). And it is Philodemus' definition that in the end proves to be cumbrous and unwieldy, in part due to his failure to spell out the exact function of *poesis* and its relation to a "poem" (compare his vague "*and everything* [*else*]" in [1]). But it would be wrong to assume that Philodemus has any special interest in clarifying, to a critic's satisfaction, terms like *poesis* or *poema* or their counterparts (*hypothesis* and *synthesis*). It is difficult to take seriously the various alternatives to Neoptolemus' criteria and labels which Philodemus proposes earlier in the same column, at col. xi (xiv) 13: "he would have been better advised to call the disposition of the material (*diatheseis*) '*poesis*,' even better, to call the works '*poemata*,' and the *poeseis* 'like webs (οἷ[ον] ὑ|φη)'." Philodemus is casting wildly about, and getting nowhere in the process, probably deliberately (by offering alternatives to Neoptolemus' "far-fetched" attempt to consistently stretch a single word-radical to cover a genus and its three species[52]). Commentators have tended to take his irony for his opinion. But Philodemus, had he encountered it, would have found the definition, "*poesis* is like a web" risible; he discounts far more precise claims.[53] Positive theorizing is not part of his game; nor does he hold any brief for the principle of interpretive charity. Philodemus' prime concern, here as everywhere, is to reduce to ashes whatever theory his critical eye beholds. This alone ought to warn us against attributing too much confusion to Neoptolemus. Greenberg's well-considered doubts touch only Neoptolemus' "unfortunate use of terms," not the substance of his distinction: "it was Philodemus' opinion that Neoptolemus' statements would have been clearer or less controversial" if alternate terms had been "substituted throughout for *poema* and *poesis*."[54] The

---

[51] The confusion is partly due to the definite article τό, which can impart either a definite or indefinite (generic) sense, as context requires.

[52] As noted by Benvenga 1951 (above, n. 28), 243. It is noteworthy that when Philodemus takes over Neoptolemus' terms he immediately converts them into concrete particulars. The plurals that emerge from this recasting of Neoptolemus in col. xi (xiv) 11–16 (ποήματα, ποιήϲειϲ) are at odds with Neoptolemus' original conception of *poema* and *poesis* as categories, not instances. Does this mean that Neoptolemus never availed himself of the plural forms? Possibly col. xii (xv) 21 and esp. 28 suggest that he may have, unless these reflect Philodemus' (or Philomelus') imprecision or distortion (cf. col. xii [xv] 24, where Philodemus obtrudes a comment using ποιήματα). Such vagaries of terminology, on the other hand, are a natural extension of the singular (cf. Brink 1963, 62).

[53] The functional value of *hypothesis* (viz., thoughts) is what counts in Philodemus' eyes, despite appearances to the contrary. οἷον ὕφη may be a deliberate, ironic echo of Aristotle's οἷον ψυχή. The metaphor was put to genuine use by Dionysius of Halicarnassus (*De compositione verborum* c. 23, p. 184, 8 Usener–Radermacher)—interestingly enough, in the service of *synthesis*, not of *hypothesis*; and later by ps.-Longinus (*On the Sublime* 1.4).   [54] Greenberg 1961 (above, n. 19), 280.

problem is not one of clarity, as I see it, but of controversy; and Neoptolemus' controversial qualities ought by now to be beyond question.[55]

A second instance of a clash of perspectives around the question of analysis and the suitability of criteria occurs earlier in the same column:

> (a) And if he (Neoptolemus) calls the *ergasia* (the workmanship) '*poetike*,' *when techne is so called* (τ[ῆϲ]‖ τέχνηϲ οὕτωϲ προϲ[αγο]‖ρευομένηϲ), he is absolutely uncomprehending (ἀ[γ]νοε[ῖ]) (col. xi [xiv] 20–23).

The italicized middle clause (a genitive absolute) is doubly ambiguous. Earlier, Philodemus had reported, as we saw,

> (b) [Neoptolemus] absurdly presents the one possessed of *techne* and of the poetic *dynamis* (τὴν) δ[ύν]α|μιν . . . τὴ[ν ποι]ητι|κήν) as a [third] *eidos* of the *techne*, along with (or "alongside") *poema* and *poesis* (col. xi [xiv] 5–11).

Reading the genitive absolute in (a) as explicating the prior statement and belonging to Neoptolemus' thought (Jensen, and then Brink, took it as a parenthesis by Philodemus),[56] we can see that Philodemus is objecting not just to the identification of poetics with *ergasia* (workmanship, the elaboration of poems), but to the double-nomenclature employed by Neoptolemus. Sometimes Neoptolemus chose to call *ergasia*, sometimes *dynamis* (the skill or capacity), "*poetike*," and *techne* could migrate freely across all of these terms (as it does, for instance, at Aristotle, *Rhetoric* 1.2 1355b25: "*rhetorike* is the *dynamis* of perceiving the possible means of persuasion in everything").[57] "Poetics," in addition to being *ergasia*, is *also* "*techne*." That Neoptolemus was guilty of such terminological fluidity seems apparent from (b) alone;[58] and indeed it is hard to imagine how Neoptolemus could have avoided mentioning somewhere along the way that "poetics" is the name of the *techne* that he had set out to describe. That *techne* is, after all, a *poetike techne*. Indeed, "*poetike*" has been assumed, not implausibly, to have featured in the title to Neoptolemus' treatise; Porphyry after all mentions "*praecepta Neoptolemi τοῦ Παριανοῦ de arte poetica*."[59]

This all sounds rather confusing, but the principles are in fact quite straightforward. Here, again, Neoptolemus is making a terminological division based on an aspectual distinction. (i) Poetics *qua ergasia* is poetics *qua* the actualization of an art, as evidenced in actual poems and, we must add (since this is the offending implica-

---

[55] Walsh 1987, 68 likewise senses that it is Philodemus, and not Neoptolemus, who is responsible for the opacities of the *poesis/poema* distinction. As Neoptolemus' teaching comes to Philodemus filtered through a certain Philomelus (col. ix [xii] 10), some confusion may be inevitable. On the other hand, Philodemus in his complete confidence never suggests this possibility.

[56] προϲαγορεύειν is Philodemus' way of labelling the opponent's nomenclature, especially whenever an unusual ("catachrestic") usage is being applied or contrasted. For the distinction, see col. xv (xviii) 6; with col. xi (xiv) 21, compare col. xix (xxii) 30.

[57] Quintilian, *Inst. Or.* (2.14.11 and 13) equates, by fluctuating between, *vis* (*dynamis*), *scientia*, and *ars* (*techne*).

[58] See also Brink: "Neoptolemus . . . called that technique (sc., *ergasia*) *poietike*" (1963, 59).

[59] "*Περὶ ποιητικῆϲ*" is the title deduced by A. Rostagni, *Arte Poetica di Orazio* (Turin 1930), lxxxv. It is as good a guess as any (Boyancé 1936 [above, n. 33], 21, accepts it; cf. Varro fr. 390 Bücheler). Rostagni feels justified to assume that Neoptolemus' work was originally in verse. This seems unlikely. See further Brink 1963, 46.

tion), viewed irrespectively of the poet's actual contribution; (ii) poetics *qua techne* is simply the name of that art *qua* its being an art (irrespective of its application). Philodemus finds this absurd and no longer just strange. For him, *ergasia* implies agency ("the poet is the one who has the *dynamis* and executes his work starting from that," πο[ιη]τῆ[ν] δὲ τὸν [τ]ὴν | δύνα[μ]ιν [ἔχ]οντα καὶ ἀ|πὸ ταύτης [ἐ]ργαζό-μεἰνον, col. xi [xiv] 17–20); and agents cannot be hypostasized as parts or aspects (*eide*) of anything (col. xi [xiv] 23–26), and still less of that art (*techne*) which they possess. Neoptolemus' rejoinder obviously will not satisfy: "You don't mean that art which poets *possess*, but that art which *defines* poets relative to poetics." Neoptolemus is not redescribing his initial tripartite scheme (of three "species" and a "genus");[60] he is redescribing the genus, or rather the whole (the term "genus" misleads) in two different ways, from two perspectives. Where Neoptolemus is able to conceive of the quality of a poem's "workmanship" (its technical elaboration) as an aspect of poetics (the poetic art) quite apart from its status as the product of human agency, Philodemus is concerned to reinstate the concept (and the privileged position) of that agency.

Neoptolemus' concept is abstract and aspect-oriented. Placing the agent (the poet) alongside the *techne* that is at his disposal (and by implication, alongside the *ergasia* that he effects) is Neoptolemus' way of reinforcing, dramatically, the theoretical divisions that he is willing to carry out in order to recast common intuitions. *Ergasia*, in other words, is being viewed *qua* effectuated by the poet (this is implicit in (b)) and then per se, thanks to a further logical separation (as in (a)). The distinction is no harder to swallow than that between a poem viewed *qua* its *synthesis* (of *lexis*) and that same poem viewed now *qua* conveying or shaping *hypothesis*. Faced with either scenario, Philodemus is obviously unwilling to accept the radical divorcement that these abstractions entail, or the terminological array that Neoptolemus' stipulations involve. Neoptolemus' position may have been softened by the *dynamis/energeia* division that his terminology suggests (and to which Philodemus seems to be reacting in col. xi [xiv] 18–23). But the centerpiece of his logic is the three-way division of *techne*: as the poetic art *simpliciter*, as its possession, and as its exercise; and the intersection of this division with another, aimed at the actual work: as seen with respect to its agent, its surface verbal arrangement, and its plotted arrangement of theme. Needless to say, the scheme implies no hierarchies and no encapsulations of one aspect by another. It does not equate "workmanship" with either *poema* or *poesis* (both involve it); nor does it even suggest that these categories describe *different* skills: there is only one skill, and that is "the art of poetry" itself. In any event, this surfeit of logical subtlety proved too much for Philodemus, who refuses to give *poema* and *poesis* a comparable worth (being inclined to subsume the one under the other, as a part of a valid whole). But as we shall see, there is more to Philodemus' reaction than an aversion to sophisms. And there is more to Neoptolemus' poetic program than what has been discussed up until now.

---

[60] Cf. Brink 1963, 59, whose explanation ("required") fails to clarify why or how Neoptolemus could term the same technique both *ergasia* and *poetike*.

4. Aristotelian Heresy

Gegen Aristoteles, der die ὄψις und das μέλος nur unter die ἡδύςματα
der Tragödie rechnet: und ganz bereit das Lesedrama sanktioniert.
Nietzsche (*Sämtliche Werke. Kritische Studien Ausgabe*, ed. Colli
and Montinari 7, 78)

Paradox, and straightfaced but blatantly *outré* assertions, are the characteristic results of Neoptolemus' allowing logical divisions and common intuition to collide,[61]
as is the following claim, filtered through Philodemus' rage:

[4] Philodemus, On Poems 5 col. xii (xv) 17–22

εὑ|ήθ[ως] δὲ γέγραπται καὶ | τὸ [μ]ὴ κοινωνε[ῖν] τῶι | πο[η]τεῖ τῶν
ἁμα[ρτ]ιῶν τὰ[ς ὑπ]οθέ[ς]εις καὶ τὰ πο|ήματα . . . .

And [Neoptolemus] stupidly wrote that the *hamartia* at the level of *hypothesis*
and of *poemata* (viz., of *synthesis*) are not shared by the poet . . . .[62]

The poet, evidently, is not to be held personally accountable for mistakes in his plot-
material or his verbal composition (even if those items remain "his").[63] This dissociation is again strictly a logical and aspectual operation. Neoptolemus is trying to
make a point about the qualitative differences among formal levels in a poetic text;
these, to be isolated, must be separated off notionally from one of their actual origins,
the poet, who in turn becomes a theoretical entity and so, too, becomes, in certain
circumstances, dispensable. In this Neoptolemus is saying nothing more scandalous
than what one of his likely sources of inspiration had said, namely Aristotle. Here
we will make a quick digression and consider some "Aristotelian heresies" (against

---

[61] Jensen's view of this matter is complex. On the one hand, he seeks to mitigate the harshness of the
divisions by reconciling them to a "Dispositionsprinzip" organizing the exposition of an eisagogic (introductory) poetic treatise, following Norden's hypothesis (Jensen 1923, 101; cf. id. 1936, 318). This
is impossible to prove (as Brink showed, cf. Brink 1963, 22), and it is rendered still less probable in view
of the subtle aspectual logic that seems to be governing Neoptolemus' terms (on which, see above). On
the other hand, and this is related to the first consideration, Jensen tends to slight the theoretical rigor of
Neoptolemus, and thus to rob his categories of any innovative potential. Thus it can be said of Neoptolemus' paradoxes that they result from Philodemus' playing havoc with Neoptolemus' intentions, not
from those intentions themselves: his objections constitute "eine Verkennung der Absichten des Neoptolemus, dem sicher weniger daran lag, daß seine Dispoition der strengen Logik gerecht wurde, als daß
sie praktisch brauchbar war," etc. (Jensen 1923, 105). This is to read Neoptolemus in the proleptic light
of Horace (106), not in the far more relevant backlighting of Aristotle. It also reimports, redundantly, a
res/verba (content/form) distinction into the category of poet, where it was already laid down outside
that category: "Diesen Unterschied [Gestaltung des Stoffes versus Lebensweisheit] hatte Neoptolemus
im Sinn, wenn er sagte, daß die Fehler der Stoffe und der Gedichte nicht dieselben seien wie die des
Dichters." This may work for Horace (cf. Brink on *sapere* ad *AP* 309); but then, Horace never claimed
that the *culpa* in *res* and *verba* is not that of the *poeta*. And that is the far more radical claim (on which,
see §1 below).

[62] Literally, "*hypotheseis* and *poemata* do not share *hamartiai* (faults) with the poet."

[63] This is the sense of col. xii (xv) 13–16 **[2b]**, as tentatively reconstructed above. The overall
scheme of Neoptolemus' theory as presented here does not require him to make this inclusion in **[2b]**.

Plato and common sense) from the *Poetics,* which I will simply list, with a minimum of comment:[64]

§1 Anatomical impossibility (a horse represented with both front legs thrown forward) is *not the error* (*hamartia*) *of the poet.* "Error in the art of poetry itself (αὐτῆϲ τῆϲ ποιητικῆϲ) is of two sorts, (a) error in *the art itself* (καθ' αὑτήν), (b) error by coincidence (κατὰ ϲυμβεβηκόϲ)" (25.1460b15–16). Related to this is Aristotle's de-emphasis throughout the *Poetics* of the individual contribution of the poet, relative to the autonomous functioning of the work itself, which takes logical precedence (e.g., 1454b31: ὑπὸ τοῦ ποιητοῦ; contrast 1454a37: ἐξ αὐτοῦ τοῦ μύθου; cf. 1453b2).[65]

§2 "Without action (ἄνευ πράξεωϲ) a tragedy cannot exist, but *without characters* (ἄνευ ἠθῶν) *it may*" (6.1450a23–25; cf. 50a21–22).[66]

§3 "The potential of tragedy exists even *without a performance and actors*" (ἄνευ ἀγῶνοϲ καὶ ὑποκριτῶν, 6.1450b18–19); cf. 51a6–7: a length of time that "stands in relation to the *performance* and *perception* (πρὸϲ τοὺϲ ἀγῶναϲ καὶ τὴν αἴϲθηϲιν) *is* not "*of*" the art itself (οὐ τῆϲ τέχνηϲ ἐϲτίν)," viz., is not determined by the nature of tragedy but by extrinsic considerations; cf. 61b29: οὐκ αἰϲθανομένων.

§4 "Tragedy can produce *its own* [sc., *effect/function*] (ποιεῖ τὸ αὐτῆϲ [sc. ἔργον, τέλοϲ]) even *without movement* (ἄνευ κινήϲεωϲ), just as epic does" (26.1462a11–12). Cf. 19.1456b5–7: "These [effects] should be apparent (τὰ μὲν δεῖ φαίνεϲθαι) *without an explanation* [ἄνευ διδαϲκαλίαϲ; perhaps rather, "without *didaskalia,*" viz., *Inszenierung*], but those dependent on speech (τὰ δὲ ἐν τῷ λόγῳ) should be produced by the speaker and arise from speech."[67]

§5 "The plot should be constructed in such a way that, *even without seeing it* (καὶ ἄνευ τοῦ ὁρᾶν), someone who hears [from reading] about the incidents will

---

[64] Translations throughout are from R. Janko, *Aristotle, Poetics, with the Tractatus Coislinianus, Reconstruction of Poetics II, and the Fragments of the On Poets* (Indianapolis 1987), with occasional modifications. There are obvious drawbacks to quoting from Aristotle out of context in this way; on the other hand, the drastic outlines of his argument are perhaps best displayed when his individual statements are collected together.

[65] The connection between these passages, pointing to Aristotle's isolation and making autonomous of the poetic *techne*, is discussed in Porter 1992 (above, n. 3), 77–80. On the autonomy of technique for Aristotle, see esp. T. G. Rosenmeyer, "Design and Execution in Aristotle, *Poetics* ch. xxv," *CSCA* 6 (1973), 231–51.

[66] Halliwell (1986 [above, n. 38], 157 and 163–64) seeks to blunt the sharp edges of §2. While it is true that "Aristotle notes the possibility of dispensing with tragic characterisation, [but] he does not recommend it," it is just as true that Aristotle never softens the claim or retracts it (cf. 6.1450a25–29). The *Poetics* is sprinkled with such startling counter-intuitions. And these stand, despite any mitigating considerations we might come up with (see Janko 1984 [above, n. 33], 228–29, on *opsis*; but *ibid.,* 230–31, on *ethos*).

[67] διδαϲκαλία is perhaps best taken in its technical sense, *pace* Lucas' comment ad loc., and should be linked to §3 above (cf. the identical contrast in the sequel remark in §8). Here, as everywhere in Aristotle, the emphasis falls on the events *qua* structured plot as necessary cause of the tragic effect arising ἐκ τῶν ϲυμβαινόντων (§5), not on the contingency of their staging.

shudder and feel pity at the outcome, as someone may feel upon hearing the plot of the *Oedipus*" (14.1453b3–6). Aristotle has substituted for "phenomenal viewing" a non-phenomenal, "theoretical viewing," akin to the poet's "setting out the universal": θεωρεῖcθαι τὸ καθόλου (1455b2). In the place of vision, he substitutes the self-fulfilling "transparence" of a successfully constructed work of art (cf. (§4): "These [effects] should be apparent, τὰ μὲν δεῖ φαίνεcθαι . . ."). At its best, tragedy works its effects in the form of their synchronous, eusynoptic, and inferential "perception," ἅμα ἡ θεωρία γίνεται (1451a1).

§6 "It is obvious (φανερά: "*self-apparent*") *from reading* it [sc., tragedy] what sort it is," sc., its nature (26.1462a12–13).

§7 "The poet must be the *maker of plots rather than of meters*" (τὸν ποιητὴν μᾶλλον τῶν μύθων εἶναι δεῖ ποιητὴν ἢ τῶν μέτρων) (9.1451b27–28).

§8 (sequel to §3) "What would the speaker's function be, if the element [viz., reasoning, or the result aimed at by a speaker] were apparent even without [the use of] speech?" (τί γὰρ ἂν εἴη τοῦ λέγοντος ἔργον, εἰ φαίνοιτο ἡ ἰδέα [*idea* Lat.: ἡ δέοι Vahlen] καὶ μὴ διὰ τὸν λόγον (19.1456b7–8) or "if [the character's *dianoia*] were apparent in the way it ought to be, even without speech." Much to his regret, Aristotle must somehow, and nonetheless, address the problem of *lexis*. Here (introductory to the chapter on *lexis*) he contemplates, just for a second, a way round this hindrance. The question he asks may be rhetorical, but in his intent focus on the formal criteria of tragedy and driven by the logic of his position, Aristotle is broaching an idea that not even he can ward off. The result is yet one more paradox. Lucas expresses his own perplexity, "It remains obscure how *dianoia* is expressed if not in speech." Aristotle, serenely, can always reply: in the same way that you can have tragedy without *ethos* (but not without *praxis*).

§9 "If [a poet] puts in sequence speeches full of character, well composed in diction and reasoning, he will not achieve what was [agreed to be] the function of tragedy; a tragedy that employs these *less* adequately, but has a plot (i.e., a structure of incidents, cύcταcιν πραγμάτων), will achieve it *more*" (6.1450a29–33). Perhaps by "more" (πολὺ μᾶλλον) Aristotle is conceding the unreachable ideality of his formalism (it has the same force as κατ᾽ εὐχήν in the *Politics*)?

§10 "He himself [sc. Orestes] says what the *poet* wants, not what the *plot* [wants]" (16.1454b34–35). Euripides has therefore blundered.

It should be obvious, not just from the first and last items, how much Neoptolemus owes to Aristotle, whose bold, oracular pronouncements jar common sensibilities precisely in proportion as they represent different degrees of conceptual isolation. The "elements" or "parts" (literally, "species": *eide*) into which Aristotle analyzes tragedy are simultaneously its aspects. As *elements*, they will be found in all tragedies; but as *aspects*, they can be conceived as absent even when they are present (in cases, deficiently present), and as more or less closely tied to the defining "essence" of tragedy.[68] Aspectuality is well brought out in *Poetics* 6.1450a19–20, where Aristotle observes that "people generally are of a certain kind *in respect of their characters* (κατὰ τὰ ἤθη), but are happy or the opposite *in respect of their actions* (κατὰ τὰς πράξεις)."[69] Surely no tragedy exhibiting some action will be devoid of characters of certain kinds; but to be conceived as tragic agents, those same agents do not have to be conceived as kinds of characters. It is not to their characters but to their actions that we look when we study or receive the effects of a tragedy.

This trait—conceptual *chorismos*—is characteristic of Aristotle's thought, so we need not be shocked when it crops up again in his theory of poetry. In fact, there is continuity of the deepest kind, which is worth mentioning just briefly. Aristotle makes no bones about the logical separability of soul, *qua* the formal principle of intelligibility and the essence of an animate body. In *De anima* 3.5, the soul *qua* active intellect is "what it is"—which is to say, is precisely defined—"only when separated" (χωρισθεὶς δ᾽ ἐστὶ μόνον τοῦθ᾽ ὅπερ ἐστί, *De an.* 430a22–23); in other words, "the 'active intellect' has no corresponding bodily potentiality."[70] This is in answer to *De anima* 1.1 403a10–11: "if there is anything *idion* to the soul's actions or affections, the soul will admit of separation (ἐνδέχοιτ᾽ ἂν αὐτὴν χωρίζεσθαι)." Clearly, by 3.5 Aristotle has isolated that *idion*, the soul's proprietary and defining aspect. The language should sound familiar, not only from the *Poetics* but from Neoptolemus.[71] To these considerations, let us add Aristotle's claim that soul, so defined, stands to the rest of an organism like *techne* to *hyle* (*De anima* 430a12). This should resonate even more when we recall that for Aristotle *mythos* is the "soul" (sc., the non-"aesthetic" and "actively intellectual" part of the soul) of tragedy; it is, at the very least, separable in definition (χωριστοῦ ὄντος . . . κατὰ λόγον, *De anima* 3.4 429a11–12), the principle in virtue of which alone, viewed *per se*, a tragedy is "what it is" (*Poetics* 18.1456a7–8; 4.1449a8, αὐτὸ καθ᾽ αὐτό; καθ᾽ ἣν λέγεται τόδε τι, *De anima* 2.1 412a8–9); and this is because *mythos* is the principle of a tragedy's intelligibility, *and* the criterion of its identity as well . And while it is true that Aristotle's efforts are directed, ultimately, at the synthesis of matter with form ("enmattered" form), in reaction to the Platonic "separation" of Forms,[72] at least as much effort is spent in the Aristotelian corpus at isolating that which within these compounds (or predicated of them) gives them essence and identity. Here, Aristotle is unsparingly formalistic: essence is logically divorced from matter (ἄνευ ὕλης, *Metaphysics* Z 27.1032b14). And the trait of logical separatism is deeply ingrained. Thus it can be said that Chapter 6 of Aristotle's *Poetics* defines the "essence" (οὐσία) of tragedy

---

[68] Even the non-illustrious example of recent tragedies which "have no character" (aspectually speaking) nonetheless have all the necessary credentials to qualify as bona fide tragedies (6.1450a25).

[69] The text, bracketed by Kassel, is accepted as genuine by Gudeman and more recently by Janko. The thought is clearly genuine; see Gudeman ad loc.

[70] A. A. Long, "Soul and Body . ʼ Stoicism," *Phronesis* 27 (1992), 35. Cf. H. M. Robinson, "Mind and Body in Aristotle," *CQ* 28 (1978), esp. sections V–VI pp. 117-24; "form" as the principle of "intelligibility" is hinted at on p. 122. Further: nn. 12 and 27 above.

[71] On its probable Platonic and Academic origins, see G. Vlastos, *Socrates: Ironist and Moral Philosopher* (Ithaca and Cambridge 1991), 256–65.

[72] As stressed brilliantly by G. E. L. Owen, "Inherence," *Phronesis* 10 (1965), 97–105. *Idion* is Aristotle's way of making form inhere again.

(*synthesis* of actions or events) over against its "matter" (spectacle, song, diction, *synthesis* of meters).

Neoptolemus nowhere echoes Aristotle more closely than when he wrote [2a], "Only *synthesis* of *lexis* [is "of," i.e., defines] *poema*, but [underlying] thoughts or actions (*praxeis*) or characterizations do not" (col. xii [xv] 1–6). *Poema* is of course alien to Aristotle, as a term but not as a concept: it designates everything that the essential features of drama effectively exclude. Aristotle's tendency was to scant the *material and phenomenal* aspects of drama: song, dance, spectacle, meter, *lexis*; and to favor the formal and discursive aspects: action (*praxis*), character (as revelatory of action), thought (as revelatory of character), a fact that the shopping list from the *Poetics* above at times makes glaringly clear. The exclusive disjunction between *praxis* and *lexis* is a straightforward consequence of Aristotle's poetics; but in neither Aristotle nor Neoptolemus is the disjunction structured by considerations of content and form, *pace* Jensen, Rostagni, and others. At *Poetics* 24.1460b2–4 Aristotle shows how complete the disjunction is: "[The poet] should take great pains with diction (*lexis*) in the slack parts [of the poem], *i.e., those stressing neither character nor reasoning.*" The reason that follows is Longinian: "For, in turn, excessively brilliant diction *obscures* (ἀποκρύπτει, literally "hides") characters and their reasonings" (cf. ps.-Longinus, *On the Sublime* 17.3). Elsewhere, *lexis* exists to make known, transparently and unobtrusively, a speaker's mind. Here, however, *lexis* is not a vehicle of thought; it exists in an extraneous domain, as a material screen, and as an obstacle to a theory of poetics. Such is the scandal of language that haunts Aristotle's theory.[73]

If Neoptolemus is an Aristotelian, then it is surely in this penchant for abstraction and especially for dissociation, and not just in virtue of the critical lexicon they share.[74] Formalism tends toward sharp aspectual rather than quantitative distinctions, and in this respect Neoptolemus is Aristotle's formalist equal.[75] But there are some outstanding differences which are easily overlooked. Now if Neoptolemus were truly arguing in the spirit of Aristotle he would have written the following [2b]: "Any time you set out to compose something involving *lexis*, it is impossible to compose anything *without* those things (namely, the thoughts, the actions, and the characterizations); rather, composition of the *praxis* appears to be [a defining characteristic] of verbal arrangement" (col. xii [xv] 10–13).[76] But as the text stands, Neoptolemus did not write this, and Philodemus had to say it for him, or rather, against him. Here, it is Philodemus, not Neoptolemus, who is showing fealty to Aristotle, by reinstating the necessary presence and pre-eminence of thought, action and character, whenever anything is to be composed "in *lexis*." In doing so, Philodemus has

---

[73] The absence of enthusiasm for matters of "style" in the *Poetics* is occasionally lamented, e.g. Brink 1963, 86; cf. the Appendix on *lexis* in Halliwell 1986 (above, n. 38) and *melos* (song) receives no treatment, cf. Janko 1984 (above, n. 33), 227.

[74] See e.g. Brink 1963, 92, where he notes some terminological resemblances and differences.

[75] On Aristotle's defense of formalist perfection as *the* criterion for poetic value, see especially Rosenmeyer 1973 (above, n. 65). The emphasis there is on technique; in the treatment given here, it is on formal causes—but these two emphases are for Aristotle of a piece, and perfectly compatible.

[76] The text may have read *idion*, as Jensen and Mangoni print it (ἴδι]ο[ν), but as was argued above, the sense of "distinctive" or "defining characteristic" is carried alone by the stipulative genitive, "of." Philodemus is thus reversing a distinction of Neoptolemus'.

assimilated Aristotelian tragic criteria to the whole of poetic literature, but in this he may simply have been following a trend that is evinced a few columns earlier, in the excerpted critical history of Philomelus, a trend followed by Neoptolemus himself: "Of those whose opinions are recorded by Philomelus, some think that a poet who is evenly accomplished in the areas of plot (*mythos*), characterization (*ethopoiia*) and *lexis* is the best kind of poet; and they are saying something that is probably true" (col. ix [xii] 1–9). But unlike either Philodemus or Aristotle, Neoptolemus nowhere suggests that *synthesis* is functionally subordinate to *praxis*, even if the two can be isolated and distinguished aspectually,[77] although this is the clear implication of Philodemus' own cherished view.

Philodemus' position is that the arrangement of plot not only involves verbal arrangement, but gives logical content to it: words are not haphazardly arranged; they are arranged with plot or content consciously in mind. By contrast, there appears to be if anything a counter-Aristotelian strain detectable in Neoptolemus' poetics: (i) in the equality that he emphatically assigns to *synthesis* (if this is in fact what he does), for "Neoptolemus wrongly seemed to separate ([χωρί]ζειν) *synthesis* [of *lexis*] from thoughts/meaning, *saying that it has neither a lesser nor a greater* [*share*(?)], as we saw" (col. x [xiii] 32–xi [xiv] 4 **[2d]**), already challenging the unequal values that these elements have in Aristotle;[78] and (ii) in the implication, which Philodemus clearly senses but which from our perspective is difficult to pin down beyond a shadow of a doubt, that the undisputed primacy (the primary evaluative criterion) for Neoptolemus goes to *synthesis*, not to the discursive elements or aspects of poetry, and still less to the poet:

[5] Philodemus, *On Poems* 5 col. xii [xv] 26–29

τὸ [τοί]|νυ[ν π]ρωτεύ[ει]ν, τ[ῶν]| εἰδῶ[ν] τὰ ποιήματα λ[έ]|γων.

He said that among the [three] species [of the art] *poema* comes first.

Does **[5]** contradict the statement given as (i) just above? Perhaps only on the surface, for all of Philodemus' summaries grope toward the conclusion that for Neoptolemus *synthesis* of *lexis* appears to take precedence, at least axiologically if not logically:[79] it seems to be τὸ βέλτιον, "better," as Philodemus suggests a little further down. "If ['first' means to be] better, how is it [sc. *poema*] this more so than *poesis*?" (col. xii [xv] 33–35; Mangoni's reading). Conceptually, all three aspects may have been equal and distinct; in point of practice, *synthesis* (*poema*) seems to

---

[77] *Pace* Brink 1963, 145, who writes, "[Neoptolemus'] literary criticism reasserted the Aristotelian pre-eminence of drama and epic against influential tendencies of his own day." This is to overstate the meaning of *poesis* and to overlook its purely logical identity. Neoptolemus' *schema* applies indifferently to all genres of poetry. This does not make Neoptolemus an Aristotelian, only someone who finds Aristotle's logic an appealing, because powerful, conceptual instrument.

[78] "Share" (μερίδα) has been supplied by Jensen based on a parallel passage in col. ix (xii). The present passage is damaged and difficult to construe.

[79] Brink 1963, 73 writes that this "may be an Aristotelian way of describing the fundamental role assigned to poetic style—τὸ πρῶτον, or πρότερον, φύσει, as it were. But it seems more likely that first things also came first in treatment" (see further Brink's appendix, 75). Rather, *Neoptolemus has found an Aristotelian way of describing an un-Aristotelian view*: if style takes primacy (or even stands even with "plot"), he has reversed all the relevant hierarchies.

have been preferred, on aesthetic grounds.[80] Aristo of Chios and others made the same preference, on what grounds we are never told (col. xvi [xix] 15–19). We can assume with Brink (1963, 93) and others that Neoptolemus is a pragmatically attuned literary critic who, as poet, "took the craftsman's interest" in style. But Neoptolemus seems more likely to have been a committed theoretician, willing to allow logic to run its free course. That logic requires that *synthesis* be elevated to logical parity with *hypothesis*; this protects the standing of *synthesis*, while reflecting its increased appreciation. Concomitantly with this, the poet is reduced to a category, and attention is focused upon the work of art conceived of now as an *object*. Hence, as Philodemus disapprovingly notes and as we saw earlier, Neoptolemus defines the art of poetry (*techne*) in terms of the elaboration (*ergasia*) that constitutes a work of art (col. xi [xiv] 20–23). Probably, *hypothesis* for Neoptolemus is first and foremost a kind of *synthesis* of its own too. At any rate, his focus need have been no more pragmatic than Aristotle's showed itself to be in his *Poetics*.

Neoptolemus' securing of *poema* in his triad is, I suspect, just a symptom of the "trend" towards *synthesis* which characterizes post-Aristotelian poetics in its non-canonical form, and which Philodemus is at pains to "reconstruct" in his historical survey in Book 5 of developments in criticism from the fourth to the second centuries (or later). Philodemus' treatise, culminating in this book, has a theme and a point, one which has not yet been identified properly: it traces the isolation and ascendency of *synthesis* in criticism. Neoptolemus clearly plays a key role in this historical development, by detaching *synthesis* from its context, and by giving it an equal standing in theory, and apparently a primacy of place in his practical judgments of poems.[81] Such a "trend" naturally comes with an increasing isolation and re-evaluation of αὐτὸ τὸ ποιεῖν (col. ix [xii] 1), the production and construction of the poetic surface ("words" as opposed to "ideas," not to say *mythos*; contrast Aristotle's §7). Its direct upshot, as we shall see, is nothing less than a redefinition of poetics itself.

Be that as it may, Philodemus will have none of this trend. For him, meaning and composition go hand in hand. This is not to claim for Philodemus some innovative policy about the "inseparability" of form and content, as Rostagni maintained (following Croce and De Sanctis, and a contradictory logic; see Appendix A to this chapter). Philodemus is not advocating that form is internal to content. He says nothing like the following paraphrase of **[2b]** by Grube: "poetry is not like a dress which

---

[80] It is difficult to say whether Neoptolemus also intended a temporal primacy (if the order of the critic's exposition reflected the order of the poet's mode of composition). If so, Neoptolemus is upsetting the customary order for describing the poetic process, which begins with *selectio* and then moves on to *compositio* (see col. x [xiii] 1–9 esp. 6ff. ἔcχατον [τὴν τ]ῆc λέξεωc ἐξερ|[γαcίαν καλῶc] cυνκεῖ-c|θαι—a passage which Jensen 1923, 102 formerly assigned to Neoptolemus, and later to Heraclides Ponticus [Jensen 1936, 294]). Cf. col. iii (vi) 24: "thoughts" must be sketched out first. Neoptolemus may stand closest to Dionysius of Halicarnasus, *De compositione verborum* c. 2, p. 8, 14–15 Usener–Radermacher: *synthesis* comes second in the temporal sequence of composing, but *first in dynamis* (power and value).

[81] For a later expression of this tendency, see the *Scholia on Dionysius of Thrax's Art of Grammar* 481, 8–9 Hilgard: "*Poema* is a *phrasis* that is metrical and rhythmic, being of prior and loftier standing (ἀρχαιοτέρα καὶ cεμνοτέρα) than logical syntax." "Prior" is a sign of the felt "primacy" of *synthesis*, refracted through a naturalizing myth of temporal primacy. The *synthesis* argument is powerful not because it *eliminates* sense, but because it *confronts* sound with sense in their simultaneous, if unequal, co-presence (the position is not that meanings have no existence, but that they do not *move* us).

can be put on a particular idea, it is the very shape of it."[82] What he is doing is asserting a definition of the poetic function, as he sees it, in the traditional idiom of literary criticism, in terms of *to prepon*: that language must be appropriate to the thought expressed (this is implied); and in terms of functional dependency (here, perhaps, expressed in terms of *to idion*): the arrangement of *praxis* (*hypothesis*) is what determines verbal *synthesis*. These are in fact two faces of a single coin. On the canon of "appropriateness," which Neoptolemus appears to have eschewed or at least left to one side in his compartmentalizing poetics, and which Philodemus endeavored to retrieve, compare the following fragmentary remark by Philodemus from elsewhere in *On Poems*:

[6] *P.Herc.* 1676 col. iv 9–17 (p. 249 Sbordone; C. Romeo, *CErc* 22 [1992], 166)

καταξι|[ω̑]ν δὲ τὸν ποιητήν, ἐὰν μ[ὴ | δια]νόημματ' οἰκεῖα λάβη[ι]|| καὶ [λέ]ξεις προσηκούcαc, [ἴ|δι]όν τι ποιητικὸν ἀπ[ο|τελε]ι̑ν, κἂν παρίδη⟨ι⟩ τ[...] | [1.5 lines] ἐcτι τυφλώττον||[τοc.

He [sc. an opponent] maintains that the poet can realize a certain poetic [*idion*: "originality"] in the absence of appropriate ("fitting") thoughts and expressions to match them (literally, appropriate *lexeis*), even if (the poet?) overlooks [. . .] [1.5 lines] (but this view) is (that) of a blind man.

Here Philodemus provides us with a textbook example of the critical dogma of *to prepon*, which enforces a strict correspondence between language (*lexis*) and subject-matter (thought, *pragmata*; the constituents of an Aristotelian *praxis*), or somewhat misleadingly, between form and content. Philodemus' language has exact echoes in Aristotle, who defines appropriateness in expression as that which is "analogous" to the subject matter, τοι̑c ὑποκειμένοιc πράγμαcιν ἀνάλογον (*Rhetoric* 3.7 1408a10–11). Aristotle's definition in the *Rhetoric* is an extension of earlier conceptions of *to prepon*; later critics would follow in his wake, as does for instance Diogenes of Babylon, "The *prepon* is *lexis* that befits the subject," πρέπον δέ ἐcτι λέξιc οἰκεία τω̑ πράγματι (Diogenes Laertius 7.59). And so, apparently, does Philodemus (but not Neoptolemus).[83] Philodemus' surprising reliance on a traditional canon of criticism was acknowledged to be the case early on by Jensen, and it was later reaffirmed, with fresh arguments, by Greenberg. It is worth quoting their reactions: "Auch der zweiter Satz [from col. ix [xii] 24–27, cited in Philomelus and assented to heartily by Philodemus], *daß Ausdruck und Inhalt gleich notwendig seien, ist so allgemein gehalten,* daß es unmöglich ist, über seinen Urheber eine bestimmte Vermutung zu äußern" (Jensen 1923, 96). Greenberg came later, and so was able to direct his criticism against Rostagni (the context of this remark is the section on Neoptolemus): "[Philodemus] vehemently states his own opinion that a

---

[82] Grube 1965, 96. Cf. Russell 1981, 130, for the more standard metaphor (ornament).

[83] There are differences between Aristotle and the Stoics (cf. M. Pohlenz, "τὸ πρέπον: Ein Beitrag zur Geschichte des griechischen Geistes," *NGG*, Phil.-Hist. Kl. 16 [1933], 53–92), but the restrictions made by both do not change the overriding principle: subject-matter dictates expression. Philodemus' equivocation on the moral sense of *to prepon* at col. xxxv (xxxviii) 22–26 does not invalidate my claim about his *de facto* endorsement of *to prepon* in the Aristotelian sense.

poema cannot be composed without regard for the content it expresses. *There is nothing startling or revolutionary about this*; it is only a restatement of *to prepon*, that old *arete lexeos* which goes back at least as far as Aristotle (*Rhetoric* 1408a). Why then does Philodemus reassert it so violently? *Because it had been denied . . . .*" (Greenberg 1961 [above, n. 19], 281; emphases added). Their insights can be extended a bit further, if we look at some of the larger implications (and limits) of Philodemus' adherence to an Aristotelian critical idiom, and at Neoptolemus' ultimate rejection of that idiom.

At first sight, appropriateness would seem to imply a two-way relation between language and thought. But what is crucially brought out, particularly in the later history of the concept of *to prepon* (where its viability increasingly came under attack in some quarters), is the fact that "appropriateness" is fundamentally governed by a one-way causal logic: for it is not the case on the *prepon* doctrine that language and thought simply go together; rather, language is *conditioned* by the exigencies of thought. This "bias," if we wish to call it such (and as later critics were more ready to do), is deeply rooted in the critical tradition, as is clear from the following passage from Aristophanes' *Frogs* (Aeschylus is speaking): "It is the unrepealable law of great ideas and thoughts that they *engender* equally great words" (ἀνάγκη μεγάλων γνωμῶν καὶ διανοιῶν ἴσα καὶ τὰ ῥήματα τίκτειν, *Frogs* 1059; interestingly, a parallel with clothing follows, as at *Thesmophoriazousae* 148, where the same thought is expressed); this remains a commonplace much later, cf. Horace, *The Art of Poetry* 311: *verbaque provisam rem non invita sequentur*.[84] As was seen, Philodemus' invocation, in other passages, of the law of "appropriateness" (of language to subject matter) is consistent with his objection to the stark separation of the two components of poetic composition in Neoptolemus' system of poetics—both here (**[6]**), and at **[2d]**, where Philodemus introduced the whole of his discussion by encapsulating Neoptolemus' program: "he separates *synthesis* from thoughts."

The passage under consideration **[2b]** does no more than reiterate the dogma of appropriateness; and that dogma carries the tacit assumption that *lexis* can be appropriate to *pragmata* only by taking its cue from the subject matter, to which it is, in fact, functionally subordinate. This is, after all, what "appropriateness" and "fittingness" mean: the language gravitates to the level of the subject-matter that "underlies" it. This subordination is further implied in Philodemus' strengthening qualification, which is appended to his objection: first, he rejects the idea that *lexis* can be arranged independently of subject matter; then he adds a rider: *lexis* stands in a special relationship to *praxis*. Philodemus' wording (if it has been properly reconstructed) is not entirely self-evident, but its drift shouldn't be open to doubt. Even if Jensen's conjecture happens to be wrong, the passage in this form has enjoyed an iconic status since the day Rostagni misconstrued it.

The passage, given in **[2b]**, begins: εἰ δ' ἐν [τῆι]‖ λέξει πεποιῆcθαί τ[ι | λέ]γει, κἀνταῦθ[α νὴ Δι' ο]ὖ|κ ἔcτι τι πεποι[ῆcθαι το]ύ|των χωρίc, then the contested part follows: ἀλλ' [ἴδι]ο[ν το]ῦ | cυνκεῖcθαι [τὴν] λέξιν τὸ |[cυ]νκεῖ-

---

[84] In the more technical discussion of music in Plato's *Republic*, the sequence of impingements is more carefully articulated into three layers: aural surface, linguistic expression, thought (sc. character and subject matter); cf. 398d9: "Harmony and rhythm should *follow* the words" and the words will be appropriate to the subject matter; cf. *Republic* 400a1.

cθαι [τὴν πρᾶξ]ιν εἶ|ν]αι φαίνεταί μ[οι]. As noted earlier, [ἴδι]ο[ν] is only a conjecture, though it seems to fill out nicely the sense that the genitive carries by itself, namely its stipulative, defining sense as we found it in Neoptolemus and as Philodemus appears to be reversing it here. First, let us consider the translations and glosses this last clause has received. (a) Jensen: "sondern mit der Gestaltung des Ausdrucks scheint mir *notwendig* die der Handlung *verbunden* zu sein"; (b) Rostagni: "il modo d'esere della forma *dipende* dal modo d'essere del contenuto" (Rostagni 1955 [below, n. 108], 370; cf. 409); (c) Greenberg: "rather it seems to me that the composition of the action is an *essential part* of the composition of the *lexis*" (Greenberg 1961 [above, n. 19], 277; cf. 281, "a *poema* cannot be composed *without regard* for the content it expresses"); (d) Brink: "[Philodemus] denies that poetic expression is separable from 'action' or subject-matter expressed" (Brink 1963, 62).

The variations can be reduced to two ways of looking at the Greek, and these need not be exclusive of each other, while both can be understood to gloss Philodemus' belief that items pertaining to *hypothesis* (to "content," if you like) are ineliminable elements of any poetic artifact: οὐ|κ ἔcτι τι πεποι[ῆcθαι το]ύ|των χωρίc. Prima facie, the clause, which functions as a kind of rider on the foregoing, should not exceed the limits of the *prepon*-doctrine, nor should it state anything more than this fact of ineliminability.[85] Rostagni's version, oddly enough, seems to be most accurately expressive of the relation between "content" and "form" as Philodemus views it, even if this vitiates entirely the thesis argued by Rostagni in the same essay, namely that Philodemus is introducing a new doctrine about the essential interwovenness of content and form ("che non dovrebbe neanche la forma essere separata dal contenuto").[86] The genitival phrase in our text may simply be definitory of the dependency that Rostagni both affirmed and denied.[87] But equally, it may be a vaguer way of expressing a mutual normative requirement; if the *praxis* is well composed, the *lexis* ought to be so too, and vice versa.[88] What the phrase cannot mean is that the very articulation of language produces subject matter, because not all composed *lexeis* necessarily entail *praxeis* (as Philodemus never wearies of reminding us: it is never enough to praise the *lexis* alone),[89] whereas the reverse (that *praxeis* entail *lexeis*) is true—so trivially true, one should think, that under ordinary circumstances the point need not be made. What we have here, however, is one of those rare

---

[85] *Idion* and *oikeios* are in some contexts interchangeable in Aristotle; see Lucas at *Poetics* 13. 1452b33.

[86] Rostagni's position (*Scritti minori*, p. 409) has already been refuted by Benvenga (above, n. 28) and Greenberg (esp. Greenberg 1961 [above, n. 19], 283), both of whom reinstated the proper subordination of form to content in Philodemus. But the issue is complex, and several nuances and new emphases still need to be made.

[87] Similarly, *P.Herc.* 1676 cols. iii 26 (p. 247 Sbordone) the *ergon* of *poetike*, and col. iv 7 (p. 249 Sbordone) the *idion* of the *techne*. But in these columns it is Philodemus' unbudging conviction that the *poetikon ti*, that which is distinctively poetic, requires the classical procedures of "finding fitting thoughts and appropriate *lexeis*."

[88] For what it is worth, ἴδιον can carry this exact meaning in Aristotle; see Vlastos 1991 (above, n. 71), 217.

[89] Substituting [ἔργ]ο[ν] for [ἴδι]ο[ν] gets us no further (here the implicit sense would be, "it is the task of the one composing the *lexis* to compose the *praxis* as well," as in **[6]**).

cases in which even this "self-evident" piece of wisdom is being subjected to the severest (methodological) skepticism by Neoptolemus.

Nor can the phrase mean that the form of language (its style) is *identical* with the form of a poem's contents, which would be the stronger claim (but also one needing elaborate defense). No evidence has been produced so far to show that Philodemus had anything like this in mind, or that the language in **[2b]** can bear this meaning, with or without such independent evidence.[90] It is unclear what such a claim amounts to.[91] And in any event, it is unlikely that Philodemus would hold such an identity-thesis (identifying style and content), certainly not if it commits one to the mimetic fallacy that style must, let alone can, "resemble" contents. Compare a later column from *On Poems*: "It is completely mad [of some anonymous critic] to fumble about with [the notion of] the 'resemblance' of *lexis* to the *pragmata* pointed to" (i.e. expressed) by the poet, or his *lexis* (τελείω[c]‖ δὲ μ[αν]ικὸν τὸ παρ[α]‖ψηλαφ[ᾶ]ν ὁμοιότητα | λέξεως τοῖς δηλουμέ|νοις πράγμασιν) (col. xxxii [xxxv] 16–20). All such resemblance is logically impossible, because *lexis* and *praxis* are (in respect of form, at least) incommensurable items.[92] And wherever they do meet, they are governed, in the end, by the rules of *to prepon* (xxxii [xxxv] 31; cf. 13), as are the Theophrastean stylistic "virtues" to which Philodemus is beholden as well.

Compare his earlier affirmation that "poems must (i) be well conceived, and (ii) take appropriate words and (iii) be well elaborated in their *lexis*," (i) ν]οηθῆναι γὰρ | αὐτὰ δεῖ κα[λ]ῶc καὶ (ii) λό|γους οἰκείο[υc] λαβεῖν (iii) καὶ | κατὰ τὴν λέξιν ἐξ[ερ]|γαcθ[ῆναι καλῶc (*On Poems* 5 x [xiii] 28).[93] I think it is obvious that the three activities named here are temporally sequenced, describing the order of composition endorsed by Philodemus; and that the temporal sequence simultaneously describes evaluative priorities: "conception"—organizing the thoughts, actions, and characterizations, in short, "composing the *praxis*" or the *poesis* (the poem's "contents")—comes first, because it stands first in importance (cf. Aristotle, *Poetics* 14. 1453b3, *proteron*); appropriate diction (*to prepon*) comes second, because the prerequisite of words is subject matter (this stage classically falls under *ekloge*, selection of diction); artistic elaboration of diction predictably comes last, as a finishing

---

[90] None of the following examples really help us understand the passage in question. Athenenaeus 5.180D: "Leading off is *idion* to the lyre," τὸ γὰρ ἐξάρχειν τῆς φόρμιγγος ἴδιον; Diogenes Laertius 7.103: "Heating, not cooling, is specific to (a defining property of) heat," ἴδιον θερμοῦ τὸ θερμαίνειν, οὐ τὸ ψύχειν. Its use in col. xii (xv) may be distantly related to another, specialized (and evaluative) sense of *idion*, to be discussed below, and equivalent to "original contribution" and "poetic good" or "value" (cf. Aristotle, *Poetics* 17.1455b23: "properly part of"). And for Philodemus, the locus of this value is invariably the subject matter, not the style.

[91] An example of it may perhaps be found in *Anonymous Prolegomena to Platonic Philosophy*, ed. L. G. Westerink (Amsterdam 1962), 17 pp. 33–34.

[92] It is precisely this (justifiable) impulse to anti-reductionism that motivates Aristotle's avoidance of any easy dichotomy between language and thought, or between "form" and "content." Aristotle's operational criteria (form/*matter*), once applied, exhaust the form/content dualism, because there is nothing left over to correspond to "content." All that remains are the materials—the artistic *hyle*, e.g., the inherited myths—and the media upon which the form is (or comes) imprinted, like a "soul."

[93] Philodemus evidently finds this formulation of his opponent's view (Demetrius of Byzantium) unobjectionable in principle. The procedure—of parasitical re-formulation—is found in other parts of *On Poems*. The substance of Philodemus' view here would be identical with **[6]** above.

stroke (again, in classical sequence, this is the *synthesis* of *lexis*). Now compare Aristotle's priorities, in the *Poetics*: δεῖ δὲ τοὺς μύθους cυνιcτάναι καὶ τῇ λέξει cυναπεργάζεcθαι ὅτι μάλιcτα πρὸ ὀμμάτων τιθέμενον; "In constructing his plots [first] and [then] using diction to bring them to completion, [the poet] should put [the events] before his eyes as much as he can" (*Poetics* 17.1455a22–23).[94] First, put your plots together (i.e., *katholou*, concentrating on their logical bare bones), then truss them up ("enmatter" them) in *lexis* (καὶ τῇ λέξει cυναπεργάζεcθαι; compare Philodemus' κατὰ τὴν λέξιν ἐξ[ερ]|γαcθ[ῆναι] above, and ἐν τῆι λέξει in [7] below). Thus, εὑρίcκοι [ἂν] τὸ πρέπον, "the poet will discover *to prepon*" (*Poetics* 17. 1455a25). Philodemus' overlap with Aristotle is not restricted to matters of usage. For in restating the claims of primacy made for *praxis* in the *Poetics*, Philodemus is affirming, not abolishing or reconfiguring, the conventional dualism of language and thought (or style and content), in making form depend upon, and conform to, that which "grounds" it, as its *hypokeimenon*: content.

Elsewhere, this same bias reappears: for Philodemus, the prime factor in poetry lies precisely in the ideas and meanings (the διανοήματα) that the poem conveys, and which define the poem's identity (and, in cases, the poet's "originality"): these are, for him, *to idion*. There are differences between Aristotle and Philodemus. Aristotle's criterion of a play's (or epic's) identity is the structural identity of the plot (*Poetics* 18.1456a7–8). Its equivalent, today, would be "form" (it is a *synthesis* of *pragmata*). By any standard, Philodemus' notion of subject matter is far less sophisticated than Aristotle's. In [2b], Philodemus does make a gesture towards the *synthesis* of *praxis*. But the specific endorsement of *praxis* (and its *synthesis*) by Philodemus is unique in his preserved corpus, and probably suggests a compromise with the language introduced by Neoptolemus (or Philomelus, or his other sources): elsewhere, Philodemus will endorse the primacy of *hypothesis* (*res*) whenever it comes in for discussion, but in general he favors "thoughts," "meanings," or "underlying ideas." Here we have just one more confirmation that Philodemus' is a reactive, ad hoc poetics, revealing occasionally and desultorily the tendencies of his aesthetic tastes, which are otherwise remarkably simple and conservative. If earlier in *On Poems* 5 (col. ix [xii] 6–9, cf. 24–27), Philodemus reacts negatively to the proposition, for instance, that "something's having been poetically composed (τὸ πεποιημένον εἶναι) *carries greater weight* in poetics (πλεῖον ἰcχύειν ἐν ποιητικῆι) than its containing valuable meanings/ideas (τοῦ τὰ διανοήματα ἔχειν πολυτελῆ)—a remark that reverses Aristotle's sentiments in *Rhetoric* 3.1 1404a18, using Aristotle's very words[95]—this is because of the irrefragable value that he attaches to meaning, both in the production and in the reception of poetry (col. ix [xii] 6–9; cf. 24–27). The poet stamps his original signature on the tradition, by contributing mentally to it; in the case of a received, "unpoetic" plot-line or motif (one never poetically presented before, literally "never done"), the poet can endow these materials with a distinctively *poetic* character alone by dint of the conceptual organization that he imparts to it (rendering it, effectively, a *pepoiomenon*, a "made object," in the sense that matters most for Philodemus):

---

[94] Cf. Lucas ad loc.   [95] Cited above, n. 7.

[7] *P.Herc.* 1081, fr. ix, 27–28 (p. 205 Sbordone):

ἀπόητον ὑπόθεcιν λα|βὼν προcθῆ⟨ι⟩ τὸν ⟨ἴ⟩διον νο[ῦν] . . .[96]

Receiving an 'unpoetic' *hypothesis*, the poet adds to it *his own* (i.e., *original*) intention . . .

Here we have the key to Philodemus' view of what constitutes the essence of poetry and poetic value (*to poetikon*). He has the sense to recognize that it is not, to quote an interesting expression from *On Poems*, "*qua* poem" (καθὸ πόημα) that he values poems, since, one might say, the poem *qua* poem for Philodemus does not include meaning *qua* meaning (*On Poems* 5 col. xxii [xxv] 30, cf. col. xxix [xxxii] 18). Philodemus is borrowing his opponents' language here, and attempting to hoist them with their own petard. καθὸ πόημα appears, moreover, to reflect the technical usage of Neoptolemus, which survives into the last columns of Book 5. Hence, the meaning of the expression can be made more precise: it singles out a Neoptolemic aspectual distinction, "the poem viewed *qua* '*poema*'," in respect of its *synthesis* only;—as it must, and as "poem *qua* poem" would in any case amount to; it is unclear on what other grounds Philodemus could make this logical precision.[97] But certain predecessors in the critical tradition (e.g., Aristo) made just this distinction, and tolerantly, or "indulgently," "preferred" the *synthesis* (the poem *qua poema*).[98] And hence Philodemus' vehement opposition to the *synthesis*-doctrine, which was grounded in this very sort of dissociation and preference. What he takes to be his fatal objection to this doctrine is that the very quality of the *synthesis* of the *lexis* must itself be gauged by the mind (cf. *On Poems* 5 col. xx [xxiii] 34: τὴν cύνθεcιν αὐτὴν τῶ[ν]| λέξεων διανοίαι γνω||ριζομένην). If **[2b]** above means anything at all, it must mean something like the following excerpt from elsewhere in *On Poems*:

[8] *P.Herc.* 1676 col. i 19–24 (p. 243 Sbordone)

τὸ γὰρ ἐγλ[έγειν]| τὰc οἰκείαc [sc. λέξειc] καὶ δ[ιατιθέ]|ναι πρὸc {α} δήλωcιν τοι|ούτου νοήματος ἐπί|τηδ[εc, τὸ το]|ιοῦτ᾽ ἢ[ν ἴ]διον αὐτοῦ).

For selecting the *appropriate lexeis* and arranging them with the aim of clarifying [bringing out] such a meaning [i.e., one that renders the *pragmata* know-

---

[96] The thought is familiar. Cf. *P.Herc.* 1676 col. vi 23–27 p. 253 Sbordone, [15] below: poetry at its best consists in "ideas" or "meanings" not got from others, but produced autonomously. Cf. *On Poems* 5 col. vii (x) 24–31: in the worst of cases, "one can set forth an illogical (*alogon*) *mythos* and *hypothesis* and elaborate it poetically"; but the "best poet" is distinguished by *selectio*, i.e., he brings his rationality to the process of the selection of material itself. (See further Greenberg 1961 [above, n. 19], 274–76).

[97] It is this special usage which prompts Philodemus' self-conscious apologetics at *On Poems* 5 col. xxxv (xxxviii) 7, where *poesis*, "understood in its common acceptation (κοινῶc)" and not in the strict technical sense of Neoptolemus, is allowed to include in its scope epigrams and Sapphic verses, poetic forms which otherwise only questionably or with difficulty fall into the undisputed rank of *poesis* and not just *poema*.

[98] Cf. *On Poems* 5 col. xvi 17–18 (in Jensen's text, which approximates the apographs) and 27–30. Aristo shares many conceptual affinities with Neoptolemus (whether this is due to a direct influence, or more indirectly to their shared acceptance of the *synthesis*-doctrine). This is undoubtedly the reason why Philodemus brings them together for our contemplation in successive columns.

able, γνωcτά] aptly—this was shown to be (the poet's) *idion* (defining distinction).

This gives Philodemus' characteristic and considered view. It is the job of the rational agent in poetic production to subordinate language to meaning. Incidentally, as [8] shows, the *idion*-relation for Philodemus is primarily a relation of propriety, viz. a *prepon*-relation: the poet's distinctiveness lies in his ideas and in his selecting appropriate *lexeis* to match them.[99] Once again it seems confirmed that [2b] expresses appropriateness (functional subordination, not identity, makes for the proper relation between *synthesis* and *hypothesis*), without explicitly using the terminology, and especially the assymetries, of *to prepon*.

Later in Book 5, Philodemus tips his hand. An opponent, he complains:

[9] Philodemus, *On Poems* 5 col. xxxii (xxxv) 6–10

καὶ περὶ τῆ[c] λέ|ξεωc μόνον λαλεῖ, τὰ νο|ήματα κυριωτέραν δύ|ναμιν ἔχοντα παραπέμ|πουc[α].

speaks *only* about *lexis*, while dismissively leaving aside *thoughts, which have the far greater value [dynamis]*

This is characteristic for Philodemus. His editorial criticism of an unnamed opponent here can be aligned with his correction of Neoptolemus (cf. especially the mark of single-minded dissociation: μόνον, "only"); and it is also partially in answer to the questions Philodemus put to the critic dissected prior to Neoptolemus, Demetrius of Byzantium, who evidently failed to spell out "what is of greater importance (τί κυρι-ώτερο[ν]) in a poem, and what of lesser importance (τί λειπόμ[εν]ον)" (*On Poems* col. x [xiii] 20–22). Philodemus' own priorities should now be plain. And his objections to Neoptolemus follow from those priorities. Neoptolemus infringed Philodemus' most basic principles of poetry, not least by severing (in theory) all connection between poet and *hypothesis*.

In the eyes of Philodemus, a poet is not merely another *eidos* of the art of poetry. *Qua* rational agency he is the *fons et origo* of the creative process, properly endowed with a *dynamis*, on the basis of which he produces his art and manifests his agency. It is the poet who is the source of poetic value: he "has the *dynamis* and executes his work *starting from that*" (*On Poems* 5 col. xi [xiv] 17–20). By *dynamis* Philodemus clearly intends at least the capacity to produce original "thoughts" susceptible to appropriate expression (or else the capacity to reorder, conceptually, poetic materials handed down in the tradition); this is his departure-point for executing poetic talent, which takes less the form of poetic *ergasia* (which is the Neoptolemic hypostasis of *synthesis* that Philodemus strictly forbids), than that of an *ergazomenon* (which signifies agency). Thoughts (their conception and arrangement) come first, temporally and axiologically.

It is out of modern convenience and habit that Philodemus' "thoughts" and "meaning" have been transposed into a more familiar "content."[100] But "thoughts" in

---

[99] See Greenberg 1955, 156–57, for a brief but perceptive comment on this column.

[100] Among recent scholars, only Calogero, Boyancé (on the heels of Immisch), and Greenberg have raised strong objections to the anachronism (but not the incoherence) of the form/content distinction.

the late Hellenistic critical vocabulary of Philodemus cover more ground than one perhaps would like. By the same token, the usage is unified by an intuitively proximate, if unanalyzed, set of concepts, as well as by a (probably not wholly fortuitous) overlap in a family of terms. The very imprecision of the term suggests that "content" (in its own way imprecise) may do an injustice to its usages. "Thoughts" include and imply, and indeed at times out of sheer ambiguity may denote simultaneously: (a) the poet's "pre-conception" of his subject-matter (τὰ προνοούμενα, col. iii [vi]); (b) that pre-conception as embodied in the conceptual structure of the poem (the underlying plot and its organization, the poem's subject-matter, story, or theme), which bears the imprint of the poet's mind (his *nous*); (c) the "ideas" or "meanings" conveyed by a poem's language and *subtending* it, ἡ ὑποτεταγμένη διάνοια or νοούμενα (*On Poems* 5 col. xix [xxii]16, xxvi [xxix] 2, *P.Herc.* 228 fr. iii B Mangoni); this suffers from a further ambiguity, discussed earlier, between "meanings" of individual words and "meanings" of parts or wholes of poems ("expressions *signifying meanings*" could refer to both); this is sometimes captured by the singular, ἡ διάνοια (e.g., col. xxvii [xxx] 34), a tendentious expression that suggests that a poem is collectively expressive of a single "idea" or "meaning," or that "what the poet meant" is straightforwardly reproducible (but it may aim at no more than *hypothesis*); and (d) most ambiguously of all, particularly whenever Philodemus simply writes "the subtended" (as in col. xxvi [xxix] 6), just possibly those mental or physical objects or events to which thoughts "refer" (a connotation that anyway lies close at hand in all of the above; cf. Epicurus, *Letter to Herodotus* 37; Sextus Empiricus, *Adv. math.* 1.300).

Behind all of these near-equivalents lies an ineradicable dualism, the notion that words do not exist independently of their meanings, or of the ideas they evoke.[101] They do not exist independently because for Philodemus they coexist (or coexisted) in the mind of the poet and his poetic *dynamis*. *Dynamis* includes the capacity to conceive thoughts capable of receiving appropriate expression, and presumably it includes the capacity to give those thoughts appropriate expression too. Perhaps it is this *dynamis* which is the object of our poetic appreciation. If so, we can only arrive at an aesthetic judgment by way of assessing, separately, the quality of the "thought" and the language that conveys it, appropriately or otherwise: hence, the dualism persists. The notion that words do not exist independently of their meanings is one that Aristotle shared. But it is a too-little noticed fact that Aristotle in his *Poetics* (and, from what we may gather, in any of his other poetic writings) *nowhere* groups "thoughts" in the senses outlined above (whether these be intentions, meanings or referents) together with *praxis, pragmata,* or *mythos*.[102] Philodemus is here going, as it were, behind Aristotle's back to his predecessor, Plato. Only, in Plato's case, the "thoughts" of a poem are vague in the sense that they have no discernible content; in Philodemus' case, "thoughts" are vague because he has no positive theory that would

---

[101] Also behind this vague barrage of clear preferences lies an implicit evaluative criterion, namely that (i) "thought" is intrinsically valuable, but (ii) not all "thoughts" are equally valuable. I doubt whether (i) is intelligible in the absence of (ii); the laws of *to prepon* alone point towards (ii). Philodemus can be shown to have held both of these positions. Benvenga's insistence on Philodemus' discovery of value-neutral criteria, i.e., "un contenuto indeterminato" (Benvenga 1951 [above, n. 28], 250) is belied by his very choice of "content" over *synthesis*, a choice which comes value–laden all by itself.

[102] Pace Benvenga 1951 (above, n. 28), 194 n. 1.

tell him what they should contain. Philodemus is unwilling to take Plato's plunge, and eliminate rational purpose altogether from his view of poetry.

Unlike Plato before him and the common run of critics after him, Aristotle has *no* theory of poetic intention or meaning.[103] He takes, as it were, Plato's plunge, but he plunges into, not away from, the nature of poetry (into its rational *form*). Correspondingly, Philodemus shows little awareness of anything that might correspond to Aristotelian *dianoia*, the only "thought" which matters to Aristotle in the *Poetics* (the thought, purpose, or judgment of an individual character, aimed at action).[104] Something has happened to Aristotle's language in the course of its reception, and this critical difference should be borne in mind as we proceed.

5. *Synthesis* in Analysis: The Deformation of Matter

In reacting to Neoptolemus' approach, which makes the content (*hypothesis, praxis, meaning*) into a form (an *eidos*), Philodemus is reasserting a less potent version of Aristotle's own formalism.[105] This is startling by itself, given Philodemus' Epicurean biases (although in other respects, Aristotle's thought was widely diffused, in diluted form, in the language of criticism).[106] But is *hypothesis*, so viewed, really translatable as "content"?[107] For a clue, we might look to Aristotle, but Aristotle, in his *Poetics*, has little that corresponds to a content/form dualism. Despite Rostagni's claims to the contrary ("noi sappiamo che l'estetica di Aristotele si sarebbe perennemente dibattuta nel *dualismo di forma* e *contenuto*"),[108] the distinction is not philosophically interesting to Aristotle; and the possibility of locating the "thought" or "content" (the *dianoemata* or *dianoia*) of a composition, as Plato tried to do, is conspicuously alien to Aristotle's project.[109] The conceptual axes in the *Poetics* are not content and form, but *matter* and form,[110] and certain later critics not only

---

[103] See also Halliwell 1986 (above, n. 38), 132 n. 35; Porter 1992 (above, n. 3), 80.

[104] At col. xxxii (xxxv) 20–32 Philodemus vehemently denies that applying the *prepon* doctrine to all characters (their speech and thought) results in an absurd mimetic requirement—not because poetry cannot be widely imitative if a poet so chooses (it can: lines 28–32), but because not all mimesis is appropriate to poetry. His taste seems to have inclined towards realism (τὸ | ποίημα δ' ἐ[cτὶ] τὸ μιμού|μενον ὡc ἐνδέχεται | μάλιcτα, col. xxiii [xxvi] 13–15).

[105] As noted earlier, Philodemus may ultimately conceive of "content" and "form" as aspects. But this too is a legacy of Aristotelian (rhetorical) thought, as is their hierarchical assymetry.

[106] Philodemus' Aristotelianism is rarely noted by scholars and then only in passing. Cf. Greenberg 1961 [above, n. 19], 273 and Walsh 1987, 59 n. 8.

[107] Rightly, Brink 1963, 60 and n. 3, interpreting Greenberg 1961 (above, n. 19), 280: "Neoptolemus seems to be careful not to equate style with *poema* and content with *poesis*." Nonetheless we find on 72, "style and subject matter"; on 144, "style and content."

[108] A. Rostagni, *Scritti Minori*, vol. 1, p. 162–63; cf. 167.

[109] Aristotle's *Poetics* knows no theory of intentionality for poets or of meaning for poems (see Halliwell 1986 [above, n. 38], 56), apart from (perhaps) a theory of *tragedy's* "intentionality" (its final cause), as in §7 above (the poet's only intention for Aristotle is in effect to be the author of an Aristotelian *mythos*). We might say that for Aristotle content is form, but his hylomorphism exhausts all competing options, including the content/form scheme. On content, see Greenberg 1961 (above, n. 19), 269. See Janko 1984 (above, n. 33), 192, for the brief but acute observation that the content/form dichotomy is "transcended" in Aristotle's *Poetics*.

[110] A possible objection is that, after all, tragedy's contents can at least be named, or listed, as Aristotle does when in c. 17 he encourages poets to outline the events "in the abstract" (καθόλου): X does

recognized this, but in the counter-Aristotelian tradition they sought to challenge it, by bringing back into the picture everything that Aristotle had brushed aside as so much matter: principally, song and *lexis*, but generally, the material and phenomenal properties of aesthetic objects. (Recall that for Aristotle, phenomenal realization in a material medium is not a *necessary* feature of art: this is his aesthetic "heresy").[111] An example of this counter-trend, which probably drew some of its inspiration from Neoptolemus too, are the euphonic theories of Aristo and Crates, theories which these heterodox thinkers took over directly from critics apparently known as *kritikoi*, whom Philodemus links together for us in a clear line of succession and influence. It is against this background that we have to place Philodemus' vigorous defense of the relation that he sees obtaining between *synthesis* and *hypothesis*.

First, a reflection on the term *synthesis*. Its superficial contrast with *hypothesis* is obvious. Does it really signify "form," or even the formal aspects of a work? The answer is, in fact, No. From before Aristotle down to Dionysius of Halicarnassus and later (e.g., ps.-Longinus), *synthesis* is just the putting together (juxtaposing) of sounds and words (bits of language); it is not their form (whatever that might be), and still less a form "containing" thoughts. *Synthesis* picks out the disposition and combination of elements (*stoicheia*) in a poem, be these letters, the sounds they represent or constitute, or larger syntactic units.[112] As such, *synthesis* is poised somewhat difficulty (and intransigently) at the threshold between the formal and material aspects of language, and this is, on reflection, only natural: in fact, we have seen "*synthesis*" used of plots (*poesis*) *and* of phonic material (*poema*) already. The "trend" toward *synthesis* will aggravate, by degrees, this insight into the threshold status of the concept. On this counter-poetics, whenever it may have emerged on the scene, *synthesis* is material in a certain disposition, but not necessarily in a "form." "Form" in our sense of the term and from their perspective has to be regarded as at best an epiphenomenal concept, a construction that may be put on a *syntheton*, or else denied to obtain in it: the acceptance of form would on this view be a mere concession to a conceptual usage, not an acknowledgment of anything intrinsic to the artifact in question.[113] Aristotle's view, by contrast, is either that form is what gives shape to

---

A and B; consequently C and D occur. But so put, these events are already embraced by the *mythos*; they give a sketch, not so much of what as why, which is to say that they encompass a logic of necessary consequences (framed by an *arche* and a *telos*) and a mirror-logic of exclusions. This outline sketch, in short, falls under (§10) above: it represents *in nuce* "what the plot wants, not what the poet wants." And it is precisely this sort of distinction that a content/form theorist will not be able to draw.

[111] Realizability is; but plays can be read without being seen and still achieve their essential purpose. This is comparable to Aristotle's all-but-stated preference for line-drawings over colors (comparing 48b18–19 with 50b1–3), viz., his endorsement of a severely restricted spectrum of aesthetic possibilities. But even more to the point, Aristotle's position may be due to the fact that matter, as such, doesn't actually enter into his ontology. Cf. M. Furth, *Substance, Form and Psyche: An Aristotelian Metaphysics* (Cambridge 1988), 87: "there is in this theory no such thing as 'bare unqualified matter,'" a controversial claim); nor does matter, qualified in any interesting sense, enter in except as a stepping stone towards form; ibid., 81: "It may sound odd to us; but it seems we are being told that certain 'parts' are *proto-structural* . . ., the same nature somehow doubling as *stuff* and as *structure*." This arguably obtains to an even more emphatic degree in non-organic wholes, like tragedies, where Aristotle can conveniently overlook the materiality of language and spectacle.

[112] *Poetics* 1447a11, 58a11, 58a28. Dionysius of Halicarnassus, *De compositione verborum* c. 2, p. 6, 17-19 Usener-Radermacher.

[113] The focus here, as with Neoptolemus, is not on "diction" but on the "*synthesis*" of *lexis* as the

matter and materials, or, more radically, that material never exists in the absence of its formal or structural properties.[114] More often than not in the early history of literary criticism precisely these factors, the materiality, the sound, the texture of poems, were not only relegated to a minor status but were neglected altogether. The Critics among others sought hard to redress the balance. The rhetoric of their arguments could be alarming at times.

In its extreme version, this counter-poetics would characteristically deny form's supervenience on materials, wherever Aristotle would characteristically wish to assert it, according to the well-mapped criteria of the *Poetics* (unity, etc.). In a fragment from another papyrus, *P.Herc.* 460 fr. ix + 1073 fr. iii p. 169 Sbordone, one of the opponents (they are Critics) puts forth the remarkable claim that parrots can achieve the *idion* (the proper characteristic) of meaningful sound through mimetism, in the absence of any rational grasp of language. This is clearly an argument *in extremis*. For the Critics, the *idion* of poetry lies in the sound of the syllables, not in some (rational and formal) *heteron ti*, as Aristotle had claimed (*Metaphysics* Z 17. 1041b11). But we should note that the form/matter dichotomy, operative on both models, obviates all recourse to a form/content dichotomy. For Aristotle, content is definitively transumed into an aspect of form. cύcταcιc τῶν πραγμάτων is not equivalent to "form of the content" but to "the form inhering in the events as presented," i.e. plot. Events have no real intelligibility (causal coherence or unity) outside of the forms they take. Remove their intelligible structure (*mythos*), and only a chaotic, random succession remains (*Poetics* 6.1450a29–33). The relevant contrast to "form" in Aristotle is thus not content, but formlessness. The Critics could not agree more. Finally, on the natural teleology of the Aristotelian position, "appropriateness" is rehabilitated into a relation between matter and form, and, more importantly, of form to form. Poets will adapt the parts of a *mythos* to its logic more or less adroitly (§10). Here, *to prepon* does not signify the way language fits content; it is a synonym for the *internal* coherence of dramatic logic. But it also conceals an evaluative criterion that decides what counts as a "proper" form.[115] Staring a poem's matter in the face, and utterly unconsumed by the question of its content, the Critics will have no truck with the standards of *to prepon* as regards content either.

But here the similarities, already marked by important differences, end. Whereas for Aristotle form carries teleological weight and is the result of a supervenient top-down causation (say, in the convergence of formal and final causes: "that for the sake of which"), note how for Neoptolemus causation appears to have been neatly *eliminated*, through a conceptual stasis. Neoptolemus has liberated the poet from all causal responsibility, in the cool clinical light of analysis, whereby poetry is dissolved into its aspects. If the poet loses his centrality as the prime mover of his creations, and *poema* moves freely into the foreground, this is partly intelligible against the historical trend towards *synthesis*: with the primacy of *hypothesis*

---

matter of language. Contrast Brink 1963, 99: "The fragments of Neoptolemus suggest that he made diction, λέξιc, one of the mainstays of the technical portion of his book"; and cf. A. Ardizzoni, *Poiema: Ricerche sulla Teoria del Linguaggio Poetico nell'Antichità* (Bari 1953), 81–82, with n. 5.

[114] For supervenience, see C. Shields, "Soul and Body in Aristotle" *OSAP* 6 (1988), 103–37; for the more radical view, Furth 1988 (above, n. 111).

[115] Cf. Seneca, *Letters* 65.7: the form of a statue is said to be that which is "in" a matter (*in quo*), *and* "adapted" to it (*quae aptatur illi*).

contested, the materiality of verbal arrangement is simply given preference, but not, evidently, given causal primacy. (In the case of Neoptolemus, all notions of "propriety," or *to prepon*, evidently are abandoned too, blocked by the same conceptual stasis.)[116] In the case of the euphonic theory inspired by the Critics, centered round pleasing sound (euphony) arising from composite materials (*syntheta*), *synthesis* expresses a *material* cause that is staunchly opposed to Aristotle's formal and final causes of poetry (he had expressly written off such aspects as minority "causes" at *Poetics* 4.1448b18–19, "accomplishment (ἀπεργαςίαν), color, or some other such cause (αἰτίαν)".[117] Here, with the Critics, we are faced with a radical undoing of the content/form dualism. "Form" is unmasked as a hermeneutical construct, of simulacral status; "content" falls away, as a functional irrelevancy (τὰ νοήματα μὴ κινεῖν, "thoughts don't move" the readers of poems, *P.Herc.* 1081 fr. xxiii p. 221 Sbordone);[118] and nothing steps in to take their place. The widest implication of their argument, however, goes beyond even the issue of the materiality of language: it comes from the recognition that "form" is not inherent as a property of objects, that it is rather a perceptual property reflective of the demands of the viewing subject— in short, that its affirmation comes not freely from our intercourse with objects but ideologically and derivatively from the way objects, and indeed the whole enterprise of criticism, are perceived. At this extreme, conventionalism seeps into even the professed naturalism of the position held by the euphonist Critics.

Let us briefly take up the euphonists' theory, and then confront it with the issues which we have been discussing until now. I will treat the euphonists pretty much en bloc, focusing on the empiricist strain in Aristo and Crates that derives from the apparently more one-sided and radical positions of the so-called *kritikoi*. These Critics could be disarmingly pigeon-holed as having been concerned with the "musicality" of poetic language *simpliciter*. "Euphony," however, masks a range of concerns, with disturbing implications that reach far beyond the mere delectation of sounds. The critical procedures of the Critics, starting from empirical sensation (αἴcθηcιc), were based on a superficially phenomenalistic foundation; at a deeper level, their starting principles look physicalist and even (in ways) atomistic.[119] But ultimately, the object of their quest is not the sources of aesthetic pleasures, but the sources of aesthetic value; their program can thus be viewed as a wider ranging conceptual critique of the critical canons in ancient literary criticism. They conceived of poetry and poetic experience as material events, and the *krisis* of poems as a material act of judgment. As I have suggested elsewhere, their terminology partly comes out of the

---

[116] *Pace* Brink 1963, e96.

[117] "Cause" here means "cause" of pleasure, and it is synonymous with the material properties it elliptically names (cf. Aristotle, *Physics* 194b24)—as it also does in the language used by the Critics. Boyancé 1936 (above, n. 33), 32 identifies *poema* with the formal cause, *hypothesis* with the final cause, and hence finds nothing to equate to a material cause.

[118] Contrast Philodemus' response in another passage: the reader's mind is stirred (κεινεῖ) by the rational perception of the technically (not irrationally) produced features of poems (*P.Herc.* 1081 fr. xxxix [p. 29 Nardelli]). He has misunderstood the Critics even here (for them, poems are a compound of technique [*thesis*] and natural factors and responses [*physis*]).

[119] Cf. *P.Herc.* 228 fr. iA 7–16 Mangoni, where Crates is said to have been resolutely empiricist in his critical evaluation of poems: πάντα | δ' ἐμπείρωc [θε]ωρούμε|[ν]α κρίνεται. αἴcθηcιc is the source, pleasure the criterion, of poetic judgment.

atomistic tradition, and partly results from a sharp inversion of the standard critical terms and conventions of the Aristotelian canon of literary criticism.[120] For present purposes it will be enough to suggest that the materiality of poems for the Critics consists in the compositional nature of the verbal artifact, which is modelled—however implicitly—on the theory of atomic aggregation and configuration (*synthesis, schematismos*—concepts for arrangement dramatically opposed to "form," as they do not allow of any converse, e.g., "content").

The model on which this anti-aesthetics is based looks like the following (much of the evidence can be adduced from *On Poems* 5). Sounds (or elements, *stoicheia*, which represent letter-sounds and are in fact irreducible to either letters or sounds) are arranged in patterns (τετάχθαι [col. xx [xxiii] 14], cύνθεcθαι or cύγκειcθαι) that generate aesthetic effects, for instance euphonic sound, which is in turn "judged" (or sorted out, κρίνεcθαι) by a physical act of mind ("by the irrational faculty of hearing," col. xxi [xxiv] 3), which is to say, through sheer corporeal contact; the ear (ἀκοή) is the key organ, and it is said to be empirically skilled (τετριμμένη, col. xxiv [xxvii] 10). In practice, the Critic scans an aesthetic artifact for its (phonic) display of material micro-differences (the διαφοραί τῶν γραμμάτων, of letters, sc. *stoicheia*), as these are arranged by *thesis* and *taxis*, i.e., by *synthesis*.[121] In their ensemble, these differences of quantity and quality—they are in fact positional attributes, and endowed with relational values—constitute aesthetic qualities at a higher level (the "macro-level" of sensation in contact with a *synthesis*), where sound can be seen to be "caused" (the "elements," viz. their positionalities, are literally the "causes," *aitia*), as a surface effect, a sur-plus phenomenon, or to take their own striking terminology, an "epiphenomenon":

[10a] Philodemus *On Poems* 5 col. xx (xxiii) 26–32

ἄ]‖θλιομ μὲν γὰρ κ[αὶ τὸ τὴν]‖ ἐπι[φ]αινομένην τῆι | cυνθέcει τῶν λέξεων εὐφωνίαν εἰcάγειν καὶ | ταύτηc ἀνατιθέναι τὴν ‖[κρί]cιν τῆι τριβῆι τῆc ἀ|[κο]ῆc.

It is despicable of him [Aristo] to drag in the [idea of] euphony [that is claimed by the Critics to be] epiphenomenal to the *synthesis,* and to ascribe the *krisis* [discrimination, judgment] of [euphony] to the practice of the ear.

The sound is "epiphenomenal" to the *synthesis* of the *lexeis.* Compare the following about Crates:

[10b] Philodemus *On Poems* 5 col. xxi (xxiv) 31

τὴν ἐπιφαινομένην ‖[α]ὐ[τῆι] (sc. τῆι cυνθέcει) φωνὴ[ν] ἐπ[αι]ν[εῖ]).

He values the sound that appears on (the surface of) the *synthesis* [of the *lexeis*]

Needless to say, any conception of "appropriateness" has absolutely no place in

---

[120] Porter 1989.

[121] Cf. Crates, ap. Philod., *On Poems* 5 col. xxiv (xxvii) 22–26. Crates' theory περὶ τῶν cτοιχείων (the quantitative and qualitative properties of letter-sounds; their standing vis à vis the source and criterion of poetic *krisis*) is mentioned briefly at col. xxvi (xxix) 8ff. and is exposed elsewhere in *On Poems* (Book 2). See Porter 1989.

this alternative model of poetry. This is just one of the consequences of the embrace-
ment of "euphony" by the Critics, and of their rejection of "meaning" as a determi-
nant of aesthetic value: *synthesis* (*qua* bearer of sound) and *hypothesis* (*qua* thought/
meaning) can obviously no longer stand in any relation beyond one of happenstance.
But the same consequence also follows from their total rejection of all "formal"
properties as well: form no longer can be normatively and naturally imposed on a
material base. The flow of impingements is, in fact, reversed, with causalities pro-
ceeding, so to speak, entirely from the bottom up.[122] This blindness to appropriateness is well brought out in a parallel context, this time involving criticism of the
"*Harmonikoi.*" The case—and the criticism—is symptomatic of a basic materialism,
waged as a form of reductivism, that runs through ancient traditions of aesthetic
inquiry, and all too quietly through the modern handbooks that set out to describe
them:

[11] ps.-Plutarch, *On Music* 33

Harmonics, for instance, is the science of the genera of melodic order, of inter-
vals, *systemata*, notes ($\phi\theta\acute{o}\gamma\gamma\omega\nu$), *tonoi*, and modulations between *systemata*,
and it is unable to advance beyond this point. Hence we cannot seek to discover
through Harmonics whether the composer ($\acute{o}$ $\pi o\iota\eta\tau\acute{\eta}c$) . . . has made an appropriate choice ($o\emph{i}\kappa\epsilon\acute{\iota}\omega c$) in using the Hypodorian *tonos* at the beginning, Dorian
at the end, and Hypophrygian and Phrygian in the middle. The science of Har-
monics does not extend to such matters, and requires supplementation from
many sources, *since it has no understanding of the nature of appropriateness*
($\tau\grave{\eta}\nu$ $\gamma\grave{\alpha}\rho$ $\tau\hat{\eta}c$ $o\emph{i}\kappa\epsilon\iota\acute{o}\tau\eta\tau o c$ $\delta\acute{u}\nu\alpha\mu\iota\nu$ $\grave{a}\gamma\nu o\epsilon\hat{\iota}$).[123]

Paradoxes ensue, which can only be suggested here. To Philodemus' strident
objection that *synthesis* must contain something, must have an *idion* (specific content), the Critics reply, *synthesis* of sound is the *idion* you seek. *Idion* now captures
the *material*, as opposed to the formal, autonomy, or more to the point, the specificity
of a given artifact. *Synthesis*, so viewed, has a value that is per se and autonomous.
A poem, in effect, must be considered *qua poema* ($\kappa\alpha\theta\grave{o}$ $\pi\acute{o}\eta\mu\alpha$). Only here, the
grounds for this preference are more radically thought through than on Neopto-
lemus' triad.[124] From the following rejoinder by Philodemus—one of his prettiest
statements on poetry, incidentally—we can glimpse the mainsprings of their program, and its negative implications (elsewhere these are made more explicit):

**[12] *P.Herc.* 1676 col. vi 16–24 (p. 253 Sbordone; C. Romeo, *CErc* 22 [1992],
167)**

When life furnishes ($\chi o\rho\eta[\gamma]o[\hat{u}]\nu\tau o c$) the abundant flow of expression ($\tau\grave{\eta}\nu$

---

[122] See n. 137 below.	[123] Tr. Barker, *Greek Musical Writings*, vol. 1, pp. 239–40.

[124] It is likely that Neoptolemus is presenting either a tempered or else just logically revamped
version of the *synthesis*-doctrine (rather than inspiring it). He is conceivably attempting to sort out the
logic of the Critics' reduction of poems to whatever meets *poema*-like criteria. Later critics, such as
Andromenides and Crates, apparently found Neoptolemus' contribution useful, and so they adopted his
terms.

χύ|ϲιν τῶ[ν] λέξεων), that is when *synthesis* becomes distinctive (*idia*)[125] of poets—not empty (ἀέριοϲ) or valued *qua* in and of itself (οὐδ' ἐπαινουμένη καθ' αὐτήν; viz., *per se*) but because it presents ideas besides (π[ρο]ϲπαρί-ϲτηϲι διαν[οί]αϲ), by means of which [poets] seduce hearts and minds (literally, "produce *psychagogia*" ψ[υ]χαγωγοῦϲιν).[126]

The opposed position is quite clear. Poems, in the camp opposite Philodemus' own, are valued on the basis of *synthesis*, which in turn is valued per se (without regard for meaning, *hypothesis*, etc.). A poem's specificity, which is elusively of the moment and "punctual," is grounded in its material coordinates: *this* sound *here*. It is in its own way, sublime.[127]

[13] *P.Herc.* 1676 col. vi 2–11 (ibid.)

[καὶ τὸ τὴν μὲν | ἐπιφαι]νομένην [ε]ὐφωνί|αν ἴδιον [εἶν]αι, τὰ δὲ νοή{ι}- |⁵ματα καὶ τὰϲ λέξειϲ ἐκτὸϲ | εἶναι καὶ κοινὰ ϲυνάγεϲ|θαι δεῖ[ν, πα]ρὰ πᾶϲι μὲν ὡϲ | ἐν [ϲτήλ]ηι μέ[ν]ει τοῖϲ κρι|τικοῖ[ϲ], ἐκλιπομένην[128] δ' ἐ̓|¹⁰χει τὴ[ν ἀ]ήθι[α]ν ἐκ τῶν | εἰρημένων.

It stands as [engraved] in [stone] for all the *kritikoi* that euphony, which is "epiphenomenal,"[129] is *idion* (a property specific to a poem),[130] while the meanings and the expressions must be concluded to be external and common (*koinon*). But based on the foregoing, this is strange and deficient.

Textual uncertainties aside, the main lines of the argument opposed by Philodemus are clear. At stake is nothing less than the value of *idion*, which displaces the semantic aspects of poems: these are sacrificed to the poem's material aspect. In a nearby column (*P.Herc.* 1676 col. v), *to idion* is claimed to reside not in the production of likenesses (for these are common, *koinon*, just by virtue of being "alike," e.g., to painters and sculptors), but rather in the actual carving (glyph-work) in metal and stone, which is specific to an instance of a given art (here, plastic art). The examples are not loosely chosen; they bring out something quintessential about the felt specificities of poetry, by locating these in the materials of the medium, in the instancing of "this" material (sound-pattern) "here," as though sounds were specific to each of their auditionings. One has to imagine the phonic equivalent of a cut or scrape, unique to a given chiseled stone, and proper to its delectation as such. Such is the

---

[125] Gomperz's conjecture ἰδ[ία] perhaps ought to read ἴδ[ιον] as in line 4 of the same column.

[126] I have adopted the revisions of Romeo (above, n. 9), 167; more recent readings below, pp. 163–64, cf. 220. The passage sheds, incidentally, some light on **[2b]**. *Synthesis* for Philodemus does not, by itself, produce *hypothesis*: it is "life" which occasions thoughts (meanings), which in turn are conveyed in poems (along with the *synthesis* that is their vehicle); and it is thoughts and meanings (whatever these are supposed to be) that are poetry's prime instrument.

[127] Cf. ps.-Longinus, *On the Sublime* 1.4 for the contrast (καιρίωϲ/ἐκ τοῦ ὅλου τῶν λόγων). The sublime is punctual, epiphanic, and in its own way epiphenomenal.

[128] The reading of Romeo (above, n. 9), 117, which partially confirms Heidemann's (Sbordone's makes little sense). Where Romeo reads ἀ]ηθί[α]ν ("novelty," "strangeness"), D. Armstrong conjectures εὐ]ηθί[α]ν. The general sense may seem clear, but it is difficult to construe the text.

[129] Literally, "appears on the surface of the *synthesis*."

[130] Both synthesis *and* the resulting euphony are *idia*.

materialist aesthetic purveyed by the critics Philodemus opposes.[131] Recent thinking on sculptural aesthetics in the post-classical period suggests that this kind of attention to sensuous detail—to material, tactile contingency—was one of the distinctive features of the early "Hellenistic Baroque."[132] If so, then the Critics are at the very least entitled to an equally "baroque" theory of aesthetic contemplation.

In refashioning *to idion*, the Critics are also reaffirming its literal significance: "proper to." *To idion*, henceforth, picks out an irreducible particular, a poem's proprietary sound, or perhaps just an irreducibly experiential property, which appears at the interface of a poem and its auditioning. Introducing such a concept into aesthetic discussion has certain obvious advantages: it brings within theoretical reach a feature of artworks that simply passed unexamined within the Aristotelian framework.[133] If the identification is right, Aristo of Chios, in the middle of the third-century, embraced the poetic principles of the Critics so as to account, we are told, for ἅπαcαc τὰc ἰδιότητac τῶν λόγων, "all the *specificities* [or "peculiarities," viz., the idiosyncratic material properties] of discourse," which are the fruit of a perceptual grasp, and which no intellectual understanding can hope to touch (*On Poems* 5 col. xxi [xxiv] 9). ἰδιότηc is naturally bound up with the Neoptolemic concept of *poema*. Their late association in the grammatical scholia to Dionysius Thrax is useful by way of contrast:

[14] Scholia on Dionysius Thrax's *Art of Grammar* 450, 10 Hilgard

μέλοc ἐcτὶ ποίημα παρ᾽ ἰδιότητα ῥυθμοῦ πεποιημένον.

Melos is a poem constructed according to the peculiarity of rhythm.

In the earlier tradition of *synthesis*-criticism, this definition would be a tautology, as Philodemus is quick to point out in characteristic Philodemese: "How is it, O Corybantes, that we do not all view a poem *qua* thrilling and plucking (τ]ὸ πόημα . . . ὡ[c] τερέτιcμα καὶ κροῦμα), but rather as *lexeis* signifying thought," etc. (*P.Herc.* 1074 fr. ii + 1081 fr. viii p. 201 Sbordone). What makes a poem a poem (defines its *idion*) is what defines Neoptolemus' *poema*: "They [the Critics] wouldn't hesitate to call [things] poems just in virtue of the plucking" (κατὰ τὰ κρούματα γὰρ οὐκ ἂν φθάνοιεν οὕτω ποιήματα λέγοντεc; fr. 52 Hausrath). The disparaging image of the Corybants has venerable roots that reach at least as far back as Plato's *Ion* (534a).

The relevance of musical theory to some strands of ancient literary criticism deserves to be underscored. Another significant parallel is again found in prior musical tradition, where the *idiotes* captures the qualities of a musical *synthesis*, viewed in respect of its material components: the notes (*phthongoi*), the intervals (their differences, *diastemata*) which define their relations, and in short, the theory and mechanics of euphonics (Aristoxenus, *Elements of Harmony* 18).[134] And in this line of

---

[131] Barthes' theory of the "grain of the voice" is a contemporary version of this.

[132] See A. F. Stewart, "Narration and Illusion in the Hellenistic Baroque," in Peter Holliday, ed., *Narrative and Event in Ancient Art* (Cambridge 1993).

[133] Aristotle of course knew the concept, but he had reasons of his own not to commend it; see Owen 1965 (above, n. 72). The question whether the Critics had in mind properties of works that were only objective or compounded from objective and subject properties is too complex to be addressed in this context.

interpreting poems, meanings as such have no material specificity, no phenomenal, which is to say no sensible, counterpart: they fail to "appear," and so too, they are accorded no place in a materialist aesthetics. *Lexeis* (expressions) are a different matter. A given *lexis* is a *koinon* (common property), until it assumes a place within a given metrical and rhythmical context. As such and by itself it "has" no rhythm, although it is capable of assuming several rhythms.[135] More abstractly, but in line with the same reasoning, a given rhythm (*rhythmos*) is strictly non-identical with any *rhythmizomenon* (word or musical phrase subjected to that *rhythmos*). In one respect, that rhythm is a *koinon*, to be instantiated materially here or there (as an *idion*); in another respect, that rhythm is "one of the things that dispose (τῶν διατιθέντων) the *rhythmizomenon* in a particular way, and make it (καὶ ποιούντων) like this or like that in respect of durations (*chronoi*)" (Aristoxenus, *Elements of Rhythm* 2.5; trans. Barker). As we know from Neoptolemus, "one of those disposing things" could be argued to be ὁ ποιῶν (the poet or musical arranger); but notionally, the human agency could be separated off from the effects of its agency, the way the shape of an object could be ascribed either to the shaper's act of disposing the object's parts or else—viewed *per se*—to "the particular arrangement (διάθεcίc τιc) of those parts": for the shape "results (γενόμενον) from the way each part is disposed relative to the others (ἐκ τοῦ cχεῖν πωc ἕκαcτον αὐτῶν)" (Aristoxenus, *Elements of Rhythm* 2.5, trans. Barker), and no trace of agency needs to be expressly written into this formula of self-relatedness. Philodemus' counter to this view taken over (we may speculate) by the Critics is virtually a quotation from his rebuttal of Neoptolemus. Meanings must be reinstated to primacy:

> Yes, you can consider *synthesis* to be *idia*—not per se, *but only in virtue of the meanings* a poem presents in addition to the sounds, which meanings are the source of poetic *psychagogia* (cf. [12]).

And the "meanings" must be realigned with the concept of agency.

[15] (sequel to [12])

> οὐ παρά τινοc λαβόντεc, ἀλλ᾽ αὐτοὶ γεννήcαντεc παρ᾽ αὐτῶν (i.e., this is their *idios nous*, which puts the definitive imprimatur of "*idion*" on a poem: cf. [7]).

> [The poets] do not get [their meanings] from anyone, but produce them by themselves. . . .

The redefinition of the meaning of *idion* by the Critics is tantamount to a revision of poetic "originality," and indeed, of the entire poetic experience. An effect of the work, given "off" by it like the peals of a bell, euphony is a transient quality that appears "on" (*epi*phainomenon), and bodies forth from, the surface of a poem— a surplus effect and a superficial extravagance, towards which the whole expenditure of poetic substance is in fact directed (wastefully, in the eyes of a Philodemus).

---

[134] Cf. also Aristoxenus, *Elements of Rhythm* 8-9. Similarly, *On Poems* 5 col. xxix (xxxii) 32 (a stylistic axiom), not as in col. v (viii) (where *to idiotes* is subjoined to truth-values).

[135] See *P.Oxy.* XXXIV 2687, esp. col. ii, a treatise devoted to covering exactly this subject.

The novelty of this counter-poetical conception, and its radicalness, are measurable against the reactions of Philodemus, who represents the traditional view.

On the euphonist theory, aesthetic properties are ephemeral and evanescent. Pleasures, like sound, are mere after-images, belated effects of buried physical causes (they call them *aitia*) now laid shockingly bare by the critic. The Critics were not alone in underlining the perceptual and even simulacral status of aesthetic experience, although they do seem to have been among the very select few who imported this philosophical insight into literary critical circles. They could easily have written something like the following: "The musical notes [read: letters of the alphabet], because they are closely successive, create the *appearance* (φαντασία) of a single sound stretched out over some amount of time," although this is taken from a document in the, in many ways parallel, musical tradition.[136] In the atomist tradition, Epicurus could pronounce a strikingly similar view, in terms of the streaming of atoms (διὰ ταύτην τὴν αἰτίαν τοῦ ἑνὸϲ καὶ ϲυνεχοῦϲ τὴν φαντασίαν ἀποδιδόν-των [sc. τῶν τύπων ἀπὸ τῶν πραγμάτων], *Letter to Herodotus* 49). Lucretius' abysmal glimpse into the squirming material causes of things provides one of the most apt and poignant analogies to the procedures of the Critics, who never tire of juxtaposing physical "causes" and secondary (and more familiar) poetic effects (cf. *On the Nature of Things* 3.25–30). There is both *horror* and *voluptas* in this poetics (we witness some of this *horror* in Philodemus' response to it). It is unlikely that the Critics derived their theoretical apparatus from Epicureanism, but neither can the possibility of an indirect influence be ruled out. Philodemus' hostility to this brand of linguistic materialism raises questions about Epicurus' own commitment to materialism in the domain of language. The issues involved are too complex to be treated here.

Such, at any rate, is the double-edged thrust of linguistic materialism, or of any poetic theory that looks to the physics of its objects. Seen from "the bottom up,"[137] poetic qualities dissipate in a welter of atomistic contiguities and intervals: letter-sounds (*grammata, phonai, stoicheia*) on a page of Sappho are just so many phonemes (signifiers) severed irreparably from the meanings they would convey (signifieds), mere dots of ink or intensities of sound, light-years removed from any-thing even remotely resembling "form," let alone "content." These latter are mere "epiphenomena": they exist in the mind, or within a tradition of aesthetics that insists on resolving the dissonance between matter and form into relations of form, content, and meaning, as it does for Philodemus in *On Poems*. In the last analysis, if pressed, a Critic might concede that even the concept of "matter" is *itself* an epiphenom-enon—though of what? Here theory becomes hypercritical and attains an excruciat-ing level of *aporia*: this marks the end of theory as we know it. No, the Critics counter: here, theory *begins*.

---

[136] Heraclides Ponticus the Younger (first century A.D.), extracted from Porphyry's *Commentary on the Harmonics of Ptolemy* 31 (ed. Düring), trans. Barker 1989, vol. 2, 236.

[137] See two suggestive articles by D. Sedley, "Epicurus' Refutation of Determinism" in ΣΥΖΗΤΗ-ΣΙΣ (Naples 1988), and "Epicurean Anti-reductionism," in J. Barnes, M. Mignucci (ed.), *Matter and Metaphysics* (Napoli 1989).

Appendix A: Rostagni on Philodemus

Rostagni's position (*Scritte Minori* vol. 2: *Aesthetica* [Turin 1955] referred to below) that in his poetics Philodemus is in conflict with Aristotle is premised, if the arguments above carry any conviction, on a misreading of Aristotle: "noi sappiamo che l'estetica di Aristotele si sarebbe perennemente dibattuta nel dualismo di *forma* e *contenuto*" (pp. 162–63). His position further involves a glaring self-contradiction. Rostagni has been taken to task for what appears to be an anachronism, most penetratingly by Calogero (see below), and later by Benvenga (above, n. 28). In the present context, it is worth re-examining the frailty of Rostagni's position. He admits that for Philodemus, "il modo d'esere della forma dipenda dal modo d'essere del contenuto" (p. 409), and "che l'effetto artistico venga dal contenuto spirituale (egli dice sempre 'pensieri,' *dianoemata*)" (p. 416). This is all part of his strategy, incredibly, to make Philodemus into a worshipper of form, and a prophet *avant la lettre* of the De Sanctist and Crocean formalist aesthetics: "Nella scienza il concetto importa; nell' arte tutto è la *forma*" (p. 365), whereby content, "nel cervello dell'artista" "è diventato una forma." It may be true for Philodemus that content "takes shape" (is "formed") in the mind of the artist, but this is not to say that "everything" (i.e., meaning and expression) is extensionally identical, or even formally identical, with the same "form." All that is shown by the evidence advanced to argue that Philodemus held this position (p. 365) is that content (meaning) cannot be positively valued if the *form* (*synthesis*) is not deemed aesthetically good. That is, we can have no access even to a "good" meaning, if its expression is marred (as discussed above).[138] This is a far cry from the claim that for Philodemus (i) content is *inseparable from* form ("La vera posizione, logica, reale, assoluta è un'altra: che non dovrebbe neanche la forma [*synthesis*] essere separata dal contenuto" [sc. "thoughts"], p. 409). In analysis, they must be separated for an aesthetic judgment to go into effect; in practice, each component must pull its weight, but presumably in seamless synchrony with the other, respective component. Later (p. 416) Rostagni wishes to claim that for Philodemus (ii) content is *identical with* form: artistic effects prescind "dal contenuto solo in quanto è espresso o *formato* (πεποιημένον) [sc., in the mind of the artist: cf. the Crocean identity of "expression and intuition," p. 371]; appunto perchè (a) egli non ammette una separazione fra spirito e forma, e (b) le espressioni senza contenuto sono altrettanto assurde quanto il contenuto senza espressioni" (p. 416). This move

---

[138] Cf. *P.Herc.* 1073 col. xva (p. 137 Sbordone), a passage which may present the views of an opponent, but with which Philodemus can agree, given his general endorsement of clear expression (e.g., *On Poems* 5 col. xxvii [xxx] 6–12). Likewise it seems to me a fallacy to deduce from Philodemus' remarks on *metathesis* (rearrangement) a theory of the dependency of "content" on "form," let alone their functional identity. Philodemus holds that verbal arrangement can positively or negatively affect meaning, by clarifying or obscuring it (*P.Herc.* 1676 col. viii [p. 257 Sbordone]). As the column from 1676 shows (in its fragile reconstruction by Heidmann and Sbordone), a text and its *metathesis* give us two *syntheseis* expressive of the same *noema*, one superior aesthetically, one deficient (τὸ νό|[ημα βέ]λ-[τιον] ἢ χεῖρον γεί|νεται (Romeo: γ[εί]νεcθ]αι Heidmann) διὰ [τ]ὰς με[τ]αθέσειc). But what they precisely do not give us are two different *noemata*; and nothing else in Philodemus suggests that he believed they do. There is nothing striking about this position, except that it is consistent with the position thaken by one of his opponents, with shom Philodemus explicitly concurs (*P.Herc.* 1676 cols. vi 26–vii 7 [pp. 253ff. Sbordone]–another heavily reconstructed passage, however). Here the meaning is said (*ex hyothesi*) to be "the same" (τὸ δὲ αὐτῆc | διανοίαc); *synthesis* has properties of its own, the most important of which, for Philodemus (like others before him, though not this particular opponent), is to allow the meaning to shine through as clearly as possible, without either detracting from it or distracting us from it (*On Poems* 5 cols. xxvii [xxx] 6–12); for meaning, not *lexis* or *synthesis*, is of supreme value and effect (ibid., col. xxxii [xxxv] 6–10). For a different view of the matter, see Chapter 11 in this volume.

from (i) to (ii) is a bold collapse, and it is totally unwarranted:[139] Philodemus has no language to express what Rostagni would have him express; and if he did, Philodemus would have to say that meanings, *qua pepoemena* (poetic inventions or constructs), exhaust the content/form distinction, and make the category of *synthesis* of *lexis* superfluous. Moreover (b) jibes poorly with (a).

Nothing warrants Rostagni's move from "inseparability" (already implying separability, despite itself) to "identity." Rostagni's sole evidence for it (p. 416) is the fragment given by Jensen on p. 147 of his edition of *On Poems 5* (*P.Herc.* 1081 fr. xxiii p. 221 Sbordone):

κεινεῖ γὰρ οὐ τὰ ἀπόητα, ἀλλὰ τὰ πε|ποημένα, διανοήματα δὲ | καὶ ταῦτ' ἐςτιν, Ἡρακλεοδώ|ρου νομίζοντος ὅλως νό|ημα μὴ κεινεῖν, ἀλλ' οὐ μό|νον τὸ ἀπόητον, ὥςτε |[κα]ταγελάςτω[ς] ἐπιφέρει . . . .

For it is not poetically unformed things which move us, but things poetically formed (*pepoemena*), and these are meanings, though Heracleodorus [a Critic] holds that meaning has absolutely no power to move [us], and not only the unformed [kind], with the result that he ridiculously adduces the claim [etc.]. . . .

That thought or meaning can be poetically or rhetorically shaped (πεποημένα) or exist in its primary unshaped form (ἀπόητα) is a commonplace of criticism, and it falls under the rubric, "figures of thought": some thoughts are figured, others are not (this was debated, but Philodemus does not seem to find the distinction problematic).[140] The pendant to this rubric was a second, within the *lektikos topos*: "figures of speech" (Theophrastus' ποιά λέξις [*Scholia on Dionysius Thrax's Art of Grammar* 168, 9 (Hilgard)] or πεποιημένα λέξις, Aristotle's ἡδυςμένος λόγος or πάθη of λέξις). The two could coexist. And we have evidence that they continued to coexist in Philodemus' mind, for whom *lexis* had to adapt, as best it could, to poetic content, in a relation of "dependency." But Philodemus does not stipulate any mimetic or other relation between the *shapes* of these two things, save that both should have shape, viz., be "poetic."[141]

On his own logic, Rostagni is constrained to claim what Philodemus vehemently denies: "E diciamo che anche un'opera di scienza, in quanto espressa, è opera d'arte" (p. 367), and what Rostagni must himself later deny, in order to conform more closely to Philodemus ("Nella scienza il concetto importa; nell'arte tutto è la *forma*," p. 365). This is the trap of the content/form distinction, which must be stated only to be annulled. And this is Rostagni's insuperable dilemma: "il contenuto è una cosa unica con la forma" (*sic*!) (p. 369). No qualifications suffice to erase this contradictory logic, not even the explanation appended to it, "perchè si concreta e si determina solo con essa," which simply perpetuates what it would annul. Nor will redefining (however vaguely) the meaning of *synthesis*, from its correct meaning of "aggregato verbale" to a "pregnant" Philodemean usage ("non altrimenti che un *significato pregnante* ["quasi di 'cosa creata'"] ha in Filodemo il vocabolo *synthesis*," ibid.; emphasis added). Philodemus plainly states that good *synthesis* of *lexis* is insufficient to yield

---

[139] Cf. G. Calogero, Review of Rostagni, *Arte poetica di Orazio*, in "Italienische Arbeiten (1930) zur Antike II," *Arch. f. Gesch. der Philosophie* 40 (1931), 297–301, followed by Benvenga 1951 (above, n. 28), 242.

[140] See Spengel, *Rhetores Graeci* 3.11, 18–3.13, 20 (trans. Russell 1981). It is quite possible that "not only the unformed [kind]" above is mooted by Philodemus and not expressive of Heracleodorus' view (which may have denied the distinction, between shaped and unshaped meaning, which Philodemus presumes to exist).

[141] But we shouldn't be fooled—a poetic meaning, for Philodemus, has to meet two criteria: it is not enough to be *pepoemenon*; the meaning must exhibit a degree of richness (*euteleia*), cf. *On Poems 5* col. v (viii) 22–25 and col. xxiii (xxvi) 4–7.

good meaning (*On Poems* 5 col. xxiii [xxvi] 1–11); the very statement suggests a logical divorce between form and content that, for Philodemus, can never be superseded or suspended. In the absence of evidence to the contrary, Rostagni's argument remains an attractive, but failed, hypothesis.

Appendix B: Neoptolemus on the "poet" as *eidos*

Above we heard how the poet's faults were to be set off from those of the formal levels of a poem's composition ([4]). There we simply noted one of the most immediate aims of this conceptual device: isolation of the formal nature of a text. But it is conceivable that Neoptolemus went further than this, and was claiming that the poet's qualities, probably his moral qualities, are an irrelevancy with regard to the poetic analysis of a text, a point made previously and less trenchantly, possibly by Heraclides Ponticus, in *On Poems* 5 cols. vii–viii [x–xi]: to be distinguished are the poet *qua* (technical) producer of *synthesis* (ὁ εὖ ποιῶν) and the poet *qua* (intelligent or moral) producer of *ekloge* or *selectio* (ὁ ἀγαθὸς ποιητής), the latter implying everything connoted by "selecting and organizing meaning." Philodemus nods in agreement with this kind of distinction, and declines to agree with Neoptolemus, who probably elevated the "technical" poet to the rank of "poet, *simpliciter*," dropping in the process all the evaluative epithets of "good," etc. In this Neoptolemus is contradicting Aristophanes, *Thesmophiazousae*169 and perhaps even going further in his minimization of the poet's persona than Aristotle would have allowed.[142] This need not conflict with Neoptolemus' celebrated claim that a poem ought to give pleasure *and* instruct (be *utile* and *dulce*). What is striking about the claim is not the mention of instruction, but its balancing act with aesthetic pleasure (*terpsis, psychagogia*); and, in the light of Philodemus' criticisms, Neoptolemus' studied lack of reflection on "instruction": "What kind of benefit and edification (ὠφελήςεως καὶ χρης[ιμ]ολογίας) needs to be present [in poems] he failed to clarify . . .," in part because he did not always bother to explain his position (col. xiii [xvi] 15). Philodemus is perhaps genuinely reduced to guessing what kind would have been entailed (21–28). Our questions can be of a different order. How central to Neoptolemus' poetic theory can the "contents" of poetry have been? Is he paying lip service to a Hellenistic commonplace?[143] Is it even a foregone conclusion that the edifying effects of poems (χρηςιμολογία, ὠφέληςις) consist, for Neoptolemus, in ideas, and not in some more diffusely conceived effect of contemplating, or even enjoying, poems as poems? His claim cited above should be recalled, namely that the poet has no share in the faults of what falls under *poema* and *poesis*, and vice versa. This suggests that *hypothesis* could be analyzed in purely *formal* terms (in terms of its construction and aesthetic properties), on the model, say, presented by Aristotle in his *Poetics*. Here, too, aspectual distinctions might have been at work: "instructive" qualities (moral or other) of poems could conceivably have been submitted to a formal analysis by Neoptolemus, in terms of their poetic qualities; their non-poetic or extra-poetic worth could have been taken for granted (as an empty requirement), or left to be determined outside the realm of poetic criticism. This by itself would suggest an aestheticizing tendency, one quite remote from the crude devices of a content/form analysis, but consistent with the better known parts of Neoptolemus' program described above. And here too, the poet (as source) is something of an accident, no longer lodged at the center of poetic analysis. In any case, the complex question of morals

---

[142] Aristotle's commentary on the qualities of the poet is sparse. The few mentions of the poet's "nature" in the *Poetics* are mainly, one should think, a concession to conventional ways of conceptualizing the poet. For a judicious treatment of these, see Halliwell 1986 (above, n. 38), 82–92.

[143] Cf. Brink 1963, 129.

and aesthetics would have to wait for its more elegant and subtle (and in any event, explicit) solution in the poetic system set forth by Aristo, in the immediately adjacent columns of *On Poems*—likewise in terms of "aspectual" differences. This is, quite possibly, their conceptual "join" in Philodemus' text.[144]

Another possibility, which cannot be ruled out a priori either, is that in giving less weight to the poet Neoptolemus was de-emphasizing the *individual* nature of the poet's contribution to his own work (specifically, in the area of invention, *heuresis*) because—as Aristotle is often keen to point out earlier, and as became an incessant leitmotif among later critics, specifically among the Critics—all texts are collaborative joint ventures with the traditions that feed and sustain them, and hence, it is misleading to give an inordinately narrow focus to the powers of any single poet. Making the poet into an *eidos* (and concomitantly focusing our aesthetic gaze on the isolated *synthesis*) already goes some distance towards depersonalizing and rarifying the poet, rendering him a logical category. This new (or rather, renewed) emphasis can be looked at in two ways: as a way of reversing some of the perhaps naturally intuitive biases of literary poetics, which tends by its nature to highlight the producer over the product; or as, perhaps, a normal expression of a Hellenistic, particularly a demure, Callimachean aesthetic. Neoptolemus could be credited with either view (nor, incidentally, would his praise of Homer as the "greatest poet" in col. xiii [xvi] conflict with either of these positions: Homer just was the author of his epics). The difference here with Aristotle would be that Neoptolemus is trading in poetic originality for a notion of *textual* individuality—the focus now being diverted from the formal structure of a poem to such individual characteristics as any attention paid to the verbal texture of a poetic artifact was likely to bring to light (and as Aristo, after him, another important accessory to the "trend" toward *synthesis*, was fond of showcasing in his own poetic theory). The threat to the *idion*-relation that Philodemus senses here has to be placed in the wider context of debates about its meaning. Philodemus' own reaction is retrograde.

Appendix C: After Neoptolemus

A word on Neoptolemus' *Nachleben*. It is unclear how much impact Neoptolemus' triad had on the tradition, or to what extent it was a momentary expression of it. Dionysius of Halicarnassus is innocent of Neoptolemus' jargon. He favors *poema* over *poesis*, in the sense of "poem" or "work," most likely for the same reasons that the term *poema* received preferred status in Neoptolemus, namely its proximity to *poema* as "verse of poetry" and as concrete workmanship, the standard meaning of *poema* in criticism. By contrast, *poesis* (singular) in Dionysius usually stands for "poetry" generally. Dionysius, in other words, reverts to the standard meaning of Neoptolemus' terms, even if he shares his biases (at least in his *De compositione verborum*).

If it is right to credit Neoptolemus with the invention of the tripartite schema, his invention nonetheless sent shock waves through much of subsequent criticism (as evidenced both in Posidonius and in the Byzantine collection of scholia, stemming from an unknown date, to Dionysius Thrax). Would Philodemus consider a lyric poem by Sappho to be *poesis* (with a *hypothesis*)? *On Poems* 5 col. xxxv [xxxviii] 7–10 suggest that Philodemus would not, in the "technical" sense of the term as it had been used by Neoptolemus. The fact that Neoptolemus' usage comes back to haunt even the closing columns of *On Poems* 5 suggests the pervasiveness of his influence (presumably the anonymous opponents rebutted there postdate Crates of Mallos), or else the forcefulness with which the distinction has seared itself on Philodemus'

---

[144] See Porter 1994 (above, n. 1).

critical self-consciousness (it remains an open question just how deeply Philodemus' comprehension of Neoptolemus actually went). But the genuine importance of Neoptolemus' place in the critical history "reconstructed" *a contrario* by Philodemus or his sources lies in his exploitation of an aspectual criterion, which made it possible to assign independent powers to the material factors of poetry. This liberation of the material sign certainly made an impact on Andromenides and Crates, who seem to have been operating within some of the frames of the tradition most radically represented by the Critics. A badly damaged column (*P.Herc.* 1073 fr. i = p. 152 Jensen = p. 165 Sbordone) gives a glimmering of the ways in which Neoptolemic categories (*eide*) were possibly appropriated by these two later critics. Andromenides' criterion for poetic excellence is legible in the next column: the *ergon* of poets is not to say *what* no one has said before, but to say it *differently* from any previous instance. Such a difference is a material difference that is fundamentally voiced in the phonic substance of poems (rhythms, sounds, "brightness" of individual letters varying in quantity and quality) (*P.Herc.* 460 fr. ii = p. 167 Sbordone). Crates, in his turn, gave "pre-eminence" to the "words" (sc., to *poema*; ἡγεμο|νίαν . . . τοῖc ἔπε|[cι], *P.Herc.* 1073 fr. i 19–20 p. 165 Sbordone), while *poesis* (for him) utilizes the passions as "allies" (cf. Longinus, *On the Sublime* 17.1), and (as Andromenides also held) the poet is an *eidos* of the art. Perhaps not surprisingly, a new reading by Cecilia Mangoni (confirmed by the *disegni*) brings to light, in col. xiii [xvi] 5 of *On Poems* 5, the same term (ἡ]γεμονίαν), but the state of the papyrus forbids a secure guess as to its use by Neoptolemus here.[145]

The most famous of Neoptolemus' legacies was of course Horace's *The Art of Poetry*, according to the scholiast Porphyrion—*in quem librum congessit praecepta Neoptolemi . . . non omnia quidem sed eminentissima*. In view of the foregoing, perhaps a new assessment of this tantalizing doxography is in order, if we hope to keep straight what Horace may have learned from Philodemus, and what he may nonetheless have borrowed from Neoptolemus.[146]

[145] ἡγεμονία makes two other appearances in the fragments of *On Poems*, once clearly in connection with the qualities linked to *poema* and sound (*P.Herc.* 994 col. xxi 23 [p. 79 Sbordone]), once in an uncertain context (*P.Herc.* 994 col. xxv 4 [p. 87 Sbordone]).

[146] This discrepancy alone prompted Philippson to doubt the ascription to Neoptolemus of Parium. The chain of influence: Neoptolemus–Philodemus–Horace is disrupted at several points. This hasn't bothered modern commentators very much, though it ought to have done so. Calogero 1931 (above, n. 139) is an exception. He suggests that Philodemus' critique made no impression on Horace. It is likely that Horace was not slavishly imitating either Neoptolemus or Philodemus.

This chapter is preliminary to a monograph currently underway. I am grateful to The National Endowment for the Humanities and to the Office of the Vice-President for Research at the University of Michigan for funding which made the research and writing of this paper possible during the fall of 1989 and the summer of 1990. Special thanks are due especially to Cecilia Mangoni, Tiziano Dorandi, Elizabeth Asmis, and Thomas Rosenmeyer for (in some cases, extensive) written comments and suggestions.

8

Philodemus on Censorship, Moral Utility, and Formalism in Poetry

Elizabeth Asmis

Heraclitus thought that Homer and Archilochus should be "thrown out of the contests and flogged" (ἐκ τῶν ἀγώνων ἐκβάλλεcθαι καὶ ῥαπίζεcθαι).[1] More than four centuries later, the censor with his rod appears again in Philodemus' *On Poems*. Philodemus objects that the demand for usefulness in a poem ἐκραπίζει, "flogs out" or "expels with the rod," the most beautiful poems.[2] In the intervening centuries, Plato had proposed a sweeping program of censorship which would have eliminated most, if not all, of the best loved poems of the Greeks. Plato's influence persisted throughout the Hellenistic period; but it also prompted a strong reaction. A number of literary theorists argued for an emancipation of poetry from morality. Among them were those who demanded complete freedom of thought for the poet.

The Hellenistic debate on the morality of poems is largely lost to us for want of evidence. A basic source of information is, of course, the extant work of the poets themselves. But for details about literary theory we rely mostly on reports by later authors. Perhaps the best known testimony is Eratosthenes' claim, as told by Strabo, that every poet aims to "move the soul" (ψυχαγωγία), not to teach.[3] Eratosthenes also held that a poem should not be judged by its thought (διάνοια) and that poetry is permitted to fashion "whatever appears to it appropriate to moving the soul" (ὃ ἂν αὐτῇ φαίνηται ψυχαγωγίας οἰκεῖον).[4] Other authors reveal more about the context of Eratosthenes' remarks. By far the most informative source on the debate in which Eratosthenes was involved is Philodemus. Although Philodemus' importance has been recognized, his writings have been used only very selectively in the study of Hellenistic literary theory. The main reason for this neglect is that his writings are preserved only in fragmentary papyri. However, much more can be retrieved from

---

[1] Heraclitus 22 B 42 Diels-Kranz.

[2] Book 5 col. iv 10–18 Mangoni 1993. For Book 5 I refer throughout to the numeration of columns in her edition.

[3] Strabo 1.2.3: ποιητὴν . . . πάντα cτοχάζεcθαι ψυχαγωγίας, οὐ διδαcκαλίας.

[4] Strabo 1.2.17 (κελεύων μὴ κρίνειν πρὸς τὴν διάνοιαν τὰ ποιήματα); and 1.2.3 (τὴν ποιητικὴν γραφώδη μυθολογίαν ἀποφαίνων, ᾗ δέδοται πλάττειν, φηcίν, ὃ ἂν αὐτῇ φαίνηται ψυχαγωγίας οἰκεῖον).

the fragments than has been done. Some of the papyri which contain Philodemus' main work on poetic theory, *On Poems*, show continuous columns of text, along with isolated fragments, which reveal detailed positions and counterpositions. In this paper, I propose to start with some relatively well preserved passages belonging to Book 5 of *On Poems*, then move on to a part of this work which is less well preserved.

In *On Poems*, Philodemus does not discuss censorship or moral utility as a separate topic. The information that he provides belongs to criticisms of the positions of others. In these criticisms, Philodemus uses certain commonplace distinctions. A basic distinction is between "events" or "things," πράγματα, and "diction," λέξις; the former is the subject matter, the latter the verbal expression. The contrast between subject matter and diction is also stated as a contrast between "thought," διάνοια, and diction.[5] Diction is divided into "selection" (ἐκλογὴ τῶν λέξεων), and "composition" (cύνθεcιc τῶν λέξεων, or cύνθεcιc simply). As Philodemus shows, there was much disagreement on the importance of thought relative to diction. Some held that the excellence of a poem resides in the verbal arrangement or simply the sound effected by the words. These theorists may be called "formalists," because they held that what makes a poem good is nothing but the linguistic or phonetic form. Others held that subject matter, or thought, and diction contribute equally to a poem; and others, such as Philodemus, held that thought is more important. Those who assigned some weight to the content were divided on whether the content of a poem should be morally useful or not. The formalists held that the poet is not directly concerned with morality; and some maintained that the poet should be free to express any thought at all.

In the fifth book of *On Poems,* Philodemus mentions by name three literary theorists who demanded that a poem be morally useful: Heraclides of Pontus; Neoptolemus of Parium; and a Stoic who has been identified in the past as Aristo of Chios, but who may be a later Stoic. All three were in basic agreement with Plato that a poem should not only be pleasant but also be useful.[6] Philodemus criticizes the demand for utility both by objections directed specifically at a particular theory and by general considerations.

Heraclides of Pontus demanded that a poet should both delight the listeners and benefit them.[7] Philodemus objects that there are many kinds of benefit and Heraclides did not specify the kind. He adds that Heraclides did not specify what delight he demanded, so that "he left the goodness of the poet indeterminate in both respects."[8] Whatever benefit he did demand, Philodemus goes on, Heraclides:

> banishes (literally, expels with the rod) from goodness the most beautiful poems of the most famous poets because they provide no benefit whatsoever–in the case of some poets, most poems, in the case of others, all poems.

10   . . . διότι τὰ κά[λ-
        λιcτ[α] ποιήματα τῶν [δο-

---

[5] See Asmis 1990a.   [6] *Republic* 607D–E.

[7] Jensen first identified the opponent as Neoptolemus in his edition (1923); upon reexamination of the papyrus, he identified him as Heraclides (1936). I agree that the opponent is Heraclides; in my view, his theory is quite different from that of Neoptolemus which Philodemus presents later.

[8] Col. iii 15–iv 10.

κιμ[ω]τάτων ποητῶ[ν
διὰ τὸ μηδ᾽ ἡντινοῦν
ὠφελίαν παρασκευ[ά-
15   ζειν, ἐνίων δὲ καὶ [τὰ
πλ[εῖ]cτα, τινῶν δὲ πά[ν-
τα [τ]ῆc ἀρετῆc ἐκρ[απ]ί-
ζει.⁹

Philodemus is offended by Heraclides' censoriousness, and he indicates his disapproval by choosing the verb ἐκραπίζει, "flog and expel," to denounce it. It is not
clear whether Heraclides himself held that many famous poems do not measure up to
his standard of goodness, or whether Philodemus merely drew this inference. In any
case, Philodemus accuses Heraclides of banning most or all of the most beautiful,
most famous poems of the Greeks. This condemnation of Greek traditional poetry is
comparable in scale to Plato's banishment of Homer and his followers in the *Republic*.

Philodemus also objects that Heraclides "burdened" the poet with a precise acquaintance with all dialects, and that he also required a knowledge of geometry,
geography, sailing, and other disciplines.[10] It seems that Heraclides demanded a wide
range of knowledge, including moral knowledge. The breadth of this demand may
account for Philodemus' complaint that Heraclides did not specify the kind of utility.
Whereas Heraclides seems to have supposed that a poet benefits by whatever truths
he conveys, Philodemus objects that Heraclides should have distinguished between
the utility of geographical information, let us say, and the utility of moral truths.

Neoptolemus was long known to classical scholars mainly as the author alleged
by the grammarian Porphyrion to be the source of the "principal precepts" of
Horace's *The Art of Poetry*:[11] Philodemus offers a brief sketch of Neoptolemus'
poetics, which includes a division of the craft of poetry into three parts, the ability of
the poet, theme (ὑπόθεcιc), and verbal composition (cύνθεcιc).[12] By a rather strange
choice of terms, Neoptolemus entitled the three divisions "poet" (ποιητής), "poetry"
(ποίηcιc), and "poem" (ποίημα). In this terminology, "poem" means "verse"; and
"poetry" denotes the noetic construct, consisting of meaning.[13] Neoptolemus, therefore, recognized both the content of a poem, or "theme," and its verbal expression, or
"composition," as integral parts of the poetic craft. He also demanded that a poem
should both benefit the listeners and move them: the perfect poet, he held, must
"benefit" the listeners and "say what is useful" along with ψυχαγωγία.[14] Philo-

---

⁹ Col. iv 10–18.

[10] Col. v 11–30. Philodemus objects that a poet does not require a knowledge of "all" geometry,
geography, and so on. This criticism does not imply that Heraclides required a complete knowledge of
geometry and so on, but that, according to Philodemus, he did not draw clear limits to the knowledge he
required. The inclusion of geometry may be explained as a reference to Plato's curriculum.

[11] See Brink 1963, 43–74.   [12] Cols. xiv 5–xv 6.

[13] Neoptolemus' use of the term anticipates Posidonius' distinction between ποίημα as metrical
diction and ποίηcιc as "a poem having meaning" (Fr. 44 Edelstein). On Neoptolemus' terminology, see
N. A. Greenberg, "The Use of ποίημα and ποίηcιc," *HSCPh* 65 (1961), 263–289; Walsh 1987; Asmis
1992c.

[14] Col. xvi 8–13. Neoptolemus cites Homer as an example, but the text is unclear.

demus accuses Neoptolemus, as he did Heraclides, of not making clear what sort of benefit he demanded, "so that it is possible to understand the [benefit] that comes from wisdom and the other kinds of knowledge."[15] Wisdom is a Stoic prerequisite for utility; and, in Philodemus' view, to require wisdom is to make good poems impossible.[16] Presumably Neoptolemus, who was not a Stoic, demanded morality of a less strict kind. Possibly, Horace was influenced by Neoptolemus in recommending that a poet both please and benefit; but certainly Neoptolemus was not his only possible source.[17]

We know little about Stoic poetics; but Philodemus' Book 5 of *On Poems* adds considerable information to the few testimonies that are found elsewhere. It contains an outline of the poetic theory of a Stoic whose name appears to end in the letters]ων and who was identified by Jensen, the editor of Book 5, as Aristo of Chios.[18] This Stoic held that good poems, which he called "fine" (ἀcτεῖα) poems, must have both fine thought and fine composition; and he used the term "fine" as coextensive with χρηcτά, "useful" or "decent."[19] Like all Stoics, he understood "good" or "fine" in the sense of "morally good" and held that only what is morally good is beneficial. According to the Stoic view of moral goodness, a good poem cannot be beneficial in a strict sense except as a morally good activity. Its utility, therefore, is an intrinsic utility, reaped by the poet himself. Although this utility cannot be transferred to an external recipient, it can serve to educate the listener. A good poem, therefore, is both beneficial and educational.[20]

Philodemus responds to the demand for fine thought by objecting that "no poet has ever written or would ever write poems containing such thoughts."[21] Philodemus' point is that no poet could possibly present the sort of thought demanded by the Stoics; for that is the prerogative of a wise person, and there just are no Stoic wise persons. The Stoic, indeed, suggested that some of Antimachus' poems might fit the category of "fine" poems; but he eliminated Homer's poems from it on the ground that his poems are called "useful" (χρηcτά) "with pardon" (μετὰ cυγγνωμῆc).[22] Since we must exercise pardon, Homer's poems can only be useful or good in an imprecise sense. In response to the Stoic's strictures, Philodemus asks where he will find "wise and educational" thoughts in the poems of the ancients; and he protests that if Homer's poems do not qualify as beautiful, he does not know what poems are beautiful.[23] The Stoic accommodated technically accomplished but unwise poems in an intermediate category of poems that are neither fine nor bad; these do not presuppose moral goodness on the part of the poet.

Philodemus follows his examination of the three moralists with a criticism of a

---

[15] Col. xvi 21–28.   [16] Col. xxxviii 22–26; cf. col. xvii 20–24.

[17] *The Art of Poetry* 343–44.

[18] Jensen 1923, 128–45 included a chapter on Aristo in his edition. Jensen's identification was generally accepted. It was challenged by M. I. Parente, "Una poetica di incerto autore in Filodemo," in *Filologia e forme letterarie, Studi offerti a Francesco Della Corte*, vol. 5 (Università degli Studi di Urbino, 1987), 81–98, who argued that the author shows signs of Peripatetic and Platonic influence and so belongs most likely to the second century B.C.

[19] See esp. cols. xvii 11–14 and xvii 32–xviii 15; see Asmis 1990b.

[20] The Stoic associates an educational aim with good poems at cols. xvii 18–20 and xviii 2–3, cf. xx 2.

[21] Col. xvii 20–24.   [22] Cols. xvii 28–xviii 1.   [23] Col. xx 1–10.

formalist, Crates of Mallos. A much underrated figure in ancient literary criticism, Crates belies the oft-repeated claim that there was no science of aesthetics until the eighteenth century. Crates attempted to found a science of literary judgment that was distinct from both grammar and philosophy.[24] He proposed vocal sound ($\phi\omega\nu\dot{\eta}$) as the sole criterion of a good poem. Philodemus describes this criterion, which he elsewhere calls "euphony" ($\epsilon\dot{v}\phi\omega\nu\acute{\iota}a$) and ascribes to the "critics," as a phenomenon that supervenes on ($\dot{\epsilon}\pi\iota\phi\alpha\iota\nu o\mu\acute{\epsilon}\nu\eta$) composition.[25] For Crates, the aesthetic quality of a poem is a supervenient quality, not identical with the arrangement of letters but arising from them. Good sound is the "natural good" ($\phi v\epsilon\iota\kappa\dot{o}\nu$ $\dot{a}\gamma\alpha\theta\acute{o}\nu$) of a poem; it is not determined by rules, but inheres naturally in a poem, as recognized by the hearing.[26] In judging a poem, Crates proposed, one must not judge either the pleasantness of the sound or the thoughts. Instead, one must judge through perception the principles of good sound that inhere in a poem, "and not without thoughts, but not the thoughts themselves."[27] The critic does not judge the thoughts of a poem, even though he has an awareness of them. The aesthetic judgement of poems, therefore, is a type of judgment that is distinct from both intellectual analysis and a purely perceptual response; it consists in a recognition of principles of good sound together with an awareness of the meaning of the sounds.

In the *Laws*, Plato proposed a very different method of judging a poem. He insisted that the content of a poem must be judged, although he denied that the poet needs to be able to do so. All the poet needs to be able to judge is harmony and rhythm. For the rest, he must submit his poetry to the judgment of political leaders; they will judge whether the thought is correct.[28] In opposition to Plato, Crates holds that the person who judges a poem must not judge the content: a poem should be judged only by its form, which (as Plato, too, supposes) it is the job of the poet to supply. In effect, Crates makes the poet arbiter of his poems by freeing him from the constraint of an external, political judgment. Although Philodemus does not say so explicitly, Crates repudiates the censorship of poems by rejecting a judgment of their content.

In the last section of Book 5, Philodemus follows his teacher Zeno of Sidon in summarizing and criticizing the whole range of Greek poetic theories. Philodemus does not attach any names to the theories he lists; for his list is not a historical recounting of particular positions, but a critical analysis. He distinguishes some thirteen attempts to define the goodness of a poem: two require that a poem must be morally beneficial; and four exclude any judgment of the content.[29] The first three

[24] See Porter 1989 and Asmis 1991b.
[25] Col. ˙xxiv 31–32. Philodemus ascribes euphony to the "critics" at col. xxi 16–17, and in *P.Herc.* 1676, cols. vi (xvii) 2–9, cf. vii (xviii) 10–11 and xii (xxiii) 6–10.
[26] Cols. xxv 2–xxix 18, esp. xxv 18–19 and xxvii 17–21.
[27] Col. xxviii 19–33. Good sound exhibits rational principles ($\lambda o\gamma\iota\kappa\dot{a}$ $\theta\epsilon\omega\rho\dot{\eta}\mu\alpha\tau a$) which inhere naturally in the poem; what one recognizes through the hearing is the operation of these natural principles.
[28] *Laws* 670E, 801B–802C, and 817A–D. According to Plato, there is no need for the poet to know whether "the imitation is beautiful or not" (*Laws* 670E).
[29] The positions may be distinguished as starting at: (1) col. xxix 23; (2) xxx 6; (3) xxxi 7; (4) and (5) xxxi 33; (6) xxxii 36; (7) xxxiii 24; (8) xxxiv 33; (9) and (10) xxxv 32; (11) xxxvii 2; (12) xxxvii 24; and

theories are alike in that they define a good poem by reference to verbal composition alone. One objection that Philodemus raises against them is that they do not specify what sort of thought is required.[30] Another theory that takes account only of diction is the view that diction should fit the characters. Philodemus objects that "it talks only about diction and dismisses thoughts, which have more authoritative power (κυριώτεραν δύναμιν)."[31] Philodemus also stresses the importance of thought in connection with the view that it is the job of a poet to move the listener. He objects that this view favors "cheap" poems that rely on reversals, paradoxes, and speeches of suffering, and ignores the fact that the most effective way of creating sympathy and moving the listener is to present certain thoughts.[32]

Philodemus follows up the first three theories, which require only a certain kind of composition, with three views that demand a certain content: they demand in turn wise, beneficial, and exceptional thought. The last view differs from the others in proposing morally neutral thought.[33] Philodemus introduces the two utilitarian positions as follows:

> [Composition that] contains wise thought and delights the hearing with its elaboration must be thrown out, [it is thought], because of each component; [also, composition that] expresses beneficial, even if not wise, thought powerfully and suggestively with respect to the hearing.

33   . . . ἤ γε διάνοιαν

μ[ἐν coφ]ὴν περιέχου-

35   cαν, τῆι δὲ κατασκευῆ⟨ι⟩

τὰc ἀκοὰc τέρπουcαν ‖

1   ἐ[κ]βόλιμοc εἶ[ναι δοκεῖ,

ἐκ]ατέρου προc[όντοc καὶ

ἤ γ]ε διάνοια[ν ὠφέλιμον,

εἰ κ]αὶ μὴ coφήν, κεκ[ρατη-

5   μένωc καὶ πρὸc τ[ὴ]ν ἀ-

κοὴν ἐμφατικῶ[c] ἐκφέ-

ρουcαν . . . .[34]

The second of these two views replaces the demand for wise thought with a demand for useful thought. This is a modification of the Stoic demand for a wise content. Since, according to the Stoics, utility implies wisdom, the second opinion is not Stoic. Following Zeno, Philodemus has grouped the two theories together as sharing the same general point of view. The first fits the Stoic theory criticized earlier in Book

---

(13) xxxviii 16. Positions (4) and (5) require moral utility; positions (1), (2), (3), and (8) reject any specification of the content. See Asmis 1992b.

[30] Cols. xxix 32–36 and xxx 34–xxxi 7.   [31] Col. xxxv 6–10.

[32] Col. xxxvi 21–xxxvii 2.   [33] Cols. xxxii 36–xxxiii 24.

[34] Cols. xxxi 33–xxxii 7. The accusative participles at xxxi 35–36 and xxxii 7 need to be changed to nominatives in order to fit the syntax (as at xxx 10). It is likely that Philodemus himself is responsible for the anacoluthon by simply copying key phrases from Zeno's treatise.

5. The second could be taken as an inclusive view that embraces both Stoic and other utilitarian theories.

Against the utilitarianism of the second position, Philodemus adduces arguments that coincide in part with those he used previously against Heraclides. His first objection is that the view does not specify the kind of utility.[35] Secondly, he objects that:

[the opinion] expels with the rod many wholly beautiful poems, some of which have a content that is not beneficial and others of which contain . . ., and prefers many lesser poems, as many as contain beneficial or more beneficial [thoughts].

9   . . . πολλὰ τῶν πανκ[ά-
10   λω[ν] ἐκραπ[ίζ]ει ποιημά-
        των τὰ μέ[ν ἀ]νω[φ]ελῆ,
        τὰ [δὲ οὐδ' ἀνωφελ]ῆ περι-
        έχοντ[α, καὶ π]ολλὰ πρ[ο-
        κρίνει [τῶ]ν ἡττόνων,
15   ὅϲα τὰϲ ὠφελίμουϲ ἢ τὰϲ
        ὠφελιμωτέραϲ περιείλη-
        φε.[36]

Philodemus again uses the term ἐκραπίζει, "expels with the rod," to express his disapproval of censorship. As before, he objects that the criterion of utility banishes many extremely beautiful poems because they contain no benefit. Poems that contain no utility, he suggests, may be better than poems that contain beneficial thoughts.

Philodemus' third objection is new: "Also, even if poems benefit, they do not benefit insofar as they are poems (καθ[ὸ] π[ο]ήματ')."[37] This claim needs explanation. In his criticism of Crates, Philodemus claims that a poem "insofar as it is a poem (καθὸ πόημα) provides no natural benefit either in diction or in thought."[38] That is why, Philodemus continues, the following aims have been established: diction should imitate diction that also teaches what is useful; and the thought should belong to persons neither wise nor vulgar but in between. A poem is "that which imitates in the way it can"; and these aims imply a certain way of working out a poetic imitation. They have been established by common consent, not by decree; and we must judge the utility of a poem by them.[39] Philodemus here implicitly rejects the claim that a

[35] Col. xxxii 7–8.

[36] Col. xxxii 9–17. I adopt Jensen's text in lines 10 and 12. Mangoni reads α]ἰϲχρὰ [ποι]εῖ in place of ἐκραπ[ίζ]ει. See Asmis 1992b.

[37] Col. xxxii 17–19: καὶ διότι κἂν ὠφελῆ⟨ι⟩, καθ[ὸ] π[ο]ήματ' οὐκ ὠφε|λεῖ. Philodemus' fourth objection is: "They will say that what is most beneficial is best, although it will not be so if it is expressed in the manner of a physician" (col. xxxii 19–22). Similarly, in his criticism of Heraclides, Philodemus objected that "what is extremely beneficial will be most perfect" (col. iv 22–24).

[38] Col. xxv 30–34: καὶ γὰρ κα|θὸ πόημα φυϲικὸν οὐδὲν | οὔτε λέξεωϲ οὔτε δ[ια|ν]οήματοϲ ὠφέλημα [πα|ρ]αϲκευάζει. Jensen takes φυϲικὸν with πόημα in line 31 and translates: "ein Gedicht bringt seiner Natur nach keinen Nutzen." Although Jensen's translation captures the basic sense of Philodemus' claim, the notion of "natural poem" is obscure, whereas φυϲικόν . . . ὠφέλημα may readily be understood as a substitute for φυϲικὸν ἀγαθόν (col. xxv 18–19).

[39] Cols. xxv 34–26.20. At col. xxvi 13–15, he asserts: τὸ | ποίημα δ' ἐ[ϲτὶ] τὸ μιμού|μενον ὡϲ ἐνδέχεται.

poem must contain wise thought in order to be useful. He also implies that poem as such, "as a poem," is an imitation, and that utility is an aim that restricts the type of imitation.[40]

In *On Music* Book 4, Philodemus shows that this aim, though not incompatible with the nature of a poem, does not suit it well. He argues that if songs benefit, they do so through thoughts that are expressed poetically and that, moreover, the thoughts would be more convincing if stated in prose.[41] Musical form, he contends, weakens the force of the thoughts by the pleasure it provokes, by distracting the listener as a result of this pleasure and the sounds, by the unnatural continuity of the diction, by the places and occasions of listening, and by numerous other causes.[42] Although Philodemus deals only with musical form, the same considerations apply to poetic form without music: it weakens the force of the thought by pleasure, distraction, unnatural diction, and so on. For these reasons, prose is more suited to imparting a benefit than poetry. Although poetry may be used to teach, this is not the proper function of poetry, nor does poetry discharge this function well.

It may surprise the reader that Philodemus, an Epicurean, should defend poems that have no moral utility and may even do harm. In antiquity, Epicurus was paired with Plato as a philosopher who condemned poetry. Epicurus is said to have denounced all poetry as a "destructive lure of myths" and to have expelled poets from cities, along with Plato.[43] In place of poetry, he proposed philosophy—his own—as the education of mankind. Philodemus does not deny that poetry has done much harm. In *On Music* Book 4, Philodemus points out that the thoughts expressed in songs either do not benefit or, if they do, their benefit is small;[44] often, the thoughts harm the listener.[45] Yet Philodemus admires poems regardless of the benefit or harm they may do; and this position is not in contradiction with that of Epicurus.[46] This does not mean that Philodemus or Epicurus believed that anyone should listen to any sort of poem: poems can harm, and it would be foolish for people to submit to this harm. However, an Epicurean who is fortified with the correct beliefs would be able to withstand the harm that a poem might do, and so derive nothing but pleasure from a poem's beauty. As Philodemus indicates in *On Music*, aesthetic pleasure is a kind of utility.[47]

Philodemus agreed with formalists such as Crates, therefore, that it is not the function of poems to impart morally useful thought. But he was also strongly opposed to the formalists' particular type of antimoralism. To learn more about their views, we must move out of Book 5 of *On Poems* to more fragmentary parts of the work. The best source is *P.Herc.* 1676, as supplemented by *P.Herc.* 1074 + 1081. I shall start with a fairly well preserved, continuous sequence of columns belonging to *P.Herc.* 1676.[48] Because the text and its interpretation are often uncertain, I quote

---

[40] See Asmis 1991b.

[41] *On Music* 4 col. xx 11–17 Neubecker. Philodemus is here specifically concerned with the claim that Stesichorus and Pindar put an end to political discord by their songs.

[42] *On Music* 4 col. xxviii 24–35; cf. cols. xv 6–7 and xxvi 10–14.

[43] Frr. 229, 228 Usener.   [44] *On Music* 4 col. xxix 32–35; cf. col. v 31–37.

[45] *On Music* 4 col. vi 5–25.   [46] See esp. fr. 20 Usener.   [47] *On Music* 4 col. xviii 5–7.

[48] *P.Herc.* 1676 was partially edited by Gomperz (1891). A complete edition, with a translation, was prepared by Heidmann (1937, 1971). The papyrus was re-edited and translated, together with parts of *P.Herc.* 1074 + 1081, by Sbordone as *Tractatus Tertius* (1976). Costantina Romeo published new

the passages that I discuss. The sequence begins with a contrast between poetry and cookery:

Col. xii (i) 1–27

... that things are unknown and the diction not pleasing, as provisions bought in the marketplace are [wretched] in the case of cookery. For this is outside this [skill], but it is not outside the poetic craft to make things known. If someone takes them completely from someone else, [...] the distinctiveness [...] by composition. For this reason, [a poet who does not use] appropriate diction is outside the [poetic craft] even if the diction has provided common benefits in life. For to select appropriate diction and arrange it purposely to show such a thought was [assumed to be] distinctive of him. But what follows next is very remote from being proved as proposed.

```
1          ... τὸ τὰ πρ[άγμα-
      τα ἄγνωϲτα εἶνα[ι τὰϲ δὲ
      λέξειϲ οὐκ ἀρεϲτά[ϲ, ὡϲ
      ἐπὶ τῆϲ μαγ[ειρι]κῆ[ϲ λυ-
5     πρὰ τἀγοράϲματα· τα[ῦτα
      μὲν γὰρ ἔξω ταύ[τηϲ ἐϲτί,
      τῆϲ δὲ ποητικῆ[ϲ οὐκ ἔϲ-
      τιν ἔξω τὸ ποεῖ[ν γνωϲ-
      τὰ τὰ πράγματ[α; κἂν γὰρ
10    παντελῶϲ αὐτ[ὰ παρ' ἑ-
      τ]έρου λαμβάνη[ι τιϲ,
      τῆ⟨ι⟩ ϲυνθέϲει τα[ . . . . .
      τατου τὴν ἰδι[ότητα
      α   του· διόπερ ὁ [ποητὴϲ μὴ
15    τὰϲ λέξειϲ ο⟨ἰ⟩κείαϲ [λαβὼν
      ἐκτόϲ ἐϲτι τῆϲ π[οητικῆϲ
      κἂν α[ἰ] λέξειϲ ὠφ[ελείαϲ
      τοῦ βίου παρεϲχ[ήκωϲι
      κοινάϲ· τὸ γὰρ ἐγλ[έγειν
20    τὰϲ ο⟨ἰ⟩κείαϲ καὶ δ[ιατιθέν-
      ναι πρὸϲ {α} δήλωϲιν τοι-
      ούτου νοήματοϲ ἐπί-
      τηδ[εϲ τὸ το]ιοῦτ' ἦ[ν ἰ]δι-
```

readings in Romeo 1992b. My readings are based on Sbordone's and Romeo's readings, together with my own inspection of the papyrus in March 1994. *P.Herc.* 1074 and 1081 make up a single papyrus roll that was cut lengthwise when the papyrus was first opened. Sbordone proposed that some parts of *P.Herc.* 1676 which were previously numbered as "fragments" are sequential "columns" that precede the previously identified sequence of "columns." Unfortunately, the text of these passages is so fragmentary that there is no obvious continuity of meaning. In my discussion, I start with column 1 as previously numbered; I have added Sbordone's numbering in brackets.

$$ov \ \alpha\vec{v}\tau o\hat{v}. \ \tau\grave{o} \ \delta\grave{\epsilon} \ cv\nu[\epsilon]\chi\grave{\epsilon}c$$

25     $\tau o\acute{v}\tau\omega\iota \ \pi o\lambda\grave{v} \ \delta\iota\acute{\epsilon}c\tau\eta\kappa\epsilon$
       $\tau o\hat{v} \ \pi\rho o\kappa\epsilon\iota\mu[\acute{\epsilon}]\nu o\upsilon \ \kappa\alpha$-
       $\tau\alpha c\kappa\epsilon\upsilon\alpha c\theta\hat{\eta}\nu\alpha\iota\cdot^{49}$

The topic of discussion is what is external and what is intrinsic to the poetic craft. It is assumed that a poet deals with two matters: "things" or subject matter ($\pi\rho\acute{\alpha}\gamma$-$\mu\alpha\tau\alpha$), and diction ($\lambda\acute{\epsilon}\xi\iota c$). Philodemus writes that it is intrinsic to the poetic craft to make things known. If, indeed, the subject matter is already completely known—that is, if the poet takes the subject matter completely from someone else—his distinctive contribution consists in composition. For this reason, Philodemus states, a poet is "outside" the poetic craft if he does not take appropriate words, even if his words provide a benefit. For it is the distinctive job of the poet to select appropriate words and arrange them for the purpose of showing this kind of thought. In sum, Philodemus here puts forward the view that it is the function of the poet both to make things known and to select and arrange appropriate diction.

Taken by itself, the passage does not show what is Philodemus' own view and what is his opponent's. As the transition to the next point indicates, Philodemus agrees to some extent with his opponent. He concedes that if a poet takes the subject matter completely from someone else—for example, if he retells Homer's story of Odysseus' encounter with Polyphemus without adding any subject matter of his own —his distinctive contribution as a poet consists in verbal arrangement. This concession suggests that the opponent proposed that, in every case, the distinctive contribution of a poet is nothing but verbal arrangement. That this is the opponent's view is confirmed by subsequent columns. According to the opponent, then, everything except composition lies "outside" the skill of a poet. It is not clear whether the opponent considered it outside a poet's job to make things known; for it is not clear whether this function might be subsumed under composition. The passage also fails to show whether the opponent agreed that a poet must select appropriate diction; subsequent columns indicate that he did not.

After a considerable section of badly damaged text, Philodemus accuses his opponent of being misled; and he writes that his opponent,

Col. xiv (iii) 11–28

saying that differing craftsmen make a similar likeness in different underlying [materials], without the variation doing any harm, blames those who consider the poet from underlying [materials], even though no one considers that the poet could really [move] the soul [from underlying materials]. If, of the things that seem to this person to be underlying, but have authority over the poetic craft–for it is the function to . . . this through certain kinds of diction and speech and weavings . . .

11   . . . $\dot{\omega}c$
       $\kappa\alpha\grave{\iota} \ \tau o\grave{v}c \ \delta[\iota\alpha]\phi[\acute{\epsilon}\rho o]\nu\tau\alpha c \ \epsilon\grave{\iota}$-

---

49 Romeo reads $\kappa\alpha\grave{\iota} \mid \dot{\epsilon}\pi\grave{\iota} \ \tau\hat{\eta}c \ \mu\alpha\gamma[\epsilon\iota\rho\iota]\kappa\hat{\eta}[c \ \tau\grave{o}]\mid \pi\rho\alpha\tau\grave{\alpha} \ \langle\tau\grave{\alpha}\rangle\gamma o\rho\acute{\alpha}c\mu\alpha\tau\alpha\cdot \ \tau[o\hat{v}\tau o]$ in lines 3–5.

πῶν τεχνείτας ὁμοίαν
εἰκόνα ποιεῖν ἐν ἄλλοις
15   ὑποκειμένοις, τῆς πα-
[ρ]αλλαγῆς οὐδὲ[ν βλ]απτού-
ϲηϲ, [ἐ]πιτειμᾶ⟨ι⟩ τοῖϲ τὸν πο-
ητῆ]ν ἐκ τῶν ὑποκειμέ-
νω]ν θεω[ροῦϲιν, οὐ]θενὸϲ
20   ἐκ] τῶ[ν ὑποκει]μένων
ὄντως ἂν ψυχὴν [κεινεῖν
θεωροῦντος τὸν ποιητήν.
εἰ δὲ τῶν τούτωι δοκούν-
τω]ν ὑποκειμέ[νω]ν, κ[υ-
25   ρί]ων δὲ τῆς ποιητικῆς
ὑ]παρχόντων, ἔργον γάρ
τοῦ]το διὰ ποιῶν λέξε-
ων ἢ [καὶ] λόγ[ω]ν καὶ πλοκῶν·⁵⁰

Here Philodemus draws a clear contrast between his view and that of his opponent. The opponent blames others for judging a poet by what "underlies" poems; these things, he claims, do not move the soul. In support of this claim, the opponent draws an analogy with other crafts: it is possible to make similar likenesses out of different materials, without the difference doing any harm. Philodemus objects that what seem to his opponent to be "underlying" materials are in fact determining ("authoritative," κυρίων) factors in the poetic craft. Then he cites a reason, only the beginning of which is preserved. But it seems to coincide with the reason stated in column i: it is the function (ἔργον) of the poet to use certain kinds of words and interweave them— in other words, to select and combine diction—as a means (διά), which is presumably that of showing the thought.

The term ὑποκείμενον was regularly used, among other ways, to designate the things that "underlie" words or the "subject matter" of a text.⁵¹ This sense fits the argument on poetry here. At the same time, the materials used by craftsmen have another analogue in poetry: the poet uses not only subject matter, but also words as underlying material. Subsequent passages show that the opponent regards both subject matter and the words that express it as the underlying material of a poet. The opponent's analogy might be illustrated as follows: just as other craftsmen might use various kinds of wood, metal, or stone to make a statue of Theseus, let us say, so a poet might depict Theseus in different circumstances, such as a battle, an ambush, or a drinking party, told in different words. The splendor or vulgarity of the material makes no difference to the quality of the resemblance. An ignoble subject matter or low diction, for example, does not impair a poetic representation; for the poet does not move the listener by his materials. Philodemus objects, as he does else-

---

⁵⁰ Romeo reads ἰδί[[ων τ]ῶν in lines 24–25.
⁵¹ See, for example, Dionysius of Halicarnassus' *De compositione verborum* 16 (p. 158 Roberts).

where, that the allegedly underlying material—the thought together with the diction
—determines how good a poem is.

After a short break, Philodemus continues his criticism:

Col. xv (iv) 4–27

... creates the similarity with a different material of the person fashioning it, but
he is completely unable to achieve what is distinctive to his craft if he does not
have the appropriate material. In claiming that a poet, if he does not take appropriate thoughts and fitting diction, achieves something distinctively poetic,
even if he overlooks ... he is ... blind. [The following point was] that the poet,
too, is not hindered in respect to the function of his distinctive type of knowledge because he does not work out the [process of] moving the soul through the
thoughts and diction of speech, but through variations, so that neglecting the
appropriate underlying things ...

4   ... δι]αφερούϲη[ι] τοῦ π[λ]άτ-
5   το]ντοϲ ὕληι ποεῖ τὴν ὁ-
       μο]ιότητα, τελέωϲ δ' [ἀ]δυ-
       ν]ατεῖ τὸ τῆϲ τέχνηϲ [ἴ]δι-
       ο]ν ϲυντελεῖν, ἂν μὴ τὴν
       οἰ]κείαν ὕλην ἔχηι· καταξι-
10   ῶ]ν δὲ τὸν ποητήν, ἐὰν μ[ὴ
       δια]νοήματ' οἰκεῖα λάβη[ι
       καὶ [λέ]ξειϲ προϲηκούϲαϲ, [ἴ-
       δι]όν τι ποιητικὸν ἀπ[ο-
       τελε]ῖν, κἂν παρίδη⟨ι⟩ τ . . .
15   [   ]
       . . πάντωϲ] ἐϲτὶ τυφλώττον·
       τοϲ. ἀκόλ]ουθο[ν δ'] ἦν τὸ
       μη]δὲ τὸν π[οη]τὴν ἐμπο-
       δί]ζεϲθαι πρὸϲ τὸ τῆϲ ἰδ[ί]αϲ
20   ἐ]πιϲτήμηϲ ἔργον, ὅτι οὐ δι-
       ὰ τῶν τοῦ λόγου διανοη-
       μ]άτων καὶ λέξεων ἐξερ-
       γ]άζεται τὴν ψυχαγωγί-
       αν, ἀλλὰ διὰ παραλλαττόν-
25   των, ὥϲτε καὶ τῶν οἰκεί-
       ων ὑποκειμένων ἀμε-
       λήϲαντα τελέωϲ ἐ[πὶ] τὴν . . .

Philodemus agrees that craftsmen can fashion similar likenesses by using different
materials; but he insists that they must have appropriate materials. Whereas the opponent denies the need for appropriate thoughts and words that fit the thought, Philodemus demands them. In the second part of the passage, Philodemus suggests rather

obscurely that, according to the opponent, a poet is not impeded in his task because he does not use "the thoughts and diction of speech" to move the listener, but "variations."

Dionysius of Halicarnassus' discussion of composition helps to throw light on the issue. Using the analogy of a housebuilder and a shipmaker, he argues that just as these craftsmen construct a house or ship by putting together materials such as bricks, stones, and wood, so a poet constructs a poem by putting together parts of speech (τὰ μόρια τοῦ λόγου)—nouns, verbs, and so forth. In this process of composition, poets must consider what words fit together; they must choose the appropriate form of the word, such as plural or singular; and, if necessary, they must alter the shape of words by lengthening, curtailing, or otherwise transforming them.[52] According to Dionysius, composition is more important than the selection of words; for it can transform a banal subject matter, told in ordinary words, into the most enchanting poem.[53] To take another example, if the subject matter involves places with unprepossessing names, the poet can arrange the names in such a way as to give them grandeur.[54]

Similarly, Philodemus' opponent maintains that the material used by the poet does not impede his function (ἔργον) as a poet; for he is able to transform this material by composition. There is no need to select "appropriate" thoughts and words because the poet can shape the material so as to make a good likeness. It is not at all transparent how the thoughts and words of "speech" (τοῦ λόγου) differ from "variations" (παραλλαττόντων). But the use of λόγος suggests a contrast between "speech" in general, as consisting of nouns, verbs, and so on, and the composite linguistic structure of a poem. As Philodemus has shown, the opponent holds that a poet moves the listener by the verbal structure that he has fashioned, not by the raw materials—the subject matter and diction—that he has used. Philodemus now seems to express the same contrast by saying that the poet does not move by the thoughts and words of λόγος simply, or unpoetic language. Unless Philodemus uses "variations" tendentiously, the term does not here signify variations in the underlying material, but verbal variations in the poem's linguistic structure.

That the function of a poet consists in composition is stated in the next column:

Col. xvi (v) 3–25

. . . because, as [I said], he adduced crafts that differ but have their goal in common. For just as it is not the distinctive function of the ring engraver to make a similarity—for this is common to the sculptor and painter—but [to make a similarity] in iron and gem stones through engraving, the good not lying in this, but in making a similarity, which is common to all, in like manner it is claimed that the poet also [wishes] his distinctive function [to lie] in composition, but hunts out the good in common with thought and diction–[a good] which this person says simply does not benefit or harm at all, as he concluded from his examples . . . .

[52] *De compositione verborum* 6 (pp. 104–110 Roberts).

[53] *De compositione verborum* 3 (p. 74–80 Roberts). Dionysius' example is Telemachus' appearance at the swineherd's cottage after his return from the Peloponnese.

[54] *De compositione verborum* 16 (pp. 166–68 Roberts).

3   . . . διότι καθάπερ ε[ἶ-
πον δια]φεροὖϲα[ϲ μὲν τέ-
5   χναϲ, ἐν δὲ τῶ⟨ι⟩ κοινῶι τὸ
τέ[λο]ϲ ἐχούϲαϲ παρατέθη-
κεν. ὡ[ϲ] γὰρ [δ]ακτυλιογλύ-
φ[ο]ϲ ἴδιον ἔχων οὐ τὸ ποιεῖν ὅμο[ι]ον—κοινὸν γὰρ ἦν
10   καὶ πλ[ά]ϲτου καὶ ζωγρ[ά-
φου—[τὸ δ'] ἐν ϲιδήρω⟨ι⟩ καὶ λι-
θαρίωι διὰ τῆϲ ἐγ[γ]λυφῆϲ,
τἀγαθὸ]ν οὐκ ἐν τούτωι
κεί[με]νον, ἀλλ' ἐν τῶι ποι-
15   εῖν ὅμο[ι]ον, ὃ πάντων κοι-
νόν, ἔχει, παραπληϲί-
ωϲ ἀξιοῦτα[ι] καὶ [ὁ] ποιητὴϲ
τὸ μὲ[ν ἴδι]ον ἐν [τῆι ϲυ]ν-
θέϲει β[ούλε]ϲθαι, τὸ δ' ἀγα-
20   θὸν δι[αν]οία[ι καὶ λέ[ξει] κοι-
νῶ[ϲ] θηρεύειν, ὅ φηϲιν οὗ-
τοϲ ἁπλῶϲ μηδὲ ἐν ὠφε-
λεῖν ἢ βλάπτειν, ὥϲπερ
ἐκ τῶν παρατεθέντων
25   ϲυνῆχε[ν . . .

The discussion has now moved to the poetic "good" and morality. The opponent draws a clear distinction between the good aimed at by the poet and the moral good. The poetic good consists in the creation of a resemblance (or "similarity"). Unlike the moral good, it does not benefit at all; nor does it harm at all. The opponent illustrated his claim by examples, but these are missing from the present discussion. According to the opponent, the poet shares the goal of making a resemblance with others, such as the ring engraver, or sculptor and painter. Different artists use different materials and different methods to achieve this common goal. The ring engraver, for example, uses iron and gems as materials and engraving as a method. Similarly, the poet uses thought and diction (as previously shown) as his materials and composition as his method. Composition is the distinctive skill by which the poet accomplishes a likeness, just as engraving is the distinctive skill by which the ring engraver creates a likeness.

This analysis uses three basic causal concepts: underlying material ("in which," ὕλη), method ("through which"), and goal (τέλος).[55] The function (ἔργον) of a poet

---

[55] The three causal concepts may be regarded as an adaptation of Aristotle's theory of causation: there is an underlying material; "through which" corresponds to the moving cause; and the "goal" corresponds to Aristotle's final cause. The craftsman is, in a sense, identical with the moving cause; for he supplies, as his distinctive contribution, the composition by which the material is fashioned. At the same

is to shape the material with the goal of making a resemblance. The goal is the poetic good (ἀγαθόν). This analysis is noteworthy not only because it classifies subject matter as material, but also because it emphasizes the creativity of the poet. Like other craftsmen, the poet takes an unshaped material and fashions it. Although the craftsmen are viewed as creating resemblances, the model is omitted from the causal analysis. To the extent that it is included at all, it exists as material; and the material, it is argued, is not a constraint. As is traditional, the poet is compared to the painter; but the dominant image is that of the plastic artist. Moreover, the opponent has chosen a new type of plastic artist as his leading paradigm: the unpretentious ring engraver. The ring engraver differs from other artists in that he does fine, small-scale work—the opposite of monumental work. This change of paradigm marks an important change in the conception of poetry: the poet is viewed primarily as someone who does fine, exquisite work, not as someone who presents grand, monumental subjects. The ring engraver symbolizes the demand of Callimachus and other poets for a "slender Muse."[56]

In an earlier passage (col. iii), it was said that the variation in material does "no harm." This particular claim need not mean anything more than that the difference in material—for example, taking a lowly or vulgar material instead of a grand theme and elevated diction—does not impair the achievement of the poetic goal, which is to make a resemblance. But the claim may also have had a stronger meaning. As it now appears, the opponent holds that the poetic goal does no moral harm; and it is possible that the earlier denial of harm included the denial of moral harm. Since the poetic goal does no moral harm and the type of material makes no difference to its achievement, it follows that the use of a lowly, ignoble material, including immoral characters and vulgar diction, does no harm of any kind—moral or poetic. Similarly, the choice of a noble material, including heroic or virtuous characters and elevated diction, confers no moral benefit or poetic advantage.

In the next column, Philodemus turns to the so-called "Critics." Although the scope of the term "Critic" was controversial in ancient antiquity and continues to be under debate, "critic" may be taken to designate literary scholars who considered grammar subordinate to criticism.[57] According to Philodemus, the critics are agreed that "thoughts and diction are outside" the poetic craft, whereas the euphony that supervenes on composition is the distinctive contribution of the poet. Philodemus' opponent has maintained likewise that thoughts and diction are materials supplied from outside the poetic craft, and that the poet's craft consists in composition. How-

---

time, this analysis differs fundamentally from Aristotle's division of a poem into object, material, and manner, that is, "what" (plot, character, thought), "by" or "in" which (diction and music), and "how" (impersonation or narration) (*Poetics* 1–3, cf. 6).

[56] Callimachus *Aitia* fr. 1.24: Μοῦσαν . . . λεπταλέην; cf. *Epigram* 27.3–4.

[57] This is how Sextus Empiricus views the difference between the grammarian and the critic. He reports that, "like the rest of the critics," Tauriscus, a pupil of Crates of Mallos, subordinated grammar to criticism (*Adv. math.* 1.248). He also reports (*Adv. math.* 1.79) that Crates compared the critic to a master craftsman (ἀρχιτέκτονι) and the grammarian to a helper (ὑπηρέτῃ), and that Crates distinguished the "critic" from the "grammarian" in that the critic is "experienced in all knowledge of language (λογικῆς ἐπιστήμης)," whereas the grammarian only explains glosses, prosody, and the like. Schenkeveld 1968, 177–79 reviews some of the evidence and suggests a rather speculative reconstruction of the history of the term κριτικός.

ever, there has been no indication that the opponent was a euphonist; and clearly there were compositionalists who were not euphonists. In introducing Crates, a euphonist, in Book 5, Philodemus points out that his view differs from that of Heracleodorus and similar persons, who proposed composition as the criterion, as well as from that of Andromenides, with whom Crates thought he was in complete agreement.[58] It is, therefore, best to distinguish between the opponent and the euphonists. We shall return later to the question of the opponent's identity.

The critics, then, identified the distinctive contribution of a poet not as composition simply, but as the euphony that supervenes on composition:

Col. xvii (vi) 2–27

... that the supervening euphony is distinctive, and that thoughts and diction are outside and must be collected as things that are common, remains fixed, as on a stele, for all the critics; its truth is deficient from what has been said. For no poet has had the power to introduce the kind of sound ... to present ... into the nature of things .... When life directs the flow of diction," the distinctive composition of poets results, not as opportune or praised in itself, but because it presents in addition thoughts by which they move the soul, not taking them from someone, but generating them from themselves.

2   ... καὶ τὸ τὴν μὲν
   ἐπιφαι]νομένην [ε]ὐφωνί-
   αν ἴδιον [εἶν]αι, τὰ δὲ νοή{ι}-
5   ματα καὶ [τ]ὰς λέξεις ἐκτὸς
   εἶναι καὶ κοινὰ συνάγεс-
   θαι δεῖ[ν, πα]ρὰ πᾶсι μὲν ὡς
   ἐν [cτήλ]ηι μέ[ν]ει τοῖс κρι-
   τικοῖ[c], ἐκλιπομένην δ᾽ ἔ-
10   χει τὴ[ν ἀλ]ήθι[α]ν ἐκ τῶν
   εἰρημένων. φωνὴν μὲγ
   γὰρ οὐδεὶс ποητὴс εἴсχυ-
   cεν ἐν[πο]ῆсαι τοιαύτην,
   οἵα εἰс τὴν φύсιν
15   τῶν [ὄντων] παρα[φ]έρειν·
   τ[τὰ]c διαν[οίαс,] ἀλ-
   λ᾽ οὐ δι καὶ τὴν χύ-
   cιν τῶ[ν] λέξεων τοῦ βίου χορη[γ]ο[ῦ]ντος ἡ сύνθε-
20   сιс ἰδ[ία γε]ίνεται τῶν πο-
   ητῶν, οὐ καίριος οὐδ᾽ ἐπαι-

---

[58] Cols. xxi 27–xxii 1. Andromenides seems to be the person who maintained that it is the function of poets to "work out dialect and wording," and "not to say what no one [says] but to interpret it in the way that no one else would" (fr. 25 col. iii 2–12, translation after Sbordone).

νουμένη καθ᾽ αὑτήν, ἀλ-
λ᾽ ὅτι προ]cπαρίcτηcι διαν[οί-
αc, αἷc ψ[υ]χαγωγοῦcιν, οὐ
25   παρά τινοc λαβόντεc, ἀλ-
λ᾽ αὐτοὶ γεννήcαντεc πα-
ρ᾽ α[ὑτ]ῶν.[59]

According to the so-called critics, life proffers thoughts and diction, to which the poet adds his distinctive contribution, verbal composition, with the aim of producing "euphony."[60] Philodemus objects that composition is not praised in itself, as the critics suppose; instead, it is praised because, in addition to its phonetic properties, it presents thoughts, and these move the listener. Philodemus maintains that poets do not take these thoughts from someone else, but generate them from themselves.

Immediately after the cited passage, Philodemus makes a concession:

Cols. xvii (vi) 27–xviii (vii) 7

The most persuasive [claim] of all is this: when the thought and diction are the same, but the poems are distinctive, [the poem] is beautiful or bad in its execution because of the composition.

27   . . . τὸ δὲ τῆc αὐτῆc
δι]ανοίαc καὶ τῆc λέξεωc ‖
1   ὑπαρχ[ο]υ⟨c⟩ῶν, ἰδί[ω]ν δὲ
τ[ῶν] πο[η]μά[τω]ν, παρὰ
τ[ὴν cύ]νθε[cιν] ἢ καλὸν
ἢ μ[οχθ]ηρὸν ἀποτελε⟨ῖ⟩c-
5   θα[ι] τ[ὸ πόημα] πάντων μέ[ν
ἐcτι[ν π]ιθανώτατον τῶν
λεγομένων.

Philodemus is willing to be persuaded that if two poems have the same thought and diction, the execution is good or bad because of the verbal composition. As illustrated amply by Dionysius of Halicarnassus, Philodemus has in mind the creation of different effects by changes in the word order of a given poem.[61] Philodemus admits that composition contributes something to the goodness of a poem, without, how-

---

[59] In line 10, D. Armstrong (below, Chapter 11, p. 220 with n. 23) suggests ε]ὑηθί[αν, "folly." Romeo 1992b (cf. above, n. 48) reads οὐκ ἀέριοc in line 22, and notes that ἀλληλουχίαν can not be the right reading in lines 16–17.

[60] The wording at lines 16–19 seems to have been derived from the "critics." Like the provider of a chorus, life furnishes the poet with an abundance of materials; these continually replenish the poem's "stream of diction." Dionysius of Halicarnassus (*De compositione verborum* 23, p. 234 Roberts) uses similar language to describe the smooth style of composition: the words move along continuously like things that flow (ῥέοντα) and never stay still. The critics seems to have characterized euphonious composition as a smooth, gliding kind of composition. As Gomperz 1891, 63 n. 1 noted, the verse on Seriphos quoted by Philodemus in the next column exemplifies the smooth style as described by Dionysius.

[61] Dionysius of Halicarnassus *De compositione verborum*, see esp. chapters 3–4. Philodemus cites a verse on Seriphos, but denies that it illustrates the critics' contention.

ever, abandoning his basic position that what makes a poem good is appropriate thoughts expressed in appropriate diction. He reiterates his position as follows:

Col. xviii (vii) 12–17

That composition moves the soul by itself, without bringing in any other good, is unconvincing.

12   . . . τὸ
       δ' α[ὐ]τὴν ψυ[χα]γωγ[ε]ῖν
       cύνθεcιν κ[αθ' α]ὑτήν, ἔτε-
15   ρο[ν] οὐδὲν ε[ἰcφ]ερομέ-
       ν[η]ν ἀγαθόν, [ἀ]πίθανόν
       ἐcτι.

In the remainder of the papyrus, Philodemus focuses on change of word order. He concludes his treatment by agreeing that change of word order can destroy the charm of a verse. Then he mentions once again a single opponent, a euphonist:

Col. xxiii (xii) 6–10

But he will not conclude through this, as he thinks, that the goodness of a poem lies in euphony.

6   . . . οὐ μέντοι γε, ὡc οὖ-
       τοc οἴεται, cυνάξει διὰ τού-
       του τὸ τὴν ἀ[ρε]τὴν τοῦ πο-
       ήματ[ο]c ἐ[ν ε]ὐφωνίαι κεῖ-
10   cθαι.[62]

Although it is possible that this euphonist is the opponent who was previously attacked, the intervening discussion provided ample opportunity for Philodemus to introduce a different opponent who argued specifically in favor of euphony.[63]

Let us now return to the previous opponent. The following views may be attributed to him: (1) The poet shares the goal of making a resemblance with other craftsmen, such as the ring-engraver. (2) The poet uses thoughts and diction as underlying materials of his craft. (3) These materials lie "outside" the poetic craft, and variations in them do not impede the poet's function. (4) The distinctive function of the poet is verbal composition (cύνθεcιc). (5) The poet moves the soul (ψυχαγωγεῖ) by verbal composition, not by the underlying thoughts or diction. (6) The goal (τέλοc) of a poet and poetic good (ἀγαθόν), therefore, is the creation of a resemblance out of the underlying materials, thought and diction, by verbal composition. (7) The poetic good, being distinct from the moral good, does not benefit or harm. (8) Therefore, whatever the material used by the poet to achieve his goal, the resemblance created out of this material confers no moral benefit or harm.

This much is supported by the text. But we may venture a little further. Since the

---

[62] There is a reference to the same euphonist a little later at line 23.

[63] The previous opponent was last referred to at col. v (xvi) 25.

text contains no indication of any restriction on the material used by the poet, it is not unreasonable to conjecture that the opponent may have granted the poet the freedom to treat any subject matter at all—moral or immoral, noble or low. The columns that we have examined do not contain any statement of such an extension. But there are fragments that show that some people drew this conclusion; we shall consider them later.

Philodemus objects to this entire sequence of argument, even though he agrees in part with (1) and (7). Although he accepts the commonplace view that the aim of a poet is to make a resemblance, he rejects the opponent's use of the analogy with other crafts. Philodemus believes that it is fundamentally misguided to regard the thoughts and words of a poem as underlying materials. These so-called underlying materials are, in his view, the very constituents of a poem, which determine how good it is. That is why, according to Philodemus, a poet must select appropriate thoughts and diction at the outset; the opponent held that a poet takes the material as given and fashions them into an appropriate product. If the opponent ever agreed that a poet combines words so as to show thought, he understood this differently from Philodemus: the goodness of a poem does not reside in the thought, but in the verbal fabric that shows them. As for making things known, the opponent held that it is not the job of the poet to convey truths, but to create verbal expression. According to Philodemus, the opponent ignores the thought that is created by the verbal structure. Philodemus agrees that moral goodness is distinct from poetic goodness and that a poem as such—as imitation—does not benefit or harm. But he does not believe that the morality of a poem's thoughts—or any aspect of a poem's content—makes no difference to poetic goodness, or that it fails to benefit or harm. If a poem has a moral content, he believed, it can benefit or harm.

The opponent's analogy may be used to illustrate the difference between the opponent and Philodemus. The opponent would argue that just as the particular stone used by the sculptor, for example, which may be marble or limestone, large or small, rounded or rectangular, is a prerequisite of the sculptor's art and makes no difference to the quality of the sculpture, so the particular thoughts and words used by the poet make no difference to the quality of the poem; what matters is how this material is fashioned. Philodemus would counter: just as the skill of the sculptor consists in both making an appropriate selection of the material and fashioning it, so the poet's skill consists in both selecting and arranging the thoughts and diction. Moreover, just as the goodness of the sculpture consists in the qualities of the stone as sculpted, so the goodness of a poem consists in the thoughts and diction as fashioned by the poet. According to Philodemus, the opponent errs in supposing that only the form, and not the combination of material and form, constitute the product.

Philodemus, indeed, casts doubt on the appropriateness of the analogy altogether. In crafts such as sculpting, there is a clearly identifiable material which might be said to remain from the beginning to the end of the craftsman's activity. In the case of poems, however, there is a clear difference between the preexistent, non-poetic thought and the thought presented by the poem. According to Philodemus, the latter is generated by the poet, not given to him from outside. Even when a theme is given to the poet from "outside," the poet alters it in the process of fashioning it. Similarly, diction is changed in the process of poetic creation. Thus a distinction needs to be made between two kinds of thoughts and diction: external, underlying thoughts and words; and the thoughts and words that make up the poem. According to Philodemus, the opponent reduces the second kind to the first, and so fails to recognize that what makes a poem distinctive is not the verbal composition in itself, but the thoughts and words that belong to it.

I shall now proceed to fragments that show details related to the opponent's position. The fragments belong to *P.Herc.* 1676 and another papyrus, *P.Herc.* 1074 + 1081, which is either continuous with *P.Herc.* 1676 or, at any rate, closely related in content.[64] Although the previous analysis of the opponent's view involves some reconstruction, it may serve as a kind of base position, assignable to a single individual. The context of the details that I shall now consider is much less clear.

First, let us return to Heracleodorus. In a fragment belonging to *P.Herc.* 1676, Philodemus mentions that Heracleodorus argued "on behalf of unclarity" (ὑπὲρ τῆς ἀσαφείας). The same sentence contains the claim that "even though poems are unclear, they move the soul (ψυχαγωγεῖν)"; presumably this is part of Heracleodorus' position.[65] In another fragment, which belongs to *P.Herc.* 1074 +1081, Philodemus criticizes Heracleodorus for supposing that thoughts do not move the listener at all:

> For unpoetic [thoughts] do not move, but those that have been put into poetry, and these too are thoughts, even though Heracleodorus believes that thought altogether fails to move, not just unpoetic thought, so that he ridiculously . . .

22   . . . κεινεῖ
γὰρ οὐ τὰ ἀπόητα, ἀλλὰ τὰ πεποημένα, διανοήματα δὲ
25   καὶ ταῦτ' ἔστιν, Ἡρακλεοδώ-
ρου νομίζοντος ὅλως νό-
ημα μὴ κείνειν, ἀλλ' οὐ μόνον τὸ ἀπόητον, ὥστε
κα]ταγελάστω[ς] . . . .[66]

Just like the opponent of the continuous columns, Heracleodorus believes that the thought of a poem does not move the listener. This follows from the claim, which

---

[64] Hausrath 1889, 229 proposed that *P.Herc.* 1081 col. xii (= first half of col. iii, Tract. Tert. Sbordone) fits a lacuna of *P.Herc.* 1676, and he conjectured that when the roll was opened *P.Herc.* 1676 was "torn away" from *P.Herc.* 1074 + 1081 which was written in the same hand (Crönert's hand g). His conjecture was rejected by Gomperz 1891, 51 n. 1, but accepted by Sbordone 1976, XXI. Both Heidmann 1971, 93 and Sbordone accept Hausrath's interleafing of *P.Herc.* 1081 col. xii with *P.Herc.* 1676. Sbordone 1976, XXI and 226–33 fits two other fragments from *P.Herc.* 1074 + 1081 into *P.Herc.* 1676; but the textual support for these intercalations is extremely slim. Sbordone 1976 edited *P.Herc.* 1676, together with the *P.Herc.* 1074 + 1081 which was written in the same hand, as "Tractatus Tertius." The remainder of *P.Herc.* 1074 + 1081, written in Crönert's hand b, was edited by Nardelli 1983 as "Trattato D."

[65] *P.Herc.* 1676 col. iii 22–29 Sbordone. One kind of unclarity (ἀσάφεια) discussed by Philodemus is allegory: he protests that some people, for example Crates, want to have the poet say something other than the obvious meaning immediately starting with the "wrath" (*P.Herc.* 1676 col. ii 18–25 Sbordone). Philodemus mentions the wrath of Achilles again at *P.Herc.* 1676 col. v 25 Sbordone.

[66] *P.Herc.* 1081 fr. n 3–10 Sbordone.

Heracleodorus shares with our earlier opponent, that it is a poet's job to provide composition. Heracleodorus' defence of unclarity fits this position: it is not the task of a poet to set out thoughts, and listeners can be moved by unclear thoughts. The two references to Heracleodorus in *P.Herc.* 1676 and *P.Herc.* 1074 + 1081, and the overlap with our opponent's position, suggest that the opponent may indeed be Heracleodorus, as others have argued.[67] The fragmentary nature of the papyri permits no certainty. But, to judge by Philodemus' reference to Heracleodorus in book 5, he was a leader among the compositionalists, and Philodemus may well have submitted his position to detailed examination in *P.Herc.* 1676.

We know from Philodemus' *On Poems* Book 5 that the compositionalists disagreed among themselves whether a poem should be clear. Some required clarity (τὸ cαφῶc, cαφήνεια) together with conciseness (τὸ cυντόμωc).[68] Others substituted vividness (τὸ ἐναργῶc, ἐνάργεια) and suggestiveness (τὸ ἐμφατικῶc) as qualities of composition.[69] Against the demand for clarity, Philodemus objects that not every kind of clarity is permitted to poets "nor is the permitted kind believed to suit all thoughts."[70] It is possible that the latter objection alludes to the beliefs of Heracleodorus. His defence of unclarity is a shift from the traditional view that speech, λόγοc, should be clear. Aristotle, Theophrastus, the Stoics, and Epicurus all proposed clarity as a basic requirement of speech, although they implicitly modified this view by admitting figures such as metaphor. In response to their position, formalists such as Heracleodorus argued that poetic speech need not be clear because intellectual opacity does not diminish the emotional effectiveness of a poem.

Clarity is the implied topic of another fragment of *P.Herc.* 1074 + 1081, which deals with the question whether the thought of a poem needs to be known. Philodemus criticizes an unidentified opponent as follows:

> Even if the thought is wholly unknown, [he] says that it does no harm at all if the poet does not fall away from his own good. How is it, O Corybantes, that all of us think of a poem not as twanging and clatter, but as diction that signifies thought as a result of being composed in some way, just as speech is not by nature . . . if the thought is wholly unknown.

> 1   κἂν ὅλωc ἀγνο[ῆτα]ι τὸ νο-
>   ούμενον, λέ[γει] μ[η]δὲ ἐν

---

[67] Gomoll 1936, 375–80 and Schenkeveld 1968, 194–95 both identify the opponent as Heracleodorus. Gomoll also argues that he was one of the "Critics" and that Philodemus, after discussing the Critics in general, returns to him in col. xii(xxiii). Schenkeveld cautions that it is unclear, even though probable, that Heracleodorus was a critic. Although I agree that the opponent discussed in columns i–v (xii–xvii) of *P.Herc.* 1676 may be Heracleodorus, I consider it unlikely (as suggested above) that he was one of the Critics.

[68] Col. xxxi 7–10. These qualities form part of the Stoics' five-fold canon of stylistic qualities (Diogenes Laertius 7.59): purity of Greek, clarity, conciseness, appropriateness (πρέπον), and elaboration (κατασκευή). The Stoics added cυντομία to the four qualities proposed by Theophrastus (Cicero *Orator* 79).

[69] Col. xxx 6–10. As the attested definitions of these terms show (for example, at *Ad Herennium* 4.67–68), vividness is distinct from clarity, and to speak ἐμφατικῶc is to intend something more than the surface meaning.

[70] Col. xxxi 28–32, including: οὔτε | τῆc cυνχωρουμένηc | ἅπαcι τοῖc νοουμένοιc | ἁρμόττειν δοκούcηc.

βλάπτειν εἰ [κατ]ὰ τὸ ἴδιον
ἀγαθὸν ὁ ποη[τὴ]ϲ μὴ ἀπο-
5 πίπτει. τίνα γ[ε τ]ρόπον, ὦ
Κορύβαντεϲ, ὅ[λωϲ τ]ὸ πόημα
πάντεϲ οὐχ ὡ[ϲ] τερέτιϲμα
καὶ κροῦμα νο[ο]ῦμε[ν], ἀλλὰ λέξειϲ ἐκ τοῦ [π]ωϲ ϲυντί-
10 θεϲθαι διανόημα ϲημαι-
νούϲαϲ, οἷον ὁ [λό]γοϲ οὐ πέφυκεν, ἂν ὅλω[ϲ ἀ]γνοῆται
τὸ νοούμεν[ον . . . .⁷¹

The expression "does no harm" was prominent in the continuous columns of *P.Herc.*
1676: the opponent claimed that variations in the material "do no harm" (column iii)
and that the poetic good "does not benefit or harm at all" (col. v). The opponents
of this fragment, dubbed "Corybantes," maintain that a poet's failure to make the
thought known "does no harm at all." Like the previous opponent, they distinguish
the poetic good from the content of a poem and identify the function of a poet with
composition. Philodemus objects that a poem is not just noise–of the sort that carries
away the Corybantes–but that the words of a poem are put together in a way that
signifies thought. It is not the case, he implies, that if the thought of a poem is unknown, there is no impairment of the poetic good. Similarly, Philodemus pointed out
in column i of *P.Herc.* 1676 that it is the task of a poet to put together words so as to
show thought and that it is not outside his craft to make things known. The text of this
column did not show whether this was Philodemus' view or his opponent's. This
fragment shows that either the opponent or someone who shared his basic position
denied that a poet needs to make the thought known.

A long and well preserved fragment of *P.Herc.* 1074 + 1081 deals with originality
of subject matter:

> . . . that . . . is a . . . poet he has simply adduced similarities to what he wishes,
> he has not proved that he is of this sort, since there is much difference in the
> kinds of knowledge. Nevertheless, just as in cases involving the handicrafts we
> do not think a person worse insofar as he worked out beautifully a material that
> he supplied from a different craftsman, so neither do we think a poet worse if,
> upon taking a non-poetic theme, he adds his own interpretation. We hold this not
> only in the case of small [themes], but not even when he has taken the [story] of
> Troy or Thebes in common from someone else and takes it apart, as it were, and,
> upon arranging it again somehow, invests it with his own elaboration. Seeing
> that Sophocles and Euripides and many others have written about Thyestes, and
> about Paris and Menelaus, and about Electra and numerous other [events], we

---

⁷¹ *P.Herc.* 1074 + 1081 fr. c col. ii 1–13 Sbordone. I read ἀγνο[ῆτα]ι in line 1 instead of the editors'
ἀγνο[ήϲη]ι; the same form occurs in line 12. In line 2, I suggest λέ[γει] instead of λέ[γων]. In line 6, I
have provisionally inserted Hausrath's ὅ[λωϲ], even though there doesn't seem to be enough room for
these letters. The end of the passage should be supplemented with an infinitive dependent on πέφυκεν.
I am very doubtful whether *P.Herc.* 1081 col. 5b (= *HV²* vol. 7, p. 83 dext.) belongs here, as Sbordone
proposes.

do not think that in this respect some are better and others worse, but often those who took [the themes] are better than those who used them previously, if they bring in the poetic good more . . .

14   . . . εἶνα[ι
15   ποιητὴν ὅμοια μόνο[ν
          ὧι βούλεται παρατέθη-
          κεν, οὐκ ἀποδέδειχεν ὅ-
          τι τοιοῦτος, ἐν ταῖς ἐπιστή-
          μαις διαφορᾶς πολλῆς ὑ-
20   παρχούσης. ἀλλ' ὅμως κα-
          θάπερ ἐπὶ τῶν κατὰ τὰς
          χειρουργίας οὐχ ἡγούμε-
          θα χείρω{ι} παρ' ὅσον ὑφέ{μ}-
          μενος ὕλην ἑτέρου τε-
25   χνείτου καλῶς ἠργάσα-
          το, οὕτως οὐδὲ ποιητὴν ἐ-
          ὰν ἀπόητον ὑπόθεσιν λα-
28   βὼν προσθῆ⟨ι⟩ τὸν ⟨ἴ⟩διον νο[ῦν, ∥
1   χείρω νομίζομεν, καὶ
          οὐκ ἐπὶ τῶν μεικρῶν
          μόνον οὕτως ἔχομεν,
          ἀλλ' οὐδ' ἂν τὰ κατ' Εἴλιον
5   ἢ] Θήβας κοινῶς παρ' ἑτέ-
          ρου λαβὼν ὥσπερ διαλύ-
          σηι, καί πως πάλι cυντά-
          ξας ἰδίαν κατασκευὴν
          περιθῆ⟨ι⟩. τὰ γοῦν περὶ τὸν
10   Θυέcτην καὶ τὰ περὶ τὸν
          Πάριν κ[αὶ Μενέλα]ον καὶ
          τὰ περὶ τὴν Ἠλέκτραν
          καὶ πλεῖον' ἄλλα Cοφ[ο]κλέ-
          α καὶ Εὐριπίδην καὶ πολ-
15   λοὺς ἄλλους γεγραφότας
          ὁρ]ῶντες, οὐ νομίζομεν
          κατὰ γὰρ τοιοῦτο τοὺς
          μὲν εἶναι βελτείους, τοὺς
          δὲ χείρους, ἀλλὰ πολλά-
20   κι τοὺς εἰληφότας ἀμεί-
          νους τῶν προκεχρημέ-
          νων, ἂν τὸ ποιητικὸν ἀ-

γαθὸν μᾶλλον εἰϲε[νέγ-
κ]ωνται.[72]

Like the opponent of the continuous columns of *P.Herc.* 1676, this opponent uses an analogy with other skills. Philodemus objects that his comparisons are arbitrary: there is a great difference, he protests, in the kinds of knowledge. But Philodemus makes a concession: just as in the handicrafts we don't consider a craftsman worse for taking his material from another craftsman, we do not think a poet worse for taking a theme from someone else. In these circumstances, what makes a poet or other craftsman good or bad is not the material, but its elaboration. Philodemus considers two kinds of poetic theme: the poet may take a theme that has not been worked out poetically before and add his own insights; or he may take a theme treated by previous poets, such as the story of Troy, and rearrange it. In both cases, the poet adds originality to his subject matter by his elaboration. Philodemus exemplifies the second type of theme by large, traditional themes. In his analogy, the opponent appears to direct special attention to small themes, derived from non-poetic sources. These sources may be exemplified by painters, historians, geographers, astronomers, and so on. This focus agrees with the preference of Callimachus and other poets for small themes and the narrow, untrodden path, and for their extensive use of learned material supplied by others.[73] It also agrees with our previous opponent's exaltation of small-scale work (col. v).

It is noteworthy that what others might regard as original subject matter is treated by this opponent as derived from another: a subject that has not been treated poetically before is traced to a nonpoetic source. This perspective agrees with our earlier opponent's claim that a poet, like other craftsmen, takes his subject matter from outside. On this view, any subject matter is borrowed, whether from a poet or from a non-poetic source, and the originality of a poem's thought consists entirely in the working out of a given subject matter.

Another fragment belonging to *P.Herc.* 1074+1081 touches on the same topic, with similar details. Philodemus claims that poetry differs from another area of expertise, which is not identified:

> . . . entirely different in poetry. [This craft] has no need to create any of its material for itself, whereas they claim that poetry sometimes fashions even a common theme for itself, and divides both it and the given theme, and discovers particular thoughts and diction out of . . .

> 2 . . . παραλλάττον ὅλωϲ
> ἐν ποιητικῆι. τὴν μὲν

---

[72] *P.Herc.* 1081, fr. e cols. i 14–ii 24 Sbordone. Sbordone's text at col. i 12–17 is: [πρὸϲ δὲ τὸ δο]|κοῦν ὅτι β[έλτιϲτον] ὁμολογοῦ[με]ν εἶνα[ι]‖ ποιητὴν ⟨ὃϲ⟩ ὅμοια μόνο[ν]‖ ὧι βούλεται παρατέ-θη|κεν. Sbordone translates: "Quanto poi all' opinione che eccellente poeta concordiamo essere colui che abbia allestito solo cose simili a cio che vuol (rappresentare)." This reading, however, rests on the supplement ⟨ὃϲ⟩, as well as a doubtful interpretation of lines 15–17, which would more naturally be taken to mean "he cited similarities to what he wants," i.e. he (the opponent) picked out just the similarities that he wanted (in constructing his analogies).

[73] On Callimachus' preference for small, new themes, see *Epigram* 28 and *Aitia* fr. 1.25–28, cf. *Epigram* 8.

γὰρ οὐθὲν δεῖ τῆϲ ὕληϲ

5   ἑαυτῆ⟨ι⟩ γεννᾶν, τὴν δὲ ποη-
τικὴν ἀξιοῦϲι καὶ τὴν
κοινὴν ὑπόθεϲιν ἔϲτιν
ὅτε πλάττειν αὐτῆ⟨ι⟩, καὶ
μερ[ί]ζειν ταύτην τε καὶ

10   τὴν δεδομένην, καὶ τὰ
κατὰ μέροϲ εὑρίϲκειν δι-
ανοήματα καὶ λέξειϲ ἐκ . . . .[74]

Again, Philodemus objects to an analogy concerning the poetic craft. He points out that whereas a certain skill to which poetry is compared has no need to create any of its material, poetry is creative. "They," the opponents, claim that "poetry" sometimes fashions a new common theme, divides both newly fashioned and given themes, and discovers particular thoughts and diction. This analysis supplements the previously cited description of how a poet deals with a large, common theme. In addition to rearranging a given common theme, poets sometimes fashion a common theme of their own, divide a theme into parts, and add new thoughts and diction. Philodemus turns this description against his opponents. In the very ways in which they say that poets fashion a given material, Philodemus contends, poets create their own material. The unidentified skill might be a skill such as sculpting or any other handicraft, in which the craftsman works with a given, physical material.

Our earlier opponent distinguished the moral good from the poetic good; but there was no discussion of the morality of a poem's content. Several fragments belonging to *P.Herc.* 1074+1081 deal with the relationship of morally good or bad content to the poetic good. In one well preserved passage, Philodemus has all of Greece bear witness that the morality of the content makes no difference to the goodness of a poem:

> . . . Greece. Apart from this, [Greece] used to admire Archilochus, Hipponax, Semonides, and some things in Homer, Euripides and other poets that are associated with base characters and are written about base deeds; and it used to deride things associated with decent characters, and hearing about decent events, it was persuaded in this way; and [Greece] supposed that a good poet is one who worked out, as I said, whatever thought he took from others or put forward himself, and perhaps a base person who conveyed decent thoughts but did not embellish . . .

1   . . . τὴν Ἑλ-
λάδα. ἀλλ᾽ ἔξω τούτων
Ἀρχίλοχον ἐθαύμαζε
καὶ τὸν Ἱππώνακτα

5   καὶ τὸν Cημωνίδην,
καὶ τῶν παρ᾽ Ὁμήρωι

[74] *P.Herc.* 1081 col. vii 2–12 Sbordone of Tractatus Tertius.

καὶ Εὐρειπίδει καὶ τοῖϲ
ἄλλοιϲ ποιηταῖϲ ἔνια,
πονηροῖϲ προϲώποιϲ
10 περικείμενα καὶ περὶ
πονηρῶν πραγμάτων
γεγραμμένα, καὶ κατε-
γέλα χρηϲτοῖϲ περικεί-
μενα, καὶ περὶ χρηϲτῶν
15 ἀκούουϲα πραγμάτων
οὕτωϲ ἐπέπειϲτο, καὶ
ποητὴν μὲν ἀγαθὸν ὑ-
πελάμβανε τὸν ἐξεργα-
ϲάμενον, ὡϲ ἔφην, ὁποῖ-
20 όν ποτ' ἂν διανόημα λά-
βηι παρ' ἑτέρων ἢ αὐτὸϲ
προθῆται, τάχα δὲ ἄνθρω-
πον πονηρὸν καὶ τόν-
δ' ἐνέγκαντα διανοή-
25 ματα χρηϲτά, μὴ καλ-
λωπίϲαντα δ' οὕτω . . . .[75]

The Greeks of the past, Philodemus writes, admired poets for the execution of the subject matter, regardless of the moral goodness or badness of the subject matter. They admired Archilochus, Hipponax, and Semonides, who were notorious for heaping abuse on their enemies; they also admired some depictions of scoundrels and base deeds in the poems of Homer, Euripides, and others, and scorned some presentations of decent characters and deeds. In short, the Greeks welcomed any thought whatsoever, whether the poet took it from someone else or invented it himself, so long as it was worked out well.

This assessment of Greek poetic taste agrees, in the first place, with that of Plato. In the *Republic*, Plato likens Homer and his followers to versatile magicians who enchant their audience by producing any image at all. Like a person who goes around with a mirror, Homer and the other poets imitate all kinds of crafts and all kinds of people, without discrimination; they produce appearances of anything at all, twice removed from the truth, and enthrall their listeners by these images, whatever they are.[76] Philodemus describes the same versatility and enchantment: the poets of the past used to present any thought at all, and the public admired their skill regardless of subject matter.

Plato sought to replace this indiscriminate imitation and enchantment with morally truthful and beneficial poetry. In the Hellenistic period, some persons called for a return to the earlier, premoral stage of poetic judgment. Although the immediate

---

[75] *PHerc.* 1074 fr. f col. iii 1–26 Sbordone. At line 11 Sbordone's γραμμάτων is an erratum for πραγμάτων; in line 24, δ' should not be bracketed.

[76] See esp. *Republic* 397A, 398A, 596C, 598B–C; cf. *Sophist* 234B.

context of Philodemus' passage is lost, its description of the earlier Greeks implies that some Hellenistic theorists agreed with them. The opponent of our continuous columns provides a theoretical underpinning for their position by arguing that verbal execution alone makes a poem good or bad, and that variations in subject matter do not impede the achievement of poetic goodness. If he did not restrict the variations in subject matter, our opponent was one of those who called for a return to an era of poetic enchantment in which a poet was permitted to present any thought at all. Eratosthenes, as cited at the beginning of this paper, may be included among those who called for such a return.[77] His claim that poetry is allowed to fashion "whatever appears" to it suitable to move the listener is directly opposed to Plato's condemnation of the indiscriminate appearances of poetry.

There are two more fragments belonging to *P.Herc.* 1074+1081 that defend immorality in poetry. One contains a clear statement of the irrelevance of morality to poetic merit. Like the previous fragment, it defends Euripides:

> . . . and [they] say that the poem [is] not base, and that a bad thought will not harm at all—as Euripides will not harm—nor a decent thought benefit—as Chaeremon will not benefit. For the fact that a non-poetic thought is decent or bad is dragged into poetic goodness, and for this neither he nor Philiscus nor the other two comic . . .

13   . . . [οὐ-

δὲ πονηρόν φα[ϲιν εἶναι

15   τὸ πόημ[α], καὶ μηδ[ὲ ἐν

βλάψειν τὸ φαῦλον—ὡ[ϲ

οὐδ' Εὐρειπίδην—δια[νό-

ημα, μηδ' ὠφελήϲ[ειν

τὸ χρηϲτόν—ὡϲ οὐδὲ [Χαι-

20   ρήμονα—. παρέλκεται γ[ὰρ

τὸ χρηϲτὸν ἢ φαῦλο[ν

εἶναι διανόημα τ[ὸ] ἀ[πό-

ητον εἰϲ ποιητικὴν [ἀ-

ρετήν, καὶ ἐπὶ τοῦτ' ο[ὐ-

25   χ οὗτος οὐδ[ὲ] Φίλιϲκο[ϲ

οὐδ' οἱ λοιπο[ὶ] δύο κω[μικοί . . . .[78]

Again, the phrase "does no harm" occurs. This time it is claimed that morally bad thought will not harm at all, just as good thought will not benefit. Like the opponent attacked in the continuous columns of *P.Herc.* 1676, these opponents draw a distinction between moral and poetic goodness. They maintain that just as a poet does not harm or benefit, neither does a poetic thought harm or benefit, with the explanation that the moral goodness or badness of a thought is "dragged into" poetic goodness. In

---

[77] See nn. 3 and 4 above.

[78] *P.Herc.* 1081 fr. h 13–26 Sbordone. I supply φα[ϲιν] in place of Sbordone's φα[μεν], μηδ[ὲ ἐν] in place of μηδ[ένα], and ὠφελήϲ[ειν] in place of ὠφελήϲ[αι]. The phrase μηδ[ὲ ἐν] occurs at *P.Herc.* 1074+1081 fr. c col. ii 2–3 Sbordone, and *P.Herc.* 1676 col. v (xvi) 22–23.

their view, morality should be left out of the judgment of whether a poem is good or bad. For when a morally good or bad thought is put into poetic form, it acquires a different, non-moral type of goodness or badness, which is without benefit or harm. A poem that represents morally bad persons and deeds, therefore, is not itself morally bad; and neither the poet nor the poetic thought harms or benefits. Although Euripides represents characters and actions that are wicked, neither he nor his poetry harms the listener. Likewise, Chaeremon does not benefit by the morally upright situations of his tragedies.[79]

In column v of *P.Herc.* 1676, Philodemus mentioned that his opponent showed with examples that the poetic good does not harm or benefit at all. The opponent might have used the examples that occur in this fragment and in the preceding fragment. If he did, he held that morally good or bad thought, when put into poetry, does not benefit or harm. In that case, he did indeed make the extension that is not actually stated in the continuous columns, but which follows logically upon the attested claims; that is, he granted the poet the freedom to present any thought at all.

Neither this nor the preceding fragment tells us Philodemus' position.[80] As we saw earlier, he agrees that a poem should not be judged by the moral utility of its content and that, as a poem, it does not benefit or harm. However, Philodemus also rejected the claim that the content of a poem is external to the poetic craft; in his view, thoughts, together with their moral value, are crucially relevant to the goodness of a poem. He did not agree, therefore, that, whatever the thought, the execution makes a poem good or bad. Moreover, he held that insofar as a poem presents morally good or bad persons or deeds, it can be beneficial or harmful. In short, according to Philodemus, moral goodness and badness are not "dragged" into the judgment of a poem, but cannot be ignored in judging either the goodness of a poem or its benefit or harm.

Philodemus shows his disapproval in the last fragment presented here:

> Further, elsewhere he says that [decent poems] provided sayings and thoughts that were elaborated in connection with certain base [characters], nor would a decent thought benefit and a base thought harm if it were taken as belonging to the poem and the poet. Perhaps someone will call a poem that is highly illustrious because of praiseworthy execution "decent," and a poem that has blameworthy execution "base." For that is said shamelessly by some people.

11   ἔ]τι δ᾽ [ἐν ἄλ]λοις φηcὶ τά
        γε] χ[ρηcτὰ παρε]cχηκέναι
        ῥήcειc καὶ δ[ι]ανοίαc

---

[79] According to Aristotle (*Rhetoric* 3.12), Chaeremon, a tragedian of the fourth century, had a style suitable for reading rather than for dramatic performance. Philodemus' reference suggests that he liked to preach.

[80] If φα[μεν], as supplied by Sbordone, is read in place of φα[cιν] (line 14), then Philodemus would be stating his own position. Although it is possible that Philodemus is in superficial agreement with the way the position is stated in this fragment, the language and concepts suggest that the assertions were made by his opponents. Along with reading φα[μεν], Sbordone assigns a different meaning to the fragment than I do. He translates παρέλκεται as "si trasferisce" and seems to attribute to Philodemus the view that the moral goodness or badness of a thought is carried over into poetic goodness. Apart from disturbing the coherence of the argument, this interpretation seems to me to to ignore the connotation of forcedness in παρέλκεται (cf. Philodemus' use of this term at *On Music* 4 col. xxvi 9–10).

κατεcκευαcμέναc περὶ
15   πονη[ρῶ]ν τινων, μ[η]δ᾽ ἂν
       ὠφελεῖν τὸ χρηcτὸν δι-
       ανόημα καὶ βλάπτειν
       τὸ πονηρὸν εἰ λαμβάνοι-
       θ᾽ ὡc ποήματοc καὶ ποη-
20   τοῦ. τάχα γὰρ τὸ διὰ τῆc
       ἐπαινετῆc ἐξ[εργα]cίαc
       ἐπιφαν[έcτατον πόη]μα
       χρηcτόν, τὸ δ᾽ ἐκ τῆc ψεκ-
       τῆc πονηρὸν ἀνακαλεῖ
25   τιc. [ἐ]κεῖνο γὰρ ὑπό τι-
       νων ἀναιδῶc λέγεται·[81]

Here, the opponent admits that the thought of a poem may benefit or harm. But in these cases, he argues, the poetic purpose is ignored; if the thought is regarded as belonging to the poem or poet, it does not benefit or harm. The opponent also seems to admit that there are morally good and bad poems; but he undercuts this admission, as he undercuts the claim that poetic thought may benefit or harm, by invoking the poetic context. Philodemus responds that one might as well call a poem that has praiseworthy execution "decent" (χρηcτόν) and its opposite "base" (πονηρόν). The opponent, he implies, ignores the meaning of moral terms when he denies that poetic thought is morally good ("decent") or bad ("base"), or that it benefits or harms. If a poem is not to be called "decent" or "base" because of its thought, why not call it so because of its execution? Philodemus says that some people have indeed used the terms "decent" (χρηcτόν) and "base" ("bad," πονηρόν) in this way. To him, this nomenclature is shameless. We may disagree; for in ordinary Greek, these terms admit of a non-moral usage. On the other hand, Philodemus' point is that the opponent ignores the fact that poems are a way of expressing moral thought; and this point has some force.

Let us now return to the opponent of columns i–v of *P.Herc.* 1676. An examination of the fragments of *P.Herc.* 1676 and *P.Herc.* 1074 + 1081 has suggested a number of ways in which his position may be filled out. The additional details (marked by superscripts) may be combined with the base position as follows: (1) The poet shares the goal of making a resemblance with other craftsmen, such as the ring engraver. (2) The poet uses thoughts and diction as underlying materials of his craft. (3) These materials lie "outside" the poetic craft; and variations in them do not impede the poet's task. (3′) The thought of a poem is supplied by a nonpoetic source or by other poems. (4) The distinctive function of the poet is verbal composition. (5) The poet moves the soul by verbal composition, not by the underlying thoughts or diction. (5′) The thought of a poem need not be clear. (5″) The thought of a poem need not be comprehensible. (6) The goal of a poet and poetic good is the creation of a resemblance out of the underlying materials, thought and diction, by verbal compo-

---

[81] *P.Herc.* 1081 fr. f col. ii 11–26 Sbordone.

sition. (7) The poetic good, being distinct from the moral good, does not benefit or harm. (8) Therefore, whatever the material used by the poet to achieve his goal, the resemblance created out of this material confers no moral benefit or harm. (8′) A poet may represent anything at all.

We know that Hellenistic thinkers proposed many variations on the views included in this sketch. The combined view that I have outlined may well be an amalgam of various views. But it is possible that a single person held all of the above views. The supplements fit logically upon the base position, and the text suggests places of insertion. If a single person did hold all the above views, the obvious candidate is Heracleodorus.[82]

[82] A shorter version of this paper was delivered at a panel on Philodemus at the meeting of the American Philological Association, December 1989. I benefitted from the comments made the panelists and other participants, and I am particularly grateful to Diskin Clay, Dirk Obbink, James Porter, and David Sider for their criticisms and suggestions.

9

Philodemus on the Technicity of Rhetoric

David Blank

It is one thing to attack the practice of an art or arts as useless or even harmful and quite another to say that a certain practice is not an art at all, but rather a mere knack, and then to claim that any attempt to make that practice into an art will fail. In his attacks on the liberal arts, Sextus Empiricus employs both these arguments, claiming, for example, that rhetoric teaches falsehood, that it does not achieve its end of persuasion with any regularity, and that if it is considered as a science, its principles (words, propositions, etc.) are non-existent. He informs us (*Adv. math.* 6.4–5; cf. 1.1) that Epicureans argue dogmatically that an art is not necessary for happiness, but is rather harmful, while others aporetically attack the fundamental principles of an art, thereby destroying it entirely.

The transition between these attacks is helped by the fact that most Greek definitions of *techne* specified that an art must be useful, as did the definition attributed to the Epicureans: "art is a method accomplishing what is useful for life"[1] and their claim that in fact it was need that gave rise to the arts in the first place.[2]

But just how clear is it that the Epicureans insisted that *technai* had to be useful; and insofar as they did so insist, for what or whom do *technai* have to be useful?

In a passage drawn from an Epicurean source, Sextus says (*Adv. math.* 1.49–52) that there are two arts of grammar: lower grammar or "grammatistic," the art of reading and writing the letters; and special, deeper or more perfected grammar, which deals with the origin and nature of language, as well as with the works of prose-writers and poets. Even Epicurus, he says, accepted that grammatistic was useful and even necessary, not just for philosophers, but for all men: for it is obvious that the end of every *techne* is something useful for life; some arts arose mainly to avoid ills (such as medicine), others to find what is helpful (such as navigation). Yet, when Sextus says that Epicureans attack the liberal arts as not necessary or as contributing nothing to happiness or wisdom, that is not to say that they are not *technai*, although Sextus incorporates them into his own attacks with just that result. All the

---

[1] Scholia to Dionysius Thrax 108.27 = Epicurus fr. 227b Usener, 205 Arrighetti: οἱ μὲν Ἐπικού-ρειοι οὕτως ὁρίζονται τὴν τέχνην· τέχνη ἐcτὶ μέθοδος ἐνεργοῦca τῷ βίῳ τὸ cυμφέρον.

[2] Cf. Diogenes of Oenoanda fr. 12 col. ii 8–10 Smith: πάcac (sc. τὰc τέχναc) γὰρ ἐγέν|νηcαν αἱ χρεῖαι καὶ πε|ριπτώcειc and Lucretius, *On the Nature of Things* 5.1029.

Epicurean need mean by this is that philosophy is the only thing truly useful for happiness. Thus, when the Epicurean distinguishes the two kinds of grammatical *techne*, he says that grammatistic is necessary, while special grammar is useless or even harmful; he does not necessarily mean that special grammar is not even a *techne*.

When Philodemus, in his treatise *On Rhetoric*, defines the usual or preconceptive meaning of *techne* as "a faculty or disposition arising from observation of certain common and fundamental things which extend through most particular instances, a faculty which grasps and produces an effect such as only a few who have not learned the art can accomplish, and doing this firmly and surely, rather than conjecturally,"[3] he expressly leaves aside the question of a *techne*'s utility, although he is conscious of its belonging in this context. On the basis of this definition, Philodemus comes to the remarkable conclusion that sophistic rhetoric, of all things, is a *techne*, while rhetoric proper (i.e., forensic) and political rhetoric are not *technai*. This conclusion is surprising in light of, for example, Philodemus' own book *On Household Management* (col. xxiii 22ff.), where the best way of making money is said to be to receive gratitude and reverence in return for λόγοι φιλόcοφοι, which are true, free of strife and turmoil, given that the result of cοφιcτικοὶ καὶ ἀγωνιcτικοί (λόγοι) is no better than the result of δημοκοπικοὶ καὶ cυκοφαντικοί (λόγοι). Obviously, such a conclusion could only be reached by leaving aside any requirement that a *techne* be useful.

We have been conditioned by our reading of Plato and Sextus to assume in a discussion of whether x-ική is a *techne* or not that: if one concludes that it is useful, then it will be said to be a *techne*; and if one concludes that it is a *techne*, then one will also claim that one ought to have it. That this is not simply true for Philodemus is clear from the above treatment of sophistic, as well as from *On Household Management*. There Philodemus argues that, as there are two kinds of cookery, a non-technical sort adequate for one's own needs, as well as a technical sort, so are there also two sorts of household management. The philosopher, who wants to have the means to satisfy not only his natural and necessary desires, but his natural and unnecessary ones as well, but who also knows the proper measure of wealth which derives from the limit of natural desire, will have the non-technical knowledge of household management; to have the technical kind would be to place an unseemly emphasis on the acquisition of wealth and would take away from the time available for friends and philosophy (cols. xii 5ff., xiii 11ff., xvii 2ff.).

We are beginning to see that the Epicurean has a varied arsenal of contrasts he can put to use in dealing with *technai*: (1) He can speak of a useful *techne* vs. one which is useless or harmful. (2) He can distinguish a layman's knowledge of a subject, which the philosopher might want or need, from the technical knowledge of a

---

[3] Philodemus, *On Rhetoric* 2 in *P.Herc.* 1674 col. xxxviii p. 123, 5–19 Longo: νοεῖ|ται τοίνυν καὶ λέγεται |[τ]έχνη παρὰ τοῖ[c] Ἕλλη|cι̣[ν ἕ]ξιc ἢ διάθ[ε]cι[c] ἀπὸ | παρ[α]τηρή[c]εω[c τιν]ῶν | κοινῶν καὶ [c]τοι[χειω][[ν]]|δῶν, ἃ διὰ πλειόν[ω]ν δι|ήκει τῶν ἐπὶ μέ[ρ]ο[υc], κα|ταλαμβάνουcά [τ]ι̣ καὶ |[c]υντελοῦcα τοιοῦτον,| οἷον ὁμοίωc τῶν μὴ | μαθόντων ἔ[νιοι], ἐcτη|κότωc καὶ βε-[βαί]ωc [οὐ|δ]ὲ cτοχαcτι[κῶc]. See Barnes 1986, 2–22 for another possible restoration at the end of this quotation: βε[βαί]ωc [ἢ | τ]ε cτοχαcτι[κῶc], which yields a wider inclusion for the province of rhetoric: "doing this firmly and surely, or even conjecturally."

professional, which the philosopher would not, at least in every case, want. (3) In a related comparison, he can contrast the casual way a layman or philosopher might engage in an activity, just for pleasure, with the concentrated and distracting way a professional engages in the same activity, striving for perfection. For example, Philodemus notes that small-minded people with nothing to do sometimes amuse themselves by working hard to learn to play a musical instrument, not seeing how much public musical performance goes on around them, an unnecessary pleasure which is laborious and shuts us off from the most important activities conducing to our well being.[4] Dionysius of Halicarnassus notes that "The doctrine that 'writing,' as Epicurus himself says, 'is no trouble to those who do not aim at the ever-varying standard' was meant to forestall the charge of gross laziness and stupidity."[5] (4) He can contrast the form of a *techne* which is in agreement with the proleptic use of its name with another form which takes off from a derived, catachrestic sense of the name. For example, lower grammar derives from *gramma* meaning "letter" or "elementary sound," while special grammar derives from the same sense of *gramma* "by extension"; geometry derives originally from land-measurement, but is now applied to theory regarding φυcικώτερα; medicine (ἰατρική) derives from the extraction of poisons (ἰοί);[6] the simple arithmetic of the many is opposed to the modern theoretical arithmetic.[7] (5) Following along these lines, he can distinguish the more practical or general *techne* from its more mathematical, technical, theoretical or special version. (6) Drawing on several of the previous distinctions, he can contrast the use of a *techne* for pleasure with any claim its technical counterpart might make to be useful for education or for character-building. Thus, Sextus' arguments against musical ἦθος are drawn from the Epicureans (*Adv. math.* 6.19ff.), as are his arguments to the effect that since poems contain equal numbers of morally good and bad statements, it is not grammar which is educational, but philosophy, which alone can judge which statements are good and which are bad (*Adv. math.* 1.277ff.; cf. 299).

So, it seems that the Epicurean recognizes *technai* in areas where there are things which can be necessary, useful, or pleasant, although each *techne* itself—or at least one of its forms—may not be helpful in getting these good things, since it has become too specialized, theoretical, or technical. What will get the good things will be, in some instances a lower form of the *techne*, in others a non-technical competence, and in others philosophy itself.

This result finds confirmation in Lucretius' description of the history of culture. In every instance of progress Lucretius records a beginning in nature and utility or need (e.g., *On the Nature of Things* 5.1028f.), followed by a development which at best is no better than the first state and at worst brings greed, strife, and war: First, people poisoned themselves out of ignorance; later they learned how to poison others

---

[4] Philodemus, *On Music* 4 col. xxxvii 9–xxxviii 12 Neubecker.

[5] Dionysius of Harlicarnassus, *De compositione verborum* 24 (= Epicurus fr. 230 Usener): τὸ γὰρ "οὐκ ἐπιπόνου τοῦ γράφειν ὄντος," ὡς Ἐπίκουρος λέγει, "τοῖς μὴ cτοχαζομένοις τοῦ πυκνὰ μεταπίπτοντος κριτηρίου" πολλῆς ἀργίας ἦν καὶ cκαιότητος ἀλεξιφάρμακον (translation Roberts).

[6] Sextus Empiricus, *Adv. math.* 1.45–48; cf. 5.1–2 on astrology as observation useful for navigation and agriculture vs. astrology as the casting of horoscopes.

[7] Proclus, *On the First Book of the Elements of Euclid* 25.15ff. Friedlein.

(5.1007f.).[8] First, our images led to notions of gods; our later reasoning about them led to superstition and misery (5.1161ff., 1194ff.). First, bronze was more valued and gold rejected because of its uselessness; now the situation is reversed (5.1241ff.). Especially telling is the story of the origin of music and dance (5.1379ff.): men learned from the birds how to sing and please the ear; they had a good time after their picnics, when they would please their bodies without great effort, especially in good weather, when they would begin to dance without *numerus* (5.1401), which made them smile and laugh and helped them stay awake; even now guards continue this practice, and they have learned to keep the *numeri* (5.1409), but they do not enjoy their activity one bit more than did their primitive ancestors. I cannot help but see in *numerus* a reference to the way in which theory can spoil the utility of a *techne*. Lucretius' general conclusion is that humanity labors in vain and, the more it develops the arts, the more it is led into misery and war (5.1430ff.).

Now let us look more closely at the *technai* Philodemus mentions in *On Rhetoric*. Among exact arts he names grammatistic, music, painting, and sculpture; medicine and navigation he names among conjectural arts. Grammatistic is named three times as a model art,[9] as is sculpture,[10] while music is named twice,[11] and poetics also puts in an appearance.[12] Let us examine each of these arts.

First we look at sculpture. It is fairly obvious that representational portrait sculpture has a method for achieving its ends and criteria by which its products can be judged. Philodemus conjures up an opponent who says: "Just as when you see a beautiful sculpture you would say without proof (χωρὶς λόγου) that it is a work of art, in the same way you will speak of the works of the politicians once you have examined them."[13] Philodemus agrees that we just recognize a work of art without proof, but then denies that this could apply to politics, which has no method.[14] The idea that we immediately recognize the artistic nature of a statue accords with Epicurus' insistence in the case of language, which he regards as an art, on using words in their first and foremost, immediately recognizable senses, that is according to their προλήψεις. Immediate recognition of a statue as a work of art also fits with Lucretius' account of the way in which we are moved by the senses through the mediation of *imagines* (*On the Nature of Things* 4.877–906: walking comes from *imagines* of walking which in turn come from *simulacra meandi*). The point is, I think, that the recognition of a work of art is a purely mechanical process. We see something and images from it impinge upon the soul atoms which are responsible for sensation. Certain patterns of moving sensory-soul atoms correspond to patterns all of us already have (the *prolepseis*) and cause us to feel pleasure. This immediacy—taken together, I assume, with the presence of a highly successful method—legitimates

[8] Cf. below, p. 214 n. 10, and for the text here see the note in M. F. Smith's Loeb edition ad loc.

[9] Philodemus, *On Rhetoric* 2 col. xxxviii 32 p. 123 Longo), xli 12 (p. 129 Longo), xliii 4 (p. 133 Longo, here: γραμματική).

[10] Cols. xix 16ff. p. 83 Longo, xxxviii 34 p. 123 Longo, xliii 4 p. 133 Longo.

[11] Cols. xxxviii 32 p. 123 Longo, xli 12 p. 129 Longo.

[12] *P.Herc.* 1672 col. xxii 39 p. 219 Longo.

[13] *On Rhetoric* 2 in *P.Herc.* 1674 col xix 16 p. 83 Longo.

[14] *On Rhetoric* 2 col. xix 26–33 p. 83 Longo: οὐ[δὲ]‖ πιθανόν ἐcτιν, εἰ καὶ | χ[ω]ρὶc λόγου γνοίη τιc ‖[ὅ]τι τέχ[νη]c ἔργα ταῦ|τ' ἐcτιν, εἰ πε[ρὶ] τῶν πο|λειτικῶν ἔρ[γ]ων τ[αὐτὰ] πα|[ρα]τιθέαcιν, οὐδ' [ὅ]‖τα[ν ὁ] περὶ τ[ούτ]ων πολ[ὺν] νοῦν ἔχων. . . .

sculpture as an Epicurean art; what Philodemus leaves out here is that the judgment of whether the sculpture is a good or bad work of art will be made by the mind, not by the eye.

Unlike the agents of visual sensation, sound particles lack mediating images and are not capable of moving the human soul.[15] Yet music, per se, is considered by Philodemus strictly as sound, which is irrational (*alogon*) and affects only the auditory sense-organs. For the elements characteristic of music are melody and rhythm, and neither can affect the character, actions, thought, mood or opinion: they cannot stop a dispute, they provide no help, can't cheer one up. They do, however, produce pleasure.

When music has an effect on our souls, it does this not *qua* music, but insofar as it contains poetry, texts, or thought.[16] The method of musical art allows one to compose pleasing songs with great regularity, which is why Philodemus includes music among the exact sciences. As also with poetry, however, any ethical content of a song stands outside the realm of the art. Ethical content has to do with the thought of a song and will be judged by philosophy, not the art of music. Further, what is good or bad in a musical composition will be judged by philosophy, not by the sense of hearing.[17]

Right through the book *On Music* Philodemus is concerned with distinguishing the irrational province of musical *techne* from two other spheres, that of *poesis*, which is responsible for whatever persuasion is accomplished by lyrics, and that of *doxa*, which determines, for example, whether we approve or disapprove of, say, the chromatic division of the tetrachord.

This seems as it should be: certain Epicurean and hence Philodemean arts should be codifications of rules about how to have a certain effect on the irrational senses. Glancing back at the Epicurean and Philodemean definitions of art, we find nothing which goes against this very simple notion. τέχνη is a μέθοδος effecting something useful for life; it is not a cύcτημα ἐκ καταλήψεων cυγγεγυμναcμένων; it consists in some general rules which can be applied to specific cases, and its effect is not what

---

[15] *On Music* 4 col. iii10–42 Neubecker: ἐπειδήπερ | οὐ[δ]ἐν μέλοc καθὸ μέλοc | ἄλογον ὑπάρχον ψυχὴν | οὔτ᾽ ἐξ ἀκεινήτου καὶ ἡcυχα|ζούc[ηc] ἐγείρει καὶ ἄγει πρὸc | τὴν κατ[ὰ φ]ύcιν ἐν ἤ[θ]ει διά|θεcιν, οὔτ᾽ ἐξ ἀ[τ]τούcηc καὶ φε|ρο[μ]ένηc π[ρὸc ὅτ]ι δήποτε | πρα[ύ]νει καὶ εἰc ἠρεμίαν κα|θίcτηcιν, οὐδ᾽ ἀπ᾽ ἄλληc ὀρ|μῆc ἐπ᾽ ἄλλην ἀποcτρέφ[ειν]|| οἷόν [τ᾽ ἐcτὶ]ν οὐδὲ τὴν ὑπάρ|χου-[cα]ν διάθεcιν εἰc αὔξη|cιν [ἄγ]ειν καὶ ἐλάττωcιν. [δι]όπερ οὐδὲ καθ᾽ | αὑτὰc ἔ[χουcι] διαφόρωc οὐδὲ | κατὰ τὴν [ἀ]λλήλαιc μεῖξιν | οὐδὲ τὰ[c] ἔ[να]ντίαc ἀλλή{λ}|λαιc διαθέ[c]ειc ὅcον ἐπὶ τοῖ[c]|| πρὸc ἀκοὴν ἐπα[ι]cθήμα|cιν ω{   }μ[   ]των ἔcτιν | δημιουρ[γεῖν].

[16] *On Music* 4 cols. xix14–xx 14 Neubecker: τίνα τρόπον δύ|ναται πα[ύ]ειν ἄλογα μέλη | λογι-κὴν διαφοράν . . . εὐχερὲc εὐ[ρ]εῖν πολὺ πι|θανώτερον τὸν [μ]ὲν περι|cπᾶν μουcικαῖc [ψ]υχαγω-γί|αιc προαιρούμενον . . . κ[αὶ δ]ιὰ λόγων | ἀιδομένων πει[θό]μενον αὐτοὺc . . . διὰ λόγων | κατεcκευαcμένων ποιη|τικῶc ἔ[πε]ιcαν, οὐ διὰ μελῶν, and *On Music* 4 col. xxix Neubecker: κ[α]ὶ κα|θ᾽ ὃ [μὲν μ]ουcικοὶ τὰ ἀc[ήμ]α[ν|τ]α, κ[αθ᾽] ὃ δὲ ποιηταὶ πεποιη|κέ[ναι] τοὺc λόγουc . . . [ἐπεὶ] τὸ πᾶν πο[ιεῖ]|τ[αι ὅφ]ελοc [ἀ]πὸ δια[νοι]ῶν, |[τὰ μέλ]η ψιλὰ καὶ τοὺc ῥυ|[θ]μοὺc [ὠφε-λ]εῖν φημ[ι οὐδέν]||.

[17] *On Music* 4 col. ii 9–15 Neubecker: . . . ἐπὶ δὲ τῶν ἀκοῶν οὐ|δ᾽ ἔcτιν ὅλωc διαφορά τιc, ἀλ|λὰ πᾶcαι τὰc ὁμοίαc τῶν | ὁμ[οί]ων μελῶν ἀντι[λή|ψ]ειc ποιοῦνται καὶ τὰc ἡδο|νὰc παραπληcί-ουc ἀπολαμβάνουcιν, and cf. *On Music* 4 col. xxii 12ff. criticizing Diogenes of Babylon's comparison of music to arts such as *kritike, grammatike* and *hypokritike*: οὐ μόνον ἀγνοεῖ καθό|cον ὡc ἐν μέλεcι καὶ ῥυθμοῖc | πρέποντοc καὶ ἀπρεποῦc ὄντ|ο[c] καὶ καλοῦ καὶ αἰcχροῦ | κριτικὴν αὐτῶν ἀπέ-λειπε | θεωρίαν, ἀλλὰ καὶ καθό|cον, εἴ τι τοιοῦτον ἦν, οὐχὶ | τοῖc φιλοcοφοῦcιν ἀπεδίδου | τὴν κρίcιν . . . .

is absolutely proper to the art: you don't need art, e.g., to speak well and clearly, but merely to do that *consistently*.[18]

Furthermore, *technai* should not contain any reference to the judgment of good or bad effects—these δόξαι belong to διάνοια alone. Yet anyone reading Philodemus' *On Poems* will find that work mostly taken up with how to judge the good poem, and the criteria to be applied are by no means restricted to the sound qualities of the poem, though there is some tendency to treat them separately; they also refer frequently to a poem's thought.

Two passages from *On Poems* can help us get a handle on this difference:[19]

(1) . . . ἰδιοβαρβαριζόντων ἕτερος ‖[αὐ]τῶν, τοῦ μὲν ἡδέως ‖[ἡ]μᾶς ἀκού-
ειν, τοῦ δὲ τά|ναντ[ί]α, κἂν διὰ μηδὲν | ἕτερον ἢ διὰ τὸ(ν) ἦχον γεί|νηται
καὶ ἐ[πὶ] τῆς ἀηδό|νος καὶ τῶν ἄ[λ]λων ὀρ|νέων, πῶς ἀ[πο]δεικτι|κόν
ἐcτι τοῦ τὸν ἐκ τῆς | ἀρθρώcεως ἦχον ἀπ[ο]‖τελεῖν τινα χάριν, περιc|[π]ᾶ-
cθαι δ' ὑπ' [ἄ]λ[λ]ων τι[νῶν; λέ]γει γ]ὰρ ἐπὶ [τ]ῶν βαρβαριζόν|[τ]ων
ὑπ[ὸ] τοῦ διὰ τὴν ἀρ|[θρ]ωc[ιν ἦχ]ου τὴ[ν] ἡδο|[ν]ὴν ἔξω χεῖν, καὶ τὴν
‖[ἀλ]λοτριότη[τ]α cυμβαί|[ν]ειν. ἀλλ' [ἡ] ἄρθ[ρω]cιc [τῆς | ἀλ]λοτριότη-
τ[οc α]ὐτῆ[c]‖ οὐκ [ἔ]cτιν [αἰ]τία, καὶ | cυμφορὰν [ἐ]δεικνύ|ομεν καὶ διὰ
τὰc ἀρθρώ‖[c]ειc λέγειν παρακολου|θεῖν, καὶ ταύτηι δυcχερ[[ἐ]c εἶνα[ι]
λαμβάν[ειν τι ἡδο]‖νῶν, οὐδ' εἶναι πρός (τι) κακῶc;

(2) . . . ψεύ]δετ' ἀναλ[όγως, λέγων]‖ ἕτερον δι' [αὐτῆc εἶναι]‖ τὸν ἦχον,
ὥ[c γίνεται]‖ ἐπὶ τῆc ἀη[δόνος καὶ ἐ]|πὶ τῶν ἄλλων ὀρνέων. | οὕτω τοίνυν
καὶ ἐπὶ | τῶν ἑλληνιζόντων ὁ | μὲν ἦχος ἀποτελεῖ τὸ | ἴδιον κατὰ τὴν
δ[ι]ά[λεκτον]‖—ἢ δεινὸν ἂν εἴη [τὰ ἴ]δι|α τὸν ἑλληνισμὸν ἀπο|cτερεῖ-
cθαι—περιcπᾶ|ται δ' ἴcως ὑπὸ ἄλλων ‖[τ]ινῶν . . . .

(1) . . . that the sound is particular in the case of Greek-speakers, and different from them in the case of speakers of a given barbarian tongue, but we hear the first with pleasure, the second with the opposite feeling. Even if 'it (sc. pleasure) comes about for no other reason than because of the sound in the case of both the nightingale and the other birds,' how does this prove his claim that 'the sound resulting from the articulation (of speech) affords a certain pleasure, but is distracted by some other factors'?

(2) . . . is false analogously, when he says that 'it is different on account of the sound itself, as happens in the case of nightingales and the other birds. So, therefore, in the case of people speaking Greek, the sound creates what is characteristic in terms of the sense' (it would indeed be dreadful for Greek to be deprived of its characteristics!), 'but it is perhaps distracted by some other factors, as when Sophocles speaks of getting ready to put to sea "the sailors furled

---

[18] *On Rhetoric* 5 col. ii (vol. 2 p. 192 Sudhaus): πολλάκιc ἐκ τῆc τέχνηc | ἐπιγείνεται· διὸ καὶ λί[αν λέ]|γει μέν τιc ἄφρον· εἰ cαφῶc, | καὶ πιcτικῶc, διὰ δὲ [το]ῦ|το καὶ καλῶc φύcει, χά|ριν δὲ τοῦ καὶ πολλάκιc τούτου τυγχάνειν τ[έ]‖χνηc δεῖται.

[19] (1) *On Poems* Treatise A col. vi 1–vii 1 p. 49 Sbordone, and (2) Treatise B 23 col. ii 1–12 p. 161 Sbordone.

(sc. raised) the fig-iron (sc. anchor) of the ship" (fr. 761). For we are brought to what the poet intends, not to the fruit, although perhaps some blow impinges upon one's hearing, in which one might rather have understood the fruit.' (translation R. Janko)

Philodemus argues against someone who wants to conclude from the unpleasant experience of someone speaking incorrect Greek (with "barbarisms") that articulation is what makes sound pleasant, as well as making it intelligible (the example of birds' speech is given). Philodemus argues, on the contrary, that the only purpose of articulation is to make sound into language, to make it intelligible. For Philodemus, therefore, there can be no Stoic distinction between *lexis* as the articulate sound which may or may not be intelligible (e.g., βλίτυρι) and *logos* which is intelligent, articulated sound. The "speech" of birds is, for Philodemus, only apparently articulate.

Thus, as soon as language is involved, the elements and the locus of the effects are no longer irrational: unlike melody and rhythm, poetry does not just remain in the ear, and while pleasure is irrational, persuasion is not. The result is that in grammar, poetry and rhetoric the artistic and philosophical considerations are to a great extent necessarily mixed. Perhaps this is in part why Philodemus writes *On Poems* instead of *On Poetry*.

Grammatistic is the art of reading and writing, teaching the letters or sounds and their combinations (Sextus Empiricus, *Adv. math.* 1.49); it is useful for life. Further, it has, according to Philodemus, a firmly established and reliable method. It was higher grammar which was attacked by Sextus and Epicurus, but probably not for the same reasons. We will see that Epicurus' attacks all stem from his conception of the prime importance and priority of philosophy.[20] Sextus characterizes this objectionable "grammar in the specific sense" as dealing with the discovery and nature of sounds and letters. Epicurus had his own theories about the invention and nature of language (*Letter to Herodotus* 37–8, 75–6), so it could not have been this interest per se which he attacked. Epicurus' own treatment of language, however, is not part of grammar but of philosophy or physiology. I would guess, then, that Epicurus attacked grammar for dealing with subjects for which it had no appropriate or adequate method, rather than leaving them to philosophy.

Looking at Epicurus' own theory of language, we see another reason to attack grammar. Grammarians study the language of poetry, including its glosses, metaphors, and tropes. They make a business out of the obscure. Epicurus, on the other hand, derived from his physiology, particularly the doctrine of προλήψεις, a philosophy which insisted that words be used in their ordinary and clear senses and that clarity was the only goal of writing.[21] Indeed, we are informed that the sage will not practice oratory using the artifices of style.[22]

A third reason for Epicurus to criticize grammar is seen in grammarians' claims to find in poems many useful theorems and much wisdom, some of which was then

---

[20] Cf. De Lacy and De Lacy 1978, 199: "It is when rhetoric tries to do the job of philosophy that Philodemus condemns it."

[21] Diogenes Laertius 10.13: κέχρηται δὲ λέξει κυρίᾳ κατὰ τῶν πραγμάτων, ἣν ὅτι ἰδιωτάτη ἐστίν, Ἀριστοφάνης ὁ γραμματικὸς αἰτιᾶται. σαφὴς δ᾽ ἦν οὕτως ὡς ἐν τῷ Περὶ ῥητορικῆς ἀξιοῖ μηδὲν ἄλλο ἢ σαφήνειαν ἀπαιτεῖν.

[22] Diogenes Laertius 10.118 = Epicurus fr. 565 Usener: οὐδὲ ῥητορεύσειν καλῶς.

taken over by philosophers. It is grammar, they claim, which finds and interprets these theorems, and which is therefore useful (Sextus Empiricus, *Adv. math.* 1.270). Sextus' replies to such claims come largely from the Epicureans. Chief among them is the statement that, since poetry's wisdom is stated without proof and often mixed in with false ideas, it is not grammar which is useful but philosophy, which alone can distinguish the good from the bad.[23]

The Epicurean would have distinguished between an *entechnos* study of grammar on the one hand and philosophy on the other, but these two studies would be related to one another. For unlike the case of music, whose proper elements are strictly irrational and affect only the irrational sense of hearing, grammar's proper elements are necessarily rational and logical in character and effect. This is the purport of the passages we have examined from *On Poems*: it is not the articulation which makes Hellenism pleasant and barbarism unpleasant. The Epicurean cannot accept the Stoic distinction between *lexis* (articulate speech, whether meaningful or not) and *logos* (meaningful articulate speech), for the sole function of articulation is to make language. Language, for its part, can be apprehended only by means of what underlies its sounds, the προλήψεις.[24]

Thus, the very subject of grammar relates to *logos* and thought. Here it is difficult to make such neat distinctions as Philodemus does in the case of music, where pleasure is auditory and comes from the properly musical elements of melody and rhythm, while attitudes and judgments are rational and come from the text of the song. On the contrary language is only language because of its effect on our *dianoia*.

Poetics is the art of composing beautiful poems (*On Poems* 5 col. xxxiv [xxxvii] 4–12). It shares with sophistic rhetoric and medicine the fact that it has method, but not much (*P.Herc.* 1672 col. xxii 39 p. 219 Longo). This method goes toward the composition (σύνθεσις) of beautiful poetry, but it is not so strict as to allow for a *scala naturalis* of lovely and unlovely sounds, etc., as Crates wanted.[25] Treatises on poetry ought not to list particular characteristics of the good poem, but rather concentrate on the general principles and in this way express the προλήψεις[26] and common notions attached to terms like "good poem."[27]

---

[23] Sextus Empiricus, *Adv. math.* 1.279–280: poems say both good and bad things without proof, and so may be harmful, διακρινομένων δὲ αὐτῶν, καὶ τῶν μὲν ἀθετουμένων τῶν δὲ προκρινομένων, χρειώδης γίνεται οὐχ ἡ γραμματικὴ ἀλλ' ἡ διακρίνειν δυναμένη φιλοσοφία. Cf. 296: . . . φιλόσοφοι δὲ καὶ οἱ λοιποὶ συγγραφεῖς διδάσκουσι τὰ ὠφέλιμα τῶν πραγμάτων, οὐ δεόμεθα γραμματικῆς.

[24] *On Rhetoric* fr. incertum in *Herculanensium Voluminum*, Collectio altera, vol. 8 p. 170–72, vol. 2 p. 190 Sudhaus: ο]ὐ μὴν πραγματι|κὴν ποιεῖται τὴν cκ[έ]|ψιν ἀλλ' ἤτοι παρὰ | τὴν ἀδιαληψίαν ὦ[ν]| ταῖς ὀνομασίαις ὑπ[ο]|τάττει διανοημάτ[ων | cυ]νιcταμένην ἢ πρὸ | αὐτῆς καὶ τὰς ἐν ταῖς [. . Cf. also: *On Poems*, Treatise B col. xxvi 1–2 τὴν δ' ὑπο|[τετα]γμένην ἔνν[οιαν] ; ibid. col. xxvi 13 [ὑ]ποτεταγμένον; Epicurus, *Letter to Herodotus* 37 τὰ ὑποτεταγμένα τοῖς φθόγγοις; Diogenes Laertius 10.33 παντὶ οὖν ὀνόματι τὸ πρώτως ὑποτεταγμένον (and Epicurus, *On Nature* 28: 6 I 11; 10 Ib; 13 VII 4 Sedley; Philodemus, *On Household Management* col. xii 14 Jensen.

[25] *On Poems*, Tractatus Tertius in *P.Herc.* 1676 col. xi, cf. Schenkeveld 1968, 193; *On Poems* 5 col. xxvi 7 with its reference to *On Poems* 2.

[26] *On Poems* 5 col. xxvii 25–33 in Jensen's text (= col. xxx 25–33 Mangoni 1993, whose numeration of columns I give in parentheses throughout): οὐ | προ[cῆκ]εν οὖν ἐν ταῖ[c]|| ὑπο[θή]καις ἐξαριθμεῖ-c|θαι κατὰ μέρος, ἀλλὰ τὸ διῆ|κον λέγειν. ἂν δὲ διὰ τού|των μόνως οἰώμεθα τὰς | π[ρο]λήψεις ἐκτυποῦcθαι, | πάντ' ἂν [ἀ]ναθετέον τῶι| γένει, [ἀλλ' οὐ] τοῖς ἀριθμοῖς.

[27] *On Poems* 5 col. xxx (xxxiii) 32: [καὶ μ]ὴν οὔτε παρε|φάπτεται τ[ῆc κ]οινῆc | ἐννο[ί]ας [οὔτε] προει|λήφαμεν ταύτην ἀρετὴν | ποιήματος.

With regard to the distinctions we have been examining in relation to music and grammar, poetry is again a complex case. As poetry is composed of words, the only part of it which affects just ἀκοή is the rhythm, which gives pleasure to our hearing,[28] but which—as everything else in a poem—is *judged* by *dianoia* .[29] "Apart from the fact that by the position and order of the letters various sounds reach us, the ἀκοή is not involved" (*On Poems* 5 col. xxiv [xxvii] 21ff.). The Stoic is wrong, according to Philodemus (*On Poems* 5 col. xx [xxiii] 21ff.) to think that good composition (cύνθεcιc) is judged by a trained ear. Rather, composition, its epiphenomenon of *euphonia*, and the actual putting together of the words of a poem are judged to be good or bad solely by reason. It is not sound which gives pleasure in the composition of a poem, Philodemus says,[30] but rather the *lexis*. Further, where we cannot recognize the *dianoia*, we can not even say we are dealing with a poem (*On Poems* 5 col. xix [xxii] 13ff.). So the good poem involves both *mimesis* (note that music is said not to be imitative by itself) of the *lexis* which only by the way teaches useful things, and thought which is between the wise and the vulgar.[31]

The goal of rhetoric is to persuade through a rhetorical *logos*,[32] not through some other means.[33] Just what the persuasiveness of a rhetorical *logos* consists in, however, is difficult to get out of the remains of Philodemus. We have just seen Philodemus distinguish "rhetorically" from "dialectically" and "drastically," exemplifying the latter by Phryne's use of beauty and music as tools of persuasion. So we need to distinguish the means of argument from the rhetorical *logos*; but we can not, for example, just refer to the sound qualities of a speech, for we are dealing with a *logos*, which for Philodemus can not be separated out into intelligible and unintelligible parts. It is clear, however, that the orator's ability to achieve the goal of persuasion with some regularity by applying rules is what makes sophistic rhetoric an art for Philodemus.

The rejection of political and the retention of sophistic rhetoric presents certain analogies with the treatment of the above arts. In particular, it is very like the rejec-

---

[28] *On Poems* 5 col. xxiii (xxvi) 32: οὐδέν ἐcτι μα[ρτ]υ|ρούμενον ὑπὸ τῆc ἀ[κο]|ῆc εἰc τοῦτο [the non-existence of *themata*], τοῖc ὅλο[ιc]| οὐδενὸc τῶν ἐν ποιή[μ]α|τι κρίcιν ἐχούcηc οὐδὲ | μὰ Δία τερπ[ομ]ένη[c π]λὴν | ὑπὸ ρυθμοῦ [τοῦ ποήμα|τοc . . . .

[29] *On Poems* Treatise A col. b 7–13 p. 25 Sbordone: πάντα | πλὴν τούτου διδόcθω{ι} | τό γ[ε] ἐφ' ἡμᾶc [ε]ἶναι· cτί]χον {δὲ} καὶ cτροφὴν εὔρυ|θμον ἢ ἄ[ρ]υθμον [ὁ]μο[ί]|ωc διανο[ῆc]αι κατὰ μέ|ροc τὴν ἀ[κοή]ν.

[30] *On Poems* 5 col. xxvi (xxix) 30ff.: τ[ῶι]|| μὴ τέρπειν ἦχον ἐν | cυνθέcει ποήματοc.

[31] *On Poems* 5 col. xxii (xxv) 30: [κα]ὶ γὰρ κα|θὸ πόημα φυcικὸν οὐδὲν | οὔτε λέξεωc οὔτε δ[ια|ν]οήματοc ὠφέλημα [πα|ρ]αcκευάζει. διὰ τοῦτ[ο]| δ[ὲ] τῆc ἀρετῆc ἐcτηκότεc || ὑπόκεινται cκ[οπ]οί, τῆι | μὲν λέξει τὸ μ[εμι]μῆc|θαι τὴν ὠφέλι[μα] προc|διδάcκουcαν, τῆc δὲ δι|ανοίαc τὸ μεταξὺ μετ[εcχη]||κέναι τῆc τῶν cοφῶν | καὶ τῆc τῶν χυδαίων, | καὶ ταῦτ' ἔcτιν, ἄν τε νο|μίcηι τιc ἄν τε μή, καὶ | κριτέον ἐπὶ τ[αῦ]τ' ἐπα|νάγοντας.

[32] *On Rhetoric* 2 col. i 26 p. 45 Longo: . . . τήν τε πλε[ο]να|[ζο]μένην ἱcτορ[ία]ν κα[ὶ |[τρι]βήν, ὅταν οἱ λε[γόμε|νοι τεχνῖται προcλάβω|c[ι]ν τῶν τελῶν τ[ι, π]α|ράγο]υcιν· τό τέ διὰ [λόγου]| ῥητορικοῦ πείθειν [τ]έ|λ[ο]c ἐcτὶ τῆc ῥ[ητορ]ικ[ῆ]c |[οὐ τ]ὸ [πε]ίθειν . . . .

[33] *On Rhetoric* 2 col. ii 1 p. 47 Longo: [πείθει] μέν, οὐ πείθει δὲ |[ῥητορι]κῶc ἀλλὰ διαλεκ|τικῶc [ἢ] δ[ρ]αc[τι]κῶc, ὡc καὶ Φρύνη καὶ ὥρα[ι]|[κ]αὶ μουcικῆι πείθει μέν, | οὐ ῥητορικῶc δὲ π[οιε]ῖ |[τὰc κα]ταcκευάc. εἰ δέ | πωc ὁ λόγοc [δ]ύναταί τι | προcάγειν ἀληθέc, τῶν | ἀ[τ]έχνων οὐ[δ]ὲ εἰc ἐν | τῶι[ι] τῆc τέχνηc ἔργωι | νικᾶι τὸν τε[χ]ν[είτην], ἐν | δὲ τῶι τῆc ῥητορικῆc |[οὐδὲ τοῦ]το καθολικόν.

tion of what Sextus calls higher grammar (which is replaced by philosophy) and the retention of grammatistic as an art. Grammatistic teaches the basics of clear expression and provides a method of reliably achieving a useful goal. Sophistic rhetoric, the art of writing speeches, giving displays and shaping treatises,[34] is a formalistic art with method, but not much of it.[35] Further, since philosophers and others must often speak or write,[36] the art is useful, but it must avoid over-elaboration.

But politics is not even an art to one who just looks at politicians' deeds (*On Rhetoric* 2 col. xix 19ff p. 83 Longo). It has no method, nor does it accomplish its aims reliably or even for the most part (*On Rhetoric* 2 col. xxvii, citing Epicurus).[37] It is rather an ἐμπειρία ἀπό τινος τριβῆς καὶ τῶν ἐν ταῖς πόλεσιν ἱστορίας (*On Rhetoric* 2 in *P.Herc.* 1672 col. xxii 1 p. 217 Longo). Further, it cannot tell what a person should do, what things he should choose or avoid in order to be happy: that is the job of φυσιολογία (*On Rhetoric* 2 in *P.Herc.* 1672 col. xxii 7–25 p. 217 Longo, quoting Metrodorus: "πότερον οὖν τὴν ῥη|τορικὴν δύναμιν λέγει[ν] | τις βλέ-πων ἐπὶ τὴν διάγνω|σιν τοῦ[του,]' ὃ πρακτέον ἐστὶν τῶι μέλ|λοντι εὐδαίμον[ι] εἶναί τε | κ[α]ὶ ἔσεσθαι καὶ [οὐ πρακτέον,]] καὶ ταύτην φησὶν ἀπὸ φυσ[ι]ο-|λογίας παραγείνεσθαι, ἢ [κ]αὶ | τὴν πολειτικὴν ἐμπειρίαν, | καθ' ἣν ἐκ τριβῆς καὶ ἱστορί|ας τῶν πόλεως πραγμάτων | συνορώ|η ἄν τις οὐ κακῶς | τὰ πλήθ'ει συμφέροντα;" | . . . "τί γὰρ [ὑ]|πόκειται, ὃ θεωρεία π[οι]εῖ, | ὥσπερ ἡ περὶ τὰς αἱρέσεις | καὶ φυγὰς ἢ καὶ περὶ τὰς πολει|τικὰς ἐκ τῆς ἱστορίας πα|ρακολουθή-σεις;"). As we have seen in poetics, these judgments will be made by philosophy according to our προλήψεις of good and bad (*On Rhetoric* 1 p. 255.10–20 Sudhaus).

Now, what is the rhetoric which makes *logos* able to persuade rhetorically? It seems that nature has given us the capacity to speak,[38] but then *techne* has given the capacity to speak well, that is persuasively. Put another way, if one speaks clearly, one speaks persuasively, and because of this also well by nature.[39] Philodemus believes there is one naturally correct language (*On Rhetoric* 4 col. vii, vol. 1 p. 151 Sudhaus: εἷς φυσικῶς καλὸς λόγος), and sophistic is the transmissible method of using this language to write clear treatises. It could be seen as a sort of continuation of grammatistic.

As such, sophistic rhetoric would obviously be useful and have a method of its own. It would also correspond to Epicurus' own ideals of style, recalling the words

---

[34] Cf. *On Rhetoric* 2 in *P.Herc.* 1674 col. xxxvii 22–24 p. 121 Longo λόγων γ[ρ]αφὰς | κ[αὶ ἐπι]δείξεις; *P.Herc.* 1672 col. xxii 33–34 p. 219 Longo καὶ τὰς τῶν | λόγων δ[ι]αθέσεις.

[35] *P.Herc.* 1672 col. xxii 36 p. 219 Longo: φαμὲν τοίνυν | τὸ μεθοδ̣[ι]κὸν ἔχειν αὐτήν, | οὐ πολὺ δὲ καθάπ[ερ] οὐδὲ τὴν | ποιητ[ι]κήν . . . .

[36] Diogenes Laertius 120a = Epicurus fr. 563–4 Usener: συγγράμματα καταλείψειν· οὐ πανηγυ-ριεῖν δέ.   [37] Cf. above, note 3.

[38] *On Rhetoric* fr. incertum in *Herculanenium Voluminum*, Collectio altera vol. 9, fol. 11–14 i, vol. 2 p. 190 Sudhaus: ὁμ[ο]ίως, τέχνη δ' ἐγένε|το τοῦ καλῶς, ὃ καὶ ἐκ[ά]|λλουν το[ῦ πι]στικῶς, [ἡ τέ]|χνη δ' ἐγ[έ]νετο τοῦ καλῶς·| ὥστε καὶ τὸ λέγειν ἡ φ[ύ|c]ιc ἔδωκεν, τὸ δὲ καλῶς |[λ]έγειν ἡ τέχνη, and *On Rhetoric* 4 vol. 2 p. 191 Sudhaus: [ὅπως δή]πο[τε] καὶ ὡς ἔτ[υχ]εν καὶ | φύσεως ἔργον, τὸ δὲ κα|λῶς τέχνης· ἐμοὶ μὲν | γὰρ καὶ τοῦτο φαίνεται, | σὺ δὲ καὶ αὐτὸς κρείνεις δύ|νασθαι παρὰ σοῦ. —πᾶσαι [α]ἱ λε[γό]μεναι στοχαστικαὶ | τ[έχ]να[ι], ὧν τὰ μὲν θεω|ρή[μ]α[θ'] ἔστηκεν [τὰ δ]ὲ τέ|[λη οὐχ] ἔστηκ[εν].

[39] *On Rhetoric* 5 vol. 2 p. 192 Sudhaus: πολλάκις ἐκ τῆς τέχνης | ἐπιγείνεται· διὸ καὶ λί[αν λέ]γει μέν τις ἄφρον· εἰ σαφῶς, | καὶ πιστικῶς, διὰ δὲ [το]ῦ|το καὶ καλῶς φύσει, χά|ριν δὲ τοῦ καὶ πολλάκις τούτου τυνχάνειν τ[έ]||χνης δεῖται.

of the master's own *On Rhetoric* (Diogenes Laertius 10.13) to the effect that σαφή-νεια was the only goal of speaking and writing. Philodemus says that *technai* flourished in early societies before there were any *technologiai* (*On Rhetoric* 1 col. viii 8 p. 59 Longo). This is in line with what Lucretius tells us about the history of humankind. In the *Letter to Herodotus* (75), Epicurus wrote that reasoning clarified and added new discoveries to the irrational lessons given by nature, then he gives an example of this development in the development of languages. I suggest that Philodemus' account of arts is a version of Epicurus' account. Grammatistic is a more or less natural development of the ability to speak, the codification of the one naturally correct language. Sophistic rhetoric is the result of applying reason to make this language the best vehicle for clear expression. As such, sophistic rhetoric should be an art Epicurus could have accepted.

10
How to Read Poetry about Gods

Dirk Obbink

1. Epicurus' Maiden Voyage

Diogenes Laertius preserves two contrasting case studies of how Epicurus came to philosophy. While both come equipped with authoritative pedigrees (and one of these impeccable), neither version is particular compelling, especially given of the hodge-podge nature of Diogenes' biography[1] and the working methods of Hellenistic biographers. To make matters worse, the two accounts appear to be mutually exclusive. Taken together, however, the two anecdotes epitomize in its complexity and ambivalence the Epicurean attitude toward traditional literature, poetry, and *paideia*.

On good Epicurean authority, Diogenes first relates that Epicurus turned to philosophy as a youth out of disgust at the schoolmasters because they could not tell him the meaning of Chaos in Hesiod.[2] We are to think of a precocious Epicurus in his perplexity coming upon the description of Chaos in the reading of Hesiod set for him by his schoolmaster (*Theogony* 116 "and first there was Chaos").[3] When the grammar teachers fail miserably one after another in their attempts to answer the question: "What, then, preceded Chaos?" he goes off in a huff to the philosophers. Epicurus would certainly not have been the first to query the primacy of Chaos: religious

---

[1] Philodemus provided Diogenes with at least some of his information about the Epicurean School: at 10.24 Philodemus is named as the authority for the encomium of the Epicurean Polyaenus, and at 10.3 a debt to Book 10 of Philodemus' *Syntaxis of Philosophers* is prominently acknowleged. Gigante 1995, chapter 2 with n. 13 sets out the case that Diogenes' *Lives of the Philosophers* in ten books is based on the structure of Philodemus' *Syntaxis*; see also his article "Biografia e dossografia in Diogene Laerzio," *Elenchos* 7 (1986), 25–34.

[2] Diogenes Laertius 10.2: "Apollodorus the Epicurean [second century B.C. head of the School] in the first book of his *Life of Epicurus* says that Epicurus turned to philosophy because he despised the schoolmasters, since they were unable to explain to him the passage about Chaos in Hesiod," Ἀπολλό-δωρος δ' ὁ Ἐπικούρειος ἐν τῷ πρώτῳ περὶ τοῦ Ἐπικούρου βίον φησὶν ἐλθεῖν αὐτὸν ἐπὶ φιλοσο-φίαν καταγνόντα τῶν γραμματιστῶν, ἐπειδὴ μὴ ἐδυνήθησαν ἑρμηνεῦσαι αὐτῷ τὰ περὶ τοῦ παρ' Ἡσιόδῳ χάους. I have drawn freely on the excellent commentary on the passage by Laks 1976, 36-38.

[3] *Theogony* 116 (first line after the hymnic prooemium and beginning of the cosmogony proper) ἦ τοι μὲν πρώτιστα Χάος γένετο, cf. 123 ἐκ Χάεος δ' Ἔρεβός τε μέλαινά τε Νὺξ ἐγένοντο, "from Chaos next were born Erebus and dark Night."

exegetes, rhapsodes, and wise men, perhaps going back to Hesiod himself, had been for centuries proposing λύϲειϲ, "solutions" to that problem. And Epicurus would of course have had good reason for questioning the import of Hesiod's verses.[4] After all, the passage from the *Theogony* posits a primal cosmogonic entity, thus violating the Epicurean principle of *nihil e nihilo*.[5] According to the story, the schoolmasters' understanding of the poem stalls within several verses of the beginning of the cosmogony. Hesiod does not fare much better: his poetry cannot be said to withstand scrutiny.

The incident might be taken to exemplify Epicurus' alleged condemnation of poetry in general, were it not for the fact that Epicurus could hardly have cared about the passage in Hesiod, had he not considered Hesiod's poetry a relevant object of interest in the first place.[6] Why else require philosophers to explain it or answer the questions it raises? Epicurus' heated rejection of the schoolmasters' explanations and the ensuing conversion to philosophy presuppose a prior attachment and keen commitment to scrutiny (or what amounts to grammatical analysis, i.e. reading and interpretation at the most basic level of sense) of the earliest Greek poetry with an eye to its cosmological, physical and ethical implications. I argue further that this preoccupation with early Greek poetry, however ambivalent and ultimately ill-advised on the Epicurean view, is similarly paralleled in Epicurus' later physical works, in Lucretius' poem, and in Philodemus' *On Piety*. In Diogenes' story, as in Philodemus and Lucretius, the Epicurean is shown to rival his grammar teachers in zetematic inquiry into canonical poetic texts. It is not explicitly said that Hesiod's statement is to be ignored altogether; rather, it is implied that the traditional methods of the schoolmasters (γραμματιϲταί, here elementary teachers in the reading

---

[4] It was presumably the schoolmasters' failure to reach an acceptable consensus on the ζήτηϲιϲ as to what preceded Chaos in the cosmogony, that is supposed to have provoked Epicurus' impatience. Chaos is also mentioned at *Theogony* 700 ("astounding heat seized Chaos" when Zeus attacked the Titans), and at 814 (the Titans now live "beyond gloomy Chaos"). But these are less likely to have been the young Epicurus' objects of inquiry, since of course Chaos, once born, is not *nihil*. On the role of Chaos in the early philosophical tradition see L. A. Cordo, *XAOΣ. Zur Ursprungsvorstellung bei den Griechen*, Beiträge zur Philosophie 101 (Idstein 1989), especially chapter 3. The figure is turned against Epicurus by adversaries representing Epicurean τὸ κενόν, "void" as "Chaotic" according to Seneca, *Epistle* 72,9 *in Epicureum illud chaos decidunt inane sine termino*.

[5] See Sextus Empiricus, *Adv. math.* 10.18, where the anecdote about Epicurus' altercation with his teachers over the priority of Chaos in Hesiod is retold in precisely this form to illustrate the problematic of establishing the existence of ϲῶμα "body," κενόν "void," and τόποϲ "place," as well as motion, coming to be, and passing away. The point is made by Laks 1976, 37: "la lecture critique d'un texte "culturel," comme celui d'Hésiode, doit l'interroger sur ses fondemonts mêmes, c'est-à-dire traiter comme philosophème le principe qu'il postule . . . . La question sur la nature du chaos hésiodique se confond avec la question philosophique de l'origine."

[6] Given the later Epicurean interest in poetry, demonstrated by six books of Lucretius, Philodemus' reputation as a poet, and the recent discovery of copies of Ennius and Lucretius in the Villa of the Papyri, one wonders whether this was not one of the occasions, as Philodemus relates in *On Anger*, when Epicurus only *appeared* to be angry: cols. xxxiv 31–xxxv 5 Indelli: the wise person may give the appearance (φαντασία) of an angry person, but not for long, and if he gives it for long he "is not deeply angry, though virtually seems so." Even Epicurus, he adds, gave some people the appearance of being angry: see J. Annas, "Epicurean Emotions," *GRBS* 30 (1989), 145-64; J. Procopé, "Epicureans on Anger," in *PHILANTHROPIA KAI EUSEBEIA. Festschrift für Albrecht Dihle zum 70. Geburtstag*, edd. G. W. Most, H. Petersmann, and A. M. Ritter (Göttingen 1993), 363-86.

of literature) are philosophically worthless.[7] The story depicts the "passage about Chaos in Hesiod" serving as an ἀφορμή, "starting point" into inquiry over origins in the budding philosophical career of the young Epicurus, much as Philodemus will later tell one of the Pisones that the passages about kingship in Homer serve as ἀφορμαί, "starting points" for the correct study of government.[8]

Diogenes immediately relates a second account of Epicurus' conversion to philosophy, a scandalous counterpart to the first, Epicurean one, providing the kind of contrast between the real Epicurus and his shameless detractors (of which there had been no shortage) with which the Epicureans were fond of representing Epicurus' intellectual development. In this version the second century B.C. biographer and satyrist Hermippus is credited with having said that Epicurus was originally himself an elementary schoolteacher (γραμματοδιδάσκαλος) who, after encountering the books of Democritus, eagerly took up philosophy.[9] Hermippus' version (patently derived from a misreading of a line from Timon of Phlius' *Silloi*) inverts the immediately preceding anecdote about the passage on Chaos in Hesiod. In this version Epicurus himself is cast in the rôle of the schoolteacher, self-deluded through a

---

[7] Rather than, as Laks 1976, 37 has it, a strict "refus de la spéculation de type théologique et hésiodique." On the terms γραμματιστὴς "school teacher" and γραμματοδιδάσκαλος "teacher of letters" see R. Cribiore, "Writing, Teachers and Students in Greco-Roman Egypt" (diss. Columbia 1993).

[8] Philodemus, *On the Good King According to Homer* col. xliii 15–20 p. 109 Dorandi εἰ δέ τινας παραλελοί|παμε]ν τῶν ἀφ[ορμῶν, ὦ Πεί|σων, ἅς ἔστι παρ' Ὁμήρου λα|βεῖν εἰς ἐπανόρθωσιν δυ|να⟨ς⟩τε[εῶν], καὶ τ[ῶν] πα[ρα]|δε[ιγμά]των, ". . . if we have passed over any of the starting points, Piso, which one can take from Homer to serve as corrections to government (or to an ethical tendency toward governorship?), and of the models . . . ." For the background on ἀφορμαί, "starting points" in philosophical instruction (not to be mistaken on the Epicurean view for philosophy itself) see Wilamowitz on Euripides, *Heracles* 236; Sextus Empiricus, *Adv. gramm.* 270: the grammarians assert that poetry furnishes many ἀφορμαί to wisdom and happiness, but (say) that without grammar it is not possible to discern what they really mean; therefore (they say) grammar is useful. On ἐπανορθώσεις "corrections" (cf. διόρθωσις), rectifications of statements in poetry made at a basic grammatical level of reading see Plutarch, *How Young People should Read Poetry* 22B δεῖ δὲ μηδὲ τὰς . . . παραλιπεῖν ἀφορμὰς πρὸς τὴν ἐπανόρθωσιν, cf. 24B, 29D, 33D, 34B (where the notion of correction is extended to amendment of the text), and Aristotle, *Rhet.* 5.10.3-7 (cf. 1.13.13-16) where the concept of equity (ἐπιείκεια) serves as a corrective (ἐπανόρθωμα) to the error inherent in the law because of its generality. Horace's instructions to the young Pisones in *The Art of Poetry* may be similarly compared, as in Armstrong 1994; cf. below, Chapter 12.

[9] Diogenes Laertius 10.3 φησὶ δ' Ἕρμιππος γραμματοδιδάσκαλον αὐτὸν γεγενῆσθαι, ἔπειτα μέντοι περιτυχόντα τοῖς Δημοκρίτου βιβλίοις, ἐπὶ φιλοσοφίαν ᾆξαι, "Hermippus says that Epicurus once had been an elementary school teacher, and then, after he encountered the books of Democritus, pursued philosophy eagerly." Hermippus' γραμματοδιδάσκαλον is pretty clearly a willful confusion of Timon's γραμμαδιδασκαλίδης, "d'une lignée de maîtres d'école" (Laks), which Diogenes quotes next (10.3 = *Supplementum Hellenisticum*, edd. H. Lloyd-Jones and P. Parsons, Texte und Kommentar 11 [Berlin 1983] no. 825). Epicurus' father Neocles was thought to have been a schoolteacher (Cicero, *On the Nature of the Gods* 1.72 *ut opinor ludi magister fuit*), and sons often inherited their father's occupation. Bailey following Bignone takes γραμμαδιδασκαλίδης to mean "enfant-teacher," i.e. "teacher of infants," according to the "generally contemptuous sense in which these terminations are imployed by the comedians." But Diogenes relates later (10.4) that Epicurus was reported by others to have assisted his father Neocles in elementary school teaching for a miserable pittance (cὺν τῷ πατρὶ γράμματα διδάσκειν λυπροῦ τινος μιcθαρίου, an obvious doublet of Demosthenes' characterization of Aeschines at *De corona* 259-60, since here it is said of Epicurus as well that he "used to go round from house to house with his mother reading out the purification prayers").

professional and pedantic obsession with letters (γράμματα) into pursuing the materialist Democritus' written teaching about the elemental building blocks of nature (γράμματα), and taking it over as his own.[10] In both stories Epicurus never quite divests himself of the influence of γραμματιστική, "elementary grammar," which centered on the teaching of the writing of letters, elementary reading, and glossological explication of the canonical authors, especially poets, beginning with Homer and Hesiod. Diogenes' two versions of Epicurus' first sailing in philosophy may be ahistorical yet not untrue, insofar as they, taken together, accurately exemplify an attitude present in Epicurus' thought toward traditional literature, poetry, and *paideia*. They may be contradictory, but they are not uncomplimentary. They complement each other with a whimsical playfulness characteristic of the ancient biographical tradition. For they are juxtaposed in such a way that Epicurus' addiction to the written teachings of Democritus about atomism (or "grammatism," as it were) in the second version supplies the resolution to the *aporia* (left unanswered in the first story) of Epicurus' question about the primacy of elements in the poetry of Hesiod.[11] Ironically Epicurus himself claimed to have had no teacher.[12]

Not surprisingly, the poetry at stake in Epicurus' case is mythographic poetry, dealing, like most traditional poetry, with origins and the status of gods and heroes. Much of Democritus' work similarly centered on origins: cultural, anthropological, physical. In what follows I will argue that a fascination with the reading of traditional literature within the educational curriculum, and with the act of poetic composition that we find in the later Epicurean tradition (in the cases of Philodemus and Lucretius), may be traced back in some form to Epicurus himself as a natural outcome of his views on the development of human culture, particularly regarding the formation of language and ideas about the gods. I adduce some new evidence from Philodemus' treatise *On Piety* that both Epicurus and his later exponents considered a more than casual familiarity with the history of traditional poetry conducive to at least one aspect of philosophy. I also avail myself more generally of this text as one that has been completely ignored for the evidence it offers regarding a kind of literary criticism practiced by the Epicureans. This neglect can only be called remarkable in view of the fact that over half of the extant treatise deals with the poets' portrayal of the

[10] For letters (γράμματα) used to signal the doctrines of the atomists see e.g. Aristotle, *Metaphysics* A4 985b17, *On Coming to Be and Passing Away* A1 315b14, both cited by Laks 1976, 37. For the analogy between the letters of the alphabet and the physical building blocks of the atomists, see Cicero, *On the Nature of the Gods* 2.93, where the Stoic Lucilius infers that the Epicurean, who thinks that atoms can fortuitously combine to produce our elaborately structured world, must also think that "a countless number of copies of the alphabet, shaken up and thrown out on the ground, could produce the *Annals* of Ennius, all ready for the reader. I doubt whether this would produce even a single verse." See further the essay of Armstrong in this volume, Chapter 11, below.

[11] So Laks 1976, 37: "Démocrite représente la voie propre d'Epicure, la solution des atomes et du vide, finalement retenue pour répondre à la question que les interprètes d'Hésiode n'avaient pas su résoudre."

[12] Diogenes Laertius 10.13: Epicurus in his *Letter to Eurylochus* denies that he heard, i.e. was a student (or: denies he heard a reading of the teachings) of Nausiphanes and Praxiphanes, and declares that he was his own teacher (ἀκοῦcαι . . . ἑαυτοῦ); Cicero, *On the Nature of the Gods* 1.72 *cum quidem gloriaretur, ut videmus in scriptis, se magistrum habuisse nullum*, "since he boasts, as we read in his writings, that he had never had a teacher." Cf. Athen. 13.588A (= fr. 117 Usener); Cic. *De fin.* 1.25–26 and 71–72.

gods. While *On Piety* does not deal with most of the technicalities of Hellenistic poetic theory encountered in the remains of Philodemus' five books on poetry, nevertheless its particular brand of literary criticism is paralleled, for example, in one prominent branch of the Hellenistic scholia to Homer, in the mythographic writers, and in Longinus.

2. Epicurus' Theory of Poetry

For reasons connected with the Epicurean view of the development of language (primarily as natural, and later by the accretion of convention)[13] and the ban on *paideia* in philosophical education, it is clear that the Epicureans did not have a constructive theory of poetry, i.e., of why or how to produce acceptable philosophical poetry. Epicurus is said to have held that "it is only the wise who can converse properly of music and poetry," but that "the sage would not compose poems as a serious activity (ἐνεργείᾳ).[14] To Pythocles he wrote: "Hoist the sails of your ship," (itself an echo of Circe's instructions to Odysseus to flee the Sirens) "and, my blessed man, steer clear of every form of conventional education" (fr. 89 Arrighetti). And he told Apelles to consider himself blessed, because he "had started out pure of every form of conventional education" (fr. 43 Arrighetti). But apart from this generally untheorized and anecdotally preserved rejection of poetry, did Epicurus, unlike his later adherent Philodemus, have no theory of poetry at all?

Before addressing that question directly, we may take note of another reason for Epicurean hesitations over the advisability of studying or composing poetry: namely that, like Hesiod's, most ancient poetry dealt in some fashion with origins, gods, and myths, employed traditional invocations, epithets, cultic *topoi,* and the like. For Epicurus not only insisted on clear expression (cαφήνεια),[15] i.e. using words in accordance with their primary mental images and being aware of their current meanings: he also set an especially high premium on speaking correctly about the divine. Having one's gods properly sorted out is a prerequisite for doing philosophy correctly (hence the primacy given in the Epicurean curriculum to *Kyria Doxa* 1) and for facilitating the ὠφέλεια which Epicurus thought the gods provided to humans. It is also necessary, if the Long–Sedley view of Epicurean theology is correct, for the gods' very existence.[16] It is beyond dispute that Epicurus held that what we say about

---

[13] See D. N. Sedley, "Epicurus, On Nature Book XXVIII," *CErc* 3 (1973), 5–83. Cf. above, p. 62.

[14] Diogenes Laertius 10.121 = Epicurus frr. 568–69 Usener; on the text, however, see above Chapter 1 n. 1.

[15] According to Diogenes Laertius 10.13 Epicurus said in his *On Rhetoric* that cαφήνεια is the only goal of speaking and writing: ἀξιοῖ μηδὲν ἄλλο ἢ cαφήνειαν ἀπαιτεῖν.

[16] See Long and Sedley 1987 vol. 1, 144–49. That the gods are constituted, according to Epicurus, by our (materially formed) ideas of them, and that their material existence consists solely in this, was a view known to Cicero. For modern reformulations see G. Schömann, *Schediasma de Epicuri theologia* vol. 4 (Greifswald 1864) 346; F. A. Lange, *Geschichte des Materialismus*, 2nd ed., vol. 1 (Iserlohn 1873), 76–77; J. Bollack, *La Pensée du Plaisir* (Paris 1975), 236–38; D. N. Sedley, *CR* 29 (1979), 82–84; A. A. Long "Epicureans and Stoics," in *Classical Mediterranean Spirituality*, ed. A. H. Armstrong (New York 1986), 135–53 at 142–145. Added support is adduced in D. Obbink, "The Atheism of Epicurus," *GRBS* 30 (1989), 187–223; cautious approbation in P.G. Woodward, "Star gods in Philodemus, PHerc. 152/

the gods is in part responsible for what we think about them, and that it is only in the form of our ideas that the gods themselves can benefit or harm us. In his *Letter to Herodotus* 77, for example, Epicurus lays down very specific restrictions on the kind of ὀνόματα to be attributed to the gods, against the penalty of mental disquiet.[17]

For this reason Epicurus has a considerable stake in what people in the the course of human history had to say about gods, and the contexts in which they said it. One source of such statements available to Epicurus were the writings of philosophers before Socrates, who speculated about cultural origins, and we can be certain that Epicurus noticed these, as the second anecdote related by Diogenes and other evidence intimate. Another source will have been the prayers, oaths, hymns, charms, curses, and other, more traditional forms of religious discourse known from Greek cult and culture. The compositions of the earliest Greek philosophers themselves had been closely bound up with these traditional forms of speech, especially poetry: for the Greek philosophical tradition had long consisted of a cultural and intellectual commentary on problematic poetic texts, both written and unwritten. Furthermore, many pre-Socratic philosophers like Empedocles, Parmenides, and Xenophanes[18] had actually adopted for their revelatory discourse the rhapsode's traditional poetic form of a hymnic proem, placing themselves in direct competition and symbiosis with the mythological tradition. While not all ancient poetry was concerned with gods (iambus being a prominent exception), there is good reason to think that the primary criterion of serious traditional poetry was a text touching on divine figures familiar from myth and cult or with a performance, festival, symposium, or other celebration conducted in their honor. In addition, and more important for Epicurus' view of human history, is the fact that the philosophical tradition regularly accorded pride of place to serious religious poetry (i.e., hymn) as the oldest form of poetry known to Greek culture.[19]

3. Poetry in *On Piety*

If we frame Epicurus' theory of poetry as at least in part a reflection of his views on the epistemic status of early poetry (as the story about his anxiety over the priority of Hesiod's Chaos implies), we have of course to turn to our later sources, since the

---

157," *CErc* 19 (1989), 29–48. Contra: J. Mansfeld, "Aspects of Epicurean Theology," *Mnemosyne* 46 (1993) 172–210.

[17] "In all the terms with which we set forth our conceptions of such blessedness (i.e., the gods), we must preserve them in all their holiness lest from our expressions there grow opinions that deny this majesty. Otherwise these contradictions will cause the greatest confusion in our souls." Epicurus discussed the matter in *On Nature* 12 and 13, to which this chapter of the *Letter to Herodotus* corresponds. I am aware that this does not necessarily mean that Epicurus thinks the gods consist *only* of such images. But it is remarkable that everything extant that Epicurus did say about the gods pertains explicitly to our ideas of them, or to the images which constitute such ideas. The standard counter-example (tirelessly propounded, for example, by Mansfeld [above, n. 16], 178–182) that according to Epicurus the gods are ζῷα "living beings," is explicitly said by Epicurus to pertain to how we are instructed to *think* of the gods as existing: *Letter to Menoeceus* 123: τὸν θεὸν ζῷον . . . . νομίζων . . . ὡς ἡ κοινὴ τοῦ θεοῦ νόησις ὑπεγράφη . . . πρόσαπτε.

[18] For Heraclitus see L. Koenen, "Der erste Satz bei Heraklit und Herodot," *ZPE* 97 (1993), 95-96.

[19] So Aristotle, *Poet.* 1448b27 where it is said to have antedated even Homer and epic, with iambic lampoon representing a second, equally ancient line of development for non-serious types of poetry.

works in which Epicurus might have discussed the matter have perished.[20] New information on this point emerges from Philodemus' *On Piety*. It reveals that the Epicureans did have a fully developed theory of how the earliest form of poetry, poetry about gods, had come to exist in the course of human history. This theory they traced to Epicurus himself. Philodemus' account outlines the Epicurean position on the invention of poetry in human history and puts forth an argument about poetry's alleged benefit in the development of human culture. It emerges clearly that, in order to make the case, this project required of the Epicurean a more than passing familiarity with traditional poetic texts.

Most of the papyrus texts of Philodemus' *On Piety* have been available in some form since Gomperz's edition of 1866, and the text has received continuous and expert editorial attention in the interim.[21] But insights into the structure of the papyrus roll have made it possible to link more columns, or parts of columns than before. You can now read two or even three continuous columns without a lacuna, where before we could only read one or half of one.[22] It would be overly optimistic to pretend that the new method completely restores the composition to its original continuous form. It is rather like being able to see the skeletal reconstruction of a dinosaur, instead of a mere pile of bones. We can with some degree of certainty envisage the living, breathing beast, but never actually see it. There is, of course, a real gain produced in seeing for the first time the extant columns in their original order rather than the chaotic disorder in which they have come down to us. As a result it is possible to discern the plan of the treatise as a unified, organic whole, divided into two parts, which I will try to summarize.[23]

4. The Invention of Mythographic Poetry

Expounding a view of piety as a natural concomitant to virtue, Philodemus in *On Piety* explains first how Epicurus and his followers upheld the existence of gods in their arguments and acts of cult, both public and private. Epicurus is quoted directly from numerous works: *On Holiness, On Gods*, letters to known addressees, and specific books of *On Nature*.[24] Philodemus says that in Book 13 of *On Nature* Epicurus

---

[20] Epicurus probably discussed the matter in his account of human history in *On Nature* 12; perhaps also in the lost portions of Book 28. We know that in *On Rhetoric* Epicurus discussed the "beguiling" encomiastic displays of orators delivered in competitions at festivals, characterized by stylistic devices of poetry, noting specifically that they were not concerned with contemporary events or pressing matters such as war or peace discussed in speeches in assemblies (fr. 53 Us. = 20.4 Arrighetti; new text by J. Hammerstaedt in *CErc* 22 [1992], 26-31).

[21] In particular the work of Albert Henrichs and Wolfgang Luppe (see n. 40 below).

[22] For some results of the new method of restoring the order of columns in Herculaneum rolls opened by the process of *scorzatura* see Obbink 1986; id., 1989 (above, n. 16); Delattre 1989; Janko 1991b; id. 1992a; id. 1993.

[23] For the text of first, philosophical part, see D. Obbink, *Philodemus On Piety: Critical Text with Commentary 1* (Oxford, forthcoming). For the second part, on the criticism of the poets, see Schober 1988 as modified by Henrichs 1972 and 1975; on the criticism of the Stoics, see Henrichs 1974; on the pre-Socratics, see A. Henrichs, "Two Doxographical Notes: Democritus and Prodicus on Religion", *HSCPh* 79 (1975), 93-123.

[24] Apart from a quotation from *On Nature* 4 in Philodemus' *On Death*, Philodemus' *On Piety* is virtually the only treatise among the books from the Herculaneum library to present such citations from

explains how there can exist a "cause of punishment and security" stemming from the gods to humans (*On Piety* 1041–49). Poetry enters the cultural scene early on, playing a minor role in Epicurus' theory of the degeneration of belief in gods in human history. In Book 12 of *On Nature* he is reported to have said that the "first humans" originally formed ideas of the gods as existing,[25] but later contaminated these with ideas about fear and death in the context of prayers, sacrifices, processions, and poetic performances: "for no longer are their happiness stemming from every source and their insusceptibility to destruction preserved."[26] Later in the first half of the treatise Philodemus contrasts Epicurus' view with another, perhaps rival account of the rise of false beliefs about the gods. According to the rival account the belief in gods was due to the fact that early philosophers and *theologoi* told false *muthoi* about the gods in order to frighten ignorant evil-doers into obedience.

In order to relate this passage, couched as it is in Philodemus' intractable Greek, to Epicurus' own views, it will be convenient to summarize it briefly in context. Philodemus is explaining rather laboriously that his opponents did not attack the religious *actions* of Epicurus (since Epicurus could be easily exonerated on this point: Philodemus has just finished retailing a long list of acts of public and private cult by Epicureans). Rather the opponents fastened upon what Epicurus *said* about the gods. But they are not successful in attacking his "words alone" either, as Philodemus goes on to show, comparing Epicurus' representation of the gods with that of his philosophical predecessors:[27]

οὐ|δεὶς γὰρ ὡς εἶπε[ἴ]ν | τῶν ὠφε[λ]εῖν καὶ | βλάπτειν εἰρηκό|των φιλοσό-
φων | τοὺς θεοὺς ὁμο[ία]ς | τοῖς χυδαίοις ὑπ[έ]λι|πε[ν] τὰς ὠφελ[ί]ας
| καὶ τὰς βλάβας· [ἔνι]|οι δ' οὐδὲ βλάπ[τει]ν | ὅλως ἔφασαν αὐτούς,
| ὡσαύτως δ' [οὐ]δὲ | προςδεῖςθαι τού||[των] παρ' ἄδεια[ν. |ἀπά]την δὲ
με[γά]||λην κα]τὰ τῶν [ἄλλων | παρ]έχοντες ε[ἰς δει]|νὰς ἀδικίας ἑ[πο]-
|μένως ἄιττου[ςι]|| τὰς κρυφαίους, {α}| τὸν ὑπονοούμε|νον ἄπαντα γινώ-
ς|κειν οὐκέτι φο|βούμενοι. δι' ὃ {ν}| ςιωπᾶν ἀςφαλές|τερον ἐ[τύγ]χαν[εν.]||
ταῦτα [δ' ἐπομ]ένως | ἐποίο[υν οἱ δί]και|οι τῶν [θεολ]όγων | καὶ φιλοσό-
φων· οὐ | γὰρ ἐλά[νθα]νεν τά|ληθὲς αὐτούς, ἀλλὰ τὰς | κακουργίας ὑπὸ |

Epicurus' *magnum opus On Nature*, in spite of the authority of that work in the Epicurean tradition (it was apparently followed closely by both Lucretius and Diogenes of Oenoanda) and the fact that the library yielded multiple copies of some of its books—and these are written in some of the oldest hands to be found among the Herculaneum papyri. This is an oddity for which I can unfortunately offer no explanation.

[25] Philodemus, *On Piety* 225–31 Obbink κἀν τῶι δω|δεκάτ[ω]ι περὶ φ[ύ]|ς[ε]ω[ς το]ὺς πρώ-
τους | φη[ςὶν ἀ]νθρώπους | ἐπὶ ν[οή]ματα ⟨τῶν ἔ⟩ξω | βα⟨ί⟩νειν ἀφθάρτων φύςεων· εἶναι γὰρ
. . . . For the text see Obbink 1989 (above, n. 16), 196–197; cf. J. Mansfeld, *Mnemosyne* 46 (1993), 178 n.12.

[26] Philodemus, *On Piety* 265–70 Obbink. For poetic performances in this context see 296-307. As explained above, the order of columns in Gomperz's edition is not that of the original treatise.

[27] Philodemus, *On Piety* 1176-1217. Where my text differs from that of Gomperz, the readings and restorations are my own. Constraints of space prohibit me from giving a full critical apparatus here. Sublinear asterisks mark those letters editorially changed from the nineteenth century copy where the original papyrus does not exist to verify the text.

τῶν μύθων ἀνα|cτελλομένας θε|ωροῦντες τῶι ἐ|πικρέμας[θ]αι τοῖς | ἀνοη-
⟨το⟩τέροις τὴν ὐ|ποψίαν, [ἴ]να μὴ τὸν ||[ὅλον βί]ον [θ]ηριώδη ||[παρ]έχω-
μεν, [κ]ἀλ|[λωc τ]ὸ δυςμενές . . . .

For virtually none of the philosophers who have said that the gods do good and
harm represented that good and harm similar to laymen, whereas some (i.e.,
other philosophers) said that that they do no harm at all, and similarly that they
have no need at all of these things (sc. good and harm) out of freedom of fear.
And preparing an immense deception against the rest, they subsequently rush
into terrible, hidden injustices, since they no longer feared anyone believed to
be all-knowing. Therefore it was safer to keep silent. Consequently that was
what those of the theologians and philosophers who were just did. For the truth
did not escape them, but, since they observed that evil deeds were held in check
by the tales because foreboding hung over the more foolish of mankind, in order
that we might not render life as a whole a beastly form of existence, and since
otherwise the hostility . . . they . . . (the sentence breaks off here).

In other words, some of Epicurus' predecessors had held (as did Epicurus) that the
gods do harm and benefit to humans, but denied that this harm and benefit were like
of the literal, mythic sort represented by common, less philosophically respectable
beliefs about the gods (οὐ . . . ὀμο[ία]c | τοῖς χυδαίοις).[28] Still other philosophers
said that the gods harmed no one; thus they (the earliest philosophers) turned to
injustice, since they no longer believed in an omniscient divinity. As a result, philosophers and *theologoi* deployed false stories (*mythoi*) about the gods in order to exert
their own control over the foolish.

This passage bears a striking similarity to, and familiarity with the famous fragment of the satyr play *Sisyphus*, attributed alternately in antiquity to Critias and
Euripides.[29] A comparison with Lucretius' account of the origin of religion in *On the
Nature of Things* 5.1161–1240 confirms the proposal[30] of Marcello Gigante that Lucretius 5.1188 *in caeloque deum sedes et templa locarunt* indeed recycles Critias'
Sisyphus lines 27ff. ναίειν δ' ἔφαςκε τοὺς θεοὺς ἐνταῦθ'. We now know that in
addition to Lucretius' allusion to the speech of Sisyphus in *On the Nature of Things*,
there was another in Philodemus' *On Piety*. As a result, a common source in Epicurus' *On Nature* 12 as transmitting a representation of Critias' portrait of Sisyphus
looks likely, especially in view of Philodemus' report, earlier in the treatise, that:[31]

---

[28] The point is that, for this reason, Epicurus cannot be faulted for saying that (a) the gods do good
and harm to humans, but that (b) they do not do so in the way commonly believed by people or as they
are portrayed in myths.

[29] Critias 43 F 19 in *Tragicorum Graecorum fragmenta*, edd. B. Snell and S. Radt, vol. 1, (Göttingen
1971), especially line 26 in which ψευδεῖ καλύψας τὴν ἀλήθειαν λόγῳ which corresponds to οὐ | γὰρ
ἐλά[νθα]νεν τἀληθὲς αὐτούς in the passage from Philodemus quoted above. On the authorship of the
speech of Sisyphus, see below, n. 31.

[30] M. Gigante, "Lucretius Sisyphum Critiae est imitatus," *Dionysio* 20.3–4 (1957), 97–98.

[31] Philodemus, *On Piety* 519–41 Obbink, a fuller text of Epicurus fr. 87 Usener = 27.2 Arrighetti
with new readings and restorations. On the authorship of the speech of Sisyphus, see A. Dihle, "Das
Statyrspiel 'Sisyphus'," *Hermes* 105 (1977), 28–42 who advocates the authorship of Euripides. But as
W. Burkert, *Greek Religion*, transl. J. Raffan (Cambridge, Mass. 1985), 314 with n. 22 noted, he overlooked the evidence of Philodemus, *On Piety* p. 112 Gomperz = Epicurus fr. 87 Usener (quoted above)

καὶ πᾶcαν μ[ανίαν Ἐ]|πίκουροc ἐμ[έμψα]|το τοῖc τὸ [θεῖον ἐ]|κ τῶν
ὄντων [ἀναι]|ροῦcιν, ὡc κἀ[ν τῶι]| δωδεκάτω[ι Προ]|δίκωι καὶ Δια[γό-
ραι]| καὶ Ῑκριτίαι κἄ[λλοιc]| μέμφ[εται] φὰc πα[ρα]|κόπτειν καὶ μ[αίνε-
c]|θαι, καὶ βακχεύου|cιν αὐτοὺc [εἰ]κά[ζει,˙ κε]|λεύc[αc μ]ὴ πρᾶγμα
ἡ|μεῖν παρέχειν οὐ|δ᾽ ἐνοχλεῖν. κα[ὶ γὰρ]| παραγραμμίζ[ουcι]| τὰ τ[ῶ]ν
θεῶν [ὀνόμα]|τά, [κα]θάπερ Ἀν[τιc]|θέ[νηc] τὸ κοινό[τατον]| ὑποτίνων
ἀν[αιρεῖ]| τὰ κατὰ μέροc [τῆι θέ]|cει καὶ διά τι[νοc ἀπά]|τηc ἔτι πρό-
τ[ερον.

Epicurus reproached for their complete madness people who eliminate the divine from existing things,[32] as in Book 12 (of *On Nature*) he reproaches
Prodicus, Diagoras, and Critias among others, saying that they rave like luna-
tics, and he likens them to Bacchant revelers, admonishing them as well to stop
causing trouble and disturbing us. For they[33] even explain the names of the gods
by transposing letters,[34] just as Antisthenes[35] eliminates what is commonly accepted[36] in suggesting that individual names exist by convention[37] or even earlier[38] through some act of deceit.

Philodemus even agrees on certain points with the rival view about the invention
of *mythoi* in early history. But he goes on in *On Piety* to argue that the attempt of early
humans to secure justice in this way was *not* ultimately in fact successful, because of
their own disbelief in the gods and their fear of other humans' finding out and harm-
ing them. Over time they neglected to fabricate lies about gods in the interest of

as testimony specifically associating Critias with atheism and antedating Satyrus and the Hellenistic
biographers. Cf. M. R. Lefkowitz, "Was Euripides an Atheist?" *SIFC* 5 (1987), 149–166; ead., "'Impiety' and 'Atheism' in Euripides' Dramas," *CQ* 39 (1989), 70–82; ead., "Commentary on Vlastos," *Proceedings of the Boston Area Colloquium in Ancient Philosophy* 5 (1991), 239–46. H. Yunis, "The Debate
on Undetected Crime and an Undetected Fragment from Euripides' Sisyphos," *ZPE* 75 (1988), 39–46
reasserts the authorship of Euripides and dismisses the relevance of Epicurus, arguing that it is unlikely
that Epicurus was thinking of the speech of Sisyphus, since the fragment of Epicurus (as presented
without context in fr. 87 Usener) does not deal specifically with undetected crime; see also D. V.
Panchenko, "Euripid ili Kriti?," *VDI* 1980 no. 1 (1980), 144–61; M. Winiarczyk, "Nochmals das Satyr-
spiel 'Sisyphos'," *WS* 100 (1987), 35–45; and M. Davies, "Sisyphus and the Invention of Religion,
('Critias' *TrGF* 1(43) F 19 = B 25 DK)," *BICS* 36 (1989), 16–32.

[32] i.e. who deny or imply that they deny that the gods exist.

[33] Prodicus, Diagoras, and Critias.

[34] Literally: "they transpose the letters in the names of the gods" (in order to explain the origin of
belief in them).

[35] Cf. Philodemus, *On Piety* p. 72 Gomperz: π]αρ᾽ Ἀντιc|θένει δ᾽ ἐν μὲν [τ]ῶι | Φυcικῶι λέγεται
τὸ | κατὰ νόμον εἶναι | πολλοὺc θεούc, κα[τὰ δὲ φύcιν ἕν[α (fr. 39A Decleva-Caizzi = Cicero, *On the
Nature of the Gods* 1.32): "In Antisthenes in his *Physics* it is said that many gods exist by convention, but
only one in reality." On the title of Antisthenes' work see Philodemus, Πρὸc τοὺc [---] (the rest of the
title is missing) fr. 110 in A. Angeli, *Agli Amici di Scuola (PHerc. 1005)*, La Scuola di Epicuro 7 (Napoli
1988) with her note on pp. 232–33, a passage which probably discussed Epicurus' acquaintance with this
work of Antisthenes (cf. fr. 111; Philodemus, *On the Stoics* col. xiii 1ff. Dorandi).

[36] The most common, most general conception (or name?) of the gods.

[37] By invoking convention or institution of belief *(thesis)* in explanation of belief in gods.

[38] Earlier in cultural history when, according to Critias, some people had tricked others into believ-
ing in gods for the purpose of political control.

protecting their countries or themselves, but did so merely in conformity with current trends in fashion, both arbitrary and irrational:[39]

διόπερ οὐ τῇ[ν ἐ]‖ποχὴν ἀναιρ[οῦν]‖τεc ἀδικίαν ἀ[ν]‖τειcάγουcιν ἀ[ν]‖τὶ τῆc δικαιο[cύ]‖νηc, μόνην δ' [ἐ]‖‖ξεργαζόμενοι τὴν | ἀcφάλειαν ἢ τὴν ἑ|αυτῶν παρὰ τῶν | πολλῶν ἢ τὴν ἐκεί|νων παρ' ἀλλήλων | ἀλλὰ τὸ φαινόμε|νον ἕκαcτοι πᾶcιν | ἐ[πιτρέπουτ]εc· [ο]ἱ δὲ | μύθουc μὲν εἰcῆγον | ἀμέλει καὶ τερατεί|αc, οὔτε δὲ τοῖc πρό|τερον ἐδόκουν ἐοι|κότα ταῦτ' εἰcφέρειν | οὔτε cωτηρίαc αἴτ[ια]‖ πολειτείαc· cὺν | δὲ ⟨τῶι⟩ cυμπεριφέ-[ρεc]‖θαι μὲν ταῖc τ[ότε]‖ ἐνϊcχνούcα[ιc δόξαιc,]‖ ἅμα διὰ τὴ[ν ἀνω]‖μα-λίαν καὶ [τὴν μανί]‖αν ἐπινοεῖν ο[ὐχ ὡc ἀ]‖cεβεῖc ἐδόκουν | μόνον ἀλλὰ καὶ φε|νακιcταί.
_*

For this reason, they substitute injustice for justice not by eliminating skepticism (ἐποχή), and securing mere safety either for themselves from the multitude or for the latter from each other, but by each leaving to everyone else what was evident. But the others | of course introduced mind-boggling tales of terror, and did not seem to be introducing these things either in the same way as their predecessors or as the sources of security to states; and what with, on the one hand conforming to currently prevailing opinions, on the other hand at the same time conceiving inconsistency and madness, they seemed not only impious but also dishonest.

Philodemus defends this Epicurean reconstruction of cultural history with a variety of arguments. Some are analogical. One of his major contentions in its support is that the entire history of Greek mythological poetry (i.e., most Greek poetry) from Homer and Orpheus to Menander and Callimachus bears out this deformation and degeneration of humankind's *prolepsis* of the divine, various Sophistic, Socratic, and Stoic attempts to rescue poetry at the expense of clarity in language notwithstanding. The poets, mythographers, and philosophers, he repeatedly complains, reduce the gods to some entity or principle, or equate one or more of them with some other divinity. The mass of resulting contradictions shows that they cannot all be right. Calling air Zeus or Demeter Earth is deemed not only an abuse of language (according to Epicurus' admonition to use words in their clearest, most immediate senses), but equivalent to atheism. Poetic myths about the gods, and their interpretations at the hand of opportunistic philosophers and politicians, historically have served for the most part to obscure naturally formed conceptions, while lulling us into a false sense of security in the hope that potential wrongdoers will believe the poets' myths and so refrain from injustice.

---

[39] Philodemus, *On Piety* 2145–74 Obbink. See also the discussion of L. Perelli, "Epicuro e la dottrina di Crizia sull' origine della religione," *RFIC* 83 (1955), 29–56. Further on μῦθοc, see below, n. 58.

5. The Epicurean Poetic Syllabus

Philodemus undertakes to support these contentions in detail by amassing the famous catalogue of poets which immediately follows in the treatise.[40] The list has an interesting organization:[41] for instance, poems positing a primal cosmogonic entity are listed first in the catalogue: the author of the *Titanomachia* is criticized for having said that all things come from Aether; Acusilaus, because he said that *all things came from Chaos*. Fortunately, the exact transition to this section is preserved (*On Piety* 2480–2509 Obbink):

[κατάρ]‖ξομαι δ᾽ ἀπὸ τ[ῶν ‖ cεμ]νῶν θεολόγων ‖[καὶ π]οητῶν, ἐπει‖[δὴ μ]άλιcτα τούτουc ‖[ἐγκω]μιάζουcιν οἱ ‖[κατ]α[τρ]έχοντεc ἡ‖[μῶ]ν ὡc ἀcεβῆ καὶ ‖[ἀcύ]μφορα τοῖc ἀν‖[θρώ]ποιc δογματι‖[ζόν]των. ἀξιῶ δ᾽ ὅ‖[τι π]αν[ε]χθίcτουc ‖[αὐτοὺc] ὡc χορὸν ‖[διαδ]οῦναι πρὸc ὅ‖[λον] χρόνον οὐ πό‖[νοc] ἀνωφελὴc ἔcται ‖[πα]ντάπαcιν οὔτε ‖[μα]κρόc. ἐντυγχά‖[νω] δὲ καὶ τοῖc ἀκρει‖[βέcι]ν ἐμ παντὶ μη‖[δὲν] cυκοφαντεῖν, ἐ‖[ὰ]ν εὕρω[cι]ν ἐνηλ⟨λ⟩α‖[γμ]ένον ὄνομα. διὰ ‖[γὰρ] τὸ πλ[ῆ]θοc ἐκ[δό]‖cεω[ν, μᾶλ]λον δ᾽ εἰκ[ό]‖τωc διὰ τὸ cπεύδε[ιν | μ᾽ ἵν]α που μὴ φανῶ [τὸν | πο]λὺν προcε‖δρεύ[[cαι] τοιούτοιc χρόνον ‖[οὐκ] ἀπώμοτον ὃ λέ‖[γ]ω γεγονέναι·

So I will begin with the self-important theologians and poets, since they are the ones who are especially praised by those who attack us, on the grounds we (sc. Epicureans) are setting forth views impious and disadvantageous to mankind. And I think it would not be a useless labor in general nor a long one to display them as archenemies for all time in a *choros*.[42] And I appeal to those concerned with accuracy under all circumstances not to raise any quibbles against me, in case they find instances of words (i.e. in citations) which have been changed (i.e. mistakenly, cf. below, p. 222). For due to the multitude of editions, or more likely because of my anxiety that I should not appear to have spent much of my time on such matters, I cannot swear that what I say has not happened.

Philodemus tells us that the task before him of surveying the poets championed by his Stoic opponents as keeping wrongdoers in check, is a "labor neither useless nor (too) long." Here [μα]κρός is the supplement of Bücheler. If correct, Philodemus is striking an ironic note. For the catalogue of poets that follows is very long.[43] Several

---

[40] In the second part of *On Piety*. For the text see Schober 1988; Henrichs 1972; id. 1975; and numerous articles by W. Luppe.

[41] Cicero summarizes the section criticizing the poets at *On the Nature of the Gods* 1.42, immediately following the mention of Diogenes of Babylons' *On Athena*; where the original material and grouping may be glimpsed: (1) *inflammatos et libidine furentis deos*, (2) *bella proelia pugnas vulnera* (note the asyndetic catalogue style), (3) *odia praeterea discidia discordias*, (4) *ortus interritus* (including Athena's?), (5) *querellas lamentationes*, (6) *effusas in omni interperantia libidines*, (7) *adulteria vincula*, (8) *cum humano genere concubitus mortalisque ex inmortali procreatos*.

[42] i.e., *in toto*, altogether as a group. For the metaphor see Philodemus, *On Rhetoric* vol. 1 p. 237,5–6 Sudhaus: ὡc ὁ τῶν πολιτευομένων | χορός "like the crowd of politicians."

[43] Daniel Delattre suggests to me that we should restore οὔτε ‖[μι]κρός here (which would accurately describe the extent of the catalogue), or οὔτε ‖[πι]κρός "neither useless nor bitter" (cf. Lucretius,

dozen poets are named and quoted or paraphrased and criticized. Philodemus contends that the devolution of the conception of god in the development of poetry was ultimately detrimental to humankind. The more counter-examples he can cite, the stronger his argument. For no one would refrain from wrongdoing out of fear of such gods as so many poets represent, as his Stoic opponents claimed they would (thus they are said, in the passage just quoted, to have charged the Epicureans with "setting forth views impious and disadvantageous to mankind").

The exact source of Philodemus' citations of the poets is open to question. One wonders whether he read all the poets, historians, and philosophers who are cited for their representations of the gods in this section. Were some of their books once present in the villa at Herculaneum, alongside those of Ennius and Lucretius? Albert Henrichs isolated numerous correspondences with the known fragments of the lost treatise *On Gods* of the second century B.C. mythographer Apollodorus of Athens, suggesting that Philodemus or his source might have mined the references in summary form from that mythological handbook.[44] Another possibility is that Diogenes of Babylon's *On Athena* provided both Apollodorus and Philodemus' teacher Zeno of Sidon (whose habitual attacks on Diogenes Philodemus often summarizes in his writings) with their mythographic material.[45] This is recommended by the fact that many of Philodemus' citations of the poets are paralleled in the final section of *On Piety*, where the Stoic philosophers are criticized (and Diogenes of Babylon is the last named) for claiming that their own doctrines are not inconsistent with the same views said earlier to be instantiated by the poets.[46]

ἐν δὲ τῶ[ι] δευ|τέρ[ωι] τά τε εἰc Ὀρφέ|α [καὶ] Μουcαῖον ἀνα|φερ[όμ]ενα
καὶ τὰ | παρ᾽ [Ὁ]μήρωι καὶ Ἡ|cιόδω[ι] καὶ Εὐριπί|δη καὶ ποιητα[ῖ]c
ἀλ|λοιc [ὣ]c καὶ Κλεάν|θης [πει]ρᾶται c[υ]οι|κειοῦ[ν] ταῖc δόξ[αι]c αὐ-
τῶ[ν]· ἅπαντά [τ᾽] ἐc|τὶν [αἰθ]ήρ, ὁ αὐτὸ[c]|| ὢν κ[αὶ] πατὴρ καὶ |[υἱ]όc,
[ὣ]c κἂν τῶι |[πρ]ώτωι μὴ μά|[χ]εcθα[ι] τὸ τὴν Ῥέ||[α]ν καὶ μητέρα
τ[οῦ]|| Διὸc εἶναι καὶ θυγ[α]||τέρα. τὰc δ᾽ αὐτὰc |[π]οιεῖται c[υ]νοικει|[ώ-
cε]ιc κἂν τῶι Περ[ὶ]|| Χαρίτων κ[αὶ] τὸν | Δία νόμον φηcὶ⟨ν⟩ εἶναι καὶ
τὰc Χάριταc | τὰc ἡμετέ[ρ]αc κα|ταρχὰc καὶ τὰc ἀν|ταποδόcειc τῶν |
εὐε[ρ]γεcιῶν.

On the Nature of Things 1.940–41 *perpotet amarum / absinthi laticem*). Note that Philodemus does not say either that the "choreography" of poets that follows is either useful (cυμφέρον, ὠφελής) nor sweet (ἡδύc, Lucr. 1.947 *quasi musaeo dulci contingere melle*); there is no claim that a τέχνη "systematic art" for the analysis of its poetic content is available to the philosopher. Perhaps Philodemus means that the elenchus of poets is at least potentially useful for philosophy and attractive in itself. He explicitly states his concern not to seem to be spending too much time on such matters. Yet this is at least partly belied by the extent, detail, and erudition of the catalogue that follows. See below, however, on the type of argument deployed.

[44] Henrichs 1975, following J. Dietze, "Die mythologischen Quellen für Philodemos Schrift περὶ εὐcεβείαc," *Jahrbuch für Philologie* 153 (1896), 218–226.

[45] Cicero's list (quoted above, n. 41) obviously reflects the polemical bias of his Epicurean source, but all the topics have in common that they illustrate the passions: Diogenes of Babylon's *On Athena* may have been a treatise on psychology rather than theology.

[46] For the text, see Henrichs 1974, 17-18 (*P.Herc.* 1428 col. 6,16-7,12). For Diogenes of Babylon's *On Athena* see col. 8,14ff (Henrichs 1974, 19-21); Cicero, *On the Nature of the Gods* 1.41; *Att.* 13.39.2.

In the second book, like Cleanthes, he (sc. Chrysippus) tries to accommodate the things attributed to Orpheus and Musaeus, and the things found in Homer, Hesiod, Euripides and other poets, to their (sc. the Stoics') views.[47] And all things are aether, which is both father and son, just as in the first book he says that there is no contradiction in Rhea's being both mother and daughter of Zeus. And he makes the same identifications in his book *On the Graces*, where he says that Zeus is the law and the Graces sacrificial offerings and exchanges of favors.

Thus Philodemus' (and Zeno's) acquaintance with the poets cited in *On Piety* was not at first hand. Nevertheless, a particular kind of familiarity with the poets is clearly required in order to make the Epicurean case (see below). The work concludes with a catalogue, adapted by Cicero in *On the Nature of the Gods* 1, of such attempts on the part of philosophers from Thales to Diogenes of Babylon, with whom the cata-logue ends, to interpret the statements of the poets as not inconsistent with their own philosophical doctrines. The Stoics' attempts to interpret the ravings of the poets in an acceptable philosophical way is argued by Philodemus to be equally risible.

This brings us back to Epicurus, and to the question of the Master's original stake in the argument over the poets' representations of the gods. For Philodemus de-scribes the work as a whole in the closing words of *On Piety*, in what is very likely an expanded form of the title itself,[48] as "the *logos* about piety according to Epicurus":

P.Herc. 1428 col. 15,13–23 (Henrichs 1974, 25–26)

13	ὥc-	So this part of the out-
	τε καὶ τοῦ μέρ[ο]υc	line set forth at the start
	τούτου τῆc δ[ιαι]ρέ-	having been sufficiently
16	cεωc τῆc κατ' ἀρχὰc	treated, it would now be
	ἐκτ[ε]θείcηc ἀπο-	the appropriate time to
	χρώντω[c ἐ]ξε[ι]ργαc-	*paragraphein* at this point
	μένου καιρὸc ἂν εἴ-	the Epicurean account of
20	η{ι} τὸν περὶ τῆc εὐ-	the topic of piety.
	cεβείαc λόγον τῆc	
	κατ' Ἐπίκουρον αὐ-	
	τοῦ παραγράφε[ι]ν.	

No doubt a fair part of the treatise's main argument—the historical and ethical com-

---

[47] Long 1992, 49-50 points out that in Cicero's version of this sentence at *On the Nature of the Gods* 1.41 *in secundo autem volt Orphei Musaei Hesiodi Homerique fabellas accommodare ad ea quae ipse primo de deis inmortalibus dixerit, ut etiam veterrimi poetae, qui haec ne suspicati quidem sunt* (var. lect., Long: *sint* alii), *Stoici fuisse videantur*, the *ut* clause is represented nowhere in Philodemus, but was added by Cicero. In other words, Cicero has deliberately over-polemicized his rendition, making his Epicurean spokesman accuse Chrysippus and Cleanthes of something they never did: namely claim that the old poets had themselves been Stoics. As Long notes, Philodemus says only that the Stoics accom-modate τά τε εἰc Ὀρφέ|α [καὶ] Μουcαῖον ἀνα|φερ[όμ]ενα, "the things attributed to Orpheus and Musaeus" (i.e. divine names and myths), not that they made the poets (or pre-Socratics) out to be Stoics themselves. According to the Stoics, the poetic citations instantiate and construct κοιναὶ ἔννοιαι: see Obbink 1992, esp. 216-25.

[48] Unfortunately both the exact title and the name of the author which appeared in the colophon following this column are lost. "Philodemus" and "On Piety" are reasonable, not certain, guesses.

ponent–derives from Epicurus' *On Nature* Books 12 and 13, from which he is quoted in the passage discussed above as having spoken very disapprovingly of the rival theories on this point of Prodicus, Diagoras, and Critias (fr. 87 Usener). Judged from his *Letter to Herodotus* 77, Epicurus there also discussed the proper use of expressions for the gods.[49] The Epicurean anthropology is synthesized from Books 12 and 13 of Epicurus' *On Nature*; some of the language of the anthropological section ("our life being turned to that of beasts") is directly paralleled in fragments of his later contemporaries Colotes and Hermarchus. But obviously Epicurus did not attack the later figures Chrysippus and Diogenes of Babylon, let alone analyze the mythical content of the later poetry of Menander, Euphorion, and Callimachus mentioned by Philodemus.[50] The catalogue of poets, drawing as it does on Eudemus (for the cosmogonies and philosophical authors)[51] and the mythographer Apollodorus of Athens or Diogenes of Babylon, must have been the compilation and innovation of later Epicureans, Philodemus and/or his teacher Zeno.

As already noted, the most remarkable feature of the catalogue of poets and philosophers is its length. In spite of Philodemus' intention, expressed in the transitional passage quoted above, "not to spend too much time on such matters," the catalogue of poets extends to over 75 extant columns (the original probably contained 140), with the critique of pre-Socratic philosophers occupying 20 columns and the final attack on Stoic thinkers another 15 columns (all of which survive in complete or fragmentary form).

In the case of the poets in particular[52] the list is virtually unbroken by digression or philosophical analysis. Philodemus catalogues authors by thematic category, usually paraphrasing their poetic texts, though on occasion in direct quotation, but always in a highly abbreviated, tachygraphic form—whether in order to include as many examples as possible, or or in order to minimize risk of ethical harm or cultural seduction to the potential Epicurean through too much exposure to the original poetic text.[53] I offer as an example the following representative column:[54]

ληϲτῶν ἀλ[ῶναι	1	
ε̄· γράφει· καὶ Π[ίνδα-	*Hymn. Hom. Bacch.* (7), 7-9	
ροϲ δὲ διέρχ[εται	Pindar fr. 267 S.-M.	
περὶ τῆϲ λη[ϲτεί-		
αϲ. λέγουϲιν [δέ τι-	5	
νεϲ, οὓϲ καὶ Μέ[ναν-	Menander fr. 841 Körte	
δροϲ παραινί[ττε-		

---

[49] ὀνόματα, cf. Philodemus, *On Piety* 536f Obbink, quoted above, p. 198.

[50] Epicurus may well have mentioned the poetry of Diagoras (see below), as I have argued; he seems to have alluded to that of Critias (see above, p. 197).   [51] See Henrichs 1972, 78 n. 28.

[52] The level of argument directed toward the pre-Socratics and the Stoics is about as rigorous or, as we might say, "propaedeutic." This is perhaps indicative of the level of audience for whom the work was intended, no doubt including the author's actual or potential patron(s).

[53] It is very likely, however, that the Epicurean compilers found the poetic citations already highly abbreviated in the lists of examples enumerated in the writings of their Stoic opponents (see above, p. 201 with n. 45).

[54] My revision of Schober 1988, 87-88 (*P.Herc.* 1088 fr. 6). Cf. O. Musso, *ZPE* 22 (1976) 37; Luppe 1985a.

ται, κα[ὶ τ]ὴν Ἑ[κάτην
ὀπαδὸ[ν Ἄρ]τέ[μιδος
εἶναι, Δήμη[τρος   10
δὲ λάτριν Εὐρι[πίδης,
Ὅμηρος δ᾽ ἐν τ[οῖς   *Hymn. Cer.* 438–40
ὕμ]νοις· "πρόπ[ολον
καὶ [ὀ]πάονα" [αὐτῆς,
Κόρ]ης δὲ τροφ[όν· καὶ   15
Σαπ]φὼ{ι} δὲ τὴ[ν Πειθὼ   Sappho fr. inc. 23 L.-P.
"χρυςοφάη θερ[άπαι-
ν]αν Ἀφροδείτ[ας".
παρ᾽ Ὁμήρω⟨ι⟩ δ᾽ ὁ [Πρω-   *Od.* 4, 886
τ]εύς ἐς[τι] Ποσ[ειδά-   20
ω]νος ὑπ[οδμώς, πα-
ρὰ δὲ τῶι ποή[σαν-
• τι τὴν Δανα[ΐδα   Danais F 3 Davies
μητρὸς τῶν θ[εῶν
θ]εράπον[τ]ες [οἱ Κου-   25
ρῆτες. Στης[ίμβρο-   Stesimbrotus *FGrHist* 107 F 16
τος δὲ Ἄρτεμ[ιν αὐ-
τῆς καὶ Ἀθην[ᾶν
ὀπαδοὺ[ς . .(.)] π[. . || 29

[Homer in his Hymns] writes (*Hymn to Dionysus* [7]) that [Dionysus] was cap-
tured [by] pirates. And Pindar narrates about the episode of piracy (fr. 267 S.-
M.). And some, whom Menander hints at (fr. 841 Körte), say that Hecate too is
a handmaid of Artemis, or of Demeter as Euripides has it, and Homer in the
Hymns says (*Hymn to Demeter* 438–40) that she (sc. Hecate) is her (sc. Demeter's) "attendant and handmaid," while she (sc. Hecate) is the nurse of Kore.
And Sappho (says) (fr. inc. 23 L.-P.) that [Peitho? Hebe?] is the "attendant of
Aphrodite, shining with gold." And in Homer (*Od.* 4, 886) Proteus is enslaved
to Poseidon; and according to the author of the *Danais* the Curetes are servants
of the mother of the gods (i.e. Rhea?). And Stesimbrotus [makes] Artemis and
Athena her servants.

In spite of the abbreviated, tachygraphic quality of the citations, the poetic testimonies are, of course, extremely valuable. The fragment of Sappho is otherwise un-
attested. A quotation of the *Homeric Hymn to Demeter* is quite rare. But what little
comment we get in the text by way of philosophical analysis is of a fairly pedestrian,
unspecialized nature such as might derive from the grammatical school-tradition as
represented, for example, in our bT scholia to the *Iliad*. Philodemus' point is a basic
one: namely that all such representations are beneath the dignity of a divinity. The
criterion employed throughout is what is πρέπον ("appropriate") to say about
the gods according to the restrictions set forth in Epicurus' *Kyria Doxa* 1 and the

Letter to Menoeceus 123. An unusually extended example of such analysis is the following:[55]

τὸν ‖[δ᾽ Ἑρ]μῆν ὅτι τετρά|[γω]νον ἄνωθεν πα|ραδεδώκαςιν θεω|ροῦμεν.
καίτοι τὸ | μὲν ἢ γεννηθῆναι | τὴν μορφὴν ἄτο|πον ἢ τῶν μερῶν | ὕςτερόν
τινι δυς|τυχῆςαι τὴν κακί|αν ἐκφεύγειν δύνα|ται, τὸ δὲ [πο]νηρο|τάτουc
ε[ἰςάγ]ειν θε|οὺς ἄνωθ[εν] ἐκ γε|νετῆς ὑπερβολὰς | ἔςτιν οὐκ ἀπολει|πόν-
των ἀςεβείας. ‖[ἆρ᾽] οὐχ Ὅμηρος μὲν ‖[Δι]ὸς υἱὸν ὄντα τὸν Ἄ|[ρη] καὶ
ἄφρονα καὶ ἀ|[θέ]μιςτον καὶ μιαι|φόνον καὶ φίλεριν | καὶ φιλόμαχον
εἰς|[ή]γαγεν καὶ καθόλου ‖[τοι]οῦτον οἷον οἱ cυν|[γεν]έςτατ[οι ψ]έγου-
‖[ςιν;

And we observe that people have traditionally represented Hermes as rectangular (i.e. as a herm). And yet to be born with an odd shape, or suffer mutilation to any of one's parts later, need not involve any wickedness; but to represent the gods as most depraved right from their birth is a sign of those who lack nothing (i.e. are second to none) in their insurpassable impiety. Or does Homer not represent Ares, the son of Zeus, as foolish, lawless, murderous, a lover of strife and battle, and generally such a one as his closest relations disparage?

A brief criticism along these lines sometimes follows the poetic citations in Philodemus' catalogue, specifying how the poetic statement conflicts with the Epicurean conception by depicting the gods as, for example, fighting in battle, becoming wounded, engaging in sexual immorality, associating with humans, and so on. Certainly no very sophisticated philosophical armature is required to make such basic points. But the overall, cumulative effect of the catalogue is to construct a detailed portrait of Epicurean divinity by dwelling at great length on what the gods are most certainly *not*.[56] What Philodemus gives, in negative form, is a list of the most characteristic attributes of the Epicurean gods.

The extent and character of this Epicurean poetic syllabus shows that a knowledge of mythological poetry could be regarded in this way as conducive to philosophy and the virtue of piety. This consists in a kind of basic familiarity with, though not technical, poetic expertise in, some of the basic texts in the mythological tradition. We hear nothing of euphony, synthesis, *dianoiai*, metrics, or any of the other topics with which Philodemus' extant technical writings on poetry are filled. But the Epicurean's familiarity with the content and genre of poetic texts should be extensive enough, Philodemus' catalogue suggests, to bring out the vacuity of the conceptions of divinity to which traditional mythological poetry had descended over time, to (negatively) sketch out the Epicurean conception of divinity, and to demonstrate the historical devolution of the first humans' originally clear concept of the divine, without at the same time extending to exactitude in names, citations, and quotations, or to technical expertise in the composition of such poetry. Later Epicurean poetic practice can be seen to exhibit a similar attitude and procedure: Lucretius in his own allusive

---

[55] For the text see Schober 1988, 84 (*N* 1088 fr. 10). On τὸ πρέπον in Epicurean theology and Lucretius in particular see Reiche 1971, an article which repays much study.

[56] That authentic Epicurean theology is presented, albeit in negative form, in this part of *On Piety*, is the suggestion of Henrichs 1972, 83; cf. Philodemus, *Epigram* 29 Gow–Page = 21 Gigante (*AP* 1.234).

fashion similarly "sampled" much of ancient poetry ranging from Homer, Hesiod, Empedocles, and Euripides to their later and more fashionable imitators Callimachus and Ennius, incorporating it in his own poem while drawing special attention, in a mimetic process akin to parody, to the philosophical shortcomings of its mythic content. Might not a desire to construct just such a demonstration have been sufficient justification for Lucretius' casting his Epicurean manifesto in poetic form in the first instance?[57]

6. Goal and Target in Epicurean Polemic

For the reasons given above it would be a misrepresentation of the text to say that Philodemus' account in this part of *On Piety* is an attack on poetry *per se*. And, as we shall see, even certain types of poetry about gods were actually approved by the Epicureans. On the other hand poetry, especially poetry of a traditional, mythographic nature, cannot be said to come away unscathed from the exercise. A useful distinction may thus be made here and elsewhere in dealing with the complex argumentative strategies found in Philodemus' polemical repertoire. In modern parlance, we should say that mythographic poetry is the *target* of Philodemus' or Lucretius' criticism (i.e. the immediate and most obvious vehicle of attention), whereas the *goal* of their endeavor is any expositor of a philosophical view that the poets are adduced to instantiate. That is to say, ostensible criticism directed toward the *target* serves, by a familiar Hellenistic device of indirection and deflection, to get more bitingly at the ultimate *goal* of one's criticism: the Stoics for Philodemus, Academics and pre-Socratics for Lucretius. For this reason it would be a mistake to represent the main thrust of Philodemus' *On Piety* as an attack on poetry or even mythographic poetry *per se*, rather than an anti-commentary on a particular Stoic view appealing to such poetry for support. Epicurean rejection of myth per se was unequivocal.[58]

---

[57] Cf. M. J. Edwards, "Treading the aether: Lucretius, *De Rerum Natura* 1.62–79," *CQ* 40 (1990) 465–69. On Lucretius as a Hellenistic poet see E. J. Kenney, "Doctus Lucretius," *Mnemosyne* 23 (1970) 366–92; for Philodemus' poetry, see the essay by Sider in this volume, Chapter 4, above.

[58] *On Piety* 2158-9 Obbink (quoted above, p. 199) [o]ἵ δὲ | μύθουc μὲν εἰcῆγον: some early humans irrationally introduced myths in conformity to poetic fashion, so that before long poets failed to preserve clear ideas of the gods, as at *P.Herc.* 1609 fr. 4,6-7 (Schober 1988, 98: some ἐμύθε|[υ]cαν that Epimetheus, not Pandora, opened the jar of evils for mankind); *P.Herc.* 1428 fr. 18b,2-8 (Schober 1988, 114 = Diogenes of Apollonia T 6 Laks = *VS* 64 A 8 foolishly praised Homer for speaking "not fictitiously, μυθικῶc, but truthfully about divinity" since he thought that air was the same as Zeus, whom Homer says knows all: Διογέ|νης ἐπαι[νεῖ] τὸν Ὃ|μηρον ὡc ο[ὐ] μυθικ[ῶc]|| ἀλλ᾽ ἀληθῶc ὑπὲρ το[ῦ]|| θείου διειλεγμένον· | τὸν ἀέρα γὰρ αὐτὸν | Δία νομίζειν φηcὶν | ἐπειδὴ πᾶν εἰδέ|ναι τὸν Δία λέγει καὶ-at which point the text breaks off). Epicurus' use of the word μῦθοc, though hardly straightforward, is negative in the main: *Letter to Herodotus* 81 ("they" are always expecting or imagining some everlasting misery, such as is depicted in μῦθοι); *To Pythocles* 87 (of rigid adherence to single cause theory); ib. 104 ὁ μῦθοc ἀπέcτω (an intriguing asseveration); ib. 116 (τοῦ μύθου ἐκβήcῃ if you keep these things in mind); *To Menoeceus* 134 (better to follow ὁ περὶ θεῶν μῦθοc than be enslaved to the εἱμαρμένη of the φυcικοί, "for the former suggests an expectation of placating the gods by worship, whereas the latter involves a necessity that is implacable", ὁ μὲν γὰρ ἐλπίδα παραιτήcεωc ὑπογράφει θεῶν διὰ τιμῆc, ἡ δὲ ἀπαραίτητον ἔχει τὴν ἀνάγκην, i.e. merely the lesser of two evils, though note here the relatively positive estimation of τιμὴ καὶ παραίτηcιc θεῶν); thus at Plutarch, *On the Cessation of Oracles* 420B Epicureans are said to have called πρόνοια a μῦθοc; cf. *Kyria Doxa* 12 (one cannot dispel fear about

Perhaps surprisingly, the only exceptions allowed in Philodemus' catalogue of proscribed poetry are pious hymns to the gods. Philodemus digresses from his attack on Chrysippus and Diogenes to compare them negatively with a famous atheist–Diagoras. He notes that, as opposed to the anecdotal biographical tradition, Diagoras' attested writings consisted of pious hymns to the gods:[59]

ὥϲτ᾽ ἔγωγε [κ]ἂν | τεθαρ[ρ]ηκότωϲ εἴπαι|μι τούτουϲ Διαγόρου |[μ]ᾶλλον
πλημμελεῖν· | ὁ μὲν γὰρ ἔπαιξεν, εἴ|περ ἄρα καὶ τοῦθ᾽ ὑ[γι]έϲ | ἐϲτ[ι]ν
ἀλλ᾽ οὐκ ἐπενή|νεκται, καθάπ[ερ ἐ]ν | τοῖϲ Μα[ν]τινέων ῎Εθε|[ϲ]ιν ᾽Αρι-
ϲτόξενόϲ φη|ϲιν. ἐν δὲ τῆι ποιήϲει | τῆι μόνηι δοκούϲῃ | κατ᾽ ἀλήθειαν ὑπ᾽
αὐ|τοῦ γεγράφθαι τ[ο]ῖϲ ὅ|λοιϲ οὐ[δ]ὲν ἀϲεβὲϲ πα|ρενέφ[ην]εν ἀλλ᾽ ἔϲτιν
| εὔφημοϲ ὡϲ [π]οιητὴϲ | εἰϲ τὸ δ[α]ιμόνιον, κα|θάπερ ἄλλα τε μαρτυ|ρεῖ
καὶ τὸ γεγρα[μ]μέ|νον εἰϲ ᾽Αριάνθην τὸν | ᾽Αργεῖον "θεὸϲ θεὸϲ | πρὸ
παντὸϲ ἔργου | βροτείο[υ] νωμᾶι φρέ|να ὑπερτάταν" καὶ | τὸ εἰϲ Νικόδω-
ρον | τὸν Μαντινέα "κα|τὰ δαίμονα καὶ τύχαν | τὰ πάντα βροτοῖϲιν
| ἐκτελεῖϲθαι." τὰ πα|ραπλήϲια δ᾽ αὐτῶι || περι[έ]χει [καὶ τ]ὸ Μαν|τι-
νέω[ν] ἐνκώμιον. οὗτοι δὲ θεοὺϲ ἐν τοῖϲ |[ϲ]υνγράμμαϲιν ἐπο|νομάζον-
τε[ϲ] ἀνῃι|ρουν ἐξεργαϲτ[ι]κῶϲ | τοῖϲ πράγμαϲι[ν] καὶ με|τὰ ϲπουδῆϲ,
ἀ[νε]λευ|θερώτεροι γινόμε|νοι Φιλίππου καὶ τῶν | ἄλλων τῶν ἁπλῶϲ τὸ
θ[εῖο]ν ἀ[ν]αιρούντων.

So that I would indeed exclaim that they (viz., the Stoics) err worse than Diagoras. For he composed frivolously (if this is indeed his work and not spurious, as Aristoxenus says in his *Customs of the Mantineans*. Yet in the poetry which alone is considered genuinely to have been written by him, throughout he does not imply anything impious, but speaks piously, as befits a poet, about the gods, as is shown by other poems (*PMG* 738) addressed to Arianthes of Argos: "A god there is, indeed a god who preserves above every mortal deed a surpassing intellect;" and the poem addressed to Nikodorus the Mantinean: "By god and fate are all things brought to pass for mortals;" and similar things are to be found in his *Encomium of the Mantineans*). But they (i.e. the Stoics), while naming the gods in their writings, subtly and deliberately eliminate them in effect, thus being baser than Philippus[60] and those who deny the gods outright.

important things if one does not know nature in general, but instead ὑποπτευόμενόν τι τῶν κατὰ τοὺϲ μύθουϲ); Colotes branded Arcesilaus' ὁ περὶ ἐποχῆϲ λόγοϲ as a μῦθοϲ (Plutarch, *Against Colotes* 1124B); Heraclitus, *Homeric Allegories* 4.2-4 (Epic. fr. 229 Us., on which see the essay of Asmis in this volume, Chapter 2, above) states that Epicurus "purified himself of all poetry at one stroke as being a destructive lure of μῦθοι" (ἅπαϲαν ὁμοῦ ποιητικὴν ὥϲπερ ὀλέθριον μύθων δέλεαρ ἀϲοφιούμενοϲ), yet further charged that Epicurus stole his doctrine of pleasure as the goal of life from Homer, *Od.* 9.6-7, 11, thus attesting at least one myth credited in part by Epicurus; Colotes against Plato's myths ap. Proclus, *Commentary on Plato's Republic* 2.113, 116 Kroll, cf. Epic. fr. 229 (no διδαϲκαλία to be found in Homer's μῦθοι); Origen, *Against Celsus* 1.20 extr., where stories about the gods are referred to as μῦθοι κενοί. See also Philodemus, *On Signs* col. 38,11 with the De Lacys' note on the translation ad loc. (probably against Stoic appeal to myths). Cf. already Critias *VS* 81 B 6.10 γλώϲϲαϲ λύουϲιν εἰϲ αἰϲχροὺϲ μύθουϲ.   [59] *P.Herc.* 1428 cols. xi 5–xii 10; for the text see Henrichs 1974, 21–22.
[60] An atheist of unknown identity.

Diagoras' lyric hymns were not the only poems known to have been approved by Epicureans.[61] But the preference here for a particular *genre* as an acceptable, traditionally recognized mode of poetic speech in which to talk about gods, reflects Philodemus' interest elsewhere in the concept of genre and theory of literary kinds.[62] This same concern is evident in Philodemus' careful choice of a specific, single genre for his own poetic efforts: namely, elegant epigrams with generally non-technical, or ironic, satyrical philosophical content. No poetic genre could be further removed in tone and theme from the narrative, dramatic and lyric mythological poetry criticized in *On Piety*. This is not of course to say that Philodemus' epigrams are devoid of religious content. The festival celebration of the sacred Epicurean *eikades* is the subject of one of these poems.[63] And in another, Philodemus employs standard hymnic form to invoke Ino's son Melicertes, Leucothea (= Ino), a chorus of Nereids, Poseidon, Waves (*Κύματα*), and the Thracian wind Zephyr:[64]

> Ἰνοῦς ὦ Μελικέρτα cύ τε γλαυκὴ μεδέουcα
> Λευκοθέη πόντου δαῖμον ἀλεξίκακε
> Νηρήδων τε χοροὶ καὶ Κύματα καὶ cύ, Πόcειδον,
> καὶ Θρῆιξ Ἀνέμων πρηΰτατε Ζέφυρε,
> ἵλαοί με φέροιτε διὰ πλατὺ κῦμα φυγόντα
> cῷον ἐπὶ γλυκερὴν ἠόνα Πειραέωc.

Melekertes son of Ino, Leukothea the grey ruler of the open sea and divine averter of troubles, choruses of Nereids, Waves,[65] and you Poseidon, and Thracian Zephyros the gentlest of the Winds, graciously may you bear me safely across a calm sea in my flight to the sweet shore of Peiraeus.

This poem is well within keeping of Philodemus' remarks about the hymnic poetry of Diagoras discussed above, as it parallels the Epicurean defense of such traditional religious forms as prayer, oath, sacrifice, and mystery initiation elaborated by Philodemus in the first part of *On Piety*.[66] The Roman Lucretius may be an Epicurean

---

[61] In her treatment of Philodemus' attempt to rehabilitate Homer in *On the Good King According to Homer* for the political pursuits of its addressee, Asmis 1991b, 1–45 shows that Epicurus cited with approval Odysseus' words on poetry at the banquet at Phaeacia (*Odyssey* 9.5–11): see *Homeric Problems* 79 and 4 (= Epicurus fr. 229 Usener): ἄπαcαν ὁμοῦ ποιητικὴν ὥcπερ ὀλέθριον μύθων δέλεαρ ἀφοcιούμενος. According to the Lamprias catalogue, Plutarch wrote a treatise (now lost) entitled ὅτι παραδοξότερα οἱ Ἐπικούρειοι τῶν ποιητῶν λέγουcι (no. 143), though of course this does not necessarily mean that he attacked them for using quotations from the poets in support of their teachings, as he did the Stoics in his extant treatise by the homonymous title.

[62] In *On Poems*: Asmis 1992c; in *On Music*: classifcation of types of Greek poetry in Philodemus, *On Music* cols. iv 2–vii 22 (cf. x 6; xxxv 2) Neubecker, together with the repeated assertion there that only certain subjects, styles, and contexts of performance are appropriate to religious poetry as a genre.

[63] *Palatine Anthology* 11.44 (Philodemus, *Epigram* 27 Sider = 20 Gigante = 23 Gow and Page), discussed by D. Sider above, Chapter 4, where the text is given.

[64] *Palatine Anthology* 6.349 (Philodemus, *Epigram* 34 Sider = 16 Gigante = 19 Gow and Page). Text and translation from the forthcoming edition by D. Sider. For an historical, autobiographical reading of this poem (as the prayer of a philosophically naïve Philodemus, on the eve of his arrival at Athens to study with Zeno the Epicurean) see Gigante 1995, Chapter 3.

[65] For Waves as divinities (since "waves of Nereids" makes for an odd phrase) see Cicero, *On the Nature of the Gods* 3.51 (Gigante proposes χεύματα "streams").

[66] See Obbink 1989 (above, n. 16); Clay 1986.

anomaly in taking a dim view of prayer and sacrifice, just as he seems to command a virtually anomalous, exception-that-proves-the-rule status as the sole Epicurean expositor of acceptable Epicurean philosophical poetry. But Lucretius himself adopts a traditional hymnic prooemion for the opening of his own poem, perhaps in imitation of an important philosophical forebearer—Empedocles.[67] Lucretius' and Philodemus' hymnic invocations were apparently not heretical. Lucretius' choice of hymn for the opening of his Epicurean poem reflects not only current fashions in Hellenistic poetry, and the topicality of Empedocles and Hesiod in Republican Latin poetry, but also current Epicurean research stemming ultimately from Epicurus' own interests.

For this reason it is no surprise that the story discussed at the beginning of this chapter about Epicurus' anxiety over the meaning of Chaos in Hesiod, and his subsequent conversion to philosophy, carries with it a very respectable pedigree. It derives from no hostile source, eager to generalize Epicurean suspicions about the detrimental effect of mythological poetry on the idea of God in human history into a condemnation of poetry *per se*. For Diogenes tells us that it was related in the biography of Epicurus (Περὶ τοῦ Ἐπικούρου βίου) by the late second-century Epicurean Apollodorus.[68] Of course, this does not in itself mean that it is historically true: the anecdote could have been fabricated as part of the School's later tradition. It would be interesting to see the incident as part of an intellectual biography of Epicurus adopted by the School, charting a second sailing for the Master at around the ripe age of fourteen (much like the one that Socrates in the *Phaedo* outlines for his early career, after having read the books of Anaxagoras), exhorting the reader to an emulation of the Master's philosophic vocation after a studied consideration of mythological poetry. Such poetry occupies a curious position in the Epicurean syllabus. It certainly can not be said to be absent, as it is in Plato's philosophic utopia. The chance to scrutinize and criticize it in detail and to incorporate both it and its criticism allusively in one's teaching and writing (without specializing in either its grammatical analysis or its composition), will have attracted not a few, as it must have attracted Lucretius and Philodemus. In a curious reversal of Lucretius' famous image, it is the seductive enticement of philosophical learning which leads in the end to the sweetened cup of poetry.[69]

---

[67] So according to D. Sedley, "The Proems of Empedocles and Lucretius," *GRBS* 30 (1989), 269-96.

[68] Diogenes Laertius 10.2, with the commentary of Laks 1976, 37-38.

[69] Earlier versions of this paper were delivered at the Congresso Internazionale l'Epicureismo Greco e Romano in May 1993 and at Duke University Classics Department in March 1994. I am grateful to Myles Burnyeat, André Laks, and Cecilia Mangoni for useful discussion and much-deserved criticism.

11

The Impossibility of Metathesis: Philodemus and Lucretius on Form and Content in Poetry[1]

David Armstrong

All of us know well enough that the stars and the elements once had magical and divine qualities ascribed to them, and the sober sciences of "astronomy" and "chemistry" were difficult for any but the most determinedly scientific minds to separate from astrology and alchemy. That the mere elements of literacy, the letters of the alphabet themselves, were once equally involved with magic in the popular mind is not so familiar a thought. But, if we think of it, most of us have smiled at the derivation of the word "glamour" by which the medieval Scots expressed their awe at the magical science of *grammata,* and can remember, if we think of it, that "abracadabra" expresses the belief that the letters of the alphabet read in order cast a spell.

This belief is attested throughout the Greek, Roman, and medieval worlds. The occurrence of Greek alphabets inscribed on archaic shields from the sixth century B.C. onwards (just as the runic alphabet appears on the shields and swords of medieval warriors), and Latin alphabets inscribed round the walls of Pompeian houses, together with many similar phenomena, proves that the alphabet itself had from the beginning in popular belief a magical and apotropaic value.[2] Every student of ancient

---

[1] Nearly all my quotations are from book 5 (ed. Jensen, 1923, with the new column numeration of Mangoni 1993 given in parentheses) and Herculaneum Papyrus 1676 (= with other papyri, Sbordone, *Tractatus Tertius* in *Richerche sui Papiri Ercolanesi* 2, Naples 1976). Where I refer to Greenberg's discussion of some other fragment I have indicated its place in Sbordone's or other more recent publications of the texts.

[2] Cf. A. Dieterich, "ABC Denkmäler," *RhM* 56 (1901), 77–109; more fully F. Dornseiff, *Das Alphabet in Mystik und Magik,* 2nd ed. (Leipzig 1925). Dieterich points out with astonishment at the end of his article that the consecration of a Roman Catholic church in his day, according to the *Pontificale Romanum* of 1896, still included the solemn drawing on its floor in ashes with the bishop's crozier of the entire Greek and Latin alphabets in an X meeting in the middle at M (one remembers Diels' contemporary theory that *elementum* comes from LMN, the sacred center-point of the Latin alphabet), followed by a prayer forbidding Satan to enter the holy place and distract worshippers' thoughts. Cf. such comparable phenomena as the Orthodox Church's (still recited) Akathist Hymns to the Saviour and to the Virgin and many others whose alphabetical form, including sacred acrostics on the model of the even more ancient

magic knows that written charms of all periods often include the alphabet, or elements of it, rearranged in nonsense-combinations; and (more importantly) that the very fact of writing out a curse or *carmen* in letters makes it more permanent and noxious than merely uttering it in sounds.

Thus Plato's move of using the Greek word for a letter of the alphabet, cτοιχεῖον, first as a metaphor (τὰ πρῶτα οἰονπερεὶ cτοιχεῖα, *Theatetus* 201ε) and then as a regular word both for the elements of the material universe and for the letters as elements of speech—a move which was first imitated for the Latin word *elementum* in the first century B.C. by Cicero and Lucretius[3]—had for ancient readers a magical resonance we can only recapture by historical thinking. It makes the writer that arranges and combines these elements into coherent speech a godlike figure, an analogue of the Demiurge. Letters are like the minima of matter, Plato says in the *Cratylus*. From them, as a painting is made from simple colors, the intellect constructs first words and then organized discourse. "Having properly examined all these points [the nature of each of the letters], we will understand how to apply each with reference to fitness, whether we must use one letter to refer to one thing, or mix many together. Just as painters, when they wish to make a likeness, sometimes only use red and sometimes some other color and sometimes mix many together, when they are getting together an image of a human being or something else of that kind, so also we shall apply *stoicheia*, letters, to things, either one by one as required, or many together, forming syllables, as we call them, and from syllables nouns and verbs; and then again from nouns and verbs together forming something large, beautiful, and whole, like the living thing in my example of painting, so here a *logos*, by onomastics or rhetoric or whatever the art in question is." (*Cratylus* 424D5–425A5) So, in the metaphor Plato is here using, the *kosmos* or arrangement of a *logos* or literary composition is made to proceed from letters as minima, as something very like the geometrical elements of the *Timaeus*, and then from syllables and words as something like molecules; just as the painter arranges elements and combinations, first of pure meaningless color, then of small-scale units of drawing, by art to make a complete representation of a much larger whole.

According to Aristotle, this metaphor (without the word *stoicheion*) was equally familiar to the first atomists, Leucippus and Democritus. The crucial texts are from Aristotle:

(1) [Leucippus and Democritus] say the differences in the elements are the causes of all other qualities. These differences, they say, are three—shape and order and position. For they say that what is is differentiated only by "rhythm" (ῥυcμός) and "inter-contact" (διαθιγή) and "turning" (τροπή); and of those, rhythm is shape (cχῆμα), inter-contact is order (τάξιc), and turning is position

---

"Alphabetic Psalms" such as the 119th, still shows forth a reminiscence of the ancient protective magic of letters in the modern world.

[3] The classic, and still important, treatment of cτοιχεῖον and *elementum* is H. Diels, *Elementum* (Leipzig 1899); see also W. Burkert, "*ΣΤΟΙΧΕΙΟΝ*. Eine semasiologische Studie," *Philologus* 103 (1959), 167–97. For cτοιχεῖον the derivation from cτείχω is of course crucial to the symbolism: both the letters (considered as separate items just γράμματα) and the physical elements are thus given the character of members of a deliberately arranged row or series.

($\theta \acute{\epsilon} c\iota c$); for A differs from N in shape, AN from NA in order, and Z from N in position.[4] (*Metaphysics* 1.4, 985b12–19).

(2) Democritus and Leucippus, however, postulate the "figures," and make alteration and coming-to-be result from them. They explain coming-to-be and passing away by their dissociation and association, but alteration by their grouping and position. And since they thought that the truth lay in the appearance, and the appearances are conflicting and infinitely many, they made the "figures" infinite in number. Hence —owing to the changes of the compound— *the same* thing seems different to different people; it is transposed by a small additional ingredient, and appears utterly other by the transposition of a single constituent ($\acute{\epsilon}\nu\grave{o}c$ $\mu\epsilon\tau\alpha\kappa\iota\nu\eta\theta\acute{\epsilon}\nu\tau oc$). For Tragedy and Comedy are both composed of *the same* letters. (*On Coming into Being and Passing Away* 1.2 315b6–15: both translations from Barnes 1984: emphasis his).

As in the universe, so also in the poem. The whole can be radically changed by the *metakinesis*, or moving-round, or *metathesis*, the shifting-round in place, of a single *stoicheion*, or even more a single word, for "Tragedy and Comedy are both composed of *the same* letters." These passages have been treated mostly as evidence for the atomic theory, not the literary theory of the atomists.[5] But obviously, to the extent that the atomists directed their attention to the literary side of this analogy, there are implications for an atomistic poetics also.

In fact, these texts from Aristotle need not be taken alone. Did Democritus himself pursue this metaphor further as a literary critic, rather than merely using it to illustrate his physics? There is, to suggest that he did, the famous fragment 21 Diels–Kranz, that "since Homer's nature was divinely inspired, he succeeded in *building, as architect, a kosmos out of all kinds of words*" ($^{"}O\mu\eta\rho oc$ $\phi\acute{v}c\epsilon\omega c$ $\lambda\alpha\chi\grave{\omega}\nu$ $\theta\epsilon\alpha\zeta o\acute{v}$-$c\eta c$ $\acute{\epsilon}\pi\acute{\epsilon}\omega\nu$ $\kappa\acute{o}c\mu o\nu$ $\acute{\epsilon}\tau\epsilon\kappa\tau\acute{\eta}\nu\alpha\tau o$ $\pi\alpha\nu\tau o\acute{\iota}\omega\nu$). Instead of being a piece of elegant belletristic imagery (as it is often taken to be),[6] the fragment fits well with the theory

---

[4] $\tau\acute{\alpha}\xi\iota c$ and $\theta\acute{\epsilon}c\iota c$ $\tau\hat{\omega}\nu$ $\gamma\rho\alpha\mu\mu\acute{\alpha}\tau\omega\nu$ are used in this sense by Philodemus at *On Poems* 5 col. xxiv (xxvii) 21–25.

[5] Apparently Diels 1879 (above, n. 3), 14 was the first to suggest a kinship between Lucretius' analogy of letters and atoms (see below) and those cited by Aristotle from Democritus and Leucippus. For a more recent discussion of the passages from Aristotle see H. Wismann, "Atomos Idea," *Neue Hefte für Philosophie* 15–16 (1979), 34–52, arguing that Democritus' and Leucippus' atoms were considerably more mystical and less (in the modern sense) materialist entities, as one would expect from Pre-Socratics, than those of Epicurus. If that is so, the analogy they drew between atomic structure and the organization of (semi-corporeal) sound into (incorporeal) meaning and meaningful structure in language is all the more profound. The passages from Aristotle have also been discussed for their purely literary implications, first by J. M. Snyder, *Puns and Poetry in Lucretius' De Rerum Natura* (Amsterdam 1980) and more recently by Porter (n. 29 below) and Ivano Dionigi, *Lucrezio, le Parole e le Cose* (Bologna 1988, n. 36 below).

[6] Not only belletristic but inconsistent (because of its reference to inspiration) with his materialism. E.g. W. K. C. Guthrie, *History of Greek Philosophy* vol. 2, 477: "How one longs to know more about this remarkable man than the scattered remnants of his achievement allow! Did he permit his delight in great poetry to carry him away, and forget for a moment the strict rationalism of his theories?" *Immo vero.* Neither this statement nor Democritus' belief that poets create these *kosmoi* under the influence of inspiration and a $\acute{\iota}\epsilon\rho\grave{o}\nu$ $\pi\nu\epsilon\hat{v}\mu\alpha$ (B 17, 18, 21 Diels–Kranz) is inconsistent with his theory of the universe. After all we need not know any more about Democritus' "gods" than we do to know that he, like any

that he considered the metaphor useful for literary criticism. Homer is the divinely inspired *architect* of a *kosmos* built from all kinds of words, i.e., he is like what a creator god would be if there were one. If there are not all kinds of letters, there are at least, to parallel Democritus' theory of the infinite varieties of *ideai*, as he called his atoms, all kinds of *words*, ἔπη παντοῖα. (An Epicurean, by contrast, holds that the number of atomic shapes is limited, like those of the *letters*, which he can therefore use instead of words as analogues for how the universe is formed from atoms. This, as we will see, is the analogy Lucretius uses instead.) But both the *atoms* of letters and the *molecules* of words—for the early atomists, and as we will see, for the Epicureans of the first century B.C. like Zeno and Philodemus—are elements, *stoicheia*, from which the artist divinely inspired builds and arranges his unique *kosmos*. Thus we can see from the coherent unity of a poem, built up from small and themselves meaningless elements, by analogy how our own *kosmos* is constructed.[7]

If we ask what the ontological status of such an art of arrangement of letters and words into a grander order might be, we must appeal to the analogy of Democritus' description of music. Music to him is a recently developed art ἐκ τοῦ περιεῦντος, *ex abundantia;* that is, it is produced by the development of civilization and is not necessary to human life from its origins onward (fr. 144 Diels–Kranz, from Philodemus' *On Music*). However, it has natural origins in our primitive experience, namely of birdsong (154 Diels–Kranz), though even at that period and in its primitive simplicity it was not so necessary as the arts of weaving and mending we learned from spiders and of housebuilding we learned from swallows.

A similar story would no doubt be told of all the fine arts if we had Democritus' complete account of them.[8] Whether Epicurus copied this schema we have no idea. But since Philodemus' entire argument in his *On Rhetoric* is devoted to establishing that Epicurus either asserted or did not deny that there was a *techne* of rhetoric, it must be that he had something to say about the arts that acknowledged their existence and development.[9] So it seems most probable that Lucretius' account of the origin and

---

other pre-Romantic, thought that the godlike, including the inspired power of the poet to create an imaginary world of sounds, is in every way the reverse of what is disorderly or chaotic.

[7] In using the phrase κόσμον ἐπέων Democritus was borrowing from Parmenides (δόξας δ' ἀπὸ τοῦδε βροτείας / μάνθανε κόσμον ἐμῶν ἐπέων ἀπατηλὸν ἀκούων, B 8.52 Diels–Kranz) and Solon (who describes himself in the second line of his Salamis elegy as κόσμον ἐπέων ᾠδὴν ἀντ' ἀγορῆς θέμενος). But he has creatively changed the meaning of the word by combining it with the verb ἐτεκτή-νατο, which makes Homer an architect as well as a poet, and brings in the meaning "universe" as well as "ornament" or "poetic arrangement" which does not attach to κόσμος in the passages Democritus is imitating. I am grateful to Andrew Ford for suggesting these passages as relevant to my argument and to Diskin Clay for clarifying their relationship in the discussion afterwards. This fragment is not discussed in Jane M. Snyder's otherwise excellent catalogue of Democritean source material for Lucretius' analogy of *elementa* in physics with those in language and literature (Snyder 1980 [above, n. 5], 31=51): but other fragments show that Democritus did indeed like to rearrange letters so the almost-same was not *the same*. Cf. the pun μὴ μᾶλλον τὸ δὲν ἤ τὸ μηδὲν εἶναι, B 156 Diels–Kranz, or the etymology γυνή–γονή, B 122 (Snyder 1980 [above, n. 5], 47f).

[8] Plato, apparently echoing Democritus' definition in the words οὐκέτι τοῦ ἀναγκαίου ἕνεκα ἐν ταῖς πόλεσιν, gives a fuller catalogue of such arts: hunting and fishing, painting, music, and practioners such as poets and rhapsodes, actors, dancers, cosmeticians (*Republic* 373B).

[9] The best conjectural account of what this might have been is in Asmis 1991a; she notes (cf. Asmis 1992b,158) that there is no evidence for Epicurean speculations on poetics between Epicurus and Zeno of Sidon, but thinks it plausible that they existed. I would not disagree. An interesting text by the undated

development of the arts in *On the Nature of Things* 5, which is in essence the same as that of Democritus, has the sanction not only of the School but probably of its founder.

Lucretius agrees with Democritus about music in both points. We find in 5.1379–1415 that man learned vocal music from the birds and wind instruments from the music of the winds, and that these in a simple form were the pleasures of rustic festivals. But now that civilization has come, our sophisticated *vigiles musici* (probably now *poetae*) keep to the same measures (i.e., use the same hexameters, iambs, and so on) as were used in primitive times: Lucretius is conscious that the very meter he writes in is age-old.[10] But they take no more pleasure in their sophisticated and slaved-over poetry than the first men enjoyed in their simple instinctive verses. It is only that "better things discovered later on change and spoil our feelings for all the

Epicurean Diogenianus (cited in Eusebius for several opinions) seems to have dropped out of the debate currently. It presents a line of argument not in Philodemus so far, but paralleled by his insistence (see below) that poetry imitates the speech and thought of those in between the totally uneducated and the truly wise, and that poetry need give only the appearance of truth, not the reality, to succeed. Diogenianus is arguing against Chrysippus' ascription of philosophical wisdom to Homer: "And it is quite in keeping for the poet, who does not promise to tell us the truth about the nature of things, but imitates the characters and experiences and opinions of all sorts of people, to say things that are contradictory; but it is not in keeping for the philosopher either to say contradictory things or for this very reason to use a poet as evidence" (Eusebius, *Praeparatio evangelica* 6. 8.7).

[10] Surely then this must be the correct interpretation of *vigiles* in *On the Nature of Things* 5.1408:

1405	et *vigilantibus* hinc aderant sollacia somno,
	ducere multimodis voces et flectere cantus
	et supera calamos unco percurrere labro;
	unde etiam *vigiles* nunc haec accepta tuentur
	et numerum servare genus didicere, neque hilo
1410	maiorem interea capiunt dulcedini' fructum
	quam silvestre genus capiebat terrigenarum.
	nam quod adest praesto, nisi quid cognovimus ante
	suavius, in primis placet et pollere videtur,
	posterior fere melior res illa reperta
1415	perdit et immutat sensus ad pristina quaeque. (5. 1405–1415)

See the two notes from the variorum edition of Havercamp ("1408 *Vigiles*: *Castrenses intelligo*, Faber; *Ego vero curis aegros*; *ut* 1405 *Vigilantibus*, Creech." Creech's would seem obviously the better interpretation; cf. Rolfe Humphries: "men who must keep awake"). Unfortunately, following Faber, Munro, Bailey, Costa and other commentators say flatly that *vigiles* are civil or military watchmen. These notes are nonsense. What would make the watchmen's street or camp cries at night, the ancient equivalent of "twelve o' clock and all's well," artistically so much superior to the whole musical armory of early man beguiling *his* own sleeplessness at night? Or how could these watchmen be required to know anything about meter ("numerum servare genus")? If we are dealing with the Hellenistic idea of *vigilata carmina*, like Lucretius' own claim *noctes vigilare serenas* in writing poetry, *On the Nature of Things* 1. 142 (cf. most recently Rudd on Horace *Epistles* 2.2. 54 *ni melius dormire putem quam scribere versus*), the entire passage is much clearer. The argument continues, after all, that so also we gave up eating acorns (for the art of cookery) and grass and leaf couches (for furniture) and beasts' skins for purple robes and gold, none of which feed us better or make us more comfortable or warmer at least according to the mere needs of nature, and merely provoke wars between us for more possessions to boot (5.1416–1435). Therefore the *vigiles* of today, though some of their musical or poetic measures are the same as of old, must offer us something of great elegance, comparable to purple vs. skins, elegant furniture vs. grass and leaf couches, etc. They must then be *vigiles poetae,* the composers of much more intellectually structured, i.e., *vigilata, carmina* than those of primitive man.

old things" (5.1414–1415). Apparently Lucretius means both music and poetry by *carmina* in this passage, and compares the sophistication of Hellenistic poetry, as much as of Hellenistic music, with the simplicity of early times. If so, he held the same theory of poetry's status as a civilized art that came into being *ex abundantia* as he did of music's status.

Certainly it goes a certain distance to support this conclusion that Lucretius tells us the invention of poetry as we know it came shortly after the discovery of both cities and commerce and of the *elementa* or letters:

> iam valides saepti degebant turribus aevum
> et divisa colebatur discretaque tellus;
> tum mare velivolis florebat †propter odores,†
> auxilia ac socios iam pacto foedere habebant,
> carminibus *cum res gestas* coepere poetae
> tradere: *nec multo prius sunt elementa reperta*. (5.1440–5)

So for Lucretius, as for Democritus, the essence of civilized poetry is no longer oral, or sonic, but to be found in the play of written letters, *elementa,* on the page. It is reasonable, therefore, to investigate how the Epicurean intellectuals of the first century may have expanded these hints from the atomists to account for the status and nature of the fine arts and poetry in particular, and the sort of civilized intellectual pleasure they can give the wise man.

Lucretius in his sketch of the origin of arts in Book 5 seems to fill out a Democritean pattern, fully authorized by Epicurus, by which they are divided into those primitive and necessary for life and those that are adornments produced by the progress of civilization. Lucretius' contemporary, Philodemus of Gadara, in the surviving fragments of his treatises on music, rhetoric, and poetics does not discuss origins at great length (though in *On Music* he cites Democritus' theory of the origins of music ἐκ τοῦ περιεῦντος, in civilized elaboration and not in necessity, with evident approval). What he has to say, however, still agrees with Lucretius' implication about all three that they are *artes ex abundantia.* If Lucretius takes at least his own poem seriously as protreptic, philosophical, and educative, he still sees modern *carmina* as this kind of "unnecessary" art, and poetry as a refinement of speech basically inconceivable without letters, writing, and a written record. Philodemus similarly sees no reason to take any of the three as anything but self-regarding arts whose moral and intellectual content is to be seen as non-existent or secondary, and whose proper pleasure is a purely intellectual one, unnecessary but harmless, which lies in understanding and appreciating their arrangement of material for and in itself.

To music Philodemus denies—as did many composers of the dodecaphonic school, and many theoretical music analysts of the Schenker school, in our own century—any moral or emotional value. All such ascriptions are for him purely subjective, usually an illusion created by the accompanying text and not really inherent in the music. But music is an art. In *On Rhetoric* (vol. 1 pp. 10,33, 17,24, 40,18 Sudhaus) Philodemus everywhere concedes it the status of a precise art, a *techne*, or *episteme*, producing exact results which pupils in turn can be taught to produce; but in *On Music* he compares it, significantly, to the art of cookery, the prime example to him, as to Lucretius, of a civilized pleasure developed from and superadded to a natural or necessary one.[11] A pure art, therefore, of arranging tones and rhythms into a structure complete in itself, and one to whose definition emotional and moral effects are superfluous.

Music is thus a purely formal art, with no appeal to the intellect (except perhaps in the study of how to produce it, which Philodemus ranks very low as a science), and no mimetic value at all: it is a pleasure of the senses and like them is ἄλογος, irrational, and ἀκοῆς μόνον, belonging to the sense of hearing alone.

Rhetoric, Philodemus claims even more audaciously, though an art, is an art neither of political science nor of persuasion (though cf. above, p. 186), because political science and persuasion need not achieve their ends by rhetoric and are consequently not part of the definition of it; also because the truest form of rhetoric is epideictic, that is belletristic display-prose, in which politics and persuasion are not in question, only entertainment. Still (though his master Zeno of Sidon had been blamed for going beyond what was authorized by Epicurus' words in saying so) rhetoric *is* an art, and a real one. It is only, however, the art of arranging words in ways beautiful and striking in themselves.[12]

Philodemus' definition of *poetry* has a family similarity to the other two which is most striking. Poetry, unlike music, *is* an imitative art and to the full extent language can imitate, τὸ μιμούμενον ὡς ἐνδέχεται (*On Poems* 5 col. xxiii [xxvi] 13–15). But here too, moral usefulness does not get us to any satisfactory definition, for poetry may be good poetry and have none, or be positively damaging from a moral point of view, or quite contrary to fact and false in its statements: it makes no difference (*On Poems* 5 col. i [iv] 1–21). Even if certain poems do contain things profitable to read, it is not *as poetry* that they profit us: κἂν ὠφελεῖ καθὸ ποήματ' οὐκ ὠφελεῖ (*On Poems* 5 col. xxix [xxxii] 17–20).[13] And at any rate poetry is powerless to finish perfectly the technical exposition of any scientific subject it takes up: that is the business of prose (*On Poems* 5 col. i [iv] 21–31). Faithfulness to truth is not a criterion of the good poem; for nothing prevents there being truths which it profits us nothing to know (like Homer's arming scenes, or, one instinctively adds, many of the subjects of Philodemus' own chosen genre as a poet, the epigram). But they can be made into good poetry nonetheless (*On Poems* 5 col. ii [v] 6–11). Philodemus is not impressed by Aristotle's or his successors' feeling that mythical subjects somehow represent reality better than history: "Why is it necessary to represent reality (τὸ πραττόμενον) clearly and briefly, when many things not simply false but purely

---

[11] Music is no more a *techne* involving ethics or mimesis *than cookery*, Philodemus claims: *On Music* 4 col. iii 24–35 Kemke; cf. v 25. But certainly that too implies that music is a *techne*. Cf. the account of his theory in Warren Anderson, *Ethos and Education in Greek Music* (Cambridge 1966), 153–76. It is probably not an accident that in the surviving texts of *On Poems* Philodemus twice compares poets to cooks (Tractatus Tertius fr. xi 1–8, cf. Greenberg 1955, 121 with n. 128, 155 with n. 26; above, 156f. with n. 49). The metaphor is used, slightly altered, to good effect by Horace (*Epistles* 2.2.58–64) in the character of a host trying to please all his guests with different poetic food. This may well be another instance of Philodemus' influence on Horace. It startled Porphyrio (*mire iam dramatico charactere tamquam ad ipsos convivas loquitur, unumquemque eorum appellans id poscentem, quod ceteris displicet*), who had no access to its source.   [12] Cf. the valuable summary in Grube 1965, 199–204.

[13] Similarly, Philodemus says in denying any ethical or mimetic value to music οὐδὲν μέλος καθὸ μέλος, ἄλογον ὑπάρχον, ψυχήν . . . ἐγείρει (*On Music* 4 col. iii 5ff. Kemke).

mythical are represented in the poets?" he asks, in refutation of a critic who was inclined to prefer didactic subjects to mythical ones (*On Poems* 5 col. iv [vii] 6–13), and at the same time making clear his indifference to Aristotle's excuses for myth: only the illusion of truth is necessary to poetry. The coherence of a poem's plot—if it is a work of fiction that has one, which it need not be—is not in question or part of the definition of poetry either; that too it might as well share with prose. Nor can the *definiens* of poetry be *any* other characteristic which could as well apply to prose— clarity, concision, vividness, etc.[14] Nor are the secrets of poetry to be found in some such hierarchical or teleological theory of genres as Aristotle's in which epic and tragedy hold the highest place: poetry in essence is the same in all genres, and rigid distinctions between them are impossible.[15]

Nor is poetry beautiful because its music appeals to the mere irrational sense of hearing: it is *not* an irrational or sensual pleasure produced by mere music that we find in poetry, but a purely intellectual pleasure, one not appreciated by the ear but by reason, λόγῳ (*On Poems* 5 col. xx [xxiii] 21–xxvi [xxix], xxiii [xxvi] 29–xxiv [xxvii] 11).[16] Nor is Hellenistic learning essential to good poetry, for many good poets (including Philodemus himself, to judge from both his prose and his verse) possessed it and many did not. Nor is knowledge, study, and imitation of great models any essential criterion of poetry or the poet, otherwise where would Homer and Sophocles have found a way to begin? (*On Poems* 5 col. xxx [xxxiii] 24–32).

The chief positive elements of Philodemus' definition are three. First, what is *considered* good poetry *is* good poetry. An Epicurean can have a secure *ennoia,* or general perception of common truth, of this fact which he shares with all (educated) mankind, and any definition by which what are called good poems, Homer's especially, are "bad"—because they disagree with ethical, scientific, or other truth—must fail.[17] The person who takes these "good" poems for granted as part of the canon may know two further things. One is that the "fixed goal," as Philodemus emphatically calls it, of poetry is (*On Poems* 5 col. xxiii [xxvi] 1–7) τῆι | μὲν λέξει τὸ μ[εμι]μεῖ-c|θαι τὴν ὠφέλι[μα] προc|διδάcκουcαν, τῆc δὲ δι|ανοίαc τὸ μεταξὺ μετ[εcχη]|-κέναι τῆc τῶν coφῶν | καὶ τῆc τῶν χυδαίων, "in the words, to imitate perfectly that diction which contains useful teaching *in addition* (i.e. to being attractive: so far as I can find, the preposition in προcδιδάcκειν is never simply redundant)[18] and to

---

[14] See the excellent reconstruction of *On Poems* 5 col. iv (vii) 13–25 in Mangoni 1988, and her discussion of parallel passages.

[15] Greenberg 1955, 125–29, 175–76: "Philodemus has attempted to show that the various genres are not rigidly distinguished and that the poetic element is common to them all. Hence, one may seek general criteria for the excellence of poetry, without regard for the individual genres of poetry. This last is the program of Book 5 . . ." (p. 129). But cf. above, p. 208f.

[16] Philodemus argues this point forcefully and at length against two enemies, the *kritikoi* who thought the pleasure of beautiful sounds the quintessence of poetry and paid as little attention as possible to the thought, and Crates of Mallos, who radically divided the judgment of these same beautiful sounds from the content, both arguing that the trained hearing is judge; see Greenberg 1955 *passim* and particularly his summary at 273–75. I agree with Porter 1989, 153 and 156, that the dative (of means) λόγῳ is in fact contrasted to judgment by the irrational ear in *both* passages. For the second passage see the objections of Asmis 1992b, 153 n. 33.   [17] Cf. Greenberg 1955, 271.

[18] "which incidentally teaches the beneficial" (Greenberg 1955, 83). But note that poetry should only *imitate perfectly* or *successfully* (that must be the sense of the perfect infinitive) this sort of instructive speech; it need not be in fact beneficial.

keep perfectly to a mean between the thoughts appropriate to the wise (or philosophical) and the thoughts appropriate to laymen." Philodemus is highly emphatic about
this ("and that's so," he continues, "whether any particular person thinks so or not,
and people *have* to criticize with this in mind"). This can apparently be cashed out as
saying that poetry has the air of instructing us in—no matter what—as long as it
draws us in by the promise of telling us something to experience its peculiar pleasure;
for there is in fact "*qua* poetry (καθὸ πόημα) no natural usefulness either in its
speech or its thought" (*On Poems* 2 col. xxii 30–xxiii 3 Janko). Poetry has necessarily, therefore, a subject it imitates by mimesis, and we are made to feel we learn about
this subject in experiencing the poem. But in reality Lucretius' celebrated metaphor
about the cup is reversed: the apparently "useful" things are in reality only there to
draw us in to the enjoyment of the poetry, and the cup is smeared with instruction that
we may be made to drink the honey of the poem itself. Or an imitation of instruction,
at least, for in Philodemus' view the poetic version of any subject will only be
instructive or accurate (if at all) to a degree appropriate to lay speakers and lay hearers, not professional students of philosophy or any other topic. There, as Michael
Wigodsky argues in Chapter 5, is the essential difference between him and Lucretius;
though probably even Lucretius would have claimed no more than a protreptic value,
not that of technical philosophical perfection, for his poem.

As for the poem itself, Philodemus' third and most distinctive doctrine is that if
it does not necessarily involve the hard work of Hellenistic learning and study
(though he was of course himself as learned as any Alexandrian critic or poet of his
age), its poetry must be very elaborately worked on, in and for itself. The thought
must be communicable, and not boringly technical like a scientific treatise (e.g.,
mathematics), but "the choice of expressions and their *careful arrangement for the
purpose of presenting clearly a specific rational content*" (*P.Herc.* 1676 fr. xi 19–24)
is the proper task of the poet. Their arrangement is not for the ear, but for the mind,
and the whole must be experienced as something so unified that it makes irrelevant
the attempt to separate its composition at the level of single lines, the poetry or
ποίημα, in practical criticism from the consideration of its arrangement as a whole,
the poem or ποίησις. As he puts it, "anyone who assumes that the thought of the
poet is unchanged if a different verbal idiom is used praises or blames it at random
(εἰκαίως)."[19]

Philodemus is willing to be so radical on this point as to claim that any treatise
simply dividing the subject into poetry, poem, and poet is wrongly conceived from
the outset. To Philodemus, the third division, the poet, is mostly an illusion: the poet
and his training are only visible to be criticized in the poetry and poem anyway. More
crucially, even where such a division is convenient, these subjects will continually
"bleed" into each other: for the whole poem is like a web or tapestry (οἷον ὕφη) of
which the separate bits of poetry are the small parts or "works" (ἔργα).[20] In a crucial

---

[19] *P.Herc.* 1676 Tractatus Tertius fr. ix 22–28 p. 237 Sbordone [ἤ]με[ῖ]ς δὲ τὸν | δ[ε]χό[με-
ν]ον ἀμετάθ[ε]|τ[ο]ν [ἄλλ]ης ϲυνηθεία[ϲ | ὑ]παρχ[ούϲ]ης τὸν νο[ῦν]| τῶ[ν] π[ο]ητῶν, εἰκ(αίωϲ)
|[ἐ]παινεῖν ἐροῦμεν ἢ [περι]|κόπτειν.

[20] *On Poems* 5 col. x (xiii) 32–xii (xv) 6. Perhaps Philodemus means something more like ἐργαϲίαι
by this last word at col. xi (xiv) 15 ("workings out," that is of individual passages), cf. LSJ s.v. ἔργον 3b
and the use of ἐργαϲίαν at col. xi (xiv) 20.

text which has fascinated critics for decades,[21] it develops that style and content are reciprocals, ἴδια, of each other in Philodemus' view:

> It is amazing of (Neoptolemus) to claim that only the subject belongs to *poesis*, when the *poema* and everything else in general belong to it; for the (entire) *poesis* is also "poetry," for example the *Iliad*, but the first thirty lines of it are "poetry," but not a *poesis*: and that only the composition (cύνθεcιc) of the diction belongs to "poetry," [but not the?] . . . thought . . . action and character-drawing; but if he claims anything is perfectly composed (πεποιῆcθαι) in the diction, even there it is impossible for it to be perfectly composed apart from these things, but the composition (cυγκεῖcθαι) of the action seems to me a function (ἴδιον) of the composition of the diction (*On Poems* 5 col. xi [xiv] 26–xii [xv] 14).

This striking statement is paralleled by declarations that sound and sense can never be criticized apart, and must be criticized by reason, not by irrational sense-perception such as that of beautiful sound apart from meaning, just as it was *logos* and intention in the poet that united them to produce their effect on the mind: "Either it is reasonable (πρὸc λόγον, a play on Philodemus' view that the senses are ἄλογα) that the words acquire their meaning through hearing, or it is true that one must praise the thought (διανοούμενα) in poetry (ποήμαcιν), and not, when we praise the composition (cύνθεcιν), rip that bodily apart (ἀποcπᾶν) from the content (τῶν ὑπο-τεταγμένων)" (*On Poems* 5 col. xxv [xxviii] 33–xxvi [xxix] 7). For Philodemus' poetics sound, at first hearing, New Critical. But they are innocent of the Coleridgian distinction between the mechanical fancies of the intellect and the subconscious, organic inspiration of the imagination in which New Critical theories of organic unity in works of art originate. They are wholly intellectualist and intentionalist (as Greenberg 1955, 176 puts it, Philodemus refutes all non-intellectual criticism of poetry in favor of the view "that the poet can deliberately and consciously compose effective poetry"). In that sense, strikingly modern as some of his intuitions about the esthetics of poetic form can seem, Philodemus' aesthetic theory is entirely classical.

Moreover, in the discussion of poetic borrowing which takes up the first half of *P.Herc.* 1676 (Sbordone's Tractatus Tertius), Philodemus makes it clear that there is no sense in speaking of *the same* subject, when treated by two different poets, because every individual treatment makes the subject itself different and *idion* to its creator. This is said in several different ways, but in particular at *P.Herc.* 1676 Tractatus Tertius col. v 26–vi 27 p. 251f. Sbordone, a passage which exemplifies Philodemus' occasional bursts of genuine eloquence and personal conviction in the

---

[21] A text which has been considerably altered by recent examination: Mangoni 1991, 76f. The passage I translate now reads (Mangoni 1993, cols. xiv 26–xv 14): θ[α]υμα[cτὸ]ν δ' αὐ|τοῦ καὶ [τὸ] τῆ[c] ποήcεω[c]| εἶναι τ[ὴ]ν ὑπόθεcιν [μ]ό|νον, καὶ τοῦ ποήματο[c καὶ]| πάντων ὅλωc τῆc ποήc[ε]|ωc ὄντων· ἡ μὲν [γ]ὰρ πό|ηcιc καὶ π[όημά γ' ἐcτιν,]| οἷον ἡ Ἰλι[άc], οἱ δ[ὲ πρῶτοι]| cτίχοι τρι[ά-κ]οντα τα[ύ]τηc | πόημα μ[έ]ν, οὐ μέντοι ποί||ηcιc· καὶ τὸ πoή[ματοc μό]|νον τὴν [cύνθεcιν τῆc] λέξεωc μ[ετέχειν ......]|νac διανοί[αc ......]| καὶ πράξειc καὶ [προcω]ποποιί[αc]. εἰ δ' ἐν [τῆι]| λέξει πε[π]οιῆcθαί [τι | λέ]γει., κἀνταῦ[θα νή Δι' οὐ]|κ ἔcτι τι πεποι[ῆcθαι το]ύ|των χωρίc, ἀλλ' [ἴδι]ο[ν το]ῦ | cυνκεῖcθαι [τὴν] λέξιν τὸ | cυνκεῖcθαι ⟨τὴν⟩ [πρᾶξ]ιν εἶ[ν]αι φαίνεταί μ[οι.] See also Chapter 12 below, where this text is discussed.

middle of pages and pages of prose so careless as to sound like a seminar transcribed from shorthand notes of his teaching as given *viva voce*. I give the Greek, indicating restorations and doubtful letters; but the restorations are (one may hope) not all that doubtful (the papyrus has twice been edited carefully, by Heidmann and by Sbordone).

[τὸ] τοίνυν τοὺc | ποητὰc τὰ[γα]θὸν παρ' ἐτέ|ρων λαβόντας καὶ πάνυ (ca. 3–4 words missing) [τὴν c]ύνθε[cιν μόνην ἰδίαν]| ἐργάζεc[θαι, καὶ τὸ τὴν μὲν | ἐπιφαι]νομένην [ε]ὐφωνί|αν ἴδιον [εῖν]αι, τὰ δὲ νοή|ματα καὶ [τ]ὰc λέξειc ἐκτὸc | εἶναι καὶ κοινὰ cυνάγεc|θαι δεῖ[ν, πα]ρὰ πᾶcι μὲν ὡc | ἐν [cτήλ]ηι μέ[ν]ει τοῖc κρι|τικοῖ[c], βλεπο[μ]ένην δ' ἔ|χει τὴ[ν ε]ὐηθί[α]ν (scripsi: ἀλ]ηθί[α]ν edd.) ἐκ τῶν | εἰρημένων· φωνὴν μὲγ | γὰρ οὐδεὶc ποητὴc εἴcχυ|cεν ἐν[πο]ῆcαι τοιαύτην, | δυνα[μέν]ην εἰc τὴν φύcιν | τῶν ὄ[ντων] παρ[αφέ]ρειν· | τε[. . .]c διαν[. . .]c ἀλ|λ' οὐδ[. . .]cε²² καὶ τὴν χύ|cιν τῶ[ν] λέξεων τοῦ βί|ου χορη[γ]ο[ῦ]ντοc ἡ cύνθε|cιc ἰδ[ία γε]ίνεται τῶν πο|ητῶν, οὐ καίριοc οὐδ' ἐπαι|νουμένη καθ' αὐτήν, ἀλ|λ' ὅτι π[ρο]-cπαρίcτηcι διαν[οί]|αc, αἷc ψ[υ]χαγωγοῦcιν, οὐ | παρά τινοc λαβόντεc, ἀλ|λ' αὐτοὶ γεννήcαντεc πα|ρ' α[ὐτ]ῶν .

And with regard to the statement that the poets appropriate what is good in them from others, and entirely (*ca. 3–4 words missing*) and create only the composition as their own, and that the beautiful sound that is revealed is their own, but the thoughts and words are things supplied externally and must be considered common property, this statement is as it were written on stone for all the *kritikoi*, but it follows from what we have said that its absurdity²³ is obvious. For on the one hand no poet has ever had the power to create such a sound as would compare with the nature of real things; but it is only after life itself²⁴ has supplied them with (*several words missing*) and mutual coherence of their thoughts and the fluency and copiousness of their expressions that the poets' composition becomes truly their own, not felicitous nor praiseworthy in and of itself, but because it establishes in addition to itself (*prosparistesi*)²⁵ the thoughts with which they command our attention, not taking them over from some other person, but generating them from within themselves.²⁶

---

²² My reading in lines 16–17 from autopsy is τε[. . . . .]c διαν[. . .]c αλλουδ[. . . .]cε. But O supplies ιω after ουδ (not in N; cf. Sbordone ad loc.).

²³ I read (and verified) ε]ὐηθί[αν here, a favorite word in Philodemian polemic, and not the usual ἀλ]ηθί[αν, since the traces of the upsilon are clearly visible on the *disegni* reproduced by Sbordone.

²⁴ The translation of part of the opening phrase of this sentence, in Greenberg 1955: "when the poet, like a chorus-master of life" (164) is wrong; but Greenberg has correctly appreciated that this is a crucial passage to Philodemus' theory (275–6).

²⁵ Mistranslated and taken as plural in Greenberg 1955, 162 "since (poets) also require the thoughts in order to effect psychagogy." προcπαρίcτημι is quite rare, and this use not recorded in LSJ. But cf. προcδιδάcκουcαν at *On Poems* 5 col. xxiii (xxvi) 1–7, discussed above with n. 18.

²⁶ Text after Heidmann, *CErc* 7 (1977), Romeo 1992b, with the clarification of my new reading (see n. 22). Romeo, who reports that ἀλληλουχία can not be read in lines 16–17, supplements: τέ[θηκε τὰ]c διαν[οία]c ἀλλ' οὐ δ[ιώικη]cε, "the adversary has laid down thoughts but not disposed them rationally." But the absence of any δὲ after the μὲν γάρ of lines 11–12 makes me hesitate to adopt this.

The grandeur of style of which Philodemus is occasionally capable[27] shows nowhere more clearly than here. Intentionalist as his poetics essentially is, it does not envisage the possibility, either for the poet or for the critic, of *separating* the style from the thought or the subject in any way or at any level. For style to Philodemus, and this is the most distinctive difference between his theory and those of the other ancient critics, has no virtue of its own apart from the whole of which it is part. Once they have been through the poet's mind and become his own handiwork, the thought and subject as well as the style are then entirely his own, and to call the subject the identical thought or subject if it is written up in a different style is entirely superficial. Sophocles' version of a legend and Euripides' are not two treatments of the same subject,[28] though it may be convenient (*grosso modo*) to put it that way, but poems on two different subjects that are not *the same* any more than are their words.

Philodemus is certainly willing to apply this principle at the molecular, and probably also at the atomistic level. No surviving passage does more than suggest that he held Democritus' doctrine about transposition of letters affecting meaning and the whole, as we will see Lucretius does.[29] Philodemus' criticism of Crates' views on what effect the arrangement of letters and their *metatheses* may or may not have on poetry was contained, he tells us, in the second book of *On Poems* (col. xxvi 8–18). Our current fragments give us little clue to Philodemus' own view so far. But we can know one thing about what it must have been. He so vociferously objects that *no* aspect of poetic arrangement, including this aspect most particularly, offers us mere irrational and sensuous pleasure, that he must certainly have considered that the proprieties of letter-arrangement and effect, like those of word arrangement, are to be judged by the reason, λόγῳ, and have impact instead on the content and the thought; just as he argues the smallest rearrangement of word-order also does.

Thus the second half of the Tractatus Tertius is devoted entirely to attacking what Philodemus considers the plausible but erroneous practice of *metathesis,* that is, showing the excellence or lack of it in a passage of poetry by rearranging the *words* and considering how the passage has been made worse in rhythm or sound. Philodemus believes that the thought is always somehow affected. The question comes up, he says, "what it is that comes about from the *metathesis* by which we are pleased or

---

[27] Philippson rightly points out several such striking passages in his article "Philodemos," *RE* 19.2 (1938), 2444–82 at 2476.

[28] Cf. Greenberg 1955, 140–43: I agree with Jensen that this passage is Philodemus' own opinion and not one he is quoting, though the thought is not unique to him.

[29] He discusses in Tractatus Tertius col. vi 27–vii 17 a *kritikos* who admired the "euphony" of the (otherwise unknown) verse Κέριφος ἅλμῃ πόντια περίρρυτος, where one notices that the last word contains all the consonants (including the rough breathing) of the first, but objects that one's feeling (πάθος) refutes this, presumably because the expression is too pompous for the insignificant little island: see the discussion in Greenberg 1955, 168–69. This only shows that Philodemus, who uses much word and letter play in his own verse, considered it failed the equally important test of meaning, so that no ψυχαγωγία results. On Poems 5 col. xxiv (xxvii) 22–29, πλὴν | γὰρ τοῦ διαφόρους τῆι θέ||[c]ει καὶ τάξει τῶν γραμ|μάτων προσπίπτειν | φωνὰς οὐδέν ἐcτιν | πρὸς ἀκοήν, ὅ[περ οὐ]δεὶς | ἂ[ν] εἴπειε διάκ[ρις]ιν | τῆς ἐν ποιήματι φυσι|κῆς διαφορᾶς, "except for the fact that sounds fall on it that are *different by the placement and arrangement of the written letters*, there is nothing for the hearing which anyone could call a judgment of natural differences in poetry") is discussed in Porter 1989, 153–60. The "natural differences" are a theory of Crates' but the other words represent Philodemus' own view, even according to Porter's thesis, and are so discussed by Asmis 1992b, 153–54.

displeased with the effect" (*On Poems* Tractatus Tertius col. vii 18–21 p. 255 Sbor-
done) τίνος cυμ[βαί]|νοντος ἐκ τῆ[ς μ]εταθέ|cεως οἰκειού[μεθ'] ἢ δυc|χεραίνο-
μεν) "on which mode of criticism I will speak offering characteristics of the whole
process, not busying myself with the thing itself alone" (loc. cit. lines 21–25 ὑπὲρ οὗ
τρό|που τοῦ παντὸς λα[λ]ή|cω χαρακτηρικὰ παρα|διδούς, ἀλλ' οὐ περὶ αὐτὸ |
τοῦτο γινόμενος). [30]

He knows, he says, that people can offer very many different rearrangements
(ἐναλλαγαί) in the verses of Homer and Sophocles; but even here he will in every
case argue that not only the order of words but the thought itself is altered, either in
emphasis or clarity or by the introduction or abolition of some ambiguity, or even if
none of that seems plausible, that the spoiling of the meter or the greater difficulty
introduced in pronunciation and delivery will affect the thought's ability, not just the
sound's, to make its full impact on us. (*P.Herc.* 1676 Tractatus Tertius cols. xvii 2–
xviii 5).

Philodemus' doctrine, then, goes even farther than to claim Sophocles' and Euripides' *Oedipus* are simply not on *the same* subject. Indeed, Sophocles' *Oedipus* with
any verse metathesized, that is with *the same* words metathesized, would not be *the
same* poem because the thought would have been changed, not just the order of
words; and the composition can never be praised apart from the composition of the
whole. [31]

Naturally this way of looking at the unity of a poem may seem to stem ultimately
from the *Phaedrus*' doctrine of organic unity [32] (as also from Democritus and from
the passage of the *Cratylus* quoted at the beginning of this chapter). But we can see,
by comparing it with Aristotle's attempt to take over this Platonic doctrine, how
different and characteristic of atomism Philodemus' working out of it is, and why it
owes more to Democritus' analogy of the building up of a poetic *kosmos* from letters
and words. In developing Plato's doctrine of organic unity in literature for his own
purposes Aristotle uses, indeed, the same verb *metatithenai* in the *Poetics* as Democritus had used for the transposing of elements that creates a different whole from the
same elements: but he is apparently talking of very large elements of the poem,
perhaps when whole scenes when he says at *Poetics* 8.1451a33–4 that the πράγματα
must so arranged that μετατιθεμένου τινὸς μέρους ἢ ἀφαιρουμένου διαφέρεcθαι
καὶ κινεῖcθαι τὸ ὅλον. His discussion of style gives no hint that what he considers
essentially the same sentiment, transposed in some single verse into different words,
would affect or be relevant to the whole. But Philodemus is militant that this happens. For Philodemus the thought or the subject in different words is simply not *the
same* but a different subject or thought. This, I think, Aristotle would never have said.
But two hundred intervening years of hard Hellenistic study of poetry word by word

[30] Philodemus believes that poetics is a matter of general principles, not anthologies of illustrative
examples discussed for themselves (though he occasionally cites examples also): cf. Greenberg 96–9.

[31] Cf. Greenberg 1955, 275–76, and his "Metathesis as an instrument in the criticism of poetry,"
TAPA 89 (1958), 262–70 at 265–67.

[32] Cf. especially the criticism of the verses on the tomb of Midas which can be rearranged without
any damage (οὐδὲν διαφέρει πρῶτον ἢ ὕcτατόν τι λέγεcθαι) because they are bad poetry (*Phaedrus*
264D).

resulted in Philodemus' being able to take a much more radical and fundamental view of what constitutes the unity of a poem.[33]

In my view, then, Philodemus' doctrine of poetics is more or less the same as that of Democritus, a coherent and organic exposition with obvious analogies to the atomist universe. He holds that poetry, like music and rhetoric, is a civilized art, an art of words, in which the proper pleasure (whatever information or emotional experience we may be given as a by-product of the art) is the appreciation of arrangement and unity built up (as in the universe) from the tiniest elements into a coherent whole. Its proper pleasure is an unnecessary but unforbidden one, in Epicurean terms: that of intellectual appreciation of beauty of form. Philodemus is unambiguous about this: poetry is appreciated λόγῳ, by reason, not by what he continually calls the irrational (ἄλογος) ear. One should remember that the status of the λόγῳ θεωρητόν (provided it is correctly understood) in the Epicurean intellectual universe is ontologically quite high. This rational pleasure is not that of learning morally or intellectually useful truth; therefore it can reside only in the appreciation by the trained critic of poetry's coherence. So also our appreciation of rhetoric is that of understanding the cleverness with words are arranged for epideictic show, and (no doubt) our appreciation of music comes, not from emotional catharsis or inner moral harmonies produced in us or disturbed, but simply from appreciation of the coherence of pure rhythm and sound. Perhaps Philodemus would have said, as Lucretius says of music, that the primitive hearers of poems, e.g., of Homer, may have experienced no less pleasure than the professorial intellectual and critic he conjures up as the "trained" hearer of poetry; but that is what the pleasure of poetry is for civilized and intelligent hearers, that of watching a unique *kosmos* of meanings grow up from the untransposable arrangement of its words.

Philodemus may well have expanded and added to this doctrine, but it is certainly in outline older than himself. In assessing its possible impact in the history of literary criticism it is of the highest importance to point out that in its complete form it probably was elaborated by his and Cicero's brilliant teacher Zeno of Sidon in the previous generation. Strictly speaking we only know from Philodemus' *On Rhetoric* that Zeno held that it was orthodox for Epicureans to believe that rhetoric was an art, though only a literary and not a political art, and that in Zeno's generation this roused controversy with other Epicureans outside Athens who considered that the Master gave no hint this was so. It has seemed obvious to most scholars, however, that Zeno also is responsible for Philodemus' theory that rhetoric is the art of neither politics nor persuasion, but of "pure" belles-lettres. This in turn seems organically connected in form with Philodemus' similar views on music and poetics, and these are therefore likely to originate with Zeno also.[34] We know, in fact, that Philodemus did consult a treatise of Zeno's, perhaps the περὶ ποιημάτων χρήςεως, for his poetics, at least for

[33] Here I should say that I find it impossible, though I have learned much from this article in details, to agree with James Porter's main thesis (Porter 1989), that Philodemus' poetics are *not* atomistic, in contrast to Crates', which are; cf. Asmis 1992b, 154 n. 35.

[34] Sedley 1989 has most recently discussed Philodemus' dependence on or allegiance to Zeno, arguing indeed for a near-total lack of originality in Philodemus' arguments where any doctrine learned from his master is concerned. This view may go a little beyond the evidence but not much.

various anonymous views he refutes at the end of the fifth book (*On Poems* 5 col. xxvi [xxix] 19–23, cf. Greenberg 1955, 93f.), though that does not absolutely prove Philodemus owed the substance of his own views, as I believe, to Zeno also. Zeno would then be the one to have taken hints from Democritus, where he found none in Epicurus, when asked to speculate about the place of music, rhetoric, and poetry not merely in the historical development of the arts but in the current studies of the Epicurean school, and to have expanded them into a coherent theory of his own. We know that Philodemus taught the literary men of the generation of Horace and Vergil (Varius and Tucca, Quintilius Varus, Vergil, probably Horace also) at his school in Naples.[35] In my opinion his view both of the accidental and arbitrary nature of poetry's moral teaching (perhaps good, but that is in no way essential), and of the crucial role of word-arrangement, had its impact on them. If I am right in ascribing Philodemus' atomist poetics in outline to Zeno, it will have had its impact on the generation of Lucretius, Catullus, and Cicero no less.

Diels found in a passage of Cicero's *On the Nature of the Gods* (2.93–94) an argument that the Democritean metaphor of the universe as an arrangement of atoms–letters was revived in Cicero's youth and violently critized by Posidonius, the most probable source of this part of Book 2: "If a man thinks it can happen that a *kosmos* arises in all its order and beauty from the fortuitous concourse of atoms, I do not understand why the same man should not think that if innumerable of the twenty–one forms of letters, of gold or some other material, were collected somehow, one could dump them all onto the ground and a legible copy of the *Annals* of Ennius would result, though I hardly believe fortune could bring it about even to the extent of one verse . . . ." No doubt Posidonius used the *Iliad* for his example instead, but we seem to hear here his criticism of the Democritean analogy (atoms–letters, *kosmos*–poem) as revived in his own day *by Zeno* (just as we know from Proclus' commentary on the *Elements* of Euclid that Posidonius refuted with violent indignation Zeno's criticisms of Euclidean geometry).[36] In this case, the metaphor and most of the whole theory I have outlined will have been as well known to Lucretius as to Philodemus himself: it will have been the poetics of the contemporary Epicureans at Athens, though not Epicurus' own, since he almost certainly had none. Posidonius'

[35] The evidence for Philodemus' personal, philosophical, and poetic influence on Horace and his contemporaries has long been known and discussed (though not with particular reference to the *Poetics*): cf. e.g. G. L. Hendrickson, "An epigram of Philodemus and two Latin congeners," *AJPh* 39 (1918), 27–43, and Tait 1941. Therefore there is especial delight in finding that Tucca, Varius, Quintilius, and Vergil are all addressed by name in a newly-deciphered passage of Philodemus (Gigante and Capasso 1989, 3–6), giving new life to Servius' theory that Vergil, *Eclogue* 6 is an allegory of Vergil and his friends at the Naples school; and that Philodemus owned both an Ennius and a Lucretius, the latter a handsomely written presentation copy (Kleve 1989 and 1990).

[36] Diels 1899 (above, n. 3), 1–14 showed that it is very improbable Epicurus himself used the Democritean metaphor of the *kosmos* of letters and words formed by a poem, and that it is more likely that the Epicureans of Posidonius' own time had revived it—as I would argue, in their effort to supply Epicureanism with a positive theory of poetics which had previously been lacking. Posidonius' criticism stuck in the ancient mind, to judge from Plutarch, *Moralia* 399e (where the literary work to result from the fortuitous concourse of letters is ironically the *Kyriai Doxai*). Perhaps Zeno's original mentioned words along with letters as elements from which the poetic *kosmos* is formed, to judge from Longinus ap. Proclus *In Timaeum* 42, where the criticism occurs that the atoms can no more form a cosmos by themselves than various *words and expressions* (ὀνόματα καὶ ῥήματα) can form a speech (λόγος).

objection brings to mind the still much discussed analogy of the monkeys, the type-writers, and *Hamlet*; and one might imagine Lucretius and Philodemus replying that one gets a certain amount of meaning out of both nature and poetry—but not immortality and not salvation from care and pain.

Everyone knows what would then be at stake: that the striking theory of Paul Friedländer, worked out so much further and in such detail by Jane Snyder in her *Puns and Poetry in Lucretius'* De Rerum Natura (Snyder 1980), is essentially correct and fully justified by Philodemus' text as well as Lucretius'. Most important in this context is Lucretius' own sturdy doctrine of the impossibility of metathesis in poetry, which is involved (to a degree for which there is only conjectural evidence in Philodemus) with the arrangement not just of words but also of letters of the alphabet.[37] Since Paul Friedländer brought out this feature of Lucretian poetics in 1941[38] it has become increasingly a commonplace of Lucretian criticism that the poet is considering the words he arranges into verses on his page consciously, as something like molecules made of separate atoms which are the letters of the alphabet. These are limited in number of shapes as the atoms of Epicurus were (and those of Leucippus and Democritus were not), but capable of immense though not infinite varieties of combinations. The analogy is one as old as atomism itself.

For Lucretius, there is the discussion of Snyder 1980, 31–51 (Chapter 2: "Lucretius' Analogy of the Elementa"). She discusses the progressive implications of the five striking passages in Books 1 and 2 that bring up the analogy of letters of the alphabet (*elementa*–atoms): 1. 196–98, 799–802, 907–914, 2.688–699, 1013–1021. For her thesis, that Lucretius' poetry is full of puns and respelled words, her discussion is entirely adequate.[39] But that this theory is full of implications for the larger unity and coherence of a poetic *kosmos* built of such literary atoms–elements–letters, and that Lucretius is alluding directly to the impossibility of the same kind of metathesis as Philodemus deplores, she does not bring out. So we shall cover the same ground with that in mind.

In the first of these passages, Lucretius merely argues that it is as logical to suppose that there are many *elementa*, atoms, common to things, *res*, as it is that a

---

[37] That Philodemus could speak, using atomistic language, of how letters strike the hearing as different in arrangement and placement ($\tau \acute{\alpha} \xi \iota c$ and $\theta \acute{\epsilon} c \iota c$), at the same time objecting (against Crates) that it is not the hearing but the $\lambda \acute{o} \gamma o c$ that judges what Crates called the "natural differences" ($\phi \upsilon c \iota \kappa \alpha \grave{\iota} \delta \iota \alpha \phi o \rho \alpha \acute{\iota}$) in poetry, is clear from *On Poems* 5 col. xxiv (xxvii) 13–xxv (xxviii) 4: so Porter 1989, 159–60 and Asmis 1992b, 53–54.

[38] Paul Friedländer, "Pattern of Sound and Atomistic Theory in Lucretius," *AJPh* 62 (1941), 16–34. Cf. David West, *The Imagery and Poetry of Lucretius* (Edinburgh 1969), 94–114, though it seems a pity that West thought first of Varronian etymology as a reference point and only secondarily of the atomistic analogy as a justification for the "puns" he finds (97).

[39] A recent writer has much expanded this discussion: J. Ferguson, "Epicurean language-theory and Lucretian practice," *LCM* 12.7 (1987), 100–104. Snyder herself has interestingly demonstrated the validity of her theory for Philodemus' own surviving poetry, which is full of significant play on words and letters: "The poetry of Philodemus the Epicurean," *CJ* 68 (1973), 346–53. Dionigi 1988 (above, n. 5) carries this study still further, and to great effect; the doubts such Lucretius scholars as West, Dalzell and Schrijvers have expressed about Snyder's and Friedländer's thesis seem to me to be put out of court by his arguments. I would only add that the discovery of a copy of Lucretius in Philodemus' library adds to the probability that his and Lucretius' poetics were not any more radically different than the rest of their philosophy.

few letters make up many different words in his verses (*On the Nature of Things* 1.196–98):

> ut potius multis communia corpora rebus
> multa putes esse, ut verbis elementa videmus,
> quam sine principiis rem ullam existere posse.

This is a brief and simple statement of the comparison, yet it brings out the connection *elementa–verba–res* clearly enough. The second is more elaborate. If one could take away a few atoms, Lucretius argues, and add a few others, and change their order (801 *ordine mutato*) and motion, fire would become air (799–802). It is therefore of great moment in what order the atoms are bound up, and with what others; for *the same* atoms *form* sky, sea, land, rivers, sun, crops, trees, living animals (820–821):

> namque eadem caelum mare terras flumina solem
> *constituunt*, eadem fruges arbusta animantis

"but only when mingled and moving with different things in different ways. Indeed scattered abroad in my verses you see many letters common to many words, and yet you must needs grant the verses and words are unlike both in sense and in the ring of their sound. So great is the power of letters by a mere change of order" (and *they* do not even have motion, Lucretius implies):

> quin etiam passim nostris in versibus ipsis
> multa elementa vides multis communia verbis,
> cum tamen inter se versus ac verba necessest
> confiteare *et re et sonitu* distare *sonanti*:
> tantum elementa queunt permutato *ordine solo*. (823–827)

It will be noted that Lucretius, like Philodemus, makes metathesis affect not just sound but also meaning (*et re et sonitu*).

In the third passage, Lucretius is explaining fire (897ff.). Now though *ignis* is not really inside *ligna, insitus lignis,* the seeds of heat are there. This proves that:

> permagni referre eadem primordia saepe
> cum quibus et quali positura contineantur
> et quos inter se dent motus accipiantque;
> atque eadem paulo inter se mutata creare
> *ignis* et *lignum*; quo pacto verba quoque ipsa
> inter se paulo mutatis sunt elementis,
> cum *ligna* atque *ignis* distincta voce notemus. (908–914)

This is no mere pun, but a crucial doctrine of Lucretius' of central importance to his whole theory of the poetic use of language, and is echoed in dozens of word plays of a similar kind throughout the poem.

The fourth passage, 2.688–699, does not add much to the doctrine except to emphasize the *similarities* in words in verses instead of, as in the third, the *differences*, as an analogy to the make-up of things from atoms. But the fifth and last Lucretian passage seems to us most of all the five to insist on the impossibility of the least metathesis, as something changing the *res* themselves. It is of great importance how the letters occur in his verses, for the same ones *signify* sky, sea, land, rivers, sun, crops, trees, living animals. He quotes himself, from the earlier passage, but changes the verb now from "form," *constituunt,* to "signify," *significant,* echoing also the important phrase *ordine mutato* from 801. What happens in the cosmos at large is in every way analogous to what happens in literature:

> quin etiam refert nostris in versibus ipsis
> cum quibus et *quali sint ordine* quaeque locata;
> namque eadem caelum mare terras flumina solem
> *significant,* eadem fruges arbusta animantis;
> si non omnia sunt, at multo maxima pars est
> consimilis; verum positura discrepitant res.
> sic ipsis in rebus item iam materiai
> concursus motus ordo positura figurae
> cum permutantur, *mutari res quoque* debet.

In letters, then, as in atoms, the *positura* is everything and can not be changed, for then the *res* themselves will be altered. More factors, indeed, enter into the changes of matter that are caused by the motion of its elements in addition, but otherwise the analogy of literature and atoms is perfect. Most importantly, at 2.1004–22 he emphasizes that though all things are created from like atoms, the order or arrangement is crucial, as in Philodemus: for "even in my verses it is important how each letter is combined with others, and in what order it is placed . . . for though the letters are alike, it is by position and placement the things or subject, *res,* sound different: *positura discrepitant res.* So also in *res,* material things themselves, when joinings, motions, orders, positions, shapes—*concursus, motus, ordo, positura, figurae*—change, the *res* themselves must alter—*mutari res quoque debent.*" This passage is parallel with Philodemus' contention that the thought is always altered by the rearrangement of the words. Lucretius shows that he knew as well as Philodemus that subject, *res,* and style, *verba* and *versus,* are inseparable functions one of the other. Compare his doctrine, quoted earlier, that poetry is a first-fruit of the invention of the written alphabet at a relatively high stage of civilization—that its graphic form is essential to it—and the outlines of a fully stated Epicurean–atomistic theory of poetry, worked out in cold prose by Philodemus as in poetry by Lucretius, are before us.[40] But Lucretius is equally adamant that the meaning and thought are always altered by the mutation, not just the sound.

---

[40] The atomists (if my contention about them is correct) were not the only ones in antiquity to read a kind of mystical analogy of the world into the symbolism of the alphabet; ancient elementary education, with its disproportionately long time spent on learning the alphabet and the possibilities of its combination into syllables, produced this kind of thinking as a natural result. ". . . no wonder," says H. Marrou, *History of Education in Antiquity,* trans. George Lamb (New York 1956), 211 "a kind of religious awe surrounded these first 'elements'–cτοιχεῖα! (The letters of the alphabet, it must be remembered, were used for figures and musical notes as well.) As samples of this religious awe, the historian will note with interest the strange belief that the letters of the alphabet were symbolic of the 'cosmic elements,' the seven vowels being associated with the seven notes of the scale and the seven angles presiding over the seven planets; they were thus used to make charms and amulets, for since they had the marvellous power to reveal man's thoughts they must be full of a mysterious magic potency." (211).

These passages add up to more, then, than mere legitimating texts for a search for word-play and etymological play and play with rearranged letters forming different words, like Snyder's or F. M. Ahl's in his *Metaformations* (see below, with n. 44). Justified as both these scholars are in seeing such techniques in Lucretius, is Lucretius to be taken seriously as saying like Philodemus and in Philodemus' sense that these metatheses affect the whole structure of discourse, the entire *res* that arises from the *verba* of poetry and is bound up with it? Certainly Friedländer (1941, above, n. 38. 132), no New Critic, is betrayed at the end of his article into thinking just that way:

> Another Tennyson could imagine the Roman poet haunted by the crowd of sounds, smooth or harsh, struggling and craving for each other, cajoling or wounding the ear, deceiving or telling the truth, forming words, and words into verses, and verses into the most extraordinary poem of Rome.

Here Friedländer has without effort laid down a view of Lucretius' doctrine of the metathesis of letters within words and verses which entirely parallels Philodemus' doctrine of the fusion of style and subject to the point that metathesis of words would damage the meaning and through it the whole poem, not just the play of letters within it. As Horace puts it in the passage Prof. Oberhelman and I analyze below in Chapter 12, that would give us a *disiectus poeta*.[41] It seems to us that the family relationship of these two doctrines is not coincidental. Epicureanism supplied an aestheticist and formalist point of view on literature (or at least what a modern would call by those names) that both Philodemus and Lucretius shared, and which influenced Lucretius, Horace, and Vergil quite as deeply as Callimachus and the Alexandrians influenced them. Lucretius gives us this theory as it relates to metathesis of letters, Philodemus' surviving text only as it relates to metathesis of words. But both are true Epicureans in that they appeal to a concept of surface textuality, and hidden appropriatenesses and deeper significances of both meaning and form beneath it, which is the literary analogy of atomist doctrine in physics.

Metathesis, then, turns out to be a key-concept in an atomistic poetics which exhibits important points of analogy with many modern systems of criticism. But we know that Zeno was one of the few Epicureans who showed profound originality in developing the Master's doctrines, and in refuting those of other schools; thus his refutations of Euclid, as von Fritz shows in his interesting *RE* article on Zeno, were not mere carping, but foreshadowed however casually (he did not bother to develop them systematically) the founding insights of post-Euclidean geometry in the nineteenth century. No longer able to appeal to universally accepted values as a measure of the worth of poetic discourse (Philodemus, unlike Aristotle, could not do this amid the skepticism and syncretism of his own day, the first century B.C.), such critics turned to readings of texts-in-themselves for their subtexts and their intertextualities

---

[41] Indeed, Friedländer is not in the least hesitant to conjecture that not only Philodemus' but even Democritus' doctrine in his lost Περὶ εὐφώνων καὶ δυςφώνων γραμμάτων (B 18b Diels) dealt in basically the same terms as does Lucretius with the importance of metathesis of letters to meaning; Friedländer 1941 (above, n. 38), 30 n. 25; cf. Snyder 1973 (above, n. 39), 46–51. If this is so, that would be one more indication that before Lucretius, Zeno of Sidon had had recourse to Democritus to fill out an Epicurean-atomist poetics.

with other texts, in short to purely aesthetic considerations of form and of thought as they exist solely to benefit the poem καθ' αὐτό, in itself.[42] It is evident to me from this exploration that, if Philodemus' theories had been available to him (and really they have only been securely available to talk about since Sbordone's texts were published in 1971 and 1976), Saussure would have found his exploration of letter-play and word-play in Latin poetry a far less maddening experience.[43] Saussure was certainly investigating something that happens in poetry to make metathesis impossible, the presence of what he called hypograms—respellings, re-presentations of all the letters, of some important word, so that the alliterations and assonances are generated by key-words in a passage—in pursuit of something Philodemus too wanted to discover, namely *differentia* of poetic speech that would show once for all why poetry is so much more artistic and so much more dependent on the exact form of its own words for its effect than any prose, even the most elaborate, can be.

This was a worthwhile effort, and that Latin poetry deals in this sort of thing and in quantity no one can doubt. What has now been so extensively shown for Lucretius by the authors cited above, and for Latin poetry in general in the pioneering study of F. M. Ahl,[44] is brilliantly indicated in an example sent Saussure in 1908 by one of the few scholars who sympathized with his investigations, A. Meillet. It is from Horace, *Odes* 4.2.1–4:

> PINDARUm quisquis studet aemulari,
> Iulle, ceratis ope Daedalea
> NItitur PINnis vitreo DAtuRUS
> NOmINA ponTo.

---

[42] Asmis 1992b elucidates very strikingly the theory of poetry as inherent in pure sonic effect held by Crates, as yet another variety of the same kind of purely formal, aesthetic and value-neutral criticism of poetry practised by Zeno and Philodemus themselves. One might have expected *a priori* that much Hellenistic criticism of the arts would be in this vein.

[43] For a description of Saussure's fascinating exploration of Latin anagrams, see Jean Starobinski, *Les mot sous les mots: les anagrammes de Ferdinand de Saussure* (Paris: Gallimard 1971), trans. Olivia Emmet as *Words upon Words: the anagrams of Ferdinand de Saussure* (New Haven 1979). I refer to the translation. Cf. particularly ch. 5, "In Pursuit of the Proof," 97–123, a hilarious account of Saussure's difficulties in getting other scholars to take his investigations of anagrams, or as he called them hypograms, in Latin poetry seriously. Crucial to understanding the history of perceptions like Saussure's in modern literature, linguistics, and psychology is M. Pierssens' difficult but rewarding study *La tour de Babil* (Paris 1976), trans. C. Lovitt as *The Power of Babel: a study of logophilia* (London 1980).

[44] F. M. Ahl, *Metaformations: Soundplay and wordplay in Ovid and other classical poets* (Ithaca 1985). Again, as in West's case (West 1969, n. 38 above), it seems a sadly missed opportunity that the author bases his theoretical exposition on Varronian etymology, and not in Epicurean atomism, which alone of ancient theories of language discards the fiction that such play is etymological in the strict sense of the word. So few of Ahl's excellent examples really imply etymology, which is a diachronic process, rather than a synchronic relation between words and letters present in the same text. This perception of related significance on a synchronic level is, I think, really at the heart of ancient "etymology" anyway, and belies its fiction of a temporal process of linguistic development; this seems to me to be excellently pointed out by Pierssens 1980 (above, note 43), xii: "To ["paragrammatism"] we owe the *eradication of a conventional punctuation of time,* from Cratylus to Virgil . . . an eternal present of the sign is invented, forever borne by languages" (my emphasis). The ancient "etymologists" are not really thinking historically, but in terms of the same kind of magic of letters and meaning as is analyzed by the writers quoted in n. 2 above.

Not only is PINDARUS in the third line, but the other name of the addressee in the vocative, ANTONI, is in the fourth, as Meillet noted;[45] and, as Meillet did not note, there is a delightful evocation of the idea of the names themselves *collapsing into the sea* along with the over-ambitious poet. Meaning supports the play. Any rearrangement, as Philodemus (and Lucretius) postulate, would affect and damage the thought, not just the sound.

Whether, indeed, one could ever stop finding such effects by merely looking in Horace "at random" is the question. Two examples of types of word arrangement and letter arrangement whose effect (I think) no one could fail to acknowledge as intentional are pictorial word-order (or what L. P. Wilkinson calls "metaphor from word-order"[46]) and emphasis of key-words at the end of a line by spelling them out before they appear. The first phenomenon is unusually frequent in Horace, e.g. the mixing of words to indicate the mixing of the music of lyre and winds in:

> sonante mixtum tibiis carmen lyra,
> hac Dorium, illis barbarum (*Epode* 9.5–6),

or Maecenas as Horace's endangered friend trapped among the triremes in:

> ibis Liburnis inter alta navium,
> *amice,* propugnacula (*Epode* 1.1.1–2)

or the moon shining out among the stars in:

> velut inter ignis
> *luna* minores (*Odes* 1.12. 47–8).

or, just from the very first Ode, the Marsic boar bursting through the smooth net:

> seu rupit teretes *Marsus aper* plagas (*Odes* 1.1.28)

and the frightened sailor surrounded by the Myrtoan sea:

> Myrtoum *pavidus nauta secet* mare. (*Odes* 1.1.14).

The second, a kind of exquisite hypogram by which the last line of a word is prepared and delicately emphasized (there are many other kinds in Horace), seems not to have been studied much, but is frequent, and obvious enough when pointed out; e.g.:

> ARTE MATERNA RApidOs <u>MORANTEM</u> (*Odes* 1.12.9)

> OMNE capax mOvet urNa <u>NOMEN</u> (*Odes* 3.1.16)

> THEssalO viCTORE ET adEmpTus <u>HECTOR</u> (*Odes* 2.4.10)

> PortUS aLEXandrEa <u>SUPPLEX</u> (*Odes* 4.14.35)

Or even, very beautifully, twice in succeeding lines:

---

[45] Starobinski 1971 (above, n. 43), 127. Meillet added: "The whole *p* grouping is striking, and the intertwining of Pindarus and Antoni. Found simply by looking into the text *at random.*"

[46] *Golden Latin Artistry* (Cambridge 1963), 65f. He illustrates it with Lucretius' wonderful *qui capite ipse sua in statuit vestigia sese* at *On the Nature of Things* 4.472, and Horace's entwining of Achilles' human and divine natures in *invicte mortalis dea nate puer Thetide* (*Epode* 13.12).

QUis TE REdonaviT QUIRITEM
dis patriis itALOQuE CAELO (*Odes* 2.7.3–4)

This is not the place to give exhaustive lists of examples; but clearly Horace thought of his poems as mosaics of unrearrangeable words and letters building up complex thought pictures; clearly this sort of thing results from his study of Philodemus' and Lucretius' poetics. This is what he meant not just by the discussion of word-order in *Satires* 1.4 but by the lines in *The Art of Poetry* about *callida iunctura*:

dixeris egregie, noTum si callida verbum
reddiderit iunctura noVum (*The Art of Poetry* 45–6)

where he makes the whole thought depend not simply on the placement of words but of the changing of a single letter within them. From such small elements are built up such secure, solid, and stable poetic wholes: *tam obscura de re tam lucida carmina pangit.*

Pierssens' book (see n. 43) shows that the recognition of the possibilities of anagram and hypogram and "paragrammatism" for the creation of strange subtexts and the subversion of surface meaning has seemed to many modern poets and theorists almost like a manifestation of insanity and madness.What I think is most attractive about the Epicurean poetic I have been attempting to recover from Horace, Philodemus, Lucretius, and the atomists is that it apparently looks to these poets and philosophers merely like one more manifestation of the poetic process, subsumed under the purely artistic theory that a poem is in all its details the one right, self-consistent way to say something. That rightness extends all the way down from the level of *poesis* to the very minima of expression at the level of *poema*, including not just the arrangement of the words but that of the letters, in an order not just musically but intellectually rewarding and significant. Paragrammatism on significant keywords, and word-order indissoluble by metathesis, and arrangement of a whole work in Plato's organically flowing and indissoluble order of topics, are plainly to them merely three aspects of the poet's work that contribute to each other; one feels no air of madness or paradox or deconstruction of the universe in Horace's or Lucretius' pictorial word-orderings or their elegant paragrammatisms. The poet is always in control; in modern terms, his effects down to the smallest level are produced by a poetic that can only be understood as completely intentionalist. Perhaps the difference in their enthusiastic reaction to such a doctrine and that of the modern poets and intellectuals Pierssens describes is accounted for by the fact that the subtext of the world presented by modern atomic and particle physics was still new, terrifying, and unsettling earlier in this century; whereas that presented by Democritus, Leucippus and Epicurus was hundreds of years old in Lucretius' and Horace's day; and paragrammatic "etymologies" and the notion of letters as semi-animate entities with a strange faculty for forming realities of their own were hundreds of years older in Greek literature than the atomists themselves who drew the analogy.

I conclude by saying that I have always wished that a doctrine of poetics that corresponds more nearly to what I understand to be the compositional practice of actual ancient poets than most previously known ancient literary criticism could be extracted from the remains of antiquity. We would then be less reduced to describing in terms of our own theories of composition and literary unity the coherence and deep suggestiveness of ancient poems, uncomfortably supposing that these virtues were achieved by their creators out of mere instinct and a feeling for the fitness of things. If my argument is right and not mere wish-fulfillment, the Herculaneum papyri have given us this doctrine. Horace and Vergil, for example, learned from Philodemus' school a theory justifying and encouraging their uncanny ability to arrange in indissolubly perfect order the letters, sounds, words and verses of their poems into a greater whole. They learned from Philodemus that the intellectual appreciation of this arrangement and order was the source of the true pleasure of poetry. They learned that poets create an utterly different *kosmos* of words on an utterly different subject every time they write about what to a superficial glance are *the same* shepherds, *the same* faithless lovers. Their subject might or might not have instructive or moral implications; that was indifferent. For "instructing" the reader about early Rome, about the virtues of Aeneas or Augustus, or about the dissolution of their own latest unhappy love affair was only an accidental by-product of poetry, the result of its being an imitative art which has by consequence to imitate something. Thus, Philodemus taught them, they were not so much responsible for the "truth" of their presentation (though a certain kind of non-technical "truth" may as well be found there as not, and may, though it need not, instruct the reader in addition), as for the perfection of its form in the smallest detail and the coherence of every detail with larger effects. Much, I think, about their attitudes and their beliefs about the question of "sincerity" in poetry may be explained on this theory. Certainly the common points between the poetic theories of Zeno, Philodemus, Lucretius, and Horace deserve to be studied at much further length.[47]

[47] In this article I am deeply indepted to the work of Nathan Greenberg, especially Greenberg 1955 (diss. Harvard, only recently made available to the general public). There is much need for an updating of the translation given in this book of all the significant fragments of Philodemus' *On Poems* known to that date, in view of later work and new readings in the papyri. But its exposition of Philodemus' views is superb and surprisingly little outdated by thirty-five years of further work on the text. Besides the translation, Greenberg's exposition has two more great virtues: of summarizing a great deal of German and Italian work devoted not so much to the exposition of Philodemus' views, but his opponents', in admirably clear, concise, and logical form; and of presenting a still unrivalled and remarkably cogent exposition of Philodemus' system in and for itself. It is not too much to say that if this work had been published thirty-five years ago, Philodemus' *On Poems* would have been the subject of a much livelier scholarly debate in recent decades. Since I first gave a version of this paper in 1989, Elizabeth Asmis has further elucidated book 5 and other texts from the *On Poems* both textually and philosophically. So also the recent issues of the Cronache Ercolanesi, with the splendid work of (in particular) Constantina Romeo, Cecilia Mangoni, and Richard Janko on the *On Poems,* Daniel Delattre on the *On Music* and Jürgen Hammerstaedt on the *Rhetoric* have added much to our knowledge. And the next decade will obviously add much more. But it is clear from these discoveries that Greenberg and other earlier researchers already appreciated the *general* nature of Philodemus' Epicurean aesthetics correctly. Some crucially important additions to our knowledge of the text, especially in book 5 of the *On Poems* that I have utilized are: those recorded in Porter 1989; Mangoni 1991; Romeo 1992b, in which along with many excellent new readings and conjectures a number of Jensen's overambitious reconstructions are shown to collapse before the evidence of autopsy and the *disegni* combined. I was able to consult Cecilia Mangoni's authoritative new text (Mangoni 1993), which appeared as this volume was going to press, and to incorporate her already published readings. I am very grateful for the assistance and criticisms of Dirk Obbink, Richard Janko, and my students at the University of Texas at Austin (especially Ned Tuck and Victor Caston); remaining errors are entirely my own.

12

Satire as Poetry and the Impossibility of Metathesis in Horace's *Satires*

Steven Oberhelman and David Armstrong

The Text: *Satires* 1.4.38b–62

38   . . . agedum, pauca accipe contra.
      primum ego me illorum dederim quibus esse poetas
40   excerpam numero; neque enim concludere versum
      dixeris esse satis; neque si qui scribat uti nos
      sermoni propiora, putes hunc esse poetam.
      ingenium cui sit, cui mens divinior atque os
      magna sonaturum, des nominis huius honorem.
45   idcirco quidam comoedia necne poema
      esset quaesivere, quod acer spiritus ac vis
      nec verbis nec rebus inest, nisi quod pede certo
      differt sermoni, sermo merus. "at pater ardens
      saevit, quod meretrice nepos insanus amica
50   filius uxorem grandi cum dote recuset,
      ebrius, ac, magnum quod dedecus, ambulet ante
      noctem cum facibus." numquid Pomponius istis
      audiret leviora, pater si viveret? ergo
      non satis est puris versum perscribere verbis,
55   quem si dissoluas, quivis stomachetur eodem,
      quo personatus pacto pater. his, ego quae nunc,
      olim, quae scripsit Lucilius, eripias si
      tempora certa modosque, et quod prius ordine verbum est
      posterius facias, praeponens ultima primis,
60   non, ut si solvas "postquam Discordia taetra
      Belli ferratos postis portasque refregit,"
      invenias etiam disiecti membra poetae.
63   hactenus haec: alias iustum sit necne poema
64/65   . . . quaeram . . . hoc genus scribendi.

Horace rejects the title of poet. He does not himself possess the natural talent, inspired soul, and voice that utters the grand style.[1] His satires are so *sermoni propiora* (42a) that not only are they are not true poetry (*iustum . . . poema*, 63b) but, if the word-order is transposed and the metrical constraints removed, only prose would remain (53–62). Furthermore, satire, like comedy, falls into the middle of a hierarchy of genres: mimes and fables (*Satires* 10.5bff.) occupy the lowest positions; epic, tragedy, and lyric, the highest (*Satires* 4.56b–62).[2] Only after Horace had set aside the hexameter *sermo* and taken up the lyric form did he assume the title of *vates*, *princeps*, and *Musarum sacerdos*;[3] the hexameters, on the other hand, were verses he simply scrawled (*illudo*, 4.139a) whenever the leisure was afforded him (*ubi quid datur oti*, 4.138b–39a) to indulge in the literary game (*haec ego ludo, Satires* 10.37b).[4]

---

[1] On this passage and the terms employed by Horace in 43–44, see A. Kiessling and R. Heinze, *Q. Horatius Flaccus. Satiren* (Berlin 1959[7]) ad 39 and 43–44. Unless otherwise indicated, all references in this article are to book 1 of the *Satires*. Earlier versions of this paper were delivered in 1990 at the University of Texas of Austin.

[2] Horace limits his literary critical discussions to these genres in *Epistles* 2.1 and *The Art of Poetry*: see Brink 1963, 202–09, 221. Our contention in this paper is that Horace, while admitting that satire's diction and style may vary by its inherent purpose (10.11–15), insists that satire is poetry. Satire of course is not epic or tragedy (on this possible meaning of *magna* in 4.44, see P. Lejay, *Œuvres d'Horace. Satirae* [Paris 1911] ad 44), but any verse qualifies as good poetry (*pulchra poemata, bona carmina*) if written well and in accordance with Horace's exacting standards.

[3] On Horace as *princeps* in *Odes* 3.10 see J. E. G. Zetzel, "The Poetics of Patronage in the Late First Century B.C.," in Barbara Gold, ed., *Literary and Artistic Patronage in Ancient Rome* (Austin 1982), 92–93, 96; Zetzel is attacked by E. Badian in his review in *CPh* 80 (1985), 352 but see D. Armstrong, "*Horatius Eques et Scriba*: Satires 1.6 and 2.7," *TAPA* 116 (1986), 285–88. In *Epistles* 1.19 Horace does claim primacy in lyric and iambic poetry, applying such terms as *princeps* (21b), *dux* (23a), and *primus* (23b) to himself, and *non prius* (32b) and *immemorata* (33b) to his verse.

[4] Cf. *Satires* 2.1.12–15, *Epistles* 1.1.10 (*versus et cetera ludicra pono*); cf. also *Epistles* 2.1.250ff.:

> nec sermones ego mallem
> repentis per humum quam res componere gestas
> terrarum situs et flumina dicere et arces
> montibus impositas et barbara regna, tuisque
> auspiciis totum confecta duella per orbem,
> claustraque custodem pacis cohibentia Ianum,
> et formidatam Parthis te principe Romam,
> si quantum cuperem possem quoque.

This tongue-in-cheek humor ("I really cannot write epic verses," followed by superb epic verses!) reappears in *Satires* 2.1.12–15:

> cupidum, pater optime, vires
> deficiunt; neque enim quivis horrentia pilis
> agmina nec fracta pereuntis cuspide Gallos
> aut labentis equo describat vulnera Parthi.

Cf. *The Art of Poetry* 306, and *Epistles* 2.1.111; 2.2.57, 2.2.141–44. Scholars typically take Horace's professed humility at face value: C. Witke, *Latin Satire: The Structure of Persuasion* (Leiden 1970), 56–59 and Brink 1963, 182, cf. 242: ". . . Horace's 'writing' applies to poetry but not to the quasi-poetry of his satires or epistles. So far as Horace is concerned (not so far as others are concerned) *scribere* then applies to his lyric verse, his incursion into poetry proper." But M. J. McGann, "The Three Worlds of Horace's *Satires*," in C. D. N. Costa, ed., *Horace* (London 1973), 85–86, 91, rightly insists that such phrases by Horace can not be taken seriously; cf. K. Reckford, *Horace* (New York 1968), 22.

So Horace's comments are nearly always interpreted. But such a reading is valid only if the present text, and with it sections of the second literary satire that conclude the book, Satire 10, are taken at the surface layer of textuality. And one must be wary of accepting Horace's words at face value.[5] A close scrutiny is warranted in a poet whose "sense of irony and ambiguity"[6] permeates his work, especially the satires; who was sensitive to the placement of words and their sounds as they affect textuality; who, most importantly, structured his poem, the hexameters and odes alike, into the organized unity of the scroll, the *liber*.[7] In fact it will be demonstrated here that Horace is asserting in the above passage his right, as a satirist, to the rank of poets; that this passage gains important further meaning when read as part of the *liber*, that is, of *Satires* Book 1, and throws light on Horace's literary critical ideas on *res/verba* and *ars/ingenium*—ideas for which Horace was greatly indebted to Philodemus and the Epicurean school.

That Horace was influenced by, and probably knew Philodemus, has been taken for granted (see Chapter 11); at this point, it seems appropriate to set forth some of the evidence for a direct contact between the philosopher/poet and the satirist. First of all, that Philodemus' poetry and philosophy were well known and influential in the Roman literary and social circles of the first century B.C. has never been questioned.[8] The *locus classicus* is Cicero's *Against Piso* 68–72, where Cicero implies that Philodemus, for an Epicurean, showed unusual interest in artistic matters and that both Philodemus and his poetry were perfectly known to every educated member of his audience.[9] It used to be doubted that Philodemus' poetic theories allowed for a fully philosophical poem and consequently that he would have approved of Lucretius. But the recent discovery in Philodemus' library of a copy of Lucretius along with a copy of Ennius[10] must, until further evidence appears, be taken to mean that Philodemus, most uncharacteristically for a Greek resident of Rome, attempted to understand

---

[5] For the persona of Horace in his satires, see now K. Freudenberg, *The Walking Muse: Horace on the Theory of Satire* (Princeton 1993), 3–8. Freudenberg, in his 1989 dissertation on which his book is based, reached independently many of the same conclusions as we had asserted in our 1988 and 1990 papers; we gratefully acknowledge his discussion of our work in *The Walking Muse*.

[6] J. E. G. Zetzel, "Horace's *Liber Sermonum*: The Structure of Ambiguity," *Arethusa* 13.1 (1980), 71.

[7] On the satires and sequential reading, see Zetzel 1980 (above, n. 5) and nn. 13–18 below; cf. Zetzel 1982 (above, n. 3), 94–95. For the *Odes* see now D. Porter, *Horace's Poetic Journey: A Reading of Odes 1–3* (Princeton 1987); M. Santirocco, *Unity and Design in Horace's Odes* (Chapel Hill 1986), especially the valuable bibliography to chapter 1 ("Horace's *Odes* and the Ancient Poetry Book") on 177–185; M. C. J. Putnam, *Artifices of Eternity: Horace's Fourth Book of Odes* (Ithaca and London 1986); L. Edmonds, *From a Sabine Farm. Reading Horace, Odes 1.9* (Chapel Hill 1992); and G. Davis, *Polyhymnia. The Rhetoric of Horatian Lyric Discourse* (Berkeley, Los Angeles, Oxford 1991).

[8] Jensen, "Die Bibliothek von Herculaneum," *Bonner Jahrbücher* 135, 56; Barra 1973, 247–60; Tait 1941, 5–7. For Philodemus' poetry, see J. Snyder, "The Poetry of Philodemus the Epicurean," *CJ* 68 (1973/74), 346–53 and D. Sider, "The Love Poetry of Philodemus," *AJPh* 108 (1987), 310–24, with bibliography at 310 n. 1.

[9] See Appendix III in R. G. Nisbet's 1961 Oxford edition (183–86); Tait 1941, 5–7; Gigante 1983, 35–53. For Philodemus and Piso, see Sider 1987 (above, n. 8), 322 n. 42 and Asmis 1990a, 2372 with n. 10. Cicero has a much more favorable report of Philodemus in *De finibus* 2.19: *familiares nostros, credo, Sironem dicis et Philodemum, cum optimos viros, tum homines doctissimos,* on which see G. L. Hendrickson, "Philodemus and Two Latin Congeners," *AJPh* 39 (1918), 34ff. Tait 1941, 5–7 offers good reasons for Cicero's attack on Philodemus in *Against Piso* being rather mild.

[10] Kleve 1989 and 1990.

Latin literature, both prose and poetry. We also know that Philodemus was intimately connected with the Neapolitan circle of poets that collected around Siro, namely, Vergil, Plotius Tucca, Varius Rufus, and Quintilius Varus.[11] Körte recognized that in the fragments of two of Philodemus' works—the *On envy* and the *On avarice*—were the names of the poets Varius Rufus and Quintilius Varus;[12] both poets were members of the Epicurean circle in Naples.[13] Körte conjectured the names of Vergil and Horace from the fragments and was supported in this by Crönert,[14] although Jensen argued that Plotius could just as easily be read in place of Horatius.[15] Gigante and Capasso[16] have now read the names of all four poets—Vergil, Plotius, Varius, and Quintilius—as addressees of another of Philodemus' works, the *On virtues and vices* (*P.Herc. Paris.* 2). All these dedicatory references prove that Philodemus knew personally the Epicurean circle of poets in Naples, a circle aptly described by Probus: *vixit [Vergilius] pluribus annis liberali in otio, secutus Epicuri sectam, insigni concordia et familiaritate usus Quintili, Tuccae et Vari* (*Life of Vergil*, p. 43 Diehl). Since these poets numbered among Horace's most intimate friends and, in fact, are mentioned, often as a group, by Horace (*Satires* 1.5.40, 1.10.44–45; *Odes* 1.24), it is reasonable to assume that Horace knew Philodemus as well.[17] Moreover, Philodemus was the literary client of L. Calpurnius Piso, whose villa was the center of Epicurean activity in southern Italy,[18] and it cannot be a coincidence that Horace addresses to this Piso's son and grandsons his *The Art of Poetry*, a work written from an Epicurean point of view and, as will be shown below, based on many of Philodemus' theories in his *On Poems*.[19] It would be reasonable then to proceed in this article on the assumption that at least some of the keys to understanding Horace's poetic theory are to be found in the papyrus fragments at Herculaneum.[20]

---

[11] Tait 1941, 110ff.

[12] A. Körte, "Augusteer bei Philodem," *RhM* 45 (1890), 172–77. The fragments are *P.Herc.* 1082 col. xi 1–2 and *P.Herc.* 253 fr. xii 4–5.   [13] Hendrickson 1918 (above, n. 9), 36ff.

[14] W. Crönert, *Kolotes und Menedemus* (Leipzig 1906), 127.

[15] Jensen (above, n. 8), 56–57.   [16] Gigante and Capasso 1989.

[17] B. Frischer, *At Tu Aureus Esto. Eine Interpretation von Vergils 7. Ekloge* (Bonn 1975), 168–71; Asmis (above, n. 9), 2373; Freudenberg (above, n. 5), 140. The phrase *liberali in otio* in Probus' text is probably to be taken literally. We know that the other poets were quite wealthy and powerful Romans, and given that these poets were addressees of Philodemus, it is reasonable to assume that Vergil's presence as an addressee is proof of his own social, economic, and literary position during this time.

[18] See M. Gigante, *Filodemo in Italia* (Firenze 1990), 17–18.

[19] We accept Frischer's date of the late 20s, although we are by no means willing to accept his theory of *The Art of Poetry* as a mock didactic poem: *Shifting Paradigms. New Approaches to Horace's Ars Poetica* (Atlanta 1991). Cf. D. Armstrong, *Horace* (New Haven 1989), 154. For further discussion on the identity of the *Pisones*, see R. Syme, "The Sons of Piso the Pontifex," *AJPh* 101 (1980), 338–40 (= Ronald Syme, *The Roman Papers*, ed. A. Birley [Oxford 1984], 1230–32) and Brink 1963, 239–44.

[20] Philodemus as a *poet* exerted a great influence on Horace. This is not the place to review the evidence, since our concern is with the relationship between Horace's satires (and *The Art of Poetry*) and Philodemus' poetic and philosophical theories. For Philodemus' poetry and its role in shaping Horace's poetry, see, e.g., Tait 1941, 64ff.; N. DeWitt, "The Parresiastic Poems of Horace," *AJPh* 60 (1939), 85–92; Jensen (above, n. 8), 57ff.; Hendrickson 1918 (above, n. 9), 31ff.; Freudenberg 1993 (above, n. 5), 18, 88ff.; Armstrong 1986 (above, n. 3), 78f., 82. Horace quotes Philodemus at *S.* 1.2.120–24 (for which see Freudenberg 1993, 195–97), a fact that Hendrickson adduces as proof of a personal relationship (pp. 36–37). Gigante 1989, 129–51, referencing the same passage, asserts (147–48) that by coupling Philodemus with Callimachus, Horace reckoned the two as equal models for Augustan poets ("Filodemo è un

Scholars typically have seen *Satires* 1.4 as Horace's response to the critical reception of the publication of the first three satires, with their attacks on living persons.[21] In turn, the supposed occasion for *Satires* 1.10 was the hostile reaction to the censure of Lucilius' style which Horace had published in 1.4.[22] These positions are based on the notion that the poems were published to a wide reading audience over an extended period of time, that we know or can guess the chronological sequence in which each was written or published, above all that each poem is discrete and separable from any sequential reading of the scroll, the *liber*, as it is unrolled or recited.

But no textual or extratextual evidence exists to make such views more plausible than the hypothesis that *Satires* 1 forms a typical "Augustan poetry book" which should be read and considered as a whole. The allusions to each of satires 1–3 in Satire 4, and the allusion back to 4 at the opening of 10, are textual markers that work better to serve a poetic chronology, that of a continuous reading beginning with Satire 1 and ending with 10, than an imaginary historical one:[23] the first thirty–five lines of Satire 4 summarize for the reader or listener the previous three poems, which are assumed to be still fresh in the mind, and the opening of Satire 10 re-opens a discussion which, as we will show, Horace purposely left unfinished in 4 so he could finish it here. If we may take Horace at his own word in at least several passages, he himself stated that the readership of his satires was limited to the select few and it is unlikely that he would have responded to a widespread reaction if one occurred.[24] In our opinion, there is no evidence to support the hypothesis that the satires were published in "installments," and not as a *liber*. The only chronology of Book 1, in other words, is the reading of the scroll, of the words that strike the eye as the scroll is unrolled or that fall upon the ear when recited in the reading performance, of the thematic and verbal threads between what is being read and what has preceded and will follow.[25] And lest anyone think this beyond the capacity of an ancient audience,

---

modello nella stessa misura di Callimaco," 150). This appraisal seems excessive; Tait 1941, esp. 86f., 108ff. is more cautious.

[21] So Lejay (above, n. 2), 96; Kiessling–Heinze 1959 (above, n. 1), xxi; W. Wili, *Horaz und die augusteische Kultur* (Basel 1948), 71; Brink 1963 (above, n. 2), 156–64; G. L. Hendrickson first suggested that the occasion of 1.4 was not an attack by angry critics: "Horace, *Serm.* 1.4: A Protest and a Programme," *AJPh* 21 (1900), 121–42; Hendrickson later was strongly challenged by N. Rudd: "Had Horace Been Criticized? A Study of *Serm.* 1.4," *AJPh* 76 (1955), 165–75; "The Poet's Defense," *CQ* 49 (1955), 142–56; and *The Satires of Horace* (Cambridge 1966), 88–89. See Freudenberg 1993 (above, n. 5), 52ff.

[22] Lejay 1911 (above, n. 2), 250; Kiessling–Heinze 1959 (above, n. 1), 155–56; Brink 1963, 165–71; Rudd 1966 (above, n. 7), 92. Cf. C. A. van Rooy, "Arrangement and Structure of Satires in Horace, *Sermones*, Book I: Satires I, 4 and I, 10," *A.Class.* 13 (1970), 8 (hereafter cited as van Rooy 1970a).

[23] For example, 4.26–32 looks back to the opening two satires; 4.48–49 to 2.20; 4.81–84 to satire 3; 4.92 is repeated from 2.27. The advice offered to Horace by his father (4.107–26) alludes to sections of the previous three satires, e.g. 1.73–79, 2.16–19, 55–57. The *nempe . . . dixi* of 10.1 denotes, according to commentators, a lengthy period of time between publication of Satire 4 and the writing of 10; we will discuss this phrase below.

[24] *Satires* 4.22–23 (on which see Zetzel 1980 [above, n. 6] 63–64), 72–73, 10.22–23. Philodemus also advocated the reading of poetry by a narrow audience; see Greenberg 1955, 84, 274–75.

[25] W. Kroll, *Studien zum Verständnis der römischen Literatur*, 2nd ed. (Stuttgart 1964), 226–27, who follows W. Port, "Die Anordnung in Gedichtbüchern augusteischer Zeit," *Philologus* 81 (1926), 280–308 and 427–68. For more recent work in this area see Zetzel 1980 (above, n. 6), 59–61; H. Dettmer, *Horace: A Study in Structure* (Hildesheim 1983), 1–75; W. Nethercut, rev. of Santirocco's *Unity and*

it should be noted that the first book of *Satires* is less than 1,000 lines in length, which approximates a single book in epic or a Greek play, and could surely be performed in the course of an afternoon or evening reading. Horace himself intimates that the ten satires should be considered a book: "I, puer, atque meo citus haec *subscribe libello*" (*Satires* 1.10.92).

This theory of the first book as a unit to be read and comprehended together is borne out by much modern scholarship. Scholars have long recognized patterns of arrangement of poems in Book 1,[26] noting such structural patterns as interlocking rings,[27] division by halves,[28] triads,[29] conjunct pairs,[30] disjunct pairs,[31] and chiastic pairs.[32] Now in our view 1.4 must be discussed within the context of a reading of the *liber* as a whole. Thus *Satires* 1.4.38b–63 should be seen as the continuation of structural, thematic, and verbal textual layers within the fourth satire itself and of the preceding three and the subsequent six. But Satire 10 also relates to 4 as a chiastic pair. That is, Horace intentionally breaks off the discussion of satire as poetry at 4.63, suspending it in poetic time, only to resume it at the opening of the tenth satire. But later on the tenth satire also completes and parallels the discussion of the public impact of satire which supplied the opening thought of Satire 4; there the question of the public role of the satirist (lines 7b–21) was brought up in the opposite order, so that we could say Horace introduces these topics in Satire 4 in the order *ab* and in Satire 10 in the order *ba*.

Within itself Satire 4 possesses a remarkably tight structure and unity.[33] It begins

---

Design, in *Helios* 14.1 (1987), 64–65. This manner of reading ignores E. Fraenkel's rule that all the material needed to interpret a Horatian satire is contained within that poem: E. Fraenkel, *Horace* (Oxford 1957), 26, 208–209, who is criticized by N. Rudd, "Professor Fraenkel's Horace," *Hermathena* 91 (1958), 46–48; cf. D. Armstrong, "Horace, *Satires* 1, 1–3: A Structural Study," *Arion* 3 (1964), 86.

[26] Zetzel 1980 (above, n. 6), 81: "[The *Liber Sermonum*] is a work of literature, not of history . . . It is not necessary—indeed it is harmful—to take the poems as straightforward statements with only a surface reading . . . One can not, under any circumstances, accept as objective truth anything in the poems." Cf. I. M. Le M. DuQuesnay, "Horace and Maecenas: The Propaganda Value of *Sermones* I," in T. Woodman and D. West, eds., *Poetry and Politics in the Age of Augustus* (Cambridge 1984), 20–21, who holds that all the poems should be dated between 38 and the winter of 36/35 and were published as a group of ten. See the discussion in Freudenberg 1993 (above, n. 5), 198–211.

[27] Port 1926 (above, n. 25), 288–91. Cf. C. Rambaux, "La composition d'ensemble du livre I des *Satires* d'Horace," *REL* 49 (1971), 179–204.

[28] F. Boll, "Die Anordnung im zweiten Buch von Horaz' *Satiren*," *Hermes* 48 (1913), 145, who accepts the structure by halves for Book 1 versus his more symmetrical scheme for Book 2.

[29] Armstrong 1964 (above, n. 25), 86–96. Cf. K. Büchner, *Horaz* (Wiesbaden 1962), 123–24; Wili 1948 (above, n. 7), 95–96; Rudd 1966 (above, n. 2), 1–35; W. Ludwig, "Die Komposition der beiden Satirenbücher des Horaz," *Poetica* 2 (1968), 304–35.

[30] W. S. Anderson, "The Form, Purpose, and Position of Horace's *Satire* I, 8," *AJPh* 93 (1972), 10–13, and the following articles by C. A. van Rooy: "Arrangement and Structure of *Satires* in Horace, *Sermones*, Book I, with More Special Reference to *Satires* 1–4," *A.Class.* 11 (1968), 38–72; "Arrangement and Structure of *Satires* in Horace, *Sermones*, Book I: *Satires* 5 and 6," *A.Class.* 13 (1970), 45–59 (hereafter cited as van Rooy 1970b); "Arrangement and Structure of *Satires* in Horace, *Sermones*, Book I: *Satires* 9 and 10," *A.Class.* 15 (1972), 37–52.

[31] van Rooy 1968 (above, n. 30), and "Arrangement and Structure of *Satires* in Horace, *Sermones*, Book I: *Satire* 7 as Related to *Satires* 10 and 8," *A.Class.* 14 (1971), 67–90; cf. Rambaux 1971 (above, n. 27), 180–81.

[32] Port 1926 (above, n. 26), 289; Büchner 1962 (above, n. 29), 124; van Rooy 1970a (above, n. 22) and Freudenberg 1993 (above, n. 5), 96ff.

[33] C. Dessen, "The Poetic Unity of Horace's *Serm.*, 1.4," *AJPh* 88 (1967), 78–81.

with alternating sections on the moral function of satire and its artistic form.[34] The opening eight verses state the moral purpose and spirit of satire in the context of Lucilius' poetry, all the while echoing thematically and verbally the previous satire;[35] next follows an attack on Lucilius' defects in style (8b–21a), then yet another, fuller description of the moral function of the genre (21b–38a). The vices alluded to in lines 3–4 and 25–33 have been mentioned specifically elsewhere (3.106) or have constituted the main themes of each of the three opening satires. While van Rooy has made a strong case for linking Satires 3 and 4, the fourth Satire also relates to Satires 1 and 2 in one important way. In the preliminary sections of Satire 4, Lucilius is attacked for an undisciplined, uncontrolled, and unstructured style: he is *vitiosus*, a term that nicely describes qualities both ethical/moral and literary (cf. *Ad Herennium* 1.11 and Cicero, *De oratore* 3.105). The term is thus a verbal bridge between the ethical principles of Satires 1–3 and the literary principles discussed in Satire 4. The interweaving throughout 4.1–38a of ethical and literary *vitia* stresses the contrasts control/lack of control, form/formlessness which so constitute the theme of these four satires that the poems in fact form a semantic and contextual unit.[36] With these issues of moral *vitia* (vis-à-vis ethics) and literary *vitia* (vis-à-vis Lucilius' verse-making) thus delineated, Horace makes his first-person entrance in verse 39.

Verses 38b–63 of Satire 4 are ostensibly a reply to the second of two complaints in verse 33: "omnes hi metuunt versus, *odere poetas.*" Thus Horace apparently diffuses, or clouds, the issue by claiming in 39–44 that he is no poet, and therefore should inspire little fear.[37] But this verse, 33, should not be taken too literally as it serves only to set up Horace's discussions of satire as an art (39–62, with Satire 10) and as vocation (4.64ff.) Still, the emphasis in this line on *poeta* and *versus*, both in the key positions in the hexameter, is significant. It takes the reader not only forward to verses 38b–63 and Satire 10, but also back to the opening twenty-five lines, where the questions of what constitutes a *poeta* and what qualities make *versus* poetic were being considered. In fact, it turns out, the issue of *poeta* and *poema*, or poetry, informs all of Satire 4. Horace begins the poem by labelling the Greek comic writers Aristophanes, Cratinus, and Eupolis *poetae*; they fulfilled both functions of the satirist, that of the good writer (*poetae*) and that of public satirist of actual characters (3–5). Moreover, *poetae* in line 1 and the "multa *poetarum* . . . manus" at the closure of the poem (141a) create a ring-composition. Whatever theories Horace may pretend to consider about whether comic poets and satirists are poets or not, both are firmly identified as such at the beginning and the end of this poem. In between, we see the word *poeta* four times (33, 39, 42, 62), while *poema* occurs twice (45, 63). In each instance *poeta* or *poema* is fixed emphatically in the final position in the hexameter line, as it is also in line 1 (in 141a *poetarum* is placed, with equal emphasis, before the caesura). By such intra- and intertextual weaving, word-placements, and ring-composition, the concepts "poetry" and "poet" are kept constantly before us as they relate to two quite different personalities—Lucilius, or rather the persona "Lucilius" in the satire, and Horace. The dichotomy thus formulated and then redefined and

[34] Fraenkel 1957 (above, n. 25), 126; cf. van Rooy 1970a (above, n. 23), 58–68.

[35] van Rooy 1970a (above, n. 22), 57–61; cf. Kiessling-Heinze 1959 (above, n. 1), 45–46.

[36] Armstrong 1964 (above, n. 25), especially pp. 91–94.

[37] Kiessling–Heinze 1959 (above, n. 1) ad 39; cf. Freudenberg 1993 (above, n. 5), 125–26 n. 34 on past opinions on these lines.

reconceptualized through the literary-critical principles of *ars/ingenium* and *res/ verba* is in fact resolved in Horace's favor: he *is* a poet, he *is* writing poetry.

And now to analyze the true meaning of the passage with which we began. Line 38b, "agedum, pauca accipe contra," recalls Lucilius' "summatim tamen experiar rescribere paucis" (1063 Warmington). The placement of Horace's revision of the Lucilian pleonasm can not be coincidental, for thereby not only is Lucilius established securely in the continuing discussion, but Horace's brevity is itself a commentary on the garrulity of Lucilius, providing a subtle reminder in small of how a disciplined *poeta* works. (So also on the largest scale, Satire 5, the Journey to Brundisium, is to be considered a reworking in the hundred-line form of a topic that took Lucilius, in his own Journey satire, several hundred lines to complete.) Horace proceeds apparently to seclude himself from the ranks of poets; reserve that title, he says, for those with *ingenium*, inspiration, and a high style.[38] His own poetry he calls too pedestrian and colloquial—nothing more than prose, like Lucilius' verses. Lines 46–48 imply that satire, like comedy, lacks the *acer spiritus ac vis* of the *res* and *verba* characterizing good poetry. True poetry (*iustum . . . poema*, 63) belongs rather to the epic poets like Ennius. Horace's own verse may be competent, but it is not poetry.[39]

A closer reading of the textual layers of lines 38b–63 of Satire 4, however, reveals a different story. First of all, it is clear that in lines 39ff. Horace considers *ingenium* an essential quality of the *poeta*. The debate for centuries among literary circles had centered on the relationship between *ars* and *ingenium*. Horace here seems to resolve the problem by deciding in favor of *ingenium* (40–44); further, he states that because he lacks this trait he is not a poet. But while the surface text seems explicitly to make this assertion, Horace carefully manipulates the structure and syntax so as to situate himself among the ranks of *poetae*, by elision and other types of significant word-placement, and also by the strategic use of subjunctives.

We note first that Horace elides the word *primum* into *ego* and *me* into *illorum*, placing the unit *millorum* emphatically at the caesura: "primum ego me illorum | dederim quibus esse poetas." Is he not thereby implying what he seems to deny? The unit *millorum is* to be equated with *dederim quibus esse poetas*. So Horace, like other *poetae*, does possess *ingenium*, and even (*primego*) among the first!

W. S. Anderson, who more than any other scholar has advanced the cause of Horace's satires as true poetry, alone has commented on this elision. Anderson, however, believes that the elision is meant to heighten the differences between Horace's *sermo* and the higher forms of poetry:[40]

> As if to emphasize the difference between *sermo* and epic, Horace does unorthodox things with his verse. In the first line (39) he pushes three pronouns

---

[38] Lejay 1911 (above, n. 2) ad 44 would have Horace not stressing the poet's *ingenium*, but the poet's ability to write the higher genres.

[39] So says Brink 1963, 161; cf. Dettmer 1983 (above, n. 25), 35–36, and G. C. Fiske, *Lucilius and Horace: A Study in the Classical Tradition of Imitation* (Madison 1920), 287–89.

[40] W. S. Anderson, *Essays on Roman Satire* (Princeton 1982), 24–25. In all fairness to this scholar, Anderson reaches the same conclusion that we offer below: that the satires of Horace must be considered poetry. Anderson's ideas on the poetic quality of the satires remain overlooked by most Horatian scholars.

together with such apparent awkwardness that he has to elide *ego* and *me* and distort good prose and indeed poetic word-order. An elision of a monosyllable (*me*) reminds one of comedy and Lucilius . . . By eliding both *ego* and *me*, Horace obliges us to feel the effacement of the lesser versifier by those august poets (*illorum*).

Now such posturing by Horace as insignificant poet suits the stereotypical interpretations of Horace of older scholarship, the *humilis persona*, but the newer Horace that is emerging from recent studies, the Horace confident and self-assured from his earliest days, even before he met Maecenas, until the end of his life, would not flee the ranks of poets—he would join them.[41] And so he does, with the elision. Now a member of the *manus*, he summons its aid when, at the conclusion of the poem, he defends his right to compose poetry: "*multa poetarum* veniat *manus* auxilio quae/ sit mihi (nam multo plures *sumus*)" (141–42a). The *sumus* shows that we have interpreted the elision correctly: Horace belongs to the poets, and says so, implicitly in line 39, explicitly in line 142. It is not (or it does not seem to us) just a matter, as so often, of one sensitively conceived reason for an elision being as good as another. Horace's reason for *primego millorum* was to undercut the surface meaning of his text.[42]

In fact the subjunctives *dixeris*, *putes*, *des*, and (most probably) *excerpam*, which allows itself to be construed either as future or subjunctive,[43] also tell us that Horace, when refusing the crown of poet, is talking about potentiality, what someone *might think*, not fact, what is factually true.[44] Now the ancient scholiasts gloss this passage with flat indicatives: "id est: non dico, me esse poetam";[45] and "sensus est autem: primum omnium ego me non pono in ⟨nu⟩mero eorum, quos consentio poetas esse."[46] But the passage translates more plausibly as "First I *might* (if I wished)

---

[41] For a reappraisal of Horace's persona in this context, see Armstrong 1986 (above, n. 3), 255–88.

[42] Horace often plays this game of word-elision and word-sound affecting thematic content. For example, in the opening three lines of Book 1 of the *Epistles*:

> prima dicte mihi, summa dicende Camena,
> spectatum satis et donatum iam rude quaeris,
> Maecenas, iterum antiquo me includere ludo.

After the opening line's anagram *Camena* for Maecenas, Horace proceeds to fulfill Maecenas's request by including himself in the gladiatorial school through the elison of *me* into *includere*; moreover, the word-sound reinforces the elision: *mincLUDere LUDo*. Even Horace's positioning of a single word can speak volumes. In 1.9, the "bore" symbolizes everything that Horace detests in moral and literary principles (the themes of Satires 4 and 10): the man is uncontrolled, superfluous, garrulous, false in friendship, possessed with an unrealistic view of his faults and good points, and, as will be pointed out below, symbolic of the Neoteric school. The latter association is made clear by the placement of the notorious Neoteric Hermogenes: *invideat quod et Hermogenes ego canto* (1.9.25). The coupling Hermogenes–*ego* offers succinctly Horace's thoughts on this man's literary ability.

[43] Lejay 1911 (above, n. 2) ad loc. comments: "excerpam: subjonctif comme tous les verbes de ce passage, pour exprimer la possibilité, l'hypothèse: 'si par aventure tu me comptes parmi les poètes.'"

[44] Cf. L. Mueller, *Quintus Horatius Flaccus, Satiren und Episteln* (Wien 1891) vol. 1, 57, and Otto Schönberger, *Horaz. Satiren und Episteln* (Berlin 1976), who translates as follows: "Fürs erste möchte ich mich aus der Zahl derer ausnehmen, denen ich zugestcho, dass sie Dichter sind."

[45] *Acronis et Porphyrionis commentarii in Q. Horatium Flaccum*, ed. F. Havthal (Amsterdam 1966) ad 4.39.

[46] *Pomponi Porfyrionis commentum in Horatium Flaccum*, ed. A. Holder (Hildesheim 1967) ad

exclude myself from the number of those I *would grant* to be poets; for you *might not grant* that to write verse is enough, and if one were to write, as I do, what resembles common speech, you *might give* the honour of this name to those who have *ingenium* (etc.) . . . for which reason some have asked (indicative) whether comedy *would or would not be* (*esset necne*) poetry,"[47] and so on. The whole question, in other words, is a theoretical one.

Now the critics, who ask "whether comedy would or would not be poetry," give a reason, it is true, which is in the indicative: "quod acer spiritus ac vis / nec verbis nec rebus inest, nisi quod pede certo/ differt sermoni, sermo merus": "Because there is neither sharp spirit and power in the words nor the subject, mere talk, except insofar as it differs from talk by metre." However, as we saw, Horace is not one of those critics, as far as comedy is concerned: line 1 stated firmly that Eupolis, Aristophanes, and Cratinus *are* poets (and later, it will turn out at *Satires* 10.40–42a that Horace's friend the comic poet Fundanius is one also). Again, that this is the critics' statement, not Horace's, is patent from the fact that the language of comedy is obviously capable of what they deny to it: the speech of the *pater* and the *quivis*, that special kind of language described by *saevit* and *stomachetur*, is full of those very qualities described with a characteristically delightful alliteration (which would disappear if you rearranged the words) in line 46: "ACeR SpIRitVs AC VIS." The examples and verbs Horace selects here imply that comedy can indeed have a spirited language.

Finally, and most importantly, the meaning of lines 56–62 of Satire 4 is not straightforward either. In fact, the ambiguities, humor, and irony of this passage make any literal meaning difficult to fix on: but one can be certain on closer examination that Horace is again *not* saying that satire is not poetry, just as he did not say that about comedy in the previous passage; he is clearly implying the reverse. First of all, commentators have failed to appreciate Horace's placement of *non* in line 60. The reader of the Latin *liber* or the listener at the performance would hesitate in determining the function of *non*: this is what Horace has gone to such lengths to achieve by his unusual word-order. Does it go with the protasis or the apodosis—that is, *non invenias* or *non ut si*? If one takes the apparently reasonable solution offered by all commentators, that *non* goes with *invenias*, the lengthy postponement almost severs the connection. Because Horace was one of the most careful of all Latin writers in placement of words, this delay of the negation must be intentional. Does it offer an intentional ambiguity? If *non* is to be taken with *ut si* even as a subaudition, we would be offered the alternative meaning that if the word-order of Horace's own verses or Lucilius' in satire were changed, and the meter removed, one would indeed find a torn-apart poet, "as one would not if" one did the same thing to Ennius' lines. Line 60, then, would mean: ". . . not so, however, if you were to do the same to, say,

---

4.39. This tense is used also by K. Quinn, *Texts and Contexts. The Roman Writers and their Audience* (London 1979): "In the first place I exclude myself from the list of those I'd call poets."

[47] Anderson 1982 (above, n. 40), 24 translates as a pure future: "In the first place, I shall exclude myself from the number of those who I have conceded are poets." Cf. the translation by R. Ghiotto, *Quinto Orazio Flacco, Le Satire* (Roma 1978): "Prima di tutto mi toglierò dal numero di quelli cui darei nome di poeti."

Ennius . . . ."[48] This interpretation may not be so far-fetched, given what Horace professes to think, throughout the satires and epistles, of the literary poetic qualities of the early Roman poets.[49]

Before the reader supposes that we are pressing a possible ambiguity until it screams in order to get the meaning we want, let us bring up two important points: the subject of this passage is metathesis, the rearrangement of words to show whether something is or is not "poetic"; and the diction, syntax, and word-order both of Horace's own words and the Ennius quotation are such as to cause interpretative problems even if we ignore the ambiguity of that *non* in line 60. The word-order and syntax of what Horace says in lines 55b–62 are highly contorted and at the farthest possible distance from the order normal in common speech. This is paradoxical, for the passage itself says that in satire word-order does not matter except to satisfy meter. Or, more accurately, the passage brings up in a series of subjunctives (*eripias, facias, solvas, invenias*) the possibility that word-order *might* not matter; yet the order and arrangement belie that idea at every point. On the other hand, the quotation from Ennius is equally paradoxical, because, as all the commentators note with puzzlement, there is not a single "poetic" word in the quotation, while the word-order is exactly that of standard Ciceronian prose!

To particularize: it has been supposed that Horace believed that a true poem is revealed by the poetic diction inherent in it and the indissoluble perfection of its word-order. But Horace has chosen as an example of true poetry a quotation from Ennius not full of old-fashioned and obsolete "poetic" Latin, as he easily might have done, but one made of words all in contemporary common use: "postquam Discordia taetra / belli ferratos postes portasque refregit." Moreover, a formidable paradox lies in the word-order of Ennius' lines, which is a perfectly commonplace prose arrangement of subject-accusative–verb, not a Golden Line or any other word-order reserved in Latin specially to poetry. It does, however, contrast sharply with the convoluted, distorted word-order of Horace's own verses describing and *mirroring as they do so* what metathesis would be, the process of putting words out of their normal order. In other words, Horace's lines, as they stand in the text, are metathesized from an imaginary prose text. The result? Time is reversed: "ego quae *nunc, olim* quae scripsit Lucilius"; order is reversed: "quod *prius* ordine verbum *posterius*"; last is literally put before first, "praeponens *ultima primis.*" What we have now is a poetic text that cannot be metathesized without destroying both poetry and poet.

To put it another way: if we *do* metathesize—that is, put Horace into the un-metathesized imaginary text and metathesize the prosaic Ennius lines—much is lost in Horace but little in Ennius. If one allows a Ciceronian apology for the metaphor,

---

[48] Horace's inclusion of Lucilius on a par with himself in lines 56–57 is pure irony, given Horace's comments, still fresh in the mind or ears of the audience, on Lucilius' style (or lack thereof).

[49] Cf. 10.54–55, 10.64–67, where Lucilius is praised as *limatior* than the poets preceding him, which statement says much about Horace's feelings on the style of these early poets; cf. *Epistles* 2.1.50ff., 2.117ff.; *The Art of Poetry* 251–74, 285–94, with Brink's commentary on these verses: C. O. Brink, *Horace on Poetry, II: The Ars Poetica* (Cambridge 1971), 295–309, 318–24, 497–99. Brink, *Horace on Poetry, III: Epistles Book II* (Cambridge 1982), 470 remarks: "[Horace] dismisses archaic verse because it does not make what in his own view appears as an artistic unity; he regards it as incoherent, imperfect, poetry."

where in fact would the sense of a poet torn apart appear in the sentence "postquam taetra Discordia resolvit, ut ita dicam, ferratos postes portasque belli . . ."? And how much of Horace's delicate effects would still appear in "si his, quae olim scripsit Lucilius, quae nunc ego, eripias tempora certa modosque, et posterius facias verbum quod prius est ordine, praeponens primis ultima, non invenias membra poetae, etiam disiecti, ut si solvas" etc.?[50] The paradox is that Horace has lost vastly more than Ennius by the transposition, though they are both poets and are both destroyed by it—made to vanish. Here, then, we see in fact that metathesis will abolish both poetry and poet. And consequently we may well be justified in suggesting in addition that the meaning "invenias membra poetae, etiam disiecti, ut si solvas Enni versus non (sc. invenias)" is there as a possibility. No solution is given in the indicative: instead, Horace merely promises one later: "hactenus haec; *alias* iustum sit necne poema . . . quaeram."

To summarize what Horace is doing here. The text seems to state that Horace's satire is poetry only because of meter and word-order and that Ennius' lines are poetry even without meter and word-order. But we must beware of this surface reading in an author like Horace, where texts may at any one moment be undercut by humorous undertones and ironic slippage. In fact, Horace's subtext (if we so choose to call it) may well assert that Ennius, at least in the lines quoted, lives up no better than Lucilius to Horace's poetic ideal. If we transpose Ennius' text, what have we left? Nothing more than the same pedestrian sentence with a different word-order. Is this metathesized sentence still poetry? Perhaps, perhaps not. It is, if Horace considered it poetry in the first place; but, as we saw above, the ambiguous placement of *non* and the string of subjunctives—not to mention Horace's overall opinion of early Latin poets—may give just the opposite answer. And what of Horace's own lines? As they presently stand in the text, they are an *exemplum* of metathesized poetry. And when read, the word-order is bewildering, but the poetic effects of individual words and phrases pervade everywhere. And if we metathesize what may be called the metathesized, all this deliberate structure of text is destroyed. What Horace has accomplished, with his usual humorous irony, is to prove how a real poetic text cannot be metathesized without injury. Granted, if we try to remove the meter and reinstate the "normal" word-order, we will get a prosaic sentence—just as we would with the Ennius passage. But the delicious humor is that Horace's metathesized lines (53b–62 in the present text) are *poetic*—Ennius' lines are not. By means of this passage, therefore, Horace has managed to prove on the *subtextual* level two important literary critical points: that metathesis will destroy good poetry (and so Horace's satires are good poetry), and that Ennius' verse, while poetry, is not good poetry because the effects of metathesis are minimal.

Horace's views on metathesis are directly related to Philodemus', which were set forth elsewhere in this volume (above, pp. 210–32). To restate in simple terms, Philodemus objected to the tactic of metathesis because any change in style, any change in expression, results in a change in thought:[51]

---

[50] Or "non invenias etiam membra poetae disiecti": any transposition makes it impossible for *etiam* to continue performing its double function.

[51] Greenberg 1955, 153f., 176, 275–76. See, too, his "Metathesis as an Instrument in the Criticism of Poetry," *TAPA* 89 (1958), 267, for Philodemus' criticism of the practice of rearrangement of words to

P.Herc. 1676 fr. ix = Treatise C col. ix Sbordone

22   [ἠ]με[ἰ]c δὲ τὸν [
      δ[ε]χό[μεν]ον ἀμετάθ[ε-
      τ[ο]ν [ἄλλ]ηc cυνηθεία[c
25   ὑ]παρχ[ούc]ηc τὸν νο[ῦν
      τῶ[ν] π[ο]ητῶν, εἰκαίωc
      ἐ]παινεῖν ἐροῦμεν ἢ [περι-
      κόπτειν.

But we will say that the man . . . who accepts that the thought of the poet is unchanged (*ametatheton*), if another form of speech is used, is praising or blaming it to no purpose.

P.Herc. 1676 col. vi = Treatise C col. xvii Sbordone (cf. *CErc* 22 [1992], 167)

17   τὴν χύ-
      cιν τῶ[ν] λέξεων τοῦ βί-
      ου χορη[γ]ο[ῦ]ντοc ἡ cύνθε-
20   cιc ἰδ[ία γε]ίνεται τῶν πο-
      ητῶν, οὐ καίριοc οὐδ᾽ ἐπαι-
      νουμένη καθ᾽ αὑτήν, ἀλ-
      λ᾽ ὅτι π[ρο]cπαρίcτηcι διαν[οί-
      αc, αἷc ψ[υ]χαγωγοῦcιν, οὐ
25   παρά τινοc λαβόντεc, ἀλ-
      λ᾽ αὐτοὶ γεννήcαντεc πα-
      ρ᾽ α[ὑτ]ῶν.

. . . but it is when life itself supplies and abundance of diction, that the composition becomes something the poets' own (*idia*), not appropriate and not to be praised in and for itself but because it establishes and creates in addition the thoughts by which they entertain us, not taking them over from someone else but generating them entirely out of themselves.

If good poetry is actualized only by expression and the proper interrelation of form and content, then it is destroyed by a change in either the form or the content. Metathesis with its rearrangement, therefore, is impossible in the case of good poetry. This poetic theory, based on atomistic views, is apparent also in Lucretius' *elementa–verba–res* connection. As Lucretius writes, atoms (*elementa*) make up things (*res*) by their "concursus, motus, ordo, positura, figurae" (*On the Nature of Things* 1.684ff.); any change in any one of these qualities results in a change of nature. (Compare Lucretius' account of colors in 2.757ff.) Likewise a change in the order, position, and arrangement of the letters (*elementa*) of words (*verba*) causes

---

study rhetorical effect as having larger than local effects on a poem, and for his insistence that any change of reading—even in Homer, where the variant readings that existed in his own day were brought up against him—(*P.Herc.* 1676, cols. vii 17–ix 18) affected the poem importantly in some way.

those words to be changed in meaning and even in sound (euphony) (*On the Nature of Things* 1.822–27):

> quin etiam passim nostris in versibus ipsis
> multa elementa vides multis communia verbis,
> cum tamen inter se versus ac verba necessest
> confiteare et re et sonitu distare sonanti.
> tantum elementa queunt permutato ordine solo.

Metathesis as practiced by the *kritikoi* whom Philodemus refutes,[52] since it involves, to use Lucretius' words, a change in the *positura* and *ordo* of the *elementa* and *verba*, destroys the poetry by effecting a change in thought and content:[53]

P.Herc. 1676 fr. xii = col. i Sbordone

```
 7    τῆϲ δὲ ποητικῆ[ϲ οὐκ ἔϲ-
      τιν ἔξω τὸ ποεῖ[ν γνωϲ-
      τὰ τὰ πράγματ[α· κᾶν γὰρ
10    παντελῶϲ αὐτ[ὰ παρ' ἑ-
      τ]έρου λαμβάνῃ[ι τιϲ,
      τῇ⟨ι⟩ ϲυνθέϲει κατ[ακτᾶ-
      τα⟨ι⟩ που τὴν ἰδι[ότητα τοῦ πο-
      ητοῦ · διόπερ ὁ [ποητὴϲ μὴ
15    τὰϲ λέξειϲ οἰκείαϲ [λαβὼν
      ἐκτόϲ ἐϲτι τῆϲ τ[έχνηϲ
```

---

[52] For the identity of these *kritikoi*, see Dorandi 1990a, 2341–42. Cf. Greenberg 1955, 269–70.

[53] Not all combinations of *elementa* are possible according to Lucretius (*On the Nature of Things* 2.700–07):

> nec tamen omnimodis conecti posse putandum est
> omnia. nam vulgo fieri portenta videres,
> semiferas hominum species existere et altos
> interdum ramos egigni corpore vivo,
> multaque conecti terrestria membra marinis,
> tum flammam taetro spirantis ore Chimaeras
> pascere naturam per terras omniparentis.

We would see a reflection of this imagery in the opening five lines of Horace's *The Art of Poetry* (for the traditional provenance of the imagery see D. Armstrong, *Toward a Theory of Structure in Horace* [diss. University of Texas 1968] 32ff.):

> humano capite cervicem pictor equinam
> iungere si velit, et varias inducere plumas
> undique collatis membris, ut turpiter atrum
> desinat in piscem mulier formosa superne,
> spectatum admissi risum teneatis, amici?

These statements about the absurdity of certain combinations and the need for proper unity (n. the *iungere* in line 2), themes of *The Art of Poetry*, may well be grounded in atomistic theory, given that the canvassings of the visual arts by Brink and other commentators have not given us a satisfactory explanation of this origin. We shall return to the word *iungere* and Epicurean physics below in a discussion of *The Art of Poetry* 46ff.

κἂν ἀ[ἴ] λέξεις ὠφ[ελείας
τοῦ βίου παρεςχ[ήκωςι
κοινάς· τὸ γὰρ ἐγλ[έγειν
20   τὰς οἰκείας καὶ δ[ιατιθέ-
ναι πρὸς {α} δήλωςιν τοι-
ούτου νοήματος ἐπί-
τηδ[ες τὸ το]ιοῦτ' ἢ[ν ἴ]δι-
ον αὐτοῦ.

It is not outside the province of poetry to present content clearly; but even when
a poet appropriates content completely from another, it is in the composition
of the style (*synthesis*) that he achieves the individuality (*idiotes*) of the poet.
Therefore, the poet who does not use expressions suited to his subject (*lexeis
oikeias*) is outside of the art, even if his words offer usefulness for common life,
because selecting the right expressions and arranging them to clarify just this
particular rational content (as we saw) was his especial (*idion*) task . . .

The rest of Satire 4 deals with satire's *res; verba*, style, is suspended in poetic
time until Satire 10.[54] At 10.1, less than five hundred lines later, Horace summons
back *verba* vis-à-vis Lucilius with *nempe . . . dixi* ("Well, yes, of course, I said . . .").
The *nempe* then does not introduce a spirited response by Horace to critics who had
read 1.4 after separate publication. It serves as a poetic chronological and structural
link to Satire 4, as a correlative, as it were, with the *alias* of 4.63, thereby fulfilling his
promise to answer the question posed in 4.39–62.[55] The difference is that now the
primary emphasis in Satire 10 will be on *ars* and *verba*, not *ingenium* and *res*, as the
latter qualities had been discussed adequately in Satire 4. What Horace has accomplished is a distinction on the textual level of what he would never separate otherwise: *res* from *verba, ars* from *ingenium*. A sequential reading, however, restores the
connection: though *verba* and *ars* are not left untouched in Satire 4, *ingenium* is the
focus of 39–62 and *res* of 63–141; in Satire 10 it is the reverse, as *ingenium* and *res*
are not left untouched but *verba* and *ars* supply the focus.

The pairs *ars/ingenium, res/verba*, and Lucilius/Horace inform to varying degrees the intervening Satires 5–9. For example, in Satire 5, Horace puts into poetic
practice his criticisms of Lucilius' style and excessive verse-making in such a way
that the poem may be viewed on one level as an artistic commentary.[56] The position
of Satire 9, the famous "bore" poem, is intentional: we are prepared for Horace's

[54] Fraenkel 1957 (above, n. 25), 126–29, and van Rooy 1968 (above, n. 30), 56–68.

[55] Like other scholars, we, of course, do not accept as genuine the eight lines prefixed to the opening
of Satire 10. N. Rudd, "*Libertas* and *Facetus*," *Mnemosyne* 10 (1957), 319–36 gives an overview of the
evidence; full bibliography in E. Burck, "Nachwort und bibliographische Nachträge," in Kiessling–
Heinze 1959 (above, n. 1), 411. We should point out that *nempe* also serves to highlight the sloppy verse-
making of Lucilius. The *nempe* is elided into *incomposito*, thus giving the meaning of "to be sure,
without any order." The primary function of *nempe*, however, is, coupled with *dixi*, to signify that Satire
10 picks up where Satire 4 had left off (at line 63). Freudenberg 1993 (above, n. 5), 164ff. assumes a new
audience for 1.10; we disagree with this view, for reasons given here.

[56] For Horace's revision of Lucilius' travelogue, see Fraenkel (above, n. 25), 105–12, and Rudd
1966 (above, n. 21), 54–64.

literary criticism in the next poem through the running battle with this obnoxious person.[57] The "bore" implicates himself as a member of the Neoterics, a group that evidently admired Lucilius[58] and included Hermogenes, already mentioned at 3.129 and 4.72 and to appear three times in the next satire (5.18, 80, 90). The unprincipled "bore," endowed with no moral or literary qualities of value, seeks entry into the literary circle of skilled poets and mentions Viscus and Varius (9.22–23). These same poets are evoked by Horace in his recitation of members of his and Maecenas' circle at 10.81–90a. In both these passages the circle is surrounded, flanked in the text by Hermogenes and others of the Neoteric group: the military language in satire 9, which Anderson has pointed out, underscores the fact that literary battle lines have been drawn. But as Horace reassures us, the approaches cannot be breached. The defences of the circle are impenetrable to poetasters who lack *ars*;[59] the Neoteric school, with all its connotations of Lucilius, has no place in Horace's universe of real poetry, since all were not in tune with the ideas on poetry and poetry writing that Horace espoused. No accident therefore that the closure of Satire 9 is "sic me serva-vit Apollo." This Latin translation of one of Lucilius' Greek tags[60] is both a poetic comment on Lucilius and a link to the opening of the literary-critical Satire 10. Once again Lucilius and Horatian criteria of *ars* are paired; and with this pair so formulated, Horace commences his discussion in Satire 10 of the stylistic requirements of satire *qua* poetry.[61]

Satire 10, with its concentration on style, is the continuation of the *res/verba* discussion initiated in Satire 4. There, the opening thirty-eight lines comprised alternating, short sections on the moral and stylistic aspects of satire. In line 39 *primum* introduced a discussion of style within the context of *ingenium*; the discussion was then interrupted in line 63 so that Horace could devote the remainder of the poem to the *res* of satire, that is, its moral themes and Horace's justifications for writing in this genre. In the final poem Horace resumes his thoughts on *verba*, the stylistic standards of good poetry, which now ambiguously includes satire. *Res* and *verba* may be severed in a linear progression; but Horace has placed a marker, a *vide infra*, in 4.63 to prevent a real distinction between the two. The chiastic pair 4 and 10, in other words, preserves the unity of *res/verba*.

Verba in Satire 10, however, are in fact not isolated from *res*. The opening four lines couple style with content:

[57] For 1.9 in relation to 1.10, see V. Buchheit, "Homerparodie und Literaturkritik in Horazens Sat. I 7 und I 9," *Gymnasium* 85 (1968), 519–55, and van Rooy 1972 (above, n. 30).

[58] On the Neoterics, Lucilius, and Horace, see Rudd 1966 (above, n. 21), 118–24.

[59] On the military language see W. S. Anderson, "Horace the Unwilling Warrior, Satires I, 9," *AJPh* 77 (1956), 148–66, summarized by Rudd 1966 (above, n. 21), 79–80. In this context the *doctus* used by Horace to describe his circle of friends (10.87; cf. 9.50–52a) is a sardonic comment on the *doctus* applied to the "bore" (9.7) and the Neoteric group (10.19).

[60] 267 Warmington. On this line see Buchheit 1968 (above, n. 57), 532–42, who relates it to Horace's criticism of Greek words mixed with Latin (10.20–30); cf. Rudd 1966 (above, n. 21), 113, and Anderson 1982 (above, n. 40), 84–89.

[61] While Buchheit 1968 (above, n. 57) and van Rooy 1972 (above, n. 30) can be cautiously recommended for specific links between Satires 9 and 10, the reader will gain a better understanding of Horace's interweaving of themes and images ("gleitende Uebergänge") from U. Knoche, "Betrachtungen über Horazens Kunst der satirischen Gesprächsführung," *Philologus* 90 (1935), 372–90 and 469–82.

nempe *incomposito* dixi *pede currere versus*
Lucili. quis tam Lucili fautor inepte est
ut non hoc fateatur? at idem, quod *sale multo*
urbem defricuit, charta laudatur eadem.

Each component, *res* and *verba*, is essential to good poetry, and thus the closure of
Satire 4 with *res* and of Satire 10 with *verba*. But of course the conclusion of 10 and
of the whole book is much more assured: Horace the satirist calls himself at the end
of 4 one of the poets, *multo plures sumus*, but by the end of 10 the band of poets to
which he belongs is not just numerically greater, like the *Iudaeorum turba,* but both
socially and artistically immensely the superior of their opponents in literature.
Nonetheless the effect is the same: by bringing in himself as a member of the band at
the end of both satires, Horace is effecting as it were the association of the satirical
poeta with both *res* and *verba*.

    Res/verba as an organic whole was part of Horace's poetic creed throughout his
career. It was not of course a new concept in Latin literary tradition. Cato the Elder's
maxim was "rem tene, verba sequentur" (Jordan, p. 80). Cicero, as we saw, insisted
on an essential interdependence of *res* and *verba* which makes their separation for
purposes of literary discussion only a practical convenience that does injustice to
literary reality (*De oratore* 3.19). In doing so, he probably is acknowledging the
Epicurean theory of Philodemus.[62] *Res/verba*, too, is at the root of Horace's attack on
Lucilius. In Horace's opinion, *res* and *verba* are so linked to the creative and conscious artistic processes of the poet (*ingenium* and *ars*, on which see *The Art of
Poetry* 294–308, 408–18) as to render them inseparable from these processes and
from each other.[63] Poetry, in other words, is *ars* and *ingenium* and *res* and *verba*
interwoven into a unity, the "simplex dumtaxat et unum" of *The Art of Poetry* 23.[64]
Poet, style, content—these interrelated and interdependent factors result in *iustum
poema*.[65] Horace's source for this ideal of unity is, we have demonstrated in the first
of these studies, the poetics explicit in Philodemus of Gadara and implicit in
Lucretius. Here it is enough to say that Philodemus had criticized Neoptolemus not
only for separating style from content, but also for making the poet a third separately
treatable aspect of a triad *poema–poesis–poetes*:

καὶ | ταύτης (sc. τῆς ποιητικῆς) εἶδος λέγειν | τὸν [ποι]ητὴ[ν] καταγέ-
[λ]α[c]||τον· θ[α]υμα[cτὸ]ν δ' αὐ|τοῦ καὶ [τὸ] τῆ[c] ποιήcεω[c]| εἶναι
τ[ὴ]ν ὑπόθεcιν [μ]ό|νον, καὶ τοῦ ποήματο[c καὶ]| πάντων ὅλωc τῆc ποή-
c[ε]||ωc ὄντων. ἡ μὲν [γ]ὰρ πό|ηcιc καὶ π[όημά γ' ἐcτίν,]|| οἷον ἡ Ἰλι[άc,]
οἱ δ[ὲ πρῶτοι]|| cτίχοι τρι[άκ]οντα τα[ύ]τηc | πόημα μ[έ]ν, οὐ μέντοι
ποί||[η]cιc· καὶ τὸ ποή[ματοc μό]|νον τὴν [cύνθεcιν τῆc]|| λέξεωc μ[ετέ-

---

[62] See Greenberg 1955, 6, 38, for Philodemus' views on the inseparability of form and content. The
connection between Cicero and Philodemus was first advocated by A. Rostagni in *Scritti Minori,* 2
(Turino 1955), 372–93, which is summarized in Grube 1965, 199 n. 2; above, pp. 143–45.

[63] Cf. Greenberg 1955, 54ff. for Philodemus' similar views.

[64] This runs counter to the traditional stereotype of *The Art of Poetry* as a sloppy and structurally
incoherent poem. Armstrong 1968 (above, n. 53), 63 asserts that *The Art of Poetry* "reveals, by its own
tightly interconnected structure of discourse, exactly what is meant by *simplex et unum.*"

[65] Cf. Greek text of *On Poems* 5 col. xvii (xx).

χειν .....]|ναс διανοί[αс .....]| καὶ πράξειс καὶ π[ροсω]|ποποιί[αс.] εἰ
δ’ ἐν [τῆι]| λέξει πε[π]οιῆсθαί τ[ι | πρέ]πει (Jensen, λέ]γει Mangoni),
κἀνταῦθ[α νὴ Δί’ οὐ]|κ ἔсτι τι πεποι[ῆсθαι το]ύ|των χωρίс, ἀλλ’ [ἴδι]ο[ν
το]ῦ | сυνκεῖсθαι [τὴν] λέξιν τὸ |[сυ]νκεῖсθαι ⟨τὴν⟩ πράξ]ιν (or: τάξ]ιν?)
εἷ[ν]αι φαίνεταί μ[οι· ἐῶ δὲ] (Mangoni, τὸ δὲ] Jensen) καὶ |[τὸ] ποι[ητοῦ
ταῦ]τα (Mangoni, [τοῦ ποιητοῦ ταῦ]τα Jensen) καὶ |[δὴ] καὶ τὴν ὑπ[όθ]ε-
сιν καὶ | τ[ὴν с]ύνθ[ε]сιν. [ὁ γ]ὰρ πάν|τ[α ποι]ῶν οὗτ[όс ἐс]τιν (Mangoni,
[εἶν]αι παν|τ[ὶ δῆλ]ον οὗτ[όс φηс]ιν Jensen). εὐ|ήθ[ωс] δὲ γέγραπται καὶ
| τὸ [μ]ὴ κοινωνε[ῖν] τῶι | πο[ιητῆ]ι (Jensen, πο[η]τεῖ Mangoni) τῶν
ἁμα[ρτ]ιῶν | τὰ[с ὑ]ποθέ[с]ειс καὶ τὰ πο|ήμα[τα·] πονηρὰ γὰρ ἔсτιν | ὅτε
[γί]νετα[ι] ποιήματα | κα[ὶ ὑπ]οθέсε[ι]с φαῦλαι ποι|ημ[άτων] (Jensen,
ποι|ήс[εω]ν Mangoni) ἀφαρμαρ[τά]νον|το[с τοῦ] ποιητοῦ. (*On Poems* 5
cols. xi 23–xii 26 = cols. xiv 23–xv 26 Mangoni: Jensen's text, as modified,
except where indicated, by Mangoni 1993)

To call the poet a subdivision of the art of poetics is ridiculous. It is astonishing
of him also (Neoptolemus) to make the subject alone belong to *poesis* since the
poema and everything else in general are part of it also; for a *poesis* is also a
poema, for example the *Iliad*; but the first thirty verses are just *poema*, but not
poesis. And (it is also astonishing of Neoptolemus) to claim the composition of
the diction belongs to *poema (one word missing)* thoughts *(several words missing)* the action and the character-drawing; because if something must be perfectly composed at the level of diction, it isn't possible to be perfectly composed
apart from these things, but I believe the composition of the action (or: arrangement, *taxis*) to be a function of the composition of the diction; and I pass over
the fact that these things are all the poet's, and also *both* the subject *and* the
diction: for he is the one creating them all; but it's silly to claim that the poet's
faults are not the same as those of the subject and of the poetry. For there
are times when bad poetry and bad subjects both come about because the poet
missed the mark.

Horace echoes this in *The Art of Poetry* 38–47a:

38   sumite materiam vestris, qui scribitis, aequam
      viribus, et versate diu, quid ferre recusent,
40   quid valeant umeri. cui lecta potenter erit res,
      nec facundia deseret hunc nec lucidus ordo.
      ordinis haec virtus erit et venus, aut ego fallor,
      ut iam nunc dicat iam nunc debentia dici,
      pleraque differat et praesens in tempus omittat;
45   in verbis etiam tenuis cautusque serendis
      dixeris egregie notum si callida verbum
      reddiderit iunctura novum.

In order for a poem to achieve the organic unity of *res* and *verba*, it must first be
conceptualized and realized by the poet's *natura* (= *ingenium*; here adumbrated in

"aequam *viribus*" and "lecta *potenter*") and then subjected to *ars* (the techniques of study and work offered here in *The Art of Poetry* as well as in the other literary epistles and satires). When any one of these four qualities is deficient, the *unum*, the poem's unity, remains unachieved.[66] Notice also that Horace observes Philodemus' reservations about these being separate subjects by treating all four at once.

A key word in the passage from *The Art of Poetry* quoted above is *iunctura*, meaning "the joinery of all the elements, large and small, of a work of art, which makes, for example, a traditional story taken from the *Iliad* something new and perfectly your own."[67] *Iungo/iungere* and *sero/series* transform material into good poetry:

> [A bad artist's] *iuncturae* fail of their effect, because there is no *series*. Nor (to extrapolate a little further) do such an artist's *iuncturae* add either *novitas* or *honor* (line 244) to the material he organizes. But this can be done by the artist who commands his material, and who knows how to set it forth as a whole. *Series* and *iunctura* together . . . are the agents of this transformation: *series* (or its equivalent, *lucidus ordo*) by creating a sense that everything is being said in the right place; *iunctura* by adding to the meaning, by creating a semantic gap between juxtapositions of words, phrases, whole segments of a poem, and enlisting the reader's aid to fill it in.[68]

One is reminded here of the interlocking of *elementa* (atoms) in Epicurean physics that Lucretius describes as constituting *res*. The best *iunctura* is achieved by the perfect interlocking of *elementa* (*On the Nature of Things* 6.1084–86):

> quorum ita texturae ceciderunt mutua contra,
> ut cava conveniant plenis haec illius illa
> huiusque inter se, *iunctura* haec optima constat.

Lucretius' example is iron (*On the Nature of Things* 6.1005–11):

> hoc ubi inanitur spatium multusque vacefit
> in medio locus, extemplo primordia ferri
> in vacuum prolapsa cadunt *coniuncta*, fit utque
> anulus ipse sequatur eatque ita corpore toto.
> nec res ulla magis *primordibus* ex *elementis*
> indupedita suis arte *conexa* cohaeret
> quam validi ferri natura et frigidus horror.

To put this in poetic/philosophical terms, the *synthesis* (combination, composition of style) of the *elementa* (atoms, letters), along with the *positura* and *ordo* of the *elementa* (*primordia*, which is a translation of the Greek *stoicheia*), transforms *materia* (substance, content) into an *unum*. Metathesis, according to Philodemus and Lucretius as well as Horace, causes a rearrangement of the *elementa* and thus severs the

---

[66] Brink 1971 (above, n. 49), 122: "In relating *ars* and *materia* to talent (*natura*) [Horace] breaks down the artificial distinctions of textbooks. The ultimate achievement of poetic art—a poem in which words and thoughts have an indissoluble organic unity—justifies the poet's choice of his task. But, paradoxically, the choice of task can be justified only by the native talent of the chooser."

[67] Armstrong 1968 (above, n. 53), 45–46.   [68] Armstrong 1968 (above, n. 53), 46.

callida iunctura of the *unum* and causes newness (*novum*). What had been a concrete and unified thought and content has been eliminated by new interlocking order (*iungere* and *serere*). As commentators have noted, *iunctura* is a surprising literary critical term and does not appear in this sense before Horace.[69] But its use by Horace will not be by happenstance if we consider *iunctura* in Epicurean atomistic terms.

In Book 1 of the *Satires* the same doctrine of the need for the unity of *res* and *verba* obtains. *Satires* 1.4.39–44 requires *ingenium* of the *poeta*.[70] *Ars* is a major topic throughout the two literary satires (e.g., *Satires* 4.8–21, 10.1–35, 51–74a). Because no person can be a poet who lacks *ars* or *ingenium*, because unity in *res* and *verba* will not result, Horace would claim, on this basis, not that satire is not poetry— it is—but that Lucilius was *pro tanto* not a *poeta*. That Lucilius possessed insufficient *ars* is obvious from the criticisms in Satires 4 and 10. Lucilius simply could not write good verse. He lacked discipline, structure, careful thought, proper diction, any semblance of formal finish. Lucilius of course is praised for the content of his satires, that is, his *res* (10.3b–5), but *res* alone does not qualify verse as true (*iustum*) poetry.[71]

Lucilius was prevented from integrating his *verba* into a unified whole, not merely because of his lack of *ars*, that Callimachean ideal of meticulous, painstaking polish and discipline[72] (which for Horace is identical with the labor of making every small detail of word-arrangement and even letter-arrangement contribute, as Philodemus prescribed, to the effect of the whole). Lucilius' *ingenium* was also inferior. Horace had already questioned Lucilius' *ingenium* at 4.12–13a: "piger scribendi ferre laborem, / scribendi recte." Granted, Horace compliments Lucilius for his wit and keen perception ("facetus, / emunctae naris," 4.7b–8a), but these are not necessarily qualities of *poetic* talent; besides, these two attributes, stated in but three words, are offset by the subsequent thirteen lines of sustained criticism.

At 10.56–64, a crucial passage which brings all our oppositions, *res/verba*, *ars/ingenium*, Horace/Lucilius together in one, Horace is more direct about Lucilius' *ingenium*.[73] Philodemus had thought that the *res* are a function (*idion*) of the *verba*,

---

[69] According to the *Thesaurus linguae Latinae*, the word is older than Horace; it is used once in Caesar as an architectural term. Varro's reference to it is too short to permit us to determine what he means. Later poets accepted Horace's use of it; see, e.g., Persius 5.14, on which see R. A. Harvey, *A Commentary on Persius* (Leiden 1981), 129–31.

[70] L. P. Wilkinson, *Horace and his Lyric Poetry* (Cambridge 1968), 89 associates 4.39–44 with the *ingenium* of *Art of Poetry* 323.

[71] For Horace's opinions of Lucilius' style see now Freudenberg (above, n. 5), 13 n. 28, 158ff., 179ff.; Freudenberg 1993 opines (p. 173) that Horace was Lucilius' greatest admirer—a statement that we do not accept with enthusiasm, although we grant that Horace took his predecessor as his model for transforming the satire genre.

[72] The bibliography on Callimachean principles in Horace's literary criticism is enormous. We refer the reader to F. Wehrli, "Horaz und Kallimachos," *MH* 1 (1944), 69–76; W. Wimmel, *Kallimachos in Rom. Die Nachfolge seines apologetischen Dichtens in der Augusteerzeit* (Weisbaden 1960), 148–67; J. V. Cody, *Horace and Callimachean Aesthetics* (Brussels 1976), especially 24–27; J. J. Clauss, "Allusion and Structure in Horace Satire 2.1: The Callimachean Response," *TAPA* 115 (1985), 197–206; Brink 1963, 159–61, 181–82, 195–96, 219–20, 255–56, who correctly points out that the only Callimachean principle Horace agreed with was the need for a high degree of formal finish and craftsmanship; and Freudenberg 1993 (above, n. 5), 104ff. and ch. 4.

[73] See the remarks of Greenberg 1955, 43ff. on Philodemus' views concerning style, composition, content, and the poet.

and vice versa. Horace also sweeps the scale from the largest to the smallest elements in this passage. He asks whether Lucilius' own *natura* (*ingenium*) or his *res*, subject matter, was at fault for the lack of *ars* which made his style so ineffective (*Satires* 1.10.56–64):

> quid vetat et nosmet Lucili scripta legentis
> quaerere, num illius, num rerum dura negarit
> versiculos natura magis factos et euntis
> mollius, ac si quis pedibus quid claudere senis,
> hoc tantum contentus, amet scripsisse ducentos
> ante cibum versus, totidem cenatus, Etrusci
> quale fuit Cassi rapido ferventius amni
> ingenium, capsis quem fama est esse librisque
> ambustum propriis?

Given that Horace had already defended Lucilius' *res* directly at the beginning of the poem and indirectly through the justification of his own satire in 4.64ff., the choice of answers offered is an illusion. The answer to Horace's question is obvious: nothing was wrong with the *res* Lucilius chose, but rather Lucilius lacked real *ingenium* and therefore *ars*. This is further implied by the conjunction of the *ingenium* of Lucilius with that of the hack poet Cassius in the lines quoted above. Finally, the lines are a response to *Satires* 1.4.9–13:

> nam fuit hoc vitiosus: in hora saepe *ducentos*,
> ut magnum, *versus* dictabat stans pede in uno.
> cum *flueret* lutulentus, erat quod tollere velles;
> *garrullus atque piger scribendi ferre laborem,*
> *scribendi recte*; nam ut multum, nil moror.

The issue of Lucilius' *ars* is closed.[74]

The passage just quoted shows that word-play and word-arrangement of the kind that makes metathesis impossible never stops in Horace. These lines are an example, as *quid* is indeed "closed up" between the words "si quis pedibus . . . claudere senis." In this context, we can appreciate the word-play and verbal ambiguities in 10.46–49, verses often taken as a praise of Lucilius:

> hoc erat, experto frustra Varrone Atacino
> atque quibusdam aliis, melius quod scribere possem,
> inventore minor; neque ego illi detrahere ausim
> haerentem capiti cum multa laude coronam.

Horace here pays homage to Lucilius: the excessive number of elisions in line 48b (*nequ(e) eg(o) illi detraher(e) ausim*) proves that Horace can play Lucilius' game. Horace also takes a humble pose by stating that he is *minor*. But is he *minor* in an artistic sense? No: he already had taken Lucilius to task for his sloppy workmanship, especially as compared with his own verses. Rather he is, by word-play, *minor* in

---

[74] Needless to say, we cannot support Rudd's contention (1966 [above, n. 21], 89): in "spite of his (sc. Lucilius') inferior craftsmanship and polish we are still meant to think of Lucilius as a poet." van Rooy 1968 (above, n. 30), 59 agrees.

both chronology and *inventio*, but not absolutely so. The ambiguity of the subjunctive "neque . . . ausim" is like that of the subjunctive verbs in 4.39–62; it makes one wonder whether Horace is being serious in this passage too. An elision of *ego* into *illi* (Lucilius), an elision which recalls that in 4.39a (*millorum*), reinforces the doubt. The elided unit *egilli* precedes a verbal unit denoting an opposite motion, *detrahere ausim*. Horace will, and yet at the same time will not, elide/conflict with Lucilius: he would not strip the crown from him but he would still contend for glory by grabbing onto his predecessor by elision. Thus while Lucilius may still be praised as *inventor*, Horace can still struggle with him for equal honor as *perfector* of the genre.

If Lucilius is not a poet according to Horace's scheme, that is, if Lucilius displays no poetic unity of *res/verba* through deficiencies in both *ars* and *ingenium*, how would Horace rate Horace? The answer to this question is self-evident. First of all, Horace's application of *ars* throughout his poetry is so well documented that no further comment is required.[75] The literary and moral criticism balanced inter- and intratextually throughout the poems of Book 1 of the *Satires* prove that Horace devoted equal care to *res* and *verba*. What, finally, of *ingenium*—the quality which in an equilibrium with *ars* constitutes the *virtus* of the poet?[76] The implication of the elision *millorum* in *Satires* 1.4.38–44, with the specific characterization of *illorum* as possessors of *ingenium*, is completed in the fine "cloud of witnesses" of 10.81–90a: Horace is indeed one of the men of *ingenium*, the company of poets and critics to whom he, the satirist, belongs as one of them. Satires 4 and 10, therefore, do not just address issues of literary criticism and the qualities of satiric writing; they also yield a portrait of Horace as the *poeta perfectus* (*The Art of Poetry* 347–476)—one whose poetic excellence and charm, *virtus et venus*, derive from *ars* and *ingenium* that create a unique unity that any metathesis would destroy, the unity of *res* and *verba*. The result may look simple, but a person would discover the limits of his own *ars* and *ingenium* who tried to equal it (*The Art of Poetry* 240–42):

> ex noto fictum carmen sequar, ut sibi quivis
> speret idem, sudet multum frustraque laboret
> ausus idem.

Much of the secret of this perfection of *poeta* is to be found in the subtleties of both word order, apparently simple to the eye but in fact inalterable and perfect, and letter-arrangement in the visual text on the page. Such subtleties and poetic theory are what Horace describes in *Satires* 1.4 and what he learned from the Epicurean circles of Philodemus and Lucretius.

---

[75] But see, e.g., J. F. D'Alton, *Roman Literary Theory and Criticism. A Study in Tendencies* (London 1931), 374–95; S. Commager, *The Odes of Horace: A Critical Study* (New Haven 1962), 23–49; Brink 1963, 158–71, 186–90, 218–19; Rudd 1966 (above, n. 21), chapter 4; Brink 1971 (above, n. 49), passim, especially 75–194; Anderson 1982 (above, n. 40), 13–28; Brink 1982 (above, n. 49), 328–60, 457–58, 469–70.

[76] See Brink 1971 (above, n. 49), ad 408–18 (pp. 394–95) and 453–76 (pp. 421–22).

Appendix 1
Philodemus, *On Poems* Book 5

Translated by David Armstrong from the edition of Cecilia Mangoni, Naples (Bibliopolis), 1993

Mangoni's text—as I have verified by reading the sources (*P.Herc.* 1425 and 1538 and the N and O *disegni* of them) in Naples and Oxford in summer 1993—is an immense improvement on the previous text, that of C. Jensen (Berlin, 1923). I did this work as part of a NEH Translation Grant, directed by Richard Janko, David Blank, and Dirk Obbink, which will result in a text with English translation and notes of *On Poems, On Music,* and *On Rhetoric.* So much speculative Greek of Jensen's has been removed and replaced by Mangoni with either excellent Greek of Philodemus' own or honestly admitted lacunae that the effect is like that of a darkened monument or painting newly and splendidly cleaned. Where I differ from her text or interpretation I have indicated this in a note. The headings I have added indicate (a) current opinion, as represented in Mangoni's preface, on the structure of the surviving part of Book 5, and (b) my own personal opinion—which is more adventurous in some respects than Mangoni's—of what positive axioms about poetics of Philodemus' own can be gleaned from his criticism of other critics.

What Jensen, whose fragment and column numbers are those of N, the Naples transcript) numbers as "fr." i and ii are numbered by Mangoni cols. i and iii. In Jensen and N there then follow "columns" i–xxxvi. The *disegnatore* of O, the Oxford transcript, numbered these "fragments" cols. i and ii, resulting in 38 columns in all. Mangoni agrees with him but has added what can be deciphered with the aid of the microscope (a little) of the column that came in between the two, now numbered in her edition col. ii. The result is that her column numbers are (after iii) those of Jensen and N +3 (e.g. Jensen's and N's col. i = Mangoni col. iv, their col. xii = Mangoni col. xv). With relation to O, they are O +1 (O col. iii = Mangoni col. iv and so on up to the final column, O xxxviii = Jensen and N xxxvi = Mangoni xxxix). For the convenience of readers comparing Jensen's edition, which follows the numbering of N but also gives (inadequate) reproductions of O, I list all three.

1. The Literary Criticism of Heraclides Ponticus:[1] No definition of poetry that is not proper to poetry itself alone is meaningful; therefore "educational," "moral," "useful," and the like are useless terms in poetics. Poetry is not suitable for a true technical presentation of any complicated scientific or philosophical topic and cannot be "useful" in this manner either. Nor is profound scholarly learning necessary to the poet

M(angoni), col. i = O i = N–J(ensen) fr. i: . . . And many philosophers, the greatest most of all, similarly would not be educational in [the kinds of education he specified].[2] Nor do the teachers of rhetoric make this promise, nor any of the comparable kinds of education. If he claims that in general none of the poets use apodeictic demonstrations (formal proofs) in their own person or their characters'. . . will command . . . of philosophers . . . of the other . . . kinds of education . . . . and many prose discourses are educational, for instance protreptic, epainetic, consolatory, and admonitory discourses; they have not the same form as those that are properly called apodeictic . . .

M col. ii (not in O, N, or Jensen) (otherwise unintelligible: lines 25–6:) . . . Empedocles . . . wrote . . .[3] from the good poets . . . facts (*pragmata*) (line 34, end) . . . of the good . . .

M Col. iii (=O ii=N–J fr. ii) poets . . . facts . . . now, Homer understood his facts, but if as (a philosopher? an educator?) I wonder, for which reason also . . . (I wonder?) (what[4] he claims is?) right conduct ([προς]ήκειν), if Homer *is* educational. And in saying that others ought, as we mentioned . . . he means that others proceed the same way, and particularly Heraclides, as we mentioned; now Heraclides . . . for saying that . . . the poet . . . the hearers, but profit the . . . if on the one hand he meant profit them in moral virtue, it is obvious from the things said before; . . . fell into . . . or it is not possible . . . if he thought otherwise, . . .

M col. iv (=O iii=N–J col. i) . . . wretched man, because though there are many ways of profiting, he did not define which of them we demand from the *poet*, and did not show by what means and what pleasure he pleases, but in both aspects left the excellence of the poet undefined.[5] Also, the finest poetry of the most famous poets, since it gives no profit whatever—of some poets, indeed, the majority of their poetry, and of several poets all of it—he expels from excellence altogether. For why need I mention those poems that do the greatest harm that is in their power (ὅϲον ἐφ᾽ [αὐτοῖϲ]) to do people? Or that by this reasoning, the most excellently useful poetry will be the most perfect; but no one can ([δύ]νacθαι) be useful through his knowledge of medicine or philosophy or many another science if he attempts to reach the

---

[1] Philodemus most probably set forth the opinions he is about to criticise in the lost first half of the book, as appears from the frequent "as we mentioned," "as we noticed," and the like. As our text opens he is criticising an unknown adversary, and then turns to Heraclides (Ponticus). It is possible that Heraclides' opinions are being criticised all the way to section 2 (col. xii), or that the name of another critic or two has vanished in the many lacunas.

[2] Mangoni's text (showing ΠΑΙΔΕΥ) excludes Jensen's τοιαύταιϲ [αἱϲ εἴρη]κε παιδεί[αιϲ . .]. Perhaps παιδεύ[ϲεϲιν, especially since O (both the original and the Oxford 1825 engraving of it) shows traces of a sigma, or omicron, and space for four more letters after the upsilon.

[3] Thus Philodemus was evidently considering the possibility of didactic poetry, such as Empedocles', as Mangoni notes ad loc.

[4] On the pap. the letter Mangoni reads as Π is ΤΙ, so Jensen's τί [φηϲιν προϲ]ήκειν may just be right.

[5] The adversary, Heraclides (Ponticus), has argued for the usefulness of poetry in some such terms as Horace's *omne tulit punctum qui miscuit utile dulci.*

height of perfection with poetic craftsmanship (ἐπ᾽ ἄκρον ἐλαύνοντα μετὰ ποιητικῆς ἐξερ-γασίας)![6] And indeed, writing that the poet 'who pleases, but does not profit, is poetic, but
M col. v (=O iv=N–J ii) ignorant of reality (πράγματα), he appears to think that every
representation of reality is profitable; which is patently false. For if some such representation
is unprofitable, nothing prevents a poet from knowing the subject and representing it poetically without profiting us a bit. Also he strangely loads down the good poet with the accurate
and complete study of the forms of speech that belong to dialect, though that dialect in which
he chooses to write is sufficient; and by not . . . to have the knowledge of music; and by such
a person's . . . in all ways; and in general to the poets (should belong) all of geometry, and
geography, and . . . and seamanship . . . necessary . . . though what belongs . . . and in general
everything not merely the province of handicraft.[7]
    M vi (=O v=N–J iii) . . . but rather . . . of handicraft. If . . . possible . . .

*Stylistic definitions which would do equally well for prose are not helpful in
poetics, because they ignore what makes poetry poetry. Philodemus' objections to a theory that "the poet" should have certain priorities in plan-
ning his poem, and that a theory of dignity and importance in subject
differentiates poetry from prose*

(. . . he says that) the first and least[8] of things to work out in advance is concision and . . . ,
but in the thoughts (persuasiveness) and vividness, and both these belong to the art and the
poet. What does "first" mean, one must enquire, and what does "least"? If "first" is just a term
for the things to be thought out first,[9] I am at a loss why this should be brought in ahead of
many other requisites. And I wonder why he calls concision and vividness least, although
nothing . . .
    M vii (=O vi=N–J iv) . . . (if he called that) the best thing, how is that at the same time the
least? how are vividness and concision better than any other of the things that belong to
poetics? Why is it necessary to represent the subject-matter (τὸ πραττόμενον) vividly *and
convincingly,* when many things not simply false but completely mythical are represented in
the poets with the utmost vividness? And why should one make a problem of whether both
these things belong to the art and the poet? Because on the one hand that is nothing peculiar
(to poets and to the art of poetry), but (good) prose-writers strive for concision and vividness
also;[10] and besides, *through* the art and *from* the poet come in this manner not just these things
(qualities) but simply everything that is excellent ([δια]φαίνεται)[11] (in poetry). Then he says
in addition that the poet puts into the solider and greater kind of poetry, in addition to the
qualities mentioned, splendor and weight, not shabbiness and flimsiness, and "this is the
handiwork and business (κατὰ τὴν χεῖρα καὶ τὴν πραγματείαν) of the poet, dealing as
material (ὕλη)

    [6] Or "but no one is profited ([ὄ]ναςθαι) by medicine, philosophy, or many other disciplines if he tries
to reach perfection in them with only their *poetic* presentation" (Jensen).
    [7] Not all of Jensen's reconstruction can be justified from the papyrus, but the meaning is little
changed: the adversary recommended all the branches of learning mentioned as necessary for the education of the perfect poet.
    [8] The context is unclear: cf. Greenberg 1955, 26.   [9] i.e. before beginning to write.
    [10] Mangoni's (or rather the text's) reading makes sense where there was little before ("For it is not
obscure, but very clear to those who create brevity and clarity that it is by art and through the poet,"
Greenberg 1955, 27 translates Jensen's text).
    [11] Or perhaps just "is to be seen." Cf. col. xv 16f. below (note 20); in Philodemus' highly intentional-
ist poetics the art (*techne*) is the source, and the poet the creator, of everything in the poem.

M viii (=O vii=N–J v) with a rich supply of personages (πρόςωπα) and their manners (ἤθη) and inquiry into particular myths and plots and the truths and unique qualities of each." Now, I ask, what does he call "solider and greater poetry? . . .

. . . and so how is poetry "without vigour" (μὴ εὔτονα) different from the "tumid" (ὀγκώδη)? and why do only these kinds of poetry and the middle genre need splendor? how is there a plot (or "subject": ὑπόθεcιc) "even in middling poetry, but most in solid ones" and what sort of plot is weighty and not flimsy? I am sure there should be no shabbiness nor flimsiness in any poem, nor in these sorts either. Why, according to this, what is there, by Zeus, that could not offer us unique stories and a plot and truths and particular qualities too![12] Richness . . . the truth of these things . . . in fictions . . .

M ix (=O viii=N–J vi) . . . How does the statement that "this belongs to the handwork and industry of the poet" differs from saying that "it is part of the art and of the poet?" Why he put "handiwork" first I do not understand. And what are we to understand by "the material" with which (the poet) deals? And indeed . . . a person explain[ing? i.e. telling (stories) in conversation?][13] expresses particular stories, and a plot, and truth. And why he put in truth in addition, nevertheless, I cannot understand.

M x (=O ix=N–J vii) . . . and then a thousand other excellences must belong to the . . . beside those . . . of poetry and prose both. And the subject matter . . .

Some positive things to say: writing good verse does not make a poet, though it is important; perfect composition is more important than any particular kind of content; style and content are equal elements

But that we need along with writing good poetry (τὸ εὖ ποιεῖν) also the . . .[14] of the good poet, and that he that writes well differs from the good poet, I entirely accept. For someone can take some unreasonable myth or plot and work it out poetically, and there have been such poets; but the good and perfect poet is one who is thought of (as making) a choice (ἐκλογή) of these (i.e. subjects) also.[15]

Now that the . . . (should be) such as we find in Homer and Sophocles . . . .

M xi (=O X=N–J viii) . . . I accept that the fact that some play the flute who are not good flute-players corresponds to the fact that he who writes good poetry is different from the good poet. And there is nothing forced in his calling in musicians to witness of that. To claim that (a) "correctly making this distinction divides the subject matter (of poetics) in two" (διαcτέλλειν τὰ προcόντα)

M xii (=O xi=N–J ix) and that (b) "the composition itself of poetry (αὐτὸ τὸ ποιεῖν) could not take a lesser part (than the subject matter), but what belongs to that is even a greater part," I think means the same as that it is more important in poetics to be perfectly composed and arranged (τὸ πεποιημένον εἶναι) than to be rich in thought (τοῦ τὰ διανοήματ' ἔχειν πολυτελῆ).[16]

---

[12] i. e. how could any of this differentiate poetry from prose? Mangoni seems right here to print the text as reconstructed by Rostagni (cf. Greenberg 1955, 31 and n. 1), not Jensen's "Would not Ti[maios] (of Tauromenium, i.e. history in general) offer us . . . ."

[13] If ΕΞΗΓΟΥΜ in the gap stands for the present participle ἐξηγούμενος.

[14] We have only the letters τουcτ . ‖[. . . .] τοῦ ἀγαθοῦ ποιητοῦ. Perhaps τοὺc τό[[πουc ("argomenti," Mangoni) or τοὺc τύ|[πουc ("the general concepts," i.e. those one has of the poet, M. Wigodsky).

[15] ἐκλογὴ ὀνομάτων =delectus verborum is the usual phrase for choice of diction, so Philodemus would be taking a word from the vocabulary of diction or style, *poema,* and applying it to large structure, *poesis,* instead.   [16] As Philodemus also thinks.

2. Critics transcribed by Philomelus.[17] Another variation of the objection that the definitions of "excellence" in most literary criticism does not exclude prose

Now of those whose opinions are transcribed in Philomelus, those on the one hand who think that the person who has equal efficacy in plot-creation, in the other aspects of character-creation, and in style is the best poet are no doubt saying something true, but are not really defining the good *poet*. Because one might set this forth as the excellence of a composer of mimes, of a teller of miraculous tales (*aretalogos*), or in general of a prose-writer. But that the style and the content are of equal essentiality (παραπληcίωc ἀναγκαῖα) is reasonable. Praxiphanes, on the other hand, says something different in Book one of his *On Poetry*: that sometimes even when the subject is . . . (*line missing*). And then Demetrios of Byzantium

M xiii (=O xii=N–J x) wrote still other things, since he claims that one must first get the contents elegantly thought out, and then dress them in words that are not inappropriate to the underlying thought, and finally work out the style of the diction beautifully . . . we may understand that those are the principal topics of his writings. For to believe that is the stamp of the good poet is surpassingly silly. He is not in any way whatever inquiring what is good poetry, nor even what is more important to it and less, but what part of it should happen first and second and last, though he could have made that fit . . . (all the genres?): for they all have to be well thought out and find appropriate words and be worked out well in respect of style.

3. Neoptolemus of Parium. The Aristotelian division style–content–author is meaningless, as content is as much a function of style as of anything else, and therefore not separably discussable; and similarly neither is "the author" a separable category from the other two

But now Neoptolemus[18] in particular seems wrong to separate the composition of the style (cύνθεcιc τῆc λέξεωc)

M xiv (=Oxiii=N–J xi) from the thoughts (διανοήματα), calling it neither a lesser part nor a greater, as we saw. And then, absurdly, he takes the person who has the art (τέχνη) and the capacity of exercising it in poetry (δύναμιc ποητική) and makes him a division of the art besides *poema* and *poesis*. How is this? He ought rather to have called the *diathesis*[19] *poesis*; or better, the *poemata* the working and weaving (ἔργα) and the *poieseis*, so to speak, the things woven (οἷον ὕφη) and the *poetes* the man who has the faculty (of working and weaving) and works according to it; and he goes wrong calling the working itself poetics, when that is rather the name of the craft; while to call the poet a subdivision of this is ridiculous. It is astonishing of him to say that only the subject (ὑπόθεcιc) belongs to *poesis*, since the *poema*

---

[17] Otherwise unknown. Philomelus' summary probably offered at least the opinions of the Peripatetic Praxiphanes of Mitylene (c. 300 B.C., a pupil of Theophrastus), Demetrius of Byzantium (another Peripatetic probably of later date), and may also have summarized Neoptolemus, "Aristo" and Crates (Mangoni 1993, 47–52).

[18] The reading [Νεοπ]τόλεμος—the Aristotelian critic Neoptolemus of Parium, according to Porphyrio the source of the principal topics of Horace's *The Art of Poetry*—is confirmed by Mangoni and is visible in the papyrus, as Jensen reported.

[19] Composition and arrangement of the whole work; in rhetoric sometimes also opposed to *heuresis*, invention of the topic.

and everything in general belong to that; for a *poesis* is also *poema,* for instance the *Iliad,* but its first thirty verses are *poema* but not *poesis.*

M xv (=O xiv=N–J xii) And also that only the composition of the diction has to do with *poema,* and not, rather, also the thought [and arrangement?] and action and character-portrayal. For if it is fitting that something should be perfectly composed in the diction, by Zeus there also it is not possible for that to happen without these things, but the composition of the action (τὸ ϲυνκεῖϲθαι ⟨τὴν⟩ [πράξ]ιν) appears to me a function (ἴδιον) of the composition of the diction (τοῦ ϲυνκεῖϲθαι τὴν λέξιν).[20] I pass over the fact that these things also belong to "poet," both the subject *and* the composition; for he is the man who creates everything in the poem (ὁ γὰρ πάντα ποιῶν οὗτός ἐϲτιν).[21] And it is stupid to have written that the defects of the subject and the poetry are not shared by the poet. For bad poetry and bad choice of subject do sometimes happen because the poet is making mistakes. And that the *poema* is first of the divisions . . . was not clever of him. If he meant that the *poema* is first in (temporal) order, that was entirely strange talk. If it is the best, why is it best rather than the *poesis,* which in fact

M xvi (=O xv=N–J xiii) embraces that (*poema*) also?[22] If he was contrasting the stylistic finish of the poem (τὸ πεποι[ῆϲθαι]) with the thoughts ([διανο]ήματα), he said the same earlier. He claims that there is a primacy or . . . and that he will put into . . . for the perfect poet along with his entertaining qualities to benefit his hearers and tell them useful things, and that Homer (both pleases and profits?); but did not undertake to show that he does in fact profit, and how . . . (pleases?) besides profiting . . . has written . . . was the greatest poet. And what kind of profit ought to be there and what kinds of useful lessons ought to be given us he has not clarified, so that one could even understand that he means the usefulness and good teachings that come from philosophy (ϲοφία) and the other sciences (ἐπιϲτῆμαι).[23]

4. A (Stoic?) critic. More against the moral definition of poetry

Now as for the follower of the Stoics . . . ( ]on or]ton?)[24] . . .

M xvii (=O xvi=N–J xiv) (on) poetry, that as a composer of treatises he is . . . contradictory, petulant, verbose and full of falsehood I cannot deny.

What is so clever in setting up against good and bad poetry the "neither good nor bad"? Or in calling" good" poetry that which has excellent composition and morally good thought (διάνοια), and (defining) "morally good thought" with "for the most part when they display good thoughts and deeds or give us poetry that is of educational value," when none of the poets has written poetry containing (περιέχοντα) such thoughts nor could ever possibly do so? But he claims he accepts not only that sort of thing (as good), but also when the poets discover new inventions peculiar to themselves about their subject, "by which reasoning," he

[20] Again Philodemus takes a phrase more usual in speaking of diction (τὸ ϲυνκεῖϲθαι τὴν λέξιν = ϲύνθεϲιϲ λέξεωϲ = *iunctura verborum*) and applies it to larger structure: cf. note 14 above.

[21] Cf. note 10 above.

[22] i.e. "of which that is only a part?" Mangoni's text, following the papyrus, here again makes far better sense than Jensen's misreading "to which he has joined it."

[23] So Neoptolemus also, like Heraclides, believed in *qui miscuit utile dulci,* but Philodemus' "so one could even understand" means that Neoptolemus did *not* (at least explicitly) commit the error of requiring the poet to know philosophy and the sciences.

[24] Perhaps a name ending in -ων followed here (and in O what looks like the crossbar of a tau can be seen before the omega and nu), but the text is too uncertain to justify Jensen's idea that the Stoic Ariston of Chios is meant. In the translation, I have used the translation by Asmis 1990b, 197–200 of cols. xvi 28–xxiv 21, mostly from Jensen's edition, for comparison. But Mangoni's discoveries in the text require changes in numerous places.

continues, "we will say that some things of Antimachus are educational. . . . Also, although with reservations we say that Homer's and Archilochus' poems are good poems,

M xviii (=O xvii=N–J xv) that only poetry containing wise and educational thought is unambiguously and perhaps even more, perhaps, even, in the only proper sense 'good'; while those others are so called in an imprecise sense (καταχρηστικῶς)." And in fact (καὶ δὴ γάρ) he would have agreed that the words "useful," "good," "excellent" are predicated of thoughts, and styles, and poetry, sometimes in a strict sense, sometimes in an imprecise sense.[25] But surely it is counterfeit to add that that which is well composed, but embraces a thought that is bizarre (ἀλλόκοτος) and off the track of our common understanding (παρεκβεβηκυῖαν τὸν κοινὸν νοῦν), is useless, like the (καθάπερ τά):

> First he put on his greaves, round his calves[26]

"Bizarre" had not been mentioned as a category; only "not-good" and "bad" thought had been mentioned. And how can a consistent thinker say that Antimachus' poetry . . .

M xix (=O xviii=N–J xvi) . . . contain . . . who could . . . good (thought) . . .

And then he thinks himself very wise to say, that that which has neither good nor bad technique is not good as a whole but neither good nor bad, but in a particular respect only (good or bad), most often in style. They call this sort of thing "artistically . . .," . . . again about composition. And indeed, though saying that certain poetry is not excellent, but "neither excellent nor incompetent," he still claims it is good in some particular respect. He says the thought is neither excellent nor bad, so that really he is saying that the composition is in some particular respect perfectly good, and especially in respect to composition.[27] . . . (if) he was calling . . . (the thought of such poems as Homer's?) . . . neither good

M xx (=O xix=N–J xvii) nor bad, what poetry was he leaving us that has these wise and educational thoughts, and which of the ancients' works did he suppose contains them? In general, if a man will not call these good poetry, I cannot see what he *will* call good. I realize some folks would say that art is "what resembles the works of Antimachus." . . . (well then) let that—since there's all authority given to everybody—be their statement. Antimachus' works are written with the praiseworthy kind of art, cities and places being in them in such

---

[25] Philodemus seems to mean that he himself agrees with the propositions in this last sentence, and that for him the proper definition of "good," etc. belongs to philosophy or other arts and sciences, as for his adversary; but the transferred sense of "good" belongs to poetry that is good *qua* poetry, which has nothing to do with "good" *per se*: Cf. column xviii ad fin.–xix init. below.

[26] The first verse of several descriptions of heroes arming themselves, *Iliad* 3. 330ff = (more or less) *ll.*17ff, 16.131ff, 19.369ff. In Mangoni's interpretation this and the rest of the description of how to put on armor apparently struck the adversary as well-composed but completely trivial and without ethical value; but the sentence is very difficult to understand unless, as Asmis 1990b, 175 argues, Philodemus' Stoic adversary believed the description to be *factually* improbable. Asmis' argument from Aristophanes *Frogs* 1034–41 may not work (Homer, says Dionysus, does not teach you to put your armor on so well that so-and-so in the audience was prevented from putting on his helmet first and then putting the crest on the helmet). And Mangoni objects that the Homeric scholiasts observe nothing peculiar in these descriptions, But cf. Leaf on *Iliad* 3.330: "(In these four descriptions) (t)he six pieces of armor are always mentioned in the same order, in which they would naturally be put on, *except that we would expect the helmet to be donned before the shield was taken on the arm.*" (Italics mine). Perhaps "Ariston" referred to some such "Homeric problem" brought up about the description as a whole. Philodemus in the later part of rolls (as here) is frequently alluding telegraphically to something more fully set out earlier. At any rate the unambiguous word *allokotos* suggests there was some "Homeric problem" behind "Ariston's" criticism.

[27] As Mangoni notes there is a space left after this word, frequently (not always) indicating the end of a sentence. Philodemus would mean that "Ariston" is guilty of tautology by not specifying further what purely poetic "goodness" is.

beautiful harmony and placed in such excellent order, something one could indeed even call useful.[28]

Bad or indifferent composition makes poetry worthless

I object to what he says next: that poetry which has neither good composition, nor good thought, is neither good nor bad, because he does not give us an example. It seems to me amazing that, if the composition is not good, and the thought not good nor poetic, the poetry is not bad.

M xxi (=O xx=N–J xviii) I approve, however, when he says that that which has good content but bad composition is bad, and that to be bad, bad composition is enough.[29]

Against those who define poetry by its special appeal to the ear

But that for goodness, good composition is not enough, but we need beautiful sound and thought-content and many other things also (is nonsense?) . . . and dragged in all atangle with (cυνεπενήνεχθαι) the groundless (theory of) "beautiful sounds" of the *kritikoi*,[30] if we remember what we said before.

Against the moral definition

I disagree even more with his statement that some ancient poems good in some respect, especially in their composition, are as a whole bad. Because when I take these words in their usual sense, I find nothing more incomprehensible than the notion that things good in some respect are as a whole bad. It is stranger still to say this: "what is not in accordance with the *technai,* even if finely composed, is bad" and that "most of the poems of the greatest poets are neither fine nor good, since they are written in contravention of

M xxii (=O xxi=N–J xix) the one sole *techne* properly so called that belongs to them,[31] but there are poems well composed by other poets in accordance with (the rules of) some arts and in contradiction to others; and particularly when (the contradiction) concerns something *recherché* and not easily accessible, and the poetic working out is fine, some such poems are perfectly good; but when there is no such particular respect then we could say it over (repeat the same estimate[32])." So also, as for his dictum that when we can not say whether a thought underlies, we cannot say whether it is poetry or not: though because he seemed to scout that notion earlier,[33] he is far from agreeing with himself, *that* is true enough, I think. But how can he say, that in cases where we know that a thought underlies, but do not know whether it

---

[28] These last three sentences are apparently meant sarcastically: Philodemus means that if the consequence of "Ariston's" moral theory of poetry is to admire Antimachus more than Homer that is a sufficient refutation of it.

[29] So Philodemus also believes. But it is clear throughout, and from what follows, that if "good" content is defined educationally or morally, he does not believe the converse at all, that "bad" content makes even well-composed poetry bad.

[30] "Ariston" (like Crates and the *kritikoi*) separated the sensual experience of beautiful sound in poetry, whose critic is the ear, from the intellectual experience of the thought or subject, whose critic is the mind.

[31] Mangoni has here replaced another senseless reading of Jensen's with a more accurate text. As she explains, "Ariston" meant that the thoughts of the great classic poets were unacceptable, whatever their style.   [32] The restoration of this last phrase may not be right.

[33] And agree with the euphonists that poetry can consist in the mere musical sound.

corresponds to ordinary human understanding or not, we should suspend our judgment of good or bad; but, in the case of things that are clearly against ordinary human understanding put them down as in the same class as the[34] so-called "bizarre" statements? if he called such cases poetry at all. It also seems to me silly, to say that people with any sort of sense . . .

Composition and thought are one in poetry, and their appreciation is an exercise of reason and the mind, not merely the senses

M xxiii (=O xxii=N–J xx) of an artistic (*technikon*) *poema* . . . praise the composition . . . not know the thought . . . of what is well composed, it is unintelligible . . . if to take them as good. Now because sometimes just the sounds are so becomingly arranged, that they fit what we recognize as good composition, some people claim that the composition is good without knowing the thought, some even when there is not a thought there or it is incoherent. But it is laughable for him to lay down that even good *composition* is not recognizable through reason, but just the exercise of one's hearing. It is wretched when he introduces the notion of that euphony that arises by the composition of the style and ascribes the criticism of it to the exercise of hearing, and more wretched still to take the composition itself of the words, which is recognized by thought (διάνοια).

M xxiv (=O xxiii=N–J xxi) as being good or bad, and ascribe it to the reasonless (ἄλογος) sense of hearing that has no business with its successes and failures, and claim that it is not recognized by reason (λόγος) how all the particular properties of words (λόγοι) can be brought out to expression.[35] Now because of this, even if . . . they refer . . . to those "well-trained" in poetry[36] not, however . . . (will we ignore?) . . . the thoughts, since neither in lyric poems . . . paintings like this fellow, who likens to the physical exercise (φυσικὴ τριβή) of hearing and sight the composition, which is a thing entirely opposite.[37]

5. Against Crates of Mallos

And now since our arguments against this critic have been set in order, it is time to look over Crates' theories. Now Crates does not take the same point of view as Heracleodoros and those like him; for he[38] does not praise the composition (σύνθεσις), but the sound (φωνή) that results from it. Nor as Andromenides, though he believes that he is agreeing with him.

M xxv (=O xxiv=N–J xxii) . . . in every respect in everything he has said.

[34] Or "adduce as examples the . . ." (Mangoni).

[35] For Philodemus, the very word *logos,* "reason," "word," implies that poetry, the art of *logoi,* has no sort of "wordless" music appealing only to the senses.

[36] τετριμμένοι, as if their training were merely physical (a τρίβη).

[37] "Ariston" offered (probably) the analogy of the appreciation of painting by eye, separating that from an criticism of the subject of the painting. But the criticism of poetic composition in Philodemus' view involves not just the enjoyment of beautiful sound, but also the exercise of mind and reason for both poet and critic.

[38] Annick Monet proposes ἐπ[αι]ν[οῦ]ϲιν κ]αὶ ("*they* do not praise"). Cf. above, p. 96 n. 170. Heracleodoros and Andromenides are both known nearly solely from Philodemus. Cf. Mangoni 1993, 275–79. Andromenides' dictum that "to a poet belong the elaborations of dialect and vocabulary, and a poet's work is not to say what no one else could say, but to express it as none other could express it" (Mangoni 1993, 277 from Tr. B. fr. xxv col. iii 5–12) is a perfect antithesis of Philodemus' doctrine that change of expression is change of thought and content. For this whole section I am greatly indebted to the analysis of Asmis 1992b, though again using Mangoni's text in place of Jensen's.

Against judgment by critical rule

Now if on the one hand he meant the Epicureans in his riddling way by "those philosophers who think there are rules, that one must always look to to judge," and who laid down the other things he (Crates) wrote out, that is nonsense. That has become clear and will become clearer in what follows. If he means others, they partly said truth and partly falsehood and partly left things out. They left entirely out the notions of good and bad *poema* and *poesis*; they told the truth claiming that there is no natural good in poetry (*if* they said it, for what he gives is unclear).[39] And they lied if they said there are only rules and no generally accessible (κοινή) judgment about good and bad poetry, but one for some kinds and another for others, as in the judgment of what is legally permissible (or: according to custom) (νόμιμα).

An ideal definition of poetic speech and style

And indeed *qua* poetry, poetry offers no natural use (φυcικὸν ὠφέλημα) of either the style (λέξιc) or the thought (διανόημα). For which reason there *are* established, underlying goals (ἐcτηκότεc ὑπόκεινται cκόποι)

M xxvi (=O xxv=N–J xxiii) for its excellence: that in diction it should successfully imitate speech that teaches useful things as a byproduct (τὴν ὠφέλιμα προcδιδάcκουcαν [λέξιν]), and in the thought or content, that which is in between the thinking of the technical expert and of the layman, and that is so whether someone decides to think so or not, and it is on that basis one must judge. For I pass over the fact, that also any mimesis or imitation in such artistic style—and poetry *is* that which imitates to the degree the medium allows (τὸ μιμούμενον ὡc ἐνδέχεται)—and especially in that artistic style, ought to allow of a judgment common to all, not by a series of rules for layers down of rules.[40]

Against euphony

And it was ridiculous of (Crates) himself, to have said that these are the only (two) notions that there have been about good poetry, and that one of these is [the view] of the philosophers,[41] and to write that it is implausible that there should be rules (θέματα), and that the *hearing* witnesses to that. For though we too are willing to testify that there are not rules, nothing whatever is witnessed by our (sense of) hearing to this purpose, because in general our hearing really possesses the judgment of nothing in poetry, nor does our hearing

M xxvii (=Oxxvi=N–J xxiv) take pleasure in anything, by Zeus, but the *rhythm* . . . (of the sounds?). . . . If he said this also, that it is not plausible to praise the *thought* (διάνοια),[42] such a thing being not part of the art (ἄτεχνον) (this he says against the "kritikoi") he would avert their objections,[43] since they too agree that the composition is in fact not part of the art by

---

[39] Philodemus could not agree more that there is no natural good, φυcικὸν ἀγαθόν, in poetry.

[40] This paragraph presents some of Philodemus' own positive views with unusual emphasis.

[41] That is, the one requiring judgment by rules, as opposed to Crates' view. From the next words to col. xxviii 13 I have compared the text and translation of Porter 1989, 153–57.

[42] Porter and Asmis well compare a passage already cited by Jensen, *P.Herc.* 228 fr. iA 7–16, giving the positive statement of Crates' doctrine: "everything is judged by being viewed empirically; for neither is it plausible that there are rules, since the hearing witnesses to this, nor *whenever our sense-perceptions are pleased,* is it right to go on and praise the thought immediately (εὐθύc), since that is not part of the art."

[43] "rifiuterebbe la loro tesi" (Mangoni), but can παραιτο[ῖτ᾽]ἄν have so strong a meaning? "In an appeal to the critics" (Asmis); the verb is unfortunately still ambiguous in Hellenistic Greek: between "deprecate" and "refuse," "avoid."

reason (?),[44] but understood by the trained hearing; which is why[45] they praise the thought. For the rest . . . to say what he himself is claiming (?) is silly because it exceeds the truth and because of his claiming to know that the natural differentia of poetry are discerned through the hearing. For except for the fact that sounds strike us as different through the arrangement and placement (θέcει καὶ τάξει) of the letters, there is nothing to do with the hearing that anyone would call a distinguishing of natural differences in poetry. But if that is what he was saying, then he was playing with words without intending anything special after all. If the pleasure from poetry occurs in the hearing, how can he say the following correctly: "a poem is not judged to be good

M xxviii (=O xxvii=N–J xxv) when it has pleased the hearing, but when it is worked out according to the reasonable rules of the art"; for if one dismisses the rest (of his theories), there would then be realized, according to these rules of the art, that which is composed so as to please the hearing, but even if it were not (realized according to these rules), it would also please the hearing! Therefore (he claims) there belongs to the art of poetry the art of criticism also, though it (the poem?) is judged by (the) pleasure (it gives).

There are not many rules, he claims, and so many things in poetry must be judged by each rule; this is forced and set forth rather mindlessly.[46]

And this, that "one ought not to judge in poetry [just] the things pleasant to the senses, nor the thought (διάνοια), but judge through the senses the rational propositions present by nature (τὰ λογικὰ θεωρήματα τὰ φύcει ὑπάρχοντα δι' αἰcθήcεωc κρίνειν), though not without the thoughts (τὰ νοούμενα), yet not judging the thoughts [in and for themselves]," is blind and hairsplitting and false, unless one is to take it that these rational propositions *are* present by nature.[47]

Another statement that style is inseparable from content

For either it is reasonable that the words acquire their content of meaning through the hearing only (διὰ τῆc ἀκοῆc τὰc λέξειc παραδέχεcθαι τὴν διάνοιαν), or it is true that in poetics we must judge the thoughts (νοούμενα),

M xxix (=O xxviii=N–J xxvi) and never, when we praise the composition (cύνθεcιc), rip that bodily apart (ἀποcπᾶν) from the underlying meanings (τά ὑποτεταγμένα).[48]

Now as for what he says about the letters of the alphabet (cτοιχεῖα), on which he says depends the judgment of what is good poetry, what sort of folly that is full of, and how great

---

[44] Probably some such emendation as "and not understood" is necessary before "by reason" (see Mangoni's apparatus).   [45] Reading ⟨δι⟩όπερ (Porter, Asmis).

[46] A convincing explanation of how Philodemus extracted this paradox from Crates' text or his summary of it has not yet been given, though Asmis 1992b, 159 is probably right in contending that Crates did not really believe any judgment by rule could be made (cf. Mangoni ad loc.).

[47] The view Philodemus criticizes has been made fairly clear by Jensen 1923, 146–73, and is summarized well in Greenberg 1955, 88–89. The Stoic theory of language divides it sharply into φωνή (physical sound) and λεκτόν (meaning, a rare non-material entity in the Stoic universe). Crates thought that a poem should have enough pure sonic beauty to appeal to the trained ear (this first postulate he thought dealt with many topics put separately by non-Stoic critics); that its language should survive the examination of a Stoic grammarian trained in the *techne* of words; and that its meanings (perhaps, as Jensen argues, Stoic-allegorical ones present "by nature," or divine inspiration) should reflect some kind of philosophical truth. For other views cf. Mangoni ad loc., Asmis 1992b, 155–57.

[48] Cf. Epicurus, *Letter to Herodotus* 37 τὰ ὑποτεταγμένα τοῖc φθόγγοιc, "the ideas underlying the sound of words" (it surprises Epicurus that his language can be misinterpreted and ψευδὴc ὑποτετάχθαι δόξα ταῖc λέξεcιν ἐκείναιc); but "Aristo" may have used the word also, cf. col. xxii above and Mangoni 1993, 103. This is a crucial statement of Philodemus' theory of the inseparability of form and content. Asmis 1992b, 159 seems to me to stretch the Greek too far in offering a different translation that makes the alternatives into complementary statements both reflecting Crates' view.

it is, we have established in the second book of this work, because it concerns *poema* generally, and have decided not to repeat here; so that I need only refute the doctrines found in
Zeno,[49] and bring this already rather long work to a close.

6. The *doxai* listed by Zeno

Against an effort to combine euphony and educational content

1. Now the opinion, that it is the excellence of *poema* when the composition pleases the
hearing or flows well and also expresses the thought masterfully, is false, in that it is not the
composition of poetry that pleases the ear, and it does not define this excellence in terms of
what and what sort of thought should be expressed; and what 'masterfully'

 M xxx (=O xxix=N–J xxvii) and what 'well' means in such cases we are equally left
ignorant; and also because there is a certain kind of prose of which that is equally the excellence, as some might claim.   2. That the composition of the diction should signify clearly
and emphatically the underlying thought is a common excellence of all prose. And in general
this statement touches upon nothing specifically pertaining to the excellence of poetry and
particularly of its composition. And the statement only deigns to mention "vividly" and "ex-
pressively" and "briefly" as though it could not be perfectly awful and possess all these properties, "clearly" and "becomingly" and all the other virtues being equally necessary.

Against cut-and-dried treatises on poetics arranged by topic

So therefore it is not right to enumerate (virtues of poetry) in a didactic treatise one by one, but
to state the general principle that runs through it (οὐ . . . ἐξαριθμεῖcθαι κατὰ μέροc, ἀλλὰ
τὸ δίκον λέγειν); or, if we think that the notions (προλήψειc) can only be represented by
these particulars, nevertheless everything should be expounded with reference to the general
principle (τῷ γένει), not to the enumerated particulars (ἀλλ᾽ οὐ τοῖc ἀρίθμοιc). And the
question of what certain sort the underlying thought should be in poetry,

 M xxxi (=O xxx=N–J xxviii) is one that in general these men and most of those we
examined before and shall examine next are far from answering fully.

Against theories that suit prose as well as poetry

3. Now the "composition clearly and briefly revealing the underlying thought and keeping to
the poetic character," except for bidding one keep to the "poetic character," will also extend
over to prose, where the definition would be [keeping to] "the prosaic character;" but neither
definition really characterizes anything. In addition this has the requirement of expressing
everything briefly, though in some cases one should practice that, and in some cases dwell on
the same thing at length, and in some cases even resort to periphrasis; and that clarity should
accompany everything seems neither to be always possible to poets nor where possible to fit
all their thoughts.   4. When another speaks of "a composition that embraces wise thought
and pleases the hearing with its arrangement"

 M xxxii (=O xxxi=N–J xxix) we may reject this, even when both are in fact present,[50] and

---

 [49] i.e. of Sidon, the Epicurean, of whom Philodemus was a disciple: that is, in yet another summary,
this time by Zeno, of others' opinions on poetic excellence, whose contents have been set forth in the
earlier part of the book. The opinions (δόξαι) given are this time listed without author; for the thirteen
opinions and their provenance cf. Mangoni 1993, 78–79 and especially the exposition of Asmis 1992a,
esp. 395–96. Jensen's text made the sequence of opinions listed much more difficult to distinguish.

 [50] Another improved reading of Mangoni's. Presumably even if both excellences were there we
would simply be back with the doctrine of Crates and the *kritikoi*. Cf. note 58 below.

that   5. "the composition should express a thought that is useful, even though not strictly wise, forcefully and in a way to impress the hearing" because (a) he does not define "useful for what;" and (b) he jettisons so much of the most beautiful poetry, some of which is useless, some even (morally harmful?) . . ., and prefers so much inferior poetry that embraces useful or comparatively more useful thoughts; and (c) even if poems are useful, they are *not* useful *qua* poems (κἂν ὠφελεῖ, καθὸ ποήματ᾽ οὐκ ὠφελεῖ)[51]; and (d) they will say that the most useful is the best poem, though it will *not* be the best poem if it is [a medical poem] expressed [in the] medically [best way]. And the word "forcefully" needs exegesis, and the phrase "in a way to impress the hearing" is not only unclear, but without meaning; and one will not look for "impressively" any more than "clearly" and also at times "concisely" and "becomingly" and "elegantly" and "adorned" with many another property. And the definition will seem in general to be in common with that of epidictic[52] speeches (in prose).   6. The sentence

M xxxiii (=O xxxii=N–J xxx) "composition of diction that teaches something more through poetry, or one that at least resembles that" does not explain, teach more than what? If he means "more than non-technical discourse" he excludes much good poetry from goodness, if "more than prose" he is elevating much bad poetry to goodness. For even bad poems "teach something more" through poetry. But that all poetic composition should be "*similar* (ὁμοιω-μένην) to that which teaches something more"[53] is said truly of all poetic composition insofar as it is praiseworthy. So the statement either introduces a false distinction or is identical with the previous statement (i.e. that poetry should have wise thoughts and please the ear).

Poetry is not the imitation of great models

Now concerning   7. "good imitation of Homer and similar traditional poets," that will not seem to make Homer and such as him good poets, since they did not imitate themselves; and it neither grasps the common notion of good poetry nor do we understand that to be the excellence of poetry; it allows . . .

M xxxiv (=O xxxiii=N–J xxxi) . . . nothing. . . . And one could go on and say thus that justice is the imitation of Aristides, and goodness that of Phocion, and wisdom that of Epicurus, and political virtue that of Pericles, and painting that of Apelles, and similarly about the rest, and oppositely about the vices; and that makes the criticism of good poetry totally rule-bound and no more accurately defined. Besides to imitate Homer and Euripides and similarly admired poets in all things does not seem reasonable; for probably we will not be able even to recognize what imitates them as they ought fittingly to be imitated, if we do not have knowledge of what is fitting. But then nothing is sillier than those who define thus; for *we* will inquire what that is that made certain poets admired, and in what respects one must rightly imitate them.

Against conventionalist conceptions of "to prepon" and of the telos of poetry

And it is no better in any way   8. "to produce a diction fitting to
M xxxv (=O xxxiv=N–J xxxii) the characters one introduces," for that is common to

---

[51] Yet another statement of Philodemus' doctrine that good poetry may incidentally express some improving or educational truth, but that is no part of its *definiens* as poetry.

[52] The true restoration in line 35 must surely be [ἐπι]δεικτικῶν λόγων, not Jensen's [ἀπο]δεικτι-κῶν (suggested to him, probably, by the discussion of apodeictic or logical reasoning in col. i Mangoni); i.e. Philodemus' "true" or epidictic (purely literary) rhetoric.

[53] In col. xxvi Philodemus specified that the diction should *imitate* (μιμεῖcθαι) speech that teaches something more, so the distinction, if very precise, is consistent (cf. Mangoni ad loc.)

prose, or at least to history and dialogue; and that is a way of talking only about diction, leaving aside the thoughts, which have a more commanding power . . . . . . that such and such a diction fits gods and heroes, is for fools, and also to say that it is better to imitate the appropriate diction; and completely mad to try and feel out a similarity of the diction to the things themselves that are depicted. Even if one is supposed to understand a similarity of the thought also, or the scribe left that out,[54] to ascribe to *poetics* the understanding of what sort of diction belongs to each character is madness. But *through* poetry, it is entirely possible to imitate whatever one wants to imitate fittingly.[55]   9. Now that which claims (the virtue of poetry) is the ability to draw the hearer even

M xxxvi (=O xxxv=N–J xxxiii) with paradoxical or surprising stories, and that which claims   10. that one should move only the educated, give a definition that is again common to certain kinds of prose.

Really, only the intelligent critic understands poetry

Besides, the first of these two makes poetical excellence impossible; or if by 'the hearer' it means the understanding hearer, it is the same definition as the next, for only the educated *do* understand, and most particularly where beauty is in question.[56] The second definition is more endurable, but both, surely, give only as the "end," if one needs to call it that, what the good poem can *do* ; but what that (good poem) is and by what means it can move us they do not teach. And thus many mediocre poems, which by peripeties and paradoxologies and pathetic speeches move us, they seem to prefer to perfectly written poems which hardly need to deal in these things. And (the hearers) sympathize most and are stirred most when there are thoughts present also, but the virtue of poetry for them has come about through some excess thing which results through poetic elaboration (ἐν τῷ διὰ τῆς κατασκευῆς παρεπιφαινο-μένῳ περίττῳ). 11. But if someone

M xxxvii (=O xxxvi=N–J xxxiv) said that the excellence of the poet is being able to compose all his poetry well, he was thereby just acknowledging the problem. For in fact when we ask who is the good poet, we are asking how, composing his poetry, he composes it well; and he just tells us, "well." If he expects him to do that in all genres of poetry, he leaves excellence as something that never occurred. For no one has been able to write every genre of poetry well; and as I think, it is impossible (for indeed it could not be). Besides, no poet has ever even achieved this consistent excellence in one single genre.   12. If it is "the capacity of composing a *poesis* which has excellence," that is less disconcerting; but we have to know in advance what is the excellence of *poesis*. Having seen this it will then be obvious that he who creates this will be the good poet, and we will call that the excellence of the perfect poet . . .

M xxxviiii (=O xxxvii=N–J xxxv) . . . then according to this argument, we can not know of those who have done this, if they had the virtue of the poet; for if he means *poesis* of any kind, the epigrammatists' and Sappho's included, that just means that the good poet is the composer of good poetry, *poemata*, which we grasped "before Theognis was born."[57]

---

[54] ἢ γραφεὺς παραλέλοιπε. Philodemus' expression indicates his suspicion that his copy of Zeno's handbook may not be perfect.

[55] Again, Philodemus has made a fine distinction: "fitting" portrayal of character is possible in other media than poetry, and consequently does not give a definition of this particular medium. But good poetry may (or may not) achieve this, just as it may (or may not) teach moral excellence.

[56] Philodemus shares the opinion that only the educated understand what poetry is about; consequently (9) would fail because even the best poetry cannot expect to enchant every hearer.

[57] Proverbial for "ages ago" or "as something obvious." Philodemus considers (12) superior to (11), because the ability to compose an excellent *poesis* or poetic whole includes (as he said earlier) the ability to compose excellent *poemata* also. Interestingly, he does not consider his own poetic genre, the epigram, or the lyric large enough to achieve a complete *poesis*, but only *poema*.

13. And of those who demand (of the poet) the ability to keep to what is fitting ($\pi\rho\acute{\epsilon}\pi o\nu$) in all genres of *poesis* we should say, that the poet must offer much beside this. If they mean the full philosophical sense of "fitting" they are describing an excellence unknown in reality and impossible to acquire; or if that which "fits" each character and subject, the same problem, because in some things it is possible for the poet to keep to what is fitting, and in some he neither knows nor could find out; but if something "fitting" to the *poesis,* of the previous . . .

M xxxix (=O xxxviii=N–J xxxvi) . . . from poetry . . . all that . . . will compose well; but then if they understand by *poesis* the ability to compose fittingly, they do not tell us how he composes in composing fittingly. And how the others fail, one may easily grasp from our previous explanations.

Philodemus
On Poetry
The Fifth Book

Supplement:
P.Herc. 228, frr. 1 and 3 Mangoni (published in *CErc* 19, 1989, 179–86).

Six fragments exist (in N *disegni* only: one actual papyrus survives in illegible state, indicating the others were *scorze,* destroyed outward as they were made). Three are about some other subject than poetics, and perhaps (*pace* Mangoni 186) do not come from the same context or even roll as the other three. Frr. 1, 3, and 6 are about poetics; but nothing can be made of 6. Frr. 1 and 3, whether from Book 5 of the *On Poems* or not, are respectively an exposition without criticism of Crates' views as set forth in xxvi 25–xxvii 21, and a setting forth of the views listed in Zeno of Sidon's handbook, numbered as 3–6 above, in the same order as Philodemus refutes them, but without criticism.

228 fr. 1 Mangoni: . . . the poetic character; everything is judged by being viewed empirically; for neither is it plausible that there are rules, since the hearing witnesses to this, nor *whenever our sense-perceptions are pleased,* is it right to go on and praise the thought immediately ($\epsilon\mathring{v}\theta\acute{v}c$), since . . . (that) is not part of the art. Besides . . . to say that the physical difference that exists in poetry is judged by hearing, but the poetry is judged good . . . .

228 fr. 3 M (a composition, [$c\acute{v}\nu\theta\epsilon c\iota c$])   3. clearly and briefly expressing the content without violating the poetic character; and others,   4. that it is composition that embraces wise thought; or others (say it is)   4a.[58] a composition that does this while delighting the ear through artistic elaboration; and others,   5. a composition which expresses useful, even if not philosophical, thought masterfully and, for the hearing, strikingly; others   6. that which teaches in addition something further through poetry, or resembles such composition; and others . . . .

---

[58] Philodemus has treated this as one proposition at col. xxxi 7–10 above, though "even when both are in fact present" may reflect his awareness that Zeno presented "composition with wise thought" and "composition with wise thought and delighting the ear" as two separate options.

Appendix 2
Philodemus on Poetics, Music, and Rhetoric: A Classified Bibliography

Abbreviations

ANRW   *Aufstieg und Niedergang der römischen Welt*
CErc   *Cronache Ercolanesi*
Ricerche   F. Sbordone, ed., *Ricerche sui Papiri Ercolanesi* 1–4 (Naples 1969–83)
SIFC   *Studi italiani di filologia classica*
ΣΥΖΗΤΗΣΙΣ   *ΣΥΖΗΤΗΣΙΣ: Studi sull'epicureismo greco e romano offerti a Marcello Gigante* (Naples 1983)

Bibliographical and lexicographical resources

Berkowitz, L. and K. A. Squitier 1990. *Thesaurus Linguae Graecae Canon of Greek Authors and Works*, 3rd ed. (Oxford).
Capasso, M. 1989. "Primo supplemento al *Catalogo dei Papiri Ercolanesi*," *CErc* 19: 193–265.
Capasso, M. 1991. *Manuale di papirologia ercolanese* (Lecce).
Gigante, M. ed. 1979. *Catalogo dei Papiri Ercolanesi* (Naples).
Usener, H. 1977. *Glossarium Epicureum*, ed. M. Gigante (Rome).
Vooys, C. J. 1934/41. *Lexicon Philodemeum* vol. 1 (Purmerend 1934); vol. 2, with D. A. van Krevelen (Amsterdam 1941).

Philodemus: general

Asmis, E. 1990a. "Philodemus' Epicureanism," *ANRW* 2, 36.4: 2369–408.
Dorandi, T. 1990a. "Filodemo: gli orientamenti della ricerca attuale," *ANRW* 2, 36.4: 2328–68.
Gigante, M., 1995. *Philodemus in Italy: The Books from Herculaneum* (Ann Arbor).
Gigante, M. 1983. *Ricerche filodemee*, 2nd ed. (Naples).
Long, A. A. and D. N. Sedley 1987. *The Hellenistic Philosophers*, 2 vols. (Cambridge).

Philodemus and Roman poetry

Barra, G. 1973. "Filodemo di Gadara e le lettere latine," *Vichiana* 2: 247–60.

Barra, G. 1977/78. "Osservazioni sulla "Poetica" di Filodemo e di Lucrezio," *Annali della Facoltà di Lettere e Filosofia dell'Università di Napoli* 20: 87–104.

Gigante, M. 1984. *Virgilio e la Campania* (Naples).

Gigante, M. 1989. "Filodemo tra poesia e prosa," *SIFC* 7: 129–51.

Gigante M. and M. Capasso 1989. "Il ritorno di Virgilio a Ercolano," *SIFC* 7: 3–6.

Gigante, M. 1992b. "Philodemo e l'epigramma," *CErc* 22: 5–8.

Kleve, K. 1989. "Lucretius in Herculaneum," *CErc* 19: 5–27.

Kleve, K. 1990. "Ennius in Herculaneum," *CErc* 20: 5–16.

Kleve, K. 1991. "Lucretius from the Ashes: Lucretius and Ennius in Herculaneum," *The Norwegian Institute at Athens* 1991: 57–64.

Tait, J. I. M. 1941. "Philodemus' Influence on the Latin Poets," (diss. Bryn Mawr).

Scribal hands and orthography

Cavallo, G. 1983. *Libri Scritture Scribi a Ercolano*, *CErc* suppl. 1 (Naples).

Crönert, W. 1903. *Memoria Graeca Herculanensis* (Leipzig).

McNamee, K. 1992. *Sigla and Select Marginalia in Greek Literary Papyri* (Brussels).

Textual reconstruction (Delattre/Obbink method)

Delattre, D. 1989. "Philodème, *De la Musique*: livre IV, colonnes 40* à 109*," *CErc* 19: 49–143.

Delattre, D. 1993. "Philodème, *De la Musique*," (diss. Sorbonne).

Dorandi, T. 1992a. "Papiri ercolanesi tra 'scorzatura' e 'svolgimento'," *CErc* 22: 179–80.

Frosén, J. and D. Hagedorn 1990. *Die verkohlten Papyri aus Bubastos (Pap. Bub.)*, Papyrologica Coloniensia 15 (Opladen).

Janko, R. 1991b. "*Philodemus resartus*: progress in reconstructing the philosophical papyri from Herculaneum," *Proceedings of the Boston Area Colloquium in Ancient Philosophy* 7: 271–308.

Janko, R. 1992a: "A first join between *PHerc*. 411 and 1583 (Philodemus, *On Music* IV)," *CErc* 22: 123–29.

Janko, R. 1993. "Introducing the Philodemus Translation Project: reconstructing the On Poems," *Proceedings of the XXth International Congress of Papyrology, Copenhagen 1992* (Copenhagen): 367–81.

Obbink, D. 1986. "Philodemus, *De pietate* I," (diss. Stanford).

New unrolling technique (K. Kleve)

Capasso, M. and A. Angeli 1989. "Papiri aperti con metodo osloense (1989–91)," *CErc* 19: 265–70.

Kleve, K. 1989. "Lucretius in Herculaneum," *CErc* 19: 5–27.

Kleve, K. 1990. "Ennius in Herculaneum," *CErc* 20: 5–16.

Kleve, K., A. Angeli, M. Capasso et al. 1991. "Three technical guides to the Papyri of Herculaneum," *CErc* 21: 111–24.

POEMS: Philodemus, *On Poems* (*De poematis*, Περὶ ποιημάτων); in five books

General

Asmis, E. 1991a. "Epicurean Poetics," *Proceedings of the Boston Area Colloquium in Ancient Philosophy* 7, 1991: 63–93, 104–105 = Chapter 2.

Asmis, E. 1991b. "Philodemus' Poetic Theory and *On the Good King According to Homer*," *CA* 10: 1–45.

Dorandi, T. 1992c. "Per una ricomposizione dello scritto di Filodemo *Sulla poetica*," *ZPE* 91: 29–46.

Gomoll, H. 1936. "Herakleodoros und die *kritikoi* bei Philodem," *Philologus* 91: 373–84.

Gomperz, T. 1993. *Theodor Gomperz. Eine auswahl herculanischer kleiner Schriften (1864– 1909)*, ed. T. Dorandi, Philosophia antiqua 59 (Leiden).

Greenberg, N. A. 1955. "The Poetic Theory of Philodemus," (diss. Harvard, publ. New York 1990).

Grube, G. M. A. 1965. *The Greek and Roman Critics* (London): 193–200, esp. 193f.

Innes, D. 1989. "Philodemus," in *The Cambridge History of Literary Criticism I: Classical Criticism*, ed. G. A. Kennedy (Cambridge): 215–19.

Meijering, R. 1987. *Literary and Rhetorical Theories in Greek Scholia* (Groningen).

Nardelli, M. L. 1982. "Euripide nella 'Poetica' di Filodemo," in *La Regione sotterrata dal Vesuvio* (Naples): 471–92.

Romeo, C. 1983. "Filodemo: La Poetica," in *ΣΥΖΗΤΗΣΙΣ*, vol. 2: 565–83.

Rostagni, A. 1955. "Filodemo contro l'estetica antica," in *Scritti minori*, vol. 1 (Turin): 394– 446.

Russell, D. A. 1981. *Criticism in Antiquity* (London).

Sbordone, F. 1969b. *Contributo alla Poetica degli Antichi* (Naples 1969, ed. 1, 1961).

Sbordone, F. 1983. *Sui Papiri della Poetica di Filodemo* (Naples).

Schenkeveld, D. M. 1968. "*Hoi kritikoi* in Philodemus," *Mnemosyne* 21: 176–214.

Schenkeveld, D. M. 1982. "Studies in the History of Ancient Linguistics I," *Mnemosyne* 35: 248–67.

Schenkeveld, D. M. 1984. "Studies in the History of Ancient Linguistics II," *Mnemosyne* 37: 291–353.

Schenkeveld, D. M. 1990. "Studies in the History of Ancient Linguistics III," *Mnemosyne* 43: 86–108, 289–306.

Main Texts

Philodemus, On Poems *1 or 2 (Treatise B [= Tractatus alter], papyri 460, 1073; papyrus 444; Treatise E, papyrus 466)*

Asmis, E. 1992b. "Crates on Poetic Criticism," *Phoenix* 46: 138–69.

Janko, R. 1991b. "*Philodemus resartus*: progress in reconstructing the philosophical papyri from Herculaneum," *Proceedings of the Boston Area Colloquium in Ancient Philosophy* 7, 1991: 271–308.

Janko, R. 1993. "Introducing the Philodemus Translation Project: reconstructing the *On Poems*," *Proceedings of the XXth International Congress of Papyrology, Copenhagen 1992* (Copenhagen): 367–81.

Nardelli, M. L. 1983. "Due Trattati filodemei 'Sulla Poetica'," in *Ricerche* 4.

Rispoli, G. M. 1981. "Suono ed articulazione nella teoria epicurea del linguaggio," *Proceedings of the XVIth International Congress of Papyrology* (Chico): 173–81.

Rispoli, G. M. 1986. "Eufonia ed ermeneutica: origine ed evoluzione di un metodo filologico," *Koinonia* 10: 134–43.

Rispoli, G. M. 1987. "Eufonia ed poetica in testi ercolanesi," *Linguistica e filologia: Atti del VII Convegno Internazionale di Linguisti* (Brescia): 461–78.

Romeo, C. 1988. *Demetrio Lacone: Sulla Poesia*, La scuola di Epicuro 9 (Naples).

Sbordone, F. 1976. "*ΦΙΛΟΔΗΜΟΥ ΠΕΡΙ ΠΟΙΗΜΑΤΩΝ* Tractatus Tres," in *Ricerche* 2 (for Treatise B).

Sbordone, F. 1983. *Sui Papiri della Poetica di Filodemo* (Naples) (for *P.Herc.* 444).

Philodemus, On Poems 1 or 2(?) (Treatise D, P.Herc. 1074a, 1081a)

Hausrath, A. 1889. *Philodemi Peri poiematon libri secundi quae videntur fragmenta* (Leipzig).

Janko, R. 1991b. "*Philodemus resartus*: progress in reconstructing the philosophical papyri from Herculaneum," *Proceedings of the Boston Area Colloquium in Ancient Philosophy* 7, 1991: 271–308.

Mette, H. J. 1979. "Zu Philodem *Peri poiematon*," *Zeitschrift für Papyrologie und Epigraphik* 34: 59–63.

Nardelli, M. L. 1983. "Due Trattati filodemei 'Sulla Poetica'," in *Ricer-che* 4 (For text of Treatise D).

Romeo, C. 1981. "Sofrone nei Papiri ercolanesi: *PHerc.* 1081 e 1014," *Proceedings of the XVIth International Congress of Papyrology* (Chico): 183–90.

Philodemus, On Poems 2 or 3 (Treatises A [= Tractatus primus] and C [= Tractatus tertius], P.Herc. 994, 1074b, 1081b, 1676, 1677):

Gigante, M. 1992a. "Lucrezio: il piacere della forma," *RIL* 125: 21–31.

Gomperz, T. 1891. "Philodem und die ästhetischen Schriften der herculanischen Bibliothek," *Sitzungsberichte der Akademie der Wissenschaften in Wien, Phil.-Hist. Kl.* 123: 1–88.

Hausrath, A. 1889. *Philodemi Peri poiematon libri secundi quae videntur fragmenta* (Leipzig).

Heidmann, J. 1937. *Der Papyrus 1676 der herculanensischen Bibliothek (Philodemus Peri Poiêmatôn)* (Bonn), repr. in *CErc* 1 (1971): 90–111 (for Treatise C fin.).

Nardelli, M. L. 1979. "Papiri della 'Poetica' di Filodemo," *CErc* 9: 137–40.

Nardelli, M. L. 1981. "*PHerc.* 1676: contenuti di un libro dell'opera filodemea *Sulla Poetica*," *Proceedings of the XVIth International Congress of Papyrology* (Chico): 163–71.

Nardelli, M. L. 1982b. "*PHerc.* 994 col. x," *CErc* 12: 135–36.

Porter, J. 1989. "Philodemus on Material Difference," *CErc* 19: 149–70.

Romeo, C. 1992a. "Il *PHerc.* 1677: un libro della Poetica di Filodemo," *Proceedings of the XIXth International Congress of Papyrology*, vol. 1 (Cairo): 173–78.

Romeo, C. 1992b. "Per una nuova edizione del *PHerc.* 1676: un libro della Poetica di Filodemo," *CErc* 22: 163–67.

Romeo, C. 1992c. "Un contributo inedito di Filodemo alla critica omerica (*PHerc.* 1677 coll. v–vii)," in M. Capasso, ed., *Papiri letterari greci e latini* (Lecce): 193–202.

Rutherford, I. 1990. "Philodemus, *Peri poiematon* Tractatus tertius, fr. e, col. i, ll. 23–4,"
        Zeitschrift für Papyrologie und Epigraphik 82: 58.
Sbordone, F. 1976. "*ΦΙΛΟΔΗΜΟΥ ΠΕΡΙ ΠΟΙΗΜΑΤΩΝ* Tractatus Tres," in *Ricerche* 2
        (for texts of Treatises A and C).
Schächter, R. 1926. "Philodemi *peri poiematon* l. II fragmenta ex *VH* X collecta," *Eos* 29:
        15–28.

Philodemus, On Poems *3 or unknown Book*

Dürr, E. 1990. "Una Testimonianza su Euripide in un papiro ercolanese inedito," in *Miscella-
        nea Papirologica in occasione del bicentenario dell'edizione della Charta Borgiana*
        (Florence): 42f.
Dürr, E. 1992. "I resti del *PHerc*. 1736 (Filodemo, *Poetica*?)," *CErc* 22: 139–56.
Spina, L. 1988. "Un Papiro inedito della collezione ercolanese: *PHerc*. 1403," *Vichiana* 17:
        99–108, and *Proceedings of the XVIIth International Congress of Papyrology* (Ath-
        ens): 399–407.

Philodemus, On Poems *4*

Janko, R. 1991a. "Philodemus' *On Poems* and Aristotle's *On Poets*," *CErc* 21: 5–64 (super-
        sedes Sbordone's text).
Mesturini, A. M. 1990. "Puntualizzazioni sul Tractatus Coislinianus," *Maia* 42: 237–47.
Romeo, C. 1980. "Nicola Lucignano e i papiri ercolanesi," *Contributi alla Storia dell'Offi-
        cina dei Papiri, I Quaderni della Biblioteca Nazionale di Napoli* 5.2 (Naples).
Sbordone, F. 1969. "Il quarto libro del περὶ ποιημάτων di Filodemo," in *Ricerche* 1: 287–
        372.

Philodemus, On Poems *4 or 5* (P.Herc. *1581)*

Janko, R. 1991a. "Philodemus'.*On Poems* and Aristotle's *On Poets*," *CErc* 21: 5–64.
Janko, R. 1992b. "From catharsis to the Aristotelian mean," in A. Rorty, ed., *Essays on Ari-
        stotle's Poetics* (Princeton): 341–58.
Nardelli, M. L. 1978. "La catarsi poetica nel *PHerc*. 1581," *CErc* 8 (1978): 96–103.

Philodemus, On Poems *5(?)* (P.Herc. *228, 403, 408)*

Coppola, C. 1983. "Frammenti inediti del *PHerc*. 228," *CErc* 13: 103–4.
Greenberg, N. A. 1955. "The Poetic Theory of Philodemus," (diss. Harvard, publ. New York
        1990) (for *PHerc*. 403).
Jensen, C. 1934. "Aristoteles in der *Auge* des Machon," *RhM* 83: 194–99.
Mangoni, C. 1989. "Il *PHerc*. 228," *CErc* 19: 179–86 (supersedes text of Coppola).
Mangoni, C. 1992a. "Il *PHerc*. 407 della *Poetica* di Filodemo," *CErc* 22: 131-37.

Philodemus, On Poems *5* (PHerc. *1425, 1538)*

Asmis, E. 1990b. "The Poetic Theory of the Stoic 'Aristo'," *Apeiron* 23: 147–201.
Asmis, E. 1992a. "An Epicurean Survey of Poetic Theories," *CQ* 42: 395–415.
Asmis, E. 1992b. "Crates on Poetic Criticism," *Phoenix* 46: 138–69.
Asmis, E. 1992c. "Neoptolemus and the classification of poetry," *CPh* 87: 206–31.

Brink, C. O. 1963. *Horace on Poetry. Prolegomena to the Literary Epistles* (Cambridge) 43–152.

Isnardi Parente, M. 1987. "Una Poetica di incerto autore in Filodemo," in *Filologia e forme letterarie: Studi offerti a F. della Corte*, vol. 5 (Urbino): 81–98.

Jensen, C. 1923. *Philodemus Über die Gedichte, Fünftes Buch* (Berlin).

Jensen, C. 1936. "Herakleides von Pontos bei Philodem und Horaz," *Sitzungsberichte der Preussischen Akademie von Wissenschaften*, Phil.-Hist. Kl., 292–320.

Mangoni, C. 1988. "Prosa e poesia nel V libro della *Poetica* di Filodemo," *CErc* 18: 127–38.

Mangoni, C. 1991. "Nuove letture nei *PHerc*. 1425 e 1538 del V libro della *Poetica* di Filodemo," *CErc* 21: 65–82.

Mangoni, C. 1992b. "Metodi argomentativi nel V libro *peri poiêmatôn* di Filodemo di Gadara," *Proceedings of the XIXth International Congress of Papyrology* vol. 1 (Cairo): 161–72.

Mangoni, C. 1993. *Filodemo, La Poesia V, La scuola di Epicuro* 14 (Naples).

Mette, H. J. 1981, "Neoptolemos von Parion," *RhM* 123: 1–24.

Porter, J. 1989. "Philodemus on Material Difference," *CErc* 19: 149–70.

Rutherford, I. 1988. "*Emphasis* in ancient literary criticism and the Tractatus Coislinianus," *Maia* 40: 125-29.

Sbordone, F. 1981. "La Poetica oraziona alla luce dei studi piú recenti," *ANRW* 2, 31.3: 1866–1920, esp. 1871ff.

Walsh, G. B. 1987. "Philodemus on the terminology of Neoptolemus," *Mnemosyne* 40: 56–68.

MUSIC: Philodemus *On Music* (*De musica*, Περὶ μουcικῆc); only book 4 survives

General

Anderson, A. 1966. *Ethos and Education in Greek Music* (Cambridge, Mass.).

Barker, A. 1984/89. *Ancient Musical Writings*: vol. 1, *The Musician and his Art* (Cambridge 1984); vol. 2, *Harmonic and Acoustic Theory* (Cambridge 1989).

Delattre, D. 1991. "Une 'citation' stoïcienne des *Lois* de Platon (II 669B–E) de Platon dans les *Commentaires sur la Musique* de Philodème?," *Revue d'histoire des textes* 21: 1–17.

Delattre, D. 1992. "Combien des livres comptaient les *Commentaires sur la Musique* de Philodème?," in M. Capasso, ed., *Papiri letterari greci e latini* (Lecce): 181–91.

Delattre, D. 1993. "Philodème, *De la Musique*," (diss. Sorbonne).

Janko, R. 1992a. "A first join between *PHerc*. 411 and 1583 (Philodemus, *On Music* IV)," *CErc* 22: 123-29.

Longo Auricchio, F. 1983. "Filodemo: La *Retorica* e la *Musica*," in *ΣΥΖΗΤΗΣΙΣ*, vol. 2: 562–64.

Pöhlmann, E. 1991. Reviews of Neubecker 1986 and Delattre 1989, *Gnomon* 63: 481–86.

Rispoli, G. M. 1969. "Il primo libro del *Peri Mousikes* di Filodemo," in *Ricerche* 1: 25–286.

Rispoli, G. M. 1986. "Eufonia ed ermeneutica: origine ed evoluzione di un metodo filologico," *Koinonia* 10: 134–43.

Rispoli, G. M. 1991. "Elementi di fisica e di etica epicurea nella teoria musicale di Filodemo di Gadara," in Wallace and MacLachlan 1991: 69-103.

Wallace, R. W. 1991a. "Musica e filosofia nell'antichità," in Wallace and MacLachlan 1991: 1-6.

Wallace, R. W. 1991b. "Damone di Oa ed i suoi successori: un'analisi delle fonti," in Wallace and MacLachlan 1991: 30-53.
van Krevelen, D. A. 1939. *Philodemus: De Muziek* (Hilversum).

Main Text

Philodemus On Music *4*

Kemke, I. 1884. *Philodemi De Musica librorum quae exstant* (Leipzig), now mostly replaced for the second half of Book 4 by:
Neubecker, A. J. 1986. *Philodem. Über die Musik, Viertes Buch*, La scuola di Epicuro 4 (Naples), revised in part by:
Delattre, D. 1989. "Philodème, *De la Musique*: livre IV, colonnes 40* à 109*," *CErc* 19: 49–143.

Remainder in:

Rispoli, G. M. 1969. "Il primo libro del *Peri Mousikes* di Filodemo," in *Ricerche* 1: 25–286.

RHETORIC: Philodemus, *On Rhetoric* (*De rhetorica*, Περὶ ῥητορικῆς) in seven books

General

Dorandi, T. 1990b. "Per una ricomposizione dello scritto filodemeo *Sulla retorica*," *Zeitschrift für Papyrologie und Epigraphik* 82: 59–87.
Hubbell, H. M. 1920. "The *Rhetorica* of Philodemus," *Transactions of the Connecticut Academy of Arts and Sciences* 23: 243–382.
Kleve K. and F. Longo Auricchio 1992. "Honey from the Garden of Epicurus," in M. Capasso, ed., *Papiri letterari greci e latini* (Lecce): 211–26.
Longo Auricchio, F. 1983. "Filodemo: La *Retorica* e la *Musica*," in *ΣΥΖΗΤΗΣΙΣ*, vol. 2: 553–65.
Sudhaus, S. 1892/96. *Philodemi Volumina Rhetorica* (Leipzig).
Sudhaus, S. 1895. *Philodemi Volumina Rhetorica: Supplementum* (Leipzig).

Main Text

Sudhaus, S. 1892/96. *Philodemi Volumina Rhetorica*, 2 vols. (Leipzig).
Partial English translation and paraphrase of Sudhaus' edition in Hubbell, H. M. 1920. "The *Rhetorica* of Philodemus," *Transactions of the Connecticut Academy of Arts and Sciences* 23: 243–382.
However, the order of books adopted by Sudhaus has recently been revised on the basis of Dorandi 1990b, and large sections of Sudhaus' edition have been replaced by more accurate editions, as follows:

Philodemus, On Rhetoric *1–2*

Longo Auricchio, F. 1977. Φιλοδήμου Περὶ ῥητορικῆς *libros primum et secundum ed.
F. Longo Auricchio*, in *Ricerche* 3: 2–277 with Italian translation (re-edits Sudhaus,

vol. 1, 1–46) + Sudhaus, vol. 2, 180–90, with the corrections of Hammerstaedt 1992: 117. Partial English translation in Hubbell 1920: 265–93. On the technicity of rhetoric; authenticity of Epicurus' view that epideictic rhetoric is an art.

Barnes, J. 1986. "Is rhetoric an art?," *darg Newsletter (Univ. of Calgary)* 2: 2–22.

Ferrario, M. 1981. "La Concezione della retorica da Epicuro a Filodemo," *Proceedings of the XVIth International Congress of Papyrology* (Chico): 145–52.

Hammerstaedt, J. 1992. "Der Schlussteil von Philodems drittem Buch über Rhetorik," *CErc* 22: 9–117.

Longo Auricchio, F. 1984. "Epicureismo e scetticismo sulla retorica," *Atti del XVII Congresso della Papirologia*, vol. 2 (Naples): 453–72.

Longo Auricchio, F. 1985. "Testimonianze dalla "Retorica" di Filodemo sulla concezione dell'oratoria nei primi maestri epicurei," *CErc* 15: 31–61.

Longo Auricchio F. and A. Tepedino Guerra 1981. "Aspetti e problemi della dissidenza epicurea," *CErc* 11: 25–40.

Sedley, D. N. 1989. "Philosophical allegiance in the Greco-Roman world," in M. Griffin and J. Barnes, edd., *Philosophia Togata* (Oxford): 97–119.

Philodemus, On Rhetoric *3 = Sudhaus' "Hypomnematicum" (P.Herc. 1426; first draft: 1506)*

Contains synopsis of books 4–7. For first half of book see Sudhaus, vol. 2: 196–239. For second half: Hammerstaedt 1992 re-edits Sudhaus 1892/96, vol. 2: 239–71. Partial translation in Hubbell 1920: 346–64.

Hammerstaedt, J. 1992. "Der Schlussteil von Philodems drittem Buch über Rhetorik," *CErc* 22: 9–117 (reedits Sudhaus 1892/96, vol. 2: 239–302).

Obbink, D. and P. A. Vander Waerdt 1991. "Diogenes of Babylon: The Stoic Sage in the City of Fools," *GRBS* 32: 355–96.

Philodemus, On Rhetoric *4 (P.Herc. 1423, 1007/1673)*

Comparison of rhetoric with philosophy. Text: Sudhaus 1892/96, vol. 1: 147–225. Partial translation in Hubbell 1920: 293–305.

Gaines, R. 1982. "Qualities of rhetorical expression in Philodemus," *TAPA* 112: 71–81.

Romeo, C. 1992b. "Per una nuova edizione del *PHerc*. 1676: un libro della Poetica di Filodemo," *CErc* 22: 163–67 (discusses *Rhet.* 4).

Rutherford, I. 1988. "*Emphasis* in ancient literary criticism and the Tractatus Coislinianus," *Maia* 40: 125–29 (discusses *Rhet.* 4).

Philodemus, On Rhetoric *5 = Sudhaus' book 6 (P.Herc. 832/1015)*

Criticism of schools that accepted rhetoric as an art, including Nausiphanes and Aristotle. Text: Sudhaus 1892/96, vol. 1: 270–325 (rev. vol. 2: 1–64). Partial translation in Hubbell 1920: 318–32.

Philodemus, On Rhetoric 6 = *Sudhaus' book 7* (P.Herc. *1004)*

Attack on Stoic political rhetoric. Text: Sudhaus 1892/96, vol. 1: 325–85 with the corrections
of Cappelluzzo 1976. Partial translation in Hubbell 1920: 332–41.

Cappelluzzo, M. G. 1976. "Per una nuova edizione di un libro della *Retorica* di Filodemo
(*PHerc*. 1004)," *CErc* 6: 69–76.

Philodemus, On Rhetoric 7 = *Sudhaus' Book 5* (P.Herc. *1669)*

Criticism of a rhetorical handbook; educational value of rhetoric: text in Ferrario 1980 (re-
edits Sudhaus 1892/96, vol. 1: 131–67). Partial translation in Hubbell 1920: 305–18.

Angeli, A. 1992. "La critica di Filodemo a Socrate nel quinto libro della Retorica," *Proceedings of the XIXth International Congress of Papyrology*, vol. 1 (Cairo): 135–46.

Ferrario, M. 1974. "Verso una nuova edizione del quinto libro della *Retorica* di Filodemo,"
CErc 4: 93–96.

Ferrario, M. 1980. "Frammenti del quinto libro della *Retorica* di Filodemo (*PHerc*. 1669),"
CErc 10: 55–124.

Ferrario, M. 1988. "Per una nuova edizione del quinto libro della *Retorica* di Filodemo,"
Proceedings of the XVIIIth International Congress of Papyrology, vol. 1 (Athens):
167–84.

Editions of Other Works by Philodemus

Philodemus' Poetry

Epigrams

Gigante, M. 1988a. *Filodemo, Epigrammi scelti*, 2nd ed. (Naples).

Cameron, A. 1993. *The Greek Anthology from Meleager to Planudes* (Oxford).

Gow, A. S. F. and D. L. Page 1968. *The Greek Anthology. The Garland of Philip* (Cambridge),
vol. 1: 1350–69; vol. 2: 371–400 (contains English translation).

Kaibel, G. 1885. *Philodemi Gadarensis Epigrammata* (Greifswald).

Sider, D. *The Epigrams of Philodemus: Introduction, Text, and Commentary* (forthcoming).

Philodemus' Homeric Criticism

Homer on the Good King (De bono rege, Περὶ τοῦ καθ' Ὅμηρον ἀγαθοῦ βασιλέως)
(P.Herc. *1507)*

Dorandi, T. 1982a. *Filodemo. Il buon re secondo Omero, Edizione, traduzione e commento*,
La scuola di Epicuro 3 (Naples); English translation in:

Asmis, E. 1991b. "Philodemus' Poetic Theory and *On the Good King According to Homer*,"
CA 10: 1–45.

Murray, O. 1965. "Philodemus On the Good King According to Homer," *JRS* 55: 161-82.

Murray, O. 1984. "Rileggendo *Il buon re secondo Omero*," *CErc* 14: 157-60.

History of Philosophy (Cύνταξιc τῶν φιλοcόφων)

Philodemus, Index Academicorum *(P.*Herc. *1021 and 164, book number unknown)*

Dorandi, T. 1991. *Filodemo, Storia dei Filosofi* [.]. *Platone e l'Academia*, La scuola di
Epicuro 12 (Naples).

Philodemus, Index Stoicorum *(P.Herc. 1018)*

Dorandi, T. 1994. *Storia dei filosofi. La Stoa da Zenone a Panezio: PHerc. 1018,* Philosophia antiqua 60 (Leiden), replaces:
Traversa, A. 1952. *Index Stoicorum Herculanensis* (Genoa).

Philodemus, On the Stoics *(De Stoicis, Περὶ τῶν Cτωικῶν) (P.Herc. 339 and 155)*

Dorandi, T. 1982b. "Filodemo. Gli stoici (*PHerc*. 155 e 339)," *CErc* 12: 91–133.

On Epicurus and Epicureans

Philodemus (?), On Epicurus *(De Epicuro, Περὶ 'Επικούρου) (P.Herc. 176)*

Vogliano, A. 1928. *Epicuri et Epicureorum scripta in herculanensibus papyris servata* (Berlin): 23–75.
Angeli, A. 1988b. "La scuola epicurea di Lampsaco nel *PHerc*. 176 (fr. 5 coll. I, IV, VIII–XXIII)," *CErc* 18: 27–51.

Philodemus (?), Against the . . . *(Πρὸc τοὺc [---], rest of title lost) (P.Herc. 1005)*

Angeli, A. 1988a. *Filodemo. Agli amici di scuola (PHerc. 1005),* La scuola di Epicuro 7 (Naples).

Epicurean Memoires *(Πραγματεῖαι μνημάτων) (P.Herc. 1418, 1027)*

Spina, L. 1977. "Il trattato di Filodemo su Epicuro e altri (*PHerc*. 1418)," *CErc* 7: 43–83.
Capasso, M. 1988. *Carneisco, Il Secondo libro del Filista (P.Herc. 1027),* La scuola di Epicuro 10 (Naples).

Ethical Works

Philodemus, On Anger *(De ira, Περὶ ὀργῆc) (P.Herc. 182)*

Indelli, G. 1988. *Filodemo. L'ira,* La scuola di Epicuro 5 (Naples).

Philodemus, On Flattery *(De garulitate, Περὶ κολακείαc) (P.Herc. 222)*

Gargiulo, T. 1981. "*PHerc*. 222: Filodemo sull'adulazione," *CErc* 11: 103–27.

Philodemus, On Freedom of Speech *(De libertate dicendi, Περὶ παρρηcίαc, from* On Types of Life, *Περὶ ἠθῶν καὶ βίων) (P.Herc. 1471)*

Olivieri, A. 1914. *Philodemi περὶ παρρηcίαc libellus* (Leipzig).

Philodemus, On Vices and Virtues *(De vitiis, Περὶ κακιῶν καὶ τῶν ἀντικειμένων ἀρετῶν) (P.Herc. 1008)*

Jensen, C. 1911. *Philodemi περὶ κακιῶν liber decimus* (Leipzig).

Philodemus, On Household Management *(De oeconomia, Περὶ οἰκονομίας = Book 9 of* On Vices and Virtues*) (P.Herc. 1424)*

Jensen, C. 1907. *Philodemi περὶ οἰκονομίας qui dicitur libellus* (Leipzig).

Philodemus, On Death *(De morte, Περὶ θανάτου) (P.Herc. 1050); only Book 4 survives*

Kuiper, T. 1925. *Philodemus Over den Dood* (Amsterdam) except beginning and end as revised by Gigante 1983, 115–234.

The Ethical Treatise edited by Comparetti (P.Herc. 1251)

Schmid, W. 1939. *Ethica Epicurea. Pap. Herc. 1251,* Studia Herculanensia 1 (Leipzig).

The Epicurean Protreptic Treatise P.Herc. 346

Capasso, M. 1982. *Trattato etico epicureo (PHerc. 346)* (Naples).

Theological Works

Demetrius of Laconia, On Gods *(De dis, Περὶ θεῶν)*

Renna, E. 1982, "Nuove letture nel *PHerc.* 1055 (libro incerto di Demetrio Lacone)," *CErc* 12: 43–49.
Renna, E. 1983. "Per la teologia epicurea in Demetrio," *CErc* 13: 25–28.

Philodemus, On Gods *(De dis, Περὶ θεῶν), Book 1 (P.Herc. 26)*

Diels, H. 1916. *Philodemus Über die Götter, Erstes Buch,* Abhandlungen der Königlich Preussischen Akademie der Wissenschaften, Philosophisch-historische Klasse Nr. 7 (Text und Erläuterung).

Book 3 (P.Herc. 152/157)

Diels, H. 1917. *Philodemus Über die Götter, Drittes Buch,* Abhandlungen der Königlich Preussischen Akademie der Wissenschaften, Nr. 4 (Text) und 6 (Erläuterung).

Philodemus (?), On Piety *(De pietate, Περὶ εὐσεβείας)*

Obbink, D. *Philodemus On Piety: Critical Text with Commentary 1* (forthcoming Oxford) (for the philosophical part).
Schober, A. 1988. "Philodemi περὶ εὐσεβείας libelli partem priorem restituit Adolf Schober," diss. ined. Königsberg 1923, publ. *CErc* 18 (1988): 67–125, except for those columns re-edited by A. Henrichs and W. Luppe, especially Henrichs, A. 1975, "Philodems De Pietate als mythographische Quelle," *CErc* 5: 5–38 (for the critique of poets).
Gomperz, T. 1866. *Philodem Über Frömmigkeit,* Herculanische Studien, Zweites Heft (Leipzig): 63–76 (for the critique of the pre-Socratic philosophers).
Henrichs, A. 1974. "Die Kritik der Stoischen Theologie im PHerc. 1428," *CErc* 4: 5–32, with German translation (for the critique of the Stoic philosophers).

Logic and Epistemology

Philodemus, On Signs *(De signis, Περὶ cημειώcεων) (P.Herc. 1065)*

De Lacy, P. H. and E. A. De Lacy 1978. *Philodemus, On Methods of Inference*, La scuola di Epicuro 1 (Naples) with English translation.

Polystratus, On Irrational Contempt for Popular Thinking *(Περὶ ἀλόγου καταφρονή-cεωc)*

Indelli, G. 1978. *Polistrato. Sul disprezzo irrazionale delle opinioni popolari*, Edizione, traduzione e commento, La scuola di Epicuro 2 (Naples).

Other Epicurean works on Poetic, Rhetorical, and Philological Criticism

Demetrius of Laconia, On Poems, On Rhetoric, *on Epicurean Texts:*

Puglia, E. 1982. "La filologia degli Epicurei," *CErc* 12: 19–34.
Puglia, E. 1988. *Demetrio Lacone, Aporie testuali ed esegetiche in Epicuro (PHerc. 1012)*, La scuola di Epicuro 8 (Naples).
Romeo, C. 1988. *Demetrio Lacone: Sulla Poesia*, La scuola di Epicuro 9 (Naples).
Gigante, M. 1988b. "Testimonianze su Demetrio Lacone," in Puglia 1988:13–23.

Other Latin Poetry from Herculaneum

Poem on the Battle of Actium

Main Text

Garuti, I. 1958. *C. Rabirius, Bellum Actiacum e papyro Herculanensi 817* (Bologna).

See also:

Courtney, E. 1993. *The Fragmentary Latin Poets* (Oxford): 334–40 with selections and excellent discussion.
Gigante, M. 1991. "Virgilio e i suoi amici tra Napoli e Ercolano," *Atti e Memorie dell'Accademia Nazionale Virgiliana*, NS 59: 87-125.
Immarco Bonvolontà, R. 1984. "Per una nuova edizione del PHerc. 817," *Atti del XVII Congresso Internazionale di Papirologia*, vol. 2 (Naples): 583–90.
Immarco, R. 1992. "La collona VI del carme *De bello Actiaco (PHerc. 817)*," in *Papiri letterari greci e latini*, Papyrologica Lupiensia 1 (Lecce): 239–48.
Zecchini, G. 1988. "Osservazione storiographiche sul *Carmen de bello Actiaco (PHerc. 817)*," in *Proceedings of the XVIII International Congress of Papyrology, Athens 1986*, vol. 1 (Athens): 291–98.
Malcovati, E. 1943. *Cicerone e la poesia* (Pavia) (on Saufeius).
Howe, H. M. 1948. "Epicurean Philosophers in the Roman Republic," (diss. Madison, Wisc.).
Howe, H. M. 1951. "Amafinius, Lucretius and Cicero," *AJPh* 72: 57–62.
Gigante, M., 1994. *Philodemus in Italy: The Books from Herculaneum* (Ann Arbor).

General Bibliography

Anderson, A. 1966. *Ethos and Education in Greek Music* (Cambridge, Mass.).

Angeli, A. 1988a. *Filodemo. Agli amici di scuola (PHerc. 1005)*, La scuola di Epicuro 7 (Naples).

Angeli, A. 1988b. "La scuola epicurea di Lampsaco nel *PHerc*. 176 (fr. 5 coll. I, IV, VIII–XXIII)," *CErc* 18: 27–51.

Angeli, A. 1992. "La critica di Filodemo a Socrate nel quinto libro della Retorica," *Proceedings of the XIXth International Congress of Papyrology*, vol. 1 (Cairo): 135–46.

Armstrong, D. 1994. "The Addressees of the 'Ars poetica': Herculaneum, Epicurean Protreptic and the Pisones," *MD* 31.

Arrighetti, G. 1973. *Epicuro, Opere*, 2nd ed. (Torino).

Asmis, E. 1990a. "Philodemus' Epicureanism," *ANRW* 2, 36.4: 2369–408.

Asmis, E. 1990b. "The Poetic Theory of the Stoic 'Aristo'," *Apeiron* 23: 147–201.

Asmis, E. 1991a. "Epicurean Poetics," *Proceedings of the Boston Area Colloquium in Ancient Philosophy* 7, 1991: 63–93 and 104–105 = Chapter 2.

Asmis, E. 1991b. "Philodemus' Poetic Theory and *On the Good King According to Homer,*" *CA* 10: 1–45.

Asmis, E. 1992a. "An Epicurean Survey of Poetic Theories," *CQ* 42: 395–415.

Asmis, E. 1992b. "Crates on Poetic Criticism," *Phoenix* 46: 138–69.

Asmis, E. 1992c. "Neoptolemus and the classification of poetry," *CPh* 87: 206–31.

Barker, A. 1984/89. *Greek Musical Writings*, 2 vols. (Cambridge 1984/89).

Barnes, J. 1986. "Is rhetoric an art?," *darg Newsletter (Univ. of Calgary)* 2: 2–22.

Barra, G. 1973 "Filodemo di Gadara e le lettere latine," *Vichiana* 2: 247–60.

Barra, G. 1977/78. "Osservazioni sulla "Poetica" di Filodemo e di Lucrezio," *Annali della Facoltà di Lettere e Filosofia dell'Università di Napoli* 20: 87–104.

Berkowitz, L. and K. A. Squitier 1990. L. Berkowitz and K.A. Squitier, *Thesaurus Linguae Graecae Canon of Greek Authors and Works*, 3rd ed. (Oxford).

Brink, C. O. 1963. *Horace on Poetry, I. Prolegomena to the Literary Epistles* (Cambridge).

Brunck, R. F. P. 1772–76. *Analecta Veterum Poetarum Graecorum* (Strassburg).

Cameron, A. 1993. *The Greek Anthology from Meleager to Planudes* (Oxford).

Capasso, M. 1982. *Trattato etico epicureo (PHerc. 346)* (Naples).

Capasso, M. 1989. "Primo supplemento al *Catalogo dei Papiri Ercolanesi,*" *CErc* 19: 193–265.

Capasso, M. 1991. *Manuale di papirologia ercolanese* (Lecce).

Capasso, M., ed. 1992. *Papiri letterari greci e latini*, Papyrologica Lupiensia 1 (Lecce).

Capasso, M. 1993. "Epicarmo nei papiri ercolanesi," in *Ercolano*: 295-300.

Capasso M. and A. Angeli 1989. "Papiri aperti con metodo osloense (1989–91)," *CErc* 19: 265–70.

Cappelluzzo, M. G. 1976. "Per una nuova edizione di un libro della *Retorica* di Filodemo (*P.Herc.* 1004)," *CErc* 6: 69–76.

Cavallo, G. 1983: *Libri Scritture Scribi a Ercolano, CErc* suppl. 1 (Naples).

Clay, D. 1983. *Lucretius and Epicurus* (Ithaca).

Clay, D. 1986. "The Cults of Epicurus," *CErc* 16: 11–28.

Coppola, C. 1988. "Frammenti inediti del *PHerc.* 228," *CErc* 13: 103f.

Crönert, W. 1903. *Memoria Graeca Herculanensis* (Leipzig).

De Lacy, P. H. and E. A. De Lacy 1978. *Philodemus, On Methods of Inference*, La scuola di Epicuro 1 (Naples).

Delattre, D. 1989. "Philodème, *De la Musique*: livre IV, colonnes 40* à 109*," *CErc* 19: 49–143.

Delattre, D. 1991. "Une 'citation' stoïcienne des *Lois* de Platon (II 669B–E) de Platon dans les *Commentaires sur la Musique* de Philodème?," *Revue d'histoire des textes* 21: 1–17.

Delattre, D. 1992. "Combien des livres comptaient les *Commentaires sur la Musique* de Philodème?," in M. Capasso, ed., *Papiri letterari greci e latini* (Lecce): 181–91.

Delattre, D. 1993. "Philodème, *De la Musique*," (diss. Sorbonne)

Diels, H., 1916. *Philodemus Über die Götter, Erstes Buch*, Abhandlungen der Königlich Preussischen Akademie der Wissenschaften, Philosophisch-historische Klasse Nr. 7 (Text und Erläuterung).

Diels, H. 1917. *Philodemus Über die Götter, Drittes Buch*, Abhandlungen der Königlich Preussischen Akademie der Wissenschaften, Nr. 4 (Text) und 6 (Erläuterung).

Diels, H. and W. Kranz 1952. *Die Fragmente der Vorsokratiker* 1-3 (Berlin).

Dorandi, T. 1982a. *Filodemo. Il buon re secondo Omero, Edizione, traduzione e commento*, La scuola di Epicuro 3 (Naples).

Dorandi, T. 1982b. "Filodemo. Gli stoici (*PHerc.* 155 e 339)," *CErc* 12: 91–133.

Dorandi, T. 1990a. "Filodemo: gli orientamenti della ricerca attuale," *ANRW* 2, 36.4: 2328–68.

Dorandi, T. 1990b. "Per una ricomposizione dello scritto filodemeo Sulla retorica," *ZPE* 82: 59–87.

Dorandi, T. 1991. *Filodemo, Storia dei Filosofi* [.]. *Platone e l'Academia*, La scuola di Epicuro 12 (Naples).

Dorandi, T. 1992a. "Papiri ercolanesi tra 'scorzatura' e 'svolgimento'," *CErc* 22: 179–80.

Dorandi, T. 1992b. "Dichtender Philosoph und philosophierender Dichter: Das literarische Schaffen des Epikureers Philodem von Gadara," *WJA* 18: 183-93.

Dürr, E. 1990. "Una Testimonianza su Euripide in un papiro ercolanese inedito," in *Miscellanea Papirologica in occasione del bicentenario dell'edizione della Charta Borgiana* (Florence): 42f.

Dürr, E. 1992. "I resti del *PHerc.* 1736 (Filodemo, *Poetica?*)," *CErc* 22: 139–56.

Eden, K. 1986. *Poetic and Legal Fiction in the Aristotelian Tradition* (Princeton).

Ercolano 1993. Ercolano 1738-1988: 250 anni di ricerca archeologica. Atti del Convengo Internazionale Ravello-Ercolano-Napoli-Pompei, ed. L. Franchi dell'Orto (Rome).

Ferrario, M. 1974. "Verso una nuova edizione del quinto libro della *Retorica* di Filodemo," *CErc* 4: 93–96.

Ferrario, M. 1980. "Frammenti del quinto libro della *Retorica* di Filodemo (*P.Herc.* 1669)," *CErc* 10: 55–124.

Ferrario, M. 1981. "La Concezione della retorica da Epicuro a Filodemo," *Proceedings of the XVIth International Congress of Papyrology* (Chico).

Ferrario, M. 1988. "Per una nuova edizione del quinto libro della *Retorica* di Filodemo," *Proceedings of the XVIIIth International Congress of Papyrology*, vol. 1 (Athens): 167–84.

Fowler, D. P. 1989. "Lucretius and Politics," in Griffin and Barnes 1989: 120-50.

Frosén, J. and D. Hagedorn 1990. *Die verkohlten Papyri aus Bubastos (Pap. Bub.)*, Papyrologica Coloniensia 15 (Opladen).

Gaines, R. 1982. "Qualities of rhetorical expression in Philodemus," *TAPA* 112: 71–81.

Gargiulo, T. 1981. "*PHerc.* 222: Filodemo sull'adulazione," *CErc* 11: 103–27.

Gigante, M., ed. 1979. *Catalogo dei Papiri Ercolanesi* (Naples).

Gigante, M. 1983. *Ricerche filodemee*, 2nd ed. (Naples).

Gigante, M. 1984. *Virgilio e la Campania* (Naples).

Gigante, M. 1988a. *Filodemo, Epigrammi scelti*, 2nd ed. (Naples).

Gigante, M. 1988b. "Testimonianze su Demetrio Lacone," in Puglia 1988: 13–23.

Gigante, M. 1989. "Filodemo tra poesia e prosa," *SIFC* 7 (1989) 129–51.

Gigante, M. 1991. "Virgilio e i suoi amici tra Napoli e Ercolano," *Atti e Memorie dell'Accademia Nazionale Virgiliana*, NS 59: 87-125.

Gigante, M. 1992a. "Lucrezio: il piacere della forma," *RIL* 125: 21–31.

Gigante, M. 1992b. "Philodemo e l'epigramma," *CErc* 22: 5–8.

Gigante, M. 1995. *Philodemus in Italy: The Books from Herculaneum* (Ann Arbor).

Gigante, M. and M. Capasso 1989. "Il ritorno di Virgilio a Ercolano," *SIFC* 7: 3–6.

Gomoll, H. 1936. "Herakleodoros und die *kritikoi* bei Philodem," *Philologus* 91: 373–84.

Gomperz, T. 1866. *Philodem Über Frömmigkeit*, Herculanische Studien, Zweites Heft (Leipzig).

Gomperz, T. 1891. "Philodem und die ästhetischen Schriften der herculanischen Bibliothek," *Sitzungsberichte der Akademie der Wissenschaften in Wien, Phil.-Hist. Kl.* 123: 1–88.

Gomperz, T. 1993. *Theodor Gomperz. Eine auswahl herculanischer kleiner Schriften (1864–1909)*, ed. T. Dorandi, Philosophia antiqua 59 (Leiden).

Gow, A. S. F. and D. L. Page 1968. *The Greek Anthology. The Garland of Philip*, 2 vols. (Cambridge).

Greenberg, N. A. 1955. "The Poetic Theory of Philodemus," (diss. Harvard, publ. New York 1990).

Greenberg, N. A. 1958. "Metathesis as an Instrument in the Criticism of Poetry," *TAPA* 89: 262–70.

Greenberg, N. A. 1961. "The Use of *POIEMA* and *POIESIS*," *HSCPh* 45: 263–89.

Griffin, M. and J. Barnes 1989. *Philosophia Togata: Essays on Philosophy and Roman Society* (Oxford).

Grube, G. M. A. 1965. *The Greek and Roman Critics* (London).

Hammerstaedt, J. 1992. "Der Schlussteil von Philodems drittem Buch über Rhetorik," *CErc* 22: 9-117.

Hausrath, A. 1889. *Philodemi* Peri poiematon *libri secundi quae videntur fragmenta* (Leipzig).

Heidmann, J. 1937. *Der Papyrus 1676 der herculanensischen Bibliothek (Philodemus Peri Poiematon)* (Bonn 1937), publ. in *CErc* 1 (1971): 90–111.

Henrichs, A. 1972. "Toward a New Edition of Philodemus' Treatise *On Piety*," *GRBS* 13: 67–98.

Henrichs, A. 1974. "Die Kritik der Stoischen Theologie im PHerc. 1428," *CErc* 4: 5–32.

Henrichs, A. 1975. "Philodems De Pietate als mythographische Quelle," *CErc* 5: 5–38.

Hubbell, H. M. 1920. "The *Rhetorica* of Philodemus," *Transactions of the Connecticut Academy of Arts and Sciences* 23: 243–382.

Indelli, G. 1978. *Polistrato. Sul disprezzo irrazionale delle opinioni popolari*, Edizione, traduzione e commento, La scuola di Epicuro 2 (Naples).

Indelli, G. 1988. *Filodemo. L'ira*, La scuola di Epicuro 5 (1988).

Innes, D. 1989. "Philodemus," in *The Cambridge History of Literary Criticism I: Classical Criticism*, ed. G. A. Kennedy (Cambridge): 215–19.

Isnardi Parente, M. 1987. "Una Poetica di incerto autore in Filodemo," in *Filologia e forme letterarie: Studi offerti a F. della Corte* vol. 5 (Urbino): 81–98.

Janko, R. 1991a. "Philodemus' *On Poems* and Aristotle's *On Poets*," *CErc* 21: 5–64.

Janko, R. 1991b. "*Philodemus resartus*: progress in reconstructing the philosophical papyri from Herculaneum," *Proceedings of the Boston Area Colloquium in Ancient Philosophy* 7, 1991: 271–308 (publ. 1993).

Janko, R. 1992a. "A first join between *PHerc*. 411 and 1583 (Philodemus, *On Music* IV)," *CErc* 22: 123–29.

Janko, R. 1992b. "From catharsis to the Aristotelian mean," in A. Rorty, ed., *Essays on Aristotle's Poetics* (Princeton): 341–58.

Janko, R. 1993. "Introducing the Philodemus Translation Project: reconstructing the *On Poems*," *Proceedings of the XXth International Congress of Papyrology, Copenhagen 1992* (Copenhagen): 367–81.

Jensen, C. 1907. *Philodemi περὶ οἰκονομίας qui dicitur libellus* (Leipzig).

Jensen, C. 1911. *Philodemi περὶ κακιῶν liber decimus* (Leipzig).

Jensen, C. 1923. *Philodemus Über die Gedichte, Fünftes Buch* (Berlin).

Jensen, C. 1934. "Aristoteles in der *Auge* des Machon," *RhM* 83: 194–99.

Jensen, C. 1936. "Herakleides von Pontos bei Philodem und Horaz," *Sitzungsberichte der Preussischen Akademie von Wissenschaften*, Phil.-Hist. Kl., 292–320.

Kaibel, G. 1885. *Philodemi Gadarensis Epigrammata* (Greifswald).

Kemke, I. 1884. *Philodemi De Musica librorum quae exstant* (Leipzig).

Kleve, K. 1989. "Lucretius in Herculaneum," *CErc* 19: 5–27.

Kleve, K. 1990. "Ennius in Herculaneum," *CErc* 20: 5–16.

Kleve, K. and F. Longo Auricchio 1992. "Honey from the Garden of Epicurus," in Capasso 1992: 211-26.

Kleve, K., A. Angeli, and M. Capasso et. al. 1991. "Three technical guides to the papyri of Herculaneum," *CErc* 21: 111–24.

van Krevelen, D. A. 1939. *Philodemus: De Muziek* (Hilversum).

Kuiper, T. 1925. *Philodemus Over den Dood* (Amsterdam).

Laks, A. 1976. "Édition critique et commentée de la 'Vie d'Épicure' dans Diogène Laërce (x, 1-34)," in J. Bollack and A. Laks, edd., *Études sur l'épicurisme antique*, Publications de l'Université de Lille III, Cahiers de philologie 1 (Lille): 1-118.

Lemon, L. T. and Marion J. Reis 1965. *Russian Formalist Criticism: Four Essays*, translated and with an introduction (Lincoln, Nebraska).

Long, A. A. 1992. "Stoic Readings of Homer," in R. Lamberton and J. Keaney, edd., *Homer's Ancient Readers* (Princeton): 30-66.

Long, A. A. and D. N. Sedley 1987. *The Hellenistic Philosophers*, 2 vols. (Cambridge).

Longo Auricchio, F. 1977. *Φιλοδήμου Περὶ ῥητορικῆς libros primum et secundum, in Ricerche sui Papiri Ercolanesi a c. di F. Sbordone*, vol. 3 (Naples) 2–277.

Longo Auricchio, F. 1983. "Filodemo: La *Retorica* e la *Musica*," in *ΣΥΖΗΤΗΣΙΣ*, vol. 2: 553–65.

Longo Auricchio, F. 1984. "Epicureismo e scetticismo sulla retorica," *Atti del XVII Congresso della Papirologia*, vol. 2 (Naples): 453–72.

Longo Auricchio, F. 1985. "Testimonianze dalla 'Retorica' di Filodemo sulla concezione dell'oratoria nei primi maestri epicurei," *CErc* 15: 31–61.

Longo Auricchio, F. and A. Tepedino Guerra 1981. "Aspetti e problemi della dissidenza epicurea," *CErc* 11: 25–40.

Luppe, W. 1974. "Zeus und Nemesis in den Kyprien. Die Verwandlungssage nach Pseudo-Apollodor und Philodem," *Philologus* 118: 193-202.

Luppe, W. 1984. "Epikureische Mythenkritik bei Philodem. Götterliebschaften in PHerc. 243 II and II," *CErc* 14: 109-124.

Luppe, W. 1985a. "Hekate als 'Amme' der Persephone," *ZPE* 58: 34.

Luppe, W. 1985b. "Götterfesselungen bei Hesiod, Aischylos und Euripides - Zu Philodem PHerc. 1088 III 8 ff.," *CErc* 15: 127-29.

Luppe, W. 1986a. "Leiden und Krankheiten der Götter bei Philodem de pietate 1088 1," *CErc* 16: 67-9.

Luppe, W. 1986b. "Götter-Sukzessionsmythos bei Satyros. Philodem, De Pietate 1088 VIII/IX + 433 VIa," *CErc* 16: 71-7.

Luppe, W. 1986c. "Poseidons Geliebte. Philodem, Περὶ εὐσεβείας P. Herc. 1602 VI," *Tyche* 1: 157-67.

Luppe, W. 1987. "Zu einigen Stellen in Philodem Περὶ εὐσεβείας P. Herc. 433," *APF* 33: 79-85.

Mangoni, C. 1988. "Prosa e poesia nel V libro della *Poetica* di Filodemo," *CErc* 18: 127–38.

Mangoni, C. 1989. "Il *PHerc.* 228," *CErc* 19: 179–86.

Mangoni, C. 1991. "Nuove letture nei *PHerc.* 1425 e 1538 del V libro della *Poetica* di Filodemo," *CErc* 21: 65–82.

Mangoni, C. 1992a. "Il *PHerc.* 407 della *Poetica* di Filodemo," *CErc* 22: 131–37.

Mangoni, C. 1992b. "Metodi argomentativi nel V libro *peri poiematon* di Filodemo di Gadara," *Proceedings of the XIXth International Congress of Papyrology*, vol. 1 (Cairo): 161–72.

Mangoni, C. 1993. *Filodemo, La Poesia V*, La scuola di Epicuro 14 (Naples).

McNamee, K. 1992. *Sigla and Select Marginalia in Greek Literary Papyri* (Brussels).

Meijering, R. 1987. *Literary and Rhetorical Theories in Greek Scholia* (Groningen).

Mesturini, A. M. 1990. "Puntualizzazioni sul Tractatus Coislinianus," *Maia* 42: 237–47.

Mette, H. J. 1979. "Zu Philodem *Peri poiematon*," *Zeitschrift für Papyrologie und Epigraphik* 34: 59–63.

Mette, H. J. 1981. "Neoptolemos von Parion," *RhM* 123: 1–24.

Michels, A. K. 1944. "παρρησία and the *Satires* of Horace," *CPh* 39: 173–77.

Murray, O. 1965. "Philodemus On the Good King According to Homer," *JRS* 55: 161-82.

Murray, O. 1984. "Rileggendo *Il buon re secondo Omero*," *CErc* 14: 157-60.

Nardelli, M. L. 1978. "La catarsi poetica nel *PHerc.* 1581," *CErc* 8: 96–103.

Nardelli, M. L. 1979. "Papiri della 'Poetica' di Filodemo," *CErc* 9: 137–40.

Nardelli, M. L. 1981. "*PHerc.* 1676: contenuti di un libro dell'opera filodemea *Sulla Poetica*," *Proceedings of the XVIth International Congress of Papyrology* (Chico): 163–71.

Nardelli, M. L. 1982a. "Euripide nella 'Poetica' di Filodemo," in *La Regione sotterrata dal Vesuvio* (Naples): 471–92.

Nardelli, M. L. 1982b. "*PHerc.* 994 col. x," *CErc* 12: 135–36.

Nardelli, M. L. 1983. "Due Trattati filodemei 'Sulla Poetica'," in *Ricerche sui Papiri Ercolanesi* 4 (Naples).

Neubecker, A. J. 1986. *Philodem. Über die Musik, Viertes Buch*, La scuola di Epicuro 4 (Naples).

Obbink, D. 1986. "Philodemus, *De Pietate* I," (diss. Stanford).

Obbink, D. 1992. "'What All Men Believe—Must be True': Common Conceptions and *consensio omnium* in Aristotle and Hellenistic Philosophy," *OSAP* 10 (1992): 193-231.

Obbink, D. and P. A. Vander Waerdt 1991. "Diogenes of Babylon: The Stoic Sage in the City of Fools," *GRBS* 32: 355–96.

Olivieri, A. 1914. *Philodemi περὶ παρρησίας libellus* (Leipzig).

Pöhlmann, E. 1991. Reviews of Neubecker 1986 and Delattre 1989, *Gnomon* 63: 481–86.

Puglia, E. 1988. *Demetrio Lacone, Aporie testuali ed esegetiche in Epicuro (PHerc. 1012)*, La scuola di Epicuro 8 (Naples).

Porter, J. 1989. "Philodemus on Material Difference," *CErc* 19: 149–70.

Reiche, H. 1971 "Myth and Magic in Cosmological Polemics," *RhM* 114: 296-329.

Renna, E. 1982. "Nuove letture nel *PHerc*. 1055 (libro incerto di Demetrio Lacone)," *CErc* 12: 43–49.

Renna, E. 1983. "Per la teologia epicurea in Demetrio," *CErc* 13: 25–28.

Rispoli, G. M. 1969. "Il primo libro del *Peri Mousikes* di Filodemo," in F. Sbordone, ed., *Ricerche sui Papiri Ercolanesi* 1 (Naples): 25–286.

Rispoli, G. M. 1981. "Suono ed articulazione nella teoria epicurea del linguaggio," *Proceedings of the XVIth International Congress of Papyrology* (Chico): 173–81.

Rispoli, G. M. 1986. "Eufonia ed ermeneutica: origine ed evoluzione di un metodo filologico," *Koinonia* 10: 134–43.

Rispoli, G. M. 1987. "Eufonia ed poetica in testi ercolanesi," *Linguistica e filologia: Atti del VII Convegno Internazionale di Linguisti* (Brescia): 461–78.

Rispoli, G. M. 1991. "Elementi di fisica e di etica epicurea nella teoria musicale di Filodemo di Gadara," in Wallace and MacLachlan 1991: 69-103.

Romeo, C. 1980. "Nicola Lucignano e i papiri ercolanesi," *Contributi alla Storia dell'Officina dei Papiri, I Quaderni della Biblioteca Nazionale di Napoli* 5.2 (Naples).

Romeo, C. 1981. "Sofrone nei Papiri ercolanesi: *PHerc*. 1081 e 1014," *Proceedings of the XVIth International Congress of Papyrology* (Chico): 183–90.

Romeo, C. 1983. "Filodemo: La Poetica," in *ΣΥΖΗΤΗΣΙΣ*, vol. 2: 565–83.

Romeo, C. 1988. *Demetrio Lacone: Sulla Poesia*, La scuola di Epicuro 9 (Naples).

Romeo, C. 1992a. "Il *PHerc*. 1677: un libro della Poetica di Filodemo," *Proceedings of the XIXth International Congress of Papyrology*, vol. 1 (Cairo 1992): 173–78.

Romeo, C. 1992b. "Per una nuova edizione del *PHerc*. 1676: un libro della Poetica di Filodemo," *CErc* 22: 163–67.

Romeo, C. 1992c. "Un contributo inedito di Filodemo alla critica omerica (*PHerc*. 1677 coll. v–vii)," in Capasso 1992.

Rostagni, A. 1955. "Filodemo contro l'estetica antica," in *Scritti minori*, vol. 1 (Turin): 394–446.

Russell, D. A. 1981. *Criticism in Antiquity* (London).

Rutherford, I. 1988. "*Emphasis* in ancient literary criticism and the Tractatus Coislinianus," *Maia* 40: 125–29.

Rutherford, I. 1990. "Philodemus, *Peri poiematon* Tractatus tertius, fr. e, col. i, ll. 23–24," *Zeitschrift für Papyrologie und Epigraphik* 82: 58.

Sbordone, F. 1969a. "Il quarto libro del *Peri Poiematon* di Filodemo," in F. Sbordone, ed., *Ricerche sui Papiri Ercolanesi* 1 (Naples): 287–372.

Sbordone, F. 1969b. *Contributo alla Poetica degli Antichi* (Naples, ed. 1, 1961).

Sbordone, F. 1976. "*ΦΙΛΟΔΗΜΟΥ ΠΕΡΙ ΠΟΙΗΜΑΤΩΝ* Tractatus Tres," in *Ricerche sui Papiri Ercolanesi* 2 (Naples).

Sbordone, F. 1981. "La Poetica oraziona alla luce dei studi piú recenti," *ANRW* 2, 31.3: 1866–1920.

Sbordone, F. 1983. *Sui Papiri della Poetica di Filodemo* (Naples).

Schächter, R. 1926. "Philodemi *peri poiematon* l. II fragmenta ex *VH* X collecta," *Eos* 29: 15–28.

Schenkeveld, D. M. 1968. "*Hoi kritikoi* in Philodemus," *Mnemosyne* 21: 176–214.

Schenkeveld, D. M. 1982. "Studies in the History of Ancient Linguistics I: *ΣΥΝΔΕΣΜΟΙ ΥΠΟΘΕΤΙΚΟΙ* and *Ο ΕΑΝ ΕΠΙΖΕΥΚΤΙΚΟΣ*," *Mnemosyne* 35: 248–68.

Schenkeveld, D. M. 1984. "Studies in the History of Ancient Linguistics II: Stoic and Peripatetic Kinds of Speech Act and the Distinction of Grammatical Moods," *Mnemosyne* 37: 291–353.

Schenkeveld, D. M. 1990. "Studies in the History of Ancient Linguistics III: The Stoic *ΤΕΧΝΗ ΠΕΡΙ ΦΩΝΗΣ*," *Mnemosyne* 43: 86–108 and "Studies in the History of Ancient Linguistics IV: Developments in the Study of Ancient Linguistics," 289–306.

Schmid, W. 1939. *Ethica Epicurea. Pap. Herc. 1251*, Studia Herculanensia 1 (Leipzig).

Schober, A. 1988. "Philodemi περὶ εὐσεβείας libelli partem priorem restituit Adolf Schober," diss. ined. Königsberg 1923, publ. in *CErc* 18 (1988): 67–125.

Sedley, D. N. 1989. "Philosophical allegiance in the Greco-Roman world," in Griffin and Barnes 1989: 97–119.

Sider, D. 1991. "Commentary on Asmis [1991a]," in *Proceedings of the Boston Area Colloquium in Ancient Philosophy* 7: 94-105 (publ. 1993) = Chapter 3.

Smith, M. F. 1993. *Diogenes of Oinoanda, The Epicurean Inscription*, La scuola di Epicuro, Supplemento 1 (Naples).

Spina, L. 1977. "Il trattato di Filodemo su Epicuro e altri (*PHerc.* 1418)," *CErc* 7: 43–83.

Spina, L. 1988. "Un Papiro inedito della collezione ercolanese: *PHerc.* 1403," *Vichiana* 17: 99–108 = *Proceedings of the XVIIth International Congress of Papyrology* (Athens): 399–407.

Sudhaus, S. 1892/96. *Philodemi Volumina Rhetorica*, 2 vols. (Leipzig).

Sudhaus, S. 1895. *Philodemi Volumina Rhetorica: Supplementum* (Leipzig).

ΣΥΖΗΤΗΣΙΣ. Studi sull'epicureismo greco e romano offerti a Marcello Gigante (Naples).

Tait, J. I. M. 1941. "Philodemus' Influence on the Latin Poets" (diss. Bryn Mawr).

Thomas, R. F. 1991. "'Death', Doxography, and 'Termerian Evil' (Philodemus, *Epigr.* 27 Page = *A.P.* 11.30)," *CQ* 41: 130-37.

Traversa, A. 1952. *Index Stoicorum Herculanensis* (Genoa).

Trimpi, W. 1978. "Horace's 'ut pictura poesis': The Argument for Stylistic Decorum," *Traditio* 34: 29-73.

Trimpi, W. 1983. *Muses of One Mind: The Literary Analysis of Experience and its Continuity* (Princeton).

Usener, H. 1887. *Epicurea* (Leipzig).

Usener, H. 1977. *Glossarium Epicureum*, ed. M. Gigante (Rome).

Vogliano, A. 1928. *Epicuri et Epicureorum scripta in herculanensibus papyris servata* (Berlin).

Vooys, C. J. 1934/41. *Lexicon Philodemeum*, vol. 1 (Purmerend 1934); vol. 2, with D. A. van Krevelen (Amsterdam 1941).

Wallace, R. W. 1991a. "Musica e filosofia nell'antichità," in Wallace and MacLachlan 1991: 1-6.

Wallace, R. W. 1991b. "Damone di Oa ed i suoi successori: un'analisi delle fonti," in Wallace and MacLachlan 1991: 30-53.

Wallace, R. W. and B. MacLachlan, edd. 1991. *Harmonia mundi. Musica e filosofia nell'antichità*, Biblioteca di Quaderni Urbinati di Cultura Classica 5 (Rome).

Walsh, G. B. 1987. "Philodemus on the terminology of Neoptolemus," *Mnemosyne* 40: 56–68.

Contributors

DAVID ARMSTRONG is Professor of Classics at the University of Texas at Austin.

ELIZABETH ASMIS is Professor of Classics at the University of Chicago and Editor of *Classical Philology.*

DAVID BLANK is Professor of Classics and Chair of the Department at UCLA.

DISKIN CLAY is Professor of Greek and Chair of the Department at Duke University.

RICHARD JANKO is Professor of Greek at University College, London, and Director of the NEH Philodemus Translation Project.

DIRK OBBINK is Assistant Professor of Classics at Barnard College, Columbia University, and a Fellow at the Center for Hellenic Studies, Washington D.C.

STEVEN OBERHELMAN is Professor of Classics and Head of the Department of Modern and Classical Languages at Texas A & M University and Editor of *Helios.*

JAMES PORTER is Associate Professor of Classics and Comparative Literature at the University of Michigan.

DAVID SIDER is Associate Professor of Classics at Fordham University.

MICHAEL WIGODSKY is Associate Professor of Classics at Stanford University.

Index of Passages Discussed

Greek

Latin

Index of Greek and Latin Words

First Lines of Philodemean Poems quoted

αὔριον εἰς λιτήν σε καλιάδα, φίλτατε Πείσων 46, 208 and n. 63
ἠράσθην, τίς δ' οὐχί; κεκώμακα, τίς δ' ἀμύητος 53
ἑπτὰ τριηκόντεσσιν ἐπέρχονται λυκάβαντες 53
Ξανθὼ κηρόπλαστε μυρόχροε μουσοπρόσωπε 55
ἤδη καὶ ῥόδον ἔςτι καὶ ἀκμάζων ἐρέβινθος 55
Ἰνοῦς ὦ Μελικέρτα σύ τε γλαυκὴ μεδέουσα 208 and n. 64

Greek Words

ἄγαλμα 55
ἀγόρασμα 156
ἀγών 119
ἄδηλον 63
ἀέριος 139, 164 n. 59
ἀηδών 183
ἀήθεια 139
αἰθήρ 201
αἴσθηεις 119
αἰσχρός 27 n. 67
ἀκάτιον 18 n. 18, 24
ἀκοή 186, 216, 221
ἀκούω 16
ἀκρόαμα 19
ἀλήθεια 163, 220 and n. 23
ἄλογος 216
ἀλληλουχία 164 n. 59
ἀλλοτριότης 183
ἁμαρτία 118
ἀναιρέω 199
ἀναφέρω 201
Ἀντιγένης 55
ἀνωφελής 27 n. 67
ἀοιδός 16
ἀπαιτέω 184
ἀπατή 196
ἀπεργαεία 110
ἀποδεικτικὸς λόγος 28, 34
ἀπόδειξις 25, 29 n. 77
ἀποκρύπτω 122
ἀπόλαυεις 18 n. 18
ἀπονία 44 n. 8
ἀποτελέω 183

ἄρθρωεις 183
ἀεέβεια 205
ἀετεῖον 151
ἀταραξία 43 n. 8
ἄτομος 40
ἄτοπος 205
αὔριον 46
ἀφορμή 25, 191 n. 8
ἀφοειόω 16, 19
ἀχρηετία 32

Βάκχιος 55
βαειλεύς 19 n. 22
βλάπτω 174, 196
βωμολοχία 19 n. 22

γέμω 83
γεννάω 172
γένος 81
γράμμα 142, 192
γραμματική 10, 185
γραμματιετής 191
γραμματιετική 10–11, 192
γραμματοδιδάεκαλος 191

δειπνίζω 48 and n. 30
δεῖπνον 48 n. 30
δέλεαρ 16
διάγνωεις 187
διαγωγή 24, 33
διάθεεις 115
διαθιγή 211
διαίρεεις 202

διανόημα 129
διάνοια 80, 102, 217, 220
διδαεκαλία 119
διήγημα 19 n. 22
Διονυειακός 19
διώκω 220
δόκιμος 27 n. 64
δύναμις 187

εἶδος 102–3, 105, 249
εἰκαίως 218
εἰκάς 47–8, 50
ἐκβάλλω 27, 148
ἐκλογή 90, 149
ἐκραπίζω 26–7, 148, 150
ἐλεύθερος 39
ἑλληνίζω 183
ἑλληνιεμός 183
ἐμπερία 187
ἐμφατικῶς 168
ἐναλλαγή 222
ἐνάργεια 22, 33, 35–6, 168
ἐναργῶς 22, 32, 36, 168
ἐνεργέω 22, 36
ἐνιαύειος 48–50
ἐπίδειξις 187 n. 34
ἐπιετήμη 20 n. 27, 215
ἐπιφαίνω 141, 152, 220
ἔπος 213
ἐποχή 199
ἐργάζω 220
ἐργαεία 106, 218 n. 20
ἔργον 119, 160, 218

298

Latin Words

General Index